W9-CAZ-881

STYLE (continued)

S13 MISCELLANEOUS DO'S AND DON'TS

S13.1 Letter to Instructor 433	S13.2 Formal Announcements 433–434	S13.3 Speechmaking 434	S13.4 Hedging 434	S13.5 Blustering 434	S13.6 "You" 434–435	S13.7 Defining Terms 435

RESEARCH

R1	R2	R3 QUOTATIONS		R4	R5 FOOTNOTES		R6	R7
Bibliography Cards 338–344	Note Cards 344–347	R3.1 On Cards 347–348	R3.2 In Paper 353–355	Slug Outline 349–350	R5.1 Use 355–356	R5.2 Form 358–362	Plagiarism 356–358	Final Bibliography 363

HANDBOOK AND GLOSSARY

GRAMMAR—G

G1	G2	G3	G4	G5	G6	G7 MODIFIERS		G8
Adjective–Adverb Confusion 447–449	Comma Splice 462–464	Comparative and Superlative Forms 465	Comparisons: Logical and Complete 465–466	Double Negative 467	Sentence Fragment 469–473	G7.1 Dangling 475–476	G7.2 Misplaced 476–477	Pronoun Agreement 479–480

G9	G10	G11	G12	G13	G14	G15	G16	G17
Pronoun Case 481–483	Pronoun Reference 483–484	Run-on Sentence 486–487	Tense Shift 487–488	Shift in Person 488–489	Subject–Verb Agreement 491–495	Subjunctive 495	Verbs: Principal Parts 496–498	Verbs: Sequence of Tenses 498–501

PUNCTUATION—Pn

Pn1 APOSTROPHE			Pn2	Pn3	Pn4 COMMA	
Pn1.1 Contractions 449	Pn1.2 Plurals 449	Pn1.3 Possessives 450–452	Brackets 452	Colon 454–455	Pn4.1 List or Series 455–456	Pn4.2 Independent Clauses 456

Pn4.3	Pn4.4	Pn4.5	Pn4.6	Pn4.7	Pn4.8	Pn4.9	Pn4.10
Introductory Elements 457–458	Interrupting Elements 458	Coordinate Adjectives 458–459	Nonrestrictive Modifiers and Appositives 459–460	Contrast 460	Direct Address Interjections Yes and No 461	Misreadings 461	Other 461–462

Pn5	Pn6	Pn7	Pn8	Pn9	Pn10	Pn11
Dash 467	Ellipsis 468	Period Question Mark Exclamation Point 468–469	Hyphen 473	Parentheses 478–479	Quotation Mark 484–486	Semicolon 487

OTHER CONVENTIONS—C

C1	C2	C3	C4	C5	C6	Glos
Abbreviations 446–447	Capitalization 452–454	Italics 473–474	Proofreading Symbols 474–475	Numerals 478	Spelling 489–490	Glossary 503–533

STUDENT'S BOOK OF COLLEGE ENGLISH
Third Edition

David Skwire
Cuyahoga Community College

Frances Chitwood
Cuyahoga Community College

Macmillan Publishing Co., Inc.
NEW YORK

MACMILLAN PUBLISHING CO., INC.
866 Third Avenue, New York, New York 10022

Collier Macmillan Canada, Ltd.

Library of Congress Catalog Card Number: 79-092703

ISBN 0-02-471800-9

Printing: 1 2 3 4 5 6 7 8   Year: 1 2 3 4 5 6 7 8

ACKNOWLEDGEMENTS

Acknowledgement is gratefully made to the following authors, agents, and publishers who have granted permission to use selections from their publications.

Ruth Banks, Ersa Poston, and the Estate of Theodore R. Poston for "The Revolt of the Evil Fairies." Reprinted by permission.

The Bettmann Archive, Inc., for photographs on pages ii–iii, xviii, 70, 326, 392, and 438. Reprinted by permission of The Bettmann Archive, Inc.

Curtis Brown, Ltd., for "The Blessington Method" by Stanley Ellin. Reprinted by permission of Curtis Brown, Ltd. Copyright © 1956 by Stanley Ellin.

Chatto and Windus Ltd., for "The Lottery Ticket" by Anton Chekhov, from THE WIFE AND OTHER STORIES by Anton Chekhov, translated by Constance Garnett. Copyright 1918 by Macmillan Publishing Co., Inc., renewed 1946 by Constance Garnett. Reprinted by permission of Chatto and Windus Ltd. and Mr. David Garnett; reprinted also by permission of Macmillan Publishing Co., Inc.; and for "Dulce et Decorum Est" from THE COLLECTED POEMS OF WILFRED OWEN: Edited by C. Day Lewis. Reprinted by permission of Chatto & Windus Ltd. and the Owen Estate. Reprinted also by permission of New Directions Publishing Corporation.

Delacorte Press, for "Harrison Bergeron" by Kurt Vonnegut Jr., from WELCOME TO THE MONKEY HOUSE by Kurt Vonnegut Jr. Copyright 1961 by Kurt Vonnegut Jr. Reprinted by permission of Delacorte Press and Seymour Lawrence.

Doubleday & Company, Inc., for "The Colonel's Lady" by W. Somerset Maugham. "The Colonel's Lady" from COMPLETE SHORT STORIES (CREATURES OF CIRCUMSTANCE) by W. Somerset Maugham. Copyright 1946 by Hearst Magazines, Inc.; and for THE FIRST FIVE YEARS (pp. 121–125) by Virginia E. Pomeranz with Dodi Schultz. Copyright 1973 by Virginia E. Pomeranz and Dodi Schultz. Reprinted by permission of Doubleday & Company, Inc.

E. P. Dutton, for "The Spires of Oxford" by Winifred M. Letts, from THE SPIRES OF OXFORD AND OTHER POEMS by Winifred M. Letts. Copyright 1917 by E. P. Dutton, renewal 1945 by Winifred M. Letts. Reprinted by permission of E. P. Dutton; reprinted also by permission of John Murray Ltd., London, England.

Nora Ephron, for "The Point, He Taught, Is the Point," by Nora Ephron. Copyright 1976 by Nora Ephron. Reprinted by permission of the author.

M. Evans & Company, Inc., for "Jerry Manelli's Father" by Donald E. Westlake. From DANCING AZTECS by Donald E. Westlake. Copyright © 1976 by Donald E. Westlake. Reprinted by permission of the publisher, M. Evans and Company, Inc., New York, N.Y. 10017.

Family Circle, Inc., for "How to Write a Letter That Will Get You a Job" by Nora Aguilar, copyright 1977; and for "Why Soap Operas Are So Popular" by Dan Wakefield, copyright 1976. Reprinted by permission of The Family Circle, Inc.

Farrar, Straus & Giroux, Inc., for "Charles" by Shirley Jackson, from THE LOTTERY by Shirley Jackson. Copyright 1943, 1949 by Shirley Jackson; copyright renewed 1971 by Lawrence Hyman, Barry Hyman, Mrs. Sarah Webster, and Mrs. Joanne Schnurer. Reprinted by permission of Farrar, Straus & Giroux, Inc.

Field Newspaper Syndicate for "Sweet Mystery of Life—Children" by Erma Bombeck, from AT WIT'S END by Erma Bombeck, copyright 1975. Reprinted by permission of Field Newspaper Syndicate.

CONTENTS

TO THE INSTRUCTOR

The third edition of *Student's Book of College English* features an unusually large number of new readings, including new student themes. The research paper chapter highlights two sample papers taking opposite stands on an issue of current controversy. Changes give life; few traps are more insidious for an instructor than teaching a book—or a course—from memory. The basic appeal of *Student's Book*, however, remains unchanged: it provides in a small package and at a reasonable cost thorough coverage of all the issues likely to be dealt with in a full year of Freshman English—and then supplements that coverage with readings in poetry and fiction as well as the essay, with readings by students as well as professionals.

One of the unorthodox, possibly unique, features of the first two editions of *Student's Book* was the mix wherever practicable of readings for use as models and readings for use as subjects for compositions. We believe this mix significantly increased the versatility of the book and helped account for its success. This principle has been maintained in the third edition. Users will find, for example, student and professional models of process writing, but they will also find two short stories that can profitably be studied and analyzed by students writing their own process papers.

We hope that clear prose and good sense also made their contributions to the success of earlier editions. We have tried to keep them constantly in mind in writing the current one.

We have tried to thank personally all the former students whose papers are part of this book, and we would like to take this opportunity to thank those students whom we were unable to contact before publication.

D. S.
F. C.

TO THE STUDENT
Preface and First Lesson

_____

This book is written for you. We don't say that simply to win your confidence or to make you think well of us. We've felt for a long time that most textbooks are written for your instructor.

Writing textbooks for your instructor instead of for you is natural enough, in a way. Instructors, after all, must teach from the books, and no book that makes them unhappy is going to find its way into the classroom. Still, this book is written for you. Its purpose is to help you become a better writer than you are now. We believe that if you read this book carefully and ask questions in class whenever there are points you have any trouble with, you can improve your writing significantly. Neither we nor anyone else knows how to teach you to be a great writer, but—with your active participation—we think we can teach you to handle competently any writing assignment you're likely to get.

We've tried to write this book in a straightforward, unfussy fashion. We've tried to concentrate as much as possible on being helpful about writing situations that you'll really be faced with in class. We've tried to pick reading selections that we think will interest you, as they have interested our own students, and that demonstrate writing principles you can apply to your own work. We've included a number of student writings, too, because we feel that comparing your work solely to that of experienced professionals is unprofitable and unfair. These writings were prepared by college students for classes similar to the one you're taking. Most of them are solid, honest pieces of work—but that's all. They are not intended to dazzle you with their genius, and they didn't all get A's in class either. We hope you'll use them as general points of reference, not as supreme models of excellence. We hope that you'll often outdo them in your own writing.

Now for your first lesson.

While this book will give you a great deal of information about writing, almost all of that information grows out of four simple ideas—ideas that are sufficiently important and usable to be thought of as rules. We're not peddling magic formulas, however, and we're not suggesting that a ready-made list of rules and regulations can substitute for the experiences and discoveries and sheer hard work by which writers educate themselves. No list ever made the pain of having nothing to say less painful. And people—not lists—write dramatic first sentences, come up with fresh insights, and choose the perfect word. Any rules we set down here or elsewhere are useful only because they can give direction and control to the inevitable hard work and thus increase the chances that the hard work will be worth the effort.

Don't approach the four simple ideas that follow, therefore, as representing more than important guidelines. They're starting points, but they're not eternal truths. George Orwell once drew up a list of rules for writing, the last of which was, "Break any of these rules rather than say anything outright barbarous." As a more immediate example, this book will advise you to write well-developed paragraphs and avoid sentence fragments. That's excellent advice, and we take it seriously, but just two paragraphs ago we deliberately wrote a five-word paragraph that also happened to be a sentence fragment. Enough said.

Here are the four ideas on which much of this book is based:

1. Except for a few commonsense exceptions such as recipes, technical manuals, encyclopedia articles, and certain kinds of stories, poems, and plays, *writing should state a central idea.* (We call that central idea—or position, or stand, or contention—the *thesis.*)
2. *The primary function of writing is to prove or support its thesis.*
3. *The most effective and interesting way to prove or support the thesis is to use specific facts presented in specific language.*
4. *Writing needs to be well organized. Every statement must be logically connected to the thesis.*

We'll be repeating and expanding and sometimes strongly qualifying these ideas throughout the book, but they are the heart of what we have to say. They are not obscure secrets or brand new discoveries. They are the assumptions about writing that nearly all good writers make. They are the principles that nearly all good writers try to put into practice in their own work.

In the chapters that follow, we will discuss in detail the full meaning and implications of these ideas and try to show you the most effective ways of applying them to common classroom writing assignments.

D. S.
F. C.

STUDENT'S
BOOK OF
COLLEGE
ENGLISH

Once you have found your thesis, hold on to it!

PART 1

FUNDAMENTALS

The Principles of Good Writing

1
FINDING A THESIS

2
SUPPORTING THE THESIS: LOGIC

3
PLANNING A PAPER: OUTLINING

4
WRITING A PAPER: AN OVERVIEW

CHAPTER 1

FINDING A THESIS

We'll begin by admitting that writing well isn't easy. But we believe that following some well-chosen pieces of advice can make it easier than many freshman English students expect. Our first piece of advice is *think before you write.* Much of what makes any piece of writing good takes place before the writer ever puts pen to paper. In this chapter we will discuss the kind of thinking you should do before you begin to write.

Limiting the subject. Many college composition books begin by advising the student to choose a subject, but we won't do that because we think it's needless advice. After all, no one writes in a vacuum. If you choose to write on your own, you do so because you're so interested in a subject—a sport, a vacation, a candidate, a book, a love affair—that you want to share your thoughts with others. Your enthusiasm selects your subject. If you don't actually "choose" to write but are told to do so by an instructor or employer, your general subject will usually be given to you. Your professor of world history won't simply tell you to write a paper; he will assign a ten-page paper on some effects of Islamic culture upon the Western world. Your employer won't merely ask for a report; she will ask for an analysis of your office's operations which includes recommendations for cutting costs and increasing productivity. Even when your assignment is an essay based on a personal experience, your instructor will give you a general subject: a memorable journey, an influential person, a goal, a hobby, a favorite newspaper or magazine. Choosing the subject, then, isn't really a problem.

But most subjects need to be *limited,* and that sometimes is a problem. Suppose, for instance, that your instructor is an old-fashioned type and wants you to write about your vacation. No matter how short your vacation might have been, if you set out to discuss every detail of it, you could fill a book. Since most classroom assignments call for only three hundred to one thousand words, the subject must be limited. You must decide what part of the subject you will write about. A good way to begin is to jot down memorable moments, pleasant and unpleasant. Even that list may prove to be lengthy. You might remember dancing all night and then going for a swim at sunrise, or the day your foreign car broke down in a small town where the only mechanic would service nothing but American products, or eating your first lobster, or meeting a village character, or watching the sunset over the ocean, or sleeping out under the stars, or being stuck at the top of a Ferris wheel for two hours. You might have noticed differences among motels and restaurants, or various accents might have fascinated you. Any one of these memories could make a good paper. How do you choose?

Let your major interests decide for you. If you have a sense of the comic, you might decide to write about the mechanic who couldn't help you, or about sitting high in the air on a broken Ferris wheel, or about your first attempt to get meat from a lobster shell. If you like to study people, you might decide to write about the village character, or about the people you met when you danced all night, or about the personalities of the waitresses who served you. If the way people talk interests you, the accents or colorful expressions of those you met on your journey could make a good subject for a paper. If scenery appeals to you, describe that sunset or sunrise or those stars. If you should find that no one experience is more memorable than another—and that rarely happens—flip a coin and settle on one so you can get on with writing your paper. You will probably have other opportunities to write about the remaining memories.

"All right," you may protest, "it would be easy enough to settle on a subject if I never had to write about anything but my vacation. But what about my history paper?" As a beginning student of history (or sociology or economics), you may feel that your problem is finding enough to say about any given subject, not limiting the subject. Still, we insist that almost every subject can and must be limited, even when some limiting has already been done by the instructor.

Take that assignment about the effects of Islamic culture on the West, for example. Your first reaction might well be to try to assemble any effects you could come up with, devoting one section of your paper to each effect—but that would lead to a very dull paper. Think a minute. If your instructor expects you to handle some part of that topic, you have had some preparation for it. You've probably read part of a textbook and heard lectures on the subject; you've heard class discussions about it; perhaps you've been asked to do some supplementary reading in the library. From all of these sources, you've already begun to appreciate the vastness of the subject, even before doing any further research.

As with your vacation, you can still limit the subject, and again your special interests can determine how you limit it. If, for example, you have a good understanding of architecture, you may decide to explain how the Islamic culture, forbidden by its religion to use human images, contributed to modern architecture by exploring the possibilities of geometric forms. Or you might discuss the influence on modern sculpture of geometric form as design. If you're a nursing or pre-med student, you could trace the contributions of the Islamic world to medical science. If you're an interested observer of the political scene, you might discuss the effects on early Islamic cultures of the lack of a centralized government, comparing these cultures with others of the same period that were governed by a pope or emperor. Your interests could lead to other subjects—from military strategy to love poems—and still fulfill the assignment. Any subject, then, can and must be limited before you begin to write, and your personal interests can often determine the way you limit it.

Setting your purpose. Once you've limited your subject, you need to set your purpose, and doing so involves a number of related choices.

First, you need to decide how you will treat your limited subject, what you will do with it. Will you *describe* a process—for example, how to pitch a tent? Will you *compare* two campsites? Will you *report* an event—what happened when you unwittingly pitched your tent in a cow pasture? Will you *argue* that one can have an enjoyable yet inexpensive vacation by camping in state parks?

You can't hope to write a coherent paper until you decide what you will do with your subject because that decision determines, in large measure, what you include and what you leave out. If, for example, you decide to describe how to pitch a tent, you won't discuss the deep satisfaction to be gained by sleeping under the stars or the delicious taste of a fish that you've caught yourself and cooked over an open fire. You have decided to give instructions for a particular activity, and you will do just that in the clearest manner possible. If, on the other hand, you choose to argue that camping in state parks is enjoyable, you might very well describe not only the joy of sleeping under the stars and cooking over an open fire, but also the conveniences provided to campers by the park system and the fun of meeting people in the relaxed atmosphere that a campfire creates.

A second choice is your *audience.* What kind of reader are you writing for? The answer to that question will affect the style and content of your paper.

Pretend, for a moment, that while driving your father's car to school the other day, you were stopped for speeding but were able to talk the officer out of giving you a ticket. How did you talk to the officer? Later you ran into a good friend at the snack bar. How did you describe the incident to your friend? You hadn't planned to tell your father at all, but at dinner your tongue slipped, the fact was out, and your father demanded an explanation. How did you describe the incident to your father? The kind of language, the tone of voice, even the facts selected were different in each case, weren't they?

That's the way it is with writing. The words a writer chooses and the facts a writer selects are largely determined by who will read the material. One physician writing to another physician may say,

> In the web of the patient's left thumb and forefinger, there is a 1½ centimeter slightly raised, mildly erythematous and tender, soft furuncle-appearing lesion that blanches with pressure.

The patient, in writing a letter to a close friend, may say,

> I've been in pretty good health lately—except for a little sore on my left hand. It's red and tender and looks like a boil. I suppose I should ask the doctor about it.

The audience makes a difference in what writers say and how they say it.

You may now be thinking that any discussion of audience is pointless because you know who your reader is—your English professor. In one sense, that's true, of course. But you'll write better papers if, instead of thinking of your English professor every time you begin to write, you imagine another specific kind of reader. After all, English professors are an adaptable lot, and they can assume the personalities of many different kinds of readers when they pick up your paper. So define a reader. Are you writing for a group of experts on your subject? For your classmates? For the president of your company? For readers of the editorial page of the morning paper? For readers of *Playboy? Good Housekeeping?* For the "general reader"? (See "Miscellaneous Do's and Don'ts," p. 433.) It's a good idea to approach these audiences differently. Defining the reader not only helps you decide the style and exact content of your paper, but also makes for livelier reading. Writing addressed to no one in particular instead of to real people can't be fully satisfying.

A third choice—and one closely related to defining the reader—is the author image you want to present to your reader. This image, this personality, is essential if you want the paper to read as if it were written by a human being, not by a computer. Are you a specialist writing for nonspecialists? Are you an expert writing for other experts? Are you an average citizen writing for other average citizens? Are you an employee suggesting a change in policy to the president of your company? And how do you feel about your sub-

ject? Do you love it? Do you hate it? Are you angry? Calm and reasonable? Mildly amused? Detached? Delighted? Are you optimistic?
Pessimistic? In short, what personality do you want to project?

The final choice you face is deciding how you want to affect your
audience: How do you want to make your appeal? Do you want to
amuse as well as persuade? Do you want to move the readers to
tears? Do you simply want them to understand your subject more
fully? Or perhaps follow your advice? This choice, too, is important
to the total effect of your paper.

All these choices—your treatment of the subject, your audience,
your author image, your effect on the audience—determine the purpose of your paper. And the purpose controls the style and content of
the paper—its organization, its facts, its diction, its tone.

In the following paper, for example, the writer chose to describe a
process, how to mail an electrical appliance to a service center. That
choice alone could have led to a very different—and much
duller—paper than the one he wrote. What other choices did he
make? How did those choices brighten the paper?

Just Mail It to Your Nearest Service Center
LARRY OLSON

Occasionally, an electrical appliance—a toaster, a mixer, a coffee
maker—ceases to function properly and must be got to a service
center for repair. Getting it to such a center is simple enough if the manufacturer of the appliance has one in your city and if you have access to it
by automobile. But this is not always the case.

More than likely the manufacturer's nearest center is in a distant part
of your state, or in a different state altogether. More than likely the
necessary work cannot be done by a general repair shop where you live or
by a neighborhood handyman. Each company has its own appliance de-
signs, its own parts lists.

Your only way of having the job done, then, may be by mailing the
appliance directly to the service center. Usually, you can find its address in
the literature that came with the new appliance itself. Or you can get the
address by telephone from the store where you made the purchase.

But now comes the biggest job of all—packaging the appliance, anything
from toaster to roaster, and getting it on its way.

First, you must find a strong cardboard box of appropriate size at some
kindly, familiar store and pack the appliance in the box with crumpled
newspaper, excelsior, or styrofoam materials, the kind your old Christmas
presents came packed in. (What a good idea it is to save some of these
materials for just such emergencies!)

Then you must close the carton with your own combination of wide tape and strong cord, keeping in mind that damage in transit is not covered by the manufacturer's guarantee.

On the carton, print very carefully, in large letters, the name and address of the service center, with your own name and address in the upper left-hand corner.

Write a letter telling as nearly as you can what is wrong with the appliance and where and when you bought it. Place the letter in an envelope bearing the name and address of the service center and your return address. Carefully secure it with tape to the outside of the carton, but be sure you do not cover the address you printed directly on the carton. The envelope should have its own postage stamp. (Now, if the envelope comes off, both it and the carton will still reach the service center.)

The Post Office will weigh the package for you, insure it against loss, and tell you the proper amount of postage. Now place the right number of stamps on the package. (Remember that the attached envelope must have its own stamp.) And good luck all the way!

Questions for Writing or Discussion

1. The author chose to describe the process of mailing an electrical appliance to a service center. Can you think of other ways to treat the subject of malfunctioning appliances?
2. What kind of audience do you think the author had in mind? Why do you think so?
3. What image or personality does the author project? Why do you think so?
4. What is the author's attitude toward the task he describes? Do you share it? Does the attitude affect the way you receive the instructions set forth in the paper?
5. How does the title of the paper contribute to the author's purpose?

Stating a thesis. Having limited your subject and determined your purpose, you could, in a few cases, begin organizing your material. The writer of "Just Mail It to Your Nearest Service Center," for example, chose to describe a process. All he had to do was divide the process into steps and describe each step fully in the language appropriate to his purpose. Similarly, some of the reports you must write, such as those for your chemistry class, often require merely a straightforward presentation of what happens when. Or a question on a psychology exam might call for a classification of types of schizophrenia, in which case you would put labels on each type and describe each fully. But apart from highly specialized kinds of papers such as technical descriptions and reports, we argue that *most* good writing, even classification or process papers, benefits from a central idea. The idea unifies the paper.

Think, for example, how dull and rambling a report about spending Christmas day with the family would be if you should begin with rising early in the morning and continue through brushing your teeth and dressing and so on until you report retiring at midnight. But many of the details of the day can be given life if you settle on a central idea: *Having Christmas dinner at my family's house requires nerves of steel.* Now you have a focus for the details. Mother takes the joy out of eating by constantly reminding the family that she overcooked the turkey, undercooked the peas, and forgot to make the cranberry relish. Father won't let the family eat anyhow because every fifteen minutes they must smile for his new, expensive camera and then listen to him swear at the defective flash bulbs. Kid Brother must be restrained from injuring other members of the family by shooting them with rubber bullets from his new Super-Duper Killer Gun. Grandpa drones on about how this younger generation doesn't understand the true meaning of Christmas. Sister Suzy sulks because her boyfriend didn't give her the diamond ring she had expected, while Sister Josephine complains because she didn't get a bonus from her company. Having a central idea enables you to select the details that make for a lively paper.

To be sure you have the kind of central idea that will lead to an interesting and unified paper, you still have one more step to take in the process of thinking before writing: *You must state a thesis.*

A *thesis* is the position a writer takes on an arguable point—one on which more than one opinion is possible. It is the main idea which the paper will prove. The writer's purpose is to convince the reader that this position or idea is valid. A thesis statement is a one-sentence summary of the idea the writer will defend: *Students in technical programs should be required to take some courses in the humanities,* for example; or *The registration procedure on our campus could be simplified.*

With few exceptions, the papers you will be asked to write in college will benefit enormously from a thesis. Your professors will expect you to do more than merely arrange the facts you have gleaned from a course in some logical order; they are interested in what you think about the facts. They will expect you to make some statement about the facts, to show what point you think the facts add up to. A professor of American literature won't ask you to summarize *Huckleberry Finn.* He wants to know what conclusions you reached after a careful reading of the novel: *Mark Twain's* Huckleberry Finn *is an indictment of slavery,* let's say; or *Mark Twain in* Huckleberry Finn *criticizes the violence of the pre-Civil War South.* Until you can make that kind of statement, you aren't ready to write because you don't have clearly in mind the point you will make. And if you aren't certain of what your idea is, you stand little chance of convincing a reader of its validity. It's important, therefore, to spend time thinking your idea through before you start writing. This will save time and grief in the long run.

A good thesis has five characteristics:

It can usually be stated in one complete sentence. That doesn't mean you must present the thesis statement, word for word, in the paper itself. In fact, once you start writing, you may find that you want to devote a paragraph or more to presenting the idea of your paper. Still, it's good to have a one-sentence statement in mind before you begin writing. Until you can state the idea in one sentence, you may not have it under control.

A good thesis makes a statement about *the facts.* To say that Brutus stabbed Shakespeare's Julius Caesar on the Ides of March is to state a fact. A thesis, a statement *about* the fact, might read, *Brutus succeeds in killing Caesar on the Ides of March because Caesar has grown too arrogant and proud to protect himself.*

A good thesis is limited; that is, the idea started must be one that can be clearly explained, supported, and illustrated in the space called for. A long magazine article might have as its thesis, *Contemporary soap operas appeal to all levels of society because the directors employ sophisticated camera techniques, the writers deal with current social problems, the actors have time to develop characters who become as familiar as old friends, and the plots provide a kind of suspense missing from prime-time shows.* But this won't do for a thousand-word paper; the thesis could not be developed fully in that short a space. A better thesis for a short paper might read, *Contemporary soap operas are thought-provoking because they often deal with current social problems.* An even better thesis would be, *The realistic treatment in* Ryan's Hope *of withdrawing life support from terminally ill patients effectively presented the dilemma doctors face in such cases.*

A good thesis is unified. Consider the thesis, *Computer teaching machines often get good results, but some of the programs need to be refined, and the college should not purchase the machines until the refinements have been made.* This thesis says three things about computer teaching machines: (1) They get good results; (2) they need refining; (3) they should not be purchased until the refinements are made. A writer who begins with such a thesis runs the risk of writing a three-part paper that has no central control. The point of emphasis is not clear. To emphasize that the machines should not be purchased just yet, the writer must subordinate the other points to that idea.

> Although the computer teaching machines often get good results, they should not be purchased by the college until all the programs have been refined.

To emphasize the effectiveness of the machines, the writer should subordinate the need to wait for refinements before purchase.

> Although the college should delay purchase of computer teaching machines until all programs are refined, the machines often get good results.

A good thesis is precise. It lets the reader and the writer know exactly what the paper will contain. Words such as *good, interesting, impressive,* and *many* are too vague to do the job. They say nothing about the subject: what is interesting or good to one person may appear dull or offensive to another. Don't say, "Agatha Christie's detective stories are good." Say, instead, "Agatha Christie's detective stories appeal to those who enjoy solving puzzles." Don't say, "My history class is interesting." Say, "My professor makes history easy to understand."

But enough of rules. Below is a student paper which illustrates a carefully defined thesis: *The highly organized celebration of today's Halloween deprives youngsters of the kind of joy I experienced during the Halloweens of my childhood.* As you read the paper, notice how the writer's choices of audience and author image contribute to the development of her thesis.

Too Bad About Ol' Halloween
SHIRLEY LYTTON-CANNON

As I was sitting at the kitchen table one morning last week having my second cup of coffee and staring, as usual, at the back of the cereal box which promised me that its breakfast plan could help me lose the extra ten-pound ball and chain I was dragging around with me, I noticed the note my fifth-grade son had brought home from school the day before. It gave instructions as to how Halloween is to be celebrated in our community this year. As I read it, I could just about hear his pinch-nosed principal dictating it.

1. Only children who are toddler age to the fourth grade are allowed to trick-or-treat. These children must be accompanied by a parent or another adult.
2. Trick-or-treating may be done from 5:00 P.M. to 6:00 P.M. only, and only at the houses where a porch light is burning.
3. Only manufacturer prewrapped and sealed treats may be given.
4. Children from the fifth grade and older should meet at the elementary school for a Halloween party. Admission 75 cents.

There was something that made me dislike the whole thing. It certainly didn't seem like much of a celebration to me, but then it dawned on me that Halloween is one more thing that has changed with time and circumstance. My experience of Halloween while growing up in a rural area of West Virginia was certainly different from the experience offered my son by this superorganized, unexciting little program I was about to thumbtack to our bulletin board.

There were certainly no age restrictions then. If you were too young to find your way after dark up and down the footpaths which led to the various houses, perhaps an older brother would take you out for an hour or so and then bring you home so he could get on with his own "Halloweening." In fact, many young-at-hearts would don masks belonging to the younger children and trick-or-treat homes of friends who were known for the quality of their hard cider.

A time restriction was also unknown then. If any poor soul had dared to suggest setting a time limit of 5:00 to 6:00 P.M., he would surely have been branded a sourpuss, stick-in-the-mud, spoilsport or tightwad, and probably would have paid dearly for his lack of sensitivity for many Halloween nights to come. It seems to me that the unspoken rule was that we confine our trick-or-treating to Halloween night after dark, although a few cheeky boys would occasionally make the rounds the night before also. As I remember, they didn't do too badly. It wouldn't have done much good for people to burn porch lights as a signal of some kind, for part of the fun was unscrewing light bulbs as we left.

And we would never have settled for the candy treats of today (if you care to call them treats), the generally tough little waxy-tasting blobs, all prewrapped and sealed, preferably by Price-Waterhouse, to ward off the growing number of "sickos" who hate children as well as Halloween. Our treats were mostly homemade cookies and candy, with the best being given by Mrs. Wright or Opal Morgan. Mrs. Wright gave us popcorn balls that were a deliciously sticky reminder that Christmas was near, and Opal Morgan made melt-in-your-mouth peanut butter fudge which she passed out in fat, soft, unwrapped squares to be devoured on the spot.

But I think it was item 4 of the Halloween instructions that saddened me most. As I reread the instructions telling us of the party for older children, I understood the principal's reasoning, but I was sorry that my son was probably never going to have memories of mischievous "tricking" on Halloween night. Parties are okay, but they're no match for the exhilarating feeling of sneaking around in the dark, going from house to house soaping windows, throwing handfuls of shelled corn on porches and roofs, and then running and laughing as the owners came out the door to try to catch us at our work. There were always a couple of outhouses that were tipped over on their sides each year, or sometimes we'd get black grease from the mines and paint a nice big line of grease around the seat hole. Someone painted grease on our seat one year, and if I could have found out who it was, I would have thanked him personally, because my oldest sister, Mary Lou, who was acting very grown-up and prissy in those days, made a trip to the outhouse just before her date arrived to take her out. Her screams of angry protest made a lovely Halloween.

As I recall it, we went pretty easy on the people we thought were nice and then stepped up our activity as we got to houses owned by people who were known for their contrary dispositions. Most of us kids had had run-ins with them at one time or another during the year, and since we always had to ''respect our elders,'' Halloween was the only time to get even. There was one particular man, Ol' Will Honeycutt, who seemed always to take the brunt of the tricking, and for good reason. He was the most sour, narrow-minded, loud-mouthed human being I have ever come across to this day. Every year we'd all get together and try to outdo each other in thinking of ways to fix him. One year we got fresh cow manure from the field and put it into a paper bag. Without making a sound, about six of us tiptoed onto his front porch, lit the bag with a match, pounded on the door as hard as we could, and then ran off the porch like a herd of stampeding elephants. Ol' Will came rushing out the door, saw the burning bag, and immediately stamped it out with his work boots. Lucky for him that he always wore the kind with high tops! Some pretty colorful language followed us into the dark night that year.

I guess I have never heard of a Halloween trick more creative than the one pulled off by my teenage cousins, Billy Gene, Bobby Lee, Joey, and Frankie Wisenhunt. They were all big, husky farm boys who had worked at one time or another for Ol' Will, and they knew of his disposition firsthand. That particular year they waited until about eleven o'clock when they could be sure he was sleeping, and then, carrying a bucket of whitewash, started walking toward Ol' Will's barn and a long night's work. Now Ol' Will had a wagon and a team of four black horses which he cared more about than he did for his wife and kids. The boys very quietly and expertly, I must admit, disassembled the wagon, hoisted the pieces up the side of the barn to the roof, and then reassembled and tied it across the eaves of the barn roof. When Ol' Will walked out the next morning, he not only saw his wagon perched on the roof, but inside the barn he found a team of zebras with whitewash stripes! He never did find out who the culprits were, but when I read about the people who play horrible tricks on children on Halloween, I sometimes wonder if maybe Ol' Will is back and trying to get even.

Well, that was a long time ago, and things do change—sometimes for the better, and sometimes for the worse. It really is too bad about Ol' Halloween, but not about Ol' Will.

Questions for Writing or Discussion

1. Does the writer state her thesis in one sentence? If so, where?
2. Does the writer's mention of the text on her cereal box and her need to lose weight contribute to her idea? If not, do the opening sentences contribute to the development of the paper? If so, how?
3. The writer devotes a disproportionate amount of her paper to the tricking that took place during her childhood. Do you feel that so much attention to tricking makes her paper seem unbalanced? Do you think the emphasis on her childhood experiences contributes to her purpose? If so, how?
4. What kind of audience is addressed in this paper? Why do you think so?
5. What author image does the writer present?
6. Select at least five phrases or words that are especially appropriate to the author's purpose.
7. Select at least five details that are especially appropriate to the author's purpose.

Now for another example. Below is a magazine article with a clearly defined thesis. See what you think of it.

F. Patrick Magee
LET'S HEAR IT FOR NEAT AND TIDY!

Why is it the slobs always get the good press? Is there anything more durable or lovable than the portrait of the rumpled-but-brilliant scientist rummaging through a desk piled high with books, papers, and yesterday's lunch? Or the house-bound soul scuffing about in mismatched slippers, soup-stained bathrobe, and rat's-nest hair style? Slobs, we think, are kind of like the frayed teddy bear everyone carried around as a kid. Companionable, mellow, huggable, just plain darn nice to have around.

Consider how cruel we are, by contrast, to the tidy individual. Oh, that Harriet, we taunt, what a neatness freak. Fussy. Smug. Uptight. The neat run white-gloved fingers over your window sills. Or arch a displeased nostril when the door of the ice box is opened. Odious! Then, too, we baste them in the sludge of psychological jargon. Compulsive. Manic. Anal retentive. The next time you watch "The Odd Couple," ask yourself, whom do I love? Trim, tidy Felix Unger? Or good old slobby Oscar Madison?

On behalf of the neat people of the world, I *object* to all this mindless propaganda. You see, we neatniks (and I'm proud to call myself one) don't really expect to perfect the world and then give it a glossy hard-wax shine. We just can't abide disorder. After all, aren't you *wiser* to label and file a report as soon as it comes in than to squander an afternoon hunting for it two weeks later? I see no logic in unnecessary trips to the laundromat and ironing board because it *seems* easier to let the garments fall where they may at day's end. A sloppy person just makes more drone work for him/ herself; if *I* want to waste time, I'd rather do it poolside or with popcorn and a grade-B horror movie.

Besides, have you ever actually *worked* alongside one of those supposedly cute and cuddly slobs? They always seem to be rooting around *your* desk looking for the correspondence that's actually in *their* desk beneath a 1969 copy of *U.S. News and World Report.* When they stand up to make a sales presentation, why is it their charts are in the mailroom, their notes in the bathroom, and the slide projector out in the parking lot in the trunk of their car? And how many times have you come back from lunch to hear, "A man called. I wrote his number down somewhere . . . oh, darn. But don't worry, he said he'll call back."

Worse yet, try *living* with a slob . . . a thrill only if you *enjoy* the sight of clothes strewn across floors like lilies on a frog pond. Or think it's fun when the heating of a single can of tomato soup leaves every white-faced surface in the kitchen with a pink polka-dot glow. Or relish rifling through the crazed coffee-table clutter to find your unpaid bills, personal letters, and favorite magazines. And, as if being forced to exist in involuntary squalor weren't enough, guess who always gets stuck doing the picking up, scrubbing up, and sorting out.

Actually, maybe I shouldn't be too upset that people, at least in the abstract, love slobs and hate neatniks. I mean, slobs have so very little *else* going for them. Disorganized, they fritter away energy; muddled, they antagonize wherever they go. They're sort of like a rusty old scow of a tanker steaming through life at quarter speed, spreading an oil slick behind. My only question is, where did they find such a good publicity agent?

Questions for Writing or Discussion

1. In one complete sentence, state the thesis of the article.
2. The author gives three major reasons why he doesn't like slobs. What are they? Do they support the thesis?
3. What personality does the author project? Is it appropriate to his subject?
4. The author uses a number of sentence fragments. Find five sentence fragments. Do you think they are appropriate to the author image being projected? Why, or why not?
5. What kind of audience is addressed by the article? Might slobs be a part of that audience?
6. Using Magee's article as a model, write a paper that favors slobs.

Exercise A

Which of the following items are thesis statements and which are not? Revise those that are not into acceptable thesis statements. Which of the original thesis statements are too general or too lacking in unity to make a good paper?

1. How to use less gasoline.
2. Television debates between political candidates are a waste of time.
3. Langston Hughes is a famous black poet.
4. Professor Smith is a terrible teacher.
5. Professor Smith grades unfairly.
6. Walking to class is interesting.
7. The best way to enjoy a fine wine.
8. Helpful faculty and upperclass students made my first day at college much easier than I expected.
9. The vocabulary used by *Time* requires constant trips to the dictionary. *Time* slants its reports to suit its political bias. The reports in *Time* are entertaining and informative.
10. The trouble with newspapers is that they never report good news.

Exercise B

Read the following article carefully and then, by answering the questions at the end of the article, see if you can state the thesis.

Dan Wakefield
WHY SOAP OPERAS ARE SO POPULAR

One of the most popular pastimes in America is largely regarded as a secret shame. Despite a growing (if often grudging) acknowledgement by the media that this kind of entertainment may not be all bad, many of the 20 million citizens who enjoy it every day are still reluctant to admit their habit in polite society. And yet it is not illegal, illicit or immoral.

It's soap opera.

Since the days of *Ma Perkins* and *The Romance of Helen Trent* on radio to the present era of *The Young and the Restless* and *Another World* on television, soaps have been accused of causing a staggering number of maladies, including high blood pressure, un-Americanism, shrinking of the brain, vertigo and "perversity."

Even the increasing variety of people who admit and defend their "soap"-watching face the attitude described by author Beth Gutcheon, who wrote in *MS.* magazine that "the fact that you're watching soaps isn't the sort of thing you want to get around."

The image of the typical soap viewer is that óf the cartoon housewife in her tattered bathrobe popping bonbons all day and nipping from a bottle of cooking sherry. No doubt there are fans of such description, but they can hardly be accounted representative of the vast and various audience that is tuned in to soaps today, an audience that includes men as well as women, college students and senior citizens, garage mechanics and economists, New York street-gang members and professors of literature, secretaries and civil servants (who watch on their lunch hours), artists and housewives, actors and salesmen.

If there's any more misleading cliché than that "typical" mindless, sherry-soaked fan, it's the cliché of the soap-opera programs themselves as interchangeable sagas of sobbing women wringing their dishpan hands over unrequited love for the doctor who saved their life with emergency surgery, played in the slowest drag-time dialogue with melodramatic organ music in the background and nothing but a steady supply of coffee to nourish the neurotic characters.

Most current soaps are far more sophisticated technically as well as thematically, with, for instance, "libraries" of tape-recorded orchestra music replacing the old organ trills, inventive camera work with fade-outs for flashbacks, story lines built around contemporary social and psychological problems such as child abuse, women's conflict with marriage and career, venereal disease, ecology, female frigidity and teen-age runaways.

Several years ago, *One Life to Live* shot scenes on location at New York City's Odyssey House for drug rehabilitation, letting real ex-addicts speak of their experiences, while an actress on the program played a troubled drug user. This year [1976] the new show, *Ryan's Hope,* built a moving story around the moral and legal questions of withdrawing life support from a patient who had lost all medical hope of being more than a human vegetable. But these new, more topical problems have not simply replaced the old heartaches in the teary twilight that once typified soap opera and is still believed to be its sole climate by critics who haven't watched the programs in the past five years. Certainly there are plenty of tears in the current daytime dramas, but there is also a pleasant new presence of laughter, fun and playfulness on many of the programs.

You can still find soaps that employ the old formula elements of the genre to greater or lesser degree. But the fact is there are now 14 soaps on the air, and they're as different and similar as, say, 14 popular novels might be. They share certain things in common due to limitations of time, budget, format and tradition, but their settings, themes and plots, their ambience and attitudes differ greatly and appeal to different sorts of people.

Some viewers are drawn to the social contrasts dramatized in *One Life to Live,* with its mixture of working-class Poles, socialite WASP's, middle-class blacks and Catholic nuns. Others prefer *Another World* of affluent Beautiful People elegantly dressed, discoursing about polo, painting and architecture as well as the inevitable personal problems of daily-life drama.

Soap fans today may choose, according to their own taste, the mystery-story aura of *The Edge of Night,* or the sense of home and roots reflected in

All My Children, or the psychiatric orientation of *General Hospital*, with its convincing dramatizations of doctor-patient therapy sessions. Millions still love the more old-fashioned style and feeling of *As the World Turns*, whose focus on the familiar themes of love and marriage in smalltown Midwestern America still appeals to fans after 20 years on the air. Many new viewers are enthused about the youngest soap entry that debuted last summer, *Ryan's Hope*, the first serial to be set in New York City, built around an Irish-Catholic family whose parents run the local bar and grille, and their friends and neighbors who include politicians, reporters and a canny local underworld boss. . . .

Perhaps it's not the story per se that captivates a fan but a particular actor or actress. One of the factors that has raised the quality of soaps in the past five years or so is the caliber of the cast members, many of whom have experience in Hollywood or on Broadway and find in daytime drama one of the steadiest and most lucrative sorts of theater work today, with salaries for stars going as high as $100,000 a year—and the likelihood of highly paid commercial work deriving from their high visibility and popularity with viewers.

Ruth Warrick, the actress who originally gained fame playing the first wife of "Citizen Kane" opposite Orson Welles and has appeared in 31 movies, has worked on TV soaps since the late 1950's. She says that actors and actresses who once scoffed at her doing soaps have changed their attitude: *"Now* they ask if I can help *them* get on a soap!"

Ruth also finds she gets more recognition and enthusiasm from her soap-opera roles than for her work in movies and theater. At a fashionable cocktail party for the road-company cast of *Irene* in Chicago she was politely applauded for her role in the musical until one woman cried out in recognition, "That's 'Phoebe Tyler'!" the role she plays on *All My Children*, and the place went wild.

Fans regard actors on soaps as *being* the role they play, not because of stupidity or naïveté, but because a different, more intimate relationship exists between the audience and cast of a soap than with a movie or a play. In a movie or play you see an actress play a role, and no matter how well she does it or how many times you go back to see it, she'll say the same lines, behave the same way, and her fate in the story will be the same. On soaps, however, you watch an actress or actor several times to five times a week, and every day they'll say and do different things, and maybe even their personality will change in the months and years that the story continues. An inevitable intimacy develops between the fans and the characters, a sense of closeness and kinship that you would feel for a friend or neighbor whom you see in the course of your daily life.

When I go to a movie I come back and talk about seeing, say, Mia Farrow playing the role of "Daisy Buchanan" in *The Great Gatsby*, or Al Pacino playing the role of "Michael Corleone" in *The Godfather*, but I don't think of those actors as *being* those characters. Yet, even though I know Mary Fickett, the first person to win an Emmy for acting in a soap opera, when I watch her on *All My Children*, I don't think of her as Mary Fickett playing "Nurse Ruth Martin," I think of her as "Nurse Ruth Martin." Discussing the show with other fans, I say things such as, "Do you think anyone as loyal as 'Ruth Martin' would really leave her husband for that new young guy with the beard?"

Okay, I know in my mind the difference between the player and the role on a soap, just as I'm sure Sammy Davis Jr. knows, but I understand why, when he and his wife pulled up at a stop light on Sunset Boulevard and saw in the next car the young actor Nick Benedict who plays "Phil Brent" on *All My Children*, Davis yelled over, "Hey, 'Phil,' don't marry 'Erica'!" . . .

Many people living alone find their favorite soaps provide a substitute family that serves not only as an entertainment but as a kind of nourishment, a human contact and connection. In our time of swift social change and uprootedness, people of all ages and backgrounds find in the continuing daytime dramas a sense of stability and support.

Soap watching amounts to a craze among college students, with fans gathering to watch their favorite serials in fraternity houses and dormitories and student unions on campuses as disparate as Columbia University, Wheaton College, the University of Northern Illinois, Brooklyn College, and the University of Texas. In the past few years, some soaps have even been taught as part of the curriculum in courses on popular culture at Princeton, and anthropology at Ohio State; but the students' interest isn't so much academic as social and personal. They find their favorite soaps entertaining—and fun. The fun isn't only in watching but in talking about them afterward, debating the age-old question of all good story-telling: What will happen next?

This question is one of the bases of the continuing appeal of the soaps, for if it is answered in one of the show's "story lines," it is raised in another; if one couple is reconciled, another is rudely torn asunder, posing anew the question of what will happen next. This is an element that prime-time shows can't employ, for by their very nature the answer to "what happens" must be given at the end of the half-hour or hour. Each episode is complete in itself, and each of the main characters remains the same for whatever challenge will be faced in the following week. There will be new criminals for "Kojak" to capture, but "Kojak" will remain "Kojak," just as "Mary Tyler Moore" will remain "Mary Tyler Moore," and "The Rookies" will remain "The Rookies" through all these shows, which are like a series of miniature movies starring the same character rather than like a serial. . . .

The serial form [has] . . . built-in problems . . . for . . . TV dramatists, for instance, in the recognition that for each new installment there may be new . . . viewers who are coming upon the story for the first time and so there has to be continual recapitulation of what has gone before, of what the relationships are among the characters. On the soaps this leads to a sometimes dreary retelling of events by one character to another, repetitive recitals of what happened yesterday or last week that many viewers already know. It is this necessity that leads to the frequency of those kaffeeklatsches where relatives or neighbors fill one another—and thus the audience—in as to what's going on.

Daytime serials on TV are also handicapped by low budgets, a lack of space and limited numbers of sets. One reason for the popularity of hospitals is that they provide a common, useful meeting place for a variety of characters. Many soaps now have their own restaurant where couples and friends and even large groups meet and talk. Soap producer Bud Kloss says people kid him that in Pine Valley, the fictional town of his show, "the main industry must be restaurants," because they often use a set designed as a restaurant for people to meet in.

The low budgets may handicap the producers of soaps, but they also help make them the most profitable shows on the networks. The three major networks spend an estimated $50 million a year on the 14 daily soaps in return for a gross of roughly $300 million. The lavish production of the prime-time shows means they often take a loss, and as any member of a daytime serial or its production staff is quick to point out, "We support the nighttime shows."

The nighttime dramas are flashier, prettier, more prestigious, and yet most of them come and go, are canceled quickly, replaced by another souped-up production, while the soaps plod along quietly year after year. Because they are economical to produce, and because the networks know it takes a serial a long time to build a following, they are given more time to become established—usually at least a year or two unless their initial ratings are unusually bad. All new soaps start at the bottom, and even the best take years to rise to the top (it took *All My Children* from January of 1970 until September of 1974 to gain a No. 1 rating in the Nielsens), but once they capture their audience, they're here to stay for years, maybe decades.

Because of budget restrictions, soaps rarely get to shoot outdoor scenes, which results in what both actors and writers call "dramatic claustrophobia." You often see people entering or leaving a room on a soap, but you'll wait a long time to see anyone *outside* of it, which sometimes gives *viewers* a sense of claustrophobia as well.

But once a fan is hooked, he becomes less aware and less critical of such limitations of the daytime serial. Once the viewer begins to wonder what will happen next, he tends to forget that most of the action is taking place in a series of little rooms, that the dialogue is often repetitive, that a "day" in the story may take three to five actual episodes in the program. The sets become familiar, even comforting. The habits and manners of the characters, as well as their problems, become interesting. Their moods, their reactions, the clothes they wear are recognizable and reassuring. Becoming involved in a soap is like moving to a new neighborhood. At first it's strange and confusing, but after a while you start to know the people and place, and you begin to feel at home.

Questions for Writing or Discussion

1. Soap operas were once characterized by deathbed scenes, trembling organ music, and unrealistic plots. What subject matter and techniques characterize today's soap operas?

2. What is the relationship between the actors and the viewers of soaps?
3. Why are the plots of soaps often more satisfying than those of prime-time shows?
4. What are some of the built-in problems of the serial form?
5. What is the thesis of the article?

Exercise C

For a change of pace, we provide two short stories. After you have read the stories, see if you can state a thesis about each story that could be developed into a brief paper.

Kate Chopin
A PAIR OF SILK STOCKINGS

Little Mrs. Sommers one day found herself the unexpected possessor of fifteen dollars. It seemed to her a very large amount of money, and the way in which it stuffed and bulged her worn out *porte-monnaie*[1] gave her a feeling of importance such as she had not enjoyed for years.

The question of investment was one that occupied her greatly. For a day or two she walked about apparently in a dreamy state but really absorbed in speculation and calculation. She did not wish to act hastily, to do anything she might afterward regret. But it was during the still hours of the night when she lay awake revolving plans in her mind that she seemed to see her way clearly toward a proper and judicious use of the money.

A dollar or two should be added to the price usually paid for Janie's shoes, which would insure their lasting an appreciable time longer than they usually did. She would buy so and so many yards of percale for new shirt waists for the boys and Janie and Mag. She had intended to make the old ones do by skilful patching. Mag should have another gown. She had seen some beautiful patterns, veritable bargains in the shop windows. And still there would be left enough for new stockings—two pairs apiece—and what darning that would save for a while! She would get caps for the boys and sailor-hats for the girls. The vision of her little brood looking fresh and dainty and new for once in their lives excited her and made her restless and wakeful with anticipation.

The neighbors sometimes talked of certain "better days" that little Mrs. Sommers had known before she had ever thought of being Mrs. Sommers. She herself indulged in no such morbid retrospection. She had no time—no second of time to devote to the past. The needs of the present absorbed her

---

[1]Pocketbook.

every faculty. A vision of the future like some dim, gaunt monster some-times appalled her, but luckily to-morrow never comes.

Mrs. Sommers was one who knew the value of bargains; who could stand for hours making her way inch by inch toward the desired object that was selling below cost. She could elbow her way if need be; she had learned to clutch a piece of goods and hold it and stick to it with persistence and de-termination till her turn came to be served, no matter when it came.

But that day she was a little faint and tired. She had swallowed a light luncheon—no! when she came to think of it, between getting the children fed and the place righted, and preparing herself for the shopping bout, she had actually forgotten to eat any luncheon at all!

She sat herself upon a revolving stool before a counter that was compara-tively deserted, trying to gather strength and courage to charge through an eager multitude that was besieging breast-works of shirting and figured lawn. An all-gone limp feeling had come over her and she rested her hand aimlessly upon the counter. She wore no gloves. By degrees she grew aware that her hand had encountered something very soothing, very pleasant to touch. She looked down to see that her hand lay upon a pile of silk stock-ings. A placard near by announced that they had been reduced in price from two dollars and fifty cents to one dollar and ninety-eight cents; and a young girl who stood behind the counter asked her if she wished to examine their line of silk hosiery. She smiled, just as if she had been asked to inspect a tiara of diamonds with the ultimate view of purchasing it: But she went on feeling the soft, sheeny luxurious things—with both hands now, holding them up to see them glisten, and to feel them glide serpent-like through her fingers.

Two hectic blotches came suddenly into her pale cheeks. She looked up at the girl.

"Do you think there are any eights-and-a-half among these?"

There were any number of eights-and-a-half. In fact, there were more of that size than any other. Here was a light-blue pair; there were some laven-der, some all black and various shades of tan and gray. Mrs. Sommers selected a black pair and looked at them very long and closely. She pre-tended to be examining their texture, which the clerk assured her was excellent.

"A dollar and ninety-eight cents," she mused aloud. "Well, I'll take this pair." She handed the girl a five-dollar bill and waited for her change and for her parcel. What a very small parcel it was! It seemed lost in the depths of her shabby old shopping bag.

Mrs. Sommers after that did not move in the direction of the bargain counter. She took the elevator, which carried her to an upper floor into the region of the ladies' waiting-rooms. Here, in a retired corner, she exchanged her cotton stockings for the new silk ones which she had just bought. She was not going through any acute mental process or reasoning with herself, nor was she striving to explain to her satisfaction the motive of her action. She was not thinking at all. She seemed for the time to be taking a rest from that laborious and fatiguing function and to have abandoned herself to some mechanical impulse that directed her actions and freed her of responsibility.

How good was the touch of the raw silk to her flesh! She felt like lying back in the cushioned chair and reveling for a while in the luxury of it. She did for a little while. Then she replaced her shoes, rolled the cotton stockings together and thrust them into her bag. After doing this she crossed straight over to the shoe department and took her seat to be fitted.

She was fastidious. The clerk could not make her out; he could not reconcile her shoes with her stockings, and she was not too easily pleased. She held back her skirts and turned her feet one way and her head another way as she glanced down at the polished, pointed-tipped boots. Her foot and ankle looked very pretty. She could not realize that they belonged to her and were a part of herself. She wanted an excellent and stylish fit, she told the young fellow who served her, and she did not mind the difference of a dollar or two more in the price so long as she got what she desired.

It was a long time since Mrs. Sommers had been fitted with gloves. On rare occasions when she had bought a pair they were always "bargains," so cheap that it would have been preposterous and unreasonable to have expected them to be fitted to the hand.

Now she rested her elbow on the cushion of the glove counter, and a pretty, pleasant young creature, delicate and deft of touch, drew a long-wristed "kid" over Mrs. Sommers' hand. She smoothed it down over the wrist and buttoned it neatly, and both lost themselves for a second or two in admiring contemplation of the little symmetrical gloved hand. But there were other places where money might be spent.

There were books and magazines piled up in the window of a stall a few paces down the street. Mrs. Sommers bought two high-priced magazines such as she had been accustomed to read in the days when she had been accustomed to other pleasant things. She carried them without wrapping. As well as she could she lifted her skirts at the crossings. Her stockings and boots and well fitting gloves had worked marvels in her bearing—had given her a feeling of assurance, a sense of belonging to the well-dressed multitude.

She was very hungry. Another time she would have stilled the cravings for food until reaching her own home, where she would have brewed herself a cup of tea and taken a snack of anything that was available. But the impulse that was guiding her would not suffer her to entertain any such thought.

There was a restaurant at the corner. She had never entered its doors; from the outside she had sometimes caught glimpses of spotless damask and shining crystal, and soft-stepping waiters serving people of fashion.

When she entered her appearance created no surprise, no consternation, as she had half feared it might. She seated herself at a small table alone, and an attentive waiter at once approached to take her order. She did not want a profusion; she craved a nice and tasty bite—a half dozen blue-points, a plump chop with cress, a something sweet—a crème-frappée, for instance; a glass of Rhine wine, and after all a small cup of black coffee.

While waiting to be served she removed her gloves very leisurely and laid them beside her. Then she picked up a magazine and glanced through it, cutting the pages with a blunt edge of her knife. It was all very agreeable. The damask was even more spotless than it had seemed through the window, and the crystal more sparkling. There were quiet ladies and gentlemen, who did not notice her, lunching at the small tables like her own. A soft, pleasing strain of music could be heard, and a gentle breeze was blowing through the window. She tasted a bite, and she read a word or two, and she sipped the amber wine and wiggled her toes in the silk stockings. The price of it made no difference. She counted the money out to the waiter and left an extra coin on his tray, whereupon he bowed before her as before a princess of royal blood.

There was still money in her purse, and her next temptation presented itself in the shape of a matinée poster.

It was a little later when she entered the theatre, the play had begun and the house seemed to her to be packed. But there were vacant seats here and there, and into one of them she was ushered, between brilliantly dressed women who had gone there to kill time and eat candy and display their gaudy attire. There were many others who were there solely for the play and acting. It is safe to say there was no one present who bore quite the attitude which Mrs. Sommers did to her surroundings. She gathered in the whole—stage and players and people in one wide impression, and absorbed it and enjoyed it. She laughed at the comedy and wept—she and the gaudy woman next to her wept over the tragedy. And they talked a little together over it. And the gaudy woman wiped her eyes and sniffled on a tiny square of filmy, perfumed lace and passed little Mrs. Sommers her box of candy.

The play was over, the music ceased, the crowd filed out. It was like a dream ended. People scattered in all directions. Mrs. Sommers went to the corner and waited for the cable car.

A man with keen eyes, who sat opposite to her, seemed to like the study of her small, pale face. It puzzled him to decipher what he saw there. In truth, he saw nothing—unless he were wizard enough to detect a poignant wish, a powerful longing that the cable car would never stop anywhere, but go on and on with her forever.

Questions for Writing or Discussion

1. Why is "A Pair of Silk Stockings" a better title for the story than "Mrs. Sommers' Shopping Spree"?
2. We are not told how Mrs. Sommers, who has obviously fallen on hard times, came by the fifteen dollars. Should we be told? Why, or why not?
3. What does Mrs. Sommers regard as a "judicious use of her money"? Do you agree?
4. Mrs. Sommers has at least four children, all of whom need clothes. Yet she spends all the money on luxury items for herself. Is Mrs. Sommers selfish? Why, or why not?
5. What is the effect of the author's referring to the character as "little Mrs. Sommers"?

6. Do you sympathize with Mrs. Sommers? Why?
7. Why do you think Mrs. Sommers spends the money as she does? Do you think she will later regret her shopping spree? Should she?

Kurt Vonnegut, Jr.
HARRISON BERGERON

The year was 2081, and everybody was finally equal. They weren't only equal before God and the law. They were equal every which way. Nobody was smarter than anybody else. Nobody was better looking than anybody else. Nobody was stronger or quicker than anybody else. All this equality was due to the 211th, 212th, and 213th Amendments to the Constitution, and to the unceasing vigilance of agents of the United States Handicapper General.

Some things about living still weren't quite right, though. April, for instance, still drove people crazy by not being springtime. And it was in that clammy month that the H-G men took George and Hazel Bergeron's fourteen-year-old son, Harrison, away.

It was tragic, all right, but George and Hazel couldn't think about it very hard. Hazel had a perfectly average intelligence, which meant she couldn't think about anything except in short bursts. And George, while his intelligence was way above normal, had a little mental handicap radio in his ear. He was required by law to wear it at all times. It was tuned to a government transmitter. Every twenty seconds or so, the transmitter would send out some sharp noise to keep people like George from taking unfair advantage of their brains.

George and Hazel were watching television. There were tears on Hazel's cheeks, but she'd forgotten for the moment what they were about.

On the television screen were ballerinas.

A buzzer sounded in George's head. His thoughts fled in panic, like bandits from a burglar alarm.

"That was a real pretty dance, that dance they just did," said Hazel.

"Huh?" said George.

"That dance—it was nice," said Hazel.

"Yup," said George. He tried to think a little about the ballerinas. They weren't really very good—no better than anybody else would have been, anyway. They were burdened with sashweights and bags of birdshot, and their faces were masked, so that no one, seeing a free and graceful gesture or a pretty face, would feel like something the cat drug in. George was toying with the vague notion that maybe dancers shouldn't be handicapped. But he didn't get very far with it before another noise in his ear radio scattered his thoughts.

George winced. So did two out of the eight ballerinas.

Hazel saw him wince. Having no mental handicap herself, she had to ask George what the latest sound had been.

"Sounded like somebody hitting a milk bottle with a ball peen hammer," said George.

"I'd think it would be real interesting, hearing all the different sounds," said Hazel, a little envious. "All the things they think up."

"Um," said George.

"Only, if I was Handicapper General, you know what I would do?" said Hazel. Hazel, as a matter of fact, bore a strong resemblance to the Handicapper General, a woman named Diana Moon Glampers. "If I was Diana Moon Glampers," said Hazel, "I'd have chimes on Sunday—just chimes. Kind of in honor of religion."

"I could think, if it was just chimes," said George.

"Well—maybe make 'em real loud," said Hazel. "I think I'd make a good Handicapper General."

"Good as anybody else," said George.

"Who knows better'n I do what normal is?" said Hazel.

"Right," said George. He began to think glimmeringly about his abnormal son who was now in jail, about Harrison, but a twenty-one-gun salute in his head stopped that.

"Boy!" said Hazel, "that was a doozy, wasn't it?"

It was such a doozy that George was white and trembling, and tears stood on the rims of his red eyes. Two of the eight ballerinas had collapsed to the studio floor, were holding their temples.

"All of a sudden you look so tired," said Hazel. "Why don't you stretch out on the sofa, so's you can rest your handicap bag on the pillows, honeybunch." She was referring to the forty-seven pounds of birdshot in a canvas bag, which was padlocked around George's neck. "Go on and rest the bag for a little while," she said. "I don't care if you're not equal to me for a while."

George weighed the bag with his hands. "I don't mind it," he said. "I don't notice it any more. It's just a part of me."

"You been so tired lately—kind of wore out," said Hazel. "If there was just some way we could make a little hole in the bottom of the bag, and just take out a few of them lead balls. Just a few."

"Two years in prison and two thousand dollars fine for every ball I took out," said George. "I don't call that a bargain."

"If you could take a few out when you came home from work," said Hazel. "I mean—you don't compete with anybody around here. You just set around."

"If I tried to get away with it," said George, "then other people'd get away with it—and pretty soon we'd be right back to the dark ages again, with everybody competing against everybody else. You wouldn't like that, would you?"

"I'd hate it," said Hazel.

"There you are," said George. "The minute people start cheating on laws, what do you think happens to society?"

If Hazel hadn't been able to come up with an answer to this question, George couldn't have supplied one. A siren was going off in his head.

"Reckon it'd fall all apart," said Hazel.

"What would?" said George blankly.

"Society," said Hazel uncertainly. "Wasn't that what you just said?"

"Who knows?" said George.

The television program was suddenly interrupted for a news bulletin. It wasn't clear at first as to what the bulletin was about, since the announcer, like all announcers, had a serious speech impediment. For about half a minute, and in a state of high excitement, the announcer tried to say, "Ladies and gentlemen—"

He finally gave up, handed the bulletin to a ballerina to read.

"That's all right—" Hazel said of the announcer, "he tried. That's the big thing. He tried to do the best he could with what God gave him. He should get a nice raise for trying so hard."

"Ladies and gentlemen—" said the ballerina, reading the bulletin. She must have been extraordinarily beautiful, because the mask she wore was hideous. And it was easy to see that she was the strongest and most graceful of all the dancers, for her handicap bags were as big as those worn by two-hundred-pound men.

And she had to apologize at once for her voice, which was a very unfair voice for a woman to use. Her voice was a warm, luminous, timeless melody. "Excuse me—" she said, and she began again, making her voice absolutely uncompetitive.

"Harrison Bergeron, age fourteen," she said in a grackle squawk, "has just escaped from jail, where he was held on suspicion of plotting to overthrow the government. He is a genius and an athlete, is under-handicapped, and should be regarded as extremely dangerous."

A police photograph of Harrison Bergeron was flashed on the screen upside down, then sideways, upside down again, then right side up. The picture showed the full length of Harrison against a background calibrated in feet and inches. He was exactly seven feet tall.

The rest of Harrison's appearance was Halloween and hardware. Nobody had ever born heavier handicaps. He had outgrown hindrances faster than the H-G men could think them up. Instead of a little ear radio for a mental handicap, he wore a tremendous pair of earphones, and spectacles with thick wavy lenses. The spectacles were intended to make him not only half blind, but to give him whanging headaches besides.

Scrap metal was hung all over him. Ordinarily, there was a certain symmetry, a military neatness to the handicaps issued to strong people, but Harrison looked like a walking junkyard. In the race of life, Harrison carried three hundred pounds.

And to offset his good looks, the H-G men required that he wear at all times a red rubber ball for a nose, keep his eyebrows shaved off, and cover his even white teeth with black caps at snaggle-tooth random.

"If you see this boy," said the ballerina, "do not—I repeat, do not—try to reason with him."

There was a shriek of a door being torn from its hinges.

Screams and barking cries of consternation came from the television set. The photograph of Harrison Bergeron on the screen jumped again and again, as though dancing to the tune of an earthquake.

George Bergeron correctly identified the earthquake, and well he might have—for many was the time his own home had danced to the same crashing tune. "My God—" said George, "that must be Harrison!"

The realization was blasted from his mind instantly by the sound of an automobile collision in his head.

When George could open his eyes again, the photograph of Harrison was gone. A living, breathing Harrison filled the screen.

Clanking, clownish, and huge, Harrison stood in the center of the studio. The knob of the uprooted studio door was still in his hand. Ballerinas, technicians, musicians, and announcers cowered on their knees before him, expecting to die.

"I am the Emperor!" cried Harrison. "Do you hear? I am the Emperor! Everybody must do what I say at once!" He stamped his foot and the studio shook.

"Even as I stand here—" he bellowed, "crippled, hobbled, sickened—I am a greater ruler than any man who ever lived! Now watch me become what I *can* become!"

Harrison tore the straps of his handicap harness like wet tissue paper, tore straps guaranteed to support five thousand pounds.

Harrison's scrap-iron handicaps crashed to the floor.

Harrison thrust his thumbs under the bar of the padlock that secured his head harness. The bar snapped like celery. Harrison smashed his headphones and spectacles against the wall.

He flung away his rubber-ball nose, revealed a man that would have awed Thor, the god of thunder.

"I shall now select my Empress!" he said, looking down on the cowering people. "Let the first woman who dares rise to her feet claim her mate and her throne!"

A moment passed, and then a ballerina arose, swaying like a willow.

Harrison plucked the mental handicap from her ear, snapped off her physical handicaps with marvelous delicacy. Last of all, he removed her mask.

She was blindingly beautiful.

"Now—" said Harrison, taking her hand, "shall we show the people the meaning of the word dance? Music!" he commanded.

The musicians scrambled back into their chairs, and Harrison stripped them of their handicaps, too. "Play your best," he told them, "and I'll make you barons and dukes and earls."

The music began. It was normal at first—cheap, silly, false. But Harrison snatched two musicians from their chairs, waved them like batons as he sang the music as he wanted it played. He slammed them back into their chairs.

The music began again and was much improved.

Harrison and his Empress merely listened to the music for a while—listened gravely, as though synchronizing their heartbeats with it.

They shifted their weights to their toes.

Harrison placed his big hands on the girl's tiny waist, letting her sense the weightlessness that would soon be hers.

And then in an explosion of joy and grace, into the air they sprang!

Not only were the laws of the land abandoned, but the law of gravity and the laws of motion as well.

They reeled, whirled, swiveled, flounced, capered, gamboled, and spun.

They leaped like deer on the moon.

The studio ceiling was thirty feet high, but each leap brought the dancers nearer to it.

It became their obvious intention to kiss the ceiling.

They kissed it.

And then, neutralizing gravity with love and pure will, they remained suspended in air inches below the ceiling, and they kissed each other for a long, long time.

It was then that Diana Moon Glampers, the Handicapper General, came into the studio with a double-barreled ten-gauge shotgun. She fired twice, and the Emperor and the Empress were dead before they hit the floor.

Diana Moon Glampers loaded the gun again. She aimed it at the musicians and told them they had ten seconds to get their handicaps back on.

It was then that the Bergerons' television tube burned out.

Hazel turned to comment about the blackout to George. But George had gone out into the kitchen for a can of beer.

George came back in with the beer, paused while a handicap signal shook him up. And then he sat down again.

"You been crying?" he said to Hazel.

"Yup," she said.

"What about?" he said.

"I forget," she said. "Something real sad on television."

"What was it?" he said.

"It's all kind of mixed up in my mind," said Hazel.

"Forget sad things," said George.

"I always do," said Hazel.

"That's my girl," said George. He winced. There was the sound of a riveting gun in his head.

"Gee—I could tell that one was a doozy," said Hazel.

"You can say that again," said George.

"Gee—" said Hazel, "I could tell that one was a doozy."

Questions for Writing or Discussion

1. The author writes a story of the future in which he looks at trends today that disturb him and asks what life would be like if they continue for a hundred years or so. What other stories, novels, movies, and television programs can you think of that use the same approach?

2. What specifically is the author satirizing in modern America? Do you feel he has good cause to be upset?

3. What would the author feel is a correct definition of equality? How would Diana Moon Glampers define equality?

4. Why is the name Harrison Bergeron a better choice than a name such as John Smith or Bill Jones?
5. Name all the different kinds of handicaps in the story. Does each attempt to solve a different problem?
6. Specifically, what are the bad results of the misunderstanding of equality?
7. What is symbolized by the soaring of Harrison and the ballerina to the ceiling?
8. Does the fact that Harrison declares himself an emperor justify the society's fear of him?

CHAPTER 2

SUPPORTING
THE THESIS: LOGIC

The best way to convince a reader that your idea is worth considering is to offer logical support for your thesis. Although lengthy books have been written about logic, we believe the subject doesn't need to be as intimidating as these elaborate treatments suggest. Common sense and fair play are the basic tools—and sometimes the only tools—that conscientious writers need. As far as possible, then, we will avoid fine philosophical distinctions and concentrate on the most common logical pitfalls—the basic errors in thinking that can turn up in anyone's writing.

To check your own logic and that of others, a knowledge of the two kinds of logical thinking, *induction* and *deduction,* and of the errors in logic, the *fallacies,* will be helpful.

Induction is the process of reasoning from the particular to the general. It is the process of arriving at a general conclusion about all the members of a class of persons or things after examining some members of the class. Induction is a useful tool because it isn't always practical or possible to check every member of a class before drawing your conclusion. If, for example, you develop a stomach ache every time you eat green apples, you may, without sampling every green apple in the world, safely conclude that green apples give you a stomach ache. You've made a generalization about all the members of the class *green apples* after examining some of its members. Or maybe you've noticed that for four Fridays in a row, Professor Hadley has given a pop quiz. You may draw the useful conclusion that Professor Hadley is likely to give pop quizzes on Fridays without waiting until the end of the term to see if you're right.

But induction is useful only if the conclusion about a class is drawn from a fair sampling of that class. What's fair depends on the class. You needn't stick your hand into twenty fires to conclude that fire burns; one or two fires will do. Other classes should be sampled more broadly. Conclusions about groups of people, for example, should be drawn from a large representative sampling and even then should usually be qualified with words like *tend, may, are likely,* etc. (See Hasty Generalization and Overgeneralization, pp. 35–36; see also Chapter 5, "Writing an Example Paper.")

Deduction is the process of reasoning from the general to the particular. A generalization already established—by oneself or by someone else—is applied to a specific case. Deduction, like induction, is a useful tool. You've concluded, for example, that Professor Hadley is likely to give pop quizzes on Friday. When your roommate suggests one Friday morning that you cut classes and spend the day in the park, you say, "No, I can't go today. Professor Hadley is likely to give a pop quiz, and my average can't stand a zero." You've applied your generalization (Fridays are likely days for quizzes) to a specific case (this Friday) and just may have assured yourself a passing grade in Professor Hadley's class.

In its simplest form, the deductive process is stated as a syllogism: an argument consisting of a *major premise,* a *minor premise,* and a *conclusion.*

> *Major premise:* Fridays are likely days for pop quizzes.
>
> *Minor premise:* Today is Friday.
>
> *Conclusion:* Therefore, today is a likely day for a pop quiz.

Perhaps a more sophisticated example is the syllogism implicit in the Declaration of Independence (p. 236):

> *Major premise:* Rulers who violate basic human rights should be overthrown.
>
> *Minor premise:* King George III has violated basic human rights.
>
> *Conclusion:* Therefore, King George III should be overthrown.

Syllogisms rarely appear in writing or conversation in their pure three-part form. It is far more common to find *enthymemes,* condensed syllogisms in which one or more parts are missing, the writer assuming that the missing parts are clearly understood and don't need to be stated directly.

> It's Friday, so I'd better go to Professor Hadley's class. (*Missing premise:* Fridays are likely days for quizzes in Professor Hadley's class.)
>
> I don't trust him because he's sneaky. (*Missing premise:* Sneaky people should not be trusted.)

I hate movies with violence, and this movie is teeming with violence. (*Missing conclusion:* Therefore, I hate this movie.)

Syllogisms are worth serious study primarily because they enable readers and writers to examine the often unstated, and sometimes shaky, assumptions behind otherwise convincing arguments.

For a syllogism to be taken seriously, of course, both premises must be true. It's hard to imagine a syllogism that begins with the premise "The earth is flat" leading to any valid conclusion. But even if both premises are true, the reasoning process itself may be faulty and the conclusion invalid. Consider this syllogism:

> *Major premise:* English majors read a lot of books.
>
> *Minor premise:* David reads a lot of books.
>
> *Conclusion:* Therefore, David is an English major.

Despite the true premises, the conclusion still doesn't follow. The major premise merely says, "English majors read a lot of books"; it says nothing about other people who may also read books. Logically, David *may* be an English major, but he may also be a merchant marine who kills time on shipboard by reading, an invalid who doesn't enjoy television, a desk clerk whose job is boring, or just someone who likes to read for no particular reason. The logical structure of the argument makes no more sense than this syllogism: Grass is green; her hat is green; therefore, her hat is grass.

So far, we have talked about induction and deduction as if the processes were mutually exclusive, but, in practice, they aren't. You will seldom engage in one kind of thought without using the other. When you use induction, you usually have a hunch about what generalization the facts will add up to. If you didn't, you wouldn't have a guideline for handling the facts. Consider, for example, that observation about Professor Hadley's quiz-giving tendency. If you hadn't already suspected that Hadley was a Friday-quiz-giver, you might not have noticed that the pop quizzes did occur on Friday. Some deduction, therefore, was involved in the process of reaching the generalization about pop quizzes on Friday.

Similarly, in deductive reasoning you must also employ induction. A syllogism is only as valid as both its premises. To assure sound premises, you must be sure that your evidence is both adequate and fair, and that involves induction. Induction is important, too, when you present your material. Even if yours is the best of syllogisms, you probably won't convince a reader of its worth unless you offer support for it—reasons, statistics, facts, opinions of authorities, examples. The reader's agreement or approval depends on the case you build; it depends on evidence. In the Declaration of Independence, for example, Thomas Jefferson supported his case against George III by citing twenty-eight instances in which the king had violated basic human rights. The instances came from induction.

Whether your primary tool is induction or deduction, you need to make certain that the evidence you offer isn't based on errors in logic. In other words, you should avoid the following fallacies.

POST HOC, ERGO PROPTER HOC

This impressive Latin phrase means "after this, therefore because of this." The *post hoc* fallacy takes for a cause an event which merely happened earlier: for example, *A black cat crossed my path and ten minutes later I broke my ankle; therefore, the black cat caused my broken ankle.* Unless the speaker tripped over the cat, such a statement is as unreasonable as *Night follows day; therefore, day causes night.*

The *post hoc* fallacy often appears in political discussions. Haven't you heard people say things like, "The crime rate has increased since the governor took office; I'm certainly not going to vote for him again"? Possibly the governor could be held responsible for the increased crime, but before he could logically be blamed for it, a direct connection between his policies and the crime rate would have to be proved.

To avoid *post hoc* fallacy in your own writing, think carefully about the events which immediately precede an outcome. They may have little or nothing to do with the real causes of the outcome. In Chekhov's "The Lottery Ticket" (p. 168), for example, Ivan Dmitritch, shortly after discovering that his wife does not hold the winning lottery ticket, threatens to hang himself. His despair, however, is not caused by that discovery. It is caused by new realizations about his life which have been prompted by his daydreams of great wealth. To attribute his despair to the loss of the lottery is to commit a *post hoc* fallacy.

CARD STACKING

Card stacking means using only the evidence which supports a thesis and ignoring that which contradicts or weakens it. Card stacking is dishonest and can sometimes do serious damage. Suppose, for instance, that a newspaper editor dislikes the mayor of the city. The editor could prevent the mayor's reelection simply by emphasizing reports of the administration's mistakes and playing down reports of its accomplishments. Soon, the readers of the newspaper would begin to think of the mayor as a bungler who shouldn't be reelected.

Unfair? Of course. It's also unnecessary. A reasonable thesis doesn't require card stacking. A writer can make concessions and still advance the argument: *Although the mayor has made some attempts to attract convention business, the efforts have been too few and too late,* for example. If a thesis isn't reasonable, if it requires card stacking for support, it probably isn't worth defending. A person writing about Williams's "The Use of Force" (p. 162), for example, would have to resort to card stacking to prove the thesis, *The doctor's sole reason for injuring the child is to protect her and the community from diphtheria.* The doctor wants to do that, of course, but to say that is the *only* reason for his actions is to ignore his own admission that he enjoyed hurting the child. The thesis isn't worth defending and should be changed.

SLANTING

A variation of card stacking is *slanting,* systematically using words whose connotations suggest extreme approval or disapproval of the subject. A person may be "a bag of bones" or have "a model's figure." In either case, the weight is the same, but one term suggests scorn and the other approval. Similarly, George Washington may be described as "a militant revolutionary responsible for the death of many people." Or he may be "a great military genius who led his freedom-loving people in a victorious battle against tyranny." The conscious use of slanting to sway opinion usually occurs when a writer lacks enough logical evidence to support the thesis. Used this way, it is, like card stacking, quite dishonest. But slanting should not be confused with a writer's legitimate efforts to convey admittedly personal impressions and emotions.

HASTY GENERALIZATION

One snowflake doesn't make a blizzard, nor does one experience make a universal law. That one student has cheated on the last five psychology quizzes doesn't mean that all psychology students in the school are cheaters; to say so is to make a *hasty generalization,* to draw a conclusion about a group which is based on insufficient evidence.

OVERGENERALIZATION

Overgeneralizations are similar to hasty generalizations. A hasty generalization results from drawing a conclusion about a large number on the basis of very limited evidence. Overgeneralization occurs, regardless of how much "evidence" is available, when one assumes that *all* members of a group, nationality, race, or sex have the characteristics observed in some members of that group: *"all* feminists are bra-burners"; *"all* blacks have rhythm"; *"all* Italians like spaghetti"; "the English are *always* cold and reserved"; *"never* trust a used-car salesman." Surely it's possible that some feminists wear undergarments, that some blacks can't dance, that some Italians prefer green salads, that some English people are volatile, and that at least one or two used-car salesmen are trustworthy. Words such as *all, never, always, every, true,* and *untrue* are seldom justified when dealing with the complexities of human beings and human institutions. You would do well in writing your papers to qualify potentially troublesome generalizations with words such as *some, seldom, tend, sometimes, frequently, seem, appear, often, perhaps,* and *many.* Both hasty generalizations and overgeneralizations lead to prejudice and superstition and to theses which cannot be developed logically and effectively.

NON SEQUITUR

The term means, "It does not follow." A *non sequitur* is a conclusion which does not follow from the premise:

> I always vote the Republican ticket because my great-great grandfather fought in the Union army.

Usually, *non sequiturs* occur because the writer or speaker believes there is a connection between the premise and the conclusion. In the above instance, the writer's thinking probably goes something like this:

1. The Union army served under President Abraham Lincoln, the first Republican president.

2. I believe in supporting the traditions of my ancestors.
3. Since one of my ancestors served under a Republican administration, I support that tradition by voting Republican.

The writer does see a connection, to be sure, but is it a connection worth making? One might as well argue that since our earliest ancestors ate their meat raw, we should also eat raw meat to honor family tradition.

Not all *non sequiturs* are so obviously foolish.

We all know what happened at Hiroshima. We must vote against nuclear power plants.

Here, as in the earlier example, the writer draws a conclusion without revealing the steps in the thought process which led to that conclusion, and if the audience doesn't fill in the missing steps, it may be taken in by the argument and rush out to vote down nuclear plants. The steps in the process are as follows:

1. The bomb exploded over Hiroshima produced greater man-made destruction than the world had ever known before.
2. The bomb's power derived from energy produced by the nuclear fission of atoms.
3. Nuclear plants derive their power from energy produced by the nuclear fission of atoms.
4. Nuclear power plants could explode like the atomic bomb and produce the same kind of destruction which occurred at Hiroshima.
5. Therefore, the construction of such plants should be prevented.

Once the thought process has been revealed, the audience can consider the logic of the argument. *Can* nuclear plants explode like atomic bombs? If not, the writer's conclusion is questionable and perhaps should be rejected.

In your own writing, you can avoid *non sequiturs* by revealing the connection between the premise and the conclusion and by making certain that the connection is defensible.

IGNORING THE QUESTION

In ignoring the question, the writer or speaker deliberately or unintentionally shifts emphasis from the topic under discussion. As you will see below, the question can be ignored in several ways.

Ad hominem argument. Arguing "against the man" means making an irrelevant attack on a person rather than dealing with the actual issue under discussion. Suppose, for example, that Senator Goodfellow, who has admitted to cheating on his income tax for the past five years, proposes a bill for national health insurance. It would be a fallacy to attack the bill by arguing that its proponent is guilty of tax evasion. The bill may be logical, humane, and in the best interest of the country. If it is not, what are its weaknesses? The bill, not Senator Goodfellow's problems with the Internal Revenue Service, should be the subject of discussion.

Not all personal attacks, of course, are necessarily irrelevant. If Senator Goodfellow were seeking reelection, one could logically approve of his ideas and still vote against him because his character defects indicate the danger of trusting him in a position of power and responsibility.

Students sometimes employ the *ad hominem* fallacy in discussing literary works by rejecting a work whose author does not fulfill their idea of a good person:

> One cannot be expected to take "Kubla Khan" seriously. Coleridge admitted to writing it after he had taken dope.

> It is well known that Edgar Allan Poe was an alcoholic. His stories are nothing but the fantasies of a drunken mind.

Such a practice indicates little understanding of the artistic process or of human nature. Writers of questionable character have produced inspiring works which affirm the highest values of civilization, and those affirmations deserve consideration. After all, most of us are such a mixture of good and evil, of wisdom and folly, of generosity and greed that if we waited until we found a good idea proposed by a perfect person, we should wait long indeed.

Straw man argument. The writer or speaker attributes to the opposition actions or beliefs of which the opposition is not guilty and then attacks the opposition for those actions or beliefs.

> Parents who boast of never having to spank their children should feel shame instead of pride. Discipline and socially responsible behavior are vitally important, and people who sneer at such things deserve the condemnation of all concerned citizens.

Some parents might very well be able to boast of not having to spank their children and yet also demand of their children discipline and socially responsible behavior.

Begging the question. The writer or speaker assumes in the thesis something which really needs to be proved.

Since students learn to write in high school, the college composition course is a waste of time and should be replaced by a more useful and stimulating course.

One who chooses to write a paper with that thesis has the obligation to prove that the students do learn how to write in high school.

Shifting the burden of proof. Logic requires that *he who asserts must prove.* It is not logical to say,

I believe the flu epidemic was caused by a communist conspiracy, and you can't prove it wasn't.

For the assertion to be taken seriously, reasonable proof of a conspiracy must be offered.

Circular argument. Arguing in a circle means simply restating the premise instead of giving a reason for holding the premise.

I like detective novels because mystery stories always give me great pleasure.

All that sentence says is, "I like detective novels because I like detective novels." One who begins a paper that way will be hard pressed to continue. Of greater interest would be the characteristics of the detective novels the speaker does like. Some readers like Agatha Christie's novels. How do her works differ from, say, Mickey Spillane's detective novels? Or Erle Stanley Gardner's? Surely one's taste for detective novels isn't indiscriminate. In other words, one needs a reason for liking detective novels, and to say that one likes them because they give pleasure is not to give a reason. *Why* do the novels give pleasure? An honest answer to that question will provide a workable thesis and prevent a circular argument.

EITHER/OR

In this fallacy, the writer or speaker suggests that there are only two alternatives when, in fact, there may be more.

Although I am quite ill, I must turn my term paper in tomorrow, or I will fail the course.

The writer presents only two alternatives; however, it is also possible that the instructor, recognizing the student's illness, might accept a late paper. Of course, if one is cursed with a professor who accepts no late papers, regardless of circumstances, then one actually has only two alternatives, and no fallacy exists.

ARGUMENT FROM ANALOGY

An analogy is an extended comparison. It is useful because it can clarify a difficult concept or dramatize an abstraction by comparing the unfamiliar with the familiar. But an analogy doesn't prove anything because, regardless of the number of similarities between two things, there are always some differences. One can't assume that because two things are alike in some respects, they are alike in all respects.

> Learning to write a good essay is like learning to drive a car. Beginning drivers feel overwhelmed by the number of operations they must perform to keep a car moving—controlling the brake and the accelerator, staying in their lane, watching the cars in front of them while keeping an eye on the rear-view mirror. In addition, they must observe all traffic laws. The tasks seem insurmountable. Yet, in time, some of the operations become almost automatic and the drivers relax enough that they can even look at the scenery now and then. So it is with beginning writers. At first, they wonder how they can make an outline for a paper, write clear topic sentences, develop paragraphs, provide transitions, write good introductions and conclusions, and still observe all the rules of English grammar. As with driving, part of the process eventually becomes automatic, and the writers relax enough to concentrate primarily on the ideas they wish to develop.

That comparison deals only with the similarities of feelings resulting from the two experiences and is a successful analogy because it clarifies for the beginner the experience of writing. But if one extends the comparison to encompass other demands on drivers—checking antifreeze, acquiring new windshield wipers, mounting snow tires, repairing flats, maintaining brake fluid—the analogy falls apart.

Historical analogies present a similar problem. Certainly, we can learn from history, but we can't assume that because two events are alike in some respects, the outcomes will inevitably be the same. You have probably heard the argument that the United States is on the verge of collapse because some conditions here—relaxed sexual mores, widespread demand for immediate pleasure, and political cynicism and corruption—parallel those of the Roman Empire just before its fall. The argument doesn't consider, among other things, that the forms of government differ, that the bases for the economy differ, or that the means of educating the population differ. The two societies are not alike in every respect, and one cannot assume that because one society fell, the other will also fall.

Analogy can be useful for clarifying an idea, but argument by analogy can be dangerous.

Exercise

Following are several examples of logical fallacies. Read them over and determine what type of fallacy each most strongly represents.

1. In history class today, Ron finally asked me for a date; we're going to the hockey game Friday! I'm certainly glad I brushed my teeth with Glow-Gel before I went to class.
2. Last term, there were twelve women and eight men in my algebra class. The three highest scores on the final exam were made by women, and the three lowest by men. Men just aren't good at math.
3. Of course he'll like the bagels. He's Jewish, isn't he?
4. There isn't one college graduate in Megalopolis' finance department. No wonder the city is nearly bankrupt.
5. Don't tell me you're going to vote for Joe Tinker as county auditor. The man hasn't been inside a church in the past ten years.
6. I enjoy reading Shakespeare's sonnets because I just love poetry.
7. We've got to do something to improve public spirit in this town.
8. We should either insist on daily grammar tests in all our nation's high schools or simply confess that we're no longer interested in teaching our children how to use their native language correctly.
9. I don't understand why Abraham Lincoln is considered a great president. He was a warmonger who, by government proclamation, took away the property of a large number of citizens.
10. How do you know there *aren't* UFOs?
11. You say there wasn't enough evidence to convict him. I'll never be able to understand why people like you want to see criminals roaming freely around the streets of our cities.
12. Of course the president should be elected to a second term. The country is in the midst of an economic crisis, and nobody goes around changing horses in the middle of the stream.

CHAPTER 3

PLANNING A PAPER: OUTLINING

Once you have a thesis and a general notion of how it can be supported logically, your next step is to plan the order of its development. What proof will you give first? What next? What examples will you use? Where? In some cases, the plan for your paper is set by your purpose. If, for example, you plan to describe a process, such as changing auto plates, all you have to do is to arrange the steps in the most convenient order for getting the job done. Some reports of events call for straight chronological order, and the planning involves simply grouping the details under such headings as, for example, discovering the fire, sounding the alarm, fighting the fire, and cleaning up the debris. If, however, your purpose is to convince, to develop a thesis, the plan may not be so obvious, and you will want to think carefully about the order in which you need to arrange your material.

Whatever the case, it's necessary to plan your paper before you begin to write because if you don't, you may get so involved in choosing the right words that you forget where you want to go. An outline will keep you moving in the right direction. Part 2 of this text will show you many different methods of organization and will help you write papers using each method. For the time being, let's consider the general rules of outlining, of planning a paper.

The form of an outline gives a picture of the logical relationship between the separate parts of a paper and the thesis or purpose. So begin by stating the thesis or purpose. Then indicate all major divisions of the paper with Roman numerals. Mark the support for the major divisions with capital letters and support for the subheadings with Arabic numerals. If you are planning a very long paper, you may want to make further subdivisions. To do so, next use small letters—a, b, c—and then Arabic numerals in parentheses—(1),

(2)—then small letters in parentheses—(a), (b). For short papers, the major divisions and two or three subdivisions for each will probably be adequate. Here, for example, is an outline for a short paper on how to change auto license plates.

Purpose: To show how to change auto license plates.
    I. Assemble materials
      A. Find screwdriver
      B. Find household oil
      C. Buy plastic screws
    II. Remove old plates
      A. Oil screws to loosen rust
      B. Unscrew plates
      C. Discard metal screws
    III. Mount new plates
      A. Position plate with screw holes
      B. Screw on plate using plastic screws
    IV. Break and discard old plates

The outline for a longer, more complex paper might look like this:

Purpose: To illustrate the outline for a complex paper.
    I. Major division
      A. First-level subdivision
        1. Second-level subdivision
        2. Second-level subdivision
          a. Third-level subdivision
          b. Third-level subdivision
            (1) Fourth-level subdivision
            (2) Fourth-level subdivision
      B. First-level subdivision
        1. Second-level subdivision
        2. Second-level subdivision
    II. Major division
      A. First-level subdivision
        1. Second-level subdivision
        2. Second-level subdivision
      B. First-level subdivision
        1. Second-level subdivision
          a. Third-level subdivision
          b. Third-level subdivision
        2. Second-level subdivision
          a. Third-level subdivision

        b. Third-level subdivision
          (1) Fourth-level subdivision
          (2) Fourth-level subdivision
            (a) Fifth-level subdivision
            (b) Fifth-level subdivision

Outlines are of two types, *topic outlines* and *sentence outlines.* The outline of the paper on license plates is a topic outline, one in which the writer uses just a few words or phrases to indicate the topics and subtopics the paper covers. Topic outlines are sufficient for many short papers, especially for papers that classify or present a process. Longer papers and those which develop theses often profit from sentence outlines.

To write a *sentence outline,* you must sum up in one sentence what you want to say on each topic and subtopic. The sentence doesn't merely indicate the topic; it states what is to be said about the topic. This kind of outline forces you to think through exactly what you want to say before you begin to write. By constructing a sentence outline, you will find out whether you really have proof for your position.

Below is a sentence outline for a paper arguing that the Christmas season, though commercialized, still is a time of good will.

Thesis: Although Christmas has become commercialized, the spirit of the season nevertheless survives.

I. Christmas has become commercialized.
  A. Media advertising suggests that viewers lack Christmas spirit if they don't buy, buy, buy.
    1. Commercials on children's shows imply that good parents buy expensive toys for children.
    2. Commercials on family shows imply that good friends deserve expensive gifts.
    3. Commercials on adult shows imply that affection from the opposite sex can be gained or kept only by giving expensive presents.
  B. Merchants, as early as Halloween, stand ready to satisfy desires created by advertising.
II. The spirit of Christmas survives.
  A. The desire to help the unfortunate increases at Christmas.
    1. Shoppers toss coins into Salvation Army kettles.
    2. Readers respond to newspaper pleas for aid to the needy.
    3. Schools and clubs collect food and clothing for the needy.

B. The desire to share with friends increases at Christmas.
   1. People entertain at home with food and gifts.
   2. Clubs have parties at which members exchange gifts.
   3. Fellow workers share food and gifts at office parties.
C. The desire to share with family increases at Christmas.
   1. Families travel great distances to be together at Christmas.
   2. Families who are apart mail gifts and telephone each other at Christmas.

The outlines you have looked at so far show that whether your outline is topic or sentence, it should include a statement of the thesis or purpose of the paper and an indication by means of Roman numerals of the main points to be covered in the paper. Major and minor subdivisions, indicated by letters and Arabic numerals respectively, should show how the main points will be developed. Here are other points to observe in preparing an outline:

1. *Do not make single subdivisions.* If you decide to subdivide a point, you must have at least two subdivisions. If there is a I, there must be a II; if there is an A, there must be a B. If you cannot think of two divisions, rephrase the heading so that no division is necessary.

2. *Use parallel grammatical form for headings of equal importance* to show their relationship to one another. If I reads "Assembling the ingredients," II should read "Mixing the ingredients," not "Mix the ingredients."

3. *Make sure the divisions of an outline do not overlap and that you stick to a single principle of division.* You should not, for example, discuss books in terms of *fiction, nonfiction,* and *novels* because novels are logically a subdivision of fiction. You should not discuss the branches of government in terms of *legislative, judicial, executive,* and *crooked politicians* because one might find crooked politicians in any of the branches. You should not discuss people in terms of *overweight, underweight, normal weight,* and *handsome.* Obviously, *handsome* does not belong in a division based on a principle of weight.

4. *Make sure that headings and subheadings show a proper logical relationship.* In discussing athletes, you should not establish *Babe Ruth* as one major division and *baseball players* as a second. You might, however, have *great home-run hitters* as a major division, and *Babe Ruth* and *Hank Aaron* as subdivisions.

Exercise A

Point out the faults in the following outlines:

Purpose: To classify the members of a football team by position.
I. Linemen
   A. Tackles
   B. Centers
   C. Lettermen
   D. Guards
II. Backs
   A. Scrubs
   B. Fullbacks
   C. Halfbacks
   D. Quarterbacks
III. Ends
   A. Split ends
   B. Tight ends
IV. Teams
   A. Offensive
   B. Defensive

Thesis: All my teachers make me think.
I. My English teacher
   A. Challenges logic of papers
   B. Relates reading assignments to everyday life
   C. Wears pretty clothes
II. My history teacher
   A. Gives lectures
III. My music teacher
   A. Speaks three languages
   B. Has great sense of humor

Purpose: To classify the divisions of the federal government.
I. The executive
   A. President
II. Legislative
   A. House of Representatives
   B. Senate
   C. Lawyers
III. Judicial
   A. Supreme Court
   B. Judges

Thesis: Foolish stereotypes about different nationalities distort our thinking.

    I. Italians
      A. Fat
    II. French
      A. Romantic
      B. Charming
    III. Asians
      A. Chinese
      B. Japanese

Thesis: Both Christmas and Easter are religious holidays which also provide an opportunity for secular pleasures.

    I. Both are religious holidays.
      A. Christmas observes the birth of Christ.
      B. Easter observes the Resurrection of Christ.
      C. Halloween is the eve of All Saints Day.
    II. Both provide opportunities for secular pleasures.
      A. Christmas is a time for parties and gifts.
        1. Families decorate trees.
        2. Children sing carols.
      B. Easter is a time for new clothes and egg hunts.
        1. The bunny rabbit is a symbol of Easter.
        2. Baskets are beautifully decorated.
        3. The President of the United States sponsors an egg roll on the White House lawn.

Exercise B

Below are seven statements which, if properly grouped, will develop the thesis, *It is unfair to call television "a vast wasteland."* Decide which statements should be indicated by Roman numerals and which by capital letters. Then reconstruct the entire outline.

1. Television has given Americans vivid close-ups of surgeon and patient in the operating room, of men on the surface of the moon, and of the most exotic specimens in the plant and animal world.
2. "Trashy" magazines and newspapers are much more common on drugstore racks than magazines and newspapers of a better sort.
3. Television has brought Shakespeare to unnumbered thousands who might never have seen a Shakespearean play without it.
4. Tasteless advertisements and advertisements for worthless and

even harmful products take up space in newspapers and magazines, just as they take up time on television.
5. Television, more than any other medium, has widened America's
consciousness of the major arts and sciences.
6. Television has had a principal part in the recent rise of ballet and
modern dance to a top place among the performing arts.
7. Many of the serious failings of television are failings of the media
generally.

Exercise C _____

Write a topic outline of "Too Bad About Ol' Halloween" (p. 11).

CHAPTER 4

WRITING A PAPER: AN OVERVIEW

We will show you in Part 2 of this book how to develop different kinds of papers—comparison, classification, process, etc. But before the close of Part 1, a few words about the characteristics of *all* papers seem to be in order.

THE INTRODUCTION

To begin, you need a beginning, or *introduction.* The simplest introduction identifies the subject and states the thesis. This is not to say that the bare thesis statement at the top of the outline must necessarily appear in the same (and often drab) form in the actual introduction. For example, the thesis statement for the outline of "Too Bad about Ol' Halloween" (p. 11) read, *The highly organized celebration of today's Halloween deprives youngsters of the kind of joy I experienced during the Halloweens of my childhood.* In the paper itself, the author stated her thesis this way:

> My experience of Halloween while growing up in a rural area of West Virginia was certainly different from the experience offered my son by this super-organized, unexciting little program I was about to thumbtack to our bulletin board.

Here's another example: The thesis statement on the outline for "The Right to Assume Responsibility" (p. 230) read, *Laws requiring motorcyclists to wear crash helmets are unconstitutional.* In the paper, the author wrote,

> The stereotyped motorcyclist is a hulking brute generally complaining about something. With the increasing popularity of motorcycles this stereotype is changing, but motorcyclists are still complaining. Many

states have dictated that a motorcyclist may not ride without a crash helmet. At first glance the helmet laws seem to be an insignificant issue, certainly not anything to enrage citizens; the government is merely trying to save lives. The wisdom of wearing crash helmets is not being debated. Motorcyclists maintain that the state has infringed upon their constitutional rights with this law. They are correct.

What matters is to present the *idea* of the thesis in the most interesting manner possible.

Here is a less dramatic example of an introduction that also identifies the subject and states the thesis:

> Ted Poston's "The Revolt of the Evil Fairies" (p. 172) tells of a little boy in an all-black school who, because of his ebony skin, is forced to take the undesirable role of an evil fairy in his school's annual presentation of "Prince Charming and the Sleeping Beauty"; on the night of the production, he gets revenge by wrecking the play when he lands a strong right on the chin of Prince Charming, a fairer-skinned child. Although the tale is amusing, under its comedy lies a serious criticism of a culture in which white is seen as good and black as evil.

This introduction immediately identifies the subject: the first sentence gives the author and title of the story and a brief description of its content. The next sentence states the thesis of the paper.

Sometimes, in addition to identifying the subject and stating the thesis, the introduction lists the divisions of the rest of the paper.

> In this day of the liberated female, any woman who admits to attending college to catch a husband risks alienation, hostility, and ridicule. I'm not sure that's fair. Although I firmly believe that a woman, while she is in college, should get the best education possible, I see no harm in her looking for a husband at the same time. I believe college is an ideal place for an intelligent woman to look for a mate. For one thing, it's easy to meet men in college. Then, too, college provides a setting in which friendships can grow freely and naturally into love. Besides, an educated woman surely wants a husband who shares her interests and tastes. What better place to find him than in college?

Here, the introduction identifies the subject, finding a husband while in college, and then states the thesis: *College is an ideal place for an intelligent woman to look for a mate.* The sentences following the thesis statement let you know how the argument will be advanced in the rest of the paper. You are prepared to expect the three reasons to be developed in such a way as to prove that college *is* an ideal place to find a husband.

In short papers, the one-paragraph introduction is common, but don't feel that you are always limited to one paragraph. Consider this four-paragraph introduction:

> "I don't like to do my Christmas shopping early. I enjoy the bustle of last-minute crowds."
>
> "Why should I start research for my term paper this early? I work best under pressure."
>
> "I'll replace the washer on the bathroom sink Saturday when I have time to do it properly."
>
> We recognize such statements for what they are—excuses for procrastination. We have, of course, been told from childhood that putting off until tomorrow what we can do today is bad practice, and we feel guilty about not following such good advice, so we make up excuses to justify our tendency to delay performing unpleasant tasks. But away with guilt. Away with excuses. Procrastination, far from being evil, can, in many cases, have positive effects.

The first three paragraphs give examples of the subject, procrastination. The fourth paragraph discusses the examples and then, about the time the reader probably expects a humdrum list of ways to avoid putting off tasks, offers a surprising thesis: Procrastination may be a good thing.

In a few instances, the introduction may not state the thesis at all. Look, for example, at Dan Wakefield's "Why Soap Operas Are So Popular" (p. 16). The thesis, never stated directly in the article, is the answer to the question: Why are soap operas popular? Wakefield begins to answer the question in the seventh paragraph ("Most current soaps are far more sophisticated . . ."). The introduction, the first six paragraphs, sets up the misconceptions about soap operas that he will disprove in the remainder of the article.

Or consider this introduction:

> The laundry room in my apartment building is large, clean, well-lighted, and attractively decorated. It has plenty of comfortable chairs where the residents may sit and read, talk, or sew while they wait for the efficient washers and dryers to do their work. But something strange happens in the laundry room. People don't sit in the comfortable chairs and read or talk or sew; instead, they perch precariously on the tables provided for sorting and folding clothes. They perch on these tables and stare at the glass-doored dryers, apparently fascinated by the sight of wet sheets and towels tumbling round and round in the big machines.
>
> In appliance stores, too, I have noticed groups gather before a row of ten or twelve soundless television sets, each tuned to the same channel.

Minutes before, the watchers had been busy shoppers, but now they stand transfixed before a situation comedy without sound.

And who has not felt the hypnotic power of a wood-burning fireplace? The flames, now blue, now orange, now red, leap and fall, and one stares as if fire were new to the planet.

Movement and color—the combination is compelling. One may well ask why.

This introduction, consisting of four paragraphs, identifies the subject—the attraction of movement and color—and gives three examples of the attraction, but it doesn't state the thesis. Instead, it asks a question: Why is the combination of color and movement so compelling? The answer to the question will make up the body of the paper. The thesis, the one-sentence answer to the question, need not be directly stated.

In other words, many kinds of introductions can be effective. You might, for example, occasionally try dramatizing a situation:

Sheila felt light-headed: her eyes would not focus and there was a slight hum in her ears. Her hands, wet and clammy, shook so that she could hardly write. She could not concentrate. She wanted only to run, to be away from that terrible scene.

Sheila has not just witnessed some horrible accident that she must report. She is a freshman composition student who has been told to write her first "in-class" composition. Many students will recognize Sheila's symptoms. Perhaps the following tips about writing a composition under pressure will help alleviate their pain.

The dramatization in the first paragraph attracts the reader's attention. The second paragraph explains the situation and anticipates the rest of the paper, which offers tips on writing under pressure.

Or you could use an anecdote to illustrate the subject:

Mrs. Peters was busily talking to a neighbor over the telephone one afternoon when she experienced the sudden fear that her baby son had been hurt. She told her neighbor and ran to check the baby, supposedly napping in his crib upstairs. To her horror, she found the child unconscious on the floor. Evidently he had tried to climb out of the crib but, in the attempt, had fallen on his head. Mrs. Peters' "knowing" her baby was in danger is the kind of experience many of us have had at one time or another. Yesterday, for example, I dialed a friend and, just before his telephone could ring, he picked up the receiver to call me. Both of these incidents are illustrations of the kind of thought transference known as *telepathy*.

The two anecdotes illustrate the way telepathy, the subject of this paper, functions. The remainder of the paper contains an extended definition of the term.

As you can see, introductions take various forms. The examples here by no means exhaust the possibilities, but they do illustrate some ways of getting into a subject. Whatever form you choose, it's important to remember that the introduction must interest your readers—after all, you do want them to read the remainder of the paper—and it should in some way prepare readers for what will follow.

THE BODY

You have seen from your study of outlining that the development of your purpose must be carefully planned. The body of your paper is the realization of the plan, with the outline serving, in a sense, as the table of contents. It is not, however, enough simply to discuss each division of your outline, although that is essential. You must also *lead* your readers from one section to another in such a way that they don't become confused.

Topic sentences. One method of leading your reader is to write clear topic sentences for each paragraph. A topic sentence is to a paragraph what a thesis is to a paper: it expresses the central idea of the paragraph. The remainder of the paragraph gives proof of the topic sentence. If you work from a sentence outline, you may find that the sentences indicating major divisions serve very well as topic sentences. Whether you use sentences from your outline or make up new ones, though, the topic sentences should clearly let the reader know what the idea of each paragraph is.

In the following paragraphs, James Morris describes the port of New York as seen from a helicopter. Notice how the topic sentences (indicated by *italics*) move the description along.

James Morris
From AROUND THE GREAT PORT

Seen from up there, in the bright October sunshine . . . *the city looked what it was: a landing place and a bazaar.* Every twenty minutes a ship leaves or enters New York. Every day a multitude equivalent to the population of Norway enters its business district. Eight railroad lines end their journeys in the city; expressways circle it, or stalk on stilts across its tenements. One and a half million passengers pass through Kennedy Airport in an average month—when I was there, 69,000 in a single day.

New York's qualifications are evident, too, when you see it from the air. *It might have been man-made as a port, so neatly functional is its shape and situation.* On the north-eastern coast of the United States, between latitudes 40° and 41° North, two large chunks of land stand out from the coastline like breakwaters. One is the flank of New Jersey, with its long line of reefs; the other is Long Island in the State of New York, a splendid boulevard, a hundred miles long, of sand, marsh, and grassland. These two land masses approach each other at an angle, and very nearly meet: they are separated by the entrance to New York Bay.

It is a wonderfully sheltered, secretive opening. Long Island protects it from the northern gales, the arm of sand called Sandy Hook reaches out from New Jersey to embrace its channel from the south, and the bulk of Staten Island stands like a cork in the middle. The mariner enters it sailing almost due west, but a few miles from the open sea he turns abruptly north, passes through the bottlenecks of the Narrows, leaves Staten Island on his port side, and finds himself in the glorious security of the upper bay— gales and high seas left behind, even the sea birds domesticated, as he steams snugly between Brooklyn and Bayonne toward the comforts of the metropolis.

This is the lordly front door of New York—the carriage sweep. *There is a kitchen entrance too, for between Long Island and the mainland there lies Long Island Sound, sixty miles of sheltered water linking the port with the Atlantic by a back route.* This will also take a seafarer into the upper bay, via the tidal strait called the East River, while from the American interior the noble Hudson River flows into the Bay out of the north, mingling its icy fresh waters with the salt tide of the Atlantic. Diverse other creeks and rivers debouch into New York Bay, and all around are little islands, inlets, and spits, forming a watery sort of filigree upon the large-scale charts.

In the center of this system of waters stands the island of Manhattan, the core of the port. With its long flat line of shore it provides safe wharfage for many ships: surrounded as it is by water, protected by the Narrows from the open sea, *it is a perfect site for a merchant city.*

Questions for Writing or Discussion

1. Why, according to the author, is Manhattan the "perfect site for a merchant city"?
2. How do the topic sentences contribute to the idea that Manhattan is a perfectly situated merchant city?
3. What is meant by "kitchen entrance" (paragraph 4)? Is the image appropriate to the idea being developed? Why?
4. Do you think the topic sentence of the last paragraph should be placed at the beginning of the paragraph? Why, or why not?

Topic sentences usually appear at the beginning of a paragraph:

The biographer who works from life, as Boswell did, has an extraor-dinary advantage over the biographer who works from the docu-ment. . . . He has seen his man in the flesh, he has been aware of a three-dimensional being, drawing breath and sitting in the midst of an age they both share. In his mind he retains a sharp image of his subject. He has heard the voice and seen the gesture (and even in our age no recording, no cinema picture can provide a substitute for that). The latecoming biographer hears only the rustle of the pages amid the silence of the tomb. This is explanation enough for the fact that the greatest biographies in our literature have been those which were writ-ten by men who knew their subjects and who painted them as the painter paints his picture—within a room, a street, a landscape, with a background and a context rich with its million points of contemporane-ous attachment. Boswell . . . repose[s] upon our shelves with vividness and mass and authority which later biographers cannot possess.

Leon Edel, *Literary Biography*

Sometimes, however, the best place for a topic sentence is at the end of the paragraph:

He drank noisily and chewed with his mouth open. He stuffed food into his mouth with his fingers and wiped his chin with the sleeve of his coat. He made loud, vulgar comments to the waitress, who had diffi-culty hiding her anger as other customers turned to stare. His idea of conversation was to regale his date with statistics about the World Series or facts about his expensive new car—especially its expense. *An hour with Bruce in the city's most costly restaurant made Jane wish she had dined at home alone on a tuna fish sandwich.*

A topic sentence can even appear in the middle of a paragraph:

A fire-warning detector will "smell" smoke and sound an alarm; a guided missile will "see" and pursue a radar echo or the hot engines of a bomber; a speed governor will "feel" when a shaft is spinning too fast and act to restrain it. *But . . . quotation marks are appropriate in all such cases, because these machines do not have minds and they do not perceive the world as human beings do.* Information from our eyes, ears, and other senses goes to our brains, and of some of it (by no means all) we are aware as a vivid part of our conscious experience, showing us the world we inhabit.

Nigel Calder, *The Mind of Man*

On rare occasions, the topic sentence need not be directly stated at all; it may be implied:

> Often when I find some passage in a book especially impressive—especially bright, say, or especially moving—I find myself turning to the dust jacket, if the author's picture is there, to communicate, to say a kind of "Well done." Coretta Scott King's photograph, soft, shadowed, and lovely, is on the jacket of her *My Life with Martin Luther King, Jr.* I must have turned to it a dozen times in the reading of this book.

Here, the paragraph's central idea—that Coretta Scott King's *My Life with Martin Luther King Jr.* is especially impressive—is so clear that a statement of it is unnecessary; indeed, to state it directly would mar the grace of the paragraph. Implied topic sentences are tricky, though, and should be used cautiously. An idea that seems quite clear to you may not be so clear to your reader.

To sum up, a topic sentence states the central idea of the paragraph. Because it does, it usually appears at the beginning of the paragraph to give the reader immediate notice of the new point being developed. It can, however, appear at the end or even in the middle of the paragraph. Once in a while, it can be omitted altogether. Wherever you decide to put your topic sentence, keep your readers in mind. They should not experience one second's confusion in following your thought. The central idea of every paragraph must be clear enough to lead readers easily from one point of your paper to another.

Exercise

Below is a group of short paragraphs without topic sentences. Suggest a logical topic sentence for each paragraph.

1. I anxiously boarded the Cessna 182 and patiently awaited my turn to jump. Then the moment came, and the jumpmaster yelled my name. With mixed emotions, I crawled to the door, swung my feet out and grabbed the wing strut. There I was, hanging onto an aircraft wing, three-thousand feet above ground and travelling at eighty-five miles per hour. With my feet dangling free behind me and the roar of the engine in front of me, I signalled my confidence to the jumpmaster with a smile and released my grasp from the Cessna's wing. The sense of weightlessness and freedom I experienced at that moment helped me appreciate how an eagle must feel in flight. My chute opened with a crack, and I found

myself suspended in mid-air. Looking around, I could see for miles and miles. Then I realized that something was missing. It was sound. The only sound I heard was that of my own heartbeat. All too soon the ground started coming up at me fast. Glancing at my altimeter, I noticed that I was five-hundred feet above ground. At that altitude, I prepared myself for landing. Safely on the ground, I carried my chute back to the hangar, my first jump over.

2. Both the child and the puppy must be housebroken in that they must be taught to heed the call of nature in specified areas only. This process takes time, patience, and reinforcement. Both the child and the puppy require special nourishment in the beginning. Eventually, both must be weaned from liquid food and taught to eat solids. Both the two-legged and the four-legged animal must be taught (for their safety and our sanity) what they are to touch, have, chew up, and, in general, how much mischief they are allowed to get into—and away with. The training of both human and beastie takes a lot of time, an unlimited supply of love, and unusual amounts of patience, caution, care, and understanding.

3. My sister wants to spend the family vacation at some expensive resort. Dad wants only a mountain stream and good fishing gear. Mom likes to visit old friends and sit and reminisce. I would like to say goodbye to all of them and hitchhike to California, but then we wouldn't have a family vacation.

4. The tuition at this college is the lowest in the state, but the quality of instruction is among the highest: the professors, who emphasize their roles as teachers rather than as researchers, seem dedicated to making their students learn. In addition to traditional courses, the college offers community-related courses in everything from fur-cutting to reading income-tax forms. Finally, the college is located in the center of downtown so that it can easily be reached by public transportation.

5. Two weeks after I bought my car, I parked it in front of a friend's house, and her neighbor's daughter backed into it, demolishing the left door. A month later, another friend's babysitter backed into it, demolishing the right door. Then I had two months of calm before a harried housewife ran a red light as I was crossing the intersection and removed my right fender. A few weeks later, a hit-and-run driver banged into the left tail light during the car's stay in a parking lot.

Transitions. Another way to help your reader follow your thought is to use *transitions,* words or phrases that show the logical connections between ideas. Such words as *and, but, however, there-*

fore, next, and *finally* act as signals. They say to a reader, "Here's an additional point," or "A contrast is coming up," or "Now, I'm drawing a conclusion." Transitions make connections between ideas clear and therefore easy to follow. Consider, for example, the following pairs of sentences.

Awkward: My nephew is a brat. I love him.
Better: My nephew is a brat, *but* I love him.
Awkward: The magician showed the audience that the hat was empty. He pulled a rabbit from it.
Better: *First,* the magician showed the audience that the hat was empty. *Then* he pulled a rabbit from it.

Perhaps the most natural transitions are the coordinating conjunctions: *and, or, nor, but, yet, for.*

I do not need to tell you how important the election is. *Nor* do I need to remind you to vote tomorrow.

Laura is always on one kind of diet or another. *Yet* she never seems to lose any weight.

Here are some other commonly used transitions:

second, third, finally, next;
in the first place, in the second place, in addition, besides;
furthermore, moreover, again, also, similarly;
for example, for instance, to illustrate;
on the other hand, nevertheless, conversely, instead, however, still;
therefore, consequently, as a result, accordingly;
of course, obviously, indeed.

Medicare and Blue Cross can be a blessing to an elderly person with many illnesses. The difficulty of filling out all the required forms, *however,* sometimes makes one wonder how blessed he is.

I have voted democratic all my life. It was a surprise to my children, *therefore,* when I voted for John Anderson.

Employed sensibly, transitions contribute to the smoothness of your paper. But a word of caution seems necessary: Too many transitions can be as distressing to a reader as too few. Look at this monstrosity:

The children wanted to see the animals in my woods. *However,* they made too much noise. *In the first place,* all twenty of them shouted.

Moreover, they screamed. *Furthermore,* they threw rocks into the streams. *Therefore,* birds, frogs, even bugs went rushing to the hills. *As a result,* the children saw no animals. *Nor* should they have expected to see animals after making so much noise. *Nevertheless,* I was sorry that they thought they might see what only hours of silence and days of watching ever bring to sight.

Now look at how the paragraph actually appears in *The Inland Island* by Josephine Johnson:

"Where are all your animals?" the little children cried, running . . . through the woods—twenty little children, panting, shouting, screaming, throwing rocks into the streams. Birds, frogs, even bugs went rushing to the hills. How sad that the children thought they might see what only hours of silence, days of watching ever bring to sight.

Clearly, Johnson's paragraph is better. All those transitions in the first paragraph do not help it flow; they get in the way. Use transitions, then, but use them only to signal a logical connection that would not otherwise be obvious.

Exercise

Underline every transition in this letter written by Abraham Lincoln to General Joseph Hooker in 1863.

I have placed you at the head of the Army of the Potomac. Of course I have done this upon what appears to me to be sufficient reasons. And yet I think it best for you to know that there are some things in regard to which I am not quite satisfied with you. I believe you to be a brave and skillful soldier, which, of course, I like. I also believe you do not mix politics with your profession, in which you are right. You have confidence in yourself, which is a valuable, if not an indispensable quality. You are ambitious, which, within reasonable bounds, does good rather than harm. But I think that during Gen. Burnside's command of the army, you have taken counsel of your ambition, and thwarted him as much as you could, in which you did a great wrong to the country, and to a most meritorious and honorable brother officer. I have heard, in such a way as to believe it, of your recently saying that both the army and the government needed a dictator. Of course it was not *for* this, but in spite of it, that I have given you the command. Only those generals who gain successes can set up dictators. What I now ask of you is military success, and I will risk the dictatorship. The government will support you to the utmost of its ability, which is neither more nor less than it has done and will do for all commanders. I much fear that the spirit which you have [helped] infuse into the army, of criticizing their commander, and with-holding confidence from him, will now turn upon you. I shall assist you, as far as I can, to put it down. Neither you, nor Napoleon, if he were alive again, could get any good out of an army while such a spirit pre-vails in it.

And now beware of rashness. Beware of rashness, but with energy, and sleepless vigilance, go forward, and give us victories.

In marking connections between ideas, you are not limited to single words and short phrases. Often the *topic sentence* serves both as a transition and as an indicator of the central idea of a paragraph.

> *Besides making life difficult for his parents,* Charles sent his first-grade teacher home with a nightly headache.
>
> *Although the Puritans observed a strict code of behavior,* their lives were often filled with great joy.

In sentences of this kind, the introductory adverbial phrase or clause points back to the preceding paragraph to provide a transition. At the same time, the rest of the sentence points forward to the subject matter of the paragraph for which it is the topic sentence.

Occasionally, an entire paragraph may serve as a transition. It's sometimes a good idea to stop—at a logical point, of course—and sum up what you've said so far before going on to another point. The good *transitional paragraph,* like the transitional topic sentence, points back to what has gone before and points forward to what is yet to come.

> Thus granting Professor Maly time to do a thorough and conscientious new edition of her book will add to her professional standing, bring a bit of valuable attention and some money to the college, and result in a book more helpful than ever in teaching students how to write clear English. These considerations are, I think, justification for the profes-sional leave she has requested, but I have other reasons for recommend-ing that her request for leave be granted.
>
> So much for the preparation of the surface. Now we are ready to paint.
>
> Thus, Jackie Robinson had to confront a long tradition of bigotry in the major leagues. How did he meet this challenge?
>
> With all these arguments in favor of state-run lotteries, opponents of such lotteries can still raise some valid points.

Paragraph development. Besides leading your reader from one paragraph to another, you need to be certain that the paragraphs themselves are logically and adequately developed. A paragraph, a group of related sentences developing a single topic, must be unified, coherent, and complete.

A paragraph must be *unified;* that is, all the sentences in the paragraph must develop *one* idea, the one contained in the topic sentence. Anything that doesn't contribute to the idea should be taken out. One of the following paragraphs appears exactly as it was written by Lewis Thomas, a skilled essayist whose paragraphs are beautifully unified. Which paragraph do you think Thomas wrote?

[1]Viewed from the distance of the moon, the astonishing thing about the earth . . . is that it is alive. [2]The photographs show the dry, pounded surface of the moon in the foreground, dead as an old bone. [3]Aloft, floating free beneath the moist, gleaming membrane of bright blue sky, is the rising earth, the only exuberant thing in this part of the cosmos. [4]If you could look long enough, you would see the swirling of the great drifts of white cloud, covering and uncovering the half-hidden masses of land. [5]If you had been looking for a very long, geologic time, you could have seen the continents themselves in motion, drifting apart on their crustal plates, held afloat by the fire beneath. [6]It has the organized, self-contained look of a live creature, full of information, marvelously skilled in handling the sun.

[1]Viewed from the distance of the moon, the astonishing thing about the earth . . . is that it is alive. [2]The great technological advances that made it possible for man to walk on the moon also made it possible to send photographs back to earth. [3]Such are the miracles of modern science that you sat in your living room and watched the astronauts romp, enjoying their gravity-less freedom. [4]Soon, however, you saw something much more important, the photographs of the moon. [5]The photographs show the dry, pounded surface of the moon in the foreground, dead as an old bone. [6]It is so dead you marvel that poets for centuries have hymned its praises. [7]On the other hand, aloft, floating free beneath the moist, gleaming membrane of bright blue sky, is the rising earth, the only exuberant thing in this part of the cosmos. [8]If you could look long enough, you would see the swirling of the great drifts of white cloud, covering and uncovering the half-hidden masses of land. [9]If you had been looking for a very long, geologic time, you could have seen the continents themselves in motion, drifting apart on their crustal plates, held afloat by the fire beneath. [10]It has the organized, self-contained look of a live creature, full of information, marvelously skilled in handling the sun.

The first paragraph is the real Lewis Thomas paragraph. In the second—and longer—one, sentences two, three, four, and six obviously do not advance Thomas's idea that the earth is alive. Instead, they distract the reader, and the paragraph's central idea is lost in the confusion.

A paragraph must be *coherent:* it must stick together. This means the sentences must be smoothly integrated. You can't expect your readers to follow your thought if the sentences do not have some kind of intelligible order. Is this paragraph orderly? Can you follow the writer's thought?

> Yesterday was one big disaster. When I found my right rear tire flat as a board, I laid my head on the steering wheel and wept. The burned bacon didn't help, either; especially after that cold shower, I needed a hot meal. I had worked so hard on my paper I didn't think it was fair that the professor gave me a "D" on it. Sleeping through the alarm always starts my day off wrong. And now I've got to write a twenty-page term paper for history. I should have stayed in bed.

The paragraph is a confusing mess, isn't it? But using a simple time, or chronological, order can make it coherent:

> Yesterday was one big disaster. I slept through the alarm. Late, I rushed to the bathroom. No more hot water. Teeth chattering from a cold shower, I decided to cook a hot breakfast—and burned the bacon. I gulped down some cold shredded wheat and dashed to my car. By running two traffic lights, I made it to my English class on time and eagerly waited for the professor to return our papers. I had worked hard and was sure I had made at least a "B" if not an "A." Then I saw a big red "D" at the top of my paper. It didn't seem fair. I went on to my history class, and the professor assigned a twenty-page term paper. I decided to cut my remaining classes and go home. When I got to my car and found the right rear tire flat as a board, I laid my head on the steering wheel and wept. I should have stayed in bed.

In fact, in some cases, as in the following paragraph, chronological order is essential to the point being made:

> Few men have seen as much of our history, and from such advantageous viewpoints, as Oliver Wendell Holmes, Jr. As a boy in Massachusetts he met veterans of the Revolution. He went to school in a Boston shaken by abolition. He fought through the Civil War, and it is said to have been his voice that shouted a rough warning to Lincoln when the President exposed his high hat above the ramparts at Fort Stevens. With peace Holmes became a lawyer and a great scholar. He served as a judge for half a century, first on the high bench of Massachusetts and then on the United States Supreme Court. And at the age of ninety-two, just retired, he received an early official visit from the newly elected Franklin D. Roosevelt. . . . That such a span of life should have been granted to a man so competent to use it is a rare event in the history of any nation.
>
> Louis Auchincloss, *Life, Law and Letters*

You can achieve order in a number of other ways. One of these lies in the use of space order—from left to right, from top to bottom, or, as in the following example, from near to far.

> It was a rimy morning, and very damp. I had seen the damp lying on the outside of my little window, as if some goblin had been crying there all night, and using the window for a pocket-handkerchief. Now I saw the damp lying on the bare hedges and spare grass, like a coarser sort of spiders' webs; hanging itself from twig to twig and blade to blade. On every rail and gate, wet lay clammy, and the marsh-mist was so thick, that the wooden finger on the post directing people to our village—a direction which they never accepted, for they never came there—was invisible to me until I was quite close under it. . . . The mist was heavier yet when I got out upon the marshes, so that instead of my running at everything, everything seemed to run at me. . . .
>
> Charles Dickens, *Great Expectations*

You can sometimes enumerate reasons for an action or belief.

> I have sought love, *first,* because it brings ecstasy—ecstasy so great that I could often have sacrificed all the rest of life for a few hours of this joy. I have sought it, *next,* because it relieves loneliness—that terrible loneliness in which one shivering consciousness looks over the rim of the world into the cold unfathomable lifeless abyss. I have sought it, *finally,* because in the union of love I have seen, in a mystic miniature, the prefiguring vision of the heaven that saints and poets have imagined. That is what I sought, and though it might seem too good for human life, that is what—at last—I have found.
>
> Bertrand Russell, "What I Have Lived For"

A paragraph may also depend for coherence on logical relationships. One logical relationship is that of idea and example.

> There are many expensive practices in football and men's basketball that could be eliminated without affecting in any way the revenue-producing potential of these sports. For example, there are many people who question the need to send teams to away games two or three days in advance of their event. The necessity to have the entire football and/or basketball teams removed from their dorms to a hotel or motel the night prior to a home game also seems questionable. To spend over $100,000 per year, as many schools do, for special "training tables" also seems unnecessary when nutritional meals are available (and already paid for) in the regular student dining facilities. Nor does offering up to 95 full scholarships for intercollegiate football appear logical when the sport permits only 11 players on the field at a time and when professional football teams manage to survive with squads half the size.
>
> Christine H. B. Grant, "Title IX Is a Civil Rights Issue"

Another logical relationship that can give coherence to a paragraph is that of cause and effect:

> This sentiment of retaliation is, of course, exactly what impels most offenders to do what they do. Except for racketeers, robbers, and professional criminals, the men who are arrested, convicted, and sentenced are usually out to avenge a wrong, assuage a sense of injury, or correct an injustice as they see it. Their victims are individuals whom they believe to be assailants, false friends, rivals, unfaithful spouses, cruel parents—or symbolic figures representing these individuals.
>
> Karl Menninger, *The Crime of Punishment*

Perhaps one of the most useful logical relationships you can use to achieve coherence within a paragraph is the comparison of one thing with another:

> In science fiction, which is the literature of extrapolation, there is to be found the recurrent theme of the omniscient computer which ultimately takes over the ordering of human life and affairs. Is this possible? I believe it is not; but I also believe that the arguments commonly advanced to refute this possibility are the wrong ones. . . . It is said, for example, that computers [unlike humans] "only do what they are told," that they have to be programmed for every computation they undertake. But I do not believe that I was born with an innate ability to solve quadratic equations or to identify common members of the British flora; I, too, had to be programmed for these activities, but I happened to call my programmers by different names, such as "schoolteacher," "lecturer" or "professor."
>
> W. T. Williams, "Computers as Botanists"

Use any of these methods—or any others that work—to achieve coherence. The important thing is to achieve it—to make the relationship between and among sentences clear to the reader.

A paragraph must be *complete*. Every paragraph in your paper must be adequately developed. That means using enough facts, details, examples, quotations of authorities, or reasons to support the topic sentence. Inadequate development, like lack of unity and coherence, causes confusion for the reader. Consider, for example, the difference between the following two paragraphs.

> Until a few years ago, there was a myth that the divorced woman, because of a generous alimony and child-support check, enjoyed a life of luxury and excitement. I wish that were so.
>
> The good life is supposed to begin as soon as a woman regains her freedom, or so I've been told. According to the script of the good life, a fat

alimony and child-support check will carry the divorcee until she walks into a glamorous new job filled with challenge, excitement, and a fabulous salary. She will enjoy a spacious suite of rooms in an exclusive neighborhood. Her closet will bulge with expensive clothes from the finest boutiques. A classic automobile, perhaps an El Dorado, will wait for her to turn the key and carry her to exotic places and adventures with exciting new friends. My experience has not quite hit all these high spots.

Obviously, the second paragraph is more fully developed than the first, which contains nothing but the barest statement of the idea. The second paragraph brings the idea to life by spelling out the myth of the divorced woman.

Now consider the following descriptive paragraphs:

My roommate's desk is a mess. It is covered with food, papers, clothing, and books. It is so cluttered that it took me three weeks to find my biology book, which she borrowed a month ago.

My roommate's desk is a study in chaos. An ancient Royal typewriter with a sheet of paper in the carriage dominates the desk, but it has considerable company. The remains of three wild roses, picked two weeks ago during a walk with her boyfriend, droop from a Coke bottle. The petals have long since fallen on her open dictionary where they punctuate the definitions of words beginning with "I." A box of Ritz crackers and a jar of peanut butter serve as one bookend for her textbooks; a stained coffee cup with a spoon in it and a jar of instant coffee serve as the other. A rolled-up sweat shirt leans wearily against a stack of overdue library books. A sheaf of notebook paper containing many scrawls is, she says, the rough draft for her term paper in history. A manual for writing term papers is opened to the page on footnotes, where a McDonald's hamburger wrapper acts as a bookmark, and mustard from its former contents has stained the pages. A jar which once contained cold cream now holds ten or fifteen pencils and ball-point pens. Cigarette butts overflow a large green ashtray. Under the ashtray is my biology book, which she borrowed a month ago.

As in the earlier example, the second paragraph brings the description to life by providing specific details. The vivid description of the roommate's desk enables the reader to visualize it and even to make some inferences about the character of the women. For these reasons, the fully developed second paragraph is more convincing than the first.

Not every paragraph need be so long, of course. The length of a paragraph is determined by its topic sentence. You have to decide how much material you need to develop the idea. Some ideas require more development than others, but in every case, the material should relate to the point and should be as concise as possible. In other words, you should never *pad* your writing. An intelligent reader can tell immediately if you are using words simply to fill space and will probably reject your arguments, however worthy, because of your manner. You should, then, use as many facts, details, examples, quotations, or reasons as you need to develop your point, but no more.

THE CONCLUSION

If you have written a thoughtful introduction and have tried to lead the reader, by means of topic sentences and transitions, through a logical and adequately developed body, your conclusion should be easy to write. A good conclusion gives a sense of finality, which may be achieved in one of several ways.

The easiest way to conclude a paper is to mention again its major ideas. The following paragraph concludes a paper in which the writer explains why he belongs to a book club:

> Convenience, variety, and economy—these were my reasons for joining a book club. I have not been disappointed.

Some conclusions merely restate the thesis, although in different words to avoid monotony. This is the case in " 'Why' Is Worse than 'What' " (p. 81):

> There's an explanation for everything, it's true, but some explanations are more readily acceptable than others. That's the way it is.

Some conclusions interpret the significance of the material presented in the body of the paper, as is the case in "Can People Be Judged by Their Appearance?" (p. 93):

> Since these personality characteristics depend on the growth of the layers of the little egg from which the person developed, they are very difficult to change. Nevertheless, it is important for the individual to know about these types, so that he can have at least an inkling of what to expect from those around him, and can make allowances for the different kinds of human nature, and so that he can become aware of and learn to control his own natural tendencies, which may sometimes guide him into making the same mistakes over and over again in handling his difficulties.

Other conclusions make predictions based on the material in the body of the paper.

> Pollution is a major world-wide problem against which many powerful interests are being marshaled. From the private citizens who are concerned with the type of detergent or pesticide they use to the leaders of great nations, all thinking people are involved in the environmental crisis. There is still time for humanity to resolve this problem, as people are creative, inventive, and ambitious. These qualities, which are responsible for precipitating this crisis, will be the very means for humanity's salvation.

An anecdote sometimes effectively concludes a paper. Following is the conclusion to a paper about the rewards given Dr. Jonas Salk for his polio vaccine:

> Probably the greatest tribute Dr. Salk has received was unwittingly paid by a small boy whose father, having shown his son the research center, told him that Dr. Salk invented the polio vaccine. The boy, looking puzzled, said "Daddy, what's polio?"

Quotations and questions can serve to conclude papers. Both devices are used in the conclusion to a paper urging support of the United Torch Drive:

> Samuel Johnson defined a patron as "one who looks with unconcern on a man struggling for life in the water, and when he has reached ground encumbers him with help." Shall we be merely patrons of the needy?

Forms of conclusions, like forms of introductions, vary. All conclusions, however, should be related to what has gone before. In writing your conclusions, be sure you don't present irrelevant material—ideas that have not been touched on in the body of the paper. Furthermore, all conclusions should be consistent in tone with the body of the paper. Don't let a strong argument just dwindle away because of a weak conclusion. If Patrick Henry, for example, had concluded his speech to the House of Burgesses with, "Thus, gentlemen, now that you have heard my arguments, I am sure you will agree with me that we should oppose the British crown," his words would not have been remembered. Instead, he said,

> Is life so dear, or peace so sweet, as to be purchased at the price of chains and slavery? Forbid it, Almighty God! I know not what course others may take; but as for me, give me liberty or give me death!

And all conclusions should be brief. Make the important points in the body of your paper. The conclusion should simply drive the points home.

A BRIEF NOTE ON STYLE

Finally, style. The paper should be readable. We realize, of course, that a polished style doesn't just happen when some English teacher calls for it, and we have devoted an entire section of this book to a discussion of style. But for starters—even before your teacher subjects you to a rigorous consideration of stylistic elements— you might do well to study "Miscellaneous Do's and Don'ts" (pp. 433–435).

Good ideas can seldom be communicated
without good organization.

PART 2

METHODS OF DEVELOPMENT

INTRODUCTORY NOTE
Why Different Methods?

So far, we have considered the general requirements for a good paper: every paper must have a purpose or a thesis; every paper must be logical; every paper must be organized. Now, we want to look at some requirements for particular kinds of papers.

Many writing assignments call for specific methods of development. In a psychology class, for example, you might be asked to *compare and contrast* psychosis and neurosis. In a history class, you might be asked to trace the *process* by which the Bolsheviks took power after the Russian Revolution. In a sociology class, you might be asked to *classify* the groups which make up a community, taking into consideration the level of income, education, taste, and social practices of each group. Each of these assignments requires a specific method of development, and this section of the text will show you how to meet those requirements.

Other writing assignments, though they may not call for specific methods, will profit from an intelligent combination of the methods discussed here. A definition, for instance, might require the use of comparisons, examples, and cause-and-effect methods. Thus, even though we have, for the purposes of discussion, arbitrarily established separate methods, we recognize that, more often than not, these methods will be combined.

We recognize, also, that our "rules" about methods of development are not sacred, even though we often deliver them as if we believe they were handed down by God to Moses along with the Ten Commandments. But we have discovered from our own students that at least some clearly stated guidelines are helpful to beginning writers. As you gain practice in writing, you will discover the exceptions to these guidelines that work for you.

CHAPTER 5

WRITING AN EXAMPLE PAPER

An *example* is something selected to represent, or sometimes to show the primary nature of, the larger group to which it belongs: a rattlesnake is an example of a reptile; kidnapping is an example of crime; a Pontiac is an example of General Motors products. Put another way, an example is one of many specific instances in which a generalization can prove to be true: a letter delivered two months late could be an example of the generalization that the post office provides poor service. An *example paper* is one which relies almost solely on example for support of the thesis, and learning to handle it well will help prepare you for all the kinds of papers you will be called upon to write.

Nearly all good writing depends heavily on examples as an important means of supporting ideas—and for very sound reasons. Examples give concreteness and therefore clarity to ideas. A magazine writer may say, for instance, that going to school can be frustrating, and, as a student, you nod your head in agreement. But how can you be sure that you and the writer have the same understanding of *frustration*? To you, frustration may result from the long reading assignments you find yourself plodding through, or from the difficulty of finding in the library just the right piece of information with which to finish your term paper. But when the writer goes on to tell stories about the causes of her frustration—when she writes about her inability to stand on her head in her physical education class, or her ineptness at dissecting a cat in her anatomy class, or her habitual failure to recharge the batteries of her calculator before going to her math class—you understand what the writer means by *frustration*. The examples have given to the abstract idea *frustration* not only clarity, but concreteness, and the concreteness does much to make the idea interesting.

Because concreteness and clarity are essential to good writing, even the smallest sentence sequence will often be shaped by example:

> To convince a reader, good writers usually offer proof of their generalizations. In the Declaration of Independence, for example, Thomas Jefferson cited twenty-eight violations of basic human rights to support his assertion that George III was a tyrant.

Similarly, one might develop an entire paragraph by example, sometimes in a chatty and informal manner:

> I can do almost anything to keep myself from writing. I can sharpen pencils. I can dust my desk. I can consider whether to use white or yellow paper. I can arrange my dictionary at a neat 45-degree angle to the wall. I can stare vacantly out the window, praying for inspiration. I can sharpen my pencils all over again.

The same principle applies in a more formal paragraph:

> Some of the greatest scientific discoveries are the result of inspirations caused by chance occurrences. Three brief examples can demonstrate this point. First, Archimedes' noticing the rise of the water level as he submerged himself in a tub led to the formulation of the laws of liquid displacement, the foundation of many of the laws of modern physics. Second, Sir Isaac Newton discovered the law of gravity because an apple fell on his head while he was sitting under a tree. Third, after being caught in a strong current of hot rising air while flying his gas balloon, George Alexander Whitehead thought about the occurrence and developed the fundamental principles of meteorology. These and other incidents show that many of the greatest scientific developments spring from lucky accidents that stimulate work in a specific direction.

Sentences and paragraphs may be shaped by example, but our concern in this chapter is to look at an entire paper developed by example. In such a paper, the writer offers well-developed examples to support a thesis. The success of the paper will depend largely on the quality of these illustrations and on their arrangement. We have a few tips.

First, *be specific*. Remember, the purpose of an example is to give concreteness and clarity to an idea, and you won't get either with vague language. (See "Abstract Writing and Concrete Writing," pp. 400–408.) Notice the concrete language and the specific details in the following passage from Eric Hoffer's "Cities and Nature":

I spent a good part of my life close to nature as a migratory worker, lumberjack, and placer miner. Mother Nature was breathing down my neck, so to speak, and I had the feeling that she did not want me around. I was bitten by every sort of insect, and scratched by burrs, foxtails and thorns. My clothes were torn by buckbrush and tangled manzanita. Hard clods pushed against my ribs when I lay down to rest, and grime ate its way into every pore of my body. Everything around me was telling me all the time to roll up and be gone. I was an unwanted intruder. I could never be at home in nature the way trees, flowers and birds are at home . . . in the city. I did not feel at ease until my feet touched the paved road.

The road led to the city, and I knew with every fiber of my being that the man-made world of the city was man's only home on this planet, his refuge from an inhospitable nonhuman cosmos.

Now, consider how much less vivid and therefore less interesting is the following version of Hoffer's passage:

I lived and worked outdoors for several years, and the experience taught me that the city is the preferable habitat for man. In nature, I always felt dirty and uncomfortable. Nature was inhospitable to me. I was an alien there and never felt comfortable until I turned again toward the city, the only appropriate environment for man.

Obviously, good examples use specific details expressed in concrete language.

Second, *make certain that your examples* are *examples, and that your generalization, or thesis, is one which can be proved by example.* To repeat what we have said earlier, an example is one thing selected from many to show the nature or character of the group, or it is one of many specific instances in which a generalization proves to be true. If Suzy is the only woman in your school who has dyed her hair green, you cannot generalize that green hair is a fad in your school and then cite the one case as an example, no matter how vividly you describe Suzy's new hair color. You can, however, use Suzy's green hair as an example of her eccentricity if she really is eccentric—if she exhibits several other odd characteristics. An example is one of many, and a generalization is that which is usually or frequently or generally true of its subject.

Third, *play fair.* When the subject allows, you should try to select examples that represent an honest cross-section of your subject. If you want to show, for instance, that most of the teachers in a particular school are boring lecturers, try to find examples of some who are young, some who are middle-aged, and some who are ready to retire. Again, some of your examples should be women and some men, some perhaps single teachers and some married. Your examples should also indicate a fair distribution among departments. You don't want your examples to suggest that all boring lecturers are middle-aged, married men who wear glasses and teach English; the idea is that boring teachers pop up everywhere and too often in this particular school, reflecting many different ages and backgrounds and subject areas—and even ways of being boring.

Of course, you don't always have to use several examples to make your point. Often, the best way to develop a thesis is to use one extended example. Even so, the example should be selected according to the same rules of fairness that apply to the selection of numerous examples. It must truly represent an honest cross-section of the subject. The following passage from Annie Dillard's "Heaven and Earth in Jest" does just that. In it, Dillard illustrates the mindless cruelty of nature with an unforgettable story about the death of a frog.

A couple of summers ago I was walking along the edge of the island to see what I could see in the water, and mainly to scare frogs. Frogs have an inelegant way of taking off from invisible positions on the bank just ahead of your feet, in dire panic, emitting a froggy "Yike!" and splashing into the water. Incredibly, this amused me, and, incredibly, it amuses me still. As I walked along the grassy edge of the island, I got better and better at seeing frogs both in and out of the water. I learned to recognize, slowing down, the difference in texture of the light reflected from mudbank, water, grass, or frog. Frogs were flying all around me. At the end of the island I noticed a small green frog. He was exactly half in and half out of the water, looking like a schematic diagram of an amphibian, and he didn't jump.

He didn't jump; I crept closer. At last I knelt on the island's winterkilled grass, lost, dumbstruck, staring at the frog in the creek just four feet away. He was a very small frog with wide, dull eyes. And just as I looked at him, he slowly crumpled and began to sag. The spirit vanished from his eyes as if snuffed. His skin emptied and drooped; his very skull seemed to collapse and settle like a kicked tent. He was shrinking before my eyes like a deflating football. I watched the taut, glistening skin on his shoulders ruck, and rumple, and fall. Soon, part of his skin, formless as a pricked balloon, lay in floating folds like bright scum on top of the water: it was a monstrous and terrifying thing. I gaped bewildered, appalled. An oval shadow hung in the water behind the drained frog; then the shadow glided away. The frog skin bag started to sink.

I had read about the giant water bug, but never seen one. "Giant water bug" is really the name of the creature, which is an enormous, heavy-bodied brown beetle. It eats insects, tadpoles, fish, and frogs. Its grasping forelegs are mighty and hooked inward. It seizes a victim with these legs, hugs it tight, and paralyzes it with enzymes injected during a vicious bite. That one bite is the only bite it ever takes. Through the puncture shoot the poisons that dissolve the victim's muscles and bones and organs—all but the skin—and through it the giant water bug sucks out the victim's body, reduced to a juice. This event is quite common in warm fresh water. The frog I saw was being sucked by a giant water bug. I had been kneeling on the island grass; when the unrecognizable flap of frog skin settled on the creek bottom, swaying, I stood up and brushed the knees of my pants. I couldn't catch my breath.

Of course, many carnivorous animals devour their prey alive. The usual method seems to be to subdue the victim by downing or grasping it so it can't flee, then eating it whole or in a series of bloody bites. Frogs eat everything whole, stuffing prey into their mouths with their thumbs. People have seen frogs with their wide jaws so full of live dragonflies they couldn't close them. Ants don't even have to catch their prey: in the spring they swarm over newly hatched, featherless birds in the nest and eat them tiny bite by bite.

On reading this passage, one accepts Dillard's generalization not only because the story of the frog's death is vividly told, but also because it *is* representative of the mindless cruelty of nature. In this case, one extended example makes the point. The last paragraph, with its few, quick additional examples, merely confirms what the reader has already accepted.

One extended example, then, can serve to support a thesis if the example is fully and convincingly developed. More often than not, however, you can build a stronger argument with several short examples. In that case, you need to give order to your illustrations, and that brings us to our last tip on writing an example paper.

Think about the arrangement of your examples. Sometimes the best arrangement is chronological. The illustrations in the above paragraph on p. 77 about scientific discoveries, for instance, are presented in chronological order—from the ancient to the modern world. At other times, a spatial order works best. In supporting a thesis about the kinds of television programs Americans watch, you might offer examples from several sections of the country, and the arrangement of those examples could be from east to west or from west to east.

Or consider this: Many writers like to save their best example for last in order to achieve a dramatic conclusion. Others like to use their best example first to awaken interest. Certainly, the first and last are likely to get the most attention from a reader. Since some examples are more dramatic and convincing than others, you do well to bury the weaker ones in the middle of the paper. Of course, if all your examples are excellent, you have nothing to worry about.

See what you think of the quality and arrangement of examples in the following student paper.

On Used Cars
MICHAEL C. ROSTANCE

Not all lemons grow on trees, nor can they all be found in supermarkets or in someone's refrigerator. At various times, many of them could be found in my garage disguised as used cars.

I bought my first used car from a reputable dealer. It was a beautiful MG Midget. It had everything I had ever dreamed about in a car. It had wire wheels, convertible top, leather upholstery, and wooden steering wheel. It was a real classic. Three weeks later the engine of my real classic exploded. I had purchased my first lemon.

I was short of money and in desperate need of a car, so I went to Thriftee Auto Sales in search of an inexpensive but reliable one. A smiling salesman helped me find the ideal car. It was a 1969 Chevrolet. "No rust! Listen to her purr! A real buy," he said. I bought it, and two days later the transmission fell out. I had purchased another lemon.

I was beginning to feel that auto dealers were taking advantage of me, so I decided to buy my next car from a private owner. Every day I read the classified ads in search of the perfect car. After two weeks I found the following ad: "1975 Pontiac. Excellent mechanical condition. Going overseas. Must sell." I took the car to a garage to have the engine and transmission inspected. The mechanic assured me that the car was in good shape. So I bought it, confident that this was a good buy. One month later the front axle broke. Lemons were becoming a habit.

I was having doubts that I would ever own a reliable car. A friend approached me at this time and informed me that he had a car for sale. I was sure that he would never try to cheat me, so I bought the car without hesitation. Six weeks later, the right front wheel fell off. I had purchased my last lemon.

After that I invested in a sturdy pair of shoes, and I am happy to report that after one year of service, they are still in excellent working condition.

Questions for Writing or Discussion

1. What is the thesis of the paper? Is it stated directly or is it implied?
2. How does the author arrange his examples? Is this the best way to present them? Why?
3. Select specific details from each paragraph and discuss their contribution to the paper's effectiveness.

4. Does the author play fair in his selection of examples? Why, or why not?

5. Think about your own experience with cars. Can you state a thesis which sums up your experience and allows you to present vivid examples?

Readings

The following newspaper articles show how examples can be used to achieve humor.

Erma Bombeck
SWEET MYSTERY OF LIFE—CHILDREN

My goodness, the children have only been out of school for six weeks. Time flies when you're under sedation, doesn't it?

As I was hiding from them in the back seat of the car just last week it occurred to me that I don't know children at all. I'm raising three of them and yet they remain one of life's greatest mysteries.

For example, I don't understand how come a child can climb up on the roof, scale the TV antenna and rescue the cat . . . yet cannot walk down the hallway without grabbing both walls with his grubby hands for balance.

Or how come a child can eat yellow snow, kiss the dog on the lips, chew gum that he has found in the ashtray, put his mouth over a muddy garden hose nozzle . . . and refuse to drink from a glass his brother has just used.

Why is it he can stand with one foot on first base while reaching out and plucking a baseball off the ground with the tips of his fingers . . . yet cannot pick up a piece of soap before it melts into the drain.

Explain to me how he can ride a bicycle, run, play ball, set up a camp, swing, fight a war, swim and race for eight hours . . . and has to be driven to the garbage can.

It puzzles me how a child can see a dairy bar three miles away, but cannot see a 4 x 6 rug that has scrunched up under his feet and has been dragged through two rooms.

Why is it a child can reject a hot dog with mustard served on a soft bun at home . . . yet eat six of them two hours later at 50 cents each.

How come I can trip over a kid's shoes under the kitchen sink, in the bathroom, on the front porch, under the coffee table, in the sandbox, in the car, in the clothes hamper and on the washer . . . but we can never find them when it is time to cut the grass.

Why is the sun hotter delivering papers than it is goofing around . . . when it is the same sun?

How come they can't remember what time they're supposed to be home, but they remember they did dishes a week ago Wednesday two nights in a row because we had spaghetti and a spoon got caught in the disposal and they traded off.

I'll never understand how a child can't even find his English book when it is under his right hand, but can find his mother hiding out in the back seat of a car.

Questions for Writing or Discussion

1. What is Bombeck's thesis? Is the thesis stated directly?
2. Are the examples varied enough to make the thesis believable?
3. How does the use of phrases such as "how come," "I don't understand," "why is it," and "explain to me" contribute to the development of the thesis?
4. Are any of the examples weaker than the others? If so, which ones?
5. Could the order of the examples be changed without altering the effect of the article?
6. A good writing exercise might be to develop a paper by examples which support a gentler thesis about children.

George E. Condon
"WHY" IS WORSE THAN "WHAT"

To quote one of the comforting clichés that puzzled people have been falling back on for many, many years, "There's an explanation for everything." Truer aphorism was never circulated. It is also true that sometimes the explanation is just as incredible as the actual happening.

Take the experience of the couple from Lorain [Ohio] who bought a house trailer and went on a vacation trip to Florida. All went well until the return trip home. The husband grew weary after many hours at the wheel and finally abdicated the driver's seat in favor of his wife, while he went back to the trailer and fell asleep.

It was a nervous sleep, to be sure. He had never before trusted his wife at the wheel, and he was naturally uneasy over the risks involved. When the vehicle suddenly came to an abrupt, screeching stop, he immediately assumed the worst and leaped out the back of the house trailer to see what had gone wrong.

All that had happened, actually, was that a traffic signal suddenly had turned red and the wife had found it necessary to slam on the brake. By the time the husband, dressed only in his underwear, made his exit to the street and in his slow, sleep-fogged way sized up the situation, the light had turned green and the wife blithely drove away, leaving him in the middle of the intersection in his underdrawers. That's where a police cruiser came upon him a few minutes later.

"I can explain it all, officer!" said the husband to the policeman as his shivering shanks were hustled into the cop car. No doubt he did, in time, but the explanation could not possibly have been an easy one.

Which brings us around to a related dilemma that faced a woman in Clearwater, Fla., a few weeks ago when she drove her new luxury car with less than 1,000 miles on it to Sarasota, not far away.

Sarasota is the permanent home of the Ringling Circus, of course, and she parked her car in a lot near circus headquarters while she visited an art show. When she returned to her car it immediately occurred to her that there was something different about her new automobile. The roof, so to speak, had caved in.

But the mystery was quickly cleared up by a man who had come upon the scene.

"This your car, lady? Ah, you're probably wondering what happened to the old buggy to flatten it that way, eh? Well, you see, we were moving some elephants through the lot and one of them decided to sit down."

On top of her car, of course.

But the representative of the parking lot hastened to assure her that the Ringling people would repair the car. He noted that while the car looked rather bad, most of the damage was in the rear, and it could be driven. He gave her instructions on the repair procedure to follow and she got in the battered new car and swung it towards its Clearwater home.

On the way, however, a bad traffic accident caused considerable congestion at an intersection, and the woman decided on a short cut through a shopping center's parking lot. She was making this shrewd move when a police car cornered her and an officer leaped out and approached.

"Why are you leaving the scene of that accident?" he demanded to know.

"I'm not trying to leave an accident," she replied. "I'm trying to drive around one."

The policeman nodded. He was a reasonable man.

"Uh-huh," he said agreeably, "then you wouldn't mind telling me how that car of yours got smashed flat, would you?"

Now, then, all she had to do was tell the copper that an elephant had come by and sat on her car. A simple enough explanation, surely, but one that would take a bit of telling. "It was this way, officer. You see, an elephant came along and . . ."

There's an explanation for everything, it's true, but some explanations are more readily acceptable than others. That's the way it is.

Questions for Writing or Discussion

1. Condon states the thesis of the article twice. Find both statements. Do you think repeating the thesis is a good idea? Why, or why not?

2. Bombeck uses ten examples to support her thesis; Condon uses only two. Does Condon's limited use of examples affect the credibility of his thesis? Why, or why not?

3. Discuss the effect of the paragraph consisting of only a sentence fragment, "On top of her car, of course."
4. Why does Condon not complete the sentence, "You see, an elephant came along and . . ."? (See *ellipsis*, p. 468.)
5. Can you think of two well-developed examples for a humorous paper with the thesis, "Life is filled with awkward (or embarrassing) moments"?

A long paper can be developed entirely by example. Most long papers, however, even those which make example the primary means of support, tend to combine example with other methods of development. An example paper is, after all, a sophisticated list, and a list can't go on forever. Many writers, therefore, prefer to use examples in combination with other methods of development. Marya Mannes' "The Thin Grey Line" is an argumentative essay. But as you read it, notice how heavily the author relies on examples to advance her argument. In fact, without examples, the essay would lose much of its appeal.

Marya Mannes
THE THIN GREY LINE

"Aw, they all do it," growled the cabdriver. He was talking about cops who took payoffs for winking at double parking, but his cynicism could as well have been directed at any of a dozen other instances of corruption, big-time and small-time. Moreover, the disgust in his voice was overlaid by an unspoken "So what?": the implication that since this was the way things were, there was nothing anybody could do.

Like millions of his fellow Americans, the cabdriver was probably a decent human being who had never stolen anything, broken any law or willfully injured another; somewhere, a knowledge of what was probably right had kept him from committing what was clearly wrong. But that knowledge had not kept a thin grey line that separates the two conditions from being daily greyer and thinner—to the point that it was hardly noticeable.

On one side of this line are They: the bribers, the cheaters, the chiselers, the swindlers, the extortioners. On the other side are We—both partners and victims. They and We are now so perilously close that the only mark distinguishing us is that They get caught and We don't.

The same citizen who voices his outrage at police corruption will slip the traffic cop on his block a handsome Christmas present in the belief that his car, nestled under a "No Parking" sign, will not be ticketed. The son of that nice woman next door has a habit of stealing cash from her purse because his allowance is smaller than his buddies'. Your son's friend admitted cheating at exams because "everybody does it."

Bit by bit, the resistance to and immunity against wrong that a healthy social body builds up by law and ethics and the dictation of conscience have broken down. And instead of the fighting indignation of a people outraged by those who prey on them, we have the admission of impotence: "They all do it."

Now, failure to uphold the law is no less corrupt than violation of the law. And the continuing shame of this country now is the growing number of Americans who fail to uphold and assist enforcement of the law, simply—and ignominiously—out of fear. Fear of "involvement," fear of reprisal, fear of "trouble." A man is beaten by hoodlums in plain daylight and in view of bystanders. These people not only fail to help the victim, but, like the hoodlums, flee before the police can question them. A city official knows of a colleague's bribe but does not report it. A pedestrian watches a car hit a woman but leaves the scene, to avoid giving testimony. It happens every day. And if the police get cynical at this irresponsibility, they are hardly to blame. Morale is a matter of giving support and having faith in one another; where both are lacking, "law" has become a worthless word.

How did we get this way? What started this blurring of what was once a thick black line between the lawful and the lawless? What makes a "regular guy," a decent fellow, accept a bribe? What makes a nice kid from a middle-class family take money for doing something he must know is not only illegal but wrong?

When you look into the background of an erring "kid" you will often find a comfortable home and a mother who will tell you, with tears in her eyes, that she "gave him everything." She probably did, to his everlasting damage. Fearing her son's disapproval, the indulgent mother denies him nothing except responsibility. Instead of growing up, he grows to believe that the world owes him everything.

The nice kid's father crosses the thin grey line himself in a dozen ways, day in and day out. He pads his expenses on his income-tax returns as a matter of course. As a landlord, he pays the local inspectors of the city housing authority to overlook violations in the houses he rents. When his son flunked his driving test, he gave him ten dollars to slip to the inspector on his second test. "They all do it," he said.

The nice kid is brought up with boys and girls who have no heroes except people not much older than themselves who have made the Big Time, usually in show business or in sports. Publicity and money are the halos of their stars, who range from pop singers who can't sing to ballplayers who can't read: from teen-age starlets who can't act to television performers who can't think. They may be excited by the exploits of spacemen, but the work's too tough and dangerous.

The nice kids have no heroes because they don't believe in heroes. Heroes are suckers and squares. To be a hero you have to stand out, to excel, to take risks, and above all, not only choose between right and wrong, but defend the right and fight the wrong. This means responsibility—and who needs it?

Today, no one has to take any responsibility. The psychiatrists, the sociologists, the novelists, the playwrights have gone a long way to help promote irresponsibility. Nobody really is to blame for what he does. It's

Society. It's Environment. It's a Broken Home. It's an Underprivileged Area. But it's hardly ever You.

Now we find a truckload of excuses to absolve the individual from responsibility for his actions. A fellow commits a crime because he's basically insecure, because he hated his stepmother at nine, or because his sister needs an operation. A policeman loots a store because his salary is too low. A city official accepts a payoff because it's offered to him. Members of minority groups, racial or otherwise, commit crimes because they can't get a job, or are unacceptable to the people living around them. The words "right" and "wrong" are foreign to these people.

But honesty is the best policy. Says who? Anyone willing to get laughed at. But the laugh is no laughing matter. It concerns the health and future of a nation. It involves the two-dollar illegal bettor as well as the corporation price-fixer, the college-examination cheater and payroll-padding Congressman, the expense-account chiseler, the seller of pornography and his schoolboy reader, the bribed judge and the stealing delinquent. All these people may represent a minority. But when, as it appears now, the majority excuse themselves from responsibility by accepting corruption as natural to society ("They all do it"), this society is bordering on total confusion. If the line between right and wrong is finally erased, there is no defense against the power of evil.

Before this happens— and it is by no means far away—it might be well for the schools of the nation to substitute for the much-argued issue of prayer a daily lesson in ethics, law, and responsibility to society that would strengthen the conscience as exercise strengthens muscles. And it would be even better if parents were forced to attend it. For corruption is not something you read about in the papers and leave to courts. We are all involved.

Questions for Writing or Discussion

1. What is the thesis of the essay?
2. What is the meaning of the title? Why is the line "thin"? Why "grey"?
3. What does Mannes mean by "They" and "We"? How do these terms relate to the title?
4. Mannes opens the essay with an example, the response of the cabdriver, before she begins to argue her point. Do you think she has chosen a good way to open her essay? Why, or why not?
5. What examples support the topic sentence of paragraph 6 ("And the continuing shame of this country now is the growing number of citizens who fail to uphold and assist enforcement of the law . . .")? Are these examples fair? Could they be rearranged with better effect?
6. The example of the "nice kid" continues through four para-

graphs. Do you think Mannes devotes too much space to his problem? Why, or why not?

7. Mannes says, "If the line between right and wrong is finally erased, there is no defense against the power of evil." What does the statement mean? Do the examples which precede the statement make clear why there would be no defense against evil? Why, or why not?

8. What, according to Mannes, are the causes of the problem she discusses? Do you agree? Why, or why not?

9. What solutions does Mannes suggest for solving the problem? Do you think these solutions would work? Why, or why not?

10. This essay was first published in 1964. Does it seem dated to you? Or do you think the problem is still with us? Do the examples still work?

Exercise

Develop a thesis which could enable you to use at least four of the following "wise sayings" as examples in a paragraph of about a hundred words or a brief essay.

Do unto others as you would have them do unto you.

Charity begins at home.

* * *

Still waters run deep.

A rolling stone gathers no moss.

* * *

A bird in the hand is worth two in the bush.

Nothing ventured, nothing gained.

* * *

A soft answer turneth away wrath.

The squeaking wheel gets the grease.

* * *

Better to be thought a fool than to open your mouth and remove all doubt.

Have the courage of your convictions.

* * *

Look before you leap.

He who hesitates is lost.

* * *

Leave well enough alone.
If at first you don't succeed, try, and try again.

   * * *

You can't judge a book by its cover.
What you see is what you get.

   * * *

Haste makes waste.
Seize the moment.

   * * *

Winning isn't everything; it's the only thing.
For when the One Great Scorer comes
To write against your name,
He marks—not that you won or lost—
But how you played the game.

   * * *

Many hands make light work.
Too many cooks spoil the broth.

   * * *

Absence makes the heart grow fonder.
Out of sight, out of mind.

   * * *

Patriotism is the last refuge of a scoundrel.
Breathes there a man with soul so dead
Who never to himself has said,
"This is my own,
My native land."

CHAPTER 6

WRITING A CLASSIFICATION OR DIVISION PAPER

In writing an example paper, you discovered you needed a thesis that is illustrated by a few examples. You enumerated, or made a list of, examples. Not all ideas or writing tasks lend themselves to list making, however sophisticated the list. Many subjects must be broken down into parts before they can be treated effectively; that is, the subjects must be *analyzed*. Two important techniques of analysis are *classification* and *division*.

CLASSIFICATION

You go to the library to get a book about Ernest Hemingway's novels. You find it shelved with other books of criticism on American authors. You turn to the want ads to see if there are any openings for a bookkeeper. You find notices of such jobs under the heading "Help Wanted." You want to send flowers to Aunt Mathilda, but you don't know where to call. You look in the Yellow Pages under "Florists." You want to buy cottage cheese at the supermarket. You find it in the dairy section. You aren't sure whether to let your six-year-old child go to a movie with her older brother. You check the entertainment section of the paper and, finding the film rated "G," decide to let her go.

    You can easily find your book or job listing or cottage cheese or information about movies and florists because someone has *classified* the subjects for you. *Classification* is the process by which one assigns members of a large group—ideas, people, plants, animals, books, poems, groceries, etc.—to categories on the basis of a single principle. A credit office, for example, might assign all applicants for credit (large group) to one of three categories: excellent risk, fair risk, poor risk. The assignment would be made on the basis of each applicant's ability and readiness to pay the bills when they come due (principle of classification).

Clearly, classification is essential to the credit office if the company is to remain in business. Classification is useful to others, too, because it enables them to cope with a large body of material by placing it in pigeonholes. Besides, we all like to classify. We do it naturally. Students classify their professors as boring or stimulating. Homemakers classify their cooking utensils, perhaps as those used often and those used occasionally, and place them in drawers and cupboards accordingly. But whether used for fun or for profit, classification has certain requirements, most of which you have already employed in developing outlines.

Determine the basis for classification and then apply it consistently. If you decide to classify the war poems in this chapter (pp. 100–108), you shouldn't establish as your categories realistic poems, brave warriors, and free verse. The first class is based on attitude, the second on subject matter, and the third on literary form. A logical principle would be attitudes toward war; then, the categories might be poems glorifying war, poems attacking war, and poems asserting that war does not significantly affect man or nature. If you wanted to classify the courses you are taking according to level of interest, you shouldn't establish as the categories dull, moderately interesting, and difficult. *Difficult* violates the principle of classification.

Define any terms that might be unfamiliar to the audience or that are used in a special way. Eric Berne (p. 93) finds that *mesomorphs, ectomorphs,* and *endomorphs* have distinct personalities. Since these terms are not household words, they must be defined. Similarly, suppose you make up names of categories. You might, for instance, classify joggers as red-faced wobblers, short-legged two-steppers, and long-legged striders. You must share with your reader your understanding of these made-up terms.

Decide whether you need only describe each category fully or whether, in addition to discussing the characteristics of each category, you need to list all or nearly all its members. A classification of people as overweight, underweight, and normal, for example, would require merely a complete description of each type. Readers could, on the basis of the description, decide which category the various people they meet belong to. On the other hand, a classification of the present Supreme Court justices as liberals or conservatives, besides giving the characteristics of liberal and conservative justices, should also give the names of the justices who belong to each category and some explanation of why they have been placed there.

Have a thesis. In one sense, of course, the classification itself provides a thesis. If you assert that there are three classes of teachers or four classes of pet-owners or five classes of social drinkers and can back up your assertion, you have a thesis. But you can, with certain subjects, take even stronger positions: *People* can *be judged by their appearance,* for example. (See "Can People Be Judged by Their Appearance?" p. 93.) Or you could show that one of the categories is preferable to the others, or that all the categories are silly or despicable or admirable. Having a thesis gives force and interest to your categories.

Establish some kind of order. In a few cases, you could order your categories according to time, from earliest to latest. Or, depending on your thesis, several other possibilities for ordering the categories present themselves: You might order the categories from worst to best, best to worst, least enjoyable to most enjoyable, or weakest to strongest, for example. In most listings, some members of the list are stronger or more interesting or more amusing than the others. Arrange your categories so that the weaker ones are in the middle of your paper. Hook your readers with a strong first category and leave them satisfied with an even stronger last category. The practice of ordering categories will make an important contribution to your classification papers.

See what you think of this student effort at classification.

The Snow Shovelers
THOMAS TAYLOR

The present weather conditions have brought out of their warm houses a group of persons to which I, unfortunately, belong: the snow shovelers. Although all within this group have the same task to perform, their approaches to the performance of the task differ. Three of the more interesting sub-groups are the jovial philosophers, the martyrs, and the fanatics.

The jovial philosophers view snowfall as an act of God, and they try to make the best of it. They appear soon after each snowfall ends. Cheerfully greeting their neighbors, they get down to work, which they seem to enjoy.

Typical of this type is my neighbor Steve. Bundled up and looking like a large bear, he whistles, sings, and hails his fellow workers with such profundities as "Wow! This sure is good exercise," or "Hey, you'll miss all this cool air when summer comes," or, best of all, "Ha-ha, this is fun, isn't it?" Steve derives great pleasure from both his work and his opportunity to perform before an audience, many of whom do not share his views.

The second group, the martyrs, are quite a different lot. The martyrs do not appear until the snow is at least twelve inches deep, packed down, and almost totally impassable. They grudgingly perform their jobs to an undercurrent of grunts and grumbles that are occasionally punctuated by a negative response to the philosophers' questions. They seem to believe all this work is some undeserved punishment pronounced upon them by a perverse power.

The best example of this type is my neighbor Ron. Ron is always one of the last people to begin shoveling snow. Therefore, he always has the most difficult task. With ice-chipper and shovel, he hacks away at the glacial mass in his driveway, usually after his wife has gotten stuck on the ice pack and has forced him out. He hums rather than sings. The blues comprise his entire repertoire—tunes such as "Trouble in Mind" and "Hard Times." He answers the philosopher: "Yeah, but this good exercise can give you a heart attack," or "I wouldn't miss this weather even if I were a door-to-door furnace salesman in hell." While I tend to sympathize with him, I do notice that he derives a certain masochistic satisfaction from his plight.

The third category of snow shovelers is the fanatics. At the drop of the first snowflake, they are out with shovel and broom, swinging viciously to left and right as if attacking a hated foe. These persons view the snowfall as a conspiracy directed at them by God, the government, Russian scientists, their neighbors, and especially by skiing enthusiasts with "Think Snow" bumper stickers on their cars. The scraping sounds of their shovels can be heard day or night as a barely adequate cover to the steady stream of curses that they heap upon the world in general.

I am most familiar with this grouping because it is the one to which I belong. Casting aside reason, I call forth a much stronger motivation than either good-natured acceptance or self-indulgent martyrdom. All the frustrations, hatreds, and disappointments of life are temporarily vented upon each and every hapless snowflake that dares to defile the passage from house to street. I neither sing nor converse with others and glare balefully at those who do. Because of the amount of energy employed, I, and those like me, usually do the best job. However, the true satisfaction always comes to me not, as with the others, in the doing. Oh no, the true reward comes in the early, before-going-to-work morning when I am proved to be the most rational of all in my outlook. We fanatics are right! The air is filled with the wails and moans of philosopher and martyr alike. You see, those conspirators that only we fanatics are aware of—skiiers with their psychokinesis, God with His snowfall, and the government with its snowplows—have buried the best of all our efforts. We will all be performing again tonight.

Questions for Writing or Discussion

1. What is the principle of classification in this paper?
2. Does the paper have a thesis? Is it stated directly?
3. Do you find one category more interesting than the others? Why?
4. Do you think the writer could have organized his categories differently? Why, or why not?
5. Select at least six specific details and discuss how these details give life to the paper.
6. Think of a group to which you belong, and classify the members of the group.

DIVISION

In analysis by classification, a large group is broken down into smaller groups.In analysis by *divison*, a subject usually thought of as a single unit is broken down into each one of its parts. An analysis of a stereo system, for example, requires naming and describing each of its components. An analysis of a poem requires studying each element in the poem—rhyme, meter, figures of speech, diction, image patterns, etc. An analysis of a breakfast cereal requires a listing of the number of calories and the grams of protein, carbohydrates, fat, sodium, etc. in a single serving. In analysis by division, then, each element which helps to make up the whole is treated separately.

Despite the differences between classification and division, the rules for writing the two kinds of papers are almost the same, but they are so important that they can bear repeating here:

1. Decide what the basis for division is and then apply it consistently.
2. Keep the divisions mutually exclusive.
3. Define unfamiliar terms or those which are used in a special way.
4. Have a thesis.
5. Establish some kind of order.

Readings

Following are two essays composed by professional writers. The first is presented as an example of classification and the second as an example of division. Do the writers observe the rules for classification and division laid down in this chapter?

Eric Berne
CAN PEOPLE BE JUDGED BY THEIR APPEARANCE?

Everyone knows that a human being, like a chicken, comes from an egg. At a very early stage, the human embryo forms a three-layered tube, the inside layer of which grows into the stomach and lungs, the middle layer into bones, muscles, joints, and blood vessels, and the outside layer into the skin and nervous system.

Usually these three grow about equally, so that the average human being is a fair mixture of brains, muscles, and inward organs. In some eggs, however, one layer grows more than the others, and when the angels have finished putting the child together, he may have more gut than brain, or more brain than muscle. When this happens, the individual's activities will often be mostly with the overgrown layer.

We can thus say that while the average human being is a mixture, some people are mainly "digestion-minded," some "muscle-minded," and some "brain-minded," and correspondingly digestion-bodied, muscle-bodied, or brain-bodied. The digestion-bodied people look thick; the muscle-bodied people look wide; and the brain-bodied people look long. This does not mean the taller a man is the brainier he will be. It means that if a man, even a short man, looks long rather than wide or thick, he will often be more concerned about what goes on in his mind than about what he does or what he eats; but the key factor is slenderness and not height. On the other hand, a man who gives the impression of being thick rather than long or wide will usually be more interested in a good steak than in a good idea or a good long walk.

Medical men use Greek words to describe these types of bodybuild. For the man whose body shape mostly depends on the inside layer of the egg, they use the word *endomorph*. If it depends mostly upon the middle layer, they call him a *mesomorph*. If it depends upon the outside layer, they call him an *ectomorph*. We can see the same roots in our English words "enter," "medium," and "exit," which might just as easily have been spelled, "ender," 'mesium," and "ectit."

Since the inside skin of the human egg, or endoderm, forms the inner organs of the belly, the viscera, the endomorph is usually belly-minded; since the middle skin forms the body tissues, or soma, the mesomorph is usually muscle-minded; and since the outside skin forms the brain, or cerebrum, the ectomorph is usually brain-minded. Translating this into Greek, we have the viscerotonic endomorph, the somatotonic mesomorph, and the cerebrotonic ectomorph.

Words are beautiful things to a cerebrotonic, but a viscerotonic knows you cannot eat a menu no matter what language it is printed in, and a somatotonic knows you cannot increase your chest expansion by reading a dictionary. So it is advisable to leave these words and see what kinds of people they actually apply to, remembering again that most individuals are fairly equal mixtures and that what we have to say concerns only the extremes. Up to the present, these types have been thoroughly studied only in the male sex.

Viscerotonic Endomorph. If a man is definitely a thick type rather than a broad or long type, he is likely to be round and soft, with a big chest but a bigger belly. He would rather eat than breathe comfortably. He is likely to have a wide face, short, thick neck, big thighs and upper arms, and small hands and feet. He has over-developed breasts and looks as though he were blown up a little like a balloon. His skin is soft and smooth, and when he gets bald, as he does usually quite early, he loses the hair in the middle of his head first.

The short, jolly, thickset, red-faced politician with a cigar in his mouth, who always looks as though he were about to have a stroke, is the best example of this type. The reason he often makes a good politician is that he likes people, banquets, baths, and sleep; he is easygoing, soothing, and his feelings are easy to understand.

His abdomen is big because he has lots of intestines. He likes to take in things. He likes to take in food, and affection and approval as well. Going to a banquet with people who like him is his idea of a fine time. It is important for a psychiatrist to understand the natures of such men when they come to him for advice.

Somatotonic Mesomorph. If a man is definitely a broad type rather than a thick or long type, he is likely to be rugged and have lots of muscle. He is apt to have big forearms and legs, and his chest and belly are well formed and firm, with the chest bigger than the belly. He would rather breathe than eat. He has a bony head, big shoulders, and a square jaw. His skin is thick, coarse, and elastic, and tans easily. If he gets bald, it usually starts on the front of the head.

Dick Tracy, Li'l Abner, and other men of action belong to this type. Such people make good lifeguards and construction workers. They like to put out energy. They have lots of muscles and they like to use them. They go in for adventure, exercise, fighting, and getting the upper hand. They are bold and unrestrained, and love to master the people and things around them. If the psychiatrist knows the things which give such people satisfaction, he is able to understand why they may be unhappy in certain situations.

Cerebrotonic Ectomorph. The man who is definitely a long type is likely to have thin bones and muscles. His shoulders are apt to sag and he has a flat belly with a dropped stomach, and long, weak legs. His neck and fingers are long, and his face is shaped like a long egg. His skin is thin, dry, and pale, and he rarely gets bald. He looks like an absent-minded professor and often is one.

Though such people are jumpy, they like to keep their energy and don't fancy moving around much. They would rather sit quietly by themselves and keep out of difficulties. Trouble upsets them, and they run away from it. Their friends don't understand them very well. They move jerkily and feel jerkily. The psychiatrist who understands how easily they become anxious is often able to help them get along better in the sociable and aggressive world of endomorphs and mesomorphs.

In the special cases where people definitely belong to one type or another, then, one can tell a good deal about their personalities from their appearance. When the human mind is engaged in one of its struggles with itself or with the world outside, the individual's way of handling the struggle will be partly determined by his type. If he is viscerotonic he will often want to go to a party where he can eat and drink and be in good company at a time when he might be better off attending to business; the somatotonic will want to go out and do something about it, master the situation, even if what he does is foolish and not properly figured out, while the cerebrotonic will go off by himself and think it over, when perhaps he would be better off doing something about it or seeking good company to try to forget it.

Since these personality characteristics depend on the growth of the layers of the little egg from which the person developed, they are very difficult to change. Nevertheless, it is important for the individual to know about these types, so that he can have at least an inkling of what to expect from those around him, and can make allowances for the different kinds of human nature, and so that he can become aware of and learn to control his own natural tendencies, which may sometimes guide him into making the same mistakes over and over again in handling his difficulties.

Questions for Writing or Discussion

1. Berne says that most people don't exactly fit into any one of these categories. In that case, is his classification justified?
2. Berne names each type and gives examples of each in his introduction. Do you find his introduction helpful to your understanding the subject, or do you find it repetitious?
3. Berne uses a number of Greek words in an essay written for lay readers. Does he provide adequate definitions of the terms?
4. Does Berne have a thesis in his article; that is, does he say something *about* the types?
5. At the end of each section, Berne explains why an understanding of each type is useful to a psychiatrist; the article, however, was written for lay readers, not psychiatrists. In this case, should Berne have included these explanations? Why, or why not?
6. Using Berne's categories, try your hand at classifying the members of your gym class.

Nona Aguilar
HOW TO WRITE A LETTER THAT WILL GET YOU A JOB

Whether you're just getting back into the job market after years out of it or you're looking for a better job to advance your career, you can double your chances of success by using a "tailored" letter.

What's a tailored letter? It's simply a brief letter highlighting background elements which most relate to the needs of a prospective employer. In other words, you "tailor" your experience to meet the needs of the person or company you want to work for. By following our simple guidelines, you can write a persuasive, concise letter that gets results.

Here's an example of the power of a tailored letter. My friend's mother, Mrs. Kinley, had been widowed for almost three years. She was 54 years old, her children were grown and she hadn't worked during the 29 years of her marriage. Now, with time on her hands, she wanted a job, but employment agencies discouraged her because, she was told, she didn't have skills or work experience.

Since she knew that I had always managed to rustle up a job no matter what or where, she talked to me about her problem. She realized that she didn't really want a full-time job; she had looked for one because it was the only type of work available through the agencies. And her only work experience was the hospital and Red Cross volunteer work she'd done throughout her marriage. We used that experience in composing her tailored letter, which she sent to 30 doctors (found in the "Physicians" section of the Yellow Pages).

What Were the Results? Within three days of mailing the letter, Mrs. Kinley had received four telephone calls. One wanted someone to work full time for five doctors in practice together; she declined that interview request but went on the other three.

While trying to decide which of two opportunities she might take—one of the positions wasn't offered to her after the interview—the mail brought a written reply asking her to call for an interview. On a hunch, she decided to make the call. That last interview turned out to be THE job; four days a week, from 9 to 1:30.

A postscript to the story: She received two more calls after she started working. She also got a few P.B.-O.s (Polite Brush-Offs) in the mail plus a "not right now but maybe in six months" letter. *That* is what I mean about the power of a tailored letter!

Measurable Accomplishments. Take a look at the letter Mrs. Kinley wrote. She used the Four Elements that form the basic structure of a good tailored letter: (1) an opening grabber, (2) an appeal to the self-interest of the reader, (3) a number of examples of her experience and (4) a good closing. The Four Elements are detailed . . . here, but as you can see, *specific accomplishments* are at the letter's heart. If your accomplishments are measurable in any way, you will look that much more impressive.

Here's what I mean by measurable. I landed a job teaching English in a language school in Italy. I was not a professional teacher; I had never taught in a school—obviously I had never been certified! However, one summer while I was still in high school, I started a little brush-up school in our family dining room to help three of my kid brothers and sisters. Four neighborhood kids joined my "class" and, through tutoring, I literally boosted English grades by about 13%.

The opening line of my tailored letter to the directress of the language school—the "grabber"—read: "I raised students' grades in English an aver-

Mrs. Kinley's letter

```
March 1, 19--

Marvin Willis, M.D.
488 Madison Avenue
New York, NY 10022

Dear Dr. Willis:

In the past several years, I have worked  (1)
over 6,000 hours in hospitals handling
bookkeeping and billing.

      I am writing to you because your office may
 (2)  be in need of a woman with my background and
      experience to work on a part-time basis.  If
      so, you may be interested in some of the
      things I have done.

For example, I was responsible for handling
Wednesday receipts for a volunteer-operated
hospital gift shop.

I sorted 500 pieces of patient mail per week.  (3)

I handled all bookkeeping for the gift shop,
insuring payment of suppliers and disbursement
of profits to the hospital by the 30th
of each month.

      If such experience would be valuable to your
 (4)  office to help with bookkeeping or billing, I
      would be happy to talk to you in more detail.
      My telephone number is EL 6-0000.

Sincerely yours,
```

THE FOUR ELEMENTS

1. AN OPENING GRABBER

Mrs. Kinley's letter begins with a short sentence listing a memorable figure: 6,000 hours of work experience in a hospital. This grabs the reader's interest.

2. SELF-INTEREST APPEAL

She appeals to his self-interest right away in her second sentence by letting the doctor know that those 6,000 hours are part of valuable experience which might be useful to him.

3. EXAMPLES

Mrs. Kinley gives three specific examples of accomplishments to further appeal to the self-interest of a would-be employer.

4. THE CLOSING

Mrs. Kinley does not plead for an interview. She doesn't even ask for one. Rather, she lets the recipient know she's a worthwhile professional person and that "if such experience would be valuable to your office . . ." she'd be happy to discuss it in an interview.

age of 13% during a summer-school program which I began in my neighborhood." The letter made an impression, sailing past almost 100 weighty epistles and résumés sent by teaching professionals listing schools, courses, degrees and experience in abundance. When I came in for my interview, the directress was already anxious to meet me. My letter had shown an awareness of her major problem: Finding teachers who could actually teach—and could then prove it.

Specific Accomplishments. So I can't stress it enough: *The heart of a successful tailored letter is specific accomplishments.* When your accomplishments are measurable, you look even more impressive—but don't equate *paid* with *measurable.* Mrs. Kinley does not apologize for her lack of paid business experience. That isn't even mentioned, nor is the fact that her work had been on a volunteer basis. Instead she casts all her experience in terms of *accomplishment.* Each separate accomplishment that relates to working in a medical environment is placed in its own brief, one-sentence paragraph. Indeed, the whole letter is brief, only eight sentences in all, so busy recipients—in this case doctors—are more inclined to read the letter straight through to the end.

It's important that your letter be short and crisp. Work and rework the letter so that your grabber is brief and punchy. Appeal right away to the self-interest of the recipient. In the Examples section of your letter, cover each accomplishment in one short sentence in its own paragraph. The succession of short, accomplishment-laden paragraphs makes a greater impact on the reader than long, cumbersome prose. Make your closing sharp and clean. And *don't beg* for an interview.

Finding Job Prospects. Of course, you have to find prospects for your letter!

It was easy with Mrs. Kinley: We just opened the phone book and picked physicians whose offices were convenient to her home.

If you already have a job but want a better one, you're probably aware of where and for whom you want to work. All you have to do is send letters to the companies on your "list."

If you use the help-wanted ads in the paper, send a tailored letter *instead* of a résumé, even if a résumé is asked for. All résumés tend to look alike, so your letter will stand out, considerably increasing your chances of getting an interview—*the* crucial first step toward getting a new job.

If you're interested in a particular business or industry, check with your librarian to see if a directory exists for it. There you'll find listings complete with spellings, business titles and addresses. You can also pick up your telephone and call companies or businesses. Ask for the name and correct spelling of the owner or president—if it's a small company—or the district manager, if it's a large company and you're calling the regional office in your city. If a secretary insists on knowing why you're calling before she gives the information, simply say that you're writing the man or woman a letter and need the information.

How many letters will you have to send out? That's hard to say.

When you send letters to companies that aren't specifically advertising or looking for someone, you can expect to send a lot. I did that some years ago;

I sent over 60 letters to advertising agencies. Some of the letters drew interviews; only one interview finally resulted in a job. But I only needed *one* job, and I got the job I wanted!

As a general rule, your letter is a good one when requests for an interview run about 8% to 10%. If Mrs. Kinley had received just two or three interview requests, she would have been doing fine. If she had received only one reply, or none, we'd have reworked the letter. As it turned out, she got six interview requests out of 30 letters—that's an exceptionally high 20%.

If you send a tailored letter when you know a company is hiring—for instance, in reply to a help-wanted ad—you will increase your chances of being called for an interview at least 30% to 50%, sometimes more. Once I was the only person called for an interview for an advertised editorial job, even though I had never worked on either a newspaper or a magazine in my life—there's the power of a tailored letter!

Look Professional! Once you've composed your short, punchy, accomplishment-laden letter and decided who's going to get it, make sure you're careful about three things:

First, *type*—don't handwrite—the letter, following standard business form; a secretarial handbook in your library will show you examples. Or follow the form Mrs. Kinley used.

Second, use plain white or ivory-colored stationery. Very pale, almost neutral, colors are okay too, but nothing flashy or brightly colored. I've found that it is helpful to write on monarch-sized stationery, which is smaller than the standard 8½" x 11" paper; the letter looks much more personal and invites a reading.

Finally, do *not* do anything gimmicky or "cute." I remember the laughter that erupted in an office when a job-seeking executive sent a letter with a small, sugar-filled bag carefully stapled to the top of the page. His opening line was: "I'd like to sweeten your day just a little." He came across looking foolish . . . and the boss didn't sweeten his day by calling him for an interview.

These are the basics that add up to a professional business letter. I've worked in a lot of offices and seen some pretty silly letters tumble out of the mail bag. Don't let yours be one of them; especially not if you're a woman of specific accomplishments who's ready for a job!

Questions for Writing or Discussion

1. What is the thesis of the article?
2. What is the subject that is divided?
3. What are the divisions?
4. Is each of these divisions fully developed in the article? If not, does the author find other ways of making the divisions clear?
5. Which of the divisions receives the greatest amount of attention? Why?

6. The early sections of the article make clear use of division. At what point does the article stop discussing divisions and become concerned with other issues? Now check the table of contents for this part of the book. What other "method" or methods is the author using?
7. Do you believe the section headed "Look Professional!" should have appeared before the section headed "Finding Job Prospects"? If so, why?

Exercise A

Select a person you admire—a friend or public figure, perhaps—and write a paper in which you divide the person's appeal into its separate elements.

Exercise B

Following is a group of poems on the theme of war. By establishing a single principle, you can classify these poems. Devise a system of classification that makes sense—that works—and write a paper showing how each poem fits into one of the categories.

DULCE ET DECORUM EST

> Bent double, like old beggars under sacks,
> Knock-kneed, coughing like hags, we cursed through sludge,
> Till on the haunting flares we turned our backs
> And towards our distant rest began to trudge.
> Men marched asleep. Many had lost their boots
> But limped on, blood-shod. All went lame; all blind;
> Drunk with fatigue; deaf even to the hoots
> Of tired, outstripped Five-Nines that dropped behind.
>
> Gas! Gas! Quick, boys!—An ecstasy of fumbling,
> Fitting the clumsy helmets just in time,
> But someone still was yelling out and stumbling
> And flound'ring like a man in fire or lime . . .
> Dim through the misty panes and thick green light,
> As under a green sea, I saw him drowning.

In all my dreams, before my helpless sight,
He plunges at me, guttering, choking, drowning.

If in some smothering dreams you too could pace
Behind the wagon that we flung him in,
And watch the white eyes writhing in his face,
His hanging face, like a devil's sick of sin;
If you could hear, at every jolt, the blood
Come gargling from the froth-corrupted lungs
Obscene as cancer, bitter as the cud
Of vile, incurable sores on innocent tongues,—
My friend, you would not tell with such high zest
To children ardent for some desperate glory,
The old lie: *Dulce et decorum est
Pro patria mori.*[1]

—Wilfred Owen

[1] "It is sweet and fitting to die for one's country."

"THERE WILL COME SOFT RAINS"

(WAR TIME)

There will come soft rains and the smell of the ground,
And swallows circling with their shimmering sound;

And frogs in the pools singing at night,
And wild plum-trees in tremulous white;

Robins will wear their feathery fire
Whistling their whims on a low fence-wire;

And not one will know of the war, not one
Will care at last when it is done.

Not one would mind, neither bird nor tree
If mankind perished utterly;

And Spring herself, when she woke at dawn,
Would scarcely know that we were gone.

—Sara Teasdale

TO OUR DEAD

Sleep well, heroic souls, in silence sleep,
  Lapped in the circling arms of kindly death!
  No ill can vex your slumbers, no foul breath
Of slander, hate, derision mar the deep
Repose that holds you close. Your kinsmen reap
  The harvest you have sown, while each man saith
  "So would I choose, when danger threateneth,
Let my death be as theirs." We dare not weep.

For you have scaled the starry heights of fame,
  Nor ever shrunk from peril and distress
    In fight undaunted for the conqueror's prize;
  Therefore your death, engirt with loveliness
Of simple service done for England's name,
    Shall shine like beacon-stars of sacrifice.

—*W. L. Courtney*

THE BATTLE OF BLENHEIM

It was a summer evening,
  Old Kaspar's work was done,
And he before his cottage door
  Was sitting in the sun,
And by him sported on the green
His little grandchild Wilhelmine.

She saw her brother Peterkin
  Roll something large and round,
Which he beside the rivulet
  In playing there had found;
He came to ask what he had found,
That was so large, and smooth, and round.

Old Kaspar took it from the boy,
  Who stood expectant by;
And then the old man shook his head,
  And, with a natural sigh,
"'Tis some poor fellow's skull," said he,
"Who fell in the great victory.

"I find them in the garden,
  For there's many here about;

And often when I go to plough,
  The ploughshare turns them out!
For many a thousand men," said he,
"Were slain in that great victory."

"Now tell us what 'twas all about,"
  Young Peterkin, he cries;
And little Wilhelmine looks up
  With wonder-waiting eyes;
"Now tell us all about the war,
And what they fought each other for."

"It was the English," Kaspar cried,
  "Who put the French to rout;
But what they fought each other for,
  I could not well make out;
But everybody said," quoth he,
"That 'twas a famous victory.

"My father lived at Blenheim then,
  Yon little stream hard by;
They burnt his dwelling to the ground,
  And he was forced to fly;
So with his wife and child he fled,
Nor had he where to rest his head.

"With fire and sword the country round
  Was wasted far and wide,
And many a childing mother then,
  And new-born baby died;
But things like that, you know, must be
At every famous victory.

"They say it was a shocking sight
  After the field was won;
For many thousand bodies here
  Lay rotting in the sun;
But things like that, you know, must be
After a famous victory.

"Great praise the Duke of Marlbro' won,
  And our good Prince Eugene."
"Why 'twas a very wicked thing!"
  Said little Wilhelmine.
"Nay, nay, my little girl," quoth he,
"It was a famous victory.

"And everybody praised the Duke
  Who this great fight did win."
"But what good came of it at last?"
  Quoth little Peterkin.
"Why that I cannot tell," said he.
"But 'twas a famous victory."

—*Robert Southey*

Blenheim (pronounced Blen'm) is in Bavaria. The battle took place in 1704;
France was defeated by the armies of England, Austria, and the Netherlands
under the command of the Duke of Marlborough and Prince Eugene of Austria.

WHAT WERE THEY LIKE?

1) Did the people of Viet Nam
   use lanterns of stone?
2) Did they hold ceremonies
   to reverence the opening of buds?
3) Were they inclined to quiet laughter?
4) Did they use bone and ivory,
   jade and silver, for ornament?
5) Had they an epic poem?
6) Did they distinguish between speech and singing?

1) Sir, their light hearts turned to stone.
   It is not remembered whether in gardens
   stone lanterns illumined pleasant ways.
2) Perhaps they gathered once to delight in blossom,
   but after the children were killed
   there were no more buds.
3) Sir, laughter is bitter to the burned mouth.
4) A dream ago, perhaps. Ornament is for joy.
   All the bones were charred.
5) It is not remembered. Remember,
   most were peasants; their life
   was in rice and bamboo.
   When peaceful clouds were reflected in the paddies
   and the water buffalo stepped surely along terraces,
   maybe fathers told their sons old tales.
   When bombs smashed those mirrors
   there was time only to scream.
6) There is no echo yet
   of their speech which was like a song.
   It was reported their singing resembled

the flight of moths in moonlight.
Who can say? It is silent now.

—Denise Levertov

GRASS

Pile the bodies high at Austerlitz and Waterloo. [1]
Shovel them under and let me work—
    I am the grass; I cover all.

And pile them high at Gettysburg
And pile them high at Ypres and Verdun. [2]
Shovel them under and let me work.
Two years, ten years, and passengers ask the conductor:
    What place is this?
    Where are we now?

    I am the grass.
    Let me work.

—Carl Sandburg

[1]Austerlitz is the scene of one of Napoleon's greatest victories, Waterloo the scene of his final defeat.
[2]Major battles of World War I.

TO LUCASTA, GOING TO THE WARS

Tell me not, sweet, I am unkind
    That from the nunnery
Of thy chaste breast and quiet mind,
    To war and arms I fly.

True, a new mistress now I chase,
    The first foe in the field;
And with a stronger faith embrace
    A sword, a horse, a shield.

Yet this inconstancy is such
    As you too shall adore;
I could not love thee, dear, so much,
    Loved I not Honor more.

—Richard Lovelace

BASE DETAILS

If I were fierce, and bald, and short of breath,
  I'd live with scarlet Majors at the Base,
And speed glum heroes up the line to death.
  You'd see me with my puffy petulant face,
Guzzling and gulping in the best hotel,
  Reading the Roll of Honour. "Poor young chap,"
I'd say—"I used to know his father well;
  Yes, we've lost heavily in this last scrap."
And when the war is done and youth stone dead,
I'd toddle safely home and die—in bed.

—Siegfried Sassoon

THE SPIRES OF OXFORD

I saw the spires of Oxford
  As I was passing by,
The gray spires of Oxford
  Against the pearl-gray sky.
My heart was with the Oxford men
  Who went abroad to die.

The years go fast in Oxford,
  The golden years and gay,
The hoary[1] Colleges look down
  On careless boys at play.
But when the bugles sounded war
  They put their games away.

They left the peaceful river,
  The cricket-field, the quad,
The shaven lawns of Oxford,
  To seek a bloody sod—
They gave their merry youth away
  For country and for God.

God rest you, happy gentlemen,
  Who laid your good lives down,
Who took the khaki and the gun
  Instead of cap and gown.
God bring you to a fairer place
  Than even Oxford town.

—Winifred M. Letts

[1]Gray.

IN TIME OF "THE BREAKING OF NATIONS"

1

Only a man harrowing clods
   In a slow silent walk
With an old horse that stumbles and nods
   Half asleep as they stalk.

2

Only thin smoke without flame
   From the heaps of couch-grass;
Yet this will go onward the same
   Though Dynasties pass.

3

Yonder a maid and her wight[1]
   Come whispering by;
War's annals will cloud into night
   Ere their story die.

—*Thomas Hardy*

The poem was published during World War I. The title alludes to Jeremiah 5:20: "Thou art my battle ax and weapons of war: for with thee will I break in pieces the nations, and with thee will I destroy kingdoms."

[1]Boy friend.

SHILOH[1]

A REQUIEM

(APRIL 1862)

Skimming lightly, wheeling still,
   The swallows fly low
Over the field in clouded days,
   The forest-field of Shiloh—
Over the field where April rain
Solaced the parched one stretched in pain
Through the pause of night

[1]The title refers to a Civil War battle fought in western Tennessee on April 6 and 7, 1862. Most of the terrible battle was fought around the Shiloh Baptist Church. The Union lost 13,047 men; the Confederates lost 10,694 men.

That followed the Sunday fight
　　Around the church of Shiloh—
The church so lone, the log-built one,
That echoed to many a parting groan
　　　And natural prayer
　　Of dying foemen mingled there—
Foemen at morn, but friends at eve—
　　Fame or country least their care:
(What like a bullet can undeceive!)
　　But now they lie low,
While over them the swallows skim,
　　And all is hushed at Shiloh.

.　　—Herman Melville

THE NEW ALLY[1]

Their great gray ships go plunging forth;
The waves, wind-wakened from the north,
Swarm up their bows and fall away,
And wash the air with golden spray.

Far off is flung their battle-line;
Far off their great guns flame and shine;
And we are one with them—we rise
With dawning thunder in our eyes
To join the embattled hosts that kept
Their pact with freedom while we slept!

—Harry Kemp

[1]The new ally is the United States which did not enter World War I, begun in 1914, until April 6, 1917, soon after German submarines sank three American ships.

CHAPTER 7

WRITING A PROCESS PAPER

The *process* paper describes a series of actions, changes, or functions that bring about an end or result. Probably the most familiar kind of process paper is the "how-to" paper, a step-by-step set of instructions on how to complete a particular task—how to change a tire, how to bake a cake, how to install storm windows, how to assemble a bicycle.

Although the rules for this kind of paper are simple and obvious, you should check your paper to see that you have observed them, because if you haven't, your description of the process may be useless to the reader. The rules follow.

Make certain that the explanation is complete and accurate. If, for example, you want to describe the process for baking a cake, you would mislead your reader if you omitted the instruction to grease and flour the pan. It's surprisingly easy to leave out important steps. You will be writing about a process you know extremely well, and you probably perform some steps—such as greasing a pan—without consciously thinking about them at all.

Maintain strict chronological order. Once the cake is in the oven, it is too late to tell the reader that walnuts should have been stirred into the batter.

If a particular kind of performance is called for in any part of the process, indicate its nature. Should the batter be stirred vigorously or gently? Should an applicant for a job approach the interviewer humbly, aggressively, nonchalantly? Besides indicating the nature of the action, you should also tell the reader why such action is called for. Readers are more likely to follow instructions if they understand the reason for them.

Group the steps in the process. A process may include many steps, but they can usually be grouped, in their chronological order, under logical headings—for example, *assembling ingredients, as-*

sembling utensils, mixing ingredients, cooking ingredients. A number of steps may be involved in each of these divisions, but reading the steps in groups is far less frightening and confusing to a reader than beginning with step one and ending with step nineteen.

Define any terms that might be unfamiliar to the reader or have more than one meaning. To most of us, *conceit* means extreme self-love, but to a literary scholar, it means an elaborate and extended metaphor. The scholar, when writing instructions for first-year students on analyzing a poem, would have to define the term if he wished to use it.

Have a thesis. It's possible just to present a clear set of instructions and stop. But the most interesting process papers do have theses. Few of us read car manuals or recipe books for pleasure, but we might well read the student paper "Porch Scrubbing with the Best" (p. 113) more than once, just for the fun of it. Part of the fun comes from the thesis that gives the paper focus and charm. It's a good idea, then, to try for a thesis.

> My way of changing license plates will save you time and frustration.
>
> Writing term papers can be simplified by breaking the work into steps.
>
> If you can afford a good accountant, filing income tax returns is simple.

Anticipate difficulties. One way to prevent difficulties for your readers is to warn them in advance when to expect problems:

> This step requires your constant attention.
>
> Now you will need all the strength you can muster.
>
> You'd better have a friend handy to help with this step.

Another way to anticipate difficulties is to give the readers advice on how to make the process easier or more pleasant. You're the authority on the subject, and you want to pass on to the novice any helpful tips you've gained from experience. Wearing old clothes isn't essential to the process of shampooing a carpet, of course, but you've learned from experience that dirty suds can fly and soil clothing, and you want to pass that information on. Similarly, it's possible to erase a typing error without moving the carriage away from the keys. But you've learned that this practice can lead to gummy keys and, in the case of an electric typewriter, a broken fan belt. Naturally, you want to warn against erasing over the keys.

Finally, *tell the reader what to do if something goes wrong.* In many processes, one can follow the instructions faithfully and still have problems. Prepare your reader for such cases.

If, at this point, the pecan pie is not firm when you test the center, reduce the heat to 250 degrees and cook it fifteen minutes longer.

If, even after careful proofreading, you find a misspelled word at the last minute, carefully erase the word and neatly print the correction by hand.

An introduction to a how-to paper, in addition to presenting the thesis, might state when and by whom the process would be performed. It could also list any equipment needed for performing the process, and it might briefly list the major headings or divisions of the process. Don't forget about the need for a conclusion. You want the last thought in your reader's mind to be about the process as a whole, not about the comparatively trivial final step.

Below is a student's process paper. Study it and determine whether the writer has given clear instructions on how to perform the task.

The Pit
DEBORAH BAZELIDES

Beautiful, healthy house plants are a great addition to any room because they add color and life to even the dullest corner. And they don't have to be expensive. An easy and inexpensive way to brighten up your home—and perhaps become a plant nut—is to start growing an avocado plant. Here's how.

The first step is to purchase a firm, ripe avocado from the produce department of your local grocery store. You may think of an avocado as a luxury item, but remember that you're getting both a salad and a beautiful plant out of this purchase. After you've enjoyed the avocado in a delicious salad of greens and tomatoes, wash the pit off and let it soak in a glass of warm water for several hours. The pit will have a brownish skin. Soaking will loosen the skin for easier removal. Using your fingers or a small paring knife, remove the skin from the avocado pit. Now the pit, which is pear-shaped or egg-shaped, will be a waxy flesh color. Put the clean pit in a clear glass of lukewarm water, and fill the glass so that the pit is about two-thirds covered with water.

Next, simply place the avocado pit in a warm, sunny window and leave it there. Avocados love warmth and sunshine, and they like to be talked to now and then. Every few days change the water. In a week or so, you'll notice the pit starting to split open from bottom to top. This is a good sign, but the pit is not ready to plant yet. Leave it in fresh water for now.

In about ten days, the avocado pit will be split all the way open, and it will start to develop some rigid, white roots. At this point, all you need do is be faithful, be patient, and change the water once a week. Eventually, you'll notice a brownish-green stem has started growing from the center of the split avocado pit. The stem will have tiny, semi-shiny green leaves clustered around the tip. Use a pair of scissors and clip the leaves. Cutting the leaves off at this stage will cause the plant to branch out and become full as it grows. If you don't cut the leaves back at this time, your plant will grow straight and spindly.

In anywhere from a few more days to several weeks (that's right), the stem will start branching out, and long, dark green leaves will appear. At last, it's time to plant the pit.

Planting your avocado pit is easy and doesn't have to be expensive. You don't need to buy a designer pot. All you really need is one six-inch clay pot with a hole on the bottom (the hole is for good water drainage), a handful of gravel stones, and a bag of all-purpose potting soil. Soak the clay pot in warm water. This helps the porous clay pot to hold moisture. Soaking is important. Then, take the gravel stones and cover the bottom of the clay pot with them. Add a little soil and then gently place the pit in the pot. Pack in some soil around the pit and continue filling the rest of the pot loosely with more soil. Water the avocado plant thoroughly with room-temperature water.

The plant doesn't require much care. Just keep it away from drafts. A draft will cause the plant's lush, green leaves to droop or turn brown or fall off. Give the plant a thorough watering once a week, and also mist it with room-temperature water every few days. Misting creates humidity and helps keep the bugs away. Otherwise, simply place your plant in a warm, sunny window and watch it grow.

With only a little attention now and then, your avocado plant will truly brighten up your home. Now that you've acquired a green thumb, you may want to start another avocado pit. Happy planting!

Questions for Writing and Discussion

1. What is the thesis of the paper? Where is it stated?
2. What function do expressions like "simply" and "all you need do" serve in the paper? Find other expressions that serve this function.
3. Does the writer observe all the requirements of a good process paper? Does she omit any important instruction?
4. Perhaps you, too, have found an inexpensive way to grow or make something that others might like to know about. If so, write a process paper telling how to perform the task.

Not all process papers simply give instructions. Some tell "how it works." Such papers explain the functioning of anything from an electric blender to the system by which congressional legislation is passed. Still other process papers describe "how it was done." This kind of paper could trace the process by which Walter Reed discovered the cause of yellow fever or, as in the popular *Making of the President* books, how a man came to be president. A how-it-was-done paper could even trace the process by which a person achieved a certain kind of awareness, as is the case in the following student paper.

Porch Scrubbing with the Best
SHIRLEY LYTTON-CANNON

There are a lot of famous experts around from whom we can learn a great deal, just by watching them or listening to what they have to say about their special techniques, style, or sources of information. Depending on what we want to learn, we usually give most of our attention to the how-to-do-it people who have at one time or another made their way into a newspaper column or perhaps have written a little manual or not-so-little book on how to do something. But if you want to know about scrubbing porches, your best bet is to take on-the-job training with Elizabeth Lytton.

Now, I know that as far as the media are concerned, Elizabeth Lytton doesn't even exist. But when you live in a mining camp such as National, West Virginia, it's darn hard to make a name for yourself, especially if you come from a family of twelve children, have only a fourth-grade education, and don't know much about anything except hard work, empty cupboards and cold houses. Nonetheless, make a name for herself she did. Everyone in National, as well as in the surrounding mining camps such as Riverseam, Flaggy Meadow, Edna Gas and Harmony Grove, knows that Elizabeth Lytton has the house with the greenest lawn, the most beautiful flower garden, the earliest lettuce, and most important, the cleanest porches.

It wasn't until I was about twelve years old and had my first porch-scrubbing lesson with her that I realized why clean porches were so highly respected. We were cleaning our big grey-painted cement porch with the white enamel bannisters and porch-green enamel flower boxes. She told me that the houses in the camps all have coal furnaces, so between the soot and gritty dirt pouring out of the chimneys of the houses, and the smoky fumes seeping out of the mine's slate dump, which was always burning nearby, a person really has to know what he's doing if he expects to sit on a porch and not feel as if he'll have to take a bath afterward.

We began by dragging the glider, chaise lounge, rocking chair, grass rug, and a couple of miscellaneous tables out into the back yard, during which time she minced no words in telling me exactly what she thought of certain people who smear dirt around with a damp mop and call a porch clean.

When we went into the basement to get the cleaning supplies, I expected her to whip out some magic cleaning solutions and mix her own concoction, but that wasn't exactly the case. Instead, she opened a giant-sized box of Spic-n-Span, which didn't look like a miracle worker to my inexperienced eyes, and then added triple the amount called for on the label to the biggest, hottest bucket of water into which I have ever had the ill fortune of dunking my hands. I asked her if she wanted me to get some rubber gloves, but she said something about the fact that cracks and grooves weren't about to move aside for fat rubber fingers! I think I began suspecting then that this was going to be no ordinary cleaning day.

We carried the bucket of Spic-n-Span water outside to the porch, along with two stiff-bristled scrub brushes, two mops, two brooms, and two old towels to be used for scrub rags. She hooked up the garden hose nearby, turned on the faucet, and we were ready to begin.

I guess at that point your average, everyday porch scrubber would have cleaned the floor of the porch after having wiped off the bannisters a little, and then been done with it. But not Elizabeth. She had a reputation to uphold, and she didn't get that reputation by doing things "with a lick and a promise." She told me to dip my brush into the bucket and bring as much hot cleaning water up with it as possible and start scrubbing the ceiling boards of the porch first, continuing to dip the brush into the bucket often enough to keep plenty of water on the boards. Well, we dipped and scrubbed until we cleaned not only the ceiling boards, but also the side of the house leading from the porch to the inside, as well as the carved posts that make up the bannister. That's a lot of dunking and scrubbing! We used our brooms and what was left of the water to scrub the floor of the porch. I noticed that my hands grew accustomed to the water temperature just about the time some of the skin between my fingers began to get cracked and flaky looking.

The fun part of the training came when we used the hose to rinse everything—fun, that is, until the ice cold water soaked through my penny loafers and white cotton socks.

Just about the time I figured we had to be pretty close to finished, she brought out another huge bucket of plain hot water, and we began to dip the towels into the bucket, squeeze the water out of them as much as possible, and then wipe each board clean and dry, making sure, if you please, to get all the cracks, grooves and crannies clean also. We used our mops in the same manner as the towels to finish cleaning the floor.

Finally, we repeated the whole ritual on the porch furniture and then put everything back in its proper place.

We sat down together for a while on the glider, just talking about how nice everything looked and how hard we had worked. It seemed to me that she felt more pleased with the work we had done than with the fact that it was finally finished.

During our lifetime together we were always working on something or other, and the one thing that I always noticed about her was that she never did anything halfway—whether it was sewing a dress, growing a garden, caring for a lawn, or scrubbing a porch. It was just her way to do the best she could, no matter how menial the task. She thrived on the pride that came from being the best at it. Maybe that's the secret of all experts such as Elizabeth.

Questions for Writing or Discussion

1. Besides learning how to scrub a porch, what is the more important lesson the writer learned?
2. Considering the lesson the writer learned, discuss the importance of paragraph 2.
3. How does the first sentence in the fifth paragraph help characterize the writer? Can you find other sentences which support that characterization?
4. Why is porch scrubbing a better subject to make the writer's point than, say, learning to appreciate the symbolism of *Moby-Dick* from a dedicated high school English teacher?
5. Perhaps you have had an experience which taught you something about yourself, a member of your family, or the nature of life. Trace the process by which you made the discovery.

Process writing can also be an effective tool of literary analysis. Following is a story by Shirley Jackson, "Charles." After you have read the story, study the paper that follows to see what process the student derived from the story.

Shirley Jackson
CHARLES

The day my son Laurie started kindergarten he renounced corduroy overalls with bibs and began wearing blue jeans with a belt; I watched him go off the first morning with the older girl next door, seeing clearly that an era of my life was ended, my sweet-voiced nursery-school tot replaced by a long-trousered, swaggering character who forgot to stop at the corner and wave good-bye to me.

He came home the same way, the front door slamming open, his cap on the floor, and the voice suddenly become raucous shouting, "Isn't anybody here?"

At lunch he spoke insolently to his father, spilled his baby sister's milk, and remarked that his teacher said we were not to take the name of the Lord in vain.

"How *was* school today?" I asked, elaborately casual.

"All right," he said.

"Did you learn anything?" his father asked.

Laurie regarded his father coldly. "I didn't learn nothing," he said.

"Anything," I said. "Didn't learn anything."

"The teacher spanked a boy, though," Laurie said, addressing his bread and butter. "For being fresh," he added, with his mouth full.

"What did he do?" I asked. "Who was it?"

Laurie thought. "It was Charles," he said. "He was fresh. The teacher spanked him and made him stand in a corner. He was awfully fresh."

"What did he do?" I asked again, but Laurie slid off his chair, took a cookie, and left, while his father was still saying, "See here, young man."

The next day Laurie remarked at lunch, as soon as he sat down, "Well, Charles was bad again today." He grinned enormously and said, "Today Charles hit the teacher."

"Good heavens," I said, mindful of the Lord's name, "I suppose he got spanked again?"

"He sure did," Laurie said. "Look up," he said to his father.

"What?" his father said, looking up.

"Look down," Laurie said. "Look at my thumb. Gee you're dumb." He began to laugh insanely.

"Why did Charles hit the teacher?" I asked quickly.

"Because she tried to make him color with red crayons," Laurie said. "Charles wanted to color with green crayons so he hit the teacher and she spanked him and said nobody play with Charles but everybody did."

The third day—it was Wednesday of the first week—Charles bounced a see-saw on to the head of a little girl and made her bleed, and the teacher made him stay inside all during recess. Thursday Charles had to stand in a corner during story-time because he kept pounding his feet on the floor. Friday Charles was deprived of blackboard privileges because he threw chalk.

On Saturday I remarked to my husband, "Do you think kindergarten is too unsettling for Laurie? All this toughness, and bad grammar, and this Charles boy sounds like such a bad influence."

"It'll be all right," my husband said reassuringly. "Bound to be people like Charles in the world. Might as well meet them now as later."

On Monday Laurie came home late, full of news. "Charles," he shouted as he came up the hill; I was waiting anxiously on the front steps. "Charles," Laurie yelled all the way up the hill, "Charles was bad again."

"Come right in," I said, as soon as he came close enough. "Lunch is waiting."

"You know what Charles did?" he demanded, following me through the door. "Charles yelled so in school they sent a boy in from first grade to tell the teacher she had to make Charles keep quiet, and so Charles had to stay after school. And so all the children stayed to watch him."

"What did he do?" I asked.

"He just sat there," Laurie said, climbing into his chair at the table. "Hi, Pop, y'old dust mop."

"Charles had to stay after school today," I told my husband. "Everyone stayed with him."

"What does this Charles look like?" my husband asked Laurie. "What's his other name?"

"He's bigger than me," Laurie said. "And he doesn't have any rubbers and he doesn't ever wear a jacket."

Monday night was the first Parent-Teachers meeting, and only the fact that the baby had a cold kept me from going; I wanted passionately to meet Charles's mother. On Tuesday Laurie remarked suddenly, "Our teacher had a friend come to see her in school today."

"Charles's mother?" my husband and I asked simultaneously.

"Naaah," Laurie said scornfully. "It was a man who came and made us do exercises, we had to touch our toes. Look." He climbed down from his chair and squatted down and touched his toes. "Like this," he said. He got solemnly back into his chair and said, picking up his fork, "Charles didn't even *do* exercises."

"That's fine," I said heartily. "Didn't Charles want to do exercises?"

"Naaah," Laurie said. "Charles was so fresh to the teacher's friend he wasn't *let* do exercises."

"Fresh again?" I said.

"He kicked the teacher's friend," Laurie said. "The teacher's friend told Charles to touch his toes like I just did and Charles kicked him."

"What are they going to do about Charles, do you suppose?" Laurie's father asked him.

Laurie shrugged elaborately. "Throw him out of school, I guess," he said.

Wednesday and Thursday were routine; Charles yelled during story hour and hit a boy in the stomach and made him cry. On Friday Charles stayed after school again and so did all the other children.

With the third week of kindergarten Charles was an institution in our family; the baby was being a Charles when she cried all afternoon; Laurie did a Charles when he filled his wagon full of mud and pulled it through the kitchen; even my husband, when he caught his elbow in the telephone cord and pulled telephone, ashtray, and a bowl of flowers off the table, said, after the first minute, "Looks like Charles."

During the third and fourth weeks it looked like a reformation in Charles; Laurie reported grimly at lunch on Thursday of the third week, "Charles was so good today the teacher gave him an apple."

"What?" I said, and my husband added warily, "You mean Charles?"

"Charles," Laurie said. "He gave the crayons around and he picked up the books afterward and the teacher said he was her helper."

"What happened?" I asked incredulously.

"He was her helper, that's all," Laurie said, and shrugged.

"Can this be true, about Charles?" I asked my husband that night. "Can something like this happen?"

"Wait and see," my husband said cynically. "When you've got a Charles to deal with, this may mean he's only plotting."

He seemed to be wrong. For over a week Charles was the teacher's helper; each day he handed things out and he picked things up; no one had to stay after school.

"The P.T.A. meeting's next week again," I told my husband one evening. "I'm going to find Charles's mother there."

"Ask her what happened to Charles," my husband said. "I'd like to know."

"I'd like to know myself," I said.

On Friday of that week things were back to normal. "You know what Charles did today?" Laurie demanded at the lunch table, in a voice slightly awed. "He told a little girl to say a word and she said it and the teacher washed her mouth out with soap and Charles laughed."

"What word?" his father asked unwisely, and Laurie said, "I'll have to whisper it to you, it's so bad." He got down off his chair and went around to his father. His father bend his head down and Laurie whispered joyfully. His father's eyes widened.

"Did Charles tell the little girl to say *that?*" he asked respectfully.

"She said it *twice,*" Laurie said. "Charles told her to say it *twice.*"

"What happened to Charles?" my husband asked.

"Nothing," Laurie said. "He was passing out the crayons."

Monday morning Charles abandoned the little girl and said the evil word himself three of four times, getting his mouth washed out with soap each time. He also threw chalk.

My husband came to the door with me that evening as I set out for the P.T.A. meeting. "Invite her over for a cup of tea after the meeting," he said. "I want to get a look at her."

"If only she's there," I said prayerfully.

"She'll be there," my husband said. "I don't see how they could hold a P.T.A. meeting without Charles's mother."

At the meeting I sat restlessly, scanning each comfortable matronly face, trying to determine which one hid the secret of Charles. None of them looked to me haggard enough. No one stood up in the meeting and apologized for the way her son had been acting. No one mentioned Charles.

After the meeting I identified and sought out Laurie's kindergarten teacher. She had a plate with a cup of tea and a piece of chocolate cake; I had a plate with a cup of tea and a piece of marshmallow cake. We maneuvered up to one another cautiously, and smiled.

"I've been so anxious to meet you," I said. "I'm Laurie's mother."

"We're all so interested in Laurie," she said.

"Well, he certainly likes kindergarten," I said. "He talks about it all the time."

"We had a little trouble adjusting, the first week or so," she said primly, "but now he's a fine little helper. With occasional lapses, of course."

"Laurie usually adjusts very quickly," I said. "I suppose this time it's Charles's influence."

"Charles?"

"Yes," I said, laughing, "you must have your hands full in that kindergarten, with Charles."

"Charles?" she said. "We don't have any Charles in the kindergarten."

Questions for Writing or Discussion

1. Does the story provide any indications of why Laurie invents the character of Charles?
2. How are Laurie's parents supposed to strike the reader? Are they good, bad, or in-between? Are they too permissive?
3. How does the response of Laurie's parents help perpetuate the existence of Charles?
4. Did you suspect the truth about Charles before the end of the story? If so, what started your suspicion?
5. Good authors of stories with surprise endings always play fair. They give plenty of clues, which readers tend to overlook, about the outcome of the story. Trace the process by which Shirley Jackson prepares the alert reader for the outcome of "Charles."

The Beginning of the End
HARRIET McKAY

Until the last sentence of Shirley Jackson's "Charles," I had no idea that Charles, the terror of kindergarten, was an imaginary person created by Laurie and that Charles's little monster antics were really Laurie's own antics. The author fooled me completely, but I have to admit that she played fair. She gave her readers all the clues they needed to make a sensible guess about how the story would end.

Laurie's own personality offers one set of clues. Even before classes start, Jackson lets us know that Laurie might have a lot to overcompensate for. His mother has been dressing him in cute little boy clothes and thinking of him as a "sweet-voiced nursery-school tot." It is at Laurie's own insistence that he begins wearing tough-kid blue jeans. In addition, any boy nicknamed "Laurie" is due for some problems; one doesn't need to be a sexist pig to say that boys named "Laurence" ought to be called "Larry" and that "Laurie," to put it bluntly, is a sissy name. No wonder Laurie goes overboard. He's not a little boy anymore. He has hit the big time in kindergarten, and he begins "swaggering" even before his first class.

Laurie's behavior at home after school starts is another giveaway. Charles may be a monster at school, but Laurie isn't that much better at lunchtime. After only one class, he slams the door, throws his hat on the floor, shouts, speaks "insolently," makes deliberate mistakes in grammar, doesn't look at people when he talks to them but talks to the bread and butter instead, speaks with his mouth full, leaves the table without asking permission and while his father is still talking to him. This is no sweet little tot. His doting parents might try to pin Laurie's behavior on the bad influence of Charles, but that's certainly not the only possible explanation, and that's what doting parents have always tried to do. Besides, it would be stretching things to the limit to imagine that even Charles could have that great an influence after only one morning in the same classroom with him.

Still another giveaway is Laurie's explanation for being late. It's impossible to believe that a group of kindergarten kids would voluntarily stay after school to watch a child being punished. Laurie's parents swallow this story so easily that many readers probably don't notice how fantastic the story really is—but an alert reader would have noticed.

The last clue I should have noticed is the way Laurie's parents look forward to the P.T.A. meeting so they can meet Charles's mother. They have been so poised and cool about everything that I really wonder why I did not realize that they would have to be brought down a few pegs at the end of the story. Have they ever made a serious effort to correct their son's bad manners? Have they ever told him to stay away from a rotten kid like Charles? Heavens no, they're much too enlightened. The parents think Charles is amusing, and they can't wait to meet Charles's mother so they can feel superior to her. In simple justice they deserve what they get, and I should have seen it coming.

Laurie's personality and behavior, his unbelievable explanation for being late, and his parents' complacency all give readers the clues they need to predict the surprise ending.

Questions for Writing or Discussion

1. What is the thesis of the paper? Is the thesis stated in one sentence?
2. What is the process traced in the paper?
3. What personality does the writer present to the reader? Is it appropriate to the subject matter?
4. Does the writer omit details from the story that could have strengthened her case?
5. Should a separate paragraph have been devoted to the issue of Laurie's lateness? If not, how could the issue have been treated more effectively?
6. Is the last paragraph too short? too abrupt? too dull?

Readings

The two selections that follow are good examples of process writing by professionals. Both provide clear instructions for performing useful tasks. One author, however, takes a straightforward, no-nonsense, how-to-do-it approach. The other takes a humorous approach. See which you prefer.

Carla Stephens
DROWNPROOFING

If your warm-weather plans include water sports, there's one thing you should do to make this summer safe as well as enjoyable for your family: Drownproof them!

Drowning is the second leading cause of accidental death for people between the ages of 4 and 44, according to the American National Red Cross. Twenty-eight percent of those drowned are children under 15 years old. Seven out of ten of them are boys.

Even more shocking is the fact that many of the seven thousand annual drowning victims *know how to swim*. In fact, swimmers face several hazards that non-swimmers don't. First, they may overexert themselves— especially in May and June when they're likely to expect out-of-condition bodies to perform as well as in summers past. They may also get into a situation beyond their skills. If panic takes over, tragedy may follow.

With drownproofing, on the other hand, a poor swimmer or even a non-swimmer can survive in the water twelve hours or more—even when fully clothed and in rough water.

Developed by the late Fred Lanoue, drownproofing relies on the body's ability to float when air fills the lungs. Picture yourself bobbing restfully just under the surface of the water. With a few easy movements you come up to breathe as often as necessary. That's the basic idea of drownproofing, a technique endorsed by the Red Cross, the National Safety Council and the YMCA. It's easy to learn, even for some three-year-olds. You can teach yourself and your family.

Here's how it's done: First, take a breath through your mouth. Then, holding your breath, put your face into the water and float vertically with your arms and legs dangling. Don't try to keep your head up; it weighs fifteen pounds.

When you're ready for another breath, slowly raise your arms to shoulder height. At the same time bring one leg a little forward and the other back into a position somewhat like the scissors kick. (If injury makes it necessary, drownproofing can be done with either the arm or the leg movements.) Then gently press your arms down to your sides (not backward) and bring your legs together. Keep your eyes open and raise your head until your mouth is out of the water. Exhale through your nose, your mouth or both.

Inhale through your mouth while continuing to press your arms down. But don't press too hard, for you want to keep your chin at, not above, the surface of the water. Finally, return to the resting position with your face in the water. If you sink too far, a small kick or a slight downward push of your arms, will return you to the surface.

When teaching your children, it's advisable to stand with them in shoulder-deep water. Have them bend forward to practice the breathing and arm movements. If they swallow water, be patient and encourage them to try again. Once they're comfortable with the procedure, move into deeper water near the side of the pool to coordinate the floating, breathing and body movements. Water just deep enough for them to go under is sufficient. Remember, all movements should be easy and relaxed.

If your child needs to work at the vertical float, let him practice at the side of a pool or some other spot where he'll be able to hold on. At first you might even help hold him up by placing a hand just beneath his shoulder. Have him take a breath, put his face into the water and then remove his hands from the side. As soon as he has some experience in floating remove your hand and watch.

While practicing, youngsters usually spend only about three seconds under water at first. That time should gradually increase—depending, of course, on their age. Older children may reach ten seconds, the period recommended for adults.

With a little practice your family will be drownproofed and truly ready for fun in the water.

Questions for Writing or Discussion

1. Does the article have a thesis? If so, what is it?
2. What personality does the author project? What kind of reader does she seem to have in mind? Are the personality and reader appropriate to the subject matter?
3. How many steps are involved in the process of staying afloat?
4. Does the author describe more than one process? If so, what process or processes are described besides that of staying afloat?
5. What rule of a good process paper do paragraphs two and three fulfill?
6. Do you believe you could follow these instructions? Do you think pictures would help make the process clearer?
7. Write a paper in which you describe a process which could be of benefit to someone else.

L. Rust Hills
HOW TO CARE FOR AND ABOUT ASHTRAYS

There are three truths about ashtrays that must be held self-evident before any household can achieve true happiness and security: (1) there can never really ever be too many ashtrays, because (2) there must be an ashtray, a specific ashtray, for each and every place anyone could conceivably ever want one, and (3) it must *be* there—always. No ashtray should ever be moved.

But there are forces at work against order in the world. The natural enemies of the ashtray are wives and children. Children are always putting something else in ashtrays: wadded Kleenex, pear cores, gum and gum wrappers, orange peels. And this of course means that wives take the ashtrays off to the kitchen, intending to wash them, which isn't the right way to clean ashtrays anyway, but then just leave them in the sink.

To clean ashtrays the right way, proceed as follows. Take a metal or plastic or wooden (but never a basket) wastebasket in your left hand, and a paper towel in your right. Approach the ashtray that is to be cleaned. Put the wastebasket down on the floor, and with your released left hand pick up the ashtray and dump its contents of cigarette ends, spent matches, and loose ashes (nothing else should be in an ashtray!) into the wastebasket. Then, still holding the ashtray over the basket, rub gently with the paper towel at any of the few stains or spots that may remain. Then put the ashtray carefully back into its place, pick up the wastebasket again, and approach the next ashtray to be cleaned. It should never be necessary to wash an ashtray, if it is kept clean and dry. Throughout its whole lifetime in a well-ordered household, an ashtray need never travel more than three feet from where it belongs, and never be out of place at all for more than thirty seconds.

But when children put pear cores and orange peels in ashtrays, of course none of this can be accomplished as it ought. One can't dump raw garbage into a wastepaper basket and then calmly put the basket back in the corner of the room. And the juice of the fruit moistens the ashtray so ashes stick and dry in hard spots so it may *need* to be washed. Then the ashtrays get left in the kitchen to drain dry, because no one likes to use a dishtowel to dry an ashtray. And then there's no ashtray where it's supposed to be when you want it, so you have to move one from somewhere else and gradually everything gets all upset and things in the household aren't the way they ought to be, even though it's not your fault.

Questions for Writing or Discussion

1. What is the thesis of the paper? Is this thesis too grand for a paper about cleaning ashtrays?
2. What personality does the author present? How does the thesis help reveal the personality? Is the personality appropriate to the subject matter?
3. Where does the description of the process for cleaning ashtrays begin? Where does it end? Does the description fulfill all the rules of a good process paper?
4. Does the author have a purpose other than the one announced in the title? If so, what? Is the title misleading? Is it a part of the personality the author presents?
5. What kind of reader is addressed by the article? Do you think that reader is expected to take seriously the author's assertion that wives and children are the "forces at work against order in the world"? Why, or why not?

6. Almost everyone has some pet peeve related to housekeeping. Think of some housekeeping practice that bothers you and describe a process by which you or members of your household could change or eliminate the practice.

This chapter ends with two short stories. Both lend themselves to process analysis. Read each story twice—once just for the fun of it, and again to look for the process.

Roald Dahl
THE LANDLADY

Billy Weaver had travelled down from London on the slow afternoon train, with a change at Reading on the way, and by the time he got to Bath it was about nine o'clock in the evening and the moon was coming up out of a clear, starry sky over the houses opposite the station entrance. But the air was deadly cold and the wind was like a flat blade of ice on his cheeks.

"Excuse me," he said to a porter, "but is there a fairly cheap hotel not too far away from here?"

"Try the Bell and Dragon," the porter answered, pointing down the road. "They might take you in. It's about a quarter of a mile along on the other side."

Billy thanked him and picked up his suitcase and set out to walk the quarter mile to the Bell and Dragon. He had never been to Bath before. He didn't know anyone who lived there. But Mr. Greenslade at the Head Office in London had told him it was a splendid town. "Find your own lodgings," he said, "and then go along and report to the branch manager as soon as you've got yourself settled."

Billy was seventeen years old. He was wearing a new navy-blue overcoat, a new brown trilby hat, and a new brown suit, and he was feeling fine. He walked briskly down the street. He was trying to do everything briskly these days. Briskness, he had decided, was *the* one common characteristic of all successful businessmen. The big shots up at Head Office were absolutely fantastically brisk all the time. They were amazing.

There were no shops on this wide street that he was walking along, only a line of tall houses on each side, all of them identical. They had porches and pillars and four or five steps going up to their front doors, and it was obvious that once upon a time they had been very swanky residences. But now, even in the darkness, he could see that the paint was peeling from the woodwork on their doors and windows, and that the handsome white facades were cracked and blotchy from neglect.

Suddenly, not six yards away, in a downstairs window that was brilliantly illuminated by a street lamp, Billy caught sight of a printed notice propped up against the glass in one of the upper panes. It said, "BED AND BREAKFAST."

There was a vase of yellow chrysanthemums, tall and beautiful, standing just underneath the notice.

He stopped walking. He moved a bit closer. Green curtains (some sort of velvety material) were hanging down on either side of the window. The chrysanthemums looked wonderful beside them. He went right up and peered through the glass into the room, and the first thing he saw was a bright fire burning on the hearth. On the carpet in front of the fire, a pretty little dachshund was curled up asleep, with its nose tucked into its belly. The room itself, as far as he could see in the half darkness, was filled with pleasant furniture. There was a baby-grand piano and a big sofa and several plump armchairs, and in one corner he spotted a large parrot in a cage. Animals were usually a good sign in a place like this, Billy told himself, and all in all, it looked as though it would be a pretty decent house to stay in. Certainly it would be more comfortable than the Bell and Dragon.

On the other hand, a pub would be more congenial than a boarding house. There would be beer and darts in the evenings, and lots of people to talk to, and it would be a good bit cheaper, too. He had stayed a couple of nights in a pub once before, and he had liked it. He had never stayed in any boarding houses, and to be perfectly honest, he was a tiny bit frightened of them. The name itself conjured up images of watery cabbage, rapacious landladies, and a powerful smell of kippers in the living room. After dithering about like this in the cold for two or three minutes, Billy decided that he would walk on and take a look at the Bell and Dragon before making up his mind. He turned to go.

And now a queer thing happened to him. He was in the act of stepping back and turning away from the window when all at once his eye was caught again and held in the most peculiar manner by the small notice that was there. "BED AND BREAKFAST," it said. "Bed and Breakfast, bed and breakfast, bed and breakfast." Each word was like a large black eye staring at him through the glass, holding him, compelling him, forcing him to stay where he was and not walk away from that house, and the next thing he knew he was actually moving across from the window to the front door, climbing the steps that led up to it, and reaching for the bell.

He pressed the bell. Far away in a back room, he heard it ringing, and then *at once*—it must have been at once, because he hadn't even had time to take his finger from the bell button—the door swung open and a woman was standing there. Normally, you ring a bell and you have at least a half-minute wait before the door opens. But this person was like a jack-in-the-box. He pressed the bell—and out she popped! It made him jump.

She was about forty-five or fifty years old, and the moment she saw him she gave him a warm, welcoming smile. *"Please* come in," she said pleasantly. She stepped aside, holding the door wide open, and Billy found himself automatically starting forward. The compulsion, or, more accurately, the desire to follow after her into that house was extraordinarily strong, but he held himself back.

"I saw the notice in the window," he said.

"Yes, I know."

"I was wondering about a room."

"It's *all* ready for you, my dear," she said. She had a round pink face and very gentle blue eyes.

"I was on my way to the Bell and Dragon," Billy told her. "But the notice in your window just happened to catch my eye."

"My dear boy," she said, "why don't you come in out of the cold?"

"How much do you charge?"

"Five and sixpence a night, including breakfast."

It was fantastically cheap. It was less than half of what he had been willing to pay.

"If that is too much," she added, "then perhaps I can reduce it just a tiny bit. Do you desire an egg for breakfast? Eggs are expensive at the moment. It would be sixpence less without the egg."

"Five and sixpence is fine," he answered. "I should like very much to stay here."

"I knew you would. Do come in."

She seemed terribly nice. She looked exactly like the mother of one's best school friend welcoming one into the house to stay for the Christmas holidays. Billy took off his hat and stepped over the threshold.

"Just hang it there," she said, "and let me help you with your coat."

There were no other hats or coats in the hall. There were no umbrellas, no walking sticks—nothing.

"We have it *all* to ourselves," she said, smiling at him over her shoulder as she led the way upstairs. "You see, it isn't very often I have the pleasure of taking a visitor into my little nest."

The old girl is slightly dotty, Billy told himself. But at five and sixpence a night, who gives a damn about that? "I should've thought you'd be simply swamped with applicants," he said politely.

"Oh, I am, my dear, I am. Of course I am. But the trouble is that I'm inclined to be just a teeny-weeny bit choosy and particular—if you see what I mean."

"Ah, yes."

"But I'm always ready. Everything is always ready day and night in this house, just on the off chance that an acceptable young gentleman will come along. And it is such a pleasure, my dear, such a very great pleasure when now and again I open the door and I see someone standing there who is just *exactly* right." She was halfway up the stairs, and she paused with one hand on the stair rail, turning her head and smiling down at him with pale lips. "Like you," she added, and her blue eyes travelled slowly all the way down the length of Billy's body to his feet and then up again.

On the second-floor landing, she said to him, "This floor is mine."

They climbed up another flight. "And this one is *all* yours," she said. "Here's your room. I do hope you'll like it." She took him into a small but charming front bedroom, switching on the light as she went in.

"The morning sun comes right in the window, Mr. Perkins. It is Mr. Perkins, isn't it?"

"No," he said. "It's Weaver."

"Mr. Weaver. How nice. I've put a water bottle between the sheets, to warm them up, Mr. Weaver. It's such a comfort to have a hot-water bottle in a strange bed with clean sheets, don't you agree? And you may light the gas fire at any time, if you feel chilly."

"Thank you," Billy said. "Thank you ever so much." He noticed that the bedspread had been taken off the bed and that the bedclothes had been neatly turned back on one side, all ready for someone to get in.

"I'm so glad you appeared," she said, looking earnestly into his face. "I was beginning to get worried."

"That's all right," Billy answered brightly. "You mustn't worry about me." He put his suitcase on the chair and started to open it.

"And what about supper, my dear? Did you manage to get anything to eat before you came here?"

"I'm not a bit hungry, thank you," he said. "I think I'll just go to bed as soon as possible, because tomorrow I've got to get up rather early and report to the office."

"Very well, then. I'll leave you now so that you can unpack. But before you go to bed, would you be kind enough to pop into the sitting room on the ground floor and sign the book? Everyone has to do that, because it's the law of the land, and we don't want to go breaking any laws at *this* stage in the proceedings, do we?" She gave him a little wave of the hand and went quickly out of the room and closed the door.

Now the fact that his landlady appeared to be slightly off her rocker didn't worry Billy in the least. After all, she not only was harmless—there was no question about that—but she was also quite obviously a kind and generous soul. He guessed that she had probably lost a son in the war, or something like that, and had never got over it. So a few minutes later, after unpacking his suitcase and washing his hands, he trotted downstairs to the ground floor and entered the living room. His landlady wasn't there, but the fire was glowing on the hearth, and the little dachshund was still sleeping soundly in front of it. The room was wonderfully warm and cozy. I'm a lucky fellow, he thought, rubbing his hands. This is a bit of all right.

He found the guestbook lying open on the piano, so he took out his pen and wrote down his name and address. There were only two other entries above his on the page, and as one always does with guestbooks, he started to read them. One was a Christopher Mulholland, from Cardiff. The other was Gregory W. Temple, from Bristol.

That's funny, he thought suddenly. Christopher Mulholland. It rings a bell. Now where on earth had he heard that rather unusual name before? Was it a boy at school? No. Was it one of his sister's numerous young men, perhaps, or a friend of his father's? No, no, it wasn't any of those. He glanced down again at the book.

Christopher Mulholland, 231 Cathedral Road, Cardiff
Gregory W. Temple, 27 Sycamore Drive, Bristol

As a matter of fact, now he came to think of it, he wasn't at all sure that the second name didn't have almost as much of a familiar ring about it as the first.

"Gregory Temple?" he said aloud, searching his memory. "Christopher Mulholland? . . ."

"Such charming boys," a voice behind him answered, and he turned and saw his landlady sailing into the room with a large silver tea tray in her hands. She was holding it well out in front of her and rather high up, as though the tray were a pair of reins on a frisky horse.

"They sound somehow familiar," he said.

"They do? How interesting."

"I'm almost positive I've heard those names before somewhere. Isn't that odd? Maybe it was in the newspapers. They weren't famous in any way, were they? I mean, famous cricketers or footballers or something like that?"

"Famous?" she said, setting the tea tray down on the low table in front of the sofa. "Oh, no, I don't think they were famous. But they were incredibly handsome, both of them, I can promise you that. They were tall and young and handsome, my dear, just exactly like you."

Once more, Billy glanced down at the book. "Look here," he said, noticing the dates. "This last entry is over two years old."

"It is?"

"Yes indeed. And Christopher Mulholland's is nearly a year before that—more than *three* years ago."

"Dear me," she said, shaking her head and heaving a dainty little sigh. "I would never have thought it. How time does fly away from us all, doesn't it, Mr. Wilkins?"

"It's Weaver," Billy said. "W-e-a-v-e-r."

"Oh, of course it is!" she cried, sitting down on the sofa. "How silly of me. I do apologize. In one ear and out the other, that's me, Mr. Weaver."

"You know something?" Billy said. "Something that's really quite extraordinary about all this?"

"No, dear, I don't."

"Well, you see, both of these names—Mulholland and Temple—I not only seem to remember each one of them separately, so to speak, but somehow or other, in some peculiar way, they both appear to be sort of connected together as well. As though they were both famous for the same sort of thing, if you see what I mean—like . . . well . . . like Dempsey and Tunney, for example, or Churchill and Roosevelt."

"How amusing," she said. "But come over here now dear, and sit down beside me on the sofa and I'll give you a nice cup of tea and a ginger biscuit before you go to bed."

"You really shouldn't bother," Billy said. "I didn't mean you to do anything like that." He stood by the piano, watching her as she fussed about with the cups and saucers. He noticed that she had small, white, quickly moving hands and red fingernails.

"I'm almost positive it was in the newspapers I saw them," Billy said. "I'll think of it in a second. I'm sure I will."

There is nothing more tantalizing than a thing like this that lingers just outside the borders of one's memory. He hated to give up. "Now wait a minute," he said. "Wait just a minute. Mulholland . . . Christopher Mulholland . . . wasn't *that* the name of the Eton schoolboy who was on a walking tour through the West Country and then all of a sudden—"

"Milk?" she said. "And sugar?"

"Yes, please. And then all of a sudden—"

"Eton schoolboy?" she said. "Oh, no, my dear, that can't possibly be right because *my* Mr. Mulholland was certainly not an Eton schoolboy when he came to me. He was a Cambridge undergraduate. Come over here now and sit next to me and warm yourself in front of this lovely fire. Come on. Your tea's all ready for you." She patted the empty place beside her on the sofa and sat there smiling at Billy and waiting for him to come over.

He crossed the room slowly and sat down on the edge of the sofa. She placed his teacup on the table in front of him.

"*There* we are," she said. "How nice and cozy this is, isn't it?"

Billy started sipping his tea. She did the same. For half a minute or so, neither of them spoke. But Billy knew that she was looking at him. Her body was half turned toward him, and he could feel her eyes resting on his face, watching him over the rim of her teacup. Now and again, he caught a whiff of a peculiar smell that seemed to emanate directly from her person. It was not in the least unpleasant, and it reminded him—well, he wasn't quite sure what it reminded him of. Pickled walnuts? New leather? Or was it the corridors of a hospital?

At length she said, "Mr. Mulholland was a great one for his tea. Never in my life have I seen anyone drink as much tea as dear, sweet Mr. Mulholland."

"I suppose he left fairly recently," Billy said. He was still puzzling his head about the two names. He was positive now that he had seen them in the newspapers—in the headlines.

"Left?" she said, arching her brows. "But my dear boy, he never left. He's still here. Mr. Temple is also here. They're on the fourth floor, both of them together."

Billy set his cup down slowly on the table and stared at his landlady. She smiled back at him, and then she put out one of her white hands and patted him comfortingly on the knee.

"How old are you, my dear?" she asked.

"Seventeen."

"Seventeen!" she cried. "Oh, it's the perfect age! Mr. Mulholland was also seventeen. But I think he was a trifle shorter than you are; in fact, I'm sure he was and his teeth weren't *quite* so white. You have the most beautiful teeth, Mr. Weaver, did you know that?"

"They're not as good as they look," Billy said. "They've got simply masses of fillings in them at the back."

"Mr. Temple, of course, was a little older," she said, ignoring his remark. "He was actually twenty-eight. And yet I never would have guessed it if he hadn't told me—never in my whole life. There wasn't a *blemish* on his body."

"A what?" Billy said.

"His skin was *just* like a baby's."

There was a pause. Billy picked up his teacup and took another sip of his tea, then set it down gently in its saucer. He waited for her to say something else, but she seemed to have lapsed into another of her silences. He sat there staring straight ahead of him into the far corner of the room, biting his lower lip.

"That parrot," he said at last. "You know something? It had me completely fooled when I first saw it through the window. I could have sworn it was alive."

"Alas, no longer."

"It's most terribly clever the way it's been done," he said. "It doesn't look in the least bit dead. Who did it?"

"I did."

"You did?"

"Of course," she said. "And have you met my little Basil as well?" She nodded toward the dachshund curled up so comfortably in front of the fire, and Billy looked at it, and as he did so he suddenly realized that this animal all the time had been just as silent and motionless as the parrot. He put out a hand and touched it gently on the top of its back. The back was hard and cold, and when he pushed the hair to one side with his fingers, he could see the skin underneath, grayish-black, and dry and perfectly preserved.

"Good gracious me," he said. "How absolutely fascinating." He turned away from the dog and stared with deep admiration at the little woman beside him on the sofa. "It must be most awfully difficult to do a thing like that."

"Not in the least," she said. "I stuff *all* my little pets myself when they pass away. Will you have another cup of tea?"

"No thank you," Billy said. The tea tasted faintly of bitter almonds, and he didn't care much for it.

"You did sign the book, didn't you?"

"Oh, yes."

"That's good. Because later on, if I happened to forget what you were called, then I could always come down here and look it up. I still do that almost every day with Mr. Mulholland and Mr. . . . Mr. . . . ."

"Temple," Billy said. "Gregory Temple. Excuse my asking, but haven't there been *any* other guests here except them in the last two or three years?"

Holding her teacup high in one hand, inclining her head slightly to the left, she looked up at him out of the corners of her eyes and gave him another gentle little smile.

"No, my dear," she said. "Only you."

Questions for Writing or Discussion

1. Does Billy's own character contribute in part to his destruction? Would you yourself have left the landlady's house before tea-time? Explain.

2. At the start of the story, why does the author bother telling us about the weather, Billy's method of transportation, Billy's clothing, and his attitudes toward business?
3. Does the hypnotic power of the "Bed and Breakfast" sign introduce a supernatural element out of keeping with the rest of the story?
4. Does the author play fair in preparing us for the surprise ending? (See "The Beginning of the End," p. 119.) This question is a good topic for an interesting process paper.

Ring Lardner
HAIRCUT

___

I got another barber that comes over from Carterville and helps me out Saturdays, but the rest of the time I can get along all right alone. You can see for yourself that this ain't no New York City and besides that, the most of the boys works all day and don't have no leisure to drop in here and get themselves prettied up.

You're a newcomer, ain't you? I thought I hadn't seen you round before. I hope you like it good enough to stay. As I say, we ain't no New York City or Chicago, but we have pretty good times. Not as good, though, since Jim Kendall got killed. When he was alive, him and Hod Meyers used to keep this town in an uproar. I bet they was more laughin' done here than any town its size in America.

Jim was comical, and Hod was pretty near a match for him. Since Jim's gone, Hod tries to hold his end up just the same as ever, but it's tough goin' when you ain't got nobody to kind of work with.

They used to be plenty fun in here Saturdays. This place is jam-packed Saturdays, from four o'clock on. Jim and Hod would show up right after their supper, round six o'clock. Jim would set himself down in that big chair, nearest the blue spittoon. Whoever had been settin' in that chair, why they'd get up when Jim come in and give it to him.

You'd of thought it was a reserved seat like they have sometimes in a theayter. Hod would generally always stand or walk up and down, or some Saturdays, of course, he'd be settin' in this chair part of the time, gettin' a haircut.

Well, Jim would set there a w'ile without openin' his mouth only to spit, and then finally he'd say to me, "Whitey,"—my right name, that is, my right first name, is Dick, but everybody round here calls me Whitey—Jim would say, "Whitey, your nose looks like a rosebud tonight. You must of been drinkin' some of your aw de cologne."

So I'd say, "No, Jim, but you look like you'd been drinkin' somethin' of that kind or somethin' worse."

Jim would have to laugh at that, but then he'd speak up and say, "No, I ain't had nothin' to drink, but that ain't sayin' I wouldn't like somethin'. I wouldn't even mind if it was wood alcohol."

Then Hod Meyers would say, "Neither would your wife." That would set everybody to laughin' because Jim and his wife wasn't on very good terms. She'd of divorced him only they wasn't no chance to get alimony and she didn't have no way to take care of herself and the kids. She couldn't never understand Jim. He *was* kind of rough, but a good fella at heart.

Him and Hod had all kinds of sport with Milt Sheppard. I don't suppose you've seen Milt. Well, he's got an Adam's apple that looks more like a mushmelon. So I'd be shavin' Milt and when I'd start to shave down here on his neck, Hod would holler "Hey, Whitey, wait a minute! Before you cut into it, let's make up a pool and see who can guess closest to the number of seeds."

And Jim would say, "If Milt hadn't of been so hoggish, he'd of ordered a half a cantaloupe instead of a whole one and it might not of stuck in his throat."

All the boys would roar at this and Milt himself would force a smile, though the joke was on him. Jim certainly was a card!

There's his shavin' mug, settin' on the shelf, right next to Charley Vail's. "Charles M. Vail." That's the druggist. He comes in regular for his shave, three times a week. And Jim's is the cup next to Charley's. "James H. Kendall." Jim won't need no shavin' mug no more, but I'll leave it there just the same for old time's sake. Jim certainly was a character!

Years ago, Jim used to travel for a canned goods concern over in Carterville. They sold canned goods. Jim had the whole northern half of the State and was on the road five days out of every week. He'd drop in here Saturdays and tell his experiences for that week. It was rich.

I guess he paid more attention to playin' jokes than making sales. Finally the concern let him out and he come right home here and told everybody he'd been fired instead of sayin' he'd resigned like most fellas would of.

It was a Saturday and the shop was full and Jim got up out of that chair and says, "Gentlemen, I got an important announcement to make. I been fired from my job."

Well, they asked him if he was in earnest and he said he was and nobody could think of nothin' to say till Jim finally broke the ice himself. He says, "I been sellin' canned goods and now I'm canned goods myself."

You see, the concern he'd been workin' for was a factory that made canned goods. Over in Carterville. And now Jim said he was canned himself. He was certainly a card!

Jim had a great trick that he used to play w'ile he was travelin'. For instance, he'd be ridin' on a train and they'd come to some little town like, well, like, we'll say, like Benton. Jim would look out the train window and read the signs on the stores.

For instance, they'd be a sign, "Henry Smith, Dry Goods." Well, Jim would write down the name and the name of the town and when he got to wherever he was goin' he'd mail back a postal card to Henry Smith at Benton and not sign no name to it, but he'd write on the card, well, somethin' like "Ask your wife about that book agent that spent the afternoon last week," or "Ask your Missus who kept her from gettin' lonesome the last time you was in Carterville." And he'd sign the card, "A Friend."

Of course, he never knew what really come of none of these jokes, but he could picture what *probably* happened and that was enough.

Jim didn't work very steady after he lost his position with the Carterville people. What he did earn, doin' odd jobs around town, why he spent pretty near all of it on gin and his family might of starved if the stores hadn't of carried them along. Jim's wife tried her hand at dressmakin', but they ain't nobody goin' to get rich makin' dresses in this town.

As I say, she'd of divorced Jim, only she seen that she couldn't support herself and the kids and she was always hopin' that some day Jim would cut out his habits and give her more than two or three dollars a week.

They was a time when she would go to whoever he was workin' for and ask them to give her his wages, but after she done this once or twice, he beat her to it by borrowin' most of his pay in advance. He told it all round town, how he had outfoxed his Missus. He certainly was a caution!

But he wasn't satisfied with just outwittin' her. He was sore the way she had acted, tryin' to grab off his pay. And he made up his mind he'd get even. Well, he waited till Evans's Circus was advertised to come to town. Then he told his wife and two kiddies that he was goin' to take them to the circus. The day of the circus, he told them he would get the tickets and meet them outside the entrance to the tent.

Well, he didn't have no intentions of bein' there or buyin' tickets or nothin'. He got full of gin and laid round Wright's poolroom all day. His wife and the kids waited and waited and of course he didn't show up. His wife didn't have a dime with her, or nowhere else, I guess. So she finally had to tell the kids it was all off and they cried like they wasn't never goin' to stop.

Well, it seems, w'ile they was cryin', Doc Stair came along and he asked what was the matter, but Mrs. Kendall was stubborn and wouldn't tell him, but the kids told him and he insisted on takin' them and their mother in the show. Jim found this out afterwards and it was one reason why he had it in for Doc Stair.

Doc Stair come here about a year and a half ago. He's a mighty handsome young fella and his clothes always look like he has them made to order. He goes to Detroit two or three times a year and w'ile he's there he must have a tailor take his measure and then make him a suit to order. They cost pretty near twice as much, but they fit a whole lot better than if you just bought them in a store.

For a w'ile everybody was wonderin' why a young doctor like Doc Stair should come to a town like this where we already got old Doc Gamble and Doc Foote that's both been here for years and all the practice in town was always divided between the two of them.

Then they was a story got round that Doc Stair's gal had throwed him over, a gal up in the Northern Peninsula somewheres, and the reason he come here was to hide himself away and forget it. He said himself that he thought they wasn't nothin' like general practice in a place like ours to fit a man to be a good all round doctor. And that's why he'd came.

Anyways, it wasn't long before he was makin' enough to live on, though they tell me that he never dunned nobody for what they owed him, and the folks here certainly has got the owin' habit, even in my business. If I had all that was comin' to me for just shaves alone, I could go to Carterville and put up at the Mercer for a week and see a different picture every night. For instance, they's old George Purdy—but I guess I shouldn't ought to be gossipin'.

Well, last year, our coroner died, died of the flu. Ken Beatty, that was his name. He was the coroner. So they had to choose another man to be coroner in his place and they picked Doc Stair. He laughed at first and said he didn't want it, but they made him take it. It ain't no job that anybody would fight for and what a man makes out of it in a year would just about buy seeds for their garden. Doc's the kind, though, that can't say no to nothin' if you keep at him long enough.

But I was goin' to tell you about a poor boy we got here in town—Paul Dickson. He fell out of a tree when he was about ten years old. Lit on his head and it done somethin' to him and he ain't never been right. No harm in him, but just silly. Jim Kendall used to call him cuckoo; that's a name Jim had for anybody that was off their head, only he called people's head their bean. That was another of his gags, callin' head bean and callin' crazy people cuckoo. Only poor Paul ain't crazy, but just silly.

You can imagine that Jim used to have all kinds of fun with Paul. He'd send him to the White Front Garage for a left-handed monkey wrench. Of course they ain't no such a thing as a left-handed monkey wrench.

And once we had a kind of a fair here and they was a baseball game between the fats and the leans and before the game started Jim called Paul over and sent him way down to Schrader's hardware store to get a key for the pitcher's box.

They wasn't nothin' in the way of gags that Jim couldn't think up, when he put his mind to it.

Poor Paul was always kind of suspicious of people, maybe on account of how Jim had kept foolin' him. Paul wouldn't have much to do with anybody only his own mother and Doc Stair and a girl here in town named Julie Gregg. That is, she ain't a girl no more, but pretty near thirty or over.

When Doc first come to town, Paul seemed to feel like here was a real friend and he hung round Doc's office most of the w'ile; the only time he wasn't there was when he'd go home to eat or sleep or when he seen Julie Gregg doin' her shoppin'.

When he looked out Doc's window and seen her, he'd run downstairs and join her and tag along with her to the different stores. The poor boy was crazy about Julie and she always treated him mighty nice and made him feel like he was welcome, though of course it wasn't nothin' but pity on her side.

Doc done all he could to improve Paul's mind and he told me once that he really thought the boy was gettin' better, that they was times when he was as bright and sensible as anybody else.

But I was goin' to tell you about Julie Gregg. Old Man Gregg was in the lumber business, but got to drinkin' and lost the most of his money and when he died, he didn't leave nothin' but the house and just enough insurance for the girl to skimp along on.

Her mother was a kind of a half invalid and didn't hardly ever leave the house. Julie wanted to sell the place and move somewheres else after the old man died, but the mother said she was born here and would die here. It was tough on Julie, as the young people round this town—well, she's too good for them.

She's been away to school and Chicago and New York and different places and they ain't no subject she can't talk on, where you take the rest of the young folks here and you mention anything to them outside of Gloria Swanson or Tommy Meighan and they think you're delirious. Did you see Gloria in Wages of Virtue? You missed somethin'!

Well, Doc Stair hadn't been here more than a week when he come in one day to get shaved and I recognized who he was as he had been pointed out to me, so I told him about my old lady. She's been ailin' for a couple years and either Doc Gamble or Doc Foote, neither one, seemed to be helpin' her. So he said he would come out and see her, but if she was able to get out herself, it would be better to bring her to his office where he could make a completer examination.

So I took her to his office and w'ile I was waitin' for her in the reception room, in come Julie Gregg. When somebody comes in Doc Stair's office, they's a bell that rings in his inside office so as he can tell they's somebody to see him.

So he left my old lady inside and come out to the front office and that's the first time him and Julie met and I guess it was what they call love at first sight. But it wasn't fifty-fifty. This young fella was the slickest lookin' fella she'd ever seen in this town and she went wild over him. To him she was just a young lady that wanted to see the doctor.

She'd came on about the same business I had. Her mother had been doctorin' for years with Doc Gamble and Doc Foote and without no results. So she'd heard they was a new doc in town and decided to give him a try. He promised to call and see her mother that same day.

I said a minute ago that it was love at first sight on her part. I'm not only judgin' by how she acted afterwards but how she looked at him that first day in his office. I ain't no mind reader, but it was wrote all over her face that she was gone.

Now Jim Kendall, besides bein' a jokesmith and a pretty good drinker, well, Jim was quite a lady-killer. I guess he run pretty wild durin' the time he was on the road for them Carterville people, and besides that, he'd had a couple little affairs of the heart right here in town. As I say, his wife could of divorced him, only she couldn't.

But Jim was like the majority of men, and women, too, I guess. He wanted what he couldn't get. He wanted Julie Gregg and worked his head off tryin' to land her. Only he'd of said bean instead of head.

Well, Jim's habits and his jokes didn't appeal to Julie and of course he was a married man, so he didn't have no more chance than, well, than a rabbit. That's an expression of Jim's himself. When somebody didn't have no chance to get elected or somethin', Jim would always say they didn't have no more chance than a rabbit.

He didn't make no bones about how he felt. Right in here, more than once, in front of the whole crowd, he said he was stuck on Julie and anybody that could get her for him was welcome to his house and his wife and kids included. But she wouldn't have nothin' to do with him; wouldn't even speak to him on the street. He finally seen he wasn't gettin' nowheres with his usual line so he decided to try the rough stuff. He went right up to her house one evenin' and when she opened the door he forced his way in and grabbed her. But she broke loose and before he could stop her, she run in the next room and locked the door and phoned to Joe Barnes. Joe's the marshal. Jim could hear who she was phonin' to and he beat it before Joe got there.

Joe was an old friend of Julie's pa. Joe went to Jim the next day and told him what would happen if he ever done it again.

I don't know how the news of this little affair leaked out. Chances is that Joe Barnes told his wife and she told somebody else's wife and they told their husband. Anyways, it did leak out and Hod Meyers had the nerve to kid Jim about it, right here in this shop. Jim didn't deny nothin' and kind of laughed it off and said for us all to wait; that lots of people had tried to make a monkey out of him, but he always got even.

Meanw'ile everybody in town was wise to Julie's bein' wild mad over the Doc. I don't suppose she had any idea how her face changed when him and her was together; of course she couldn't of, or she'd of kept away from him. And she didn't know that we was all noticin' how many times she made excuses to go up to his office or pass it on the other side of the street and look up in his window to see if he was there. I felt sorry for her and so did most other people.

Hod Meyers kept rubbin' it into Jim about how the Doc had cut him out. Jim didn't pay no attention to the kiddin' and you could see he was plannin' one of his jokes.

One trick Jim had was the knack of changin' his voice. He could make you think he was a girl talkin' and he could mimic any man's voice. To show you how good he was along this line, I'll tell you the joke he played on me once.

You know, in most towns of any size, when a man is dead and needs a shave, why the barber that shaves him soaks him five dollars for the job; that is, he don't soak *him*, but whoever ordered the shave. I just charge three dollars because personally I don't mind much shavin' a dead person. They lay a whole lot stiller than live customers. The only thing is that you don't feel like talkin' to them and you get kind of lonesome.

Well, about the coldest day we ever had here, two years ago last winter, the phone rung at the house w'ile I was home to dinner and I answered the phone and it was a woman's voice and she said she was Mrs. John Scott and her husband was dead and would I come out and shave him.

Old John had always been a good customer of mine. But they live seven miles out in the country, on the Streeter road. Still I didn't see how I could say no.

So I said I would be there, but would have to come in a jitney and it might cost three or four dollars besides the price of the shave. So she, or the voice, it said that was all right, so I got Frank Abbott to drive me out to the place and when I got there who should open the door but old John himself! He wasn't no more dead than, well, than a rabbit.

It didn't take no private detective to figure out who had played me this little joke. Nobody could of thought it up but Jim Kendall. He certainly was a card!

I tell you this incident just to show you how he could disguise his voice and make you believe it was somebody else talkin'. I'd of swore it was Mrs. Scott had called me. Anyways, some woman.

Well, Jim waited till he had Doc Stair's voice down pat; then he went after revenge.

He called Julie up on a night when he knew Doc was over in Carterville. She never questioned but what it was Doc's voice. Jim said he must see her that night; he couldn't wait no longer to tell her somethin'. She was all excited and told him to come to the house. But he said he was expectin' an important long distance call and wouldn't she please forget her manners for once and come to his office. He said they couldn't nothin' hurt her and nobody would see her and he just *must* talk to her a little w'ile. Well, poor Julie fell for it.

Doc always keeps a night light in his office, so it looked to Julie like they was somebody there.

Meanw'ile Jim Kendall had went to Wright's poolroom, where they was a whole gang amusin' themselves. The most of them had drank plenty of gin, and they was a rough bunch even when sober. They was always strong for Jim's jokes and when he told them to come with him and see some fun they give up their card games and pool games and followed along.

Doc's office is on the second floor. Right outside his door they's a flight of stairs leadin' to the floor above. Jim and his gang hid in the dark behind these stairs.

Well, Julie come up to Doc's door and rung the bell and they was nothin' doin'. She rung it again and she rung it seven or eight times. Then she tried the door and found it locked. Then Jim made some kind of a noise and she heard it and waited a minute, and then she says, "Is that you, Ralph?" Ralph is Doc's first name.

They was no answer and it must of came to her all of a sudden that she'd been bunked. She pretty near fell downstairs and the whole gang after her. They chased her all the way home, hollerin', "Is that you, Ralph?" and "Oh, Ralphie, dear, is that you?" Jim says he couldn't holler it himself, as he was laughin' too hard.

Poor Julie! She didn't show up here on Main Street for a long, long time afterward.

And of course Jim and his gang told everybody in town, everybody but Doc Stair. They was scared to tell him, and he might of never knowed only for Paul Dickson. The poor cuckoo, as Jim called him, he was here in the shop one night when Jim was still gloatin' yet over what he'd done to Julie.

And Paul took in as much of it as he could understand and he run to Doc with the story.

It's a cinch Doc went up in the air and swore he'd make Jim suffer. But it was a kind of a delicate thing, because if it got out that he had beat Jim up, Julie was bound to hear of it and then she'd know that Doc knew and of course knowin' that he knew would make it worse for her than ever. He was goin' to do somethin', but it took a lot of figurin'.

Well, it was a couple days later when Jim was here in the shop again, and so was the cuckoo. Jim was goin' duck-shootin' the next day and had came in lookin' for Hod Meyers to go with him. I happened to know that Hod had went over to Carterville and wouldn't be home till the end of the week. So Jim said he hated to go alone and he guessed he would call it off. Then poor Paul spoke up and said if Jim would take him he would go along. Jim thought a w'ile and then he said, well, he guessed a half-wit was better than nothin'.

I suppose he was plottin' to get Paul out in the boat and play some joke on him, like pushin' him in the water. Anyways, he said Paul could go. He asked him had he ever shot a duck and Paul said no, he'd never even had a gun in his hands. So Jim said he could set in the boat and watch him and if he behaved himself, he might lend him his gun for a couple of shots. They made a date to meet in the mornin' and that's the last I seen of Jim alive.

Next mornin', I hadn't been open more than ten minutes when Doc Stair come in. He looked kind of nervous. He asked me had I seen Paul Dickson. I said no, but I knew where he was, out duck-shootin' with Jim Kendall. So Doc says that's what he had heard, and he couldn't understand it because Paul had told him he wouldn't never have no more to do with Jim as long as he lived.

He said Paul had told him about the joke Jim had played on Julie. He said Paul had asked him what he thought of the joke and the Doc had told him that anybody that would do a thing like that ought not to be let live.

I said it had been a kind of a raw thing, but Jim just couldn't resist no kind of a joke, no matter how raw. I said I thought he was all right at heart, but just bubblin' over with mischief. Doc turned and walked out.

At noon he got a phone call from old John Scott. The lake where Jim and Paul had went shootin' is on John's place. Paul had came runnin' up to the house a few minutes before and said they'd been an accident. Jim had shot a few ducks and then give the gun to Paul and told him to try his luck. Paul hadn't never handled a gun and he was nervous. He was shakin' so hard that he couldn't control the gun. He let fire and Jim sunk back in the boat, dead.

Doc Stair, bein' the coroner, jumped in Frank Abbott's flivver and rushed out to Scott's farm. Paul and old John was down on the shore of the lake. Paul had rowed the boat to shore, but they'd left the body in it, waitin' for Doc to come.

Doc examined the body and said they might as well fetch it back to town. They was no use leavin' it there or callin' a jury, as it was a plain case of accidental shootin'.

Personally I wouldn't never leave a person shoot a gun in the same boat I was in unless I was sure they knew somethin' about guns. Jim was a sucker to leave a new beginner have his gun, let alone a half-wit. It probably served Jim right, what he got. But still we miss him round here. He certainly was a card!

Comb it wet or dry?

Questions for Writing or Discussion

1. To whom does the barber tell his story? Why is this character, who never speaks, essential to the story?
2. Do you agree with the barber that Jim Kendall "certainly was a card"? What do *you* think of Jim Kendall?
3. How intelligent is the barber? Can we trust his evaluation of events?
4. Is Paul, as the barber believes, not "crazy, but just silly"? What evidence, other than the ending of the story, do you find for your answer?
5. What is the relationship between Paul and Julie Gregg? Between Paul and Dr. Stair? Between Dr. Stair and Julie? Why are these relationships essential to the story?
6. How and why did Jim Kendall die? Was his death accidental?
7. Why is the ending of the story inevitable? The answer to that question can make an excellent paper. Trace the process by which Ring Lardner makes Kendall's death seem inevitable. Do not write a mere plot summary.

CHAPTER 8

WRITING A
DEFINITION PAPER

From time to time, you've probably found yourself engaged in a shouting match with one or more acquaintances over a question such as, which is the better rock group—Pink Floyd or The Knack. Eventually, some wise soul says, "Hey, wait a minute. What's your idea of a good rock group?" The speaker has demanded a definition of the term at the heart of the debate. When you and your friends begin to explain what you're shouting about, you may find that one person's standard for *good* is the degree of amplification the group possesses. Another may respond to the subtlety with which the group improvises on a theme. Then you realize, perhaps, either that your respective ideas of a good group are so different that you can't have a discussion or that, once a definition is understood, you have no real disagreement.

When writing, you won't have the advantage of another person's saying, "Hey, wait a minute. Don't you think you'd better define your terms?" If you want to appear reasonable in your presentation of an idea, you will sometimes have to define terms. Often, the dictionary won't be much help. It may be a good place to start, but there are times when a dictionary definition won't lead to a full understanding of a term. Take that word *good,* for example. A dictionary tells you that it means "having positive or desirable qualities," and so it does, but how does such a definition help you distinguish between one rock group and another? To do so, you could *begin* with the dictionary definition, to be sure, but you must let your reader know what you believe the positive or desirable qualities of a rock group are. You must write an *extended* definition.

No matter how solid your reasons for approving or disapproving of a person, place, thing, group, or idea, those reasons are unlikely to find acceptance with a reader if you don't define your terms. In writing the Declaration of Independence (p. 236), for example, Thomas Jefferson clearly understood the need to define a *good* government—one which secures the natural rights of "life, liberty, and the pursuit of happiness" and which derives its powers "from the consent of the 'governed"—before arguing that George III's government failed to meet those standards. Without the carefully stated definition of a good government, the long list of complaints against the British government might well have been viewed as merely an expression of dissatisfaction by a group of malcontents.

Certain kinds of terms, then, require a more extended definition than the dictionary will give. The burden is on you to explain what you mean by the term. Sometimes this extended definition may appear as a paragraph or two of a long paper. Occasionally, a definition can become a paper in itself.

What kinds of terms need defining?

Judgmental words, words which reflect opinions, need definitions. Whether subjects being discussed are *good, better, best; bad, worse, worst; beautiful, ugly; friendly, unfriendly; wise, foolish; fair, unfair;* etc., is a matter of opinion.

Specialized terms, terms with a special meaning to a given group, need definition. Almost every professional or occupational group uses specialized terms that the members of the group understand but that require explanation for those outside the group: for example, *psychosis,* a psychological term; *neoclassicism,* a literary term; *writ,* a legal term; and *gig,* a show-business term.

Abstractions, general words like *love, democracy, justice, freedom,* and *quality,* need definition.

Controversial terms like *male chauvinist, nuclear build-up,* and *affirmative action* need definition.

Slang terms like *right on, with it, cool,* and *hot* may need definition for many audiences.

You can present your extended definition in one of two ways—formally or informally.

The *formal* definition contains the three parts of a dictionary definition: the *term* itself—the word or phrase to be defined; the *class*—the large group to which the object or concept belongs; and the *differentiation*—those characteristics which distinguish it from all others in its class.

Term	Class	Differentiation
A garden	is a small plot of land	used for the cultivation of flowers, vegetables, or fruits.
Beer	is a fermented alcoholic beverage	brewed from malt and flavored with hops.
Lunch	is a meal	eaten at midday.

To write an extended formal definition, you would first need to develop a one-sentence definition of the term. In doing so, keep the following cautions in mind:

1. *Keep the class restricted.* Speak of a sonnet not as a kind of literature, but as a kind of poem.
2. *Include no important part of the term itself or its derivatives in the class or differentiation.* Don't say that "a definition is that which defines."
3. *Make certain that the sentence defines and does not simply make a statement about the term.* "Happiness is a dry martini" doesn't have the essential parts of a definition of happiness.
4. *Provide adequate differentiation to clarify the meaning.* Don't define a traitor as "one who opposes the best interests of his or her country." That definition doesn't exclude the well-meaning person who misunderstands the country's best interests and opposes from ignorance. Try, "A traitor is one who opposes the best interests of his or her country with malicious intent."
5. *Don't make the definition too restrictive.* Don't define a matinee as "a drama presented during the day." That definition doesn't include other forms of entertainment, such as ballets or concerts, which could also be held in daytime.
6. *Make sure to include the class.* Don't write, "Baseball is when nine players. . . ." Write, "Baseball is a *sport* in which nine players. . . ."

Once you have composed a one-sentence formal definition, its three parts could become the major divisions of your paper. The introduction to your paper might contain the term and its one-sentence definition. That sentence could become the thesis for your paper. Or, in addition to providing a one-sentence definition, you could also express an attitude toward the term: "Equality *ought to be* a philosophy and set of laws in which all people are given the same opportunity to achieve their own individual potential." (See "Everyone Is Equal in the Grave," p. 143.)

The next division of your paper could discuss the class, and the final division, the differentiation. In those discussions, you can make your idea clear by using specific details, by using analogies, by giving examples or telling anecdotes, and sometimes by tracing the history of the term. Often you will be able to quote or refer to the definitions others have given the term. This technique is particularly useful if experts disagree over the meaning of the term. An especially effective tool of definition is *exclusion,* showing what the term is *not:*

> *Gourmet* cooking does not mean to me the preparation of food in expensive wines; it does not mean the preparation of exotic dishes like octopus or rattlesnake; it does not mean the smothering of meat with highly caloric sauces. *Gourmet* cooking to me means the preparation of any food—whether black-eyed peas or hollandaise sauce—in such a way that the dish will be as tasty and attractive as it can be made.

In advancing your discussions of class and differentiation, you can use any method or combination of methods of development you have studied. You might, for instance, make your idea clear by further *classifying* your term. For example, in "Discipline" (p. 145), the author classifies *discipline* as *juvenile* and *adult.* You might *compare and contrast* your understanding of the term with another conception of the term. In the student paper "Everyone Is Equal in the Grave," for example, the author contrasts his understanding of *equality* with that of the futuristic society represented in Vonnegut's short story "Harrison Bergeron." You could also trace a *process.* A definition of *alcoholism,* for instance, could contain a step-by-step analysis of the process by which one becomes an alcoholic. Finally, you could, in some instances, show cause-and-effect relationships. If you were defining a *ghetto,* for example, you could make the definition more insightful by analyzing the reasons ghettos come into existence.

In the paper below, the student derives a formal definition of *equality* from his reading of "Harrison Bergeron" (p. 25).

Everyone Is Equal in the Grave
FREDERICK SPENSE

Kurt Vonnegut, Jr.'s short story "Harrison Bergeron" contrasts the misunderstanding and perversion of equality with the true meaning of the word. Equality ought to be a philosophy and set of laws in which all people are given the same opportunity to achieve their own individual potential. In the U.S.A. of 2081, equality has become a philosophy and set of laws in which everyone is forced to be the same.

The Declaration of Independence presents the principle that "all men are created equal," and various laws attempt to put the principle into practice—laws about voting, employment, housing, and so on. "Equal before God and the law" in the second sentence of the story seems to show Vonnegut's approval of this approach. "Equal every which way" is another problem, though, and the story attempts to show that a government that interprets equality in that manner is going to be a slave state.

Giving people an equal opportunity to be the best they can be is not the same as forcing people to be like everyone else. Any girl who wants to should have the chance to study ballet. That represents equality. Letting poor dancers join the ballet company and "handicapping" good dancers so everyone will be the same is the corruption of equality that has taken place in 2081.

Instead of everyone with a good voice having the same chance to become an announcer if he or she wants to, all the announcers in the world of 2081 have speech impediments. Instead of the most skilled technicians competing for jobs on the television crews so that the best person will be chosen, the crews consist of people who cannot even hold cards right side up. Instead of admitting that smart people and dumb people are different even though they have the same worth as human beings, the government installs electronic equipment to prevent the smart people using their brains for more than a few seconds at a time. Good-looking people wear masks to make them "equal" to ugly people. Strong people wear weights to make them "equal" to weak people.

Vonnegut's point is that this is not true equality, but tyranny. It is not just stupid to stifle exceptional people and create a world where being outstanding is a sin, but to do so requires a tremendous government agency whose job is to snoop and to control the smallest aspects of people's private lives. The Constitution has to be amended to make all this possible, and the Handicapper General has the authority to shoot criminals—that is, individuals—on sight.

Equality is and ought to be one of our most precious ideals. If it ever comes to mean sameness and conformity, it will not really be equality at all, only obedience and regimentation. Equality like that is the equality of the grave.

Questions for Writing or Discussion

1. What is the thesis of the paper?
2. Does the writer successfully achieve a one-sentence formal definition of the term? If so, what is·it?
3. What methods of development does the writer use in advancing his definition? Could he make his idea clear without using these methods?
4. From your reading of the story, do you believe that the definition of *equality* presented in this paper is one that Vonnegut would approve?

Here is another formal definition. See what you think of this student's one-paragraph effort.

Discipline
SHIRLEY MARLYNE

Human discipline is the setting of boundaries within which a person's actions may range. The foregoing broad definition may be subdivided into two categories: (1) the training intended to produce a specified character or pattern of behavior, *juvenile discipline,* and (2) the controlled behavior resulting from such training, *adult discipline.* Throughout their lives, human beings are subject to juvenile discipline—a spanking, the withholding of privileges, a stay in the detention room, a speeding ticket, a chiding for increased girth, a reminder to take the pills *before* meals. Of far greater importance is adult discipline because it is an internal quality, derived from an intellectual and emotional reservoir. Adult discipline allows a driver to move slowly through a traffic pinch so that other cars can get into line before him. It provides the courage to deliver a message to a crowd while suffering from terrible stage fright. The strength that comes through adult discipline permits the toiler to perform an overwhelming task in small increments and to be satisfied with the lesser rewards of gaining each sub-goal. It leads one not to seek revenge or even immediate redress for injustice. Juvenile discipline, then, is direction from outside, but adult discipline is the schooling of self.

Questions for Writing or Discussion

1. What is the formal, one-sentence definition of the term?
2. Does the writer favor one form of discipline over the other? Why do you think so? Do you agree with her choice?
3. What methods of development does the writer use in defining the term?
4. Do you understand the meaning of the term well enough to give examples—other than those used by the author—of the two kinds of discipline?

Not all terms lend themselves to the three-part formal definition. Some are better explained by *informal* definition. What is a *good teacher,* for example? Or a *bad marriage?* Or an *ideal home?* Clearly, such topics can only be defined in a subjective or personal way; your purpose is to show what the term means to you. In such instances, it is probably wise to get away from the rigidity of the formal definition and just do a good job of making your conception of the term clear, usually by describing the subject as fully as you can. By the time readers finish the paper, they should understand what the term means to you.

As with formal definitions, you can employ any method or combination of methods of development you have studied. *Examples* and *anecdotes* are especially good for explaining a term. So are *comparison, process, classification,* and *cause and effect.* The idea is to use whatever techniques come in handy to put the idea across.

One good subject for an informal definition is a word or phrase used by a group or a region of the country. In the student paper below, the author explains a term used only by members of her family.

The Grinnies
HELEN FLEMING

Until I was twelve years old, I thought everyone in the world knew about the grinnies, if I thought about the term at all—which is unlikely. After all, everyone in my family used the word quite naturally, and we understood each other. So far as I knew, it was a word like any other word—like *bath,* or *chocolate,* or *homework.* But it was my homework which led to my discovery that *grinnies* was a word not known outside my family.

My last report card had said that I was a "C" student in English, and my parents, both teachers, decided that no child of theirs would be just an average student of anything. So nightly I spelled words aloud and answered questions about the fine points of grammar. I wrote and rewrote and rewrote every composition until I convinced my mother that I could make no more improvements. And the hard work paid off. One day the teacher returned compositions, and there it was—a big, fat, bright red "A" on the top of my paper. Naturally, I was delighted, but I didn't know I was attracting attention until the teacher snapped, "Helen, what *are* you doing?"

Called suddenly out of my happy thoughts, I said, "Oh, I've got the grinnies!" The teacher and my classmates burst into laughter, and then I understood that grinnies were confined to my family. Other people were not so privileged.

And it is a privilege to have the grinnies, an uncontrollable, spontaneous state of ecstasy. Grinnies are demonstrated on the outside by sparkling eyes and a wide, wide smile—not just any smile, but one that shows the teeth and stretches the mouth to its limits. A person experiencing the grinnies appears to be all mouth. On the inside, grinnies are characterized by a feeling of joyful agitation, almost a bubbly sensation. Grinnies usually last just a few seconds, but they can come and go. Sometimes, when life seems just perfect, I have intermittent attacks of the grinnies for a whole day.

The term originated in my mother's family. Her youngest sister, Rose, who had deep dimples, often expressed her pleasure with such a grin that the dimples appeared to become permanent. When Rose was about four, she started explaining her funny look by saying, "I have the grinnies." The term caught on, and it has been an important word in our family now for two generations.

The occasion doesn't matter. Anything can bring on the grinnies—just so long as one feels great delight. When my brother finally pumped his bicycle—without training wheels—from our house to the corner and back, he came home with the grinnies. When I was little, my mother's announcement that we would have homemade ice cream for dessert always gave me the grinnies. My father had the grinnies when I was valedictorian. Grinnies can be brought on by a good meal, a sense of pride, a new friend, a telephone call from someone special, an accomplishment. Or sometimes one gets the grinnies for no reason at all: just a sudden sense of well-being can bring on a case. Whatever brings them on, an attack of the grinnies is among life's greatest pleasures.

In fact, now that I look back on the experience, I feel sorry for my seventh-grade teacher. I think it's a pity that she didn't know the word *grinnies*. It's such a useful term for saying, "I'm really, really pleased!"

Questions for Writing or Discussion

1. What is the author's attitude toward her subject?
2. Could a comprehensive understanding of the term be accomplished by a three-part formal definition of the word? Why, or why not?
3. What methods of development does the writer use in defining the term?
4. Do you understand the meaning of the term well enough to give examples—other than those used by the author—of situations which could produce the grinnies?

In another informal definition, the writer deals with a term we have all thought about and explains what the term means to her.

That Santa Claus Feeling
JUDY LOESCHER

Picture, if you will, a plump old man, with snow-white hair and a beard, dressed in a red velvet suit. Obviously, it is Santa Claus, the king of the toy scene. Behave for a full year and on the night of December 24th, this fat cat will slide down your chimney and leave all sorts of goodies.

Is this what Santa Claus is really all about? Not to me, it isn't. Santa is not really a person or being, but a feeling that surfaces every year at Christmas time. He is a feeling of good will and friendliness, a feeling of giving just for the sake of giving. Idealistic, maybe, but so be it.

Don't misunderstand me—I'm no goody-two-shoes. But during the Christmas season, I am overwhelmed by a sense of benevolence. At times, I hardly know myself. Just this past Christmas Eve, after having elbowed my way through a pack of last-minute shoppers at Gold Circle, I was hurrying to the security and emptiness of my car when I spotted something sticking out of the snow. It was not the usual beer can. It was a wallet, and not an empty one. The wallet contained three twenty dollar bills, a ten, and six singles, a Master Charge and a Bankamericard. In all honesty, if it had not been the Christmas season, I would have been tempted to keep the money and drop the wallet in the mail box. But it *was* Christmas Eve, so I called the owner and returned the wallet, money and all. The owner was, of course, overjoyed at having recovered his lost property, and I came away in a rapture of good will.

That Santa Claus feeling—how can I explain it? I often catch myself doing favors for people because I need one done for me. Occasionally, when I go to the store, for example, I will ask my neighbor on the left if there is anything I can get for her. All the while, I'll be entertaining the notion that she will babysit for me the next time I need a sitter. This scheming, self-seeking part of me disappears during the Yuletide. I can't seem to do enough for people. And sometimes I find others who also have the Santa Claus feeling. When that happens, the good will and friendliness can often last indefinitely. For example, I had lived on Elm Street for three years, and during that time I had hardly spoken to my neighbor on the right. We had exchanged maybe ten words altogether. We weren't what you would call neighborly—until this past Christmas season. Late one evening, I was outside laboring to remove eight inches of snow from my driveway so I would have half a chance of making it to school on time the next day. I jumped at the sound of a motor, and looking down the driveway, I saw my neighbor and his snow blower cleaning my drive. To reciprocate, I went over and shovelled his front porch and steps. We finished at the same time, and I invited him in for a beer. We still don't see each other often, but when we do, we manage to find a lot to talk about.

That Santa Claus feeling—sometimes I get carried away by it. Two years ago, unable to buy gifts for many family members and friends, but wishing to show them that they were thought of and cared about, I decided to bake Christmas cookies for all of them. I baked ten dozen of each of ten different kinds of cookies. I baked from nine o'clock in the morning until well past midnight for three days in a row, stopping only temporarily to care for my eighteen-month-old cookie monster or to move the fast-disappearing cookies from her reach. My house was wall-to-wall cookie crumbs and powdered sugar. The cupboards were bare; all the dishes, crusted with egg and flour, were stacked in the sink. It took me the last three weeks of my four-week break to put the house back in order and to get my daughter back on the proper diet. But this didn't really bother me. I had been able to give, and that's all that mattered. The recipients didn't even have to say thanks.

Santa is toys and candy to some, but to me he is good will and friendliness and giving. He's a nice gentleman to have around—once a year.

Questions for Writing or Discussion

1. Can you give a one-sentence definition of the writer's concept of Santa Claus?
2. What method of development does the writer use in defining the term?
3. Such a subject could be treated in an overly sentimental manner. How does the writer avoid excessive sentimentality? (In other words, how does she keep the corn under control?)

Readings

The reading selections that follow are examples of definitions. As you study them, see if you can identify the methods of development which help make them good definitions.

Karen Horney
FEAR AND ANXIETY

When a mother is afraid that her child will die when it has only a pimple or a slight cold we speak of anxiety; but if she is afraid when the child has a serious illness we call her reaction fear. If someone is afraid whenever he stands on a height or when he has to discuss a topic he knows well, we call his reaction anxiety; if someone is afraid when he loses his way high up in the mountains during a heavy thunderstorm we would speak of fear. Thus far we should have a simple and neat distinction: fear is a reaction that is proportionate to the danger one has to face, whereas anxiety is a disproportionate reaction to danger, or even a reaction to imaginary danger.

This distinction has one flaw, however, which is that the decision as to whether the reaction is proportionate depends on the average knowledge existing in the particular culture. But even if that knowledge proclaims a certain attitude to be unfounded, a neurotic will find no difficulty in giving his action a rational foundation. In fact, one might get into hopeless arguments if one told a patient that his dread of being attacked by some raving lunatic is neurotic anxiety. He would point out that his fear is realistic and would refer to occurrences of the kind he fears. The primitive would be similarly stubborn if one considered certain of his fear reactions disproportionate to the actual danger. For instance, a primitive man in a tribe which has taboos on eating certain animals is mortally frightened if by any chance he has eaten the tabooed meat. As an outside observer you would call this a disproportionate reaction, in fact an entirely unwarranted one. But knowing the tribe's beliefs concerning forbidden meat you would have to realize that the situation represents a real danger to the man, danger that the hunting or fishing grounds may be spoiled or danger of contracting an illness.

There is a difference, however, between the anxiety we find in primitives and the anxiety we consider neurotic in our culture. The content of neurotic anxiety, unlike that of the primitive, does not conform with commonly held opinions. In both the impression of a disproportionate reaction vanishes once the meaning of the anxiety is understood. There are persons, for example, who have a perpetual anxiety about dying; on the other hand, because of their sufferings they have a secret wish to die. Their various fears of death, combined with their wishful thinking with regard to death, create a strong apprehension of imminent danger. If one knows all these factors one cannot help but call their anxiety about dying an adequate reaction. Another, simplified example is seen in persons who become terrified when they find themselves near a precipice or a high window or on a high bridge. Here again, from without, the fear reaction seems to be disproportionate. But such a situation may present to them, or stir up in them, a conflict between the wish to live and the temptation for some reason or another to jump down from the heights. It is this conflict that may result in anxiety.

All these considerations suggest a change in the definition. Fear and anxiety are both proportionate reactions to danger, but in the case of fear the danger is a transparent, objective one and in the case of anxiety it is hidden and subjective. That is, the intensity of the anxiety is proportionate to the meaning the situation has for the person concerned, and the reasons why he is thus anxious are essentially unknown to him.

The practical implication of the distinction between fear and anxiety is that the attempt to argue a neurotic out of his anxiety—the method of persuasion—is useless. His anxiety concerns not the situation as it stands actually in reality, but the situation as it appears to him. The therapeutic task, therefore, can be only that of finding out the meaning certain situations have for him.

Questions for Writing or Discussion

1. How does Horney define *fear* and *anxiety?* Which term is her real concern?
2. What author image does Horney project?
3. For what audience do you think the definition was written? Why?

4. What method of development does Horney use in defining the term?
5. What does Horney think is the flaw in the usual distinction between fear and anxiety? If that distinction is flawed, why does she make it? Is the distinction necessary to her definition?
6. At what point does Horney present an acceptable distinction between the terms? Should it have been presented sooner? Why, or why not?

George E. Hollister
WITH LEGS LIKE THESE . . . WHO NEEDS WINGS?

He's half tail and half feet. The rest of him is head and beak. When he runs, he moves on blurring wheels. He can turn on a dime and leave change. He doesn't need to fly because he can run faster. He kicks dirt in a snake's face, and then eats the snake. He chases lizards, and watches hawks with one eye.

He's "Meep-meep" and a cartoon favorite of three generations. He's an odd bird, but a real one—the roadrunner.

Early southwestern settlers were surprised to see a wildly colored bird dart onto a trail, race ahead of a lone horse and rider, slide to a dusty halt and then bob and bow in salute. Scientists later labeled him *Geococcyx californianus*, a member of the cuckoo family, but settlers aptly named him "roadrunner."

Because of his foot structure, Indians of the Southwest believed he had special power. His toes form an X, with two pointed forward and two backward. This arrangement held special meaning to the Indians, who scratched duplicate X figures near new graves and, for extra protection from evil spirits, decorated infant cradleboards with roadrunner feathers.

The footprint X's are unique in a more concrete way—they show the roadrunner may take 22-inch strides in high gear. He's been clocked at fifteen miles per hour (the rate of a four-minute miler). This means his thin muscular legs are taking 12 steps every second.

The combination of fast feet and a flat, wide tail serving as rudder gives the roadrunner a double advantage over lizards and low-flying insects. He simply darts and twists after his prey, screeching into ninety-degree turns, careening around sagebrush and spurting into a straightaway as he catches his meals on the run.

In the roadrunner's hot, dry desert environment, all this hyper-activity would seem likely to dehydrate the bird. (He also frequents many plains, prairies and oak-hickory forests.) But he has adapted remarkably well to temperatures over one hundred degrees and dry winds. His biggest problem—water—is solved by careful budgeting. He rests in the shade during the hottest part of the day, and replenishes body water through his diet; he eats things like lizards, whose bodies have a high water content, and then manufactures liquid by oxidation of the food into carbon dioxide.

The remainder of his diet is no problem, mainly because he eats most anything he can catch that's smaller than he is. He prefers insects (high water content), plants, lizards, snakes, and mammals like mice and rats.

His manner of catching a snake is especially noteworthy. He dashes in circles around a coiled snake, stops within striking distance, shuffles his feet, swishes his tail in the dirt and stirs up a blinding cloud of dust.

Then begins Act II. Roadrunner ruffles his feathers to reduce penetration from a direct strike, and leaps back into a dizzying series of circles around the bewildered snake. He often reverses directions in mid-stride, catches the snake going the other way, and clouts him with his long, sharp beak. Finally, the tired, wounded snake catches several pecks to the brain and succumbs.

Eating the snake requires almost as much talent as catching it; the bird is dealing with a dinner frequently longer than itself. Roadrunner swallows his prey headfirst, forcing the snake as far down his gullet as possible. If there is excess snake, the bird simply waits for his superactive digestive juices to do their part, and in a matter of hours the snake is completely eaten.

Compared to snakes, insects are easy pickings. Most are simply snapped off mesquite and cacti, or flushed from under rocks with a tail flick. To catch cicadas, so erratic in flight that man can hardly catch them, Roadrunner simply dogs their odd flight pattern.

Roadrunner's eyesight is spectacular. He can spot a lizard skittering out of reach and watch an enemy hawk overhead at the same time. When he really wants to concentrate, he can focus all attention through one eye. Roadrunners have been observed standing entranced with head tilted sideways, one eye focused on the ground, and the other scanning the sky for airborne enemies.

In the spring, Roadrunner gets restless, grows a few sporty new feathers in his head crest and begins stepping out. When he finds a likely prospect for his affections, he starts acting like a normal roadrunner—odd. His call to establish territory is normal: his series of six or eight calls descends in pitch until the last one resembles a mourning dove's plaintive coo.

He'll offer some food, flutter his tail, shuffle his feet in another dust-stirring dance, then end the performance with a graceful bow and more coos. If the hen thinks he's acceptable, she takes the food, they dance and bow, then begin to look for a suitable place to build a nest.

Nest building, roadrunner style, usually results in a disorganized pile of sticks, feathers, old snake skins and rubble. The hen tramples a slight hollow in the center of this debris and lays three to eight white eggs at infrequent intervals. This haphazardly planned parenthood usually results in the first hatched young stumbling over a freshly laid egg or two.

It remained for Warner Brothers to enshrine the incredible roadrunner. From cartoons, the screwball bird and "meep-meep" branched out to emblems, decals and patches. And not only for the toddler set—unofficial military insignia also bear his picture.

And he's not done yet. Next time you see a whirling cloud of dust, watch for some fast soft-shoe, a little artful bobbing and weaving. In the center of that cloud will be a roadrunner, the king of the cuckoos, doing his bit to enliven your hours on the road.

Questions for Writing or Discussion

1. A bird which is half tail and half feet would have no body. What is the effect of such an exaggeration in the opening of the article?
2. Hollister discusses the bird as if it were a person. What personality does he give the bird? Does that technique help you to understand what a roadrunner is?
3. Hollister uses several methods of development in this highly informal definition. What are they?
4. What is the advantage to the reader of being told that Warner Brothers has enshrined the roadrunner?
5. Write an informal paper in which you define *law of the jungle, rat race, mutt,* or some other phrase that involves animals or terms associated with animals.

Here is a story which you can use as the basis of a definition paper. As you read the story, try to decide why Galsworthy called it "Quality."

John Galsworthy
QUALITY

I knew him from the days of my extreme youth, because he made my father's boots; inhabiting with his elder brother two little shops let into one, in a small by-street—now no more, but then most fashionably placed in the West End.

That tenement had a certain quiet distinction; there was no sign upon its face that he made for any of the Royal Family—merely his own German name of Gessler Brothers; and in the window a few pairs of boots. I remember that it always troubled me to account for those unvarying boots in the window, for he made only what was ordered, reaching nothing down, and it seemed so inconceivable that what he made could ever have failed to fit. Had he bought them to put there? That, too, seemed inconceivable. He would never have tolerated in his house leather on which he had not worked himself. Besides, they were too beautiful—the pairs of pumps, so inexpressibly slim, the patent leathers with cloth tops, making water come into one's mouth, the tall brown riding-boots with marvelous sooty glow, as if, though new, they had been worn a hundred years. Those pairs could only have been made by one who saw before him the Soul of Boot—so truly were they prototypes, incarnating the very spirit of all footwear. These thoughts, of course, came to me later, though even when I was promoted to him, at the age of perhaps fourteen, some inkling haunted me of the dignity of himself and brother. For to make boots—such boots as he made—seemed to me then, and still seems to me, mysterious and wonderful.

I remember well my shy remark, one day, while stretching out to him my youthful foot:

"Isn't it awfully hard to do, Mr. Gessler?"

And his answer, given with a sudden smile from out of the sardonic redness of his beard: "Id is an Ardt!"

Himself, he was a little as if made of leather, with his yellow crinkly face, and crinkly reddish hair and beard, and neat folds slanting down his cheeks to the corners of his mouth, and his guttural and one-toned voice; for leather is a sardonic substance, and stiff and slow of purpose. And that was the character of his face, save that his eyes, which were gray-blue, had in them the simple gravity of one secretly possessed by the Ideal. His elder brother was so very like him—though watery, paler in every way, with a great industry—that sometimes in early days I was not quite sure of him until the interview was over. Then I knew that it was he, if the words, "I will ask my brudder," had not been spoken, and that, if they had, it was the elder brother.

When one grew old and wild and ran up bills, one somehow never ran them up with Gessler Brothers. It would not have seemed becoming to go in there and stretch out one's foot to that blue iron-spectacled face, owing him for more than—say—two pairs, just the comfortable reassurance that one was still his client.

For it was not possible to go to him very often—his boots lasted terribly, having something beyond the temporary—some, as it were, essence of boot stitched into them.

One went in, not as into most shops, in the mood of: "Please serve me, and let me go!" but restfully, as one enters a church; and, sitting on the single wooden chair, waited—for there was never anybody there. Soon— over the top edge of that sort of well—rather dark, and smelling soothingly of leather—which formed the shop, there would be seen his face, or that of his elder brother, peering down. A guttural sound, and the tip-tap of bast slippers beating the narrow wooden stairs, and he would stand before one without coat, a little bent, in leather apron, with sleeves turned back, blinking—as if awakened from some dream of boots, or like an owl surprised in daylight and annoyed at this interruption.

And I would say: "How do you do, Mr. Gessler? Could you make me a pair of Russia leather boots?"

Without a word he would leave me, retiring whence he came, or into the other portion of the shop, and I would continue to rest in the wooden chair, inhaling the incense of his trade. Soon he would come back, holding in his thin, veined hand a piece of gold-brown leather. With eyes fixed on it, he would remark: "What a beaudiful biece!" When I, too, had admired it, he would speak again: "When do you wand dem?" And I would answer: "Oh! As soon as you conveniently can." And he would say: "Tomorrow fordnighd?" Or if he were his elder brother: "I will ask my brudder!"

Then I would murmur: "Thank you! Good-morning, Mr. Gessler."
"Goot-morning!" he would reply, still looking at the leather in his hand.
And as I moved to the door, I would hear the tip-tap of his bast slippers
restoring him, up the stairs, to his dream of boots. But if it were some new
kind of footgear that he had not yet made me, then indeed he would observe
ceremony—divesting me of my boot and holding it long in his hand, looking at it with eyes at once critical and loving, as if recalling the glow with
which he had created it, and rebuking the way in which one had disorganized this masterpiece. Then, placing my foot on a piece of paper, he
would two or three times tickle the outer edges with a pencil and pass his
nervous fingers over my toes, feeling himself into the heart of my requirements.

I cannot forget that day on which I had occasion to say to him: "Mr.
Gessler, that last pair of town walking-boots creaked, you know."

He looked at me for a time without replying, as if expecting me to with-
draw or qualify the statement, then said:

"Id shouldn'd 'ave greaked."

"It did, I'm afraid."

"You goddem wed before dey found demselves?"

"I don't think so."

At that he lowered his eyes, as if hunting for memory of those boots, and I
felt sorry I had mentioned this grave thing.

"Zend dem back!" he said; "I will look at dem."

A feeling of compassion for my creaking boots surged up in me, so well
could I imagine the sorrowful long curiosity of regard which he would bend
on them.

"Zome boods," he said slowly, "are bad from birdt. If I can do noding wid
dem, I dake dem off your bill."

Once (once only) I went absentmindedly into his shop in a pair of boots
bought in an emergency at some large firm's. He took my order without
showing me any leather, and I could feel his eyes penetrating the interior
integument of my foot. At last he said:

"Dose are nod my boods."

The tone was not one of anger, nor of sorrow, not even of contempt, but
there was in it something quiet that froze the blood. He put his hand down
and pressed a finger on the place where the left boot, endeavoring to be
fashionable, was not quite comfortable.

"Id 'urds you dere," he said. "Dose big virms 'ave no self-respect. Drash!"
And then, as if something had given way within him, he spoke long and
bitterly. It was the only time I ever heard him discuss the conditions and
hardships of his trade.

"Dey get id all," he said, "dey get id by adverdisement, nod by work. Dey
dake id away from us, who lofe our boods. Id gomes to this—bresently I haf
no work. Every year id gets less—you will see." And looking at his lined
face I saw things I had never noticed before, bitter things and bitter
struggle—and what a lot of gray hairs there seemed suddenly in his red
beard!

As best I could, I explained the circumstances of the purchase of those ill-omened boots. But his face and voice made a so deep impression that during the next few minutes I ordered many pairs! Nemesis fell! They lasted more terribly than ever. And I was not able conscientiously to go to him for nearly two years.

When at last I went I was surprised that outside one of the two little windows of his shop another name was painted, also that of a boot-maker—making, of course, for the Royal Family. The old familiar boots, no longer in dignified isolation, were huddled in the single window. Inside, the now contracted well of the one little shop was more scented and darker than ever. And it was longer than usual, too, before a face peered down, and the tip-tap of the bast slippers began. At last he stood before me, and, gazing through those rusty iron spectacles, said:

"Mr.——, isn'd id?"

"Ah! Mr. Gessler," I stammered, "but your boots are really *too* good, you know! See, these are quite decent still!" And I stretched out to him my foot. He looked at it.

"Yes," he said, "beople do nod wand good boods, id seems."

To get away from his reproachful eyes and voice I hastily remarked: "What have you done to your shop?"

He answered quietly: "Id was too exbensif. Do you wand some boods?"

I ordered three pairs, though I had wanted only two, and quickly left. I had, I know not quite what feeling of being part, in his mind, of a conspiracy against him; or not perhaps so much against him as against his idea of boot. One does not, I suppose, care to feel like that; for it was again many months before my next visit to his shop, paid, I remember, with the feeling: "Oh! well, I can't leave the old boy—so here goes! Perhaps it'll be his elder brother!"

For his elder brother, I knew, had not character enough to reproach me, even dumbly.

And, to my relief, in the shop there did appear to be his elder brother, handling a piece of leather.

"Well, Mr. Gessler," I said, "how are you?"

He came close, and peered at me.

"I am breddy well," he said slowly; "but my elder brudder is dead."

And I saw that it was indeed himself—but how aged and wan! And never before had I heard him mention his brother. Much shocked, I murmured: "Oh! I am sorry!"

"Yes," he answered, "he was a good man, he made a good bood; but he is dead." And he touched the top of his head, where the hair had suddenly gone as thin as it had been on that of his poor brother, to indicate, I suppose, the cause of death. "He could nod get over losing de oder shop. Do you wand any boods?" And he held up the leather in his hand: "Id's a beaudiful biece."

I ordered several pairs. It was very long before they came—but they were better than ever. One simply could not wear them out. And soon after that I went abroad.

It was over a year before I was again in London. And the first shop I went to was my old friend's. I had left a man of sixty, I came back to find one of seventy-five, pinched and worn and tremulous, who genuinely, this time, did not at first know me.

"Oh! Mr. Gessler," I said, sick at heart: "how splendid your boots are! See, I've been wearing this pair nearly all the time I've been abroad; and they're not half worn out, are they?"

He looked long at my boots—a pair of Russia leather, and his face seemed to regain its steadiness. Putting his hand on my instep, he said:

"Do dey vid you here? I 'ad trouble wid dat bair, I remember."

I assured him that they had fitted beautifully.

"Do you wand any boods?" he said. "I can make dem quickly; id is a slack dime."

I answered: "Please, please! I want boots all round—every kind!"

"I vill make a vresh model. Your food must be bigger." And with utter slowness, he traced round my foot, and felt my toes, only once looking up to say:

"Did I dell you my brudder was dead?"

To watch him was quite painful, so feeble had he grown; I was glad to get away.

I had given those boots up, when one evening they came. Opening the parcel, I set the four pairs out in a row. Then one by one I tried them on. There was no doubt about it. In shape and fit, in finish and quality of leather, they were the best he had ever made me. And in the mouth of one of the town walking-boots I found his bill. The amount was the same as usual, but it gave me quite a shock. He had never before sent it in until quarter day. I flew downstairs and wrote a check, and posted it at once with my own hand.

A week later, passing the little street, I thought I would go in and tell him how splendidly the new boots fitted. But when I came to where his shop had been, his name was gone. Still there, in the window, were the slim pumps, the patent leathers with cloth tops, the sooty riding-boots.

I went in, very much disturbed. In the two little shops—again made into one—was a young man with an English face.

"Mr. Gessler in?" I said.

He gave me a strange, ingratiating look.

"No, sir," he said, "no. But we can attend to anything with pleasure. We've taken the shop over. You've seen our name, no doubt, next door. We make for some very good people."

"Yes, yes," I said, "but Mr. Gessler?"

"Oh!" he answered; "dead."

"Dead! But I received these boots from him only last Wednesday week."

"Ah!" he said; "a shockin' go. Poor old man starved 'imself."

"Good God!"

"Slow starvation, the doctor called it! You see he went to work in such a way! Would keep the shop on; wouldn't have a soul touch his boots except himself. When he got an order, it took him such a time. People won't wait. He lost everybody. And there he'd sit, goin' on and on—I will say that for him—not a man in London made a better boot! But look at the competition! He never advertised! Would 'ave the best leather, too, and do it all 'imself. Well, there it is. What could you expect with his ideas?"

"But starvation—!"

"That may be a bit flowery, as the sayin' is—but I know myself he was sittin' over his boots day and night, to the very last. You see, I used to watch him. Never gave 'imself time to eat; never had a penny in the house. All went in rent and leather. How he lived so long I don't know. He regular let his fire go out. He was a character. But he made good boots."

"Yes," I said, "he made good boots."

Questions for Writing or Discussion

1. Why did the Gessler brothers not advertise that they made boots for the Royal Family?
2. How sympathetic do you think the author wants readers to be toward Mr. Gessler? Does the fact that he makes shoes that last forever make him more admirable or simply foolish?
3. What is the difference between the boots made by Mr. Gessler and those bought by the narrator at a larger store?
4. The only facts we learn directly about the Gessler brothers tell us that they made good shoes. What other facts are strongly implied?
5. Write a paper with specific references to the story in which you define the author's conception of "quality."

CHAPTER 9

WRITING A CAUSE AND EFFECT PAPER

Many of the papers you will be asked to write in college will require analysis of causes or circumstances which lead to a given result: Why does the cost of living continue to rise? Why do Ivan and Masha Dmitritch in "The Lottery Ticket" (p. 168) end up hating each other? Why is the sky blue? In questions of this type, the *effect* or result is given, at least briefly. Your job as a student is to analyze the causes which produce that effect.

Other assignments will require that you discuss the results of a particular cause: What are the positive and negative effects of legalizing lotteries? Discuss the effects of giving direct legislative power to the people. What is the effect of noise pollution on our bodies? In questions of this type, the *cause* is given, and you must determine the effects which might result or have resulted from that cause.

Cause-and-effect papers do not call for the rigid structure demanded of classification, process, and definition papers. Nevertheless, some logical demands must be met:

Do not confuse cause with process. A process paper tells *how* an event or product came about; a cause-and-effect paper tells *why* something happened.

Avoid the post hoc *fallacy* (p. 34). That a man lost his billfold shortly after walking under a ladder does not mean that walking under the ladder caused his loss. Similarly, that a woman lost her hearing shortly after attending a loud rock concert does not prove that her deafness is a direct result of the band's decibel level.

Do not oversimplify causes. Getting a good night's sleep before an exam doesn't cause a student to receive the highest grade in the class. The rest certainly won't do any harm, but familiarity with the material covered on the exam, intelligence, and an ability to write also have something to do with the grade. Almost all effects worth writing about have more than one cause.

Do not oversimplify effects. Even though it may be true that many people lose a lot of money by gambling on lotteries, that does not mean legalizing lotteries will result in nationwide bankruptcy.

Once you have determined the causes or effects you wish to discuss, you can organize your paper in several ways. In a paper devoted primarily to cause, the simplest pattern is to open by describing the *effect* in some detail, then to develop the reasons for that effect in the body of the paper. If, for example, you want to explain a recent rise in the cost of living, you might begin with a description of the rise (effect)—the cost of living has risen dramatically during the past three years and promises to go even higher in the coming year—before dealing with the causes. Similarly, a paper devoted primarily to effect usually begins with a description of the *cause.* If your subject is the probable effects of a proposed state lottery, you might begin with a description of the proposal itself (cause) before discussing effects.

In some cases, as when cause and effect are of approximately equal concern, you may want to present one dramatic instance of an effect to open the paper. For example, you might begin a paper on ocean pollution with a description of the sludge mass off the coast of New York City, a striking example of oil pollution. The rest of the introduction would lead into the causes, or sources, of ocean pollution in general. The first major division of what follows might list several important causes other than oil spillage, and the second major division might detail the effects of those causes: extermination of sea life, danger to public water supplies and hence to public health, and so on.

Now let's take a look at a student paper and see how the author handles cause and effect relationships.

The Popcorn Habit
MICHAEL BARTKO

It was Friday night. I had been ill, but I was beginning to recover. I knew what I had to do. I did not want this to happen again. I wished that I could avail myself of the twelve steps of Alcoholics Anonymous, but somehow they did not apply; neither could I find an addict's halfway house. I had no problem with drugs. I was not an alcoholic. There was no one to understand me or to commiserate with me. I was a popcorn freak, and I was getting sick of it. I had to try to break the habit, but how?

I know now that I must try to understand my affliction. What purpose does it serve? Why do I enjoy it so much? My life has so many problems. The way I usually deal with problems is to sit in as near a fetal position as

I can, knit my brow, grind my teeth together, and worry. I sometimes need a break from this response to problems. With popcorn, I can forget everything and enjoy many pleasurable aspects of gluttony. First, I can think of popcorn. Next, I can buy the popcorn. I can then cook the popcorn. I can listen to it pop, slowly at first, building to an intense climax as the corn forces open the lid of the pan. I can smell the enticing corn fragrance. Then, I can salt the popcorn. Finally, at last, I can eat the popcorn. Yes, it is good to lose myself in food. This is part of the answer, but why just popcorn?

There are many beautiful things about popcorn itself which cause me to love it: the way it looks, gold and white in the pan, the tempting way it smells, its flavor. It is easy to eat, but its crispness gives the illusion of chewing something solid. It is salty. It is hot.

There is yet another reason I love popcorn so much: happy memories. When I was small, my family used to gather around the radio on Sunday night and listen to the then common mystery and comedy shows. As an extra treat my father would make for us huge bowls of fresh, hot popcorn. This was his way of showing love, of making an exception to his cool deportment. We loved him for it.

The usefulness and pleasure of gluttony, the intrinsic qualities of popcorn, and the fond memories I have about it are strong reasons for continuing the habit, just as they have been strong causes for starting it. Maybe I can learn to live with it. Maybe I'll have to.

Questions for Writing or Discussion

1. What is the thesis of the paper? Where is it stated?
2. What pattern of organization does the writer employ?
3. Look for good transitional devices which help give the paper coherence.
4. Do the causes the student gives appear to be reasonable explanations for how the habit developed?
5. Think about a habit or a prejudice or an unreasonable fear that you have and write a paper which analyzes its causes.

You may find that cause-and-effect analysis is a useful tool for writing about fiction. You look at a character and say, "Why is he like that, exactly?" Then you examine the work to discover the causes for the character traits you have observed. Or you may trace the causes that lead to a crisis in a story.

Following is a story by William Carlos Williams, "The Use of Force." After you have read the story, study the paper that follows it.

William Carlos Williams
THE USE OF FORCE

They were new patients to me, all I had was the name, Olson. Please come down as soon as you can, my daughter is very sick.

When I arrived I was met by the mother, a big startled looking woman, very clean and apologetic who merely said, Is this the doctor? and let me in. In the back, she added. You must excuse us, doctor, we have her in the kitchen where it is warm. It is very damp here sometimes.

The child was fully dressed and sitting on her father's lap near the kitchen table. He tried to get up, but I motioned for him not to bother, took off my overcoat and started to look things over. I could see that they were all very nervous, eyeing me up and down distrustfully. As often, in such cases, they weren't telling me more than they had to, it was up to me to tell them; that's why they were spending three dollars on me.

The child was fairly eating me up with her cold, steady eyes, and no expression to her face whatever. She did not move and seemed, inwardly, quiet; an unusually attractive little thing, and as strong as a heifer in appearance. But her face was flushed, she was breathing rapidly, and I realized that she had a high fever. She had magnificent blonde hair, in profusion. One of those picture children often reproduced in advertising leaflets and the photogravure sections of the Sunday papers.

She's had a fever for three days, began the father and we don't know what it comes from. My wife has given her things, you know, like people do, but it don't do no good. And there's been a lot of sickness around. So we tho't you'd better look her over and tell us what is the matter.

As doctors often do I took a trial shot at it as a point of departure. Has she had a sore throat?

Both parents answered me together, No . . . No, she says her throat don't hurt her.

Does your throat hurt you? added the mother to the child. But the little girl's expression didn't change nor did she move her eyes from my face.

Have you looked?

I tried to, said the mother, but I couldn't see.

As it happens we had been having a number of cases of diphtheria in the school to which this child went during that month and we were all, quite apparently, thinking of that, though no one had as yet spoken of the thing.

Well, I said, suppose we take a look at the throat first. I smiled in my best professional manner and asking for the child's first name I said, come on, Mathilda, open your mouth and let's take a look at your throat.

Nothing doing.

Aw, come on, I coaxed, just open your mouth wide and let me take a look. Look, I said opening both hands wide, I haven't anything in my hands. Just open up and let me see.

Such a nice man, put in the mother. Look how kind he is to you. Come on, do what he tells you to. He won't hurt you.

At that I ground my teeth in disgust. If only they wouldn't use the word "hurt" I might be able to get somewhere. But I did not allow myself to be hurried or disturbed but speaking quietly and slowly I approached the child again.

As I moved my chair a little nearer suddenly with one catlike movement both her hands clawed instinctively for my eyes and she almost reached them too. In fact she knocked my glasses flying and they fell, though unbroken, several feet away from me on the kitchen floor.

Both the mother and father almost turned themselves inside out in embarrassment and apology. You bad girl, said the mother, taking her and shaking her by one arm. Look what you've done. The nice man . . .

For heaven's sake, I broke in. Don't call me a nice man to her. I'm here to look at her throat on the chance that she might have diphtheria and possibly die of it. But that's nothing to her. Look here, I said to the child, we're going to look at your throat. You're old enough to understand what I'm saying. Will you open it now by yourself or shall we have to open it for you?

Not a move. Even her expression hadn't changed. Her breaths however were coming faster and faster. Then the battle began. I had to do it. I had to have a throat culture for her own protection. But first I told the parents that it was entirely up to them. I explained the danger but said that I would not insist on a throat examination so long as they would take the responsibility.

If you don't do what the doctor says you'll have to go to the hospital, the mother admonished her severely.

Oh yeah? I had to smile to myself. After all, I had already fallen in love with the savage brat, the parents were contemptible to me. In the ensuing struggle they grew more and more abject, crushed, exhausted while she surely rose to magnificent heights of insane fury of effort bred of her terror of me.

The father tried his best, and he was a big man but the fact that she was his daughter, his shame at her behavior and his dread of hurting her made him release her just at the critical times when I had almost achieved success, till I wanted to kill him. But his dread also that she might have diphtheria made him tell me to go on, go on though he himself was almost fainting, while the mother moved back and forth behind us raising and lowering her hands in an agony of apprehension.

Put her in front of you on your lap, I ordered, and hold both her wrists.

But as soon as he did the child let out a scream. Don't, you're hurting me. Let go of my hands. Let them go I tell you. Then she shrieked terrifyingly, hysterically. Stop it! Stop it! You're killing me!

Do you think she can stand it, doctor! said the mother.

You get out, said the husband to his wife. Do you want her to die of diphtheria?

Come on now, hold her, I said.

Then I grasped the child's head with my left hand and tried to get the wooden tongue depressor between her teeth. She fought, with clenched teeth, desperately! But now I also had grown furious—at a child. I tried to hold myself down but I couldn't. I know how to expose a throat for inspection. And I did my best. When finally I got the wooden spatula behind the last teeth and just the point of it into the mouth cavity, she opened up for an instant but before I could see anything she came down again and gripping the wooden blade between her molars she reduced it to splinters before I could get it out again.

Aren't you ashamed, the mother yelled at her. Aren't you ashamed to act like that in front of the doctor?

Get me a smooth-handled spoon of some sort, I told the mother. We're going through with this. The child's mouth was already bleeding. Her tongue was cut and she was screaming in wild hysterical shrieks. Perhaps I should have desisted and come back in an hour or more. No doubt it would have been better. But I have seen at least two children lying dead in bed of neglect in such cases, and feeling that I must get a diagnosis now or never I went at it again. But the worst of it was that I too had got beyond reason. I could have torn the child apart in my own fury and enjoyed it. It was a pleasure to attack her. My face was burning with it.

The damned little brat must be protected against her own idiocy, one says to one's self at such times. Others must be protected against her. It is a social necessity. And all these things are true. But a blind fury, a feeling of adult shame, bred of a longing for muscular release are the operatives. One goes on to the end.

In a final unreasoning assault I overpowered the child's neck and jaws. I forced the heavy silver spoon back of her teeth and down her throat till she gagged. And there it was—both tonsils covered with membrane. She had fought valiantly to keep me from knowing her secret. She had been hiding that sore throat for three days at least and lying to her parents in order to escape just such an outcome as this.

Now truly she was furious. She had been on the defensive before but now she attacked. Tried to get off her father's lap and fly at me while tears of defeat blinded her eyes.

Questions for Writing or Discussion

1. Several of the doctor's comments reveal something about his character.
   a. He says of the mother and father, ". . . they weren't telling me more than they had to, it was up to me to tell them; that's why they were spending three dollars on me."
   b. "At that I ground my teeth in disgust. If only they wouldn't use the word 'hurt' I might be able to get somewhere."
   c. "I had already fallen in love with the savage brat, the parents were contemptible to me."
   d. ". . . I wanted to kill him" (the father).
   What do these quotations and the events of the last part of the story reveal about the man?

2. Why does the doctor say he was in love with the child and also call her a "damned little brat"?
3. Keeping your answers to the above questions in mind, write a paper which explains why the doctor tore the child's mouth. Fear that the child had diphtheria is only one cause.

A Complicated Case
EUNICE PAPES

William Carlos Williams' "The Use of Force" tells about a doctor who, in an attempt to examine her throat during a house call, overpowers a hysterical child, Mathilda Olson, and tears her mouth until it bleeds. Such behavior is hardly in keeping with the image of the doctor as healer. One is especially disturbed when the doctor says, "I could have torn the child apart in my own fury and enjoyed it. It was a pleasure to attack her." Is the man a sadist who stumbled into the medical profession by mistake? Possibly. For the doctor says, "Perhaps I should have desisted and come back in an hour or more. No doubt it would have been better." But he does not desist. Other elements of the story, however, suggest that the doctor is a dedicated physician whose cruelty on this occasion results from several causes.

The most obvious reason for the doctor's behavior despite the terrified child's resistance is the urgent need to obtain a throat culture. The doctor knows that several cases of diphtheria have developed in the child's school. The first duty of a physician in such a situation is to examine the patient's throat. Confronted with the possibility of that often fatal disease, any doctor who did not obtain a throat culture would be considered negligent. However, while the necessity of examining Mathilda's throat helps explain the doctor's behavior, it does not explain why he enjoys hurting the child.

The enjoyment of cruelty has other roots. One is the doctor's frustration caused by the parents of the child. Not only do they fail to help the doctor examine Mathilda, they contribute to his difficulties in several other ways. They do not trust the doctor, and they give him very little information. ("They weren't telling me more than they had to. . . .") The mother says, "He won't hurt you," putting the idea of pain in the child's mind. Later the mother moves around "raising and lowering her hands in an agony of apprehension." Mathilda must believe her terror is justified when she sees her mother in such a state. The father tries to hold the girl's hands so the doctor can examine her throat, but he lets her go just when the doctor has almost succeeded. One can almost understand why the doctor says, "The parents were contemptible to me."

The doctor does not, however, find Mathilda contemptible. He says, "I had already fallen in love with the savage brat. . . ." He describes her as "an unusually attractive little thing" who "had magnificent blonde hair, in profusion." In her struggle, she rises to "magnificent heights." The doctor admires the child, but he has reason to call her "a savage brat." She tries to claw his eyes; she knocks his glasses to the floor; she is unimpressed with his "best professional manner," refusing to cooperate. The man's pride must suffer when a mere child responds to him with such fury. His pride must require him to defeat the child. It might even cause him to enjoy seeing her suffer.

All these causes for the doctor's behavior seem reasonable enough. But something is missing. An urgent need for diagnosis, ignorant and un-cooperative parents, and lovable but resistant brats must be fairly common in a doctor's practice. Yet doctors don't ordinarily bloody children's mouths in these frustrating circumstances. Perhaps the most important cause for the doctor's behavior remains unexplored.

Before his experience with Mathilda, the doctor is, I believe, unaware of his own capacity for irrational behavior, and because he is unaware, he has no defense against it. Until he actually attacks the child, he seems almost arrogant in his self-assurance. Although he has never seen the Olsons be-fore, for example, he presumes to know what they think and how they feel. The mother is "apologetic." He "knows" the parents are spending their three dollars on him because they believe he has all the answers. He uses his "best professional manner" in addressing the child. He knows "how to expose a throat for inspection." He is apparently accustomed to being in control—of himself and of his circumstances.

Close to the surface of that control, however, is an unexamined capacity for violence. For example, he grinds his teeth "in disgust" at the mother's comments. Angry with the father's inability to hold the child, he says, "I wanted to kill him." Even so, he seems surprised that he has "grown furious—at a child." ("How could *I* become furious with a child?" he seems to say.) When he can finally admit his fury, he recognizes—maybe for the first time—the irrational elements within him. He characterizes his behavior as "beyond reason," as resulting from a "blind fury," as an "unreasoning assault." Now that he knows that he, like the rest of us, is capable of "the use of force," perhaps he will never again attack a child.

Questions for Writing or Discussion

1. What causes does the writer give for the doctor's cruelty to the child? Do you think these are the real causes? Do you have another explanation for the doctor's behavior?

2. Does the writer ignore any significant parts of the story which might contradict her analysis of the doctor's behavior?

3. The writer uses a number of quotations from the story. Do you think her use of quotations is effective? Why? Or do you think she uses too many quotations? Why?

4. Does the introduction clearly call for an analysis of causes?

Readings

Here is a group of readings in which the writers dramatize several cause-and-effect relationships. Notice what a diversity of subjects lend themselves to this approach.

BALLAD OF THE LANDLORD

Landlord, landlord,
My roof has sprung a leak.
Don't you 'member I told you about it
Way last week?

Landlord, landlord,
The steps is broken down.
When you come up yourself
It's a wonder you don't fall down.

Ten bucks you say I owe you?
Ten bucks you say is due?
Well, that's ten bucks more'n I'll pay you
Till you fix this house up new.

What? You gonna get eviction orders?
You gonna cut my heat?
You gonna take my furniture and
Throw it in the street?

Um-huh! You talking high and mighty.
Talk on—till you get through.
You ain't gonna be able to say a word
If I land my fist on you.

Police! Police!
Come and get this man!
He's trying to ruin the government
And overturn the land!

Copper's whistle!
Patrol bell!
Arrest.

Precinct Station.
Iron cell.
Headlines in press:

MAN THREATENS LANDLORD
* * *

TENANT HELD NO BAIL
      * * *

JUDGE GIVES NEGRO 90 DAYS IN COUNTY JAIL

—*Langston Hughes*

Questions for Writing or Discussion

1. Outline the sequence of happenings. Several causes bring about the first effect, and that effect in turn becomes a cause for another effect, and so on.
2. How does the author's selection of details and language make us side with the tenant rather than the landlord?

Anton Chekhov
THE LOTTERY TICKET

Ivan Dmitritch, a middle-class man who lived with his family on an income of twelve hundred a year and was very well satisfied with his lot, sat down on the sofa after supper and began reading the newspaper.

"I forgot to look at the newspaper today," his wife said to him as she cleared the table. "Look and see whether the list of drawings is there."

"Yes, it is," said Ivan Dmitritch; "but hasn't your ticket lapsed?"

"No; I took the interest on Tuesday."

"What is the number?"

"Series 9,499, number 26."

"All right . . . we will look . . . 9,499 and 26."

Ivan Dmitritch had no faith in lottery luck, and would not, as a rule, have consented to look at the lists of winning numbers, but now, as he had nothing else to do and as the newspaper was before his eyes, he passed his finger downwards along the column of numbers. And immediately, as though in mockery of his scepticism, no further than the second line from the top, his eye was caught by the figure 9,499! Unable to believe his eyes, he hurriedly dropped the paper on his knees without looking to see the number of the ticket, and, just as though some one had given him a douche of cold water, he felt an agreeable chill in the pit of the stomach; tingling and terrible and sweet!

"Masha, 9,499 is there!" he said in a hollow voice.

His wife looked at his astonished and panic-stricken face, and realized that he was not joking.

"9,499?" she asked, turning pale and dropping the folded tablecloth on the table.

"Yes, yes . . . it really is there!"

"And the number of the ticket?"

"Oh, yes! There's the number of the ticket too. But stay . . . wait! No, I say! Anyway, the number of our series is there! Anyway, you understand. . . ."

Looking at his wife, Ivan Dmitritch gave a broad, senseless smile, like a baby when a bright object is shown it. His wife smiled too; it was as pleasant to her as to him that he only mentioned the series, and did not try to find out the number of the winning ticket. To torment and tantalize oneself with hopes of possible fortune is so sweet, so thrilling!

"It is our series," said Ivan Dmitritch, after a long silence. "So there is a probability that we have won. It's only a probability, but there it is!"

"Well, now look!"

"Wait a little. We have plenty of time to be disappointed. It's on the second line from the top, so the prize is seventy-five thousand. That's not money, but power, capital! And in a minute I shall look at the list, and there—26! Eh? I say, what if we really have won?"

The husband and wife began laughing and staring at one another in silence. The possibility of winning bewildered them; they could not have said, could not have dreamed, what they both needed that seventy-five thousand for, what they would buy, where they would go. They thought only of the figures 9,499 and 75,000 and pictured them in their imagination, while somehow they could not think of the happiness itself which was so possible.

Ivan Dmitritch, holding the paper in his hand, walked several times from corner to corner, and only when he had recovered from the first impression began dreaming a little.

"And if we have won," he said—"why, it will be a new life, it will be a transformation! The ticket is yours, but if it were mine I should, first of all, of course, spend twenty-five thousand on real property in the shape of an estate; ten thousand on immediate expenses, new furnishing . . . travelling . . . paying debts, and so on. . . . The other forty thousand I would put in the bank and get interest on it."

"Yes, an estate, that would be nice," said his wife, sitting down and dropping her hands in her lap.

"Somewhere in the Tula or Oryol provinces. . . . In the first place we shouldn't need a summer villa, and besides, it would always bring in an income."

And pictures came crowding on his imagination, each more gracious and poetical than the last. And in all these pictures he saw himself well-fed, serene, healthy, felt warm, even hot! Here, after eating a summer soup, cold as ice, he lay on his back on the burning sand close to a stream or in the garden under a lime-tree. . . . It is hot. . . . His little boy and girl are crawling about near him, digging in the sand or catching ladybirds in the grass. He dozes sweetly, thinking of nothing, and feeling all over that he need not go to the office today, tomorrow, or the day after. Or, tired of lying still, he goes to the hayfield, or to the forest for mushrooms, or watches the peasants catching fish with a net. When the sun sets he takes a towel and soap and saunters to the bathing-shed, where he undresses at his leisure, slowly rubs his bare chest with his hands, and goes into the water. And in the water, near the opaque soapy circles, little fish flit to and fro and green water-weeds nod their heads. After bathing there is tea with cream and milk rolls. . . . In the evening a walk or *vint* with the neighbors.

"Yes, it would be nice to buy an estate," said his wife, also dreaming, and from her face it was evident that she was enchanted by her thoughts.

Ivan Dmitritch pictured to himself autumn with its rains, its cold evenings, and its St. Martin's summer. At that season he would have to take longer walks about the garden and beside the river, so as to get thoroughly chilled, and then drink a big glass of vodka and eat a salted mushroom or a soused cucumber, and then—drink another. . . . The children would come running from the kitchen-garden, bringing a carrot and a radish smelling of fresh earth. . . . And then, he would lie stretched full length on the sofa, and in leisurely fashion turn over the pages of some illustrated magazine, or, covering his face with it and unbuttoning his waistcoat, give himself up to slumber.

The St. Martin's summer is followed by cloudy, gloomy weather. It rains day and night, the bare trees weep, the wind is damp and cold. The dogs, the horses, the fowls—all are wet, depressed, downcast. There is nowhere to walk; one can't go out for days together; one has to pace up and down the room, looking despondently at the grey window. It is dreary!

Ivan Dmitritch stopped and looked at his wife.

"I should go abroad, you know, Masha," he said.

And he began thinking how nice it would be in late autumn to go abroad somewhere to the South of France . . . to Italy . . . to India!

"I should certainly go abroad too," his wife said. "But look at the number of the ticket!"

"Wait, wait!"

He walked about the room and went on thinking. It occurred to him: what if his wife really did go abroad? It is pleasant to travel alone, or in the society of light, careless women who live in the present, and not such as think and talk all the journey about nothing but their children, sigh, and tremble with dismay over every farthing. Ivan Dmitritch imagined his wife in the train with a multitude of parcels, baskets, and bags; she would be sighing over something, complaining that the train made her head ache, that she had spent so much money. . . . At the stations he would continually be having to run for boiling water, bread and butter. . . . She wouldn't have dinner because of its being too dear. . . .

"She would begrudge me every farthing," he thought, with a glance at his wife. "The lottery ticket is hers, not mine! Besides, what is the use of her going abroad? What does she want there? She would shut herself up in the hotel, and not let me out of her sight . . . I know!"

And for the first time in his life his mind dwelt on the fact that his wife had grown elderly and plain, and that she was saturated through and through with the smell of cooking, while he was still young, fresh, and healthy, and might well have got married again.

"Of course, all that is silly nonsense," he thought; "but . . . why should she go abroad? What would she make of it? And yet she would go, of course. . . . I can fancy. . . . In reality it is all one to her, whether it is Naples or Klin. She would only be in my way. I should be dependent upon her. I can fancy how, like a regular woman, she will lock the money up as soon as she gets it. . . . She will look after her relations and grudge me every farthing."

Ivan Dmitritch thought of her relations. All those wretched brothers and sisters and aunts and uncles would come crawling about as soon as they heard of the winning ticket, would begin whining like beggars, and fawning upon them with oily, hypocritical smiles. Wretched, detestable people! If they were given anything, they would ask for more; while if they were refused, they would swear at them, slander them, and wish them every kind of misfortune.

Ivan Dmitritch remembered his own relations, and their faces, at which he had looked impartially in the past, struck him now as repulsive and hateful.

"They are such reptiles!" he thought.

And his wife's face, too, struck him as repulsive and hateful. Anger surged up in his heart against her, and he thought malignantly:

"She knows nothing about money, and so she is stingy. If she won it she would give me a hundred rubles, and put the rest away under lock and key."

And he looked at his wife, not with a smile now, but with hatred. She glanced at him too, and also with hatred and anger. She had her own day-dreams, her own plans, her own reflections; she understood perfectly well what her husband's dreams were. She knew who would be the first to try to grab her winnings.

"It's very nice making daydreams at other people's expense!" is what her eyes expressed. "No, don't you dare!"

Her husband understood her look; hatred began stirring again in his breast, and in order to annoy his wife he glanced quickly, to spite her, at the fourth page of the newspaper and read out triumphantly:

"Series 9,499, number 46! Not 26!"

Hatred and hope both disappeared at once, and it began immediately to seem to Ivan Dmitritch and his wife that their rooms were dark and small and low-pitched, that the supper they had been eating was not doing them good, but lying heavy on their stomachs, that the evenings were long and wearisome. . . .

"What the devil's the meaning of it?" said Ivan Dmitritch, beginning to be ill-humored. "Wherever one steps there are bits of paper under one's feet, crumbs, husks. The rooms are never swept! One is simply forced to go out. Damnation take my soul entirely! I shall go and hang myself on the first aspen-tree!"

Questions for Writing or Discussion

1. The "effect" in this story is clear. The characters end up hating their lives and each other. Could this effect result only from the possibility of holding a winning lottery ticket?

2. What are the other causes behind the couple's emotions, if any? Why does the author not discuss these other causes directly? Write a paper on the underlying causes for Ivan Dmitritch's unhappiness.

Ted Poston
THE REVOLT OF THE EVIL FAIRIES

The grand dramatic offering of the Booker T. Washington Colored Grammar School was the biggest event of the year in our social life in Hopkinsville, Kentucky. It was the one occasion on which they let us use the old Cooper Opera House, and even some of the white folks came out yearly to applaud our presentation. The first two rows of the orchestra were always reserved for our white friends, and our leading colored citizens sat right behind them—with an empty row intervening, of course.

Mr. Ed Smith, our local undertaker, invariably occupied a box to the left of the house and wore his cutaway coat and striped breeches. This distinctive garb was usually reserved for those rare occasions when he officiated at the funerals of our most prominent colored citizens. Mr. Thaddeus Long, our colored mailman, once rented a tuxedo and bought a box too. But nobody paid him much mind. We knew he was just showing off.

The title of our play never varied. It was always Prince Charming and the Sleeping Beauty, but no two presentations were ever the same. Miss H. Belle LaPrade, our sixth-grade teacher, rewrote the script every season, and it was never like anything you read in the storybooks.

Miss LaPrade called it "a modern morality play of conflict between the forces of good and evil." And the forces of evil, of course, always came off second best.

The Booker T. Washington Colored Grammar School was in a state of ferment from Christmas until February, for this was the period when parts were assigned. First there was the selection of the Good Fairies and the Evil Fairies. This was very important, because the Good Fairies wore white costumes and the Evil Fairies black. And strangely enough most of the Good Fairies usually turned out to be extremely light in complexion, with straight hair and white folks' features. On rare occasions a darkskinned girl might be lucky enough to be a Good Fairy, but not one with a speaking part.

There never was any doubt about Prince Charming and the Sleeping Beauty. They were always lightskinned. And though nobody ever discussed those things openly, it was an accepted fact that a lack of pigmentation was a decided advantage in the Prince Charming and Sleeping Beauty sweepstakes.

And therein lay my personal tragedy. I made the best grades in my class, I was the leading debater, and the scion of a respected family in the community. But I could never be Prince Charming, because I was black.

In fact, every year when they started casting our grand dramatic offering my family started pricing black cheesecloth at Franklin's Department Store.

For they knew that I would be leading the forces of darkness and skulking back in the shadows—waiting to be vanquished in the third act. Mamma had experience with this sort of thing. All my brothers had finished Booker T. before me.

Not that I was alone in my disappointment. Many of my classmates felt it too. I probably just took it more to heart. Rat Joiner, for instance, could rationalize the situation. Rat was not only black; he lived on Billy Goat Hill. But Rat summed it up like this:

"If you black, you black."

I should have been able to regard the matter calmly too. For our grand dramatic offering was only a reflection of our daily community life in Hopkinsville. The yallers had the best of everything. They held most of the teaching jobs in Booker T. Washington Colored Grammar School. They were the Negro doctors, the lawyers, the insurance men. They even had a "Blue Vein Society," and if your dark skin obscured your throbbing pulse you were hardly a member of the elite.

Yet I was inconsolable the first time they turned me down for Prince Charming. That was the year they picked Roger Jackson. Roger was not only dumb; he stuttered. But he was light enough to pass for white, and that was apparently sufficient.

In all fairness, however, it must be admitted that Roger had other qualifications. His father owned the only colored saloon in town and was quite a power in local politics. In fact, Mr. Clinton Jackson had a lot to say about just who taught in the Booker T. Washington Colored Grammar School. So it was understandable that Roger should have been picked for Prince Charming.

My real heartbreak, however, came the year they picked Sarah Williams for Sleeping Beauty. I had been in love with Sarah since kindergarten. She had soft light hair, bluish-gray eyes, and a dimple which stayed in her left cheek whether she was smiling or not.

Of course Sarah never encouraged me much. She never answered any of my fervent love letters, and Rat was very scornful of my one-sided love affairs. "As long as she don't call you a black baboon," he sneered, "you'll keep on hanging around."

After Sarah was chosen for Sleeping Beauty, I went out for the Prince Charming role with all my heart. If I had declaimed boldly in previous contests, I was matchless now. If I had bothered Mamma with rehearsals at home before, I pestered her to death this time. Yes, and I purloined my sister's can of Palmer's Skin Success.

I knew the Prince's role from start to finish, having played the Head Evil Fairy opposite it for two seasons. And Prince Charming was one character whose lines Miss LaPrade never varied much in her many versions. But although I never admitted it, even to myself, I knew I was doomed from the start. They gave the part to Leonardius Wright. Leonardius, of course, was yaller.

The teachers sensed my resentment. They were most apologetic. They pointed out that I had been such a splendid Head Evil Fairy for two seasons that it would be a crime to let anybody else try the role. They reminded me that Mamma wouldn't have to buy any more cheesecloth because I could use my same old costume. They insisted that the Head Evil Fairy was even more important than Prince Charming because he was the one who cast the spell on Sleeping Beauty. So what could I do but accept?

I had never liked Leonardius Wright. He was a goody-goody, and even Mamma was always throwing him up to me. But, above all, he too was in love with Sarah Williams. And now he got a chance to kiss Sarah every day in rehearsing the awakening scene.

Well, the show must go on, even for little black boys. So I threw my soul into my part and made the Head Evil Fairy a character to be remembered. When I drew back from the couch of Sleeping Beauty and slunk away into the shadows at the approach of Prince Charming, my facial expression was indeed something to behold. When I was vanquished by the shining sword of Prince Charming in the last act, I was a little hammy perhaps—but terrific!

The attendance at our grand dramatic offering that year was the best in its history. Even the white folks overflowed the two rows reserved for them, and a few were forced to sit in the intervening one. This created a delicate situation, but everybody tactfully ignored it.

When the curtain went up on the last act, the audience was in fine fettle. Everything had gone well for me too—except for one spot in the second act. That was where Leonardius unexpectedly rapped me over the head with his sword as I slunk off into the shadows. That was not in the script, but Miss LaPrade quieted me down by saying it made a nice touch anyway. Rat said Leonardius did it on purpose.

The third act went on smoothly, though, until we came to the vanquishing scene. That was where I slunk from the shadows for the last time and challenged Prince Charming to mortal combat. The hero reached for his shining sword—a bit unsportsmanlike, I always thought, since Miss LaPrade consistently left the Head Evil Fairy unarmed—and then it happened!

Later I protested loudly—but in vain—that it was a case of self-defense. I pointed out that Leonardius had a mean look in his eye. I cited the impromptu rapping he had given my head in the second act. But nobody would listen. They just wouldn't believe that Leonardius really intended to brain me when he reached for his sword.

Anyway, he didn't succeed. For the minute I saw that evil gleam in his eye—or was it my own?—I cut loose with a right to the chin, and Prince Charming dropped his shining sword and staggered back. His astonishment lasted only a minute, though, for he lowered his head and came charging in, fists flailing. There was nothing yellow about Leonardius but his skin.

The audience thought the scrap was something new Miss LaPrade had written in. They might have kept on thinking so if Miss LaPrade hadn't been screaming so hysterically from the sidelines. And if Rat Joiner hadn't decided that this was as good a time as any to settle old scores. So he turned around and took a sock at the male Good Fairy nearest him.

When the curtain rang down, the forces of Good and Evil were locked in combat. And Sleeping Beauty was wide awake and streaking for the wings.

They rang the curtain back up fifteen minutes later, and we finished the play. I lay down and expired according to specifications but Prince Charming will probably remember my sneering corpse to his dying day. They wouldn't let me appear in the grand dramatic offering at all the next year. But I didn't care. I couldn't have been Prince Charming anyway.

Questions for Writing or Discussion

1. To what race does Miss LaPrade belong?
2. Why is it significant that the narrator made the best grades, was the leading debater, and was the son of a respected family?
3. Why do the "yallers" have the best of everything in the community?
4. Why is the Head Evil Fairy unarmed?
5. Write a paper in which you explain why the narrator "couldn't have been Prince Charming anyway."

George Orwell
SHOOTING AN ELEPHANT

In Moulmein, in Lower Burma, I was hated by large numbers of people—the only time in my life that I have been important enough for this to happen to me. I was sub-divisional police officer of the town, and in an aimless, petty kind of way anti-European feeling was very bitter. No one had the guts to raise a riot, but if a European woman went through the bazaars alone somebody would probably spit betel juice over her dress. As a police officer I was an obvious target and was baited whenever it seemed safe to do so. When a nimble Burman tripped me up on the football field and the referee (another Burman) looked the other way, the crowd yelled with hideous laughter. This happened more than once. In the end the sneering yellow faces of young men that met me everywhere, the insults hooted after me when I was at a safe distance, got badly on my nerves. The young Buddhist priests were the worst of all. There were several thousands of them in the town and none of them seemed to have anything to do except stand on street corners and jeer at Europeans.

All this was perplexing and upsetting. For at that time I had already made up my mind that imperialism was an evil thing and the sooner I chucked up my job and got out of it the better. Theoretically—and secretly, of course—I was all for the Burmese and all against their oppressors, the British. As for the job I was doing, I hated it more bitterly than I can perhaps make clear. In a job like that you see the dirty work of Empire at close quarters. The wretched prisoners huddling in the stinking cages of the lock-ups, the grey, cowed faces of the long-term convicts, the scarred buttocks of the men who had been flogged with bamboos—all these oppressed me with an intolerable sense of guilt. But I could get nothing into perspective. I was young and ill-educated and I had had to think out my problems in the utter silence that is imposed on every Englishman in the East. I did not even know that the British Empire is dying, still less did I know that it is a great deal better than the younger empires that are going to supplant it. All I knew was that I was stuck between my hatred of the empire I served and my rage against the evil-spirited little beasts who tried to make my job impossible. With one part of my mind I thought of the British Raj as an unbreakable tyranny, as something clamped down, *in saecula saeculorum*,[1] upon the will of prostrate peoples; with another part I thought that the greatest joy in the world would be to drive a bayonet into a Buddhist priest's guts. Feelings like these are the normal by-products of imperialism; ask any Anglo-Indian official, if you can catch him off duty.

One day something happened which in a roundabout way was enlightening. It was a tiny incident in itself, but it gave me a better glimpse than I had had before of the real nature of imperialism—the real motives for which despotic governments act. Early one morning the sub-inspector at a police station the other end of the town rang me up on the phone and said that an elephant was ravaging the bazaar. Would I please come and do something about it? I did not know what I could do, but I wanted to see what was happening and I got on to a pony and started out. I took my rifle, an old .44 Winchester and much too small to kill an elephant, but I thought the noise might be useful *in terrorem*.[2] Various Burmans stopped me on the way and told me about the elephant's doings. It was not, of course, a wild elephant, but a tame one which had gone "must."[3] It had been chained up as tame elephants always are when their attack of "must" is due, but on the previous night it had broken its chain and escaped. Its mahout,[4] the only person who could manage it when it was in that state, had set out in pursuit, but he had taken the wrong direction and was now twelve hours' journey away, and in the morning the elephant had suddenly reappeared in the town. The Burmese population had no weapons and were quite helpless against it. It had already destroyed somebody's bamboo hut, killed a cow and raided some fruit-stalls and devoured the stock; also it had met the municipal rubbish van, and, when the driver jumped out and took to his heels, had turned the van over and inflicted violence upon it.

The Burmese sub-inspector and some Indian constables were waiting for me in the quarter where the elephant had been seen. It was a very poor quarter, a labyrinth of squalid bamboo huts, thatched with palm-leaf, winding all over a steep hillside. I remember that it was a cloudy stuffy morning at the beginning of the rains. We began questioning the people as to where the elephant had gone, and, as usual, failed to get any definite information. That is invariably the case in the East; a story always sounds clear enough at a distance, but the nearer you get to the scene of events the vaguer it becomes. Some of the people said that the elephant had gone in one direction,

---

[1]Latin for "time out of mind."
[2]Latin for "as a warning."
[3]Period of hyperactive behavior in elephants, associated with sexual excitement.
[4]Trainer and rider.

some said that he had gone in another, some professed not even to have heard of any elephant. I had almost made up my mind that the whole story was a pack of lies, when we heard yells a little distance away. There was a loud, scandalised cry of "Go away, child! Go away this instant!"and an old woman with a switch in her hand came round the corner of a hut, violently shooing away a crowd of naked children. Some more women followed, clicking their tongues and exclaiming; evidently there was something there that the children ought not to have seen. I rounded the hut and saw a man's dead body sprawling in the mud. He was an Indian, a black Dravidian coolie, almost naked, and he could not have been dead many minutes. The people said that the elephant had come suddenly upon him round the corner of the hut, caught him with its trunk, put its foot on his back and ground him into the earth. This was the rainy season and the ground was soft, and his face had scored a trench a foot deep and a couple yards long. He was lying on his belly with arms crucified and head sharply twisted to one side. His face was coated with mud, the eyes wide open, the teeth bared and grinning with an expression of unendurable agony. (Never tell me, by the way, that the dead look peaceful. Most of the corpses I have seen looked devilish.) The friction of the great beast's foot had stripped the skin from his back as neatly as one skins a rabbit. As soon as I saw the dead man I sent an orderly to a friend's house nearby to borrow an elephant rifle. I had already sent back the pony, not wanting it to go mad with fright and throw me if it smelled the elephant.

The orderly came back in a few minutes with a rifle and five cartridges, and meanwhile some Burmans had arrived and told us that the elephant was in the paddy fields below, only a few hundred yards away. As I started forward practically the whole population of the quarter flocked out of their houses and followed me. They had seen the rifle and were all shouting excitedly that I was going to shoot the elephant. They had not shown much interest in the elephant when he was merely ravaging their homes, but it was different now that he was going to be shot. It was a bit of fun to them, as it would be to an English crowd; besides, they wanted the meat. It made me vaguely uneasy. I had no intention of shooting the elephant—I had merely sent for the rifle to defend myself if necessary—and it is always unnerving to have a crowd following you. I marched down the hill, looking and feeling a fool, with the rifle over my shoulder and an ever-growing army of people jostling at my heels. At the bottom, when you got away from the huts, there was a metalled road and beyond that a miry waste of paddy fields a thousand yards across, not yet ploughed but soggy from the first rains and dotted with coarse grass. The elephant was standing eighty yards from the road, his left side towards us. He took not the slightest notice of the crowd's approach. He was tearing up bunches of grass, beating them against his knees to clean them and stuffing them into his mouth.

I had halted on the road. As soon as I saw the elephant I knew with perfect certainty that I ought not to shoot him. It is a serious matter to shoot a working elephant—it is comparable to destroying a huge and costly piece of machinery—and obviously one ought not to do it if it can possibly be avoided. And at that distance, peacefully eating, the elephant looked no more dangerous than a cow. I thought then and I think now that his attack of "must" was already passing off; in which case he would merely wander harmlessly about until the mahout came back and caught him. Moreover, I did not in the least want to shoot him. I decided that I would watch him for a little while to make sure that he did not turn savage again, and then go home.

But at that moment I glanced round at the crowd that had followed me. It was an immense crowd, two thousand at the least and growing every minute. It blocked the road for a long distance on either side. I looked at the sea of yellow faces above the garish clothes—faces all happy and excited over this bit of fun, all certain that the elephant was going to be shot. They were watching me as they would watch a conjuror about to perform a trick. They did not like me, but with a magical rifle in my hands I was momentarily worth watching. And suddenly I realised that I should have to shoot the elephant after all. The people expected it of me and I had got to do it; I could feel their two thousand wills pressing me forward, irresistibly. And it was at this moment, as I stood there with the rifle in my hands, that I first grasped the hollowness, the futility of the white man's dominion in the East. Here was I, the white man with his gun, standing in front of the unarmed native crowd—seemingly the leading actor of the piece; but in reality I was only an absurd puppet pushed to and fro by the will of those yellow faces behind. I perceived in this moment that when the white man turns tyrant it is his own freedom that he destroys. He becomes a sort of hollow, posing dummy, the conventionalised figure of a sahib.[5] For it is the condition of his rule that he shall spend his life in trying to impress the "natives" and so in every crisis he has got to do what the "natives" expect of him. He wears a mask, and his face grows to fit it. I had got to shoot the elephant. I had committed myself to doing it when I sent for the rifle. A sahib has got to act like a sahib; he has got to appear resolute, to know his own mind and do definite things. To come all that way, rifle in hand, with two thousand people marching at my heels, and then to trail feebly away, having done nothing—no, that was impossible. The crowd would laugh at me. And my whole life, every white man's life in the East, was one long struggle not to be laughed at.

But I did not want to shoot the elephant. I watched him beating his bunch of grass against his knees, with that preoccupied grandmotherly air that elephants have. It seemed to me that it would be murder to shoot him. At that age I was not squeamish about killing animals, but I had never shot an elephant and never wanted to. (Somehow it always seems worse to kill a *large* animal.) Besides, there was the beast's owner to be considered. Alive, the elephant was worth at least a hundred pounds; dead, he would only be worth the value of his tusks—five pounds, possibly. But I had got to act quickly. I turned to some experienced-looking Burmans who had been there when we arrived, and asked them how the elephant had been behaving. They all said the same thing: he took no notice of you if you left him alone, but he might charge if you went too close to him.

It was perfectly clear to me what I ought to do. I ought to walk up to within, say, twenty-five yards of the elephant and test his behaviour. If he charged I could shoot, if he took no notice of me it would be safe to leave

---

[5]Master.

him until the mahout came back. But also I knew that I was going to do no such thing. I was a poor shot with a rifle and the ground was soft mud into which one would sink at every step. If the elephant charged and I missed him, I should have about as much chance as a toad under a steam-roller. But even then I was not thinking particularly of my own skin, only the watchful yellow faces behind. For at that moment, with the crowd watching me, I was not afraid in the ordinary sense, as I would have been if I had been alone. A white man mustn't be frightened in front of "natives"; and so, in general, he isn't frightened. The sole thought in my mind was that if anything went wrong those two thousand Burmans would see me pursued, caught, trampled on and reduced to a grinning corpse like that Indian up the hill. And if that happened it was quite probable that some of them would laugh. That would never do. There was only one alternative. I shoved the cartridges into the magazine and lay down on the road to get a better aim.

The crowd grew very still, and a deep, low, happy sigh, as of people who see the theatre curtain go up at last, breathed from innumerable throats. They were going to have their bit of fun after all. The rifle was a beautiful German thing with cross-hair sights. I did not then know that in shooting an elephant one should shoot to cut an imaginary bar running from ear-hole to ear-hole. I ought therefore, as the elephant was sideways on, to have aimed straight at his ear-hole; actually I aimed several inches in front of this, thinking the brain would be further forward.

When I pulled the trigger I did not hear the bang or feel the kick—one never does when a shot goes home—but I heard the devilish roar of glee that went up from the crowd. In that instant, in too short a time, one would have thought, even for the bullet to get there, a mysterious, terrible change had come over the elephant. He neither stirred nor fell, but every line of his body had altered. He looked suddenly stricken, shrunken, immensely old, as though the frightful impact of the bullet had paralysed him without knocking him down. At last, after what seemed a long time—it might have been five seconds, I dare say—he sagged flabbily to his knees. His mouth slobbered. An enormous senility seemed to have settled upon him. One could have imagined him thousands of years old. I fired again into the same spot. At the second shot he did not collapse but climbed with desperate slowness to his feet and stood weakly upright, with legs sagging and head drooping. I fired a third time. That was the shot that did for him. You could see the agony of it jolt his whole body and knock the last remnant of strength from his legs. But in falling he seemed for a moment to rise, for as his hind legs collapsed beneath him he seemed to tower upwards like a huge rock toppling, his trunk reaching skyward like a tree. He trumpeted, for the first and only time. And then down he came, his belly towards me, with a crash that seemed to shake the ground even where I lay.

I got up. The Burmans were already racing past me across the mud. It was obvious that the elephant would never rise again, but he was not dead. He was breathing very rhythmically with long rattling gasps, his great mound of a side painfully rising and falling. His mouth was wide open—I could see far down into caverns of pale pink throat. I waited a long time for him to die, but his breathing did not weaken. Finally I fired my two remaining shots into the spot where I thought his heart must be. The thick blood welled out of him like red velvet, but still he did not die. His body did not even jerk when the shots hit him, the tortured breathing continued without a pause. He was dying, very slowly and in great agony, but in some world remote from me where not even a bullet could damage him further. I felt that I had got to put an end to that dreadful noise. It seemed dreadful to see the great beast lying there, powerless to move and yet powerless to die, and not even to be able to finish him. I sent back for my small rifle and poured shot after shot into his heart and down his throat. They seemed to make no impression. The tortured gasps continued as steadily as the ticking of a clock.

In the end I could not stand it any longer and went away. I heard later that it took him half an hour to die. Burmans were arriving with dahs[6] and baskets even before I left, and I was told they had stripped his body almost to the bones by the afternoon.

Afterwards, of course, there were endless discussions about the shooting of the elephant. The owner was furious, but he was only an Indian and could do nothing. Besides, legally I had done the right thing, for a mad elephant has to be killed, like a mad dog, if its owner fails to control it. Among the Europeans opinion was divided. The older men said I was right, the younger men said it was a damn shame to shoot an elephant for killing a coolie, because an elephant was worth more than any damn Coringhee coolie. And afterwards I was very glad that the coolie had been killed; it put me legally in the right and it gave me a sufficient pretext for shooting the elephant. I often wondered whether any of the others grasped that I had done it solely to avoid looking a fool.

Questions for Writing or Discussion

1. What insight about the real nature of imperialism did Orwell gain from the incident?
2. Why did Orwell shoot the elephant?
3. Why did he not want to shoot the elephant?
4. Why, if Orwell's purpose is to explain his hatred of imperialism, does he devote so much space to his hatred of the Burmese?
5. In view of the insight Orwell gained, do you find the last paragraph ironic?
6. Does Orwell's statement that he had killed the elephant solely to avoid looking a fool have greater meaning than merely trying to avoid an embarrassing moment? If so, what other meaning do you find in the statement?
7. Write a paper in which you analyze the causes for Orwell's shooting the elephant. Why did he feel he *had* to shoot the elephant?

---

[6] Knives.

CHAPTER 10

WRITING A COMPARISON AND CONTRAST PAPER

A comparison shows the similarities between two or more things; a contrast shows the differences between two or more things; a comparison-contrast shows both similarities and differences. The most common kind of essay question on examinations calls for comparison-contrast. You do well, therefore, to master the techniques of this method of development.

Comparison and contrast are useful because they enable us to comprehend our world. A small boy asks his mother what an apartment is. The mother responds, "It's like our house. It has a living room, kitchen, bathroom, and bedroom. Some apartments have dining rooms and more than one bedroom—just as we do. But it's not exactly like our house. You wouldn't have your own yard to play in. And there are lots of apartments in one building, so many families live close together. An apartment is usually much smaller than a house. And you are not as free in an apartment as in a house. You wouldn't be able to run in the living room because you might bother the neighbors beneath you." The mother, by comparing and contrasting the familiar with the unfamiliar, has been able to give the child some idea of what an apartment is; she has enlarged his comprehension of the world.

Everyone uses comparisons, sometimes to explain the unfamiliar, and sometimes just to establish a superficial similarity: "He is as slow as a snail," for example. But to produce papers of significant worth, a writer should apply logical principles to the consideration of similarities and differences.

Compare and contrast according to a single principle. The average citizen might compare and contrast automobiles and airplanes as means of transportation. An engineer might deal with the same subjects in an attempt to solve the problem of air pollution. The principle in the first instance is ease of travel; in the second, pollution. In each case, the principle determines the similarities and differences discussed in the paper. The citizen concerned with ease of travel wouldn't mention the variety of colors that both airplanes and automobiles can be painted. The engineer concerned with pollution wouldn't mention the comfort of adjustable seats.

In a sense, this means developing a thesis. However, a principle for comparison-contrast usually needs to be established before the writer can arrive at a thesis: the meaning of the similarities and differences. A writer might, for example, after examining the similarities and differences according to the principle of ease of travel, establish as a thesis that travel by air is more convenient than travel by automobile.

Compare and contrast according to a single purpose. One useful purpose is to *clarify* by pointing out the similarities in apparently dissimilar things and the differences in apparently similar things. One might, for example, discuss a novel like *The Great Gatsby* and the movie version of that novel, which starred Robert Redford and Mia Farrow. The novel is generally regarded as a classic of our literature; the movie, which was extraordinarily faithful to the book, is thought by most critics to be a catastrophe. An effective paper on the two could help clarify the reasons for the success of one and the failure of the other.

A second purpose of comparison-contrast is to show the superiority of one thing over another. The writer who concludes that travel by air is more convenient than travel by automobile does that.

A third purpose of comparison-contrast is to use the two items as examples of a generalization: for instance, "That black people in America want to be thought of as individuals rather than as stereotyped representatives of causes or groups is shown in the writings of Ralph Ellison and James Baldwin."

Be fair with your comparison-contrasts. If you see an exception to the comparison you have made, mention it. This is known as *qualification*, and can often be a most effective means of winning the reader's respect and confidence.

A comparison-contrast paper can be organized in one of three ways: subject-by-subject, point-by-point, or a combination of the two.

For short papers, one of the clearest patterns of organization—for comparison *or* contrast—is the subject-by-subject pattern. If you select this pattern, you first discuss one side of the subject completely, and then you discuss the other side. You must, of course, stress the same points in discussing each side of the subject; otherwise there will be no comparison. The following outline and paper will illustrate this pattern of development.

The Gay Divorcée
BARBARA GROSS

Thesis: The life of the divorced woman is vastly different from what is represented in the myth of the gay divorcée.

    I. Elements of the myth
       A. Support
       B. Living quarters
       C. Clothes
       D. Transportation
       E. Entertainment
   II. Reality of the situation
       A. Support
       B. Living quarters
       C. Clothes
       D. Transportation
       E. Entertainment

It took twenty-five minutes to get married, and after five years, only fifteen minutes to get unmarried. "La Dolce Vita" is supposed to begin as soon as a woman regains her freedom, or so I've been told.

According to the script of "La Dolce Vita," a fat alimony-and-child-support check will carry the divorcée until she walks into a glamorous new job filled with challenge, excitement, and a fabulous salary. She will enjoy a spacious suite of rooms in an exclusive neighborhood. Her closet will bulge with expensive clothes from the very finest boutiques. A classic automobile, perhaps an El Dorado, will wait for her to turn the key and carry her to exotic places and adventures with exciting new friends.

My experience has not quite hit all these high points. When my ex and I parted company, I got the kids, the furniture, the cat and a nonexistent monthly support check.

Glamour is one word I would not use when talking about that first job I "walked into" in my newly awarded freedom. (And *grabbed* is probably a better term than *walked into*!) I was not the best prepared person to have to shoulder the support of two small children. Two and a half years as a girl Friday in a department store's accounts payable department coupled with a high school diploma and interrupted by a five-year marriage does not put one in the five-figure salary bracket; it barely gets one into the middle of four! After forty-seven interviews in which I was either overqualified for low pay jobs or underqualified for decent pay jobs, I accepted the intriguing opportunity to become a bookkeeper for a fish house. The fabulous salary I acquired with my new position barely put me over the poverty level.

Consequently, my plush apartment is a relatively comfortable upstairs of an aging two-family on the west side. It's not the Gold Coast, but then someone has to live in the inner city. And my wardrobe consists largely of leftovers from the last eight years and some hand-me-downs from a second cousin.

Six months after I was divorced, I took the plunge and learned to drive. My first car was an adventure in itself. My father purchased the marvel on wheels for fifteen dollars and after he made some "minor" repairs, he turned me loose. It took me one month and a rainy day to wreck it, and the public transportation system chauffeured me about for nearly a year afterwards.

The fish house is hardly exotic, and the bus drivers and truckers from the fish house hardly comprise a group of exciting new friends, nice folks though they are, but I've gone back to college now, and I enjoy my courses.

I've had two raises in pay since I started at the fish house, and I feel pretty good about life. Looking back over the past three years since I began "La Dolce Vita," I must say things have improved, but I still have a long way to go, Baby!

A second pattern of development is the point-by-point pattern. This pattern is most frequently used in writing long papers, but it can be employed even in a short paragraph. In it, the writer establishes one or more points of comparison or contrast and then applies those points to each side of a subject.

A Trip Back Home
SHIRLEY STURKEY

Thesis: My hometown isn't the same any more.

   I. Main street
      A. Before I left
      B. After I returned

  II. Countryside
      A. Before I left
      B. After I returned

 III. Home
      A. Before I left
      B. After I returned

Lincoln is a small town forty-five miles east of Birmingham, Alabama, and 125 miles west of Atlanta, Georgia. It is right in the middle of nowhere. The population is small and everyone knows everyone else—at least, that's the way I remembered it. Lincoln was home for me for eighteen years. After living up north for seven years in a noisy, unfriendly city, I was looking forward to going back home to quiet, friendly, and familiar surroundings. Almost immediately upon my arrival, I discovered that the "familiar" surroundings were no longer familiar to me.

I was amazed to see how a small rural town like Lincoln could blossom into a city in less than seven years. The old wooden frame buildings that once lined Main Street had been torn down, and erected in their places were brick buildings. J. C. Penney's department store and an A&P supermarket were built where the combination doctor's office and drug store once stood. Lincoln's famous landmark, the courthouse—a huge building which housed the jail, bank, and post office—was torn down. In its place and halfway down two city blocks were three separate buildings equipped with modern facilities for these agencies. As I walked up and down Main Street admiring the beautiful surroundings, it suddenly dawned on me that I hadn't recognized any of the people I saw. They were all strangers to me. While I was caught in this thought, my father arrived. I had completely forgotten he was to pick me up at the bus stop.

The leisurely, scenic drive from town to my parents' house used to take fifteen minutes. On this day it took us thirty minutes because of road construction. A crew was busy mutilating the beautiful countryside to build project housing for the increasing population. As we drove on, my father told me that Lincoln began to change when the Talladega Speedway was built about one mile from our house. The Winston 500, an annual event, attracted thousands of people to see and participate with big-name drivers like Bobby Unser, A. J. Foyt, Cale Yarborough, and others. As each year went by, more and more people stayed on in Lincoln to live the simple life.

We finally arrived home. As we drove into the yard, I could see that my sister and her husband had added two more crumb-snatchers to their family and, from the looks of her, expected to add a third any day. My mother had gained several pounds, which seemed to enhance her beauty and grace. My father looked older than I remembered, but just as kind as ever. Our old dog, Pete, was gone, but the new puppy, Andy, wagged his tail in friendly greeting.

My trip back home was at first upsetting—so much had changed. Yet between hugs and tears of joy, I thought to myself that even though my family had changed visibly, the love, warmth, and closeness we felt for each other remained unchanged. My hometown had changed considerably, but my place in my family's heart hadn't changed at all.

The point-by-point pattern and the subject-by-subject pattern are most useful for stressing only the similarities between two items or only the differences between two items. Sometimes, however, you will want to give approximately equal weight to similarities *and* differences. To do that, you may combine the above patterns, as the outline and paper below illustrate.

A Tropical Christmas
SANDRA LYNN

Thesis: It is not necessary to spend the Christmas holidays at home to enjoy them.

    I. Similarities
        A. Waking up
        B. Opening the gifts
        C. Going to church
    II. Differences
        A. Weather
           1. In Olmsted Falls, Ohio
           2. In Ft. Myers Beach, Florida
        B. Christmas tree
           1. In Olmsted Falls, Ohio
           2. In Ft. Myers Beach, Florida
        C. Christmas dinner
           1. In Olmsted Falls, Ohio
           2. In Ft. Myers Beach, Florida

For the past few years, my family and I have spent the holiday season in Florida. Many foolish people actually presume that we miss being home on Christmas Day. Nothing could be farther from the truth. It is not necessary to be at home to enjoy Christmas. To be blunt and to risk seeming snooty, a rented condominium in Ft. Myers Beach, Florida, is the best place to be on Christmas Day.

As at home, the children are up with the first ray of light that filters through the drapes. They giggle and whisper just loudly enough not to aggravate my husband and me but loudly enough to wake us up for their big event of the day—the opening of the gifts.

As at home, the beautiful gift wrappings are demolished in record time each year. Before-and-after pictures are a definite necessity; otherwise nobody would believe I spent a full day adorning the gifts with handmade name tags and glittering Christmas paper that it takes the children only twenty minutes to destroy. No matter what part of the country it is in, a mess is a mess.

As at home, the opening of gifts is followed by a battle to convince the children they must get dressed for church and to give them the assurance that their toys will still be under the tree when we return. As at home, we struggle through the Christmas morning traffic, sit through a too-long sermon, concern ourselves more with keeping the children content than we do with concentrating on the minister's words, and struggle back through the traffic, just as we did up North. But, oh, the weather! The weather and the informal way of life make for important differences between Christmas in Olmsted Falls, Ohio, and Ft. Myers Beach, Florida.

At home in Olmsted Falls it is generally bleak and cold on December twenty-fifth. Granted, a snowfall of three inches or so can be a classic addition to this holiday, but more often than not, there are only dirty, gray slush and half-melted snowmen to greet me on Christmas Day. Instinctively, I take the warmest outfit I own out of the closet.

In Ft. Myers Beach there is the sound of the beckoning surf and the warmth of the golden morning sun to greet me. In front of the balcony some fluttering seagulls signal us with sharp, shrill tones in anticipation of their breakfast—scraps from our dinner of the previous evening. By the time the gifts are opened, the mess is cleared away, and a very simple breakfast is served, the temperature is just right for sunbathing. After church, I don my red and green bathing suit as the appropriate apparel for the rest of the day.

The Christmas tree we used to purchase in Olmsted Falls was always overpriced and misshapen. I had to place the daintily designed ornaments just so on the tree, and my husband cursed while he tried to string the lights. The children were yelled at for crinkling the tinsel and reprimanded unless each strand was placed perfectly on a branch.

One of the nicest experiences in Florida is the leisurely stroll that my husband and children take along the beach to search for the inimitable tree. When they spy a grove of Whispering Pines, my husband snaps off the plumpest branch. Upon their return, they place it in a milk carton now filled with wet sand. Each of us makes several ornaments with the stipulation that most materials must come from the beach, with the exception of thread, glue, glitter, and paint. To us the finished product is a marvelous Florida Christmas tree with color-coated shells chock-full of glitter dangling from the frail stems and a spiny, unbending starfish standing rigid at the top. We fondly dub our tree the "Charley Brown Christmas Tree."

At home, for several days before and on Christmas Day, I worked like a fool cleaning and cooking. I was compelled to invite my relatives for dinner. Every corner, drawer, and cupboard had to be immaculate. The turkey had to be stuffed and basted, the sweet potatoes candied, the gravy made as smooth as possible, and the pumpkin pie baked to perfection. The table had to be set elegantly with my best linen tablecloth and napkins, and the crystal and china had to be rewashed to sparkle. By the time we sat down to eat, I was too tired to lift my fork.

In Florida, it is every person for himself. It is my vacation, and my motto is, "God helps those who help themselves." Usually my husband will bring home some hamburgers after his golf game, or we may even splurge and purchase a bucket of Kentucky Fried Chicken. A real honest-to-goodness dish is a profane word to me, and a stiff penalty is invoked on anyone not using a paper plate. In the evening, I sip on something tropical and watch the sun set over Sanibel Island.

There is only one disadvantage to a Christmas season in Florida and that is its coming to an end.

In the next paper, the writer speculates on a current fashion by giving equal weight to similarities and differences.

What's in a Name?
PAMELA FISHER

Thesis: The current fashion of giving children Biblical names represents a desire to escape the complexities of modern life.

    I. Similarities
        A. Biblical names today
        B. Biblical names in grandmother's day
    II. Differences
        A. Reason for Biblical names in grandmother's day
        B. Reason for Biblical names today

   The other day I received an announcement of the birth of Joshua Seth,
the second son of Rick and Debbie Newton. Their first son, Aaron,
Debbie's letter told me, was pleased with his baby brother. A few months
before Joshua Seth's birth, my friends Barb and Bob Grant had named their
first child Leah. Aaron, Leah, Joshua, Seth—all Biblical names. I began to
think about the number of Sarahs and Rachels, Daniels and Benjamins
who have joined the human race in the past few years. Biblical names
seem to be in fashion.
   They were fashionable, too, in my grandmother's day. Her children—
Joseph, Abigail, Jacob, Gideon, Amos, Ezekiel, and Esther—all owed their
names to my grandmother's careful study of the Bible. My grandmother,
whose name was Sarah, did not differ from most parents of her day. Go
back two or three generations in almost any family and you'll find a Josiah
or an Adam or even a Moses or a Hepzibah.
   Now we're returning to the Biblical name.
   The people of my grandmother's generation turned to the Bible for
names because the Bible was important in their daily lives. It was as
natural for them to give their children Biblical names as it was to go to
church on Sunday. Today, however, a generation of Ricks, Debbies, Marks,
Todds, Tracies, Kathies, and Lisas—a generation that has looked into the
Bible, if at all, only for its famous examples of good literature; a generation
that has rarely seen the inside of a church—turns to the Bible when naming its children.
   Does this return to Biblical names signal a return to old-time religion? I
think not. My guess is that the Marks and Ricks and Lisas—these new
parents—have turned to Biblical names as they have turned to antiques, to
"organic" foods, to natural childbirth, even to farming. Distressed by the
dangers and complexities of modern life, they seek a past they believe was
simpler and better. The names are merely a part of that past.

   The comparison-contrast paper is especially effective as a means
of writing about literature because when one literary work is com-

pared with another, the comparison often provides fresh insights into both works. If, for example, you read the following two poems separately, you would probably not derive the same meaning from them as did the student who compared them in "Two Kinds of Love."

SONNET 29

When, in disgrace with Fortune and men's eyes,
I all alone beweep my outcast state,
And trouble deaf heaven with my bootless[1] cries,
And look upon myself and curse my fate,
Wishing me like to one more rich in hope,
Featured like him, like him with friends possessed,
Desiring this man's art, and that man's scope,
With what I most enjoy contented least;
Yet in these thoughts myself almost despising,
Haply[2] I think on thee, and then my state,
Like to the lark at break of day arising
From sullen earth, sings hymns at heaven's gate;
   For thy sweet love remembered such wealth brings
   That then I scorn to change my state with kings.

—*William Shakespeare*

---

1. Futile.
2. By chance.

SONNET 130

My mistress' eyes are nothing like the sun;
Coral is far more red than her lips' red;
If snow be white, why then her breasts are dun;
If hairs be wires, black wires grow on her head.
I have seen roses damasked, red and white,
But no such roses see I in her cheeks;
And in some perfumes is there more delight
Than in the breath that from my mistress reeks.
I love to hear her speak; yet well I know
That music hath a far more pleasing sound.
I grant I never saw a goddess go:
My mistress, when she walks, treads on the ground.
   And yet, by heaven, I think my love as rare
   As any she belied with false compare.

—*William Shakespeare*

Two Kinds of Love
JULIE OLIVERA

Shakespeare's Sonnet 29, "When, in disgrace with Fortune and men's eyes," and Sonnet 130, "My mistress' eyes are nothing like the sun," both strike me as very fine love poems. Both offer great tributes to the loved person. Love comes in all shapes and sizes, however, and I think the feelings expressed in "My mistress' eyes" are more realistic and more trustworthy. I'd rather be the woman that poem was written for than the other woman.

"When, in disgrace" begins by describing a situation in which the poet feels totally depressed. Totally is no exaggeration. He hasn't had any good "fortune," people look down on him, he is jealous of other people, heaven is "deaf" to his prayers. He has little or no hope. He has few, if any, friends. The things he enjoys most mean nothing to him. He even comes close to hating himself. The second part of the poem very beautifully says that even in a foul mood like that if he just happens to "think on thee," he cheers up. He realizes, in fact, that he is one of the luckiest men in the world. He has her love, and her love makes him richer than a king in all that really matters. "For thy sweet love remembered such wealth brings / That then I scorn to change my state with kings."

Well, I'd be flattered, of course, and I might even wipe away a tear, but I'm not sure how much I would trust him. Love is a great inspiration to fall back on if one's life starts going to pieces, but it also has to exist on a day-to-day basis, through all the normal wear and tear, through all the boredom and nothing-special times. If I save a drowning person, he might say with complete sincerity that he loves and adores me, but that is no real basis for a lifelong relationship. If it takes bad times to make the poet realize how much he loves his lady, what starts happening to the love when times aren't so bad?

In "My mistress' eyes," the poet is not depressed, but confident and cheerful. He is in love just as much, but this time with a real person, not a goddess or miracle worker. If anything bothers him, it is people who have to depend on illusions and lies to make their loves seem worthwhile. He still wouldn't trade places with a king, yet he knows and gladly accepts that other women are better-looking, and that they have nicer voices, and even that they have sweeter-smelling breath. He doesn't have to turn his lady into something she isn't in order to love her.

I think this expression of love is by far the more valid one. People want to be loved for what they are, imperfections and all. If someone says he loves me, I want to feel he loves me rather than an unrealistic mental image he has of me. If all he loves is the image, the love is an insult. In direct contrast, the poet in "When, in disgrace" seems to love the woman for what she does for him, while the poet in "My mistress' eyes" loves her simply for what she is.

Between the stickiness and sweetness of the first poem and the realism of the second, I have to choose the second. Both poems are fine, but one is written for rare moods, and the other is written for a lifetime.

Questions for Writing and Discussion

1. The writer depends on the poems to communicate her own feelings about love. Are her summaries of each poem accurate and complete?
2. What pattern of development does the writer use? Can you outline the paper?
3. Has the writer produced a unified comparison-and-contrast paper, or has she written two separate essays on two separate poems?
4. Do the poems strike you as presenting two opposing attitudes? The writer assumes they were written about two different women. Could they have been written about the same woman?

Readings

The groups of readings that follow were selected to provide you with subject matter for comparison and contrast papers of your own. Questions and possible writing assignments appear at the end of each group.

THE BATTLE OF THE SEXES:
Two Stories for Comparison and Contrast

James Thurber
A COUPLE OF HAMBURGERS

It had been raining for a long time, a slow, cold rain falling out of iron-colored clouds. They had been driving since morning and they still had a hundred and thirty miles to go. It was about three o'clock in the afternoon. "I'm getting hungry," she said. He took his eyes off the wet, winding road for a fraction of a second and said, "We'll stop at a dog-wagon." She shifted her position irritably. "I wish you wouldn't call them *dog*-wagons," she said. He pressed the klaxon button and went around a slow car. "That's what they are," he said. "Dog-wagons." She waited a few seconds. "*Decent* people call them *diners*," she told him, and added, "Even if you call them diners, I don't like them." He speeded up a hill. "They have better stuff than most restaurants," he said. "Anyway, I want to get home before dark and it takes too long in a restaurant. We can stay our stomachs with a couple hamburgers." She lighted a cigarette and he asked her to light one for him. She lighted one deliberately and handed it to him. "I wish you wouldn't say 'stay our stomachs,'" she said. "You know I hate that. It's like 'sticking to your ribs.' You say that all the time." He grinned. "Good old American expressions, both of them," he said. "Like sow belly. Old pioneer term, sow belly." She sniffed. "My ancestors were pioneers, too. You don't have to be vulgar just because you were a pioneer." "Your ancestors never got as far west as mine did," he said. "The real pioneers travelled on their sow belly and got somewhere." He laughed loudly at that. She looked out at the wet trees and signs and telephone poles going by. They drove on for several miles without a word; he kept chortling every now and then.

"What's that funny sound?" she asked, suddenly. It invariably made him angry when she heard a funny sound. "What funny sound?" he demanded. "You're always hearing funny sounds." She laughed briefly. "That's what you said when the bearing burned out," she reminded him. "You'd never have noticed it if it hadn't been for me." "I noticed it, all right," he said. "Yes," she said. "When it was too late." She enjoyed bringing up the subject of the burned-out bearing whenever he got to chortling. "It was too late when *you* noticed it, as far as that goes," he said. Then, after a pause, "Well, what does it sound like *this* time? All engines make a noise running, you know." "I know all about that," she answered. "It sounds like—it sounds like a lot of safety pins being jiggled around in a tumbler." He snorted. "That's your imagination. Nothing gets the matter with a car that sounds like a lot of safety pins. I happen to know that." She tossed away her cigarette. "Oh, sure," she said. "You always happen to know everything." They drove on in silence.

"I want to stop somewhere and get something to *eat!*" she said loudly. "All right, all right!" he said. "I been watching for a dog-wagon, haven't I? There hasn't been any. I can't make you a dog-wagon." The wind blew rain in on her and she put up the window on her side all the way. "I won't stop at just any old diner," she said. "I won't stop unless it's a cute one." He looked around at her. "Unless it's a *what* one?" he shouted. "You know what I mean," she said. "I mean a decent, clean one where they don't slosh things at you. I hate to have a lot of milky coffee sloshed at me." "All right," he said. "We'll find a cute one, then. You pick it out. I wouldn't know. I might find one that was cunning but not cute." That struck him as funny and he began to chortle again. "Oh, shut up," she said.

Five miles farther along they came to a place called Sam's Diner. "Here's one," he said, slowing down. She looked it over. "I don't want to stop there," she said. "I don't like the ones that have nicknames." He brought the car to a stop at one side of the road. "Just what's the matter with the ones that have nicknames?" he asked with edgy, mock interest. "They're always Greek ones," she told him. "They're always Greek ones," he repeated after her. He set his teeth firmly together and started up again. After a time, "Good old Sam, the Greek," he said, in a singsong. "Good old Connecticut Sam Beardsley, the Greek." "You didn't see his name," she snapped. "Winthrop, then," he said. "Old Samuel Cabot Winthrop, the Greek dog-wagon man." He was getting hungry.

On the outskirts of the next town she said, as he slowed down, "It looks like a factory kind of town." He knew that she meant she wouldn't stop there. He drove on through the place. She lighted a cigarette as they pulled out into the open again. He slowed down and lighted a cigarette for himself. "Factory kind of town than *I* am!" he snarled. It was ten miles before they came to another town. "Torrington," he growled. "Happen to know there's a dog-wagon here because I stopped in it once with Bob Combs. Damn cute place, too, if you ask me." "I'm not asking you anything," she said, coldly. "You think you're *so* funny. I think I know the one you mean," she said, after a moment. "It's right in the town and it sits at an angle from the road. They're never so good, for some reason." He glared at her and almost ran up against the curb. "What the hell do you mean 'sits at an angle from the road'?" he cried. He was very hungry now. "Well, it isn't silly," she said, calmly. "I've noticed the ones that sit at an angle. They're cheaper, because they fitted them into funny little pieces of ground. The big ones parallel to the road are the best." He drove right through Torrington, his lips compressed. "Angle from the road, for God's sake!" he snarled, finally. She was looking out her window.

On the outskirts of the next town there was a diner called The Elite Diner. "This looks—" she began. "I see it, I see it!" he said. "It doesn't happen to look any cuter to me than any goddam—" She cut him off. "Don't be such a sorehead, for Lord's sake," she said. He pulled up and stopped beside the diner, and turned on her. "Listen," he said, grittingly, "I'm going to put down a couple of hamburgers in this place even if there isn't one single inch of chintz or cretonne in the whole—" "Oh, be still," she said. "You're just hungry and mean like a child. Eat your old hamburgers, what do I care?" Inside the place they sat down on stools and the counterman walked over to them, wiping up the counter top with a cloth as he did so. "What'll it be, folks?" he said. "Bad day, ain't it? Except for ducks." "I'll have a couple of—" began the husband, but his wife cut in. "I just want a pack of cigarettes," she said. He turned around slowly on his stool and stared at her as she put a dime and a nickel in the cigarette machine and ejected a package of Lucky Strikes. He turned to the counterman again. "I want a couple of hamburgers," he said. "With mustard and lots of onion. *Lots* of onion!" She hated onions. "I'll wait for you in the car," she said. He didn't answer and she went out.

He finished his hamburgers and his coffee slowly. It was terrible coffee. Then he went out to the car and got in and drove off, slowly humming "Who's Afraid of the Big Bad Wolf?" After a mile or so, "Well," he said, "what was the matter with the Elite Diner, milady?" "Didn't you *see* that cloth the man was wiping the counter with?" she demanded. "Ugh!" She shuddered. "I didn't happen to want to eat any of the counter," he said. He laughed at that comeback. "You didn't even notice it," she said. "You never notice anything. It was filthy." "I noticed they had some damn fine coffee in there," he said. "It was swell." He knew she loved good coffee. He began to hum his tune again; then he whistled it; then he began to sing it. She did not show her annoyance, but she knew that he knew she was annoyed. "Will you be kind enough to tell me what time it is?" she asked. "Big *bad* wolf, big *bad* wolf—five minutes o' five—tum-dee-*doo*-dee-dum-m-m." She settled back in her seat and took a cigarette from her case and tapped it on the case. "I'll wait till we get home," she said. "If you'll be kind enough to speed up a little." He drove on at the same speed. After a time he gave up the "Big Bad Wolf" and there was deep silence for two miles. Then suddenly he began to sing, very loudly, *H*-A-double-R-*I*-G-A-N *spells Harrr*-i-gan—" She gritted her teeth. She hated that worse than any of his songs except "Barney Google." He would go on to "Barney Google" pretty soon, she knew. Suddenly she leaned slightly forward. The straight line of her lips began to curve up ever so slightly. She heard the safety pins in the tumbler again. Only now they were louder, more insistent, ominous. He was singing too loud to hear them. "Is a *name* that *shame* has never been con-*nec*-ted with—*Harrr*-i-gan, that's *me!*" She relaxed against the back of the seat content to wait.

Mary Wilkins Freeman
THE REVOLT OF "MOTHER"

"Father!"

"What is it?"

"What are them men diggin' over there in the field for?"

There was a sudden dropping and enlarging of the lower part of the old man's face, as if some heavy weight had settled therein; he shut his mouth tight, and went on harnessing the great bay mare. He hustled the collar on to her neck with a jerk.

"Father!"

The old man slapped the saddle upon the mare's back.

"Look here, father, I want to know what them men are diggin' over in the field for, an' I'm goin' to know."

"I wish you'd go into the house, mother, an' 'tend to your own affairs," the old man said then. He ran his words together, and his speech was almost as inarticulate as a growl.

But the woman understood; it was her most native tongue.

"I ain't goin' into the house till you tell me what them men are doin' over there in the field," said she.

Then she stood waiting. She was a small woman, short and straight-waisted like a child in her brown cotton gown. Her forehead was mild and benevolent between the smooth curves of gray hair; there were meek downward lines about her nose and mouth; but her eyes, fixed upon the old man, looked as if the meekness had been the result of her own will, never of the will of another.

They were in the barn, standing before the wide open doors. The spring air, full of the smell of growing grass and unseen blossoms, came in their faces. The deep yard in front was littered with farm wagons and piles of wood; on the edges, close to the fence and the house, the grass was a vivid green, and there were some dandelions.

The old man glanced doggedly at his wife as he tightened the last buckles on the harness. She looked as immovable to him as one of the rocks in his pasture-land, bound to the earth with generations of blackberry vines. He slapped the reins over the horse, and started forth from the barn.

"*Father!*" said she.

The old man pulled up. "What is it?"

"I want to know what them men are diggin' over there in that field for."

"They're diggin' a cellar, I s'pose, if you've got to know."

"A cellar for what?"

"A barn."

"A barn? You ain't goin' to build a barn over there where we was goin' to have a house, father?"

The old man said not another word. He hurried the horse into the farm wagon, and clattered out of the yard, jouncing as sturdily on his seat as a boy.

The woman stood a moment looking after him, then she went out of the barn across a corner of the yard to the house. The house, standing at right angles with the great barn and a long reach of sheds and out-buildings, was infinitesimal compared with them. It was scarcely as commodious for people as the little boxes under the barn eaves were for doves.

A pretty girl's face, pink and delicate as a flower, was looking out of one of the house windows. She was watching three men who were digging over in the field which bounded the yard near the road line. She turned quietly when the woman entered.

"What are they digging for, mother?" said she. "Did he tell you?"

"They're diggin' for—a cellar for a new barn."

"Oh, mother, he ain't going to build another barn?"

"That's what he says."

A boy stood before the kitchen glass combing his hair. He combed slowly and painstakingly, arranging his brown hair in a smooth hillock over his forehead. He did not seem to pay any attention to the conversation.

"Sammy, did you know father was going to build a new barn?" asked the girl.

The boy combed assiduously.

"Sammy!"

He turned, and showed a face like his father's under his smooth crest of hair. "Yes, I s'pose I did," he said, reluctantly.

"How long have you known it?" asked his mother.

"'Bout three months, I guess."

"Why didn't you tell of it?"

"Didn't think 'twould do no good."

"I don't see what father wants another barn for," said the girl, in her sweet, slow voice. She turned again to the window, and stared out at the digging men in the field. Her tender, sweet face was full of a gentle distress. Her forehead was as bald and innocent as a baby's, with the light hair strained back from it in a row of curl-papers. She was quite large, but her soft curves did not look as if they covered muscles.

Her mother looked sternly at the boy. "Is he goin' to buy more cows?" said she.

The boy did not reply; he was tying his shoes.

"Sammy, I want you to tell me if he's goin' to buy more cows."

"I s'pose he is."

"How many?"

"Four, I guess."

His mother said nothing more. She went into the pantry, and there was a clatter of dishes. The boy got his cap from a nail behind the door, took an old arithmetic from the shelf, and started for school. He was lightly built, but clumsy. He went out of the yard with a curious spring in the hips, that made his loose home-made jacket tilt up in the rear.

The girl went to the sink, and began to wash the dishes that were piled up there. Her mother came promptly out of the pantry, and shoved her aside. "You wipe 'em," said she; "I'll wash. There's a good many this mornin'."

The mother plunged her hands vigorously into the water, the girl wiped the plates slowly and dreamily. "Mother," said she, "don't you think it's too bad father's going to build that new barn, much as we need a decent house to live in?"

Her mother scrubbed a dish fiercely. "You ain't found out yet we're women-folks, Nanny Penn," said she. "You ain't seen enough of men-folks yet to. One of these days you'll find it out, an' then you'll know that we know only what men-folks think we do, so far as any use of it goes, an' how we'd ought to reckon men-folks in with Providence, an' not complain of what they do any more than we do of the weather."

"I don't care; I don't believe George is anything like that, anyhow," said Nanny. Her delicate face flushed pink, her lips pouted softly, as if she were going to cry.

"You wait an' see. I guess George Eastman ain't no better than other men. You hadn't ought to judge father, though. He can't help it, 'cause he don't look at things jest the way we do. An' we've been pretty comfortable here, after all. The roof don't leak—ain't never but once—that's one thing. Father's kept it shingled right up."

"I do wish we had a parlor."

"I guess it won't hurt George Eastman any to come to see you in a nice clean kitchen. I guess a good many girls don't have as good a place as this. Nobody's ever heard me complain."

"I ain't complained either, mother."

"Well, I don't think you'd better, a good father an' a good home as you've got. S'pose your father made you go out an' work for your livin'? Lots of girls have to that ain't no stronger an' better able to than you be."

Sarah Penn washed the frying-pan with a conclusive air. She scrubbed the outside of it as faithfully as the inside. She was a masterly keeper of her box of a house. Her one living-room never seemed to have in it any of the dust which the friction of life with inanimate matter produces. She swept, and there seemed to be no dirt to go before the broom; she cleaned, and one could see no difference. She was like an artist so perfect that he has apparently no art. To-day she got out a mixing bowl and a board, and rolled some pies, and there was no more flour upon her than upon her daughter who was doing finer work. Nanny was to be married in the fall, and she was sewing on some white cambric and embroidery. She sewed industriously while her mother cooked, her soft milk-white hands and wrists showed whiter than her delicate work.

"We must have the stove moved out in the shed before long," said Mrs. Penn. "Talk about not havin' things, it's been a real blessin' to be able to put a stove up in that shed in hot weather. Father did one good thing when he fixed that stove-pipe out there."

Sarah Penn's face as she rolled her pies had that expression of meek vigor which might have characterized one of the New Testament saints. She was making mince-pies. Her husband, Adoniram Penn, liked them better than any other kind. She baked twice a week. Adoniram often liked a piece of pie between meals. She hurried this morning. It had been later than usual when she began, and she wanted to have a pie baked for dinner. However deep a resentment she might be forced to hold against her husband, she would never fail in sedulous attention to his wants.

Nobility of character manifests itself at loop-holes when it is not provided with large doors. Sarah Penn's showed itself to-day in flaky dishes of pastry. So she made the pies faithfully, while across the table she could see, when she glanced up from her work, the sight that rankled in her patient and steadfast soul—the digging of the cellar of the new barn in the place where Adoniram forty years ago had promised her their new house should stand.

The pies were done for dinner. Adoniram and Sammy were home a few minutes after twelve o'clock. The dinner was eaten with serious haste. There was never much conversation at the table in the Penn family. Adoniram asked a blessing, and they ate promptly, then rose up and went about their work.

Sammy went back to school, taking soft sly lopes out of the yard like a rabbit. He wanted a game of marbles before school, and feared his father would give him some chores to do. Adoniram hastened to the door and called after him, but he was out of sight.

"I don't see what you let him go for, mother," said he. "I wanted him to help me unload that wood."

Adoniram went to work out in the yard unloading wood from the wagon. Sarah put away the dinner dishes, while Nanny took down her curl-papers and changed her dress. She was going down to the store to buy some more embroidery and thread.

When Nanny was gone, Mrs. Penn went to the door. "Father!" she called.

"Well, what is it!"

"I want to see you jest a minute, father."

"I can't leave this wood nohow. I've got to git it unloaded an' go for a load of gravel afore two o'clock. Sammy had ought to helped me. You hadn't ought to let him go to school so early."

"I want to see you jest a minute."

"I tell ye I can't, nohow, mother."

"Father, you come here." Sarah Penn stood in the door like a queen; she held her head as if it bore a crown; there was that patience which makes authority royal in her voice. Adoniram went.

Mrs. Penn led the way into the kitchen, and pointed to a chair. "Sit down, father," said she; "I've got somethin' I want to say to you."

He sat down heavily; his face was quite stolid, but he looked at her with restive eyes. "Well, what is it, mother?"

"I want to know what you're buildin' that new barn for, father?"

"I ain't got nothin' to say about it."

"It can't be you think you need another barn?"

"I tell ye I ain't got nothin' to say about it, mother; an' I ain't goin' to say nothin'."

"Be you goin' to buy more cows?"

Adoniram did not reply; he shut his mouth tight.

"I know you be, as well as I want to. Now, father, look here"—Sarah Penn had not sat down; she stood before her husband in the humble fashion of a Scripture woman—"I'm goin' to talk real plain to you; I never have sence I married you, but I'm goin' to now. I ain't never complained, an' I ain't goin' to complain now, but I'm goin' to talk plain. You see this room here, father; you look at it well. You see there ain't no carpet on the floor, an' you see the paper is all dirty, an' droppin' off the walls. We ain't had no new paper on it for ten year, an' then I put it on myself, an' it didn't cost but ninepence a roll. You see this room, father; it's all the one I've had to work in an' eat in an' sit in sence we was married. There ain't another woman in the whole town whose husband ain't got half the means you have but what's got better. It's all the room Nanny's got to have her company in; an' there ain't one of her mates but what's got better, an' their fathers not so able as hers is. It's all the room she'll have to be married in. What would you have thought, father, if we had had our weddin' in a room no better than this? I was married in my mother's parlor, with a carpet on the floor, an' stuffed furniture, an' a mahogany card-table. An' this is all the room my daughter will have to be married in. Look here, father!"

Sarah Penn went across the room as though it were a tragic stage. She flung open a door and disclosed a tiny bedroom, only large enough for a bed and bureau, with a path between. "There, father," said she—"there's all the room I've had to sleep in forty year. All my children were born there—the two that died, an' the two that's livin'. I was sick with a fever there."

She stepped to another door and opened it. It led into the small, ill-lighted pantry. "Here," said she, "is all the buttery I've got—every place I've got for my dishes, to set away my victuals in, an' to keep my milk-pans in. Father, I've been takin' care of the milk of six cows in this place, an' now you're goin' to build a new barn, an' keep more cows, an' give me more to do in it."

She threw open another door. A narrow crooked flight of stairs wound upward from it. "There, father," said she, "I want you to look at the stairs that go up to them two unfinished chambers that are all the places our son an' daughter have had to sleep in all their lives. There ain't a prettier girl in town nor a more ladylike one than Nanny, an' that's the place she has to sleep in. It ain't so good as your horse's stall; it ain't so warm an' tight."

Sarah Penn went back and stood before her husband. "Now, father," said she, "I want to know if you think you're doin' right an' accordin' to what you profess. Here, when we was married, forty year ago, you promised me faithful that we should have a new house built in that lot over in the field before the year was out. You said you had money enough, an' you wouldn't ask me to live in no such place as this. It is forty year now, an' you've been makin' more money, an' I've been savin' of it for you ever since, an' you ain't built no house yet. You've built sheds an' cow-houses an' one new barn, an' now you're goin' to build another. Father, I want to know if you think it's right. You're lodgin' your dumb beasts better than you are your own flesh an' blood. I want to know if you think it's right."

"I ain't got nothin' to say."

"You can't say nothin' without ownin' it ain't right, father. An' there's another thing—I ain't complained; I've got along forty year, an' I s'pose I should forty more, if it wa'n't for that—if we don't have another house. Nanny she can't live with us after she's married. She'll have to go somewheres else to live away from us, an' it don't seem as if I could have it so, noways, father. She wa'n't ever strong. She's got considerable color, but there wa'n't never any backbone to her. I've always took the heft of everything off her, an' she ain't fit to keep house an' do everything herself. She'll be all worn out inside of a year. Think of her doin' all the washin' an' ironin' an' bakin' with them soft white hands an' arms, an' sweepin'! I can't have it so, noways, father."

Mrs. Penn's face was burning; her mild eyes gleamed. She had pleaded her little cause like a Webster; she had ranged from severity to pathos; but her opponent employed that obstinate silence which makes eloquence futile with mocking echoes. Adoniram arose clumsily.

"Father, ain't you got nothin' to say?" said Mrs. Penn.

"I've got to go off after that load of gravel. I can't stan' here talkin' all day."

"Father, won't you think it over, an' have a house built there instead of a barn?"

"I ain't got nothin' to say."

Adoniram shuffled out. Mrs. Penn went into her bedroom. When she came out, her eyes were red. She had a roll of unbleached cotton cloth. She spread it out on the kitchen table, and began cutting out some shirts for her husband. The men over in the field had a team to help them this afternoon; she could hear their halloos. She had a scanty pattern for the shirts; she had to plan and piece the sleeves.

Nanny came home with her embroidery, and sat down with her needlework. She had taken down her curl-papers, and there was a soft roll of fair hair like an aureole over her forehead; her face was as delicately fine and clear as porcelain. Suddenly she looked up, and the tender red flamed all over her face and neck. "Mother," said she.

"What say?"

"I've been thinking—I don't see how we're goin' to have any—wedding in this room. I'd be ashamed to have his folks come if we didn't have anybody else."

"Mebbe we can have some new paper before then; I can put it on. I guess you won't have no call to be ashamed of your belongin's."

"We might have the wedding in the new barn," said Nanny, with gentle pettishness. "Why, mother, what makes you look so?"

Mrs. Penn had started, and was staring at her with a curious expression. She turned again to her work, and spread out a pattern carefully on the cloth. "Nothin'," said she.

Presently Adoniram clattered out of the yard in his two-wheeled dump cart, standing as proudly upright as a Roman charioteer. Mrs. Penn opened the door and stood there a minute looking out; the halloos of the men sounded louder.

It seemed to her all through the spring months that she heard nothing but the halloos and the noises of saws and hammers. The new barn grew fast. It was a fine edifice for this little village. Men came on pleasant Sundays, in their meeting suits and clean shirt bosoms, and stood around it admiringly. Mrs. Penn did not speak of it, and Adoniram did not mention it to her, although sometimes, upon a return from inspecting it, he bore himself with injured dignity.

"It's a strange thing how your mother feels about the new barn," he said, confidentially, to Sammy one day.

Sammy only grunted after an odd fashion for a boy; he had learned it from his father.

The barn was all completed ready for use by the third week in July. Adoniram had planned to move his stock in on Wednesday; on Tuesday he received a letter which changed his plans. He came in with it early in the morning. "Sammy's been to the post-office," said he, "an' I've got a letter from Hiram." Hiram was Mrs. Penn's brother, who lived in Vermont.

"Well," said Mrs. Penn, "what does he say about the folks?"

"I guess they're all right. He says he thinks if I come up country right off there's a chance to buy jest the kind of a horse I want." He stared reflectively out of the window at the new barn.

Mrs. Penn was making pies. She went on clapping the rolling-pin into the crust, although she was very pale, and her heart beat loudly.

"I dun' know but what I'd better go," said Adoniram. "I hate to go off jest now, right in the midst of hayin', but the ten-acre lot's cut, an' I guess Rufus an' the others can git along without me three or four days. I can't get a horse around here to suit me, nohow, an' I've got to have another for all that wood-haulin' in the fall. I told Hiram to watch out, an' if he got wind of a good horse to let me know. I guess I'd better go."

"I'll get out your clean shirt an' collar," said Mrs. Penn calmly.

She laid out Adoniram's Sunday suit and his clean clothes on the bed in the little bedroom. She got his shaving-water and razor ready. At last she buttoned on his collar and fastened his black cravat.

Adoniram never wore his collar and cravat except on extra occasions. He held his head high, with a rasped dignity. When he was all ready, with his coat and hat brushed, and a lunch of pie and cheese in a paper bag, he hesitated on the threshold of the door. He looked at his wife, and his manner was defiantly apologetic. "If them cows come to-day, Sammy can drive 'em into the new barn," said he; "an' when they bring the hay up, they can pitch it in there."

"Well," replied Mrs. Penn.

Adoniram set his shaven face ahead and started. When he had cleared the door-step, he turned and looked back with a kind of nervous solemnity. "I shall be back by Saturday if nothin' happens," said he.

"Do be careful, father," returned his wife.

She stood in the door with Nanny at her elbow and watched him out of sight. Her eyes had a strange, doubtful expression in them; her peaceful forehead was contracted. She went in, and about her baking again. Nanny sat sewing. Her wedding-day was drawing nearer, and she was getting pale and thin with her steady sewing. Her mother kept glancing at her.

"Have you got that pain in your side this mornin'?" she asked.

"A little."

Mrs. Penn's face, as she worked, changed, her perplexed forehead smoothed, her eyes were steady, her lips firmly set. She formed a maxim for herself, although incoherently with her unlettered thoughts. "Unsolicited opportunities are the guide-posts of the Lord to the new roads of life," she repeated in effect, and she made up her mind to her course of action.

"S'posin' I *had* wrote to Hiram," she muttered once, when she was in the pantry—"s'posin' I had wrote, an' asked him if he knew of any horse? But I didn't, an' father's goin' wa'n't none of my doin'. It looks like a providence." Her voice rang out quite loud at the last.

"What you talkin' about, mother?" called Nanny.

"Nothin'."

Mrs. Penn hurried her baking; at eleven o'clock it was all done. The load of hay from the west field came slowly down the cart track, and drew up at the new barn. Mrs. Penn ran out. "Stop!" she screamed—"stop!"

The men stopped and looked; Sammy upreared from the top of the load, and stared at his mother.

"Stop!" she cried out again. "Don't you put the hay in that barn; put it in the old one."

"Why, he said to put it in here," returned one of the haymakers, wonderingly. He was a young man, a neighbor's son, whom Adoniram hired by the year to help on the farm.

"Don't you put the hay in the new barn; there's room enough in the old one, ain't there?" said Mrs. Penn.

"Room enough," returned the hired man, in his thick, rustic tones. "Didn't need the new barn, nohow, far as room's concerned. Well, I s'pose he changed his mind." He took hold of the horses' bridles.

Mrs. Penn went back to the house. Soon the kitchen windows were darkened, and a fragrance like warm honey came into the room.

Nanny laid down her work. "I thought father wanted them to put the hay into the new barn?" she said, wonderingly.

"It's all right," replied her mother.

Sammy slid down from the load of hay, and came in to see if dinner was ready.

"I ain't goin' to get a regular dinner to-day, as long as father's gone," said his mother. "I've let the fire go out. You can have some bread an' milk an' pie. I thought we could get along." She set out some bowls of milk, some bread, and a pie on the kitchen table. "You'd better eat your dinner now," said she. "You might jest as well get through with it. I want you to help me afterward."

Nanny and Sammy stared at each other. There was something strange in their mother's manner. Mrs. Penn did not eat anything herself. She went into the pantry, and they heard her moving dishes while they ate. Presently she came out with a pile of plates. She got the clothes-basket out of the shed, and packed them in it. Nanny and Sammy watched. She brought out cups and saucers, and put them in with the plates.

"What you goin' to do, mother?" inquired Nanny, in a timid voice. A sense of something unusual made her tremble, as if it were a ghost. Sammy rolled his eyes over his pie.

"You'll see what I'm goin' to do," replied Mrs. Penn.

"If you're through, Nanny, I want you to go up-stairs an' pack up your things; an' I want you, Sammy, to help me take down the bed in the bedroom."

"Oh mother, what for?" gasped Nanny.

"You'll see."

During the next few hours a feat was performed by this simple, pious New England mother which was equal in its way to Wolfe's storming of the Heights of Abraham. It took no more genius and audacity of bravery for Wolfe to cheer his wondering soldiers up those steep precipices, under the sleeping eyes of the enemy, than for Sarah Penn, at the head of her children, to move all their little household goods into the new barn while her husband was away.

Nanny and Sammy followed their mother's instructions without a murmur; indeed, they were overawed. There is a certain uncanny and superhuman quality about all such purely original undertakings as their mother's was to them. Nanny went back and forth with her light loads, and Sammy tugged with sober energy.

At five o'clock in the afternoon the little house in which the Penns had lived for forty years had emptied itself into the new barn.

Every builder builds somewhat for unknown purposes, and is in a measure a prophet. The architect of Adoniram Penn's barn, while he designed it for the comfort of four-footed animals, had planned better than he knew for the comfort of humans. Sarah Penn saw at a glance its possibilities. Those great box-stalls, with quilts hung before them, would make better bedrooms than the one she had occupied for forty years, and there was a tight carriage-room. The harness-room, with its chimney and shelves, would make a kitchen of her dreams. The great middle space would make a parlor, by-and-by, fit for a palace. Up stairs there was as much room as down. With partitions and windows, what a house would there be! Sarah looked at the row of stanchions before the allotted space for cows, and reflected that she would have her front entry there.

At six o'clock the stove was up in the harness-room, the kettle was boiling, and the table set for tea. It looked almost as home-like as the abandoned house across the yard had ever done. The young hired man milked, and Sarah directed him calmly to bring the milk to the new barn. He came gaping, dropping little blots of foam from the brimming pails on the grass. Before the next morning he had spread the story of Adoniram Penn's wife moving into the new barn all over the little village. Men assembled in the store and talked it over, women with shawls over their heads scuttled into each other's houses before their work was done. Any deviation from the ordinary course of life in this quiet town was enough to stop all progress in it. Everybody paused to look at the staid, independent figure on the side track. There was a difference of opinion with regard to her. Some held her to be insane; some, of a lawless and rebellious spirit.

Friday the minister went to see her. It was in the forenoon, and she was at the barn door shelling pease for dinner. She looked up and returned his salutation with dignity, then she went on with her work. She did not invite him in. The saintly expression of her face remained fixed, but there was an angry flush over it.

The minister stood awkwardly before her, and talked. She handled the pease as if they were bullets. At last she looked up, and her eyes showed the spirit that her meek front had covered for a lifetime.

"There ain't no use talkin', Mr. Hersey," said she. "I've thought it all over an' over, an' I believe I'm doin' what's right. I've made it the subject of prayer, an' it's betwixt me an' the Lord an' Adoniram. There ain't no call for nobody else to worry about it."

"Well, of course, if you have brought it to the Lord in prayer, and feel satisfied that you are doing right, Mrs. Penn," said the minister, helplessly. His thin gray-bearded face was pathetic. He was a sickly man; his youthful confidence had cooled; he had to scourge himself up to some of his pastoral duties as relentlessly as a Catholic ascetic, and then he was prostrated by the smart.

"I think it's right jest as much as I think it was right for our forefathers to come over from the old country 'cause they didn't have what belonged to 'em," said Mrs. Penn. She arose. The barn threshold might have been Plymouth Rock from her bearing. "I don't doubt you mean well, Mr. Hersey," said she, "but there are things people hadn't ought to interfere with. I've been a member of the church for over forty year. I've got my own mind an' my own feet, an' I'm goin' to think my own thoughts an' go my own ways, an' nobody but the Lord is goin' to dictate to me unless I've a mind to have him. Won't you come in an' set down? How is Mis' Hersey?"

"She is well, I thank you," replied the minister. He added some more perplexed apologetic remarks; then he retreated.

He could expound the intricacies of every character study in the Scriptures, he was competent to grasp the Pilgrim Fathers and all historical innovators, but Sarah Penn was beyond him. He could deal with primal cases, but parallel ones worsted him. But, after all, although it was aside from his province, he wondered more how Adoniram Penn would deal with his wife than how the Lord would. Everybody shared the wonder. When Adoniram's four new cows arrived, Sarah ordered three to be put in the old barn, the other in the house shed where the cooking-stove had stood. That added to the excitement. It was whispered that all four cows were domiciled in the house.

Towards sunset on Saturday, when Adoniram was expected home, there was a knot of men in the road near the new barn. The hired man had milked, but he still hung around the premises. Sarah Penn had supper all ready. There were brown-bread and baked beans and a custard pie; it was the supper that Adoniram loved on a Saturday night. She had on a clean calico, and she bore herself imperturbably. Nanny and Sammy kept close at her heels. Their eyes were large, and Nanny was full of nervous tremors. Still there was to them more pleasant excitement than anything else. An inborn confidence in their mother over their father asserted itself.

Sammy looked out of the harness-room window. "There he is," he announced, in an awed whisper. He and Nanny peeped around the casing. Mrs. Penn kept on about her work. The children watched Adoniram leave the new horse standing in the drive while he went to the house door. It was fastened. Then he went around to the shed. That door was seldom locked, even when the family was away. The thought how her father would be confronted by the cow flashed upon Nanny. There was a hysterical sob in her throat. Adoniram emerged from the shed and stood looking about in a dazed fashion. His lips moved; he was saying something, but they could not hear what it was. The hired man was peeping around a corner of the old barn, but nobody saw him.

Adoniram took the new horse by the bridle and led him across the yard to the new barn. Nanny and Sammy slunk close to their mother. The barn doors rolled back, and there stood Adoniram, with the long mild face of the great Canadian farm horse looking over his shoulder.

Nanny kept behind her mother, but Sammy stepped suddenly forward, and stood in front of her.

Adoniram stared at the group. "What on airth you all down here for?" said he. "What's the matter over to the house?"

"We've come here to live, father," said Sammy. His shrill voice quavered out bravely.

"What"—Adoniram sniffed—" what is it smells like cookin?" said he. He stepped forward and looked in the open door of the harness-room. Then he turned to his wife. His old bristling face was pale and frightened. "What on airth does this mean, mother?" he gasped.

"You come in here, father," said Sarah. She led the way into the harness-room and shut the door. "Now, father," said she, "you needn't be scared. I ain't crazy. There ain't nothin' to be upset over. But we've come here to live, an' we're goin' to live here. We've got jest as good a right here as new horses an' cows. The house wa'n't fit for us to live in any longer, an' I made up my mind I wa'n't goin' to stay there. I've done my duty by you forty year, an' I'm goin' to do it now; but I'm goin' to live here. You've got to put in some windows and partitions; an' you'll have to buy some furniture."

"Why, mother!" the old man gasped.

"You'd better take your coat off an' get washed—there's the wash-basin—an' then we'll have supper."

"Why, mother!"

Sammy went past the window, leading the new horse to the old barn. The old man saw him, and shook his head speechlessly. He tried to take off his coat, but his arms seemed to lack the power. His wife helped him. She poured some water into the tin basin, and put in a piece of soap. She got the comb and brush, and smoothed his thin gray hair after he had washed. Then she put the beans, hot bread, and tea on the table. Sammy came in and the family drew up. Adoniram sat looking dazedly at his plate, and they waited.

"Ain't you goin' to ask a blessin', father?" said Sarah.

And the old man bent his head and mumbled.

All through the meal he stopped eating at intervals, and stared furtively at his wife; but he ate well. The home food tasted good to him, and his old frame was too sturdily healthy to be affected by his mind. But after supper he went out, and sat down on the step of the smaller door at the right of the barn, through which he had meant his Jerseys to pass in stately file, but which Sarah designed for her front house door, and he leaned his head on his hands.

After the supper dishes were cleared away and the milk-pans washed, Sarah went out to him. The twilight was deepening. There was a clear green glow in the sky. Before them stretched the smooth level of field; in the distance was a cluster of hay-stacks like the huts of a village; the air was very cool and calm and sweet. The landscape might have been an ideal one of peace.

Sarah bent over and touched her husband on one of his thin, sinewy shoulders. "Father!"

The old man's shoulders heaved: he was weeping.

"Why, don't do so, father," said Sarah.

"I'll—put up the—partitions, an'—everything you—want, mother."

Sarah put her apron up to her face; she was overcome by her own triumph.

Adoniram was like a fortress whose walls had no active resistance, and went down the instant the right besieging tools were used. "Why, mother," he said, hoarsely, "I hadn't no idee you was so set on't as all this comes to."

Questions for Writing or Discussion

1. Almost every marriage has some underlying tensions. What are the underlying tensions in the marriages treated in these two stories?
2. In which marriage are the tensions more serious?
3. How are the tensions resolved in each marriage? Which way is better? Why?
4. Is either marriage in danger of breaking up? If so, which? Why?
5. If you had to choose one of these couples as friends, which would you choose? Why?
6. Which couple is more admirable?
7. Write a paper comparing these two short stories.

COMING OF AGE:
Two Stories for Comparison and Contrast

Katherine Mansfield
HER FIRST BALL

Exactly when the ball began Leila would have found it hard to say. Perhaps
her first real partner was the cab. It did not matter that she shared the cab
with the Sheridan girls and their brother. She sat back in her own little
corner of it, and the bolster on which her hand rested felt like the sleeve of
an unknown young man's dress suit; and away they bowled, past waltzing
lamp-posts and houses and fences and trees.

"Have you really never been to a ball before, Leila? But, my child, how too
weird—" cried the Sheridan girls.

"Our nearest neighbour was fifteen miles," said Leila softly, gently opening and shutting her fan.

Oh, dear, how hard it was to be indifferent like the others! She tried not to
smile too much; she tried not to care. But every single thing was so new and
exciting . . . Meg's tuberoses, Jose's long loop of amber, Laura's little dark
head, pushing above her white fur like a flower through snow. She would
remember for ever. It even gave her a pang to see her cousin Laurie throw
away the wisps of tissue paper he pulled from the fastenings of his new
gloves. She would like to have kept those wisps as a keepsake, as a remem-
brance. Laurie leaned forward and put his hand on Laura's knee.

"Look here, darling," he said. "The third and the ninth as usual. Twig?"[1]

Oh, how marvellous to have a brother! In her excitement Leila felt that if
there had been time, if it hadn't been impossible, she couldn't have helped
crying because she was an only child, and no brother had ever said, "Twig?"
to her; no sister would ever say, as Meg said to Jose that moment, "I've
never known your hair go up more successfully than it has to-night!"

But, of course, there was no time. They were at the drill hall already; there
were cabs in front of them and cabs behind. The road was bright on either
side with moving fan-like lights, and on the pavement gay couples seemed
to float through the air; little satin shoes chased each other like birds.

"Hold on to me, Leila; you'll get lost," said Laura.

"Come on, girls, let's make a dash for it," said Laurie.

Leila put two fingers on Laura's pink velvet cloak, and they were somehow lifted past the big golden lantern, carried along the passage, and pushed
into the little room marked "Ladies." Here the crowd was so great there was
hardly space to take off their things; the noise was deafening. Two benches
on either side were stacked high with wraps. Two old women in white
aprons ran up and down tossing fresh armfuls. And everybody was pressing
forward trying to get at the little dressing-table and mirror at the far end.

---

1. Understand?

A great quivering jet of gas lighted the ladies' room. It couldn't wait; it was dancing already. When the door opened again and there came a burst of tuning from the drill hall, it leaped almost to the ceiling.

Dark girls, fair girls were patting their hair, tying ribbons again, tucking handkerchiefs down the fronts of their bodices, smoothing marble-white gloves. And because they were all laughing it seemed to Leila that they were all lovely.

"Aren't there any invisible hair-pins?" cried a voice. "How most extraordinary! I can't see a single invisible hair-pin."

"Powder my back, there's a darling," cried someone else.

"But I must have a needle and cotton. I've torn simply miles and miles of the frill," wailed a third.

Then "Pass them along, pass them along!" The straw basket of programmes was tossed from arm to arm. Darling little pink-and-silver programmes, with pink pencils and fluffy tassels. Leila's fingers shook as she took one out of the basket. She wanted to ask someone, "Am I meant to have one too?" but she had just time to read: "Waltz 3. *Two, Two, in a Canoe.* Polka 4. *Making the Feathers Fly,*" when Meg cried, "Ready, Leila?" and they pressed their way through the crush in the passage towards the big double doors of the drill hall.

Dancing had not begun yet, but the band had stopped tuning, and the noise was so great it seemed that when it did begin to play it would never be heard. Leila, pressing close to Meg, looking over Meg's shoulder, felt that even the little quivering coloured flags strung across the ceiling were talking. She quite forgot to be shy; she forgot how in the middle of dressing she had sat down on the bed with one shoe off and one shoe on and begged her mother to ring up her cousins and say she couldn't go after all. And the rush of longing she had had to be sitting on the veranda of their forsaken upcountry home, listening to the baby owls crying "More pork" in the moonlight, was changed to a rush of joy so sweet that it was hard to bear alone. She clutched her fan, and, gazing at the gleaming, golden floor, the azaleas, the lanterns, the stage at one end with its red carpet and gilt chairs and the band in a corner, she thought breathlessly, "How heavenly; how simply heavenly!"

All the girls stood grouped together at one side of the doors, the men at the other, and the chaperones in dark dresses, smiling rather foolishly, walked with little careful steps over the polished floor towards the stage.

"This is my country cousin Leila. Be nice to her. Find her partners; she's under my wing," said Meg, going up to one girl after another.

Strange faces smiled at Leila—sweetly, vaguely. Strange voices answered. "Of course, my dear." But Leila felt the girls didn't really see her. They were looking towards the men. Why didn't the men begin? What were they waiting for? There they stood, smoothing their gloves, patting their glossy hair and smiling among themselves. Then, quite suddenly, as if they had only just made up their minds that that was what they had to do, the men came gliding over the parquet. There was a joyful flutter among the girls. A tall, fair man flew up to Meg, seized her programme, scribbled something; Meg passed him on to Leila. "May I have the pleasure?" He ducked and smiled.

There came a dark man wearing an eyeglass, then cousin Laurie with a friend, and Laura with a little freckled fellow whose tie was crooked. Then quite an old man—fat, with a big bald patch on his head—took her programme and murmured, "Let me see, let me see!" And he was a long time comparing his programme, which looked black with names, with hers. It seemed to give him so much trouble that Leila was ashamed. "Oh, please don't bother," she said eagerly. But instead of replying the fat man wrote something, glanced at her again. "Do I remember this bright little face?" he said softly. "Is it known to me of yore?" At that moment the band began playing; the fat man disappeared. He was tossed away on a great wave of music that came flying over the gleaming floor, breaking the groups up into couples, scattering them, sending them spinning. . . .

Leila had learned to dance at boarding school. Every Saturday afternoon the boarders were hurried off to a little corrugated iron mission hall where Miss Eccles (of London) held her "select" classes. But the difference between that dusty-smelling hall—with calico texts on the walls, the poor terrified little woman in a brown velvet toque with rabbit's ears thumping the cold piano, Miss Eccles poking the girls' feet with her long white wand—and this was so tremendous that Leila was sure if her partner didn't come and she had to listen to that marvellous music and to watch the others sliding, gliding over the golden floor, she would die at least, or faint, or lift her arms and fly out of one of those dark windows that showed the stars.

"Ours, I think—" Someone bowed, smiled, and offered her his arm; she hadn't to die after all. Someone's hand pressed her waist, and she floated away like a flower that is tossed into a pool.

"Quite a good floor, isn't it?" drawled a faint voice close to her ear.

"I think it's most beautifully slippery," said Leila.

"Pardon!" The faint voice sounded surprised. Leila said it again. And there was a tiny pause before the voice echoed. "Oh, quite!" and she was swung round again.

He steered so beautifully. That was the great difference between dancing with girls and men, Leila decided. Girls banged into each other, and stamped on each other's feet; the girl who was gentleman always clutched you so.

The azaleas were separate flowers no longer; they were pink and white flags streaming by.

"Were you at the Bell's last week?" the voice came again. It sounded tired. Leila wondered whether she ought to ask him if he would like to stop.

"No, this is my first dance," said she.

Her partner gave a little gasping laugh. "Oh, I say," he protested.

"Yes, it is really the first dance I've ever been to." Leila was most fervent. It was such a relief to be able to tell somebody. "You see, I've lived in the country all my life up until now. . . ."

At that moment the music stopped, and they went to sit on two chairs against the wall. Leila tucked her pink satin feet under and fanned herself, while she blissfully watched the other couples passing and disappearing through the swing doors.

"Enjoying yourself, Leila?" asked Jose, nodding her golden head.

Laura passed and gave her the faintest little wink; it made Leila wonder

for a moment whether she was quite grown up after all. Certainly her partner did not say very much. He coughed, tucked his handkerchief away,
pulled down his waistcoat, took a minute thread off his sleeve. But it didn't
matter. Almost immediately the band started, and her second partner
seemed to spring from the ceiling.

"Floor's not bad," said the new voice. Did one always begin with the
floor? And then, "Were you at the Neaves' on Tuesday?" And again Leila
explained. Perhaps it was a little strange that her partners were not more
interested. For it was thrilling. Her first ball! She was only at the beginning
of everything. It seemed to her that she had never known what the night
was like before. Up till now it had been dark, silent, beautiful very often—
oh, yes—but mournful somehow. Solemn. And now it would never be like
that again—it had opened dazzling bright.

"Care for an ice?" said her partner. And they went through the swing
doors, down the passage, to the supper room. Her cheeks burned, she was
fearfully thirsty. How sweet the ices looked on little glass plates, and how
cold the frosted spoon was, iced too! And when they came back to the hall
there was the fat man waiting for her by the door. It gave her quite a shock
again to see how old he was; he ought to have been on the stage with the
fathers and mothers. And when Leila compared him with her other partners
he looked shabby. His waistcoat was creased, there was a button off his
glove, his coat looked as if it was dusty with French chalk.

"Come along, little lady," said the fat man. He scarcely troubled to clasp
her, and they moved away so gently, it was more like walking than dancing.
But he said not a word about the floor. "Your first dance, isn't it?" he
murmured.

"How *did* you know?"

"Ah," said the fat man, "that's what it is to be old!" He wheezed faintly as
he steered her past an awkward couple. "You see, I've been doing this kind
of thing for the last thirty years."

"Thirty years?" cried Leila. Twelve years before she was born!

"It hardly bears thinking about, does it?" said the fat man gloomily. Leila
looked at his bald head, and she felt quite sorry for him.

"I think it's marvellous to be still going on," she said kindly.

"Kind little lady," said the fat man, and he pressed her a little closer, and
hummed a bar of the waltz. "Of course," he said, "you can't hope to last
anything like as long as that. No-o," said the fat man, "long before that
you'll be sitting up there on the stage, looking on, in your nice black velvet.
And these pretty arms will have turned into little short fat ones, and you'll
beat time with such a different kind of fan—a black bony one." The fat man
seemed to shudder. "And you'll smile away like the poor old dears up there,
and point to your daughter, and tell the elderly lady next to you how some
dreadful man tried to kiss her at the club ball. And your heart will ache,
ache"—the fat man squeezed her closer still, as if he really was sorry for
that poor heart—"because no one wants to kiss you now. And you'll say
how unpleasant these polished floors are to walk on, how dangerous they
are. Eh, Mademoiselle Twinkletoes?" said the fat man softly.

Leila gave a light little laugh, but she did not feel like laughing. Was it—

could it all be true? It sounded terribly true. Was this first ball only the beginning of her last ball after all? At that the music seemed to change; it sounded sad, sad; it rose upon a great sigh. Oh, how quickly things changed! Why didn't happiness last for ever? For ever wasn't a bit too long.

"I want to stop," she said in a breathless voice. The fat man led her to the door.

"No," she said, "I won't go outside. I won't sit down. I'll just stand here, thank you." She leaned against the wall, tapping with her foot, pulling up her gloves and trying to smile. But deep inside her a little girl threw her pinafore over her head and sobbed. Why had he spoiled it all?

"I say, you know," said the fat man, "you mustn't take me seriously, little lady."

"As if I should!" said Leila, tossing her small dark head and sucking her underlip. . . .

Again the couples paraded. The swing doors opened and shut. Now new music was given out by the bandmaster. But Leila didn't want to dance any more. She wanted to be home, or sitting on the veranda listening to those baby owls. When she looked through the dark windows at the stars, they had long beams like wings. . . .

But presently a soft, melting, ravishing tune began, and a young man with curly hair bowed before her. She would have to dance, out of politeness, until she could find Meg. Very stiffly she walked in the middle; very haughtily she put her hand on his sleeve. But in one minute, in one turn, her feet glided, glided. The lights, the azaleas, the dresses, the pink faces, the velvet chairs, all became one beautiful flying wheel. And when her next partner bumped into the fat man and he said, "Pardon," she smiled at him more radiantly than ever. She didn't even recognize him again.

Joyce Carol Oates
WHERE ARE YOU GOING, WHERE HAVE YOU BEEN?

To Bob Dylan

Her name was Connie. She was fifteen and she had a quick nervous giggling habit of craning her neck to glance into mirrors, or checking other people's faces to make sure her own was all right. Her mother, who noticed everything and knew everything and who hadn't much reason any longer to look at her own face, always scolded Connie about it. "Stop gawking at yourself, who are you? You think you're so pretty?" she would say. Connie would raise her eyebrows at these familiar complaints and look right through her mother, into a shadowy vision of herself as she was right at that moment: she knew she was pretty and that was everything. Her mother had been pretty once too, if you could believe those old snapshots in the album, but now her looks were gone and that was why she was always after Connie.

"Why don't you keep your room clean like your sister? How've you got your hair fixed—what the hell stinks? Hair spray? You don't see your sister using that junk."

Her sister June was twenty-four and still lived at home. She was a secretary in the high school Connie attended, and if that wasn't bad enough—with her in the same building—she was so plain and chunky and steady that Connie had to hear her praised all the time by her mother and her mother's sisters. June did this, June did that, she saved money and helped clean the house and cooked and Connie couldn't do a thing, her mind was all filled with trashy daydreams. Their father was away at work most of the time and when he came home he wanted supper and he read the newspaper at supper and after supper he went to bed. He didn't bother talking much to them, but around his bent head Connie's mother kept picking at her until Connie wished her mother were dead and she herself were dead and it were all over. "She makes me want to throw up sometimes," she complained to her friends. She had a high, breathless, amused voice which made everything she said sound a little forced, whether it was sincere or not.

There was one good thing: June went places with girlfriends of hers, girls who were just as plain and steady as she, and so when Connie wanted to do that her mother had no objections. The father of Connie's best girlfriend drove the girls the three miles to town and left them off at a shopping plaza, so that they could walk through the stores or go to a movie, and when he came to pick them up again at eleven he never bothered to ask what they had done.

They must have been familiar sights, walking around that shopping plaza in their shorts and flat ballerina slippers that always scuffed the sidewalk, with charm bracelets jingling on their thin wrists; they would lean together to whisper and laugh secretly if someone passed by who amused or interested them. Connie had long dark blond hair that drew anyone's eye to it, and she wore part of it pulled up on her head and puffed out and the rest of it she let fall down her back. She wore a pullover jersey blouse that looked one way when she was at home and another way when she was away from home. Everything about her had two sides to it, one for home and one for anywhere that was not home: her walk that could be childlike and bobbling, or languid enough to make anyone think she was hearing music in her head, her mouth which was pale and smirking most of the time, but bright and pink on these evenings out, her laugh which was cynical and drawling at home—"Ha, ha, very funny"—but high-pitched and nervous anywhere else, like the jingling of the charms on her bracelet.

Sometimes they did go shopping or to a movie, but sometimes they went across the highway, ducking fast across the busy road, to a drive-in restaurant where older kids hung out. The restaurant was shaped like a big bottle, though squatter than a real bottle, and on its cap was a revolving figure of a grinning boy who held a hamburger aloft. One night in mid-summer they ran across, breathless with daring, and right away someone leaned out a car window and invited them over, but it was just a boy from high school they didn't like. It made them feel good to be able to ignore him. They went up through the maze of parked and cruising cars to the bright-lit, fly-infested restaurant, their faces pleased and expectant as if they were entering a sacred building that loomed out of the night to give them what haven and what blessing they yearned for. They sat at the counter and crossed their legs at the ankles, their thin shoulders rigid with excitement, and listened to the music that made everything so good: the music was always in the background like music at a church service, it was something to depend upon.

A boy named Eddie came in to talk with them. He sat backward on his stool, turning himself jerkily around in semicircles and then stopping and turning again, and after awhile he asked Connie if she would like something to eat. She said she did and so she tapped her friend's arm on her way out—her friend pulled her face up into a brave droll look—and Connie said she would meet her at eleven, across the way. "I just hate to leave her like that," Connie said earnestly, but the boy said that she wouldn't be alone for long. So they went out to his car and on the way Connie couldn't help but let her eyes wander over the windshields and faces all around her, her face gleaming with a joy that had nothing to do with Eddie or even this place; it might have been the music. She drew her shoulders up and sucked in her breath with the pure pleasure of being alive, and just at that moment she happened to glance at a face just a few feet from hers. It was a boy with shaggy black hair, in a convertible jalopy painted gold. He stared at her and then his lips widened into a grin. Connie slit her eyes at him and turned away, but she couldn't help glancing back and there he was still watching her. He wagged a finger and laughed and said, "Gonna get you, baby," and Connie turned away again without Eddie noticing anything.

She spent three hours with him, at the restaurant where they ate hamburgers and drank Cokes in wax cups that were always sweating, and then down an alley a mile or so away, and when he left her off at five to eleven only the movie house was still open at the plaza. Her girlfriend was there, talking with a boy. When Connie came up the two girls smiled at each other and Connie said, "How was the movie?" and the girl said, "*You* should know." They rode off with the girl's father, sleepy and pleased, and Connie couldn't help but look at the darkened shopping plaza with its big empty parking lot and its signs that were faded and ghostly now, and over at the drive-in restaurant where cars were still circling tirelessly. She couldn't hear the music at this distance.

Next morning June asked her how the movie was and Connie said, "So-so."

She and that girl and occasionally another girl went out several times a week that way, and the rest of the time Connie spent around the house—it was summer vacation—getting in her mother's way and thinking, dreaming, about the boys she met. But all the boys fell back and dissolved into a single face that was not even a face, but an idea, a feeling, mixed up with the urgent insistent pounding of the music and the humid night air of July. Connie's mother kept dragging her back to the daylight by finding things for her to do or saying, suddenly, "What's this about the Pettinger girl?"

And Connie would say nervously, "Oh, her. That dope." She always drew thick clear lines between herself and such girls, and her mother was simple and kindly enough to believe her. Her mother was so simple, Connie thought, that it was maybe cruel to fool her so much. Her mother went scuffling around the house in old bedroom slippers and complained over the telephone to one sister about the other, then the other called up and the two of them complained about the third one. If June's name was mentioned her mother's tone was approving, and if Connie's name was mentioned it was disapproving. This did not really mean she disliked Connie, and actually Connie thought that her mother preferred her to June because she was prettier, but the two of them kept up a pretense of exasperation, a sense that they were tugging and struggling over something of little value to either of them. Sometimes, over coffee, they were almost friends, but something would come up—some vexation that was like a fly buzzing suddenly around their heads—and their faces went hard with contempt.

One Sunday Connie got up at eleven—none of them bothered with church—and washed her hair so that it could dry all day long, in the sun. Her parents and sister were going to a barbecue at an aunt's house and Connie said no, she wasn't interested, rolling her eyes to let mother know just what she thought of it. "Stay home alone then," her mother said sharply. Connie sat out back in a lawn chair and watched them drive away, her father quiet and bald, hunched around so that he could back the car out, her mother with a look that was still angry and not at all softened through the windshield, and in the back seat poor old June all dressed up as if she didn't know what a barbecue was, with all the running yelling kids and the flies. Connie sat with her eyes closed in the sun, dreaming and dazed with the warmth about her as if this were a kind of love, the caresses of love, and her mind slipped over onto thoughts of the boy she had been with the night before and how nice he had been, how sweet it always was, not the way someone like June would suppose but sweet, gentle, the way it was in movies and promised in songs; and when she opened her eyes she hardly knew where she was, the back yard ran off into weeds and a fence-line of trees and behind it the sky was perfectly blue and still. The asbestos "ranch house" that was now three years old startled her—it looked small. She shook her head as if to get awake.

It was too hot. She went inside the house and turned on the radio to drown out the quiet. She sat on the edge of her bed, barefoot, and listened for an hour and a half to a program called XYZ Sunday Jamboree, record after record of hard, fast, shrieking songs she sang along with, interspersed by exclamations from "Bobby King": "An' look here you girls at Napoleon's—Son and Charley want you to pay real close attention to this song coming up!"

And Connie paid close attention herself, bathed in a glow of slow-pulsed joy that seemed to rise mysteriously out of the music itself and lay languidly about the airless little room, breathed in and breathed out with each gentle rise and fall of her chest.

After a while she heard a car coming up the drive. She sat up at once, startled, because it couldn't be her father so soon. The gravel kept crunching all the way in from the road—the driveway was long—and Connie ran to the window. It was a car she didn't know. It was an open jalopy, painted a bright gold that caught the sunlight opaquely. Her heart began to pound and her fingers snatched at her hair, checking it, and she whispered

"Christ, Christ," wondering how bad she looked. The car came to a stop at the side door and the horn sounded four short taps as if this were a signal Connie knew.

She went into the kitchen and approached the door slowly, then hung out the screen door, her bare toes curling down off the step. There were two boys in the car and now she recognized the driver: he had shaggy, shabby black hair that looked crazy as a wig and he was grinning at her.

"I ain't late, am I?" he said.

"Who the hell do you think you are?" Connie said.

"Toldja I'd be out, didn't I?"

"I don't even know who you are."

She spoke sullenly, careful to show no interest or pleasure, and he spoke in a fast bright monotone. Connie looked past him to the other boy, taking her time. He had fair brown hair, with a lock that fell onto his forehead. His sideburns gave him a fierce, embarrassed look, but so far he hadn't even bothered to glance at her. Both boys wore sunglasses. The driver's glasses were metallic and mirrored everything in miniature.

"You wanta come for a ride?" he said.

Connie smirked and let her hair fall loose over one shoulder.

"Don'tcha like my car? New paint job," he said. "Hey."

"What?"

"You're cute."

She pretended to fidget, chasing flies away from the door.

"Don'tcha believe me, or what?" he said.

"Look, I don't even know who you are," Connie said in disgust.

"Hey, Ellie's got a radio, see. Mine's broke down." He lifted his friend's arm and showed her the little transistor the boy was holding, and now Connie began to hear the music. It was the same program that was playing inside the house.

"Bobby King?" she said.

"I listen to him all the time. I think he's great."

"He's kind of great," Connie said reluctantly.

"Listen, that guy's *great*. He knows where the action is."

Connie blushed a little, because the glasses made it impossible for her to see just what this boy was looking at. She couldn't decide if she liked him or if he was just a jerk, and so she dawdled in the doorway and wouldn't come down or go back inside. She said, "What's all that stuff painted on your car?"

"Can'tcha read it?" He opened the door very carefully, as if he was afraid it might fall off. He slid out just as carefully, planting his feet firmly on the ground, the tiny metallic world in his glasses slowing down like gelatine hardening and in the midst of it Connie's bright green blouse. "This here is my name, to begin with," he said. ARNOLD FRIEND was written in tarlike black letters on the side, with a drawing of a round grinning face that re-minded Connie of a pumpkin, except it wore sunglasses. "I wanta introduce myself, I'm Arnold Friend and that's my real name and I'm gonna be your friend, honey, and inside the car's Ellie Oscar, he's kinda shy." Ellie brought his transistor radio up to his shoulder and balanced it there. "Now these numbers are a secret code, honey," Arnold Friend explained. He read off the numbers 33, 19, 17 and raised his eyebrows at her to see what she thought of that, but she didn't think much of it. The left rear fender had been smashed and around it was written, on the gleaming gold background: DONE BY CRAZY WOMAN DRIVER. Connie had to laugh at that. Arnold Friend was pleased at her laughter and looked up at her. "Around the other side's a lot more—you wanta come and see them?"

"No."

"Why not?"

"Why should I?"

"Don'tcha wanta see what's on the car? Don'tcha wanta go for a ride?"

"I don't know."

"Why not?"

"I got things to do."

"Like what?"

"Things."

He laughed as if she had said something funny. He slapped his thighs. He was standing in a strange way, leaning back against the car as if he were balancing himself. He wasn't tall, only an inch or so taller than she would be if she came down to him. Connie liked the way he was dressed, which was the way all of them dressed: tight faded jeans stuffed into black, scuffed boots, a belt that pulled his waist in and showed how lean he was, and a white pullover shirt that was a little soiled and showed the hard small muscles of his arms and shoulders. He looked as if he probably did hard work, lifting and carrying things. Even his neck looked muscular. And his face was a familiar face, somehow: the jaw and chin and cheeks slightly darkened, because he hadn't shaved for a day or two, and the nose long and hawklike, sniffing as if she were a treat he was going to gobble up and it was all a joke.

"Connie, you ain't telling the truth. This is your day set aside for a ride with me and you know it," he said, still laughing. The way he straightened and recovered from his fit of laughing showed that it had been all fake.

"How do you know what my name is?" she said suspiciously.

"It's Connie."

"Maybe and maybe not."

"I know my Connie," he said, wagging his finger. Now she remembered him even better, back at the restaurant, and her cheeks warmed at the thought of how she sucked in her breath just at the moment she passed him—how she must have looked to him. And he had remembered her. "Ellie and I come out here especially for you," he said. "Ellie can sit in back. How about it?"

"Where?"

"Where what?"

"Where're we going?"

He looked at her. He took off the sunglasses and she saw how pale the skin around his eyes was, like holes that were not in shadow but instead in light. His eyes were like chips of broken glass that catch the light in an amiable way. He smiled. It was as if the idea of going for a ride somewhere, to some place, was a new idea to him.

"Just for a ride, Connie sweetheart."

"I never said my name was Connie," she said.

"But I know what it is. I know your name and all about you, lots of things," Arnold Friend said. He had not moved yet but stood still leaning back against the side of his jalopy. "I took a special interest in you, such a pretty girl, and found out all about you like I know your parents and sister are gone somewheres and I know where and how long they're going to be gone, and I know who you were with last night, and your best girlfriend's name is Betty. Right?"

He spoke in a simple lilting voice, exactly as if he were reciting the words to a song. His smile assured her that everything was fine. In the car Ellie turned up the volume on his radio and did not bother to look around at them.

"Ellie can sit in the back seat," Arnold Friend said. He indicated his friend with a casual jerk of his chin, as if Ellie did not count and she should not bother with him.

"How'd you find out all that stuff?" Connie said.

"Listen: Betty Schultz and Tony Fitch and Jimmy Pettinger and Nancy Pettinger," he said, in a chant. "Raymond Stanley and Bob Hutter—"

"Do you know all those kids?"

"I know everybody."

"Look, you're kidding. You're not from around here."

"Sure."

"But—how come we never saw you before?"

"Sure you saw me before," he said. He looked down at his boots, as if he were a little offended. "You just don't remember."

"I guess I'd remember you," Connie said.

"Yeah?" He looked up at this, beaming. He was pleased. He began to mark time with the music from Ellie's radio, tapping his fists lightly together. Connie looked away from his smile to the car, which was painted so bright it almost hurt her eyes to look at it. She looked at that name, ARNOLD FRIEND. And up at the front fender was an expression that was familiar—MAN THE FLYING SAUCERS. It was an expression kids had used the year before, but didn't use this year. She looked at it for a while as if the words meant something to her that she did not yet know.

"What're you thinking about? Huh?" Arnold Friend demanded. "Not worried about your hair blowing around in the car, are you?"

"No."

"Think I maybe can't drive good?"

"How do I know?"

"You're a hard girl to handle. How come?" he said. "Don't you know I'm your friend? Didn't you see me put my sign in the air when you walked by?"

"What sign?"

"My sign." And he drew an X in the air, leaning out toward her. They were maybe ten feet apart. After his hand fell back to his side the X was still in the air, almost visible. Connie let the screen door close and stood perfectly still inside it, listening to the music from her radio and the boy's blend together. She stared at Arnold Friend. He stood there so stiffly relaxed, pretending to be relaxed, with one hand idly on the door handle as if he were keeping himself up that way and had no intention of ever moving again. She recognized most things about him, the tight jeans that showed his thighs and buttocks and the greasy leather boots and the tight shirt, and even that slippery friendly smile of his, that sleepy dreamy smile that all the boys used to get across ideas they didn't want to put into words. She recognized all this and also the singsong way he talked, slightly mocking, kidding, but serious and a little melancholy, and she recognized the way he tapped one fist against the other in homage to the perpetual music behind him. But all these things did not come together.

She said suddenly, "Hey, how old are you?"

His smile faded. She could see than that he wasn't a kid, he was much older—thirty, maybe more. At this knowledge her heart began to pound faster.

"That's a crazy thing to ask. Can'tcha see I'm your own age?"

"Like hell you are."

"Or maybe a coupla years older. I'm eighteen."

"Eighteen?" she said doubtfully.

He grinned to reassure her and lines appeared at the corners of his mouth. His teeth were big and white. He grinned so broadly his eyes became slits and she saw how thick the lashes were, thick and black as if painted with a black tarlike material. Then he seemed to become embarrassed, abruptly, and looked over his shoulder at Ellie. *"Him,* he's crazy," he said. "Ain't he a riot, he's a nut, a real character." Ellie was still listening to the music. His sunglasses told nothing about what he was thinking. He wore a bright orange shirt unbuttoned halfway to show his chest, which was a pale, bluish chest and not muscular like Arnold Friend's. His shirt collar was turned up all around and the very tips of the collar pointed out past his chin as if they were protecting him. He was pressing the transistor radio up against his ear and sat there in a kind of daze, right in the sun.

"He's kinda strange," Connie said.

"Hey, she says you're kinda strange! Kinda strange!" Arnold Friend cried. He pounded on the car to get Ellie's attention. Ellie turned for the first time and Connie saw with shock that he wasn't a kid either—he had a fair, hairless face, cheeks reddened slightly as if the veins grew too close to the surface of his skin, the face of a forty-year-old baby. Connie felt a wave of dizziness rise in her at this sight and she stared at him as if waiting for something to change the shock of the moment, make it all right again. Ellie's lips kept shaping words, mumbling along with the words blasting in his ear.

"Maybe you two better go away," Connie said faintly.

"What? How come?" Arnold Friend cried. "We come out here to take you for a ride. It's Sunday." He had the voice of the man on the radio now. It was the same voice, Connie thought. "Don'tcha know it's Sunday all day and honey, no matter who you were with last night today you're with Arnold Friend and don't you forget it!—Maybe you better step out here," he said, and this last was in a different voice. It was a little flatter, as if the heat was finally getting to him.

"No. I got things to do."

"Hey."

"You two better leave."

"We ain't leaving until you come with us."

"Like hell I am—"

"Connie, don't fool around with me. I mean, I mean, don't fool *around*," he said, shaking his head. He laughed incredulously. He placed his sunglasses on top of his head, carefully, as if he were indeed wearing a wig, and brought the stems down behind his ears. Connie stared at him, another wave of dizziness and fear rising in her so that for a moment he wasn't even in focus but was just a blur, standing there against his gold car, and she had the idea that he had driven up the driveway all right but had come from nowhere before that and belonged nowhere and that everything about him and even about the music that was so familiar to her was only half real.

"If my father comes and sees you—"

"He ain't coming. He's at a barbecue."

"How do you know that?"

"Aunt Tillie's. Right now they're—uh—they're drinking. Sitting around," he said vaguely, squinting as if he were staring all the way to town and over to Aunt Tillie's back yard. Then the vision seemed to get clear and he nodded energetically. "Yeah. Sitting around. There's your sister in a blue dress, huh? And high heels, the poor sad bitch—nothing like you, sweetheart! And your mother's helping some fat woman with the corn, they're cleaning the corn—husking the corn—"

"What fat woman?" Connie cried.

"How do I know what fat woman, I don't know every goddam fat woman in the world!" Arnold laughed.

"Oh, that's Mrs. Hornby . . . Who invited her?" Connie said. She felt a little light-headed. Her breath was coming quickly.

"She's too fat. I don't like them fat. I like them the way you are, honey," he said, smiling sleepily at her. They stared at each other for a while, through the screen door. He said softly, "Now what you're going to do is this: you're going to come out that door. You're going to sit up front with me and Ellie's going to sit in the back, the hell with Ellie, right? This isn't Ellie's date. You're my date. I'm your lover, honey."

"What? You're crazy—"

"Yes, I'm your lover. You don't know what that is but you will," he said. "I know that too. I know all about you. But look: it's real nice and you couldn't ask for nobody better than me, or more polite. I always keep my word. I'll tell you how it is, I'm always nice at first, the first time. I'll hold you so tight you won't think you have to try to get away or pretend anything because you'll know you can't. And I'll come inside you where it's all secret and you'll give in to me and you'll love me—"

"Shut up! You're crazy!" Connie said. She backed away from the door. She put her hands against her ears as if she'd heard something terrible, something not meant for her. "People don't talk like that, you're crazy," she muttered. Her heart was almost too big now for her chest and its pumping made sweat break out all over her. She looked out to see Arnold Friend pause and then take a step toward the porch lurching. He almost fell. But, like a clever drunken man, he managed to catch his balance. He wobbled in his high boots and grabbed hold of one of the porch posts.

"Honey?" he said. "You still listening?"

"Get the hell out of here!"

"Be nice, honey. Listen."

"I'm going to call the police—"

He wobbled again and out of the side of his mouth came a fast spat curse, an aside not meant for her to hear. But even this "Christ!" sounded forced. Then he began to smile again. She watched this smile come, awkward as if he were smiling from inside a mask. His whole face was a mask, she thought wildly, tanned down onto his throat but then running out as if he had plastered makeup on his face but had forgotten about his throat.

"Honey—? Listen, here's how it is. I always tell the truth and I promise you this: I ain't coming in that house after you."

"You better not! I'm going to call the police if you—if you don't—"

"Honey," he said, talking right through her voice, "honey, I'm not coming in there but you are coming out here. You know why?"

She was panting. The kitchen looked like a place she had never seen before, some room she had run inside but which wasn't good enough, wasn't going to help her. The kitchen window had never had a curtain, after three years, and there were dishes in the sink for her to do—probably—and if you ran your hand across the table you'd probably feel something sticky there.

"You listening, honey? Hey?"

"—going to call the police—"

"Soon as you touch the phone I don't need to keep my promise and can come inside. You don't want that."

She rushed forward and tried to lock the door. Her fingers were shaking. "But why lock it," Arnold Friend said gently, talking right into her face. "It's just a screen door. It's just nothing." One of his boots was at a strange angle, as if his foot wasn't in it. It pointed out to the left, bent at the ankle. "I mean, anybody can break through a screen door and glass and wood and iron or anything else if he needs to, anybody at all and specially Arnold Friend. If the place got lit up with a fire honey you'd come runnin' out into my arms, right into my arms an' safe at home—like you knew I was your lover and'd stopped fooling around. I don't mind a nice shy girl but I don't like no fooling around." Part of those words were spoken with a slight rhythmic lilt, and Connie somehow recognized them—the echo of a song from last year, about a girl rushing into her boyfriend's arms and coming home again—

Connie stood barefoot on the linoleum floor, staring at him. "What do you want?" she whispered.

"I want you," he said.

"What?"

"Seen you that night and thought, that's the one, yes sir. I never needed to look any more."

"But my father's coming back. He's coming to get me. I had to wash my hair first—" She spoke in a dry, rapid voice, hardly raising it for him to hear. "No, your Daddy is not coming and yes, you had to wash your hair and you washed it for me. It's nice and shining and all for me, I thank you, sweetheart," he said, with a mock bow, but again he almost lost his balance. He had to bend and adjust his boots. Evidently his feet did not go all the way down; the boots must have been stuffed with something so that he would seem taller. Connie stared out at him and behind him Ellie in the car, who seemed to be looking off toward Connie's right into nothing. This Ellie said, pulling the words out of the air one after another as if he were just discovering them, "You want me to pull out the phone?"

"Shut your mouth and keep it shut," Arnold Friend said, his face red from bending over or maybe from embarrassment because Connie had seen his boots. "This ain't none of your business."

"What—what are you doing? What do you want?" Connie said. "If I call the police they'll get you, they'll arrest you—"

"Promise was not to come in unless you touch that phone, and I'll keep that promise," he said. He resumed his erect position and tried to force his shoulders back. He sounded like a hero in a movie, declaring something important. He spoke too loudly and it was as if he were speaking to someone behind Connie. "I ain't made plans for coming in that house where I don't belong but just for you to come out to me, the way you should. Don't you know who I am?"

"You're crazy," she whispered. She backed away from the door but did not want to go into another part of the house, as if this would give him permission to come through the door. "What do you . . . You're crazy, you . . ."

"Huh? What're you saying, honey?"

Her eyes darted everywhere in the kitchen. She could not remember what it was, this room.

"This is how it is, honey: you come out and we'll drive away, have a nice ride. But if you don't come out we're gonna wait till your people come home and then they're all going to get it."

"You want that telephone pulled out?" Ellie said. He held the radio away from his ear and grimaced, as if without the radio the air was too much for him.

"I toldja shut up, Ellie," Arnold Friend said, "you're deaf, get a hearing aid, right? Fix yourself up. This little girl's no trouble and's gonna be nice to me, so Ellie keep to yourself, this ain't your date—right? Don't hem in on me. Don't hog. Don't crush, Don't bird dog. Don't trail me," he said in a rapid meaningless voice, as if he were running through all the expressions he'd learned but was no longer sure which one of them was in style, then rushing on to new ones, making them up with his eyes closed, "Don't crawl under my fence, don't squeeze in my chipmunk hole, don't sniff my glue, suck my pop-sicle, keep your own greasy fingers on yourself!" He shaded his eyes and peered in at Connie, who was backed against the kitchen table. "Don't mind him honey he's just a creep. He's a dope. Right? I'm the boy for you and like I said you come out here nice like a lady and give me your hand, and nobody else gets hurt, I mean, your nice old bald-headed daddy and your mummy and your sister in her high heels. Because listen: why bring them in this?"

"Leave me alone," Connie whispered.

"Hey, you know that old woman down the road, the one with the chickens and stuff—you know her?"

"She's dead!"

"Dead? What? You know her?" Arnold Friend said.

"She's dead—"

"Don't you like her?"

"She's dead—she's—she isn't here any more—"

"But don't you like her, I mean, you got something against her? Some grudge or something?" Then his voice dipped as if he were conscious of a rudeness. He touched the sunglasses perched on top of his head as if to make sure they were still there. "Now you be a good girl."

"What are you going to do?"

"Just two things, or maybe three," Arnold Friend said. "But I promise it won't last long and you'll like me the way you get to like people you're close to. You will. It's all over for you here, so come on out. You don't want your people in any trouble, do you?"

She turned and bumped against a chair or something, hurting her leg, but she ran into the back room and picked up the telephone. Something roared in her ear, a tiny roaring, and she was so sick with fear that she could do nothing but listen to it—the telephone was clammy and very heavy and her fingers groped down to the dial but were too weak to touch it. She began to scream into the phone, into the roaring. She cried out, she cried for her mother, she felt her breath start jerking back and forth in her lungs as if it were something Arnold Friend were stabbing her with again and again with no tenderness. A noisy sorrowful wailing rose all about her and she was locked inside it the way she was locked inside this house.

After a while she could hear again. She was sitting on the floor with her wet back against the wall.

Arnold Friend was saying from the door. "That's a good girl. Put the phone back."

She kicked the phone away from her.

"No, honey. Pick it up. Put it back right."

She picked it up and put it back. The dial tone stopped.

"That's a good girl. Now you come outside."

She was hollow with what had been fear, but what was now just an emptiness. All that screaming had blasted it out of her. She sat, one leg cramped under her, and deep inside her brain was something like a pinpoint of light that kept going and would not let her relax. She thought, I'm not going to see my mother again. She thought, I'm not going to sleep in my bed again. Her bright green blouse was all wet.

Arnold Friend said, in a gentle-loud voice that was like a stage voice, "The place where you came from ain't there any more, and where you had in mind to go is canceled out. This place you are now—inside your daddy's house—is nothing but a cardboard box I can knock down any time. You know that and always did know it. You hear me?"

She thought, I have got to think. I have to know what to do.

"We'll go out to a nice field, out in the country here where it smells so nice and it's sunny," Arnold Friend said. "I'll have my arms tight around you so you won't need to try to get away and I'll show you what love is like, what it does. The hell with this house. It looks solid all right," he said. He ran a fingernail down the screen and the noise did not make Connie shiver, as it would have the day before. "Now put your hand on your heart, honey. Feel that? That feels solid too but we know better, be nice to me, be sweet like you can because what else is there for a girl like you but to be sweet and pretty and give in?—and get away before her people come back?"

She felt her pounding heart. Her hand seemed to enclose it. She thought for the first time in her life that it was nothing that was hers, that belonged to her, but just a pounding, living thing inside this body that wasn't really hers either.

"You don't want them to get hurt," Arnold Friend went on. "Now get up, honey. Get up all by yourself."

She stood.

"Now turn this way. That's right. Come over here to me—Ellie, put that away, didn't I tell you? You dope. You miserable creepy dope," Arnold Friend said. His words were not angry but only part of an incantation. The incantation was kindly. "Now come out through the kitchen to me honey, and let's see a smile, try it, you're a brave sweet little girl and now they're eating corn and hot dogs cooked to bursting over an outdoor fire, and they don't know one thing about you and never did and honey you're better than them because not a one of them would have done this for you."

Connie felt the linoleum under her feet; it was cool. She brushed her hair back out of her eyes. Arnold Friend let go of the post tentatively and opened his arms for her, his elbows pointing in toward each other and his wrists limp, to show that this was an embarrassed embrace and a little mocking, he didn't want to make her self-conscious.

She put out her hand against the screen. She watched herself push the door slowly open as if she were safe back somewhere in the other doorway, watching this body and this head of long hair moving out into the sunlight where Arnold Friend waited.

"My sweet little blue-eyed girl," he said, in a half-sung sigh that had nothing to do with her brown eyes but was taken up just the same by the vast sunlit reaches of the land behind him and on all sides of him, so much land that Connie had never seen before and did not recognize except to know that she was going to it.

Questions for Writing or Discussion

1. What effect does music have on both Connie and Leila?
2. In what ways are going to a ball and going to a hamburger stand similar?
3. In both stories, the young men sound bored when they talk. Why?
4. In each story, an older man awakens the girl to a truth about herself. What is the truth in each case? What do the truths have in common?
5. Connie has an older sister to whom she feels superior. Leila has cousins whom she admires for being more worldly than she. Is this difference between the two girls important?

6. Leila is eager to tell each of her partners that she has never been to a ball before. Connie tries to give the impression she has more experience than is the case. Does this difference between the two girls account for the difference in the endings of the two stories?
7. Write a paper in which you use comparison-contrast techniques to discuss the two stories as "initiation" stories.

TWO APPROACHES TO DISCIPLINING CHILDREN

Virginia E. Pomeranz with Dodi Schultz
From THE FIRST FIVE YEARS

It is important to realize that no punishment is effective unless the alternatives are understood clearly to start with. In other words, a choice must be presented: "Either you will do what I have asked you to do or you will be punished." And the consequences of the behavior in question must be understood as well.

You and I are well aware that if we toss a glass vase about on the patio it may fall on the flagstones and break; we know this because it's part of our past experience. But your three-year-old is not likely to really comprehend your warning, "Susie, don't play with that; it's breakable, and very valuable." Susie may actually be quite astonished when the vase falls from her fingers and shatters. Punishing her is not really appropriate. You simply have to explain that's what you meant, and clean it up, and say, "Next time, be careful."

When punishment *is* called for, the thing to do is administer it without delay. Small children have very short memories. "I'll tell your father when he comes home, and are you going to get it!"—when that event is six hours in the future—is ridiculous. By that time the child will have long since forgotten the exact nature of the transgression, and the punishment will be meaningless. Secondly, as they said in *The Mikado*, "let the punishment fit the crime"—at least as closely as possible.

Let us say that two-year-old Georgie is playing in the sandbox with a group of other children and he bites another child. This is a dangerous act and should be firmly discouraged. You dash right over there, grab Georgie, and get his attention; you tell him that he is not ever to do that again, and that if he disobeys you he *will be punished.* You return to the bench, keeping a keen eye on Georgie. He does it again. Lose no time: immediately remove him from the sandbox and take him home. This is an appropriate deprivation, since he probably likes to play in the sandbox. (And if the act is repeated on another occasion, you might keep him out of the sandbox for several days.) Refusing to let him watch television, or play with his crayons, would not be punishments that fit the crime.

If on the other hand, Georgie takes it into his head to scribble on the dining-room wall—again, if the subject has never come up before, you must make the alternatives clear. You might say, "You are not to do that again. You may draw on the special place on the wall in your own room, but you are not to use any other wall. If you do so again, your crayons will be taken away from you." Again, an appropriate punishment. And again, follow through if the act is repeated: take the crayons away, for at least a day or two—at which point Georgie will probably begin asking for them. He should be reminded, when the crayons are returned, of why they were taken away—and the specifics of where they may and may not be used should be repeated.

How about depriving a child of food? I don't think sending a child to bed without supper is ever a proper form of punishment. Nor do I think depriving a youngster of even a favorite food treat—e.g., ice cream for dessert—is appropriate, unless the crime itself is directly connected with food. (Desserts, in any case, should be nutritious and considered part of the meal.)

If he has deliberately, in defiance of your directives to use his spoon and eat neatly, dumped his spinach on the floor, a no-dessert punishment might be appropriate. Or if he has, earlier in the day, rammed an ice cream cone into his brother's face, you are justified in saying, "You obviously do not know how to handle ice cream properly, and you are not going to have ice cream for a few days." But I do not think it right to say, "Because you have not eaten your spinach you may not have your ice cream." Failure to ingest one food is no reason to be deprived of another.

It is, incidentally, possible in any of these situations that the error will never be repeated. Partly because the child wishes to avoid the announced punishment. But partly, too, in response to your initial displeasure. . . . Children do, basically, want to win their parents' approval. Sometimes—not always, by a long shot—the disappointment or displeasure in your voice when you indicate what has been done wrong will be sufficient deterrent.

Do not, in any event, make idle threats. We have all witnessed scenes in which an exasperated mother says irately, "Johnny, if you don't stop that this very minute, we are going right home." Johnny, giving no sign that he has heard, keeps right on doing what he is doing, and his mother's next statement is, "Now come on, Johnny, stop doing that." Now he knows that she is not going to follow through. Or rather, he does not know *what* to believe. She may pick him up and take him home within the next thirty seconds. On the other hand, she may not. She has become completely unpredictable. And she has placed the child in a dilemma. Can he rely on any threats she makes? Can he rely on any promises whatever? Johnny is going to be pretty confused, since he is left without clear cause-and-effect premises on which to operate.

There are two forms of punishment I urge you not to use.

One is yelling. Very few parents can avoid yelling entirely, and that's understandable; there will be times when your patience is exhausted, and you will find yourself instinctively raising your voice. If these occasions are rare, the child will respond immediately, because the new and different tone of voice will startle him. But if you get into the habit of screaming at your child constantly, he will totally tune you out. Which will have two results, neither one desirable.

You will be hoarse by the end of the day. And because the child will learn to scream back at you, you will no longer converse in normal, conversational tones but will be trying to outshout each other continuously. This will leave you both exhausted. And child care will become a horrible burden, instead of the pleasure it should be.

Further, since your screaming has lost all special significance, some day when you shout at him as he is starting to cross the street in front of an oncoming car, he is not going to hear you.

Secondly, physical punishment. I think hitting a child is a very poor practice, chiefly because you are, by this action, suggesting a new form of behavior that does not occur instinctively in children. If you watch a group of small children playing together—children who have neither been hit themselves nor observed older youngsters fighting—you'll find that those who behave aggressively will push, pull, and occasionally bite; but they won't hit. If *you* hit the child, you are in fact demonstrating a form of behavior to him. And if you are doing it, it must be acceptable, right? You've told him, in other connections, that you want him to act "grown up," haven't you?

You have also introduced a distinct conflict by such action. Chances are you have taken some prior opportunity to point out that bullying, whether of younger siblings or smaller playmates, is not an acceptable form of behavior. Now here you are, hitting a three-year-old. And he looks up at you and says, "If I can't hit Jimmy, because he's littler than me—then how come you, a big person, can hit little me?" There is no answer, and there is egg all over your face. If he doesn't say it, he is thinking it. He is likely to reach the conclusion that bullying is okay after all, and may turn into the terror of the neighborhood. He will of course no longer trust any pronouncements of high principle on your part.

What if the child has taken it into his head to attack *you* physically? You must not permit it; we know that it can result in deep residual feelings of guilt in the child. But don't descend to his level and hit (or scratch or bite) him back. Simply seize the child's wrist(s) firmly. Say in firm, measured tones, "You are not to do that—ever." Hang onto him for at least a full minute. The child will inevitably realize that you possess vastly superior strength. When you let him go, he will feel bad, and there will be marks on his wrists—but you will not have done him any lasting damage, either physically or psychologically.

Fitzhugh Dodson
From HOW TO PARENT

It would be nice if we could rely entirely on the natural consequences of inadequate behavior to discipline a child. Unfortunately, natural consequences are not always sufficient. Sometimes we must find artificial or arbitrary consequences to apply to the behavior of a child.

There are three main methods we can use:

1. *We can deprive the child of something important to him.*

   Suppose your five-year-old scribbles on your living room walls with crayons. Such behavior is "normal" for a two-year-old. But it is an act of hostility for a five-year-old. Unfortunately for your discipline, there are no unpleasant natural consequences for the child as a result of scribbling on the walls of your house. You have to create some artificial and arbitrary consequences which will set firm limits to the child, and, in effect, say to him: "No more of this!"

If you feel sufficiently angered when you discover it, you may immediately spank him. That is one type of artificial but unpleasant consequence for him. Or you might deprive him of some privilege, perhaps saying, "Danny, you're old enough to know not to draw on walls with crayons, so I guess you won't be allowed to use your crayons for three days. That will help to remind you that crayons are to be used on paper, not on walls."

2. *We can use social isolation by sending the child out of his social group or to his room.*

Suppose your four-year-old is disrupting the play of a group of children in your back yard. You might say to him, "Charles, I see you are not able to play well with the other children right now. You keep hitting them and causing trouble. You'll have to go to your room and play by yourself until you tell me that you're able to control your actions."

Whenever you use social isolation as a means of discipline, it is important you make it an open-ended rather than a closed-ended affair. Don't just send the child to his room, as if he had to stay there forever. The purpose of sending him to his room is not to incarcerate him indefinitely, but to enable a change in his behavior to take place. Always let him know that when his behavior is able to change and he is able to play reasonably with the other children, he can come back and play.

3. *We can spank a child.*

I want to make it clear that there is a "right" kind of spanking and a "wrong" kind. By the wrong kind I mean a cruel and sadistic beating. This fills a child with hatred, and a deep desire for revenge. This is the kind that is administered with a strap or stick or some other type of parental "weapon." Or it could also mean a humiliating slap in the face.

The right kind of spanking needs no special paraphernalia. Just the hand of the parent administered a few times on the kid's bottom. The right kind of spanking is a *positive* thing. It clears the air, and is vastly to be preferred to moralistic and guilt-inducing parental lectures.

Some of you may have heard the old saying, "Never strike a child in anger." I think that that is psychologically very poor advice, and I suggest the opposite: "Never strike a child *except* in anger."

A child can understand very well when you strike him in anger. He knows you are mad at him and he understands why. What a child cannot understand is when he disobeys mother at 10 A.M. and she tells him, "All right, young man—your father will deal with you when he gets home!" Then when Dad arrives home he is expected to administer a spanking which will "really teach the boy a lesson." That's the kind of cold-blooded spanking a child cannot either understand or forgive.

What I advocate is the "pow-wow" type of spanking: your "pow" followed by his "Wow!" Spank your child only when you are furious at him and feel like letting him have it right then. Too many mothers nowadays seem to be afraid to spank their children. They talk and nag a great deal as a substitute; they try to negotiate with a child. This is a huge mistake because it reduces their authority as parents.

What you should do is to tell your child once or perhaps twice what you want him to do or to stop doing. Then, if he refuses to obey your reasonable request, and you have become frustrated and angry, let him have it right then and there!

After spanking, your first immediate reaction may be frustration and guilt. It may bother you that you've blown your cool.

Courage, Mother, all is not lost!

You can always say to your child, in your own way: "Look Mommy goofed. I lost my temper, and I'm sorry I did." Then you can go on from there. You don't have to be "stuck" with the guilt and the frustration and the unhappy feelings.

Wait until you really feel better about the situation and about your child. It might be five minutes or five hours later. But if you feel you have blown your stack, *it's important to admit it to your child.* Above all, don't pretend to him that the sole reason you spanked him was for his benefit. That's as phony as a three-dollar bill, and he will know it.

The main purpose of spanking, although most parents don't like to admit it, is to relieve the parent's feelings of frustration. All of us need to do this from time to time when our kids get on our nerves.

If we were 100 percent perfect parents, we would all be so mature we would never need to spank our kids except in unusual or extreme situations (such as when a child runs out into the street). The point is, we are not such 100 percent perfect parents. We are not able to administer discipline calmly and serenely all the time. It would be nice if we could. But life doesn't seem to work out that way. We get fed up when our kids misbehave and we lose our cool and swat them. But that's nothing to feel guilty about. We feel better and they feel better, the air is cleared.

Both parent and child get a chance to begin again. Having gotten angry feelings out of your system, you can once more feel positive toward your child. You can then assume your rightful role of parental authority.

Some of you may feel uncomfortable with the notion I have just advanced that the main purpose of spanking is to relieve the frustrated feelings of the parent. You may still be under the illusion that the purpose of spanking is solely to influence your child in a better direction. In this case, I refer you to one of my favorite cartoons, which shows a father whaling the tar out of his little boy, saying as he whales him, "That'll teach you to hit people!" (He's right—it will!)

Nevertheless, we parents are human, and so I say "spank away" if you need to. But, hopefully, if you follow the constructive suggestions I have made on child discipline, you will find you need to spank far less frequently than you otherwise would. And as your child grows older and becomes increasingly capable of self-regulation, you should have to spank far less often.

If you are quite honest with yourself, you will find that there are times when you will lose your temper, fly off the handle at your child, and yell at him or spank him—only to realize afterwards that what he did actually should not have elicited such a violent outburst from you. You were really mad at your husband or your neighbor. Or just cranky for some unknown reason. And you took it out on your child.

What can you do in such a situation? Well, you could pretend you are a holy paragon of virtue and that your child fully deserved the scolding or spanking he got. Or you can have the courage to say something like this to your child: "Danny, mother got mad at you and scolded you. But I can see now that you didn't do anything that was really that bad. I think I was really mad at something else and I was sort of taking it out on you. So I'm sorry."

Your child will feel a wonderful warm feeling toward you for admitting you are human and fallible. This will do wonders for his self-concept—and yours!

Questions for Writing or Discussion

1. Each article has a clearly stated thesis. What is the thesis in each case? Where is it stated?
2. The authors, in each case, make assumptions about the character of parents. What are the assumptions? Which to you seems more realistic?
3. The authors, in each case, have strong views about spanking a child. What are their respective views? Which to you seems more reasonable?
4. Each article recommends specific punishments for specific offenses. What are the crimes and punishments discussed in each article?
5. Write a paper in which you show that one of these two approaches to discipline is better than the other.

CHAPTER 11

WRITING AN ARGUMENTATIVE PAPER

An argumentative paper attempts to strengthen or change an attitude of the reader, or to persuade the reader to a particular point of view by means of logic. (See pp. 31–40 for a discussion of logic.) Although writers of argumentative papers may employ emotional appeals, they place their principal faith in appealing to the understanding of their readers.

The subject matter for argumentative papers must be controversial; that is, there must be the possibility for a difference of opinion on the subject. Otherwise, there would be no need for persuasion. That does not mean, however, that the subject matter need be earth-shaking. Writers differ on how poems should be interpreted or on how cakes should be baked. In the sense that the purpose of an argumentative paper is to persuade a reader to a point of view, you have been writing argumentative papers since you began your study of English composition. In every paper you have written, you have taken a position on a subject and have offered logical reasons for holding that position.

A formal argumentative paper, however, has its own very specific requirements:

1. The writer states the problem or issue, sometimes tracing its causes.
2. In some cases the writer states the possible positions to be taken on the problem.
3. The writer states the position that the paper will take.
4. The writer offers proof that the position taken is the reasonable one to hold.
5. The writer anticipates objections to the position and refutes them.
6. The writer affirms the position and makes a final appeal.

A formal argumentative paper, also, can combine two or more of the methods of development in its organization. A defense of free speech, for example, might begin with a *definition* of the term and then review the major crises that arose in the *process* of maintaining that right in this country.

Since the Declaration of Independence is often held up as a model of a perfect argument, an analysis of it might be helpful. It begins with a statement of the problem: the United States finds it necessary to dissolve its political connections with Great Britain and assert its independence. This is followed by a definition of good government and the assertion that King George has violated the requirements of good government. This is the reason for the break with Great Britain. But Jefferson does not expect the rest of mankind simply to take his word that King George is a dreadful ruler. He offers proof in the form of twenty-eight violations of basic human rights. Then he anticipates possible criticisms of his argument: some might insist that the United States does not need to take such drastic action, that she could settle her differences in the courts; some might say that although George III is tyrannical, the United States must have friends in Great Britain who would plead her case with him. Jefferson refutes these possible criticisms and, having made his case as airtight as possible, concludes with a declaration of the country's independence.

Thomas Jefferson was, of course, a master of argumentation. Here is a student's argumentative paper on an issue that has aroused heated controversy in recent years. Read it and see what you think of his efforts.

The Right to Assume Responsibility
HUGH NICHOLES

The stereotyped motorcyclist is a hulking brute generally complaining about something. With the increasing popularity of motorcycles this stereotype is changing, but motorcyclists are still complaining. Many states have dictated that a motorcyclist may not ride without a crash helmet. At first glance the helmet laws seem to be an insignificant issue, certainly not anything to enrage citizens; the government is merely trying to save lives. The wisdom of wearing crash helmets is not being debated. Motorcyclists maintain that the state has infringed upon their constitutional rights with this law. They are correct.

A government may restrict an individual's freedom of choice if that freedom may cause other members of the public harm. By passing the helmet laws, the government has implied that the wearing of helmets is necessary to protect the public. This implication is unsupportable. A crash helmet protects only the person wearing it; it does nothing to protect bystanders in any way. A crash helmet does not in any way lessen the chances of losing control of a motorcycle, which might cause damage to the general public. In fact, a heavy cumbersome helmet may make hearing difficult or irritate the driver, which could result in damage to the general public. The only way a helmet might be of public benefit is in the protection of the passengers who are riding with the driver. It must be assumed that any passengers are on a motorcycle of their own free will; motorcycles are most impractical kidnapping vehicles. As such, the passenger enjoys the same rights and responsibilities as any motorcyclist.

It has been argued that crash helmets benefit the public indirectly. A person without a helmet who has been killed or mangled in a cycle crash is a liability to society. While this is entirely true, it is also discriminatory when applied only to motorcyclists. Since there are proportionately more deaths caused by car crashes than are caused by motorcycle crashes, and since persons killed or mangled in car crashes are also a liability to society, and since motorcyclists must wear helmets to deter such liabilities, then car drivers should be forced to wear helmets if the law is truly just. The usual response to this idea is the claim that cars offer more protection than motorcycles; riding a motorcycle is a greater risk. This may be true, but amateur mountain climbers and scuba divers would be astonished to find that taking a risk is illegal. The risk must be assumed by the motorcyclist, and it is entirely his responsibility to deal with any potential hazards.

The penalties exacted for riding without a helmet make the law even more objectionable. Not only is the rider fined, but he is cited for a moving traffic violation. From a legal point of view, the refusal to wear a crash helmet places the rider in the same category as reckless drivers, speeders, and other truly dangerous drivers. Violators of the more reasonable traffic laws endanger the general public, while offenders against helmet laws endanger only themselves; there is no valid parallel between the two types of offenses. In spite of this fact, a cyclist may lose his driver's license by repeatedly refusing to protect himself according to the state's standards, even though society does not benefit by the removal of such a person from the road. The punishment is inappropriate for what the state terms a crime.

The governments of many states have created a law which unfairly deprives motorcyclists of their right to be responsible for the safety of their own persons. Through the helmet law, citizens who ride motorcycles may be penalized. As legitimate grounds for the law do not exist, the penalties are unjust. The law should be removed from the books.

Questions for Writing or Discussion

1. Does the writer disapprove of safety helmets or only of laws that require them? Where does he make the distinction? Is the distinction important?
2. Does the writer show an awareness of the arguments that can be offered against his own position?

3. The writing throughout is fairly formal, perhaps because the writer does not want to be mistaken for the "hulking brute" stereotype of motorcyclists. Where does he introduce a note of humor to lighten the tone?
4. How convincing is the author's argument that motorcyclists are the victims of discrimination? Would he be happy if automobile drivers and mountain climbers were required to wear helmets?
5. Should laws require automobile drivers to fasten their seat belts? Would that differ in any significant way from requiring all citizens to eat balanced diets and engage in daily exercises?

The following student paper, perhaps inspired by "Strike Out Little League" (p. 233), calls for a change in attitude toward high school sports. What do you think of it?

More Participant Sports
IRIS MCDOUGAL

In many cities, villages, and other places across the country, taxpayers in increasing numbers have been rejecting levies and bond issues for public school operations and building programs. The reasons for rejection are sometimes simple-minded and sometimes complex and justified. They will not be a part of this paper. The reasons for voter support of levies and bond issues are also complex (and simple-minded) and will not be discussed here. Rather, I shall look at the situation as it is. And I shall ask what the schools themselves can do to maintain, or even improve educational opportunities while undergoing whatever belt-tightening is demanded.

No doubt, there are many areas in which small economies might be achieved. But let's start, for the purposes of this paper, with an economy of some size—an economy, too, that might actually widen educational opportunity and improve its quality.

I am speaking of the substitution of participant sports for the spectator sports that now dominate school athletic programs. We are spending large sums on the outfitting and on the training, care, and comfort of teams in interschool competition in football, basketball, soccer, track, and baseball while neglecting the musculature and physical coordination of the average student.

Along with continued programs looking ultimately to the development of professional and technical skills in the arts and sciences, in commerce and industry, we should be thinking of the future physical health and strength of the average young person. Participant sports of a kind possible in school buildings or grounds should be much more widely available than now, and participation should be required. Every public school should have more tennis, more handball, more softball, more basketball—with many single basketball backboards and nets for one-on-one set-ups. This could all be done without expensive uniforms and equipment and even continue to provide some competitiveness here and there.

There is no reason at all why the secondary schools should have formally organized varsities in every sport. There is no reason why secondary schools should provide a hunting ground for college talent scouts. There is every reason why secondary schools should help their individual students at athletic performance.

Without varsity teams, the most skilled players, the best natural athletes, would, with some faculty guidance, be happy to supervise and teach the less skilled. Athletic costs would go down (it is a myth that football revenues support everything else athletic), and education and health would be served. And the savings example might sooth the taxpayer into fewer rejections of school-board requests in the future.

Questions for Writing or Discussion

1. What is the thesis of the paper? Where is it first introduced?
2. Do you think the writer spends too much space getting into her subject? Why, or why not?
3. Does the writer show an awareness of the arguments that can be offered against her position? If so, where?
4. Does the writer offer enough proof that more participant sports would "widen educational opportunity and improve its quality"? Why do you think so?
5. Do you think the writer's beginning and ending with the taxpayer is a good device? Why, or why not?

Readings

The reading selections that follow are examples of argumentative writing. The first is a short essay by a former major league pitcher. Two are classic documents of American history. The last two are good examples of argumentative writing in popular magazines. As you study them, see if you can identify the six parts of a good argumentative paper in each.

Robin Roberts
STRIKE OUT LITTLE LEAGUE

In 1939, Little League baseball was organized by Bert and George Bebble and Carl Stotz of Williamsport, Pa. What they had in mind in organizing this kids' baseball program, I'll never know. But I'm sure they never visualized the monster it would grow into.

At least 25,000 teams, in about 5,000 leagues, compete for a chance to go to the Little League World Series in Williamsport each summer. These leagues are in more than fifteen countries, although recently the Little League organization has voted to restrict the competition to teams in the United States. If you judge the success of a program by the number of participants, it would appear that Little League has been a tremendous success. More than 600,000 boys from 8 to 12 are involved. But I say Little League is wrong—and I'll try to explain why.

If I told you and your family that I want you to help me with a project from the middle of May until the end of July, one that would totally disrupt your dinner schedule and pay nothing, you would probably tell me to get lost. That's what Little League does. Mothers or fathers or both spend four or five nights a week taking children to Little League, watching the game, coming home around 8 or 8:30 and sitting down to a late dinner.

These games are played at this hour because the adults are running the programs and this is the only time they have available. These same adults are in most cases unqualified as instructors and do not have the emotional stability to work with children of this age. The dedication and sincerity of these instructors cannot be questioned, but the purpose of this dedication should be. Youngsters eligible for Little League are of the age when their concentration lasts, at most, for five seconds—and without sustained concentration organized athletic programs are a farce.

Most instructors will never understand this. As a result there is a lot of pressure on these young people to do something that is unnatural for their age—so there will always be hollering and tremendous disappointment for most of these players. For acting their age, they are made to feel incompetent. This is a basic fault of Little League.

If you watch a Little League game, in most cases the pitchers are the most mature. They throw harder, and if they throw strikes very few batters can hit the ball. Consequently, it makes good baseball sense for most hitters to take the pitch. Don't swing. Hope for a walk. That could be a player's instruction for four years. The fun is in hitting the ball; the coach says don't swing. That may be sound baseball, but it does nothing to help a young player develop his hitting. What would seem like a basic training ground for baseball often turns out to be a program of negative thoughts that only retards a young player.

I believe more good young athletes are turned off by the pressure of organized Little League than are helped. Little Leagues have no value as a training ground for baseball fundamentals. The instruction at that age, under the pressure of an organized league program, creates more doubt and eliminates the naturalness that is most important.

If I'm going to criticize such a popular program as Little League, I'd better have some thoughts on what changes I would like to see.

First of all, I wouldn't start any programs until the school year is over. Any young student has enough of a schedule during the school year to keep busy.

These programs should be played in the afternoon—with a softball. Kids have a natural fear of a baseball; it hurts when it hits you. A softball is bigger, easier to see and easier to hit. You get to run the bases more and there isn't as much danger of injury if one gets hit with the ball. Boys and girls could play together. Different teams would be chosen every day. The instructors would be young adults home from college, or high-school graduates. The instructor could be the pitcher and the umpire at the same time. These programs could be run on public playgrounds or in schoolyards.

I guarantee that their dinner would be at the same time every night. The fathers could come home after work and relax; most of all, the kids would have a good time playing ball in a program in which hitting the ball and running the bases are the big things.

When you start talking about young people playing baseball at 13 to 15, you may have something. Organize them a little, but be careful; they are still young. But from 16 and on, work them really hard. Discipline them, organize the leagues, strive to win championships, travel all over. Give this age all the time and attention you can.

I believe Little League has done just the opposite. We've worked hard with the 8- to 12-year-olds. We overorganize them, put them under pressure they can't handle and make playing baseball seem important. When our young people reach 16 they would appreciate the attention and help from the parents, and that's when our present programs almost stop.

The whole idea of Little League baseball is wrong. There are alternatives available for more sensible programs. With the same dedication that has made the Little League such a major part of many of our lives, I'm sure we'll find the answer.

I still don't know what those three gentlemen in Williamsport had in mind when they organized Little League baseball. I'm sure they didn't want parents arguing with their children about kids' games. I'm sure they didn't want to have family meals disrupted for three months every year. I'm sure they didn't want young athletes hurting their arms pitching under pressure at such a young age. I'm sure they didn't want young boys who don't have much athletic ability made to feel that something is wrong with them because they can't play baseball. I'm sure they didn't want a group of coaches drafting the players each year for different teams. I'm sure they didn't want unqualified men working with the young players. I'm sure they didn't realize how normal it is for an 8-year-old boy to be scared of a thrown or batted baseball.

For the life of me, I can't figure out what they had in mind.

Questions for Writing or Discussion

1. The author pitched for the Philadelphia Phillies from 1948 to 1962 and was elected to the Baseball Hall of Fame in 1976. Does this information make you take his arguments more seriously or

does it make no difference? Where does the author reveal his special inside knowledge of and experience with baseball?

2. Does the author ignore any strong arguments that could be made in favor of Little League?

3. Does the author exaggerate the drawbacks of Little League?

4. Is the conclusion an effective wrap-up or does it introduce fresh points?

5. What is the function of the second paragraph, the one in which the author writes about the success of Little League?

DECLARATION OF INDEPENDENCE

In Congress, July 4, 1776
The unanimous Declaration of the thirteen
United States of America

When in the course of human events, it becomes necessary for one people to dissolve the political bands which have connected them with another, and to assume among the powers of the earth, the separate and equal station to which the Laws of Nature and of Nature's God entitle them, a decent respect to the opinions of mankind requires that they should declare the causes which impel them to the separation.

We hold these truths to be self-evident, that all men are created equal, that they are endowed by their Creator with certain unalienable rights, that among these are life, liberty and the pursuit of happiness. That to secure these rights, governments are instituted among men, deriving their just powers from the consent of the governed. That whenever any form of government becomes destructive of these ends, it is the right of the people to alter or to abolish it, and to institute new government, laying its foundation on such principles and organizing its powers in such form, as to them shall seem most likely to effect their safety and happiness. Prudence, indeed, will dictate that governments long established should not be changed for light and transient causes; and accordingly all experience hath shown, that mankind are more disposed to suffer, while evils are sufferable, than to right themselves by abolishing the forms to which they are accustomed. But when a long train of abuses and usurpations, pursuing invariably the same object evinces a design to reduce them under absolute despotism, it is their right, it is their duty, to throw off such government, and to provide new guards for their future security. Such has been the patient sufferance of these Colonies; and such is now the necessity which constrains them to alter their former systems of government. The history of the present King of Great Britain is a history of repeated injuries and usurpations, all having in direct object the establishment of an absolute tyranny over these States. To prove this, let facts be submitted to a candid world.

He has refused his assent to laws, the most wholesome and necessary for the public good.

He has forbidden his Governors to pass laws of immediate and pressing importance, unless suspended in their operation till his assent should be obtained; and when so suspended, he has utterly neglected to attend to them.

He has refused to pass other laws for the accommodation of large districts of people, unless those people would relinquish the right of representation in the Legislature, a right inestimable to them and formidable to tyrants only.

He has called together legislative bodies at places unusual, uncomfortable, and distant from the depository of their public records, for the sole purpose of fatiguing them into compliance with his measures.

He has dissolved representative houses repeatedly, for opposing with manly firmness his invasions on the rights of the people.

He has refused for a long time, after such dissolutions, to cause others to be elected; whereby the legislative powers, incapable of annihilation, have returned to the people at large for their exercise; the State remaining in the meantime exposed to all the dangers of invasion from without and convulsions within.

He has endeavoured to prevent the population of these states; for that purpose obstructing the laws of naturalization of foreigners; refusing to pass others to encourage their migration hither, and raising the conditions of new appropriations of lands.

He has obstructed the administration of justice, by refusing his assent to laws for establishing judiciary powers.

He has made judges dependent on his will alone, for the tenure of their offices, and the amount and payment of their salaries.

He has erected a multitude of new offices, and sent hither swarms of officers to harass our people, and eat out their substance.

He has kept among us, in times of peace, standing armies without the consent of our legislatures.

He has affected to render the military independent of and superior to the civil power.

He has combined with others to subject us to a jurisdiction foreign to our constitution, and unacknowledged by our laws; giving his assent to their acts of pretended legislation:

For quartering large bodies of armed troops among us:

For protecting them, by a mock trial, from punishment for any murders which they should commit on the inhabitants of these States:

For cutting off our trade with all parts of the world:

For imposing taxes on us without our consent:

For depriving us in many cases, of the benefits of trial by jury:

For transporting us beyond seas to be tried for pretended offences:

For abolishing the free system of English laws in a neighbouring Province, establishing therein an arbitrary government, and enlarging its boundaries so as to render it at once an example and fit instrument for introducing the same absolute rule into these Colonies:

For taking away our Charters, abolishing our most valuable laws, and altering fundamentally the forms of our governments:

For suspending our own Legislatures, and declaring themselves invested with power to legislate for us in all cases whatsoever.

He has abdicated government here, by declaring us out of his protection and waging war against us.

He has plundered our seas, ravaged our coasts, burnt our towns, and destroyed the lives of our people.

He is at this time transporting large armies of foreign mercenaries to complete the works of death, desolation and tyranny, already begun with circumstances of cruelty and perfidy scarcely paralleled in the most barbarous ages, and totally unworthy the head of a civilized nation.

He has constrained our fellow citizens taken captive on the high seas to bear arms against their country, to become the executioners of their friends and brethren, or to fall themselves by their hands.

He has excited domestic insurrections amongst us, and has endeavoured to bring on the inhabitants of our frontiers, the merciless Indian savages, whose known rule of warfare, is an undistinguished destruction of all ages, sexes, and conditions.

In every stage of these oppressions we have petitioned for redress in the most humble terms: our repeated petitions have been answered only by repeated injury. A prince whose character is thus marked by every act which may define a tyrant is unfit to be the ruler of a free people.

Nor have we been wanting in attention to our British brethren. We have warned them from time to time of attempts by their legislature to extend an unwarrantable jurisdiction over us. We have reminded them of the circumstances of our emigration and settlement here. We have appealed to their native justice and magnanimity, and we have conjured them by the ties of our common kindred to disavow these usurpations, which would inevitably interrupt our connections and correspondence. They too have been deaf to the voices of justice and of consanguinity. We must, therefore, acquiesce in the necessity, which denounces our separation, and hold them, as we hold the rest of mankind, enemies in war, in peace friends.

We, therefore, the Representatives of the United States of America, in General Congress assembled, appealing to the Supreme Judge of the world for the rectitude of our intentions, do, in the name, and by authority of the good people of these Colonies, solemnly publish and declare, That these United Colonies are, and of right ought to be Free and Independent States; that they are absolved from all allegiance to the British Crown, and that all political connection between them and the state of Great Britain, is and ought to be totally dissolved; and that as Free and Independent States, they have full power to levy war, conclude peace, contract alliances, establish commerce, and to do all other acts and things which Independent States may of right do. And for the support of this declaration, with a firm reliance on the protection of Divine Providence, we mutually pledge to each other our lives, our fortunes, and our sacred honor.

Questions for Writing or Discussion

1. What does the Declaration of Independence devote most of its efforts to proving?

2. What basic assumptions does it make that do not need to be proved?
3. How does the Declaration of Independence take special pains to show that it is the product of rational, responsible men rather than hotheads? This question should make a good subject for a paper.
4. Where does the language become most emotional? Is this emotion justified where it occurs, and, if so, why?

Martin Luther King, Jr.
From LETTER FROM BIRMINGHAM JAIL[1]

April 16, 1963

My Dear Fellow Clergymen:

While confined here in the Birmingham city jail, I came across your recent statement calling my present activities "unwise and untimely." Seldom do I pause to answer criticism of my work and ideas. If I sought to answer all the criticisms that cross my desk, my secretaries would have little time for anything other than such correspondence in the course of the day, and I would have no time for constructive work. But since I feel that you are men of genuine good will and that your criticisms are sincerely set forth, I want to try to answer your statement in what I hope will be patient and reasonable terms.

I think I should indicate why I am here in Birmingham, since you have been influenced by the view which argues against "outsiders coming in." I have the honor of serving as president of the Southern Christian Leadership Conference, an organization operating in every southern state, with headquarters in Atlanta, Georgia. We have some eighty-five affiliated organizations across the South, and one of them is the Alabama Christian Movement for Human Rights. Frequently we share staff, educational and financial resources with our affiliates. Several months ago the affiliate here in Birmingham asked us to be on call to engage in a nonviolent direct-action program if such were deemed necessary. We readily consented, and when the hour came we lived up to our promise. So I, along with several members of my staff, am here because I was invited here. I am here because I have organizational ties here.

[1]*Author's Note:* This response to a published statement by eight fellow clergymen from Alabama (Bishop C. C. J. Carpenter, Bishop Joseph A. Durick, Rabbi Hilton L. Grafman, Bishop Paul Hardin, Bishop Holan B. Harmon, the Reverend George M. Murray, the Reverend Edward V. Ramage and the Reverend Earl Stallings) was composed under somewhat constricting circumstances. Begun on the margins of the newspaper in which the statement appeared while I was in jail, the letter was continued on scraps of writing paper supplied by a friendly Negro trusty, and concluded on a pad my attorneys were eventually permitted to leave me. Although the text remains in substance unaltered, I have indulged in the author's prerogative of polishing it for publication.

But more basically, I am in Birmingham because injustice is here. Just as the prophets of the eighth century B.C. left their villages and carried their "thus saith the Lord" far beyond the boundaries of their home towns, and just as the Apostle Paul left his village of Tarsus and carried the gospel of Jesus Christ to the far corners of the Greco-Roman world, so am I compelled to carry the gospel of freedom beyond my own home town. Like Paul, I must constantly respond to the Macedonian call for aid.

Moreover, I am cognizant of the interrelatedness of all communities and states. I cannot sit idly by in Atlanta and not be concerned about what happens in Birmingham. Injustice anywhere is a threat to justice everywhere. We are caught in an inescapable network of mutuality, tied in a single garment of destiny. Whatever affects one directly, affects all indirectly. Never again can we afford to live with the narrow, provincial "outside agitator" idea. Anyone who lives inside the United States can never be considered an outsider anywhere within its bounds.

You deplore the demonstrations taking place in Birmingham. But your statement, I am sorry to say, fails to express a similar concern for the conditions that brought about the demonstrations. I am sure that none of you would want to rest content with the superficial kind of social analysis that deals merely with effects and does not grapple with underlying causes. It is unfortunate that demonstrations are taking place in Birmingham, but it is even more unfortunate that the city's white power structure left the Negro community with no alternative.

In any nonviolent campaign there are four basic steps: collection of the facts to determine whether injustices exist; negotiation; self-purification; and direct action. We have gone through all these steps in Birmingham. There can be no gainsaying the fact that racial injustice engulfs this community. Birmingham is probably the most thoroughly segregated city in the United States. Its ugly record of brutality is widely known. Negroes have experienced grossly unjust treatment in the courts. There have been more unsolved bombings of Negro homes and churches in Birmingham than in any other city in the nation. These are the hard, brutal facts of the case. On the basis of these conditions, Negro leaders sought to negotiate with the city fathers. But the latter consistently refused to engage in good-faith negotiation.

Then, last September, came the opportunity to talk with leaders of Birmingham's economic community. In the course of the negotiations, certain promises were made by the merchants—for example, to remove the stores' humiliating racial signs. On the basis of these promises, the Reverend Fred Shuttlesworth and the leaders of the Alabama Christian Movement for Human Rights agreed to a moratorium on all demonstrations. As the weeks and months went by, we realized that we were the victims of a broken promise. A few signs, briefly removed, returned; the others remained.

As in so many past experiences, our hopes had been blasted, and the shadow of deep disappointment settled upon us. We had no alternative except to prepare for direct action, whereby we would present our very bodies as a means of laying our case before the conscience of the local and the national community. Mindful of the difficulties involved, we decided to undertake a process of self-purification. We began a series of workshops on nonviolence, and we repeatedly asked ourselves: "Are you able to accept blows without retaliating?" "Are you able to endure the ordeal of jail?" We decided to schedule our direct-action program for the Easter season, realizing that except for Christmas, this is the main shopping period of the year. Knowing that a strong economic-withdrawal program would be the by-product of direct action, we felt that this would be the best time to bring pressure to bear on the merchants for the needed change.

Then it occurred to us that Birmingham's mayoral election was coming up in March, and we speedily decided to postpone action until after election day. When we discovered that the Commissioner of Public Safety, Eugene "Bull" Connor, had piled up enough votes to be in the runoff, we decided again to postpone action until the day after the run-off so that the demonstrations could not be used to cloud the issues. Like many others, we wanted to see Mr. Connor defeated, and to this end we endured postponement after postponement. Having aided in this community need, we felt that our direct-action program could be delayed no longer.

You may well ask: "Why direct action? Why sit-ins, marches and so forth? Isn't negotiation a better path?" You are quite right in calling for negotiation. Indeed, this is the very purpose of direct action. Nonviolent direct action seeks to create such a crisis and foster such a tension that a community which has constantly refused to negotiate is forced to confront the issue. It seeks so to dramatize the issue that it can no longer be ignored. My citing the creation of tension as part of the work of the nonviolent-resister may sound rather shocking. But I must confess that I am not afraid of the word "tension." I have earnestly opposed violent tension, but there is a type of constructive, nonviolent tension which is necessary for growth. Just as Socrates felt that it was necessary to create a tension in the mind so that individuals could rise from the bondage of myths and half-truths to the unfettered realm of creative analysis and objective appraisal, so must we see the need for nonviolent gadflies to create the kind of tension in society that will help men rise from the dark depths of prejudice and racism to the majestic heights of understanding and brotherhood.

The purpose of our direct-action program is to create a situation so crisis-packed that it will inevitably open the door to negotiation. I therefore concur with you in your call for negotiation. Too long has our beloved Southland been bogged down in a tragic effort to live in monologue rather than dialogue.

One of the basic points in your statement is that the action that I and my associates have taken in Birmingham is untimely. Some have asked: "Why didn't you give the new city administration time to act?" The only answer that I can give to this query is that the new Birmingham administration must be prodded about as much as the outgoing one, before it will act. We are sadly mistaken if we feel that the election of Albert Boutwell as mayor will bring the millennium to Birmingham. While Mr. Boutwell is a much more gentle person than Mr. Connor, they are both segregationists, dedicated to maintenance of the status quo. I have hope that Mr. Boutwell will be reasonable enough to see the futility of massive resistance to desegregation. But he will not see this without pressure from devotees of civil rights. My friends, I must say to you that we have not made a single gain in civil rights without determined legal and nonviolent pressure. Lamentably, it is an historical fact that privileged groups seldom give up their privileges voluntarily. Individuals may see the moral light and voluntarily give up their unjust posture; but, as Reinhold Niebuhr has reminded us, groups tend to be more immoral than individuals.

We know through painful experience that freedom is never voluntarily given by the oppressor; it must be demanded by the oppressed. Frankly, I have yet to engage in a direct-action campaign that was "well timed" in the view of those who have not suffered unduly from the disease of segregation. For years now I have heard the word "Wait!" It rings in the ear of every Negro with piercing familiarity. This "Wait" has almost always meant "Never." We must come to see, with one of our distinguished jurists, that "justice too long delayed is justice denied."

We have waited for more than 340 years for our constitutional and God-given rights. The nations of Asia and Africa are moving with jetlike speed toward gaining political independence, but we still creep at horse-and-buggy pace toward gaining a cup of coffee at a lunch counter. Perhaps it is easy for those who have never felt the stinging darts of segregation to say, "Wait." But when you have seen vicious mobs lynch your mothers and fathers at will and drown your sisters and brothers at whim; when you have seen hate-filled policemen curse, kick and even kill your black brothers and sisters; when you see the vast majority of your twenty million Negro brothers smothering in an airtight cage of poverty in the midst of an affluent society; when you suddenly find your tongue twisted and your speech stammering as you seek to explain to your six-year-old daughter why she can't go to the public amusement park that has just been advertised on television, and see tears welling up in her eyes when she is told that Funtown is closed to colored children, and see ominous clouds of inferiority beginning to form in her little mental sky, and see her beginning to distort her personality by developing an unconscious bitterness toward white people; when you have to concoct an answer for a five-year-old son who is asking: "Daddy, why do white people treat colored people so mean?"; when you take a cross-country drive and find it necessary to sleep night after night in the uncomfortable corners of your automobile because no motel will accept you; when you are humiliated day in and day out by nagging signs reading "white" and "colored"; when your first name becomes "nigger," your middle name becomes "boy" (however old you are) and your last name becomes "John," and your wife and mother are never given the respected title "Mrs."; when you are harried by day and haunted by night by the fact that you are a Negro, living constantly at tiptoe stance, never quite knowing what to expect next, and are plagued with inner fears and outer resentments; when you are forever fighting a degenerating sense of "nobodiness"—then you will understand why we find it difficult to wait. There comes a time when the cup of endurance runs over, and men are no longer willing to be plunged into the abyss of despair. I hope, sirs, you can understand our legitimate and unavoidable impatience.

You express a great deal of anxiety over our willingness to break laws. This is certainly a legitimate concern. Since we so diligently urge people to obey the Supreme Court's decision of 1954 outlawing segregation in the public schools, at first glance it may seem rather paradoxical for us consciously to break laws. One may well ask: "How can you advocate breaking some laws and obeying others?" The answer lies in the fact that there are two types of laws: just and unjust. I would be the first to advocate obeying just laws. One has not only a legal but a moral responsibility to obey just laws. Conversely, one has a moral responsibility to disobey unjust laws. I would agree with St. Augustine that "an unjust law is no law at all."

Now, what is the difference between the two? How does one determine whether a law is just or unjust? A just law is a man-made code that squares with the moral law or the law of God. An unjust law is a code that is out of harmony with the moral law. To put it in the terms of St. Thomas Aquinas: An unjust law is a human law that is not rooted in eternal law and natural law. Any law that uplifts human personality is just. Any law that degrades human personality is unjust. All segregation statutes are unjust because segregation distorts the soul and damages the personality. It gives the segregator a false sense of superiority and the segregated a false sense of inferiority. Segregation, to use the terminology of the Jewish philosopher Martin Buber, substitutes an "I-it" relationship for an "I-thou" relationship and ends up relegating persons to the status of things. Hence segregation is not only politically, economically and sociologically unsound, it is morally wrong and sinful. Paul Tillich has said that sin is separation. Is not segregation an existential expression of man's tragic separation, his awful estrangement, his terrible sinfulness? Thus it is that I can urge men to obey the 1954 decision of the Supreme Court, for it is morally right; and I can urge them to disobey segregation ordinances, for they are morally wrong.

Let us consider a more concrete example of just and unjust laws. An unjust law is a code that a numerical or power majority group compels a minority group to obey but does not make binding on itself. This is *difference* made legal. By the same token, a just law is a code that a majority compels a minority to follow and that it is willing to follow itself. This is *sameness* made legal.

Let me give another explanation. A law is unjust if it is inflicted on a minority that, as a result of being denied the right to vote, had no part in enacting or devising the law. Who can say that the legislature of Alabama which set up that state's segregation laws was democratically elected? Throughout Alabama all sorts of devious methods are used to prevent Negroes from becoming registered voters, and there are some counties in which, even though Negroes constitute a majority of the population, not a single Negro is registered. Can any law enacted under such circumstances be considered democratically structured?

Sometimes a law is just on its face and unjust in its application. For instance, I have been arrested on a charge of parading without a permit. Now, there is nothing wrong in having an ordinance which requires a permit for a parade. But such an ordinance becomes unjust when it is used to maintain segregation and to deny citizens the First-Amendment privilege of peaceful assembly and protest.

I hope you are able to see the distinction I am trying to point out. In no

sense do I advocate evading or defying the law, as would the rabid segrega-
tionist. That would lead to anarchy. One who breaks an unjust law must do
so openly, lovingly, and with a willingness to accept the penalty. I submit
that an individual who breaks a law that conscience tells him is unjust, and
who willingly accepts the penalty of imprisonment in order to arouse the
conscience of the community over its injustice, is in reality expressing the
highest respect for law.

Of course, there is nothing new about this kind of civil disobedience. It
was evidenced sublimely in the refusal of Shadrach, Meshach and Abednego
to obey the laws of Nebuchadnezzar, on the ground that a higher moral law
was at stake. It was practiced superbly by the early Christians, who were
willing to face hungry lions and the excruciating pain of chopping blocks
rather than submit to certain unjust laws of the Roman Empire. To a degree,
academic freedom is a reality today because Socrates practiced civil disobedience. In our own nation, the Boston Tea Party represented a massive act
of civil disobedience.

We should never forget that everything Adolf Hitler did in Germany was
"legal" and everything the Hungarian freedom fighters did in Hungary was
"illegal." It was "illegal" to aid and comfort a Jew in Hitler's Germany. Even
so, I am sure that, had I lived in Germany at the time, I would have aided
and comforted my Jewish brothers. If today I lived in a Communist country
where certain principles dear to the Christian faith are suppressed, I would
openly advocate disobeying that country's antireligious laws. . . .

Before closing I feel impelled to mention one other point in your statement that has troubled me profoundly. You warmly commended the Birmingham police force for keeping "order" and "preventing violence." I
doubt that you would have so warmly commended the police force if you
had seen its dogs sinking their teeth into unarmed, nonviolent Negroes. I
doubt that you would so quickly commend the policemen if you were to
observe their ugly and inhumane treatment of Negroes here in the city jail;
if you were to watch them push and curse old Negro women and young
Negro girls; if you were to see them slap and kick old Negro men and young
boys; if you were to observe them, as they did on two occasions, refuse to
give us food because we wanted to sing our grace together. I cannot join you
in your praise of the Birmingham police department.

It is true that the police have exercised a degree of discipline in handling
the demonstrators. In this sense they have conducted themselves rather
"nonviolently" in public. But for what purpose? To preserve the evil system
of segregation. Over the past few years I have consistently preached that
nonviolence demands that the means we use must be as pure as the ends we
seek. I have tried to make clear that it is wrong to use immoral means to
attain moral ends. But now I must affirm that it is just as wrong, or perhaps
even more so, to use moral means to preserve immoral ends. Perhaps Mr.
Connor and his policemen have been rather nonviolent in public as was
Chief Pritchett in Albany, Georgia, but they have used the moral means of
nonviolence to maintain the immoral end of racial injustice. As T. S. Eliot
has said: "The last temptation is the greatest treason: To do the right deed
for the wrong reason."

I wish you had commended the Negro sit-inners and demonstrators of Birmingham for their sublime courage, their willingness to suffer and their amazing discipline in the midst of great provocation. One day the South will recognize its real heroes. They will be the James Merediths, with the noble sense of purpose that enables them to face jeering and hostile mobs, and with the agonizing loneliness that characterizes the life of the pioneer. They will be old, oppressed, battered Negro women, symbolized in a seventy-two-year-old woman in Montgomery, Alabama, who rose up with a sense of dignity and with her people decided not to ride segregated buses, and who responded with ungrammatical profundity to one who inquired about her weariness: "My feets is tired, but my soul is at rest." They will be the young high school and college students, the young ministers of the gospel and a host of their elders, courageously and nonviolently sitting in at lunch counters, and willingly going to jail for conscience' sake. One day the South will know that when these disinherited children of God sat down at lunch counters, they were in reality standing up for what is best in the American dream and for the most sacred values in our Judaeo-Christian heritage, thereby bringing our nation back to those great wells of democracy which were dug deep by the founding fathers in their formulation of the Constitution and the Declaration of Independence.

Never before have I written so long a letter. I'm afraid it is much too long to take your precious time. I can assure you that it would have been much shorter if I had been writing from a comfortable desk, but what else can one do when he is alone in a narrow jail cell, other than write long letters, think long thoughts and pray long prayers?

If I have said anything in this letter that overstates the truth and indicates an unreasonable impatience, I beg you to forgive me. If I have said anything that understates the truth and indicates my having a patience that allows me to settle for anything less than brotherhood, I beg God to forgive me.

I hope this letter finds you strong in the faith. I also hope that circumstances will soon make it possible for me to meet each of you, not as an integrationist or a civil-rights leader but as a fellow clergyman and a Christian brother. Let us all hope that the dark clouds of racial prejudice will soon pass away and the deep fog of misunderstanding will be lifted from our fear-drenched communities, and in some not too distant tomorrow the radiant stars of love and brotherhood will shine over our great nation with all their scintillating beauty.

Yours for the cause of Peace and Brotherhood,
Martin Luther King, Jr.

Questions for Writing or Discussion

1. What difference does the author draw between violent tension and "creative tension"?
2. What is the immediate aim of the protest demonstrations? What is the long-range aim?

3. How does the author distinguish between just laws and unjust laws? Does he believe that people have the right to disobey any law with which they disagree?

4. What section of the "Letter" relies primarily on an appeal to emotion rather than on logical argument? Is the emotional appeal out of place?

5. The direct audience for the letter is a group of clergymen who had previously been sympathetic to King's cause. What elements in the "Letter" show King's awareness of this special audience?

Suzanne Britt Jordan
"I WANTS TO GO TO THE PROSE"

I'm tired—and have been for quite a while. In fact, I think I can pinpoint the exact minute at which I first felt the weariness begin. I had been teaching for three years at a community college. I had, for quite a while, overlooked ignorance, dismissed arrogance, championed fairness, emphasized motivation, boosted egos and tolerated laziness. I was, in short, the classic modern educator.

One day a student, Marylou Simmons, dropped by my office. She had not completed a single assignment and had missed perhaps 50 per cent of her classes. Her writing, what little I saw of it, was illogical, grammatically incorrect and sloppy. "Can I help you, Marylou?" I said cheerily, ever the understanding and forgiving teacher. Her lip began to tremble; her eyes grew teary. It seemed she had been having trouble with her boyfriend. "I'm sorry, but what can *I* do?" I asked. Suddenly all business, Marylou said, "Since I've been so unhappy, I thought you might want to just give me a D or an Incomplete on the course." She smiled encouragingly, even confidently. That's when the weariness set in, the moment at which I turned into a flaming conservative in matters educational. Whatever Marylou's troubles, I suddenly saw that I was not the cause, nor was I about to be the solution.

Namby-Pamby Courses   When I read about declining SAT scores, the "functional illiteracy" of our students, the namby-pamby courses, the army of child psychologists, reading aides, educational liaisons, starry-eyed administrators and bungling fools who people our school systems, my heart sinks. Public schools abide mediocre students; put 18-year-olds, who can't decide what to wear in the morning, into independent study programs; excuse every absence under the sun, and counsel, counsel, counsel. A youngster in my own school system got into a knife fight and was expelled—for one week. I noticed in the paper that bus drivers regularly see riders smoking marijuana and drinking wine on the bus at, for God's sake, 8 in the morning. I could go on, but the public knows well enough the effects of a system of education gone awry.

Consider for a moment what caused the mess. A few years ago people began demanding their rights. Fair enough. They wanted equal education under the law. I'm for it. Social consciousness was born. Right on. Now, enter the big wrong turn, the one that sent our schools into never-never land. We suddenly, naively, believed that by offering equal opportunities we could (1) make everybody happy, (2) make everybody well-adjusted, (3) forgive everybody who failed, and (4) expect gratitude to boot. When students were surly, uncooperative, whiny and apathetic, educators decided they themselves didn't know how to teach. So they made it easier on the poor, disadvantaged victims of broken homes, the misfits, the unloved. Well and good. But the catch to such lofty theories is evident. Poverty, ignorance and just plain orneriness will always abound. We look for every reason in the world for the declining test scores of our children, except for stupidity and laziness.

A Curmudgeon Speaks   I'm perfectly aware that I sound like an old curmudgeon and it frightens me more than it offends you. But I have accepted what educators can't seem to face. The function of schools, their first and primary obligation, is not to probe tender psyches, to feed and clothe the homeless, nor to be the papa and mama a kid never had. The job is to teach.

The teacher's job is to know his subject, inside out, backward, forward and every which way. Nothing unnerves a student more than to have a teacher who doesn't know his or her stuff. Incompetence they cannot abide. Neither can I.

Before educators lost their way and tried to diversify by getting into the business of molding human beings, a teacher was, ideally, someone who knew a certain body of information and conveyed it. Period. Remember crochety old Miss Dinwiddie, who could recite 40 lines of the "Aeneid" at a clip? Picture Mr. Wassleheimer, who could give a zero to a cheating student without pausing in his lecture on frog dissection. Every student knew that it wasn't wise to mess around with a teacher who had the subject down cold. They were the teachers we once despised and later admired.

I want them back, those fearsome, awe-inspiring experts. I want them back because they knew what a school was for and didn't waste any time getting on with the task at hand. They were hard, even at times unjust, but when they were through, we knew those multiplication tables blindfolded with both trembling hands tied behind our backs.

Before the schoolmasters and the administrators change, they will have to shake off the guilt, the simpering, apologetic smiles and the Freudian theories. Which is crueler? Flunking a kid who has flunked or passing a kid who has flunked? Which teaches more about the realities of life? Which, in fact, shows more respect for the child as a human being?

Just today I talked to a big blond bruiser of a football player who wants to learn the basics of grammar. I didn't tell him it was too late. You see, he was a very, very good football player, so good that he never failed a course in high school. He had written on a weekly theme, "I wants to go to the prose and come fames." He may become a pro, may even become famous, but he will probably never read a good book, write a coherent letter or read a story to his children. I will, however, flunk him if he does not learn the material in the course. My job means too much to me to sacrifice my standards and turn soft. Suppose that every time my student played football badly, the coach said it was "just a game." Suppose the coach allowed him to drink booze, stay up all night, eat poorly and play sloppily. My student would be summarily dismissed from the team or the team would lose the game. So it goes with academic courses.

Life is Real   The young people are interested, I think, in taking their knocks, just as adults must take theirs. Students deserve a fair chance, and, failing to take advantage of that chance, a straightforward dismissal. It has been said that government must guarantee equal opportunity, not equal results. I like that. Through the theoretical fog that has clouded our perceptions and blanketed our minds, we know what is equitable and right. Mother put it another way. She always said, "Life is real; life is earnest." Incidentally, she taught me Latin and never gave me air in a jug. I had to breathe on my own. So do we all.

Questions for Writing or Discussion

1. What is the thesis of the article?
2. What is the relationship between the title of the article and the thesis?
3. What is the function of the fourth paragraph, in which the author discusses the causes of the "mess"? What is the "mess"?
4. The author uses an analogy (see p. 247) in the next to the last paragraph. Does the analogy clarify her point? Is it fair? Why, or why not?
5. What is a curmudgeon? Does the author indeed sound like an old curmudgeon? If so, does the tone detract from the persuasiveness of her argument?
6. Do you agree that "young people are interested . . . in taking their knocks, just as adults take theirs"?
7. Are there, do you think, students who should be given some breaks, some special compensations? Why?

Theodore M. Bernstein
I FAVOR WHOM'S DOOM

If I have anything to say about it, the pronoun *whom* will be dropped from the English language except in one context. And I do have something to say about it in what follows.

Not only is *whom* useless and senseless; it is in addition a complicated nuisance. Think, for example, of the puzzle-solving needed to determine the proper pronoun to use in each of these sentences:

"A suspect *whom* the police identified as John Jones was arrested."

"A suspect *who* the police said was John Jones was arrested."

"*Whomever (whoever?)* she marries will not be the boss in her home."

The pronoun in the objective case form serves no purpose in the language and should be banished, except when it follows immediately after a preposition and "sounds natural" even to the masses, as in "To *whom* it may concern" or "He married the girl for *whom* he had risked his life." Except for such postprepositional uses of *whom*, forget it.

Dropping *whom* will be neither radical nor unprecedented. The wiping out of case declensions of pronouns began centuries ago. The seven Indo-European cases were reduced to four, then by the time of the Middle English period the four were cut down to three with the disappearance of the distinction between the dative and the accusative. More than a century and a half ago Noah Webster denounced *whom* as useless and argued that common sense was on the side of "*Who* did he marry?" And half a century ago H. L. Mencken in "The American Language" said, "Although the schoolma'am continues the heroic task of trying to teach the difference between *who* and *whom*, *whom* is fast vanishing from Standard American; in the vulgar language it is virtually extinct."

Mencken made a valid point when he said that *whom* was fast vanishing, but the real point is the vanishing point: How can we speed its arrival? How can we escape from this pedagogical perplexity?

It seemed to me that the first step was to find out what experts on English thought about *whom's* doom. So I drew up a list of a couple of dozen teachers, consultants on dictionaries, writers and knowledgeable linguists, striving, so far as I was able, to achieve a balance between liberals and conservatives. A copy of the foregoing argument was sent to each of them along with a letter asking each to indicate agreement or disagreement with it by a vote of "yea" or "nay" and inviting any comments the recipient cared to make. Not to keep you in suspense, the results were 6 "nays," 15 "yeas" and 4 in-betweens, most of which leaned more to the "yea" side than the "nay" side.

Among the "nay"-sayers, Prof. Lionel Trilling of Columbia University commented, "Difficult though the correct use of *whom* often is, it seems to me that the difficulty it entails is of a kind the confrontation of which tends to build character, and in our cultural situation we need all the character we can get." Other "nay"-sayers were Russell Baker, *New York Times* columnist; Herbert Brucker, former editor of The *Hartford Courant*; Rudolf Flesch, writer on English style; Marya Mannes, author and critic, and Walter W. (Red) Smith, *New York Times* sports columnist.

There isn't space to quote all 15 "yea"-sayers, but Dwight Macdonald, author and critic, said, "YES, a thousand times YES on your proposal to deep-six *whom*. One of the practical beauties of English is its delightful poverty of inflection (ditto its confining gender to sex). English has replaced French as the world's second language precisely because of its lack of such archaic frills. So do let's excise this vermiform appendix."

William F. Buckley Jr., editor of *National Review*, commented, "Your distinction is exactly correct. Where 'who' *sounds* right, it should be retained

. . . You are aware of the Leo Durocher answer to a tough question at a banquet speech? (Pause) 'Whom knows?' "*

Norman Cousins, editor of *Saturday Review,* was one of the in-betweens. "Admittedly," he said, "there are cases when insistence on correct usage is stuffy and pedantic; I see no reason why *who* shouldn't suffice. But if you abolish *whom,* as you propose, will you not therefore be judging those who use the word correctly? In this case, you are abolishing sin for the sinner but superimposing it on the virtuous."

"Naturally I agree with the general purport of your treatment of *whom,*" said another of the "in-betweens," Emeritus Prof. Albert H. Marckwardt of Princeton University, "but . . . I doubt that advocacy, in the form of a solemn pronouncement that *whom* is dead or should die, will have much effect one way or the other." Other in-betweens were David B. Guralnik, editor of *Webster's New World Dictionary,* and Jess Stein, editor of the *Random House Dictionary.*

Among the replies there is little defense of *whom* on the ground of "correctness" or necessity. There is some on the ground of discipline and building of character. But most interesting to me is the feeling suggested in two or three of the responses that the banishment of *whom* is not the kind of thing that can be legislated. It is true that changes in the language in the past have come about by themselves without anyone's doing anything about them. But does that mean that nothing can be done? Has anyone— including Mencken and Webster—ever attempted to do anything beyond commenting on the need for a change?

I propose a course of action. To begin with, I propose that teachers of English drop the obviously futile attempt to implant into pupils' minds the senseless rules about *whom.* I suggest that such bodies as the National Council of Teachers of English and the Council for Basic Education decide that such rules are null, void, useless, trouble-making and from now on to be ignored. For the present the existing textbooks can remain in use with the teachers pointing out that what the books say about *whom* is in the same class as what some of them say about the split infinitive or about ending a sentence with a preposition. But from now on the textbooks should note that those rules are archaic.

But what about the grown-up who agrees that *whom* should go, but shrinks from doing anything about the matter himself for fear the "purists" will think him ignorant? For you who feel that way I have a gimmicky solution. No matter who you are writing to don't use a *whom* except after a

---

*The other "yeas" came from Prof. Robert L. Allen, Teachers College, Columbia University; Prof. Sheridan Baker, University of Michigan; Prof. Jacques Barzun, Columbia University; Margaret M. Bryant, professor of English emeritus, City University of New York; Roy H. Copperud, the *Editor & Publisher* columnist; Prof. Bergen Evans, Northwestern University; Prof. S. I. Hayakawa, president emeritus, San Francisco State College; Jessica Mitford, author; William Morris, editor of the *American Heritage Dictionary;* Prof. Maxwell Nurnberg, New York University; Eric Partridge, English lexicographer; Prof. Mario Pei, Columbia University; and Vermont Royster, contributing editor of *The Wall Street Journal.*

preposition and, so he or she won't think you are ignorant, write at the bottom of the letter "I favor Whom's Doom except after a preposition." Better yet, get yourself a rubber stamp (cost: about $1) and stamp that declaration on your stationery.

Who knows, after enough of us have used such a stamp maybe the bumper-sticker people will grab the idea, spread it far and wide, and our cause will be whom free.

Questions for Writing or Discussion

1. What is the thesis of Bernstein's article? Where is it stated?
2. What two reasons does the author give for the position he takes?
3. How does the author handle refutation of possible objections to the position he takes? Is he fair?
4. Some arguments can end with a call for action. What course of action does Bernstein propose? Do you think he intends to be taken seriously? Why, or why not?

CHAPTER 12

WRITING A DESCRIPTIVE PAPER

"Write a description of a person or place that you know about from your own experience." An assignment of this sort may come as a welcome change of pace for you. Many English teachers give the assignment for precisely that reason. At last, you won't be writing about someone else's work. You may be asked to read some material to get an idea of how other writers have handled descriptions, but your subject will be your own. You will be comparatively free, if you wish, to let yourself go, to express yourself, and to be creative in a way most of your previous assignments have not allowed. Of course, all good writing is creative, but a descriptive theme enables you to express your emotions more directly and dramatically than elsewhere, and to use vivid, colorful language that might be inappropriate in an impersonal theme. Approached in the proper frame of mind, writing a descriptive theme is almost fun.

How do we apply the principles of good writing that this book has been hammering away at to a descriptive theme? The principles still exist, of course, despite the juicy sound of words like "creativity." Creativity does not mean formlessness, after all, and self-expression does not mean slop. What are the special elements that characterize a well-written descriptive theme? What are the special difficulties and temptations that we need to avoid? Writing will always be an elusive process, but the following comments should come in handy.

1. *Don't take inventory. You must have a thesis.* Periodically, shopkeepers need to take inventory. They itemize every single article in their store so that they will know which have sold well or poorly and will be able to order future goods intelligently. This procedure is vital to business survival, but if you try to include every

piece of information you have on your subject in a descriptive theme, you are inviting disaster.

The writer who takes inventory may begin a theme this way:

> My friend Judy is twenty years old. She is a solid C student. She has black hair, brown eyes, and weighs 115 pounds. Her family is comfortably middle-class. Judy is very nearsighted, but is vain about her appearance and often does not wear her glasses. She's been my friend for many years, and I like her a lot.

This paragraph is simply a random collection of stray facts. No logic, no principle seems to be at work here except the desire to get everything in, to take inventory. But getting everything in is a task that has no end; if the writer feels Judy's grades are worth mentioning, why decide not to mention the titles of the books she has read over the past year? Why decide that her grades were worth mentioning in the first place—or her weight, or her eyesight, or her family? Why are twenty thousand other facts about Judy not in the paper—the presents she received on her last birthday, her height, the name of her optometrist? If the writer is only taking inventory, all facts are of equal importance, which means in effect that no facts are of any importance.

A descriptive theme needs a thesis. This statement will come as no surprise to you, but it has a number of very specific consequences. It means that you must give up the effort to tell your reader everything. It means that you must think of your paper not as "A Description of Judy," but as an attempt to prove that "Judy is terribly vain," or "Many people think that Judy is a real grind, but she has a lot of fine qualities," or "Judy has no remarkable traits of any kind, and I wonder why she has been my best friend for so many years." It means that you must choose only descriptive details that are connected to your thesis, and that if it will break your heart to omit a colorful but irrelevant detail, you must change your thesis to make the detail relevant. Sometimes, of course, a simple change in phrasing can turn a seemingly irrelevant detail into something significant, and your thesis can remain unchanged. Notice how a thesis and a few additional phrases can transform the mess about Judy into a coherent start for a potentially effective paper.

> There is nothing at all special about my friend Judy. Judy is such a completely ordinary twenty-year-old woman that I often wonder how our friendship has lasted so long and stayed so warm.
>
> Just for starters, consider these totally ordinary facts about her. Physically, she has absolutely undistinguished black hair and brown eyes,

stands a normal 5 feet 4 inches, and weighs a normal 115 pounds. Scholastically, she is a solid C student. By solid, I *mean* solid. In two years at college, I can't recall her once getting a daring C− or an exciting C+. Her family—you guessed it—is comfortably middle-class, not too rich and not too poor. Even in her little flaws, Judy is just what you'd expect. Like so many people of her age, she tends to be vain about personal appearance and all too frequently tries to get by without her glasses, even though she's very nearsighted.

2. *Use lively specific details.* The most effective way of communicating an immediate sense of your subject is to use specific details—a lot of them. Don't spend as much time telling your reader that a room is old and neglected as you do telling about the squeaky floorboard right by the door, the lint collected in the coils of the radiator, the window that needs to be propped up with a sooty stick of wood. If you do the job with details, the sense of age and neglect will come through loud and clear. In many ways, the more precise the detail, the greater its potential for arousing the attention of your reader. Nothing should be beneath your notice. The condition of a man's fingernails, the name of the store where a woman buys her clothes, or a broken traffic light on a street corner can convey as much information about a man, a woman, or a neighborhood—and convey it more interestingly—than any number of generalized comments.

3. *Choose a principle of organization that will present the descriptive details in a logical sequence.* All this suggestion means is that you should have some way of determining what comes first and what comes next. The particular organizing principle you select makes little difference as long as it helps create a coherent paper. In describing a snowstorm, for instance, you might organize by *time,* presenting the storm from the first hesitant flakes, through the massive downfall, to the Christmas-card quietness at the end of the storm. In describing a landscape, you might organize by *space,* beginning with the objects farthest from the observer and working your way closer. A physical description of a person could go from top to bottom or bottom to top.

Not all principles of organization have to be anything close to this rigid. A landscape description could be built by progressing from the most ordinary details to the least ordinary details. If the top-to-bottom approach to a description of a person strikes you as dull, you might organize the paper by unattractive features and attractive features or first impressions and second impressions. The important consideration is that some clear principle is needed to give structure to the paper.

Rules mean nothing, of course, until they are applied. What do you think of this student's effort at a descriptive theme?

Thunderstorms
ELLEN REPICKY

There is something about a thunderstorm that always seems to bring out the child in me. I don't know whether it is the enormous amount of water being poured down from the heavens or the powerful thunder and lightning tearing at the skies that make me act as though the world is coming to an end, but I do know that I feel uncontrollable fear and insecurity during thunderstorms.

Usually more of a happy-go-lucky person than anything else, when I hear that a thunderstorm is heading my way, I quickly change to a timid little girl. I run to my room, shut my door, and draw the blinds. By doing this, I pretend that nothing scary is going on outside, and everything is cool. But in my mind I can picture what is happening with complete clarity. The birds have flown to a safe place of refuge. The streets look like those in a ghost town. Even the sun has managed to hide herself from this ugliness. Just about now, the air is drenched with a foul, fishy odor. The darkening gray skies are traveling at a rapid pace, and the trees are bending backwards, yielding to the almighty wind. In the distance, a faint rumbling can be heard.

Crash! Thunder roars, and to my dismay the storm has begun. By this time, I am in sheer agony. Nothing can calm me down. My whole body is shaking incessantly, and I jump with each crash of thunder. The rain is beating fiercely on my window. I try not to let it intimidate me, but it does. Within my body, my stomach is doing somersaults. My head feels as light and vulnerable as a balloon. Outside, the wind is banging the shutters in tempo with the thunder and the raindrops. Some might think that this chorus is beautiful music, but I don't. Suddenly I notice the frightening sounds have diminished, and I feel my heartbeat slow, for I know that the worst is over. And I have lived through one more thunderstorm.

I know that my actions are immature, but there is nothing I can do about them. Every time there is a thunderstorm I revert to being a helpless, hysterical child. When the sun comes back out, I laugh at myself, of course, but that lasts only until the next time. And the next time always comes.

Questions for Writing or Discussion

1. What is the thesis? Does the writer keep her thesis in mind through the body of the paper?

2. Should the writer have devoted more attention to the storm itself? Should she have devoted more attention to her feelings? Or is the proportion just about right?

3. A curious element in this paper is that the writer, particularly in paragraph two, presents a picture of what she did not see (she is hiding in her room). Why is this technique so effective?

4. What phase of the storm does the writer concentrate on most? Why?

5. In paragraph two, "The darkening gray skies are traveling at a rapid pace" seems dull and abstract. How could the phrase be enlivened?

6. Almost everyone has deep-seated fears, and the objects of those fears offer excellent topics for descriptive papers. Write a short descriptive paper about your fear of one of the following: speaking in front of an audience, darkness, insects, rats, dogs, heights, fires, getting lost, failing a course, contracting a particular illness, drowning, driving on snowy roads, flying.

Readings

The examples of description that follow show seasoned professional writers at work. Note how description is never allowed to become merely a piece of pretty writing but is used to communicate insights into people and society.

Charles Dickens
MISS MURDSTONE from "David Copperfield"

It was Miss Murdstone who was arrived, and a gloomy-looking lady she was; dark, like her brother, whom she greatly resembled in face and voice, and with very heavy eyebrows, nearly meeting over her large nose, as if, being disabled by the wrongs of her sex from wearing whiskers, she had carried them to that account. She brought with her two uncompromising hard black boxes, with her initials on the lids in hard brass nails. When she paid the coachman she took her money out of a hard steel purse, and she kept the purse in a very jail of a bag which hung upon her arm by a heavy chain, and shut up like a bite. I had never, at that time, seen such a metallic lady altogether as Miss Murdstone was.

Wilkie Collins
MARIAN HALCOMBE from "The Woman in White"

My first glance round me, as the man opened the door, disclosed a well-furnished breakfast-table, standing in the middle of a long room, with many windows in it. I looked from the table to the window farthest from me, and saw a lady standing at it, with her back turned towards me. The instant my eyes rested on her, I was struck by the rare beauty of her form, and by the unaffected grace of her attitude. Her figure was tall, yet not too tall; comely and well-developed, yet not fat; her head set on her shoulders with an easy, pliant firmness; her waist, perfection in the eyes of a man, for it occupied its natural place, it filled out its natural circle, it was visibly and delightfully undeformed by stays. She had not heard my entrance into the room; and I allowed myself the luxury of admiring her for a few moments, before I moved one of the chairs near me, as the least embarrassing means of attracting her attention. She turned towards me immediately. The easy elegance of every movement of her limbs and body as soon as she began to advance from the far end of the room, set me in a flutter of expectation to see her face clearly. She left the window—and I said to myself, The lady is dark. She moved forward a few steps—and I said to myself, The lady is young. She approached nearer—and I said to myself (with a sense of surprise which words fail me to express), The lady is ugly!

Never was the old conventional maxim, that Nature cannot err, more flatly contradicted—never was the fair promise of a lovely figure more strangely and startlingly belied by the face and head that crowned it. The lady's complexion was almost swarthy, and the dark down on her upper lip was almost a moustache. She had a large, firm, masculine mouth and jaw; prominent, piercing, resolute brown eyes; and thick, coal-black hair, growing unusually low down on her forehead. Her expression—bright, frank, and intelligent—appeared, while she was silent, to be altogether wanting in those feminine attractions of gentleness and pliability, without which the beauty of the handsomest woman alive is beauty incomplete. To see such a face as this set on shoulders that a sculptor would have longed to model—to be charmed by the modest graces of action through which the symmetrical limbs betrayed their beauty when they moved, and then to be almost repelled by the masculine form and masculine look of the features in which the perfectly shaped figure ended—was to feel a sensation oddly akin to the helpless discomfort familiar to us all in sleep, when we recognise yet cannot reconcile the anomalies and contradictions of a dream.

Questions for Writing or Discussion

1. Who makes better use of specific details, Dickens or Collins?
2. Does Collins ever "take inventory," or are all his comments related to a main idea?
3. Identify the topic sentences in the Dickens and Collins passages.

4. Write a description of an unusually good-looking or unusually ugly man or woman.

Donald E. Westlake
JERRY MANELLI'S FATHER

Jerry's father had retired two years ago from his job in a department store's warehouse out on Long Island, and as soon as he became a senior citizen his name got onto more rotten mailing lists than you could shake your fist at. Everybody wants to hustle the old folks. A running theme in all this junk mail was that retired people ought to have a hobby, take up the slack from no longer having a job. The old man had never *worked* a day in his life— he'd spent most of his laboring years trying to figure a way to slip unnoticed out of the warehouse with a sofa—but he believed this hobby thing as though the Virgin herself had come down on a cloud to give him his instructions. "Man without a hobby shrivels up and dies," he'd say. "A hobby keeps your mind active, your blood circulating, keeps you young. They've done studies, they got statistics, it's a proven thing."

Unfortunately, though, the old man had never had a hobby in his life, didn't really know what the hell a hobby was, and couldn't keep up his interest in any hobby he tried. He'd been through stamp collecting, coin collecting, matchbook collecting. He'd paid good money for a ham radio but he never used it, because, "I don't have anything to say. I don't even know those people." He'd tried making a ship in a bottle, and within half an hour he'd busted the bottle on the radiator and stalked out of the house. He was going to build a St. Patrick's Cathedral out of toothpicks, and got as far as the first step. He figured he'd become an expert on baseball statistics, but the last time he'd looked at baseball there were sixteen teams in the two major leagues and now there were hundreds. He started clipping things out of the newspapers—disaster stories or funny headlines ("Action on Building Bribes Delayed by Lack of Funds," for instance, from the *New York Times*)—and all he managed to do was cut the dining room tablecloth with the scissors, and glue his fingers together.

The old man didn't know it, and nobody would tell him, but it turned out his hobby was looking for hobbies. It was certainly keeping his mind active and his blood circulating, and if he was actually out in the park now with a homemade kite then maybe it was also keeping him young.

Questions for Writing or Discussion

1. Which sentence serves as the thesis statement.
2. How has "the old man" turned failure into success?
3. What was the intended meaning of the newspaper headline? What meaning does it seem to have in print?

4. Write a description of a relative that focuses on only one out-standing personality trait.

Nora Ephron
THE POINT, HE TAUGHT, IS THE POINT

The best teacher I ever had was named Charles Simms, and he taught jour-nalism at Beverly Hills High School in 1956 and 1957. He was young, cute in an owlish way—crew cut, glasses, etc.—and was a gymnast in the 1956 Olympics. He was also the first person any of us knew who had stereo ear-phones, and he taught us all to play mah-jong.

The first day of journalism class, Mr. Simms did what just about every journalism teacher does in the beginning—he began to teach us how to write a lead. The way this is normally done is that the teacher dictates a set of facts and the class attempts to write the first paragraph of a news story about them. Who, what, where, when, how and why. So he read us a set of facts. It went something like this: "Kenneth L. Peters, principal of Beverly Hills High School, announced today that the faculty of the high school will travel to Sacramento on Thursday for a colloquium on new teaching methods. Speaking there will be anthropologist Margaret Mead, educator Robert Maynard Hutchins, and several others." We all began typing, and after a few minutes we turned in our leads. All of them said approximately what Mr. Simms had dictated, but in the opposite order ("Margaret Mead and Robert Maynard Hutchins will address the faculty," etc.). Mr. Simms riffled through what we had turned in, smiled, looked up and said: "The lead to the story is, 'There will be no school Thursday.' "

It was an electrifying moment. *So that's it,* I realized. *It's about the point.* The classic newspaper lead of who-what-where-when-how-and-why is ut-terly meaningless if you haven't figured out what the significance of the facts is. What is the point? What does it mean? He planted those questions in my head. And for the year he taught me journalism, every day was like the first; every assignment, every story, every set of facts he provided us had a point buried in it somewhere if you looked hard enough. He turned the class into a gorgeous intellectual game, and he gave me enthusiasm for the profession that I have never lost. Also, of course, he taught me something that works just as well in life as it does in journalism.

After teaching at Beverly Hills High School for two years, Charles Simms quit and opened a chain of record stores in Los Angeles. I hope he's a mil-lionaire.

Questions for Writing or Discussion

1. Define in your own words what the author means by "the point."
2. The reading selection tells us something about Mr. Simms's

teaching techniques. Does it also give us any sense of his personality?

3. Do the details about Mr. Simms in the first paragraph contribute to the reading as a whole. Is the fact that Mr. Simms left teaching of any special significance?

4. How does Mr. Simms's lesson work "just as well in life as it does in journalism"?

5. Look back into your childhood and write a description of an adult from whom you once learned an important lesson. The adult need not be a classroom teacher.

Mark Twain (Samuel L. Clemens)
THE PROFESSIONAL

The face of the water [of the Mississippi River where the author was a steamboat pilot] in time became a wonderful book—a book that was a dead language to the uneducated passenger but which told its mind to me without reserve, delivering its most cherished secrets as clearly as if it uttered them with a voice. And it was not a book to be read once and thrown aside, for it had a new story to tell every day. Throughout the long twelve hundred miles there was never a page that was void of interest, never one that you could leave unread without loss, never one that you would want to skip, thinking you could find higher enjoyment in some other thing. There never was so wonderful a book written by man, never one whose interest was so absorbing, so unflagging, so sparklingly renewed with every reperusal. The passenger who could not read it was charmed with a peculiar sort of faint dimple on its surface (on the rare occasions when he did not overlook it altogether) but to the pilot that was an *italicized* passage; indeed it was more than that, it was a legend of the largest capitals with a string of shouting exclamation-points at the end of it, for it meant that a wreck or a rock was buried there that could tear the life out of the strongest vessel that ever floated. It is the faintest and simplest expression the water ever makes, and the most hideous to a pilot's eye. In truth, the passenger who could not read this book saw nothing but all manner of pretty pictures in it, painted by the sun and shaded by the clouds, whereas to the trained eye these were not pictures at all, but the grimmest and most dead-earnest of reading matter.

Now when I had mastered the language of this water, and had come to know every trifling feature that bordered the great river as familiarly as I knew the letters of the alphabet, I had made a valuable acquisition. But I had lost something, too. I had lost something which could never be restored to me while I lived. All the grace, the beauty, the poetry, had gone out of the majestic river! I still kept in mind a certain wonderful sunset which I witnessed when steamboating was new to me. A broad expanse of the river was turned to blood; in the middle distance the red hue brightened into gold, through which a solitary log came floating, black and conspicuous; in one place a long, slanting mark lay sparkling upon the water; in another the surface was broken by boiling, tumbling rings, that were as many-tinted as an opal; where the ruddy flush was faintest, was a smooth spot that was covered with graceful circles and radiating lines, ever so delicately traced; the shore on our left was densely wooded, and the somber shadow that fell from this forest was broken in one place by a long, ruffled trail that shone like silver; and high above the forest wall a clean-stemmed dead tree waved a single leafy bough that glowed like a flame in the unobstructed splendor that was flowing from the sun. There were graceful curves, reflected images, woody heights, soft distances; and over the whole scene, far and near, the dissolving lights drifted steadily, enriching it every passing moment with new marvels of coloring.

I stood like one bewitched. I drank it in, in a speechless rapture. The world was new to me, and I had never seen anything like this at home. But as I have said, a day came when I began to cease from noting the glories and the charms which the moon and the sun and the twilight wrought upon the river's face; another day came when I ceased altogether to note them. Then, if that sunset scene had been repeated, I should have looked upon it without rapture, and should have commented upon it, inwardly, after this fashion: "This sun means that we are going to have wind to-morrow; that floating log means that the river is rising, small thanks to it; that slanting mark on the water refers to a bluff reef which is going to kill somebody's steamboat one of these nights, if it keeps on stretching out like that; those tumbling 'boils' show a dissolving bar and a changing channel there; the lines and circles in the slick water over yonder are a warning that that troublesome place is shoaling up dangerously; that silver streak in the shadow of the forest is the 'break' from a new snag, and he has located himself in the very best place he could have found to fish for steamboats; that tall dead tree, with a single living branch, is not going to last long, and then how is a body ever going to get through this blind place at night without the friendly old landmark?"

No, the romance and beauty were all gone from the river. All the value any feature of it had for me now was the amount of usefulness it could furnish toward compassing the safe piloting of a steamboat. Since those days, I have pitied doctors from my heart. What does the lovely flush in a beauty's cheek mean to a doctor but a "break" that ripples above some deadly disease? Are not all her visible charms sown thick with what are to him the signs and symbols of hidden decay? Does he ever see her beauty at all, or doesn't he simply view her professionally and comment upon her unwholesome condition all to himself? And doesn't he sometimes wonder whether he has gained most or lost most by learning his trade?

Questions for Writing or Discussion

1. Identify all the words and phrases in paragraph one that describe the river as being a book.

2. After paragraph one, does the author ever repeat the idea of the river's being a book?
3. Which sentence or sentences first state the thesis? Where is the thesis restated?
4. In paragraph two's description of the sunset, what principle of organization determines the order in which the details are presented?
5. Do you agree with the author that increased knowledge interferes with simple emotional pleasure?
6. Write a description of a person or place emphasizing the contrast between past and present.

John Steinbeck
THE USED CAR LOT from "The Grapes of Wrath"

In the towns, on the edges of the towns, in fields, in vacant lots, the used-car yards, the wreckers' yards, the garages with blazoned signs—Used Cars, Good Used Cars. Cheap transportation, three trailers. '27 Ford, clean. Checked cars, guaranteed cars. Free radio. Car with 100 gallons of gas free. Come in and look. Used Cars. No overhead.

A lot and a house large enough for a desk and chair and a blue book. Sheaf of contracts, dog-eared, held with paper clips, and a neat pile of unused contracts. Pen—keep it full, keep it working. A sale's been lost 'cause a pen didn't work.

Those sons-of-bitches over there ain't buying. Every yard gets 'em. They're lookers. Spend all their time looking. Don't want to buy no cars; take up your time. Don't give a damn for your time. Over there, them two people—no, with the kids. Get 'em in a car. Start 'em at two hundred and work down. They look good for one and a quarter. Get 'em rolling. Get 'em out in a jalopy. Sock it to 'em! They took our time.

Owners with rolled-up sleeves. Salesmen, neat, deadly, small intent eyes watching for weaknesses.

Watch the woman's face. If the woman likes it we can screw the old man. Start 'em on that Cad'. Then you can work 'em down to that '26 Buick. 'F you start on the Buick, they'll go for a Ford. Roll up your sleeves an' get to work. This ain't gonna last forever. Show 'em that Nash while I get the slow leak pumped up on that '25 Dodge. I'll give you a Hymie when I'm ready.

What you want is transportation, ain't it? No baloney for you. Sure the upholstery is shot. Seat cushions ain't turning no wheels over.

Published in 1939, John Steinbeck's *The Grapes of Wrath* deals with the hardships of the "Okies," dispossessed farmers of Oklahoma and neighboring states who fled from the drought-created "Dust Bowl" to become migrant farm workers in California. "The Used Car Lot," Chapter 7 of the novel, presents a vivid picture of the hopeless battle to find cheap, reliable transportation for the thousand-mile trip west.

Cars lined up, noses forward, rusty noses, flat tires. Parked close together.

Like to get in to see that one? Sure, no trouble. I'll pull her out of the line.

Get 'em under obligation. Make 'em take up your time. Don't let 'em forget they're takin' your time. People are nice, mostly. They hate to put you out. Make 'em put you out, an' then sock it to 'em.

Cars lined up, Model T's, high and snotty, creaking wheel, worn bands. Buicks, Nashes, De Sotos.

Yes, sir. '22 Dodge. Best goddamn car Dodge ever made. Never wear out. Low compression. High compression got lots a sap for a while, but the metal ain't made that'll hold it for long. Plymouths, Rocknes, Stars.

Jesus, where'd that Apperson come from, the Ark? And a Chalmers and a Chandler—ain't made 'em for years. We ain't sellin' cars—rolling junk. Goddamn it, I got to get jalopies. I don't want nothing for more'n twenty-five, thirty bucks. Sell 'em for fifty, seventy-five. That's a good profit. Christ, what cut do you make on a new car? Get jalopies. I can sell 'em fast as I get 'em. Nothing over two hundred fifty. Jim, corral that old bastard on the sidewalk. Don't know his ass from a hole in the ground. Try him on that Apperson. Say, where is that Apperson? Sold? If we don't get some jalopies we got nothing to sell.

Flags, red and white, white and blue—all along the curb. Used Cars. Good Used Cars.

Today's bargain—up on the platform. Never sell it. Makes folks come in, though. If we sold that bargain at that price we'd hardly make a dime. Tell 'em it's jus' sold. Take out that yard battery before you make delivery. Put in that dumb cell. Christ, what they want for six bits? Roll up your sleeves— pitch in. This ain't gonna last. If I had enough jalopies I'd retire in six months.

Listen, Jim, I heard that Chevvy's rear end. Sounds like bustin' bottles. Squirt in a couple quarts of sawdust. Put some in the gears, too. We got to move that lemon for thirty-five dollars. Bastard cheated me on that one. I offer ten an' he jerks me to fifteen, an' then the son-of-a-bitch took the tools out. God Almighty! I wisht I had five hundred jalopies. This ain't gonna last. He don't like the tires? Tell 'im they got ten thousand in 'em, knock off a buck an' a half.

Piles of rusty ruins against the fence, rows of wrecks in back, fenders, grease-black wrecks, blocks lying on the ground and a pig weed growing up through the cylinders. Brake rods, exhausts, piled like snakes. Grease, gasoline.

See if you can't find a spark plug that ain't cracked. Christ, if I had fifty trailers at under a hundred I'd clean up. What the hell is he kickin' about? We sell 'em, but we don't push 'em home for him. That's good! Don't push 'em home. Get that one in the Monthly, I bet. You don't think he's a pros-pect? Well, kick 'im out. We got too much to do to bother with a guy that can't make up his mind. Take the right front tire off the Graham. Turn that mended side down. The rest looks swell. Got tread an' everything.

Sure! There's fifty thousan' in that ol' heap yet. Keep plenty oil in. So long. Good luck.

Lookin' for a car? What did you have in mind? See anything attracts you? I'm dry. How about a little snort a good stuff? Come on, while your wife's lookin' at that La Salle. You don't want no La Salle. Bearings shot. Uses too much oil. Got a Lincoln '24. There's a car. Run forever. Make her into a truck.

Hot sun on rusted metal. Oil on the ground. People are wandering in, bewildered, needing a car.

Wipe your feet. Don't lean on that car, it's dirty. How do you buy a car? What does it cost? Watch the children, now. I wonder how much for this one? We'll ask. It don't cost money to ask. We can ask, can't we? Can't pay a nickel over seventy-five, or there won't be enough to get to California.

God, if I could only get a hundred jalopies. I don't care if they run or not.

Tires, used, bruised tires, stacked in tall cylinders; tubes, red, gray, hanging like sausages.

Tire patch? Radiator cleaner? Spark intensifier? Drop this little pill in your gas tank and get ten extra miles to the gallon. Just paint it on—you got a new surface for fifty cents. Wipers, fan belts, gaskets? Maybe it's the valve. Get a new valve stem. What can you lose for a nickel?

All right, Joe. You soften 'em up an' shoot 'em in here. I'll close 'em, I'll deal 'em or I'll kill 'em. Don't send in no bums. I want deals.

Yes, sir, step in. You got a buy there. Yes, sir! At eighty bucks you got a buy.

I can't go no higher than fifty. The fella outside says fifty.

Fifty. Fifty! He's nuts. Paid seventy-eight fifty for that little number. Joe, you crazy fool, you tryin' to bust us? Have to can that guy. I might take sixty. Now look here, mister, I ain't got all day. I'm a business man but I ain't out to stick nobody. Got anything to trade?

Got a pair of mules I'll trade.

Mules! Hey, Joe, hear this? This guy wants to trade mules. Didn't nobody tell you this is the machine age? They don't use mules for nothing but glue no more.

Fine big mules—five and seven years old. Maybe we better look around.

Look around! You come in when we're busy, an' take up our time an' then walk out! Joe, did you know you was talkin' to pikers?

I ain't a piker. I got to get a car. We're goin' to California. I got to get a car.

Well, I'm a sucker. Joe says I'm a sucker. Says if I don't quit givin' my shirt away I'll starve to death. Tell you what I'll do—I can get five bucks apiece for them mules for dog feed.

I wouldn't want them to go for dog feed.

Well, maybe I can get ten or seven maybe. Tell you what we'll do. We'll take your mules for twenty. Wagon goes with 'em, don't it? An' you put up fifty, an' you can sign a contract to send the rest at ten dollars a month.

But you said eighty.

Didn't you never hear about carrying charges and insurance? That just boosts her a little. You'll get her all paid up in four-five months. Sign your name right here. We'll take care of ever'thing.

Well, I don't know—

Now, look here. I'm givin' you my shirt, an' you took all this time. I might a made three sales while I been talkin' to you. I'm disgusted. Yeah, sign right there. All right, sir. Joe, fill up the tank for this gentleman. We'll give him gas.

Jesus, Joe, that was a hot one! What'd we give for that jalopy? Thirty bucks—thirty-five wasn't it? I got that team, an' if I can't get seventy-five for that team, I ain't a business man. An' I got fifty cash an' a contract for forty more. Oh, I know they're not all honest, but it'll surprise you how many kick through with the rest. One guy come through with a hundred two years after I wrote him off. I bet you this guy sends the money. Christ, if I could only get five hundred jalopies! Roll up your sleeves, Joe. Go out an' soften 'em, an' send 'em in to me. You get twenty on that last deal. You ain't doing bad.

Limp flags in the afternoon sun. Today's Bargain. '29 Ford pickup, runs good.

What do you want for fifty bucks—a Zephyr?

Horsehair curling out of seat cushions, fenders battered and hammered back. Bumpers torn loose and hanging. Fancy Ford roadster with little colored lights at fender guide, at radiator cap, and three behind. Mud aprons, and a big die on the gear-shift lever. Pretty girl on tire cover, painted in color and named Cora. Afternoon sun on the dusty windshields.

Christ, I ain't had time to go out an' eat! Joe, send a kid for a hamburger.

Spattering roar of ancient engines.

There's a dumb-bunny lookin' at that Chrysler. Find out if he got any jack in his jeans. Some a these farm boys is sneaky. Soften 'em up an' roll 'em in to me, Joe. You're doin' good.

Sure, we sold it. Guarantee? We guaranteed it to be an automobile. We didn't guarantee to wet-nurse it. Now listen here, you—you bought a car, an' now you're squawkin'. I don't give a damn if you don't make payments. We ain't got your paper. We turn that over to the finance company. They'll get after you, not us. We don't hold no paper. Yeah? Well you jus' get tough an' I'll call a cop. No, we did not switch the tires. Run 'im outa here, Joe. He bought a car, an' now he ain't satisfied. How'd you think if I bought a steak an' et half an' try to bring it back? We're runnin' a business, not a charity ward. Can ya imagine that guy, Joe? Say—looka there! Got an Elk's tooth! Run over there. Let 'em glance over that '36 Pontiac. Yeah.

Square noses, round noses, rusty noses, shovel noses, and the long curves of streamlines, and the flat surfaces before streamlining. Bargains Today. Old monsters with deep upholstery—you can cut her into a truck easy. Two-wheel trailers, axles rusty in the hard afternoon sun. Used Cars. Good Used Cars. Clean, runs good. Don't pump oil.

Christ, look at 'er! Somebody took nice care of 'er.

Cadillacs, La Salles, Buicks, Plymouths, Packards, Chevvies, Fords, Pontiacs. Row on row, headlights glinting in the afternoon sun. Good Used Cars.

Soften 'em up, Joe. Jesus, I wisht I had a thousand jalopies! Get 'em ready to deal, an' I'll close 'em.

Goin' to California? Here's jus' what you need. Looks shot, but they's thousan's of miles in her.

Lined up side by side. Good Used Cars. Bargains. Clean, runs good.

Questions for Writing or Discussion

1. Steinbeck's thesis is never stated directly but is strongly felt in almost every word. What is the thesis?
2. Does the author go to unconvincing extremes? Are the buyers too innocent to believe, the dealers too evil?
3. What repeated wish is expressed by the owner of the used car lot? Where else does the author use repetition to heighten the effect of his writing?
4. Why does the author make such frequent use of sentence fragments?
5. Is the author describing one used car lot or many?
6. Using Steinbeck's impressionistic or stream-of-consciousness approach, write a description of one of the following: Christmas shopping, rush hour, a traffic jam, a crowded beach or swimming pool, an airport, an amusement park, spectators at a sporting event. Remember the need for a clear thesis.

CHAPTER 13

WRITING AN ANALYSIS OF LITERATURE

To analyze is to study a complex substance by examining one or more of its parts and then showing the relationship of each part to the whole. When you are given an assignment such as "Describe the unpleasant new insight into his own character that the doctor discovers in 'The Use of Force'" or "Explain the direct and indirect reasons for the disruption of the play in 'The Revolt of the Evil Fairies,'" you are being asked to write a literary analysis. Sometimes teachers like to assign a special form of literary analysis called "explication," in which a poem or short story is examined pretty much word by word or paragraph by paragraph to show how each element fits into the general pattern and purpose of the entire work.

We are convinced that nobody ever learned how to write a good literary analysis by reading instructions in a textbook. Your instructors have undoubtedly devoted a large portion of their professional life to analyzing literature. A few classroom sessions with your instructor, digging into specific works without worrying too much about preestablished methods and rules, will probably teach you far more than we can.

All we would like to do in this chapter is to suggest a few guidelines that should make your life easier when you have to write an analysis. We can't tell you *what* to say—that will vary with each assignment, depending on the material you are analyzing, and some subjects offer a good deal of leeway for individual interpretations and insights. In addition, whatever you say, we can't tell you very much new about *how* to say it—by this time, you should have a reasonable knowledge of the requirements for any piece of good writing. Still, we believe that the following common sense suggestions will be helpful.

267

1. *Read the material slowly.* When you need to wade through a pile of junk, fast reading is fine. When you are reading good or great literature, much of which treats complex ideas and emotions, often with complex means of expression, the intelligent approach is to read slowly. Moreover, any analysis involves the close examination of details. Fast reading can give you a general sense of the main points, but it can't prepare you to deal competently with all the concerns of a full-fledged analysis.

2. *Reread.* When you read a story or poem for the first time, you're unlikely to have any valid notion of what the author is up to. The author knows how the story is going to end, but you don't. That's why you're reading it—to find out. And since the author does know in advance what is going to happen on that last page, he or she has been making all sorts of crucial preparations earlier in the story to lead into the ending. On a first reading, those earlier pages cannot mean much to you. They can create interest or suspense, but that's about all, since you don't yet know anything of the author's purpose. Once you do understand what the author has been trying to do, and then *read the story again,* all the ingredients will begin to register in a different way, a way that is emotionally and intellectually impossible to achieve in a first reading. The seemingly separate parts of the story can now come through to you as pieces within a logical pattern. Without a sense of that logical pattern and of how all elements are related to it, your analysis will be weak and incomplete.

3. *Assume that everything is significant.* In good literature, nothing should be an accident. Each word, each character, each thought, each incident should make a contribution to the total effect the author is trying for. The contribution is sometimes obvious and direct: the author casually mentions that a car is nine years old because later on the car will break down. At other times, the contribution is indirect: the author spends a paragraph describing a glowing fireplace in order to establish a homey mood that fits in with the story's central idea—the joys of family life. As you think about the material you are going to analyze, as you brood about what you are going to say and how you are going to say it, keep in mind that *nothing is beneath your notice.* Assume that everything serves a purpose and that you have not reached a full understanding of the story, poem, or play until you clearly see the purpose that everything serves. When you come up against elements that serve no purpose, you can safely conclude that the work is imperfect. Read closely, and give serious attention to details. When you get to the writing stage, make liberal use of the details to support your comments. No matter how much actual work you have done, if you do not rely heavily on references to details, your analysis will seem to be based on vague impressions and snap judgments.

4. *Do not study details out of context.* Your response to the details of a work—a word, a phrase, a character, an incident—depends upon the work as a whole. A sentence like "Mrs. Smythe spent twenty minutes arranging the flowers in the vase" could appear in a satire of a fussy little old lady or a moving sketch of a mother preparing the house for her son's return from the army. A diploma may appear in one place as a symbol of hope and in another as a symbol of despair. Your analysis or interpretation of the flower arranging or the diploma must obviously be in harmony with the rest of the work. Keep the intentions of the whole work in mind as you consider the proper approach toward one of its parts.

One more observation: try not to let your purely personal tastes or prejudices interfere with your responses. If a writer in the context of a short story has a character light a cigarette to show nervousness, fight off any temptation to analyze the character as a stupid person who doesn't know that cigarettes are hazardous to health. If another writer presents a sympathetic and approving study of a couple who decide to stay married for the sake of the children, don't analyze the couple as victims of outmoded bourgeois morality and a repressive society. An analysis explains what is going on in a piece of literature, not what your own philosophy of life may happen to be.

Now read the following poem.

OZYMANDIAS

I met a traveller from an antique land
Who said: Two vast and trunkless legs of stone
Stand in the desert. Near them, on the sand,
Half sunk, a shattered visage lies, whose frown,
And wrinkled lip, and sneer of cold command,
Tell that its sculptor well those passions read
Which yet survive, stamped on these lifeless things,
The hand that mocked them, and the heart that fed:[1]
And on the pedestal these words appear:
"My name is Ozymandias, king of kings:
Look on my works, ye Mighty, and despair!"
Nothing beside remains. Round the decay
Of that colossal wreck, boundless and bare
The lone and level sands stretch far away.

—*Percy Bysshe Shelley*

1. The passions stamped on the broken face of the statue survive the hand (of the sculptor) that mocked them and the heart (of Ozymandias) that fed them.

The assignment given to students was "Discuss the implications of the inscription on the pedestal of the statue in Shelley's 'Ozymandias.' " What do you think of this effort?

Enough Despair to Go Around
ALAN BENJAMIN

In Percy Bysshe Shelley's "Ozymandias," we are told that the following words are inscribed on the pedestal of a broken statue in the desert: "My name is Ozymandias, king of kings:/ Look on my works, ye Mighty, and despair!" What King Ozymandias had in mind when he chose those words is dramatically different from the meaning they have now. The new meaning comes not from Ozymandias but from the passage of time.

The still visible "wrinkled lip and sneer of cold command" suggest the vanity and arrogance that motivated Ozymandias to have his statue built in the first place. The "colossal" size of the statue and Ozymandias's description of himself as "king of kings" add to the impression that he thought a great deal of himself and wanted others to do the same. We can imagine the statue being erected at the gates or in the central square of King Ozymandias's great capital city. Marble buildings gleam in the sunlight: the palace, the treasury, the temples, the monuments to military victories. Powerful and "mighty" people from all over the known world come to see the wonders of Ozymandias's kingdom. "Look on my works, ye Mighty, and despair," sneers Ozymandias. Despair because your creations, your works, will never be able to equal the magnificence of mine. Despair because when you look at my works, you can only feel a sense of the pitiful insignificance of your own.

Time passes. Time eats away marble. Buildings and statues crumble. The glorious, thriving kingdom of Ozymandias is now a desert. Two grotesque stone legs stick up in the air, and together with a "shattered visage" they are all that is left of the statue. Everything else is sand and desolation. In one sense, the inscription on the pedestal has now become meaningless, for there are no more "works" left to look on, and we can think only of how silly Ozymandias must have been. In another sense, the words are filled with a strong new meaning, stronger and far more true than Ozymandias ever dreamed. Powerful and mighty people today can look at Ozymandias's works and still despair. This time, however, they will despair not because of envy, but because they can see the eventual fate of all their own works. They will despair because, even if their own works surpass those of Ozymandias, it won't make any difference. They will despair now because they can see that all material things crumble to dust and that people who put their faith in such things are doomed to futility and disappointment.

Ozymandias originally hoped that the despair would come from petty and foolish reasons. Today it can come from more intelligent and realistic reasons. But there is still more than enough despair to go around as "the lone and level sands stretch far away."

Questions for Writing or Discussion

1. Is there a clear thesis? If so, where is it first presented?
2. Does paragraph two have a topic sentence? If not, does it need one?
3. In the next-to-last sentence of paragraph three, what does "it" refer to? Should the sentence be revised?
4. Is the writing, particularly in paragraph three, too emotional for an analysis, or does the emotional writing make the paper more interesting to read?
5. Does the last paragraph effectively summarize the writer's main points? Is the last sentence too dramatic?

SOME NOTES ON A FEW LITERARY TERMS

A number of fairly specialized words get flung about a great deal in discussing literature. Most of them have meaning and can be valuable—even indispensable—when used wisely, but sometimes they serve to show off or dress up a perfectly simple point in an atmosphere of obscurity and fraudulent importance. What follows is not intended to be a dictionary of literary terms, but rather some helpful comments on a few of the most troublesome and frequently abused terms.

Hidden meanings

A number of students are fond of using this phrase when they discuss or write about literature—and it means nothing. No writer who is any good goes around hiding meanings. Writers have enough trouble expressing them openly. The few writers who do play hide-and-seek with their readers are generally pretentious fakes. At any rate, avoid the "hidden meanings" approach to literature. Never use the phrase, as many people do, to refer to an idea or emotion that the author had no intention of concealing, but that you just didn't happen to notice on a first reading.

Moral and theme

Good literature, in general, is not pure art in the sense that a painting of a pretty landscape is pure art. Most literature attempts far more directly than such paintings to make a comment on life. In considering a story like William Carlos Williams's "The Use of Force" (p. 162), we can and should discuss artistic elements such as plot construction and dialogue, but the story is also a comment on violence and human nature. The author has "something to say." Our response to the story depends largely on how well that "something" comes through to us. Without artistry, of course, the author's comment has no chance of coming through, but the author obviously has more than artistry alone on his mind. If literature attempts to be a comment on life, the critic needs to understand that comment fully. If a work has something to say, we must ask ourselves *what* it is saying as well as how it is saying it.

A comment on life, however, is not necessarily a *moral.* In good literature, especially modern literature, it is almost never a moral. This fact confuses many inexperienced readers. For them the question of "what does it mean" or "what does it say" usually implies "what is the moral"—the direct, simple, short statement of a lesson or message to be drawn from the work. When they find no clear moral, they tend to feel cheated or frustrated. Why can't writers just come right out with it and say what they mean? Why are they so fond of hidden meanings (even if the authors of this book state that there aren't such things)? Why do they indulge in these mystifying literary games?

There are two ways of answering these questions, one simple and one not so simple. First, morals have a way of being too tidy, too catchy, and dangerously superficial. They are fine in proverbs. They are fine in children's stories and five-minute sermons. An adult mind, however, can't help being suspicious of truths that are so conveniently packaged. Life is too complicated to be handled with the complacent certainties of Aesop's *Fables* or *Poor Richard's Almanac.* Literature produced by a thoughtful writer attempts to capture some of the quality of life itself, and the preachy oversimplifications inherent in moralizing spring from distortions of life. *He who hesitates is lost; life begins at forty; it's no use crying over spilt milk*—this stuff sounds good enough, but we all know that sometimes hesitation is advisable, that a significant life can begin at any age, and that crying over spilt milk has inspired, among many other things, some immortal poetry. When you look for neat little morals in literature, you cheat yourself and you are unfair to the writer. If a writer's comment on life can be summed up in a moral, the odds are that you have wasted your time reading the entire work.

The second reason that people have trouble when they set out to find morals is that a good writer *dramatizes* ideas. The ideas, in other words, are rarely expressed directly, as they would be in a sermon or a philosophy or sociology textbook. Insofar as the writer has any ideas, they grow out of the characters the writer creates and their response to the situations the writer devises for them. Thus, because we care about the characters, the ideas register on our emotions as well as our intellects. Writers try to convey life, not merely ideas *about* life—for if the ideas are all that matter, their works are elaborate shams that should have been sermons, textbooks, or letters to the editor of their local newspapers. The good writer does not *tell* us, "Young love can be beautiful, but can create a lot of problems, too"; he writes *Romeo and Juliet*. Granted, we may get this abstract idea about love from the play, along with many other ideas just as significant, but primarily we get a far richer sense of profound concern for two human beings. William Carlos Williams does not *tell* us "The use of violence, even in the best causes, is always dangerous" or "All people have violent tendencies buried within them" or squeeze any number of other morals out of the story; he writes "The Use of Force" and shows us violence in action. He dramatizes. Those who read the story as it was meant to be read do not simply wind up feeling abstractly afraid of violence—who needs a story for that?—but cringing with shock and perhaps self-knowledge at a good man's unleashing of the terrifying urges locked inside each of us. How do you put that into a moral?

As readers and critics we are much better off in dealing with a writer's something-to-say if we think not of the moral, but of the *theme*. Life, as we have stated, is too complex to be reduced to morals, and writers attempt to dramatize life in all its depth and complexity. A theme in literature is not a moral, a message, or a piece of advice; rather, it is *the underlying issue, the basic area of permanent human experience treated by the author*. A theme does not make a statement; it names a subject. We can say that the theme or themes of *Romeo and Juliet* are love, and family, and fate, and conflicting loyalties, and reason vs. passion. We could add to the list, and a good critic could probably then find a way of linking all the separate themes into one theme that covers them all. The author offers comments on these separate themes by creating certain characters who act in certain ways. Are we really entitled to draw general morals from these themes? Almost certainly not. Romeo and Juliet are individuals, not representatives of all young lovers. Their families are feuding, as most families are not. The characters in the play face issues that are permanent ingredients of human life and respond to these issues in their own way—and *that* is why the play has something to say, not because it gives us handy hints on how to live our own lives. Discussing the ideas in literature through the concept of theme enables us to escape the tyranny of moralizing.

It enables writers to be what they are best at being: writers, not philosophers, prophets, reformers, or know-it-alls.

Symbols

A symbol is a person, place, or thing that stands for or strongly suggests something in addition to itself, generally an abstract idea more important than itself. Don't let this definition intimidate you. Symbols are not fancy literary devices that readers have to wrestle with. In fact, the daily, nonliterary lives of readers are filled, quite comfortably and naturally, with more symbols than exist in any book ever written.

A mink coat, for example, is a piece of clothing made from the pelt of an animal in the weasel family, but for many people it stands for something else: it is a symbol of success or status or good taste. People do not make sacrifices and sounds of ecstasy over the pelt of a weasel, but over a symbol. A beard, to cite another example, is a hairy growth on a man's face, but a person would have to be a recent arrival from another planet not to realize that a beard is sometimes viewed as a symbol of anything from youthful self-assertion to political radicalism. Our lives are pervaded, perhaps dominated, by symbols. Think about the different symbolic meanings everyone gives to the following: a Cadillac, a new house, money, rats, a college diploma, a trip to Europe, a crucifix, a date with a popular and good-looking woman, the American flag, a blind date, Jane Fonda, the F.B.I., Niagara Falls, Valley Forge, a fireplace.

Making symbols and reacting to symbols seem such basic ingredients of the human mind that we should hardly be astonished to find symbols in literature. Symbols have an extremely practical value to a writer, however. They enable the writer to communicate abstract concepts with the energy and vitality that can come only from specific details. Just as some people may be indifferent to abstract oratory about freedom's being a good thing but deeply moved by a visit to the Statue of Liberty, a reader may be bored or antagonistic to philosophical assertions about the passing of time but intensely impressed by the specific symbol—from a novel by Arnold Bennett—of a wedding ring almost totally embedded in the fat flesh on the finger of an old woman. Symbols of abstract ideas can often have a dramatic impact that the ideas themselves cannot, and sometimes in the hands of a master, symbols can express what might otherwise be almost inexpressible.

Our comments so far have stressed that symbols in literature are not as difficult and mysterious as they are sometimes imagined to be. Dealing with symbols is nevertheless not child's play, and four major traps lie in wait for critics—professionals no less than amateurs.

First, the symbol stands for or suggests something *in addition to* itself, *not instead of* itself. The symbolic level of a story or poem should never be allowed to dwarf the other levels—especially the basic level of people and plot. The wedding ring on the fat finger not only suggests the sadness of the passing of time, but it also tells us in a straightforward, down-to-earth, nonsymbolic fashion that the woman eats too much and hasn't taken very good care of herself.

Second, symbols are usually obvious. If a critic has to struggle to establish that something functions as a symbol, it probably was not meant to be one. Excessive ingenuity in symbol hunting is one of the worst of all critical sins. Stick to what the author clearly intends. In Hemingway's *A Farewell to Arms,* one of the lovers says that she is afraid of the rain because she dreams that it means her death. Then, when she does die and it is indeed raining, we can say that the rain is a symbol of death. This is a deliberately simple example, of course, but the principle is perfectly valid: real symbols are usually obvious because writers tend to make big productions of them.

Third, symbols should not be confused with ordinary significant details. This confusion can be the main reason a symbol hunter pounces on a nonsymbol. A symbol stands for or suggests something substantially different from itself. Rain may symbolize death. A veil may symbolize isolation. Springtime may symbolize youth, re-birth, longing, hope. If a man in a story, however, wipes his running nose with the back of his hand and doesn't cover his mouth when he coughs, we simply know that he has bad manners (in addition to a cold). The way he wipes his nose is not a symbol of bad manners, nor is the way he coughs; they *are* bad manners, details about the character that reveal something about him. A symbol is a person, place, or thing that bears little concrete resemblance to whatever it stands for or suggests; the reader must make a major mental leap to identify the symbol with its meaning. A significant detail about a person, place, or thing, on the other hand, merely conveys more information about or insight into its subject.

Fourth, nobody who writes about literature should be too eager to make a symbol stand for any one thing in particular. The most effective symbols often are not meant to work that way at all. They *stand for* nothing. They are meant to *suggest*—on an emotional level, at times a virtually subconscious level—a number of different and elusive concepts. That is precisely why symbols can be so valu-able. Herman Melville's white whale in *Moby-Dick,* to mention a single example, is surely not meant to symbolize any one idea. The whale becomes such a powerful symbol because it suggests so many ideas: evil, man's insignificance, the unchanging order of the universe, nature, God's will, and so on. Symbols are often a great writer's imaginative shortcuts for dealing with the imposing and frightening complexity of life as we know it.

Metaphors and similes

Metaphors and similes are the two most common kinds of figurative language or figures of speech. A working definition of figurative language might be language that cannot be taken literally. In one way or another, figurative language departs from the conventional meaning and expression of words to bring about special effects, usually emotional. Figurative language is a common ingredient of our speech and writing; it is basic to almost all poetry, far more so than rhyme or meter.

A simile is a comparison using *like* or *as.*

The lecture was as dry as the Sahara Desert.

The nonsmokers at the cocktail party drew themselves into a small circle, like a wagon train surrounded by Indians.

All through that dreary summer weekend, we felt as if life had turned into a slow-motion movie.

A metaphor is often defined as a comparison that does without the *like* or *as,* thus establishing a closer connection between the items compared. It is also helpful, however, to think of a metaphor as a word or phrase generally used in one frame of reference that is shifted to another frame of reference.

The lecture was a Sahara Desert of dryness.

Our lives that dreary summer weekend had turned into a slow-motion movie.

She had ice-water in her veins.

Life is a cabaret.

The president told his administrators to stonewall the opposition.

Bill is the sparkplug of his team.

We thought the new boss was going to be a tiger, but he turned out to be a pussycat.

As indicated by many of the previous examples, our daily language is filled with metaphors. A number of them are so familiar that we have to struggle to recognize their metaphorical nature.

the arms of a chair	a wallflower
a clean sweep	the legs of a table
the traffic crawled	the heart of the matter
a green rookie	it's all a whitewash
a poker face	peaches-and-cream complexion

Effective metaphors and similes enable writers to stimulate and direct the emotions of their readers, to communicate their own emotions with concrete images rather than flat, abstract statements, and thus to develop stylistic color and excitement. Readers and critics should pay particular attention to metaphorical *patterns*— metaphors sustained and developed through a whole work rather than dropped after one sentence. Many writers consciously use such patterns to achieve greater unity, consistency, and dramatic power.

Exercise

Look over the following poems. First, identify each metaphor and simile. Second, try to find any patterns running through the entire poem. Third, consider whether the metaphors and similes are effective, and why.

NOT WAVING BUT DROWNING

Nobody heard him, the dead man,
But still he lay moaning:
I was much further out than you thought
And not waving but drowning.

Poor chap, he always loved larking[1]
And now he's dead
It must have been too cold for him his heart gave way,
They said.

Oh, no no no, it was too cold always
(Still the dead one lay moaning)
I was much too far out all my life
And not waving but drowning.

—*Stevie Smith*

1. Having fun.

IF WE MUST DIE

If we must die, let it not be like hogs
Hunted and penned in an inglorious spot,
While round us bark the mad and hungry dogs,
Making their mock at our accursèd lot.
If we must die, O let us nobly die,
So that our precious blood may not be shed
In vain; then even the monsters we defy
Shall be constrained to honor us though dead!
O kinsmen we must meet the common foe!
Though far outnumbered let us show us brave,
And for their thousand blows deal one deathblow!
What though before us lies the open grave?
Like men we'll face the murderous, cowardly pack,
Pressed to the wall, dying, but fighting back!

—*Claude McKay*

BRIDAL COUCH

Follows this a narrower bed,
Wood at feet, wood at head;
Follows this a sounder sleep
Somewhat longer and too deep.

All too meanly and too soon
Waxes once and wanes our moon;
All too swiftly for each one
Falls to dark our winter sun.

Let us here then wrestle death,
Intermingled limb and breath,
Conscious both that we beget
End of rest, endless fret,

And come at last to permanence,
Tired dancers from a dance,
Yawning, and content to fall
Into any bed at all.

—*Donald J. Lloyd*

I TASTE A LIQUOR NEVER BREWED

I taste a liquor never brewed—
From Tankards scooped in Pearl—

Not all the Vats upon the Rhine
Yield such an Alcohol!

Inebriate of Air—am I—
And Debauchee of Dew—
Reeling—thro endless summer days—
From inns of Molten Blue—

When "Landlords" turn the drunken Bee
Out of the Foxglove's door—
When Butterflies—renounce their "drams"—
I shall but drink the more!

Till Seraphs swing their snowy Hats—
And Saints—to windows run—
To see the little Tippler
Leaning against the—Sun—

—*Emily Dickinson*

BATTER MY HEART, THREE-PERSONED GOD

Batter my heart, three-personed God; for you
As yet but knock, breathe, shine, and seek to mend;
That I may rise and stand, o'erthrow me, and bend[1]
Your force, to break, blow, burn, and make me new.
I, like an usurped town to another due,
Labour to admit you, but Oh, to no end;
Reason, your viceroy in me, me should defend,
But is captived, and proves weak or untrue,
Yet dearly I love you, and would be loved fain
But am betrothed unto your enemy;
Divorce me, untie or break that knot again;
Take me to you, imprison me, for I,
Except you enthrall[2] me, never shall be free,
Nor ever chaste, except you ravish me.

—*John Donne*

1. Apply.
2. Capture, enslave.

DOVER BEACH

The sea is calm tonight,
The tide is full, the moon lies fair
Upon the straits;—on the French coast, the light
Gleams and is gone; the cliffs of England stand,

Glimmering and vast, out in the tranquil bay.
Come to the window, sweet is the night air!
Only, from the long line of spray
Where the sea meets the moon-blanch'd land,
Listen! you hear the grating roar
Of pebbles which the waves draw back, and fling,
At their return, up the high strand,
Begin, and cease, and then again begin,
With tremulous cadence slow, and bring
The eternal note of sadness in.

Sophocles[1] long ago
Heard it on the Aegean, and it brought
Into his mind the turbid ebb and flow
Of human misery; we
Find also in the sound a thought,
Hearing it by this distant northern sea.

The Sea of Faith
Was once, too, at the full, and round earth's shore
Lay like the folds of a bright girdle furl'd.
But now I only hear
Its melancholy, long, withdrawing roar,
Retreating, to the breath
Of the night-wind, down the vast edges drear
And naked shingles[2] of the world.

Ah, love, let us be true
To one another! for the world, which seems
To lie before us like a land of dreams,
So various, so beautiful, so new,
Hath really neither joy, nor love, nor light,
Nor certitude, nor peace, nor help for pain;
And we are here as on a darkling plain
Swept with confused alarms of struggle and flight,
Where ignorant armies clash by night.

—*Matthew Arnold*

1. Ancient Greek writer of tragic dramas.
2. Pebbled beaches.

Tone

In speaking and in writing, tone is not only an inseparable part of meaning, but also helps to create meaning. It is one of the ways by which speakers and writers convey their attitudes toward their subjects. When people exclaim to us, "Don't use that tone of voice with me," or "I don't like your tone," they may have nothing against the literal meaning of the words we have used, but may still have perfectly valid grounds for objecting to what we have said. Depending on what we do with our voices, our silences and pauses, and the words we choose to stress, we can make our attitude (our tone) angry, impatient, amused, contemptuous, appreciative, sarcastic, and so on. Notice how each of the following can change drastically in meaning as the tone varies:

Waiter!

I'm going to the opera next week.

Yes, dear, I think you drive very, very well.

My wife just had triplets.

Late papers, as usual, will not be accepted.

It's easy enough to recognize tone in speech, but what about writing? Writers can't raise and lower their voices, at least not in the usual sense. They may underline or capitalize an occasional word for emphasis, but they can hardly express through these means the hundred shades of emphasis that human speech can. Moreover, speakers can use gestures and facial expressions to help establish tone, and these conveniences are obviously unavailable to a writer. To compensate, writers must carefully use all the resources that *are* at their command; they must manage to choose appropriate words, word order, contexts, connotations, figurative language, sounds, and rhythms. All these elements and more add up to tone. Somehow or other, as we know, writers do successfully create tone, for we feel it in everything we read. Primarily through our awareness of and response to tone, we discover if a writer wants us to feel pity or scorn—or both—for a character, hatred or fear of an idea, passionate involvement or sophisticated detachment toward a plot. Consider the differences in the poems in the last exercise: the rage and bitterness of "If We Must Die," the restrained pathos of "Not Waving but Drowning," the gentle playfulness of "I Taste a Liquor Never Brewed."

Readings

This chapter ends with a group of four short stories. The first is accompanied by a student paper which should stimulate further thought about the story and about the writing of literary analysis in general. The remaining stories present additional opportunities for writing your own papers, this time without the inspiration of other students.

Stanley Ellin
THE BLESSINGTON METHOD

Mr. Treadwell was a small, likable man who worked for a prosperous company in New York City, and whose position with the company entitled him to an office of his own. Late one afternoon of a fine day in June a visitor entered this office. The visitor was stout, well-dressed, and imposing. His complexion was smooth and pink, his small, near-sighted eyes shone cheerfully behind heavy horn-rimmed eyeglasses.

"My name," he said, after laying aside a bulky portfolio and shaking Mr. Treadwell's hand with a crushing grip, "is Bunce, and I am a representative of the Society for Gerontology. I am here to help you with your problem, Mr. Treadwell."

Mr. Treadwell sighed. "Since you are a total stranger to me, my friend," he said, "and since I have never heard of the outfit you claim to represent, and, above all, since I have no problem which could possibly concern you, I am sorry to say that I am not in the market for whatever you are peddling. Now, if you don't mind—"

"Mind?" said Bunce. "Of course, I mind. The Society for Gerontology does not try to sell anything to anybody, Mr. Treadwell. Its interests are purely philanthropic. It examines case histories, draws up reports, works toward the solution of one of the most tragic situations we face in modern society."

"Which is?"

"That should have been made obvious by the title of the organization, Mr. Treadwell. Gerontology is the study of old age and the problems concerning it. Do not confuse it with geriatrics, please. Geriatrics is concerned with the diseases of old age. Gerontology deals with old age as the problem itself."

"I'll try to keep that in mind," Mr. Treadwell said impatiently. "Meanwhile, I suppose, a small donation is in order? Five dollars, say?"

"No, no, Mr. Treadwell, not a penny, not a red cent. I quite understand that this is the traditional way of dealing with various philanthropic organizations, but the Society for Gerontology works in a different way entirely. Our objective is to help you with your problem first. Only then would we feel we have the right to make any claim on you."

"Fine," said Mr. Treadwell more amiably. "That leaves us all even. I have no problem, so you get no donation. Unless you'd rather reconsider?"

"Reconsider?" said Bunce in a pained voice. "It is you, Mr. Treadwell, and not I who must reconsider. Some of the most pitiful cases the Society deals with are those of people who have long refused to recognize or admit their problem. I have worked months on your case, Mr. Treadwell. I never dreamed you would fall into that category."

Mr. Treadwell took a deep breath. "Would you mind telling me just what you mean by that nonsense about working on my case? I was never a case for any damned society or organization in the book!"

It was the work of a moment for Bunce to whip open his portfolio and extract several sheets of paper from it.

"If you will bear with me," he said, "I should like to sum up the gist of these reports. You are forty-seven years old and in excellent health. You own a home in East Sconsett, Long Island, on which there are nine years of mortgage payments still due, and you also own a late-model car on which eighteen monthly payments are yet to be made. However, due to an excellent salary you are in prosperous circumstances. Am I correct?"

"As correct as the credit agency which gave you that report," said Mr. Treadwell.

Bunce chose to overlook this. "We will now come to the point. You have been happily married for twenty-three years, and have one daughter who was married last year and now lives with her husband in Chicago. Upon her departure from your home your father-in-law, a widower and somewhat crotchety gentleman, moved into the house and now resides with you and your wife."

Bunce's voice dropped to a low, impressive note. "He's seventy-two years old, and, outside of a touch of bursitis in his right shoulder, admits to exceptional health for his age. He has stated on several occasions that he hopes to live another twenty years, and according to actuarial statistics which my Society has on file *he has every chance of achieving this.* Now do you understand, Mr. Treadwell?"

It took a long time for the answer to come. "Yes," said Mr. Treadwell at last, almost in a whisper. "Now I understand."

"Good," said Bunce sympathetically. "Very good. The first step is always a hard one—the admission that there *is* a problem hovering over you, clouding every day that passes. Nor is there any need to ask why you make efforts to conceal it even from yourself. You wish to spare Mrs. Treadwell your unhappiness, don't you?"

Mr. Treadwell nodded.

"Would it make you feel better," asked Bunce, "if I told you that Mrs. Treadwell shared your own feelings? That she, too, feels her father's presence in her home as a burden which grows heavier each day?"

"But she can't!" said Mr. Treadwell in dismay. "She was the one who wanted him to live with us in the first place, after Sylvia got married, and we had a spare room. She pointed out how much he had done for us when we first got started, and how easy he was to get along with, and how little expense it would be—it was she who sold me on the idea. I can't believe she didn't mean it!"

"Of course, she meant it. She knew all the traditional emotions at the thought of her old father living alone somewhere, and offered all the traditional arguments on his behalf, and was sincere every moment. The trap she led you both into was the pitfall that awaits anyone who indulges in murky, sentimental thinking. Yes, indeed, I'm sometimes inclined to believe that Eve ate the apple just to make the serpent happy," said Bunce, and shook his head grimly at the thought.

"Poor Carol," groaned Mr. Treadwell. "If I had only known that she felt as miserable about this as I did—"

"Yes?" said Bunce. "What would you have done?"

Mr. Treadwell frowned. "I don't know. But there must have been something we could have figured out if we put our heads together."

"What?" Bunce asked. "Drive the man out of the house?"

"Oh, I don't mean exactly like that."

"What then?" persisted Bunce. "Send him to an institution? There are some extremely luxurious institutions for the purpose. You'd have to consider one of them, since he could not possibly be regarded as a charity case; nor, for that matter, could I imagine him taking kindly to the idea of going to a public institution."

"Who would?" said Mr. Treadwell. "And as for the expensive kind, well, I did look into the idea once, but when I found out what they'd cost I knew it was out. It would take a fortune."

"Perhaps," suggested Bunce, "he could be given an apartment of his own—a small, inexpensive place with someone to take care of him."

"As it happens, that's what he moved out of to come live with us. And on that business of someone taking care of him—you'd never believe what it costs. That is, even allowing we could find someone to suit him."

"Right!" Bunce said, and struck the desk sharply with his fist. "Right in every respect, Mr. Treadwell."

Mr. Treadwell looked at him angrily. "What do you mean—right? I had the idea you wanted to help me with this business, but you haven't come up with a thing yet. On top of that you make it sound as if we're making great progress."

"We are, Mr. Treadwell, we are. Although you weren't aware of it we have just completed the second step to your solution. The first step was the admission that there was a problem; the second step was the realization that no matter which way you turn there seems to be no logical or practical solution to the problem. In this way you are not only witnessing, you are actually participating in, the marvelous operation of The Blessington Method which, in the end, places the one possible solution squarely in your hands."

"The Blessington Method?"

"Forgive me," said Bunce. "In my enthusiasm I used a term not yet in scientific vogue. I must explain, therefore, that The Blessington Method is the term my co-workers at the Society for Gerontology have given to its course of procedure. It is so titled in honor of J. G. Blessington, the Society's founder, and one of the great men of our era. He has not achieved his proper acclaim yet, but he will. Mark my words, Mr. Treadwell, some day his name will resound louder than that of Malthus."[1]

"Funny I never heard of him," reflected Mr. Treadwell. "Usually I keep up with the newspapers. And another thing," he added, eyeing Bunce narrowly, "we never did get around to clearing up just how you happened to list me as one of your cases, and how you managed to turn up so much about me."

Bunce laughed delightedly. "It does sound mysterious when you put it like that, doesn't it? Well, there's really no mystery to it at all. You see, Mr. Treadwell, the Society has hundreds of investigators scouting this great land of ours from coast to coast, although the public at large is not aware of this. It is against the rules of the Society for any employee to reveal that he is a professional investigator—he would immediately lose effectiveness.

---

1. Robert Malthus (1766–1834) was a British economist who wrote on the problems of overpopulation.

"Nor do these, investigators start off with some specific person as their subject. Their interest lies in *any* aged person who is willing to talk about himself, and you would be astonished at how garrulous most aged people are about their most intimate affairs. That is, of course, as long as they are among strangers.

"These subjects are met at random on park benches, in saloons, in libraries—in any place conducive to comfort and conversation. The investigator befriends the subjects, draws them out—seeks, especially, to learn all he can about the younger people on whom they are dependent."

"You mean," said Mr. Treadwell with growing interest, "the people who support them."

"No, no," said Bunce. "You are making the common error of equating *dependence* and *finances*. In many cases, of course, there is a financial dependence, but that is a minor part of the picture. The important factor is that there is always an *emotional* dependence. Even where a physical distance may separate the older person from the younger, that emotional dependence is always present. It is like a current passing between them. The younger person by the mere realization that the aged exist is burdened by guilt and anger. It was his personal experience with this tragic dilemma of our times that led J. G. Blessington to his great work."

"In other words," said Mr. Treadwell, "you mean that even if the old man were not living with us, things would be just as bad for Carol and me?"

"You seem to doubt that, Mr. Treadwell. But tell me, what makes things bad for you now, to use your own phrase?"

Mr. Treadwell thought this over. "Well," he said, "I suppose it's just a case of having a third person around all the time. It gets on your nerves after a while."

"But your daughter lived as a third person in your home for over twenty years," pointed our Bunce. "Yet, I am sure you didn't have the same reaction to her."

"But that's different," Mr. Treadwell protested. "You can have fun with a kid, play with her, watch her growing up—"

"Stop right there!" said Bunce. "Now you are hitting the mark. All the years your daughter lived with you you could take pleasure in watching her grow, flower like an exciting plant, take form as an adult being. But the old man in your house can only wither and decline now, and watching that process casts a shadow on your life. Isn't that the case?"

"I suppose it is."

"In that case, do you suppose it would make any difference if he lived elsewhere? Would you be any the less aware that he was withering and declining and looking wistfully in your direction from a distance?"

"Of course not. Carol probably wouldn't sleep half the night worrying about him, and I'd have him on my mind all the time because of her. That's perfectly natural, isn't it?"

"It is, indeed, and, I am pleased to say, your recognition of that completes the third step of The Blessington Method. You now realize that it is not the *presence* of the aged subject which creates the problem, but his *existence*."

Mr. Treadwell pursed his lips thoughtfully. "I don't like the sound of that."

"Why not? It merely states the fact, doesn't it?"

"Maybe it does. But there's something about it that leaves a bad taste in the mouth. It's like saying the only way Carol and I can have our troubles settled is by the old man's dying."

"Yes," Bunce said gravely, "it is like saying that."

"Well, I don't like it—not one bit. Thinking you'd like to see somebody dead can make you feel pretty mean, and as far as I know it's never killed anybody yet."

Bunce smiled. "Hasn't it?" he said gently.

He and Mr. Treadwell studied each other in silence. Then Mr. Treadwell pulled a handkerchief from his pocket with nerveless fingers and patted his forehead with it.

"You," he said with deliberation, "are either a lunatic or a practical joker. Either way, I'd like you to clear out of here. That's fair warning."

Bunce's face was all sympathetic concern. "Mr. Treadwell," he cried, "don't you realize you were on the verge of the fourth step? Don't you see how close you were to your solution?"

Mr. Treadwell pointed to the door. "Out—before I call the police."

The expression on Bunce's face changed from concern to disgust. "Oh, come, Mr. Treadwell, you don't believe anybody would pay attention to whatever garbled and incredible story you'd concoct out of this. Please think it over carefully before you do anything rash, now or later. If the exact nature of our talk were even mentioned, you would be the only one to suffer, believe me. Meanwhile, I'll leave you my card. Anytime you wish to call on me I will be ready to serve you."

"And why should I ever want to call on you?" demanded the white-faced Mr. Treadwell.

"There are various reasons," said Bunce, "but one above all." He gathered his belongings and moved to the door. "Consider, Mr. Treadwell: anyone who has mounted the first three steps of The Blessington Method inevitably mounts the fourth. You have made remarkable progress in a short time, Mr. Treadwell—you should be calling soon."

"I'll see you in hell first," said Mr. Treadwell.

Despite this parting shot, the time that followed was a bad one for Mr. Treadwell. The trouble was that having been introduced to The Blessington Method he couldn't seem to get it out of his mind. It incited thoughts that he had to keep thrusting away with an effort, and it certainly colored his relationship with his father-in-law in an unpleasant way.

Never before had the old man seemed so obtrusive, so much in the way, and so capable of always doing or saying the thing most calculated to stir annoyance. It especially outraged Mr. Treadwell to think of this intruder in his home babbling his private affairs to perfect strangers, eagerly spilling out details of his family life to paid investigators who were only out to make trouble. And, to Mr. Treadwell in his heated state of mind, the fact that the investigators could not be identified as such did not serve as any excuse.

Within very few days Mr. Treadwell, who prided himself on being a sane and level-headed businessman, had to admit he was in a bad way. He began to see evidences of a fantastic conspiracy on every hand. He could visualize hundreds—no, thousands—of Bunces swarming into offices just like his all over the country. He could feel cold sweat starting on his forehead at the thought.

But, he told himself, the whole thing was *too* fantastic. He could prove this to himself by merely reviewing his discussion with Bunce, and so he did, dozens of times. After all, it was no more than an objective look at a social problem. Had anything been said that a *really* intelligent man should shy away from? Not at all. If he had drawn some shocking inferences, it was because the ideas were already in his mind looking for an outlet.

On the other hand—

It was with a vast relief that Mr. Treadwell finally decided to pay a visit to the Society for Gerontology. He knew what he would find there: a dingy room or two, a couple of under-paid clerical workers, the musty odor of a piddling charity operation—all of which would restore matters to their proper perspective again. He went so strongly imbued with this picture that he almost walked past the gigantic glass and aluminum tower which was the address of the Society, rode its softly humming elevator in confusion, and emerged in the anteroom of the Main Office in a daze.

And it was still in a daze that he was ushered through a vast and seemingly endless labyrinth of rooms by a sleek, long-legged young woman, and saw, as he passed, hosts of other young women, no less sleek and long-legged, multitudes of brisk, square-shouldered young men, rows of streamlined machinery clicking and chuckling in electronic glee, mountains of stainless-steel card indexes, and, over all, the bland reflection of modern indirect lighting on plastic and metal—until finally he was led into the presence of Bunce himself, and the door closed behind him.

"Impressive, isn't it?" said Bunce, obviously relishing the sight of Mr. Treadwell's stupefaction.

"Impressive?" croaked Mr. Treadwell hoarsely. "Why, I've never seen anything like it. It's a ten-million-dollar outfit!"

"And why not? Science is working day and night like some Frankenstein, Mr. Treadwell, to increase longevity past all sane limits. There are fourteen million people over sixty-five in this country right now. In twenty years their number will be increased to twenty-one million. Beyond that no one can even estimate what the figures will rise to!

"But the one bright note is that each of these aged people is surrounded by many young donors or potential donors to our Society. As the tide rises higher, we, too, flourish and grow stronger to withstand it."

Mr. Treadwell felt a chill of horror penetrate him. "Then it's true, isn't it?"

"I beg your pardon?"

"This Blessington Method you're always talking about," said Mr. Treadwell wildly. "The whole idea is just to settle things by getting rid of old people!"

"Right!" said Bunce. "That is the exact idea. And not even J. G. Blessington himself ever phrased it better. You have a way with words, Mr. Treadwell. I always admire a man who can come to the point without sentimental twaddle."

"But you can't get away with it!" said Mr. Treadwell incredulously. "You don't really believe you can get away with it, do you?"

Bunce gestured toward the expanses beyond the closed doors. "Isn't that sufficient evidence of the Society's success?"

"But all those people out there! Do they realize what's going on?"

"Like all well-trained personnel, Mr. Treadwell," said Bunce reproachfully, "they know only their own duties. What you and I are discussing here happens to be upper echelon."

Mr. Treadwell's shoulders drooped. "It's impossible," he said weakly. "It can't work."

"Come, come," Bunce said not unkindly, "you mustn't let yourself be overwhelmed. I imagine that what disturbs you most is what J. G. Blessington sometimes referred to as the Safety Factor. But look at it this way, Mr. Treadwell: isn't it perfectly natural for old people to die? Well, our Society guarantees that the deaths will appear natural. Investigations are rare—not one has ever caused us any trouble.

"More than that, you would be impressed by many of the names on our list of donors. People powerful in the political world as well as the financial world have been flocking to us. One and all, they could give glowing testimonials as to our efficiency. And remember that such important people make the Society for Gerontology invulnerable, no matter at what point it may be attacked, Mr. Treadwell. And such invulnerability extends to every single one of our sponsors, including you, should you choose to place your problem in our hands."

"But I don't have the right," Mr. Treadwell protested despairingly. "Even if I wanted to, who am I to settle things this way for anybody?"

"Aha." Bunce leaned forward intently. "But you do want to settle things?"

"Not this way."

"Can you suggest any other way?"

Mr. Treadwell was silent.

"You see," Bunce said with satisfaction, "the Society for Gerontology offers the one practical answer to the problem. Do you still reject it, Mr. Treadwell?"

"I can't see it," Mr. Treadwell said stubbornly. "It's just not right."

"Are you sure of that?"

"Of course I am!" snapped Mr. Treadwell. "Are you going to tell me that it's right and proper to go around killing people just because they're old?"

"I am telling you that very thing, Mr. Treadwell, and I ask you to look at it this way. We are living today in a world of progress, a world of producers and consumers, all doing their best to improve our common lot. The old are neither producers nor consumers, so they are only barriers to our continued progress.

"If we want to take a brief, sentimental look into the pastoral haze of yesterday we may find that once they did serve a function. While the young were out tilling the fields, the old could tend to the household. But even that function is gone today. We have a hundred better devices for tending the household, and they come far cheaper. Can you dispute that?"

"I don't know," Mr. Treadwell said doggedly. "You're arguing that people are machines, and I don't go along with that at all."

"Good heavens," said Bunce, "don't tell me that you see them as anything else! Of course, we are machines, Mr. Treadwell, all of us. Unique and wonderful machines, I grant, but machines nevertheless. Why, look at the world around you. It is a vast organism made up of replaceable parts, all striving to produce and consume, produce and consume until worn out. Should one permit the worn-out part to remain where it is? Of course not! It must be cast aside so that the organism will not be made inefficient. It is the whole organism that counts, Mr. Treadwell, not any of its individual parts. Can't you understand that?"

"I don't know," said Mr. Treadwell uncertainly. "I've never thought of it that way. It's hard to take in all at once."

"I realize that, Mr. Treadwell, but it is part of The Blessington Method that the sponsor fully appreciate the great value of his contribution in all ways—not only as it benefits him, but also in the way it benefits the entire social organism. In signing a pledge to our Society a man is truly performing the most noble act of his life."

"Pledge?" said Mr. Treadwell. "What kind of pledge?"

Bunce removed a printed form from a drawer of his desk and laid it out carefully for Mr. Treadwell's inspection. Mr. Treadwell read it and sat up sharply.

"Why, this says that I'm promising to pay you two thousand dollars in a month from now. You never said anything about that kind of money!"

"There has never been any occasion to raise the subject before this," Bunce replied. "But for some time now a committee of the Society has been examining your financial standing, and it reports that you can pay this sum without stress or strain."

"What do you mean, stress or strain?" Mr. Treadwell retorted. "Two thousand dollars is a lot of money, no matter how you look at it."

Bunce shrugged. "Every pledge is arranged in terms of the sponsor's ability to pay, Mr. Treadwell. Remember, what may seem expensive to you would certainly seem cheap to many other sponsors I have dealt with."

"And what do I get for this?"

"Within one month after you sign the pledge, the affair of your father-in-law will be disposed of. Immediately after that you will be expected to pay the pledge in full. Your name is then enrolled on our list of sponsors, and that is all there is to it."

"I don't like the idea of my name being enrolled on anything."

"I can appreciate that," said Bunce. "But may I remind you that a donation to a charitable organization such as the Society for Gerontology is tax-deductible?"

Mr. Treadwell's fingers rested lightly on the pledge. "Now just for the sake of argument," he said, "suppose someone signs one of these things and then doesn't pay up. I guess you know that a pledge like this isn't collectible under the law, don't you?"

"Yes," Bunce smiled, "and I know that a great many organizations cannot redeem pledges made to them in apparently good faith. But the Society for Gerontoloty has never met that difficulty. We avoid it by reminding all sponsors that the young, if they are careless, may die as unexpectedly as the old . . . No, no," he said, steadying the paper, "just your signature at the bottom will do."

When Mr. Treadwell's father-in-law was found drowned off the foot of East Sconsett pier three weeks later (the old man fished from the pier regularly although he had often been told by various local authorities that the fishing was poor there), the event was duly entered into the East Sconsett records as Death By Accidental Submersion, and Mr. Treadwell himself made the arrangements for an exceptionally elaborate funeral. And it was at the funeral that Mr. Treadwell first had the Thought. It was a fleeting and unpleasant thought, just disturbing enough to make him miss a step as he entered the church. In all the confusion of the moment, however, it was not too difficult to put aside.

A few days later, when he was back at his familiar desk, the Thought suddenly returned. This time it was not to be put aside so easily. It grew steadily larger and larger in his mind, until his waking hours were terrifyingly full of it, and his sleep a series of shuddering nightmares.

There was only one man who could clear up the matter for him, he knew; so he appeared at the offices of the Society for Gerontology burning with anxiety to have Bunce do so. He was hardly aware of handing over his check to Bunce and pocketing the receipt.

"There's something that's been worrying me," said Mr. Treadwell, coming straight to the point.

"Yes?"

"Well, do you remember telling me how many old people there would be around in twenty years?"

"Of course."

Mr. Treadwell loosened his collar to ease the constriction around his throat. "But don't you see? I'm going to be one of them!"

Bunce nodded. "If you take reasonably good care of yourself there's no reason why you shouldn't be," he pointed out.

"You don't get the idea," Mr. Treadwell said urgently. "I'll be in a spot then where I'll have to worry all the time about someone from this Society coming in and giving my daughter or my son-in-law ideas! That's a terrible thing to have to worry about all the rest of your life."

Bunce shook his head slowly. "You can't mean that, Mr. Treadwell."

"And why can't I?"

"Why? Well, think of your daughter, Mr. Treadwell. Are you thinking of her?"

"Yes."

"Do you see her as the lovely child who poured out her love to you in exchange for yours? The fine young woman who has just stepped over the threshold of marriage, but is always eager to visit you, eager to let you know the affection she feels for you?"

"I know that."

"And can you see in your mind's eye that manly young fellow who is her husband? Can you feel the warmth of his handclasp as he greets you? Do you know his gratitude for the financial help you give him regularly?"

"I suppose so."

"Now, honestly, Mr. Treadwell, can you imagine either of these affectionate and devoted youngsters doing a single thing—the slightest thing—to harm you?"

The constriction around Mr. Treadwell's throat miraculously eased; the chill around his heart departed.

"No," he said with conviction, "I can't."

"Splendid," said Bunce. He leaned far back in his chair and smiled with a kindly wisdom. "Hold on to that thought, Mr. Treadwell. Cherish it and keep it close at all times. It will be a solace and comfort to the very end."

Questions for Writing or Discussion

1. What are the four steps in the Blessington Method?
2. How much of a struggle does Mr. Treadwell put up before consenting to the removal of his father-in-law?
3. What contribution to the story as a whole is made by the description of the offices of the Society for Gerontology?
4. What is "the Thought" that Mr. Treadwell has in the last part of the story?
5. Explain the point of Mr. Bunce's comment: "I'm sometimes inclined to believe that Eve ate the apple just to make the serpent happy."
6. Like Vonnegut's "Harrison Bergeron" (p. 25), "The Blessington Method" uses fantasy to present some serious observations about contemporary society. What is the nature of those observations, and how valid do you think they are?

A Horror Story
STEWART BENDER

It doesn't take a great mind to realize that although Stanley Ellin's "The Blessington Method" is a readable and—for a while—amusing story, there is a serious and disturbing side to it, too. Obviously, the author is unhappy with our society's attitude toward old people and its treatment of them. He is even more unhappy, and the story is even more disturbing, however, because of the basic attitude toward life that lies behind the Society for Gerontology and Mr. Treadwell's consent to its proposal to eliminate his inconvenient old father-in-law. Without vampires, ghosts, werewolves, or body snatchers, "The Blessington Method" is a true horror story.

The heart of the horror is the assumption that pure, strict logic is the only way to think about life and people. Love, loyalty, gratitude, fond memories are all the product of "murky, sentimental thinking." Moral disgust and outrage at the idea of murder is simply "sentimental twaddle." If it's logical "to settle things by getting rid of old people," then the only course of action is to go ahead and get rid of them. When machines break down, they are "cast aside." People are machines. Q. E .D.

It is easy to see the commitment to logic of the Society and its spokes-man, Mr. Bunce. (Even the fees are determined only after careful research.) Less apparent is that the "likable" Mr. Treadwell, so "sane and level-headed," is also a person without moral principles. The entire story con-sists of Mr. Treadwell's being convinced step by step that literally putting out a contract on his father-in-law makes logical sense. When he is con-vinced, he has no personal ethical standards to fall back on, apart from some short-lived "sentimental twaddle."

One by one, all of Treadwell's objections and hesitations about the murder of his relative are refuted as being illogical. Isn't the old man in his seventies, and couldn't he die naturally at any time? Wrong! Sta-tistics show the old man is likely to live for twenty more years. Won't Treadwell's wife be sorry about her father's death? No. What about an in-stitution or apartment instead of murder? Too expensive. What about get-ting caught? No chance—just look at the record of the Society's successes and its list of influential friends. Mr. Treadwell has nothing to fall back on. There is nothing inside him.

The horror in this horror story doesn't stop with the nothingness inside Mr. Treadwell. Treadwell is just one client, after all. *Nobody* turns down the Society after reaching the third step of the Blessington Method. The Society is a multimillion dollar, highly successful, nationwide enterprise. *Everybody* is like Mr. Treadwell—his own daughter included.

"The Blessington Method" presents a picture not just of a civilization that treats elderly people badly. It presents a picture of a civilization with-out convictions, values, moral standards of any kind, a civilization where man's immortal soul has been replaced by brain waves and computers.

Questions for Writing or Discussion

1. Does the writer distort any of the facts of the story?
2. Does the writer use enough details to support his thesis adequately?
3. Does the writer omit any details that would have strengthened his argument?
4. Where is the thesis first stated?
5. Are there too many direct quotes from the story?

W. Somerset Maugham
THE COLONEL'S LADY

All this happened two or three years before the outbreak of the war.[1]
    The Peregrines were having breakfast. Though they were alone and

---

1. World War I.

the table was long they sat at opposite ends of it. From the walls George Peregrine's ancestors, painted by the fashionable painters of the day, looked down upon them. The butler brought in the morning post. There were several letters for the Colonel, business letters, *The Times* and a small parcel for his wife Evie. He looked at his letters and then, opening *The Times*, began to read it. They finished breakfast and rose from the table. He noticed that his wife hadn't opened the parcel.

"What's that?" he asked.

"Only some books."

"Shall I open it for you?"

"If you like."

He hated to cut string and so with some difficulty untied the knots.

"But they're all the same," he said when he had unwrapped the parcel. "What on earth d'you want six copies of the same book for?" He opened one of them. "Poetry." Then he looked at the title page. *When Pyramids Decay*, he read, by E. K. Hamilton. Eva Katherine Hamilton: that was his wife's maiden name. He looked at her with smiling surprise. "Have you written a book, Evie? You are a slyboots."

"I didn't think it would interest you very much. Would you like a copy?"

"Well, you know poetry isn't much in my line, but—yes, I'd like a copy; I'll read it. I'll take it along to my study. I've got a lot to do this morning."

He gathered up *The Times*, his letters and the book and went out. His study was a large and comfortable room, with a big desk, leather armchairs and what he called "trophies of the chase" on the walls. In the bookshelves were works of reference, books on farming, gardening, fishing and shooting, and books on the last war, in which he had won an M.C. and a D.S.O. For before his marriage he had been in the Welsh Guards. At the end of the war he retired and settled down to the life of a country gentleman in the spacious house, some twenty miles from Sheffield, which one of his forebears had built in the reign of George III. George Peregrine had an estate of some fifteen hundred acres which he managed with ability; he was a justice of the peace and performed his duties conscientiously. During the season he rode to hounds two days a week. He was a good shot, a golfer and though now a little over fifty could still play a hard game of tennis. He could describe himself with propriety as an all-around sportsman.

He had been putting on weight lately, but was still a fine figure of a man; tall, with grey curly hair, only just beginning to grow thin on the crown, frank blue eyes, good features and a high colour. He was a public-spirited man, chairman at any number of local organizations and, as became his class and station, a loyal member of the Conservative party. He looked upon it as his duty to see to the welfare of the people on his estate and it was a satisfaction to him to know that Evie could be trusted to tend the sick and succour the poor. He had built a cottage hospital on the outskirts of the village and paid the wages of a nurse out of his own pocket. All he asked of the recipients of his bounty was that at elections, county or general, they should vote for his candidate. He was a friendly man, affable to his inferiors, considerate with his tenants and popular with the neighbouring gentry. He would have been pleased and at the same time slightly embarrassed if someone had told him he was a jolly good fellow. That was what he wanted to be. He desired no higher praise.

It was hard luck that he had no children. He would have been an excellent father, kindly but strict, and would have brought up his sons as a gentleman's sons should be brought up, sent them to Eton, you know, taught them to fish, shoot and ride. As it was, his heir was a nephew, son of his brother killed in a motor accident, not a bad boy, but not a chip off the old block, no, sir, far from it; and would you believe it, his fool of a mother was sending him to a co-educational school. Evie had been a sad disappointment to him. Of course she was a lady, and she had a bit of money of her own; she managed the house uncommonly well and she was a good hostess. The village people adored her. She had been a pretty young thing when he married her, with a creamy skin, light brown hair and a trim figure, healthy, too, and not a bad tennis player; he couldn't understand why she'd had no children; of course she was faded now, she must be getting on for five and forty; her skin was drab, her hair had lost its sheen and she was as thin as a rail. She was always neat and suitably dressed, but she didn't seem to bother how she looked; she wore no makeup and didn't even use lipstick; sometimes at night when she dolled herself up for a party you could tell that once she'd been quite attractive, but ordinarily she was—well, the sort of woman you simply didn't notice. A nice woman, of course, a good wife, and it wasn't her fault if she was barren, but it was tough on a fellow who wanted an heir of his own loins; she hadn't any vitality, that's what was the matter with her. He supposed he'd been in love with her when he asked her to marry him, at least sufficiently in love for a man who wanted to marry and settle down, but with time he discovered that they had nothing much in common. She didn't care about hunting, and fishing bored her. Naturally they'd drifted apart. He had to do her the justice to admit that she'd never bothered him. There'd been no scenes. They had no quarrels. She seemed to take it for granted that he should go his own way. When he went up to London now and then she never wanted to come with him. He had a girl there, well, she wasn't exactly a girl, she was thirty-five if she was a day, but she was blonde and luscious and he only had to wire ahead of time and they'd dine, do a show and spend the night together. Well, a man, a healthy normal man had to have some fun in his life. The thought crossed his mind that if Evie hadn't been such a good woman she'd have been a better wife; but it was not the sort of thought that he welcomed and he put it away from him.

George Peregrine finished his *Times* and being a considerate fellow rang the bell and told the butler to take the paper to Evie. Then he looked at his watch. It was half-past ten and at eleven he had an appointment with one of his tenants. He had half an hour to spare.

"I'd better have a look at Evie's book," he said to himself.

He took it up with a smile. Evie had a lot of highbrow books in her sitting-room, not the sort of books that interested him, but if they amused her he had no objection to her reading them. He noticed that the volume he now held in his hand contained no more than ninety pages. That was all to the good. He shared Edgar Allan Poe's opinion that poems should be short. But as he turned the pages he noticed that several of Evie's had long lines of irregular length and didn't rhyme. He didn't like that. At his first school, when he was a little boy, he remembered learning a poem that began: *The boy stood on the burning deck,* and later, at Eton, one that started: *Ruin seize thee, ruthless king;* and then there was Henry V; they'd had to take that one half. He stared at Evie's pages with consternation.

"That's not what I call poetry," he said.

Fortunately it wasn't all like that. Interspersed with the pieces that looked so odd, lines of three or four words and then a line of ten or fifteen, there were little poems, quite short, that rhymed, thank God, with the lines all the same length. Several of the pages were just headed with the word *Sonnet,* and out of curiosity he counted the lines; there were fourteen of them. He read them. They seemed all right, but he didn't quite know what they were all about. He repeated to himself: *Ruin seize thee, ruthless king.*

"Poor Evie," he sighed.

At that moment the farmer he was expecting was ushered into the study, and putting the book down he made him welcome. They embarked on their business.

"I read your book, Evie," he said as they sat down to lunch. "Jolly good. Did it cost you a packet to have it printed?"

"No, I was lucky. I sent it to a publisher and he took it."

"Not much money in poetry, my dear," he said in his good-natured, hearty way.

"No, I don't suppose there is. What did Bannock want to see you about this morning?"

Bannock was the tenant who had interrupted his reading of Evie's poems.

"He's asked me to advance the money for a pedigree bull he wants to buy. He's a good man and I've half a mind to do it."

George Peregrine saw that Evie didn't want to talk about her book and he was not sorry to change the subject. He was glad she had used her maiden name on the title page; he didn't suppose anyone would ever hear about the book, but he was proud of his own unusual name and he wouldn't have liked it if some damned penny-a-liner had made fun of Evie's effort in one of the papers.

During the few weeks that followed he thought it tactful not to ask Evie any questions about her venture into verse and she never referred to it. It might have been a discreditable incident that they had silently agreed not to mention. But then a strange thing happened. He had to go to London on business and he took Daphne out to dinner. That was the name of the girl with whom he was in the habit of passing a few agreeable hours whenever he went to town.

"Oh, George," she said, "is that your wife who's written a book they're all taking about?"

"What on earth d'you mean?"

"Well, there's a fellow I know who's a critic. He took me out to dinner the other night and he had a book with him. 'Got anything for me to read?' I said. 'What's that?' 'Oh, I don't think that's your cup of tea,' he said, 'It's poetry, I've just been reviewing it.' 'No poetry for me,' I said. 'It's about the hottest stuff I ever read,' he said. 'Selling like hot cakes. And it's damned good.' "

"Who's the book by?" asked George.

"A woman called Hamilton. My friend told me that wasn't her real name. He said her real name was Peregrine. 'Funny,' I said, 'I know a fellow called Peregrine.' 'Colonel in the army,' he said. 'Lives near Sheffield.' "

"I'd just as soon you didn't talk about me to your friends," said George with a frown of vexation.

"Keep your shirt on, dearie. Who'd you take me for? I just said, 'It's not the same one.' " Daphne giggled. "My friend said: 'They say he's a regular Colonel Blimp.' "[2]

George had a keen sense of humour.

"You could tell them better than that," he laughed. "If my wife had written a book I'd be the first to know about it, wouldn't I?"

"I suppose you would."

Anyhow the matter didn't interest her and when the Colonel began to talk of other things she forgot about it. He put it out of his mind too. There was nothing to it, he decided, and that silly fool of a critic had just been pulling Daphne's leg. He was amused at the thought of her tackling that book because she had been told it was hot stuff and then finding it just a lot of stuff cut up into unequal lines.

He was a member of several clubs and next day he thought he'd lunch at one in St. James's Street. He was catching a train back to Sheffield early in the afternoon. He was sitting in a comfortable armchair having a glass of sherry before going into the dining-room when an old friend came up to him.

"Well, old boy, how's life?" he said. "How d'you like being the husband of a celebrity?"

George Peregrine looked at his friend. He thought he saw an amused twinkle in his eyes.

"I don't know what you're talking about," he answered.

"Come off it, George. Everyone knows E. K. Hamilton is your wife. Not often a book of verse has a success like that. Look here, Henry Dashwood is lunching with me. He'd like to meet you."

"Who the devil is Henry Dashwood and why should he want to meet me?"

"Oh, my dear fellow, what do you do with yourself all the time in the country? Henry's about the best critic we've got. He wrote a wonderful review on Evie's book. D'you mean to say she didn't show it to you?"

Before George could answer his friend had called a man over. A tall, thin man, with a high forehead, a beard, a long nose and a stoop, just the sort of man whom George was prepared to dislike at first sight. Introductions were effected. Henry Dashwood sat down.

"Is Mrs. Peregrine in London by any chance? I should very much like to meet her," he said.

"No, my wife doesn't like London. She prefers the country," said George stiffly.

"She wrote me a very nice letter about my review. I was pleased. You know, we critics get more kicks than halfpence. I was simply bowled over by her book. It's so fresh and original, very modern without being obscure.

---

2. Comic stereotype of British army officer.

She seems to be as much at her ease in free verse as in classical metres." Then because he was a critic he thought he should criticize. "Sometimes her ear is a trifle at fault, but you can say the same of Emily Dickinson. There are several of those short lyrics of hers that might have been written by Landor."

All this was gibberish to George Peregrine. The man was nothing but a disgusting highbrow. But the Colonel had good manners and he answered with proper civility. Henry Dashwood went on as though he hadn't spoken.

"But what makes the book so outstanding is the passion that throbs in every line. So many of these young poets are so anaemic, cold, bloodless, dully intellectual, but here you have real naked, earthy passion; of course deep, sincere emotion like that is tragic—ah, my dear Colonel, how right Heine was when he said that the poet makes little songs out of his great sorrows. You know, now and then, as I read and re-read those heart-rending pages I thought of Sappho."

This was too much for George Peregrine and he got up.

"Well, it's jolly nice of you to say such nice things about my wife's little book. I'm sure she'll be delighted. But I must bolt, I've got to catch a train and I want to get a bite of lunch."

"Damned fool," he said irritably to himself as he walked upstairs to the dining-room.

He got home in time for dinner and after Evie had gone to bed he went into his study and looked for her book. He thought he'd just glance through it again to see for himself what they were making such a fuss about, but he couldn't find it. Evie must have taken it away.

"Silly," he muttered.

He'd told her he thought it jolly good. What more could a fellow be expected to say? Well, it didn't matter. He lit his pipe and read the *Field* till he felt sleepy. But a week or so later it happened that he had to go into Sheffield for the day. He lunched there at his club. He had nearly finished when the Duke of Haverel came in. This was the great local magnate and of course the Colonel knew him, but only to say how d'you do to; and he was surprised when the Duke stopped at his table.

"We're so sorry your wife couldn't come to us for the week-end," he said, with a sort of shy cordiality. "We're expecting rather a nice lot of people."

George was taken aback. He guessed that the Haverels had asked him and Evie over for the week-end and Evie, without saying a word to him about it, had refused. He had the presence of mind to say he was sorry too.

"Better luck next time," said the Duke pleasantly and moved on.

Colonel Peregrine was very angry and when he got home he said to his wife:

"Look here, what's this about our being asked over to Haverel? Why on earth did you say we couldn't go? We've never been asked before and it's the best shooting in the country."

"I didn't think of that. I thought it would only bore you."

"Damn it all, you might at least have asked me if I wanted to go."

"I'm sorry."

He looked at her closely. There was something in her expression that he didn't quite understand. He frowned.

"I suppose *I* was asked?" he barked.

Evie flushed a little.

"Well, in point of fact you weren't."

"I call it damned rude of them to ask you without asking me."

"I suppose they thought it wasn't your sort of party. The Duchess is rather fond of writers and people like that, you know. She's having Henry Dashwood, the critic, and for some reason he wants to meet me."

"It was damned nice of you to refuse, Evie."

"It's the least I could do," she smiled. She hesitated a moment. "George, my publishers want to give a little dinner party for me one day towards the end of the month and of course they want you to come too."

"Oh, I don't think that's quite my mark. I'll come up to London with you if you like. I'll find someone to dine with."

Daphne.

"I expect it'll be very dull, but they're making rather a point of it. And the day after, the American publisher who's taken my book is giving a cocktail party at Claridge's. I'd like you to come to that if you wouldn't mind."

"Sounds like a crashing bore, but if you really want me to come I'll come."

"It would be sweet of you."

George Peregrine was dazed by the cocktail party. There were a lot of people. Some of them didn't look so bad, a few of the women were decently turned out, but the men seemed to him pretty awful. He was introduced to everybody as Colonel Peregrine, E. K. Hamilton's husband, you know. The men didn't seem to have anything to say to him, but the women gushed.

"You *must* be proud of your wife. Isn't it *wonderful!* You know, I read it right through at a sitting, I simply couldn't put it down, and when I'd finished I started again at the beginning and read it right through a second time. I was simply *thrilled.*"

The English publisher said to him:

"We've not had a success like this with a book of verse for twenty years. I've never seen such reviews."

The American publisher said to him:

"It's swell. It'll be a smash hit in America. You wait and see."

The American publisher had sent Evie a great spray of orchids. Damned ridiculous, thought George. As they came in, people were taken up to Evie and it was evident that they said flattering things to her, which she took with a pleasant smile and a word or two of thanks. She seemed a trifle flushed with excitement, but seemed quite at her ease. Though he thought the whole thing a lot of stuff and nonsense, George noted with approval that his wife was carrying it off in just the right way.

"Well, there's one thing," he said to himself, "you can see she's a lady and that's a damned sight more than you can say of anyone else here."

He drank a good many cocktails. But there was one thing that bothered him. He had a notion that some of the people he was introduced to looked at him in a rather funny sort of way, he couldn't quite make out what it meant, and once when he strolled by two women who were sitting together on a sofa he had the impression that they were talking about him and after he passed he was almost certain they tittered. He was very glad when the party came to an end.

In the taxi on their way back to their hotel Evie said to him:

"You were wonderful, dear. You made quite a hit. The girls simply raved about you; they thought you so handsome."

"Girls," he said bitterly. "Old hags."

"Were you bored, dear?"

"Stiff."

She pressed his hand in a gesture of sympathy.

"I hope you won't mind if we wait and go down by the afternoon train. I've got some things to do in the morning."

"No, that's all right. Shopping?"

"I do want to buy one or two things, but I've got to go and be photographed. I hate the idea, but they think I ought to be. For America, you know."

He said nothing. But he thought. He thought it would be a shock to the American public when they saw the portrait of the homely, dessicated little woman who was his wife. He'd always been under the impression that they liked glamour in America.

He went on thinking and next morning when Evie had gone out he went to his club and up to the library. There he looked up recent numbers of *The Times Literary Supplement,* the *New Statesman* and the *Spectator.* Presently he found reviews of Evie's book. He didn't read them very carefully, but enough to see that they were extremely favourable. Then he went to the bookseller's in Piccadilly where he occasionally bought books. He'd made up his mind that he had to read this damned thing of Evie's properly, but he didn't want to ask her what she'd done with the copy she'd given him. He'd buy one for himself. Before going in he looked in the window and the first thing he saw was a display of *When Pyramids Decay.* Damned silly title! He went in. A young man came forward and asked if he could help him.

"No, I'm just having a look round." It embarrassed him to ask for Evie's book and he thought he'd find it for himself and then take it to the salesman. But he couldn't see it anywhere and at last, finding the young man near him, he said in a carefully casual tone: "By the way, have you got a book called *When Pyramids Decay?*"

"The new edition came in this morning. I'll get a copy."

In a moment the young man returned with it. He was a short, rather stout young man, with a shock of untidy carroty hair and spectacles. George Peregrine, tall, upstanding, very military, towered over him.

"Is this a new edition then?" he asked.

"Yes, sir. The fifth. It might be a novel the way it's selling."

George Peregrine hesitated a moment.

"Why d'you suppose it's such a success? I've always been told no one reads poetry."

"Well, it's good, you know. I've read it meself." The young man, though obviously cultured, had a slight Cockney accent, and George quite instinctively adopted a patronizing attitude. "It's the story they like. Sexy, you know, but tragic."

George frowned a little. He was coming to the conclusion that the young man was rather impertinent. No one had told him anything about there being a story in the damned book and he had not gathered that from reading the reviews. The young man went on.

"Of course it's only a flash in the pan, if you know what I mean. The way I look at it, she was sort of inspired by a personal experience, like Housman was with *The Shropshire Lad.* She'll never write anything else."

"How much is the book?" said George coldly to stop his chatter. "You needn't wrap it up, I'll just slip it in my pocket."

The November morning was raw and he was wearing a greatcoat.

At the station he bought the evening papers and magazines and he and Evie settled themselves comfortably in opposite corners of a first-class carriage and read. At five o'clock they went along to the restaurant car to have tea and chatted a little. They arrived. They drove home in the car which was waiting for them. They bathed, dressed for dinner, and after dinner Evie, saying she was tired out, went to bed. She kissed him, as was her habit, on the forehead. Then he went into the hall, took Evie's book out of his greatcoat pocket and going into the study began to read it. He didn't read verse very easily and though he read with attention, every word of it, the impression he received was far from clear. Then he began at the beginning again and read it a second time. He read with increasing malaise, but he was not a stupid man and when he had finished he had a distinct understanding of what it was all about. Part of the book was in free verse, part in conventional metres, but the story it related was coherent and plain to the meanest intelligence. It was the story of a passionate love affair between an older woman, married, and a young man. George Peregrine made out the steps of it as easily as if he had been doing a sum in simple addition.

Written in the first person, it began with the tremulous surprise of the woman, past her youth, when it dawned upon her that the young man was in love with her. She hesitated to believe it. She thought she must be deceiving herself. And she was terrified when on a sudden she discovered that she was passionately in love with him. She told herself it was absurd; with the disparity of age between them nothing but unhappiness could come to her if she yielded to her emotion. She tried to prevent him from speaking, but the day came when he told her that he loved her and forced her to tell him that she loved him too. He begged her to run away with him. She couldn't leave her husband, her home; and what life could they look forward to, she an aging woman, he so young? How could she expect his love to last? She begged him to have mercy on her. But his love was impetuous. He wanted her, he wanted her with all his heart, and at last trembling, afraid, desirous, she yielded to him. Then there was a period of ecstatic happiness. The world, the dull, humdrum world of every day, blazed with glory. Love songs flowed from her pen. The woman worshipped the young, virile body of her lover. George flushed darkly when she praised his broad chest and slim flanks, the beauty of his legs and the flatness of his belly.

Hot stuff, Daphne's friend had said. It was that all right. Disgusting.

There were sad little pieces in which she lamented the emptiness of her life when, as must happen, he left her, but they ended with a cry that all she had to suffer would be worth it for the bliss that for a while had been hers. She wrote of the long, tremulous nights they passed together and the languor that lulled them to sleep in one another's arms. She wrote of the rapture of brief stolen moments when, braving all danger, their passion overwhelmed them and they surrendered to its call.

She thought it would be an affair of a few weeks, but miraculously it lasted. One of the poems referred to three years having gone by without lessening the love that filled their hearts. It looked as though he continued to press her to go away with him, far away, to a hill town in Italy, a Greek island, a walled city in Tunisia, so that they could be together always, for in another of the poems she besought him to let things be as they were. Their happiness was precarious. Perhaps it was owing to the difficulties they had to encounter and the rarity of their meetings that their love had retained for so long its first enchanting ardour. Then on a sudden the young man died. How, when or where George could not discover. There followed a long, heartbroken cry of bitter grief, grief she could not indulge in, grief that had to be hidden. She had to be cheerful, give dinner parties and go out to dinner, behave as she had always behaved, though the light had gone out of her life and she was bowed down with anguish. The last poem of all was a set of four short stanzas in which the writer, sadly resigned to her loss, thanked the dark powers that rule man's destiny that she had been privileged at least for a while to enjoy the greatest happiness that we poor human beings can ever hope to know.

It was three o'clock in the morning when George Peregrine finally put the book down. It had seemed to him that he heard Evie's voice in every line; over and over again he came upon turns of phrase he had heard her use, there were details that were as familiar to him as to her; there was no doubt about it; it was her own story she had told, and it was as plain as anything could be that she had had a lover and her lover had died. It was not anger so much that he felt, nor horror or dismay, though he was dismayed and he was horrified, but amazement. It was as inconceivable that Evie should have had a love affair, and a wildly passionate one at that, as that the trout in a glass case over the chimney piece in his study, the finest he had ever caught, should suddenly wag its tail. He understood now the meaning of the amused look he had seen in the eyes of that man he had spoken with at the club, he understood why Daphne when she was talking about the book had seemed to be enjoying a private joke, and why those two women at the cocktail party had tittered when he strolled past them.

He broke out into a sweat. Then on a sudden he was seized with fury and he jumped up to go and awake Evie and ask her sternly for an explanation. But he stopped at the door. After all what proof had he? A book. He remembered that he'd told Evie he thought it jolly good. True, he hadn't read it, but he'd pretended he had. He would look a perfect fool if he had to admit that.

"I must watch my step," he muttered.

He made up his mind to wait for two or three days and think it all over. Then he'd decide what to do. He went to bed, but he couldn't sleep for a long time.

"Evie," he kept on saying to himself, "Evie, of all people."

They met at breakfast next morning as usual. Evie was as she always was, quiet, demure and self-possessed, a middle-aged woman who made no effort to look younger than she was, a woman who had nothing of what he still called It. He looked at her as he hadn't looked at her for years. She had her usual placid serenity. Her pale blue eyes were untroubled. There was no sign of guilt on her candid brow. She made the same little casual remarks she always made.

"It's nice to get back to the country again after those two hectic days in London. What are you going to do this morning?"

It was incomprehensible.

Three days later he went to see his solicitor. Henry Blane was an old friend of George's as well as his lawyer. He had a place not far from Peregrine's and for years they had shot over one another's preserves. For two days a week he was a busy country gentleman and for the other five a busy lawyer in Sheffield. He was a tall, robust fellow, with a boisterous manner and a jovial laugh, which suggested that he liked to be looked upon essentially as a sportsman and a good fellow and only incidentally as a lawyer. But he was shrewd and worldly-wise.

"Well, George, what's brought you here today?" he boomed as the Colonel was shown into his office. "Have a good time in London? I'm taking my missus up for a few days next week. How's Evie?"

"It's about Evie I've come to see you," said Peregrine, giving him a suspicious look. "Have you read her book?"

His sensitivity had been sharpened during those last days of troubled thought and he was conscious of a faint change in the lawyer's expression. It was as though he were suddenly on his guard.

"Yes, I've read it. Great success, isn't it? Fancy Evie breaking out into poetry. Wonders will never cease."

George Peregrine was inclined to lose his temper.

"It's made me look a perfect damned fool."

"Oh, what nonsense, George! There's no harm in Evie's writing a book. You ought to be jolly proud of her."

"Don't talk such rot. It's her own story. You know it and everyone else knows it. I suppose I'm the only one doesn't know who her lover was."

"There is such a thing as imagination, old boy. There's no reason to suppose the whole thing isn't just made up."

"Look here, Henry, we've known one another all our lives. We've had all sorts of good times together. Be honest with me. Can you look me in the face and tell me you believe it's a made-up story?"

Henry Blane moved uneasily in his chair. He was disturbed by the distress in old George's voice.

"You've got no right to ask me a question like that. Ask Evie."

"I daren't," George answered after an anguished pause. "I'm afraid she'd tell me the truth."

There was an uncomfortable silence.

"Who was the chap?"

Henry Blane looked at him straight in the eye.

"I don't know, and if I did I wouldn't tell you."

"You swine. Don't you see what a position I'm in? Do you think it's very pleasant to be made absolutely ridiculous?"

The lawyer lit a cigarette and for some moments silently puffed it.

"I don't see what I can do for you," he said at last.

"You've got private detectives you employ, I suppose. I want you to put them on the job and let them find everything out."

"It's not very pretty to put detectives on one's wife, old boy; and besides, taking for granted for a moment that Evie had an affair, it was a good many years ago and I don't suppose it would be possible to find a thing. They seem to have covered their tracks pretty carefully."

"I don't care. You put the detectives on. I want to know the truth."

"I won't, George. If you're determined to do that you'd better consult someone else. And look here, even if you got evidence that Evie had been unfaithful to you what would you do with it? You'd look rather silly divorcing your wife because she'd committed adultery ten years ago."

"At all events I could have it out with her."

"You can do that now, but you know just as well as I do that if you do she'll leave you. D'you want her to do that?"

George gave him an unhappy look.

"I don't know. I always thought she'd been a damned good wife to me. She runs the house perfectly, we never have any servant trouble; she's done wonders with the garden and she's splendid with all the village people. But damn it, I have my self-respect to think of. How can I go on living with her when I know that she was grossly unfaithful to me?"

"Have you always been faithful to her?"

"More or less, you know. After all we've been married for nearly twenty-four years and Evie was never much for bed."

The solicitor slightly raised his eyebrows, but George was too intent on what he was saying to notice.

"I don't deny that I've had a bit of fun now and then. A man wants it. Women are different."

"We only have men's word for that," said Henry Blane, with a faint smile.

"Evie's absolutely the last woman I'd have suspected of kicking over the traces. I mean, she's a very fastidious, reticent woman. What on earth made her write the damned book?"

"I suppose it was a very poignant experience and perhaps it was a relief to her to get it off her chest like that."

"Well, if she had to write it why the devil didn't she write it under an assumed name?"

"She used her maiden name. I suppose she thought that was enough and it would have been if the book hadn't had this amazing boom."

George Peregrine and the lawyer were sitting opposite one another with a desk between them. George, his elbow on the desk, his cheek resting on his hand, frowned at his thought.

"It's so rotten not to know what sort of a chap he was. One can't even tell if he was by way of being a gentleman. I mean, for all I know he may have been a farmhand or a clerk in a lawyer's office."

Henry Blane did not permit himself to smile and when he answered there was in his eyes a kindly, tolerant look.

"Knowing Evie so well I think the probabilities are that he was all right. Anyhow I'm sure he wasn't a clerk in my office."

"It's been such a shock to me," the Colonel sighed. "I thought she was fond of me. She couldn't have written that book unless she hated me."

"Oh, I don't believe that. I don't think she's capable of hatred."

"You're not going to pretend that she loves me."

"No."

"Well, what does she feel for me?"

Henry Blane leaned back in his swivel chair and looked at George reflectively.

"Indifference, I should say."

The Colonel gave a little shudder and reddened.

"After all, you're not in love with her, are you?"

George Peregrine did not answer directly.

"It's been a great blow to me not to have any children, but I've never let her see that I think she's let me down. I've always been kind to her. Within reasonable limits I've tried to do my duty by her."

The lawyer passed a large hand over his mouth to conceal the smile that trembled on his lips.

"It's been such an awful shock to me," Peregrine went on. "Damn it all, even ten years ago Evie was no chicken, and God knows she wasn't much to look at. It's so ugly." He sighed deeply. "What would *you* do in my place?"

"Nothing."

George Peregrine drew himself bolt upright in his chair and he looked at Henry with the stern, set face that he must have worn when he inspected his regiment.

"I can't overlook a thing like this. I've been made a laughing-stock. I can never hold up my head again."

"Nonsense," said the lawyer sharply, and then in a pleasant, kindly manner: "Listen, old boy: the man's dead; it all happened a long while back. Forget it. Talk to people about Evie's book, rave about it, tell 'em how proud you are of her. Behave as though you had so much confidence in her, you *knew* she could never have been unfaithful to you. The world moves so quickly and people's memories are so short. They'll forget."

"I shan't forget."

"You're both middle-aged people. She probably does a great deal more for you than you think and you'd be awfully lonely without her. I don't think it matters if you don't forget. It'll be all to the good if you can get it into that thick head of yours that there's a lot more in Evie than you ever had the gumption to see."

"Damn it all, you talk as if *I* was to blame."

"No, I don't think you were to blame, but I'm not so sure that Evie was either. I don't suppose she wanted to fall in love with this boy. D'you remember those verses right at the end? The impression they gave me was that though she was shattered by his death, in a strange sort of way she welcomed it. All through she'd been aware of the fragility of the tie that bound them. He died in the full flush of his first love and had never known that love so seldom endures; he'd only known its bliss and beauty. In her own bitter grief she found solace in the thought that he'd been spared all sorrow."

"All that's a bit above my head, old boy. I see more or less what you mean."

George Peregrine stared unhappily at the inkstand on the desk. He was silent and the lawyer looked at him with curious, yet sympathetic eyes.

"Do you realize what courage she must have had never by a sign to show how dreadfully unhappy she was?" he said gently.

Colonel Peregrine sighed.

"I'm broken. I suppose you're right; it's no good crying over spilt milk and it would only make things worse if I made a fuss."

"Well?"

George Peregrine gave a pitiful little smile.

"I'll take your advice. I'll do nothing. Let them think me a damned fool and to hell with them. The truth is, I don't know what I'd do without Evie. But I'll tell you what, there's one thing I shall never understand till my dying day: What in the name of heaven did the fellow ever see in her?"

Questions for Writing or Discussion

1. Which of Colonel Peregrine's many character defects are mainly amusing, relatively harmless flaws? Which are more serious?
2. Does the Colonel have any good or likable qualities?
3. What details show that Evie has been and still is an excellent wife?
4. Why is it important to the plot that Colonel Peregrine neither likes nor understands poetry?
5. Daphne is a minor character but an important one. Why?

John Cheever
O YOUTH AND BEAUTY!

At the tag end of nearly every long, large Saturday-night party in the suburb of Shady Hill, when almost everybody who was going to play golf or tennis in the morning had gone home hours ago and the ten or twelve people remaining seemed powerless to bring the evening to an end although the gin and whiskey were running low, and here and there a woman who was sitting out her husband would have begun to drink milk; when everybody had lost track of time, and the baby sitters who were waiting at home for these diehards would have long since stretched out on the sofa and fallen into a deep sleep, to dream about cooking-contest prizes, ocean voyages, and romance; when the bellicose drunk, the crapshooter, the pianist, and the woman faced with the expiration of her hopes had all expressed themselves; when every proposal—to go to the Farquarsons' for breakfast, to go swimming, to go and wake up the Townsends, to go here and go there—died as soon as it was made, then Trace Bearden would begin to chide Cash Bentley about his age and thinning hair. The chiding was preliminary to moving the living-room furniture. Trace and Cash moved the tables and the chairs, the sofas and the fire screen, the woodbox and the footstool; and when they had finished, you wouldn't know the place. Then if the host had a revolver, he would be asked to produce it. Cash would take off his shoes and assume a starting crouch behind a sofa. Trace would fire the weapon out of an open window, and if you were new to the community and had not understood what the preparations were about, you would then realize that you were watching a hurdle race. Over the sofa went Cash, over the tables, over the fire screen and the woodbox. It was not exactly a race, since Cash ran it alone, but it was extraordinary to see this man of forty surmount so many obstacles so gracefully. There was not a piece of furniture in Shady Hill that Cash could not take in his stride. The race ended with cheers, and presently the party would break up.

Cash was, of course, an old track star, but he was never aggressive or tiresome about his brilliant past. The college where he had spent his youth had offered him a paying job on the alumni council, but he had refused it, realizing that that part of his life was ended. Cash and his wife, Louise, had two children, and they lived in a medium-cost ranchhouse on Alewives Lane. They belonged to the country club, although they could not afford it, but in the case of the Bentleys nobody ever pointed this out, and Cash was one of the best-liked men in Shady Hill. He was still slender—he was careful about his weight—and he walked to the train in the morning with a light and vigorous step that marked him as an athlete. His hair was thin, and there were mornings when his eyes looked bloodshot, but this did not detract much from a charming quality of stubborn youthfulness.

In business Cash had suffered reverses and disappointments, and the Bentleys had many money worries. They were always late with their tax payments and their mortgage payments, and the drawer of the hall table was stuffed with unpaid bills; it was always touch and go with the Bentleys and the bank. Louise looked pretty enough on Saturday night, but her life was exacting and monotonous. In the pockets of her suits, coats, and dresses there were little wads and scraps of paper on which was written: "Oleomargarine, frozen spinach, Kleenex, dog biscuit, hamburger, pepper, lard . . ." When she was still half awake in the morning, she was putting on the water for coffee and diluting the frozen orange juice. Then she would be wanted by the children. She would crawl under the bureau on her hands and knees to find a sock for Toby. She would lie flat on her belly and wriggle under the bed (getting dust up her nose) to find a shoe for Rachel. Then there were the housework, the laundry, and the cooking, as well as the demands of the children. There always seemed to be shoes to put on and shoes to take off, snowsuits to be zipped and unzipped, bottoms to be wiped, tears to be dried, and when the sun went down (she saw it set from the kitchen window) there was the supper to be cooked, the baths, the bedtime story, and the Lord's Prayer. With the sonorous words of the Our Father in a darkened room the children's day was over, but the day was far from over for Louise Bentley. There were the darning, the mending, and some ironing to do, and after sixteen years of housework she did not seem able to escape her chores even while she slept. Snowsuits, shoes, baths, and groceries seemed to have permeated her subconscious. Now and then she would speak in her sleep—so loudly that she woke her husband. "I can't *afford* veal cutlets," she said one night. Then she sighed uneasily and was quiet again.

By the standards of Shady Hill, the Bentleys were a happily married couple, but they had their ups and downs. Cash could be very touchy at times. When he came home after a bad day at the office and found that Louise, for some good reason, had not started supper, he would be ugly. "Oh, for Christ sake!" he would say, and go into the kitchen and heat up some frozen food. He drank some whiskey to relax himself during this ordeal, but it never seemed to relax him, and he usually burned the bottom out of a pan, and when they sat down for supper the dining space would be full of smoke. It was only a question of time before they were plunged into a bitter quarrel. Louise would run upstairs, throw herself onto the bed, and sob. Cash would grab the whiskey bottle and dose himself. These rows, in spite of the vigor with which Cash and Louise entered into them, were the source of a great deal of pain for both of them. Cash would sleep downstairs on the sofa, but sleep never repaired the damage, once the trouble had begun, and if they met in the morning, they would be at one another's throats in a second. Then Cash would leave for the train, and, as soon as the children had been taken to nursery school, Louise would put on her coat and cross the grass to the Beardens' house. She would cry into a cup of warmed-up coffee and tell Lucy Bearden her troubles. What was the meaning of marriage? What was the meaning of love? Lucy always suggested that Louise get a job. It would give her emotional and financial independence, and that, Lucy said, was what she needed.

The next night, things would get worse. Cash would not come home for dinner at all, but would stumble in at about eleven, and the whole sordid wrangle would be repeated, with Louise going to bed in tears upstairs and Cash again stretching out on the living-room sofa. After a few days and nights of this, Louise would decide that she was at the end of her rope. She would decide to go and stay with her married sister in Mamaroneck. She usually chose a Saturday, when Cash would be at home, for her departure. She would pack a suitcase and get her War Bonds from the desk. Then she would take a bath and put on her best slip. Cash, passing the bedroom door, would see her. Her slip was transparent, and suddenly he was all repentance, tenderness, charm, wisdom, and love. "Oh, my darling!" he would groan, and when they went downstairs to get a bite to eat about an hour later, they would be sighing and making cow eyes at one another; they would be the happiest married couple in the whole Eastern United States. It was usually at about this time that Lucy Bearden turned up with the good news that she had found a job for Louise. Lucy would ring the doorbell, and Cash, wearing a bathrobe, would let her in. She would be brief with Cash, naturally, and hurry into the dining room to tell poor Louise the good news. "Well that's very nice of you to have looked," Louise would say wanly, "but I don't think that I want a job any more. I don't think that Cash wants me to work, do you, sweetheart?" Then she would turn her big dark eyes on Cash, and you could practically smell smoke. Lucy would excuse herself hurriedly from this scene of depravity, but she never left with any hard feelings, because she had been married for nineteen years herself and she knew that every union has its ups and downs. She didn't seem to leave any wiser, either; the next time the Bentleys quarreled, she would be just as intent as ever on getting Louise a job. But these quarrels and reunions, like the hurdle race, didn't seem to lose their interest through repetition.

On a Saturday night in the spring, the Farquarsons gave the Bentleys an anniversary party. It was their seventeenth anniversary. Saturday afternoon, Louise Bentley put herself through preparations nearly as arduous as the Monday wash. She rested for an hour, by the clock, with her feet high in the air, her chin in a sling, and her eyes bathed in some astringent solution. The clay packs, the too tight girdle, and the plucking and curling and painting that went on were all aimed at rejuvenation. Feeling in the end that she had not been entirely successful, she tied a piece of veiling over her eyes—but she was a lovely woman, and all the cosmetics that she had struggled with seemed, like her veil, to be drawn transparently over a face where mature beauty and a capacity for wit and passion were undisguisable. The Farquarsons' party was nifty, and the Bentleys had a wonderful time. The only person who drank too much was Trace Bearden. Late in the party, he began to chide Cash about his thinning hair and Cash good-naturedly began to move the furniture around. Harry Farquarson had a pistol, and Trace went out onto the terrace to fire it up at the sky. Over the sofa went Cash, over the end table, over the arms of the wing chair and the fire screen. It was a piece of carving on a chest that brought him down, and down he came like a ton of bricks.

Louise screamed and ran to where he lay. He had cut a gash in his forehead, and someone made a bandage to stop the flow of blood. When he tried to get up, he stumbled and fell again, and his face turned a terrible green. Harry telephoned Dr. Parminter, Dr. Hopewell, Dr. Altman, and Dr. Barnstable, but it was two in the morning and none of them answered. Finally, a Dr. Yerkes—a total stranger—agreed to come. Yerkes was a young man—he did not seem old enough to be a doctor—and he looked around at the disordered room and the anxious company as if there was something weird about the scene. He got off on the wrong foot with Cash. "What seems to be the matter, old-timer?" he asked.

Cash's leg was broken. The doctor put a splint on it, and Harry and Trace carried the injured man out to the doctor's car. Louise followed them in her own car to the hospital, where Cash was bedded down in a ward. The doctor gave Cash a sedative, and Louise kissed him and drove home in the dawn.

Cash was in the hospital for two weeks, and when he came home he walked with a crutch and his broken leg was in a heavy cast. It was another ten days before he could limp to the morning train. "I won't be able to run the hurdle race any more, sweetheart," he told Louise sadly. She said that it didn't matter, but while it didn't matter to her, it seemed to matter to Cash. He had lost weight in the hospital. His spirits were low. He seemed discontented. He did not himself understand what had happened. He, or everything around him, seemed subtly to have changed for the worse. Even his senses seemed to conspire to damage the ingenuous world that he had enjoyed for so many years. He went into the kitchen late one night to make himself a sandwich, and when he opened the icebox door he noticed a rank smell. He dumped the spoiled meat into the garbage, but the smell clung to his nostrils. A few days later he was in the attic, looking for his old varsity sweater. There were no windows in the attic and his flashlight was dim. Kneeling on the floor to unlock a trunk, he broke a spider web with his lips. The frail web covered his mouth as if a hand had been put over it. He wiped it impatiently, but also with the feeling of having been gagged. A few nights later, he was walking down a New York side street in the rain and saw an old whore standing in a doorway. She was so sluttish and ugly that she looked like a cartoon of Death, but before he could appraise her—the instant his eyes took an impression of her crooked figure—his lips swelled, his breathing quickened, and he experienced all the other symptoms of erotic excitement. A few nights later, while he was reading *Time* in the living room, he noticed that the faded roses Louise had brought in from the garden smelled more of earth than of anything else. It was a putrid, compelling smell. He dropped the roses into a wastebasket, but not before they had reminded him of the spoiled meat, the whore, and the spider web.

He had started going to parties again, but without the hurdle race to run, the parties of his friends and neighbors seemed to him interminable and stale. He listened to their dirty jokes with an irritability that was hard for him to conceal. Even their countenances discouraged him, and, slumped in a chair, he would regard their skin and their teeth narrowly, as if he were himself a much younger man.

The brunt of his irritability fell on Louise, and it seemed to her that Cash, in losing the hurdle race, had lost the thing that preserved his equilibrium. He was rude to his friends when they stopped in for a drink. He was rude and gloomy when he and Louise went out. When Louise asked him what was the matter, he only murmured, "Nothing, nothing, nothing," and poured himself some bourbon. May and June passed, and then the first part of July, without his showing any improvement.

Then it is a summer night, a wonderful summer night. The passengers on the eight-fifteen see Shady Hill—if they notice it at all—in a bath of placid golden light. The noise of the train is muffled in the heavy foliage, and the long car windows look like a string of lighted aquarium tanks before they flicker out of sight. Up on the hill, the ladies say to one another, "Smell the grass! Smell the trees!" The Farquarsons are giving another party, and Harry has hung a sign, WHISKEY GULCH, from the rose arbor, and is wearing a chef's white hat and an apron. His guests are still drinking, and the smoke from his meat fire rises, on this windless evening, straight up into the trees.

In the clubhouse on the hill, the first of the formal dances for the young people begins around nine. On Alewives Lane sprinklers continue to play after dark. You can smell the water. The air seems as fragrant as it is dark—it is a delicious element to walk through—and most of the windows on Alewives Lane are open to it. You can see Mr. and Mrs. Bearden, as you pass, looking at their television. Joe Lockwood, the young lawyer who lives on the corner, is practicing a speech to the jury before his wife. "I intend to show you," he says, "that a man of probity, a man who reputation for honesty and reliability . . ." He waves his bare arms as he speaks. His wife goes on knitting. Mrs. Carver—Harry Farquarson's mother-in-law—glances up at the sky and asks, *"Where* did all the stars come from?" She is old and foolish, and yet she is right: Last night's stars seem to have drawn to themselves a new range of galaxies, and the night sky is not dark at all, except where there is a tear in the membrane of light. In the unsold house lots near the track a hermit thrush is singing.

The Bentleys are at home. Poor Cash has been so rude and gloomy that the Farquarsons have not asked him to their party. He sits on the sofa beside Louise, who is sewing elastic into the children's underpants. Through the open window he can hear the pleasant sounds of the summer night. There is another party, in the Rogerses' garden, behind the Bentleys'. The music from the dance drifts down the hill. The band is sketchy—saxophone, drums, and piano—and all the selections are twenty years old. The band plays "Valencia," and Cash looks tenderly toward Louise, but Louise, tonight, is a discouraging figure. The lamp picks out the gray in her hair. Her apron is stained. Her face seems colorless and drawn. Suddenly, Cash begins frenziedly to beat his feet in time to the music. He sings some gibberish—Jabajabajabajaba—to the distant saxophone. He sighs and goes into the kitchen.

Here a faint, stale smell of cooking clings to the dark. From the kitchen window Cash can see the lights and figures of the Rogerses' party. It is a young people's party. The Rogers girl has asked some friends in for dinner before the dance, and now they seem to be leaving. Cars are driving away. "I'm covered with grass stains," a girl says. "I hope the old man remembered to buy gasoline," a boy says, and a girl laughs. There is nothing on their minds but the passing summer night. Taxes and the elastic in underpants—all the unbeautiful facts of life that threaten to crush the breath out of Cash—have not touched a single figure in this garden. Then jealously seizes him—such savage and bitter jealousy that he feels ill.

He does not understand what separates him from these children in the garden next door. He has been a young man. He has been a hero. He has been adored and happy and full of animal spirits, and now he stands in a dark kitchen, deprived of his athletic prowess, his impetuousness, his good looks—of everything that means anything to him. He feels as if the figures in the next yard are the specters from some party in that past where all his tastes and desires lie, and from which he has been cruelly removed. He feels like a ghost of the summer evening. He is sick with longing. Then he hears voices in the front of the house. Louise turns on the kitchen light. "Oh, here you are," she says. "The Beardens stopped in. I think they'd like a drink."

Cash went to the front of the house to greet the Beardens. They wanted to go up to the club, for one dance. They saw, at a glance, that Cash was at loose ends, and they urged the Bentleys to come. Louise got someone to stay with the children and then went upstairs to change.

When they got to the club, they found a few friends of their age hanging around the bar, but Cash did not stay in the bar. He seemed restless and perhaps drunk. He banged into a table on his way through the lounge to the ballroom. He cut in on a young girl. He seized her too vehemently and jigged her off in an ancient two-step. She signaled openly for help to a boy in the stag line, and Cash was cut out. He walked angrily off the dance floor onto the terrace. Some young couples there withdrew from one another's arms as he pushed open the screen door. He walked to the end of the terrace, where he hoped to be alone, but here he surprised another young couple, who got up from the lawn, where they seemed to have been lying, and walked off in the dark toward the pool.

Louise remained in the bar with the Beardens. "Poor Cash is tight," she said. And then, "He told me this afternoon that he was going to paint the storm windows," she said. "Well, he mixed the paint and washed the brushes and put on some old fatigues and went into the cellar. There was a telephone call for him at around five, and when I went down to tell him, do you know what he was going? He was just sitting there in the dark with a cocktail shaker. He hadn't touched the storm windows. He was just sitting there in the dark, drinking Martinis."

"Poor Cash," Trace said.

"You ought to get a job," Lucy said. "That would give you emotional and financial independence." As she spoke, they all heard the noise of furniture being moved around in the lounge.

"Oh, my God! Louise said. "He's going to run the race. Stop him, Trace, stop him! He'll hurt himself. He'll kill himself!"

They all went to the door of the lounge. Louise again asked Trace to interfere, but she could see by Cash's face that he was way beyond remonstrating with. A few couples left the dance floor and stood watching the preparations. Trace didn't try to stop Cash—he helped him. There was no pistol, so he slammed a couple of books together for the start.

Over the sofa went Cash, over the coffee table, the lamp table, the fire screen, and the hassock. All his grace and strength seemed to have returned to him. He cleared the big sofa at the end of the room and instead of stopping there, he turned and started back over the course. His face was strained. His mouth hung open. The tendons of his neck protruded hideously. He made the hassock, the fire screen, the lamp table, and the coffee table. People held their breath when he approached the final sofa, but he cleared it and landed on his feet. There was some applause. Then he groaned and fell. Louise ran to his side. His clothes were soaked with sweat and he gasped for breath. She knelt down beside him and took his head in her lap and stroked his thin hair.

Cash had a terrible hangover on Sunday, and Louise let him sleep until it was nearly time for church. The family went off to Christ Church together at eleven, as they always did. Cash sang, prayed, and got to his knees, but the most he ever felt in church was that he stood outside the realm of God's infinite mercy, and, to tell the truth, he no more believed in the Father, the Son, and the Holy Ghost than does my bull terrier. They returned home at one to eat the overcooked meat and stony potatoes that were their customary Sunday lunch. At around five, the Parminters called up and asked them over for a drink. Louise didn't want to go, so Cash went alone. (Oh, those suburban Sunday nights, those Sunday-night blues! Those departing weekend guests, those stale cocktails, those half-dead flowers, those trips to Harmon to catch the Century, those post-mortems and pickup suppers!) It was sultry and overcast. The dog days were beginning. He drank gin with the Parminters for an hour or two and then went over to the Townsends' for a drink. The Farquarsons called up the Townsends and asked them to come over and bring Cash with them, and at the Farquarsons' they had some more drinks and ate the leftover party food. The Farquarsons were glad to see that Cash seemed like himself again. It was half past ten or eleven when he got home. Louise was upstairs, cutting out of the current copy of *Life* those scenes of mayhem, disaster, and violent death that she felt might corrupt her children. She always did this. Cash came upstairs and spoke to her and then went down again. In a little while, she heard him moving the living-room furniture around. Then he called to her, and when she went down, he was standing at the foot of the stairs in his stocking feet, holding the pistol out to her. She had never fired it before, and the directions he gave her were not much help.

"Hurry up," he said. "I can't wait all night."

He had forgotten to tell her about the safety, and when she pulled the trigger nothing happened.

"It's that little lever," he said. "Press that little lever." Then, in his impatience, he hurdled the sofa anyhow.

The pistol went off and Louise got him in midair. She shot him dead.

Questions for Writing or Discussion

1. What does the hurdle race represent to Cash?
2. What point is being made in the account of Louise's preparations for the anniversary party?
3. Why are Louise's household chores described in such minute detail while Cash's job is barely mentioned?
4. What does the author appear to dislike about upper-middle class suburban life? Does he like anything about the suburbs?
5. What do the "spoiled meat, the whore, and the spider web" and the faded roses all have in common?
6. Is the shooting at the end of the story an accident?

Flannery O'Connor
A GOOD MAN IS HARD TO FIND

The grandmother didn't want to go to Florida. She wanted to visit some of her connections in east Tennessee and she was seizing at every chance to change Bailey's mind. Bailey was the son she lived with, her only boy. He was sitting on the edge of his chair at the table, bent over the orange sports section of the *Journal.* "Now look here, Bailey," she said, "see here, read this," and she stood with one hand on her thin hip and the other rattling the newspaper at his bald head. "Here this fellow that calls himself The Misfit is aloose from the Federal Pen and headed toward Florida and you read what it says he did to these people. Just you read it. I wouldn't take my children in any direction with a criminal like that aloose in it. I couldn't answer to my conscience if I did."

Bailey didn't look up from his reading so she wheeled around then and faced the children's mother, a young woman in slacks, whose face was as broad and innocent as a cabbage and was tied around with a green head-kerchief that had two points on the top like rabbit's ears. She was sitting on the sofa, feeding the baby his apricots out of a jar. "The children have been to Florida before," the old lady said. "You all ought to take them somewhere else for a change so they would see different parts of the world and be broad. They never have been to east Tennessee."

The children's mother didn't seem to hear her but the eight-year-old boy, John Wesley, a stocky child with glasses, said, "If you don't want to go to Florida, why dontcha stay at home?" He and the little girl, June Star, were reading the funny papers on the floor.

"She wouldn't stay at home to be queen for a day," June Star said without raising her yellow head.

"Yes and what would you do if this fellow, The Misfit, caught you?" the grandmother asked.

"I'd smack his face," John Wesley said.

"She wouldn't stay at home for a million bucks," June Star said. "Afraid she'd miss something. She has to go everywhere we go."

"All right, Miss," the grandmother said. "Just remember that the next time you want me to curl your hair."

June Star said her hair was naturally curly.

The next morning the grandmother was the first one in the car, ready to go. She had her big black valise that looked like the head of a hippopotamus in one corner, and underneath it she was hiding a basket with Pitty Sing, the cat, in it. She didn't intend for the cat to be left alone in the house for three days because he would miss her too much and she was afraid he might brush against one of the gas burners and accidentally asphyxiate himself. Her son, Bailey, didn't like to arrive at a motel with a cat.

She sat in the middle of the back seat with John Wesley and June Star on either side of her. Bailey and the children's mother and the baby sat in front and they left Atlanta at eight forty-five with the mileage on the car at 55890. The grandmother wrote this down because she thought it would be interesting to say how many miles they had been when they got back. It took them twenty minutes to reach the outskirts of the city.

The old lady settled herself comfortably, removing her white cotton gloves and putting them up with her purse on the shelf in front of the back window. The children's mother still had on slacks and still had her head tied up in a green kerchief, but the grandmother had on a navy blue straw sailor hat with a bunch of white violets on the brim and a navy blue dress with a small white dot in the print. Her collars and cuffs were white organdy trimmed with lace and at her neckline she had pinned a purple spray of cloth violets containing a sachet. In case of an accident, anyone seeing her dead on the highway would know at once that she was a lady.

She said she thought it was going to be a good day for driving, neither too hot nor too cold, and she cautioned Bailey that the speed limit was fifty-five miles an hour and that the patrolmen hid themselves behind billboards and small clumps of trees and sped out after you before you had a chance to slow down. She pointed out interesting details of the scenery: Stone Mountain; the blue granite that in some places came up to both sides of the highway; the brilliant red clay banks slightly streaked with purple; and the various crops that made rows of green lace-work on the ground. The trees were full of silver-white sunlight and the meanest of them sparkled. The children were reading comic magazines and their mother had gone back to sleep.

"Let's go through Georgia fast so we won't have to look at it much," John Wesley said.

"If I were a little boy," said the grandmother, "I wouldn't talk about my native state that way. Tennessee has the mountains and Georgia has the hills."

"Tennessee is just a hillbilly dumping ground," John Wesley said, "and Georgia is a lousy state too."

"You said it," June Star said.

"In my time," said the grandmother, folding her thin veined fingers, "children were more respectful of their native states and their parents and everything else. People did right then. Oh look at the cute little picka-ninny!" she said and pointed to a Negro child standing in the door of a shack. "Wouldn't that make a picture, now?" she asked and they all turned and looked at the little Negro out of the back window. He waved.

"He didn't have any britches on," June Star said.

"He probably didn't have any," the grandmother explained. "Little niggers in the country don't have things like we do. If I could paint, I'd paint that picture," she said.

The children exchanged comic books.

The grandmother offered to hold the baby and the children's mother passed him over the front seat to her. She set him on her knee and bounced him and told him about the things they were passing. She rolled her eyes and screwed up her mouth and stuck her leathery thin face into his smooth bland one. Occasionally he gave her a faraway smile. They passed a large cotton field with five or six graves fenced in the middle of it, like a small island. "Look at the graveyard!" the grandmother said, pointing it out. "That was the old family burying ground. That belonged to the plantation."

"Where's the plantation?" John Wesley asked.

"Gone With the Wind," said the grandmother. "Ha. Ha."

When the children finished all the comic books they had brought, they opened the lunch and ate it. The grandmother ate a peanut butter sandwich and an olive and would not let the children throw the box and the paper napkins out the window. When there was nothing else to do they played a game by choosing a cloud and making the other two guess what shape it suggested. John Wesley took one the shape of a cow and June Star guessed a cow and John Wesley said, no, an automobile, and June Star said he didn't play fair, and they began to slap each other over the grandmother.

The grandmother said she would tell them a story if they would keep quiet. When she told a story, she rolled her eyes and waved her head and was very dramatic. She said once when she was a maiden lady she had been courted by a Mr. Edgar Atkins Teagarden from Jasper, Georgia. She said he was a very good-looking man and a gentleman and that he brought her a watermelon every Saturday afternoon with his initials cut in it, E. A. T. Well, one Saturday, she said, Mr. Teagarden brought the watermelon and there was nobody at home and he left it on the front porch and returned in his buggy to Jasper, but she never got the watermelon, she said, because a nigger boy ate it when he saw the initials, E. A. T.! This story tickled John Wesley's funny bone and he giggled and giggled but June Star didn't think it was any good. She said she wouldn't marry a man that just brought her a watermelon on Saturday. The grandmother said she would have done well to marry Mr. Teagarden because he was a gentleman and had bought Coca-Cola stock when it first came out and that he had died only a few years ago, a very wealthy man.

They stopped at The Tower for barbecued sandwiches. The Tower was a part stucco and part wood filling station and dance hall set in a clearing outside of Timothy. A fat man named Red Sammy Butts ran it and there were signs stuck here and there on the building and for miles up and down the highway saying, TRY RED SAMMY'S FAMOUS BARBECUE. NONE LIKE FAMOUS RED SAMMY'S! RED SAM! THE FAT BOY WITH THE HAPPY LAUGH A VETERAN! RED SAMMY'S YOUR MAN!

Red Sammy was lying on the bare ground outside The Tower with his head under a truck while a gray monkey about a foot high, chained to a small chinaberry tree, chattered nearby. The monkey sprang back into the tree and got on the highest limb as soon as he saw the children jump out of the car and run toward him.

Inside, The Tower was a long dark room with a counter at one end and tables at the other and dancing space in the middle. They all sat down at a broad table next to the nickelodeon and Red Sam's wife, a tall burnt-brown woman with hair and eyes lighter than her skin, came and took their order. The children's mother put a dime in the machine and played "The Tennessee Waltz," and the grandmother said that tune always made her want to dance. She asked Bailey if he would like to dance but he only glared at her. He didn't have a naturally sunny disposition like she did and trips made him nervous. The grandmother's brown eyes were very bright. She swayed her head from side to side and pretended she was dancing in her chair. June Star said play something she could tap to so the children's mother put in another dime and played a fast number and June Star stepped out onto the dance floor and did her tap routine.

"Ain't she cute?" Red Sam's wife said, leaning over the counter. "Would you like to come be my little girl!?"

"No I certainly wouldn't," June Star said. "I wouldn't live in a broken-down place like this for a million bucks!" and she ran back to the table.

"Ain't she cute?" the woman repeated, stretching her mouth politely.

"Aren't you ashamed?" hissed the grandmother.

Red Sam came in and told his wife to quit lounging on the counter and hurry up with these people's order. His khaki trousers reached just to his hip bones and his stomach hung over them like a sack of meal swaying under his shirt. He came over and sat down at a table nearby and let out a combination sigh and yodel. "You can't win," he said. "You can't win," and he wiped his sweating red face off with a gray handkerchief. "These days you don't know who to trust," he said. "Ain't that the truth?"

"People are certainly not nice like they used to be," said the grandmother.

"Two fellers come in here last week," Red Sammy said, "driving a Chrysler. It was a old beat-up car but it was a good one and these boys looked all right to me. Said they worked at the mill and you know I let them fellers charge the gas they bought? Now why did I do that?"

"Because you're a good man!" the grandmother said at once.

"Yes'm, I suppose so," Red Sam said as if he were struck with this answer.

His wife brought the orders, carrying the five plates all at once without a tray, two in each hand and one balanced on her arm. "It isn't a soul in this green world of God's that you can trust," she said. "And I don't count nobody out of that, not nobody," she repeated, looking at Red Sammy.

"Did you read about that criminal, The Misfit, that's escaped?" asked the grandmother.

"I wouldn't be a bit surprised if he didn't attack this place right here," said the woman. "If he hears about it being here, I wouldn't be none surprised to see him. If he hears it's two cent in the cash register, I wouldn't be at all surprised if he . . ."

"That'll do," Red Sam said. "Go bring these people their Co'-Colas," and the woman went off to get the rest of the order.

"A good man is hard to find," Red Sammy said. "Everything is getting terrible. I remember the day you could go off and leave your screen door unlatched. Not no more."

He and the grandmother discussed better times. The old lady said that in her opinion Europe was entirely to blame for the way things were now. She said the way Europe acted you would think we were made of money and Red Sam said it was no use talking about it, she was exactly right. The children ran outside into the white sunlight and looked at the monkey in the lacy chinaberry tree. He was busy catching fleas on himself and biting each one carefully between his teeth as if it were a delicacy.

They drove off again into the hot afternoon. The grandmother took cat naps and woke up every few minutes with her own snoring. Outside of Toombsboro she woke up and recalled an old plantation that she had visited in this neighborhood once when she was a young lady. She said the house had six white columns across the front and that there was an avenue of oaks leading up to it and two little wooden trellis arbors on either side in front where you sat down with your suitor after a stroll in the garden. She recalled exactly which road to turn off to get to it. She knew that Bailey would not be willing to lose any time looking at an old house, but the more she talked about it, the more she wanted to see it once again and find out if the little twin arbors were still standing. "There was a secret panel in this house," she said craftily, not telling the truth but wishing that she were, "and the story went that all the family silver was hidden in it when Sherman came through but it was never found . . .''

"Hey!" John Wesley said. "Let's go see it! We'll find it! We'll poke all the woodwork and find it! Who lives there? Where do you turn off at? Hey Pop, can't we turn off there?"

"We never have seen a house with a secret panel!" June Star shrieked. "Let's go to the house with the secret panel! Hey Pop, can't we go see the house with the secret panel!"

"It's not far from here, I know," the grandmother said. "It wouldn't take over twenty minutes."

Bailey was looking straight ahead. His jaw was as rigid as a horseshoe. "No," he said.

The children began to yell and scream that they wanted to see the house with the secret panel. John Wesley kicked the back of the front seat and June Star hung over her mother's shoulder and whined desperately into her ear that they never had any fun even on their vacation, that they would never do what THEY wanted to do. The baby began to scream and John Wesley kicked the back of the seat so hard that his father could feel the blows in his kidney.

"All right!" he shouted and drew the car to a stop at the side of the road. "Will you all shut up? Will you all just shut up for one second? If you don't shut up, we won't go anywhere."

"It would be very educational for them," the grandmother murmured.

"All right," Bailey said, "but get this: this is the only time we're going to stop for anything like this. This is the one and only time."

"The dirt road that you have to turn down is about a mile back," the grandmother directed. "I marked it when we passed."

"A dirt road," Bailey groaned.

After they had turned around and were headed toward the dirt road, the grandmother recalled other points about the house, the beautiful glass over the front doorway and the candle-lamp in the hall. John Wesley said that the secret panel was probably in the fireplace.

"You can't go inside this house," Bailey said. "You don't know who lives there."

"While you all talk to the people in front, I'll run around behind and get in a window," John Wesley suggested.

"We'll all stay in the car," his mother said.

They turned onto the dirt road and the car raced roughly along in a swirl of pink dust. The grandmother recalled the times when there were no paved roads and thirty miles was a day's journey. The dirt road was hilly and there were sudden washes in it and sharp curves on dangerous embankments. All at once they would be on a hill, looking down over the blue tops of trees for miles around, then the next minute, they would be in a red depression with the dust-coated trees looking down on them.

"This place had better turn up in a minute," Bailey said, "or I'm going to turn around."

The road looked as if no one had traveled on it in months.

"It's not much farther," the grandmother said and just as she said it, a horrible thought came to her. The thought was so embarrassing that she turned red in the face and her eyes dilated and her feet jumped up, upsetting her valise in the corner. The instant the valise moved, the newspaper top she had over the basket under it rose with a snarl and Pitty Sing, the cat, sprang onto Bailey's shoulder.

The children were thrown to the floor and their mother, clutching the baby, was thrown out the door onto the ground; the old lady was thrown into the front seat. The car turned over once and landed right-side-up in a gulch off the side of the road. Bailey remained in the driver's seat with the cat—gray-striped with a broad white face and an orange nose—clinging to his neck like a caterpillar.

As soon as the children saw they could move their arms and legs, they scrambled out of the car, shouting, "We've had an ACCIDENT!" The grandmother was curled up under the dashboard, hoping she was injured so that Bailey's wrath would not come down on her all at once. The horrible thought she had had before the accident was that the house she had remembered so vividly was not in Georgia but in Tennessee.

Bailey removed the cat from his neck with both hands and flung it out the window against the side of a pine tree. Then he got out of the car and started looking for the children's mother. She was sitting against the side of the red gutted ditch, holding the screaming baby, but she only had a cut down her face and a broken shoulder. "We've had an ACCIDENT!" the children screamed in a frenzy of delight.

"But nobody's killed," June Star said with disappointment as the grandmother limped out of the car, her hat still pinned to her head but the broken front brim standing up at a jaunty angle and the violet spray hanging off the side. They all sat down in the ditch, except the children, to recover from the shock. They were all shaking.

"Maybe a car will come along," said the children's mother hoarsely.

"I believe I have injured an organ," said the grandmother, pressing her side, but no one answered her. Bailey's teeth were clattering. He had on a yellow sport shirt with bright blue parrots designed in it and his face was as yellow as the shirt. The grandmother decided that she would not mention that the house was in Tennessee.

The road was about ten feet above and they could see only the tops of the trees on the other side of it. Behind the ditch they were sitting in there were more woods, tall and dark and deep. In a few minutes they saw a car some distance away on top of a hill, coming slowly as if the occupants were watching them. The grandmother stood up and waved both arms dramatically to attract their attention. The car continued to come on slowly, disappeared around a bend and appeared again, moving even slower, on top of the hill they had gone over. It was a big black battered hearse-like automobile. There were three men in it.

It came to a stop just over them and for some minutes, the driver looked down with a steady expressionless gaze to where they were sitting, and didn't speak. Then he turned his head and muttered something to the other two and they got out. One was a fat boy in black trousers and a red sweat shirt with a silver stallion embossed on the front of it. He moved around on the right side of them and stood staring, his mouth partly open in a kind of loose grin. The other had on khaki pants and a blue striped coat and a gray hat pulled down very low, hiding most of his face. He came around slowly on the left side. Neither spoke.

The driver got out of the car and stood by the side of it, looking down at them. He was an older man than the other two. His hair was just beginning to gray and he wore silver-rimmed spectacles that give him a scholarly look. He had a long creased face and didn't have on any shirt or undershirt. He had on blue jeans that were too tight for him and was holding a black hat and a gun. The two boys also had guns.

"We've had an ACCIDENT!" the children screamed.

The grandmother had the peculiar feeling that the bespectacled man was someone she knew. His face was as familiar to her as if she had known him all her life but she could not recall who he was. He moved away from the car and began to come down the embankment, placing his feet carefully so that he wouldn't slip. He had on tan and white shoes and no socks, and his ankles were red and thin. "Good afternoon," he said. "I see you all had you a little spill."

"We turned over twice!" said the grandmother.

"Oncet," he corrected. "We seen it happen. Try their car and see will it run, Hiram," he said quietly to the boy with the gray hat.

"What you got that gun for?" John Wesley asked. "Whatcha gonna do with that gun?"

"Lady," the man said to the children's mother, "would you mind calling them children to sit down by you? Children make me nervous. I want all you to sit down right together there where you're at."

"What are you telling US what to do for?" June Star asked.

Behind them the line of woods gaped like a dark open mouth. "Come here," said their mother.

"Look here now," Bailey began suddenly, "we're in a predicament! We're in . . ."

The grandmother shrieked. She scrambled to her feet and stood staring. "You're The Misfit!" she said. "I recognized you at once!"

"Yes'm," the man said, smiling slightly as if he were pleased in spite of himself to be known, "but it would have been better for all of you, lady, if you hadn't of reckernized me."

Bailey turned his head sharply and said something to his mother that shocked even the children. The old lady began to cry and The Misfit reddened.

"Lady," he said, "don't you get upset. Sometimes a man says things he don't mean. I don't reckon he meant to talk to you thataway."

"You wouldn't shoot a lady, would you?" the grandmother said and removed the clean handkerchief from her cuff and began to slap at her eyes with it.

The Misfit pointed the toe of his shoe into the ground and made a little hole and then covered it up again. "I would hate to have to," he said.

"Listen," the grandmother almost screamed, "I know you're a good man. You don't look a bit like you have common blood. I know you must come from nice people!"

"Yes mam," he said, "finest people in the world." When he smiled he showed a row of strong white teeth. "God never made a finer woman than my mother and my daddy's heart was pure gold," he said. The boy with the red sweat shirt had come around behind them and was standing with his gun at his hip. The Misfit squatted down on the ground. "Watch them children, Bobby Lee," he said. "You know they make me nervous." He looked at the six of them huddled together in front of him and he seemed to be embarrassed as if he couldn't think of anything to say. "Ain't a cloud in the sky," he remarked, looking up at it. "Don't see no sun but don't see no cloud neither."

"Yes, it's a beautiful day," said the grandmother. "Listen," she said, "you shouldn't call yourself The Misfit because I know you're a good man at heart. I can just look at you and tell."

"Hush!" Bailey yelled. "Hush! Everybody shut up and let me handle this!" He was squatting in the position of a runner about to sprint forward but he didn't move.

"I pre-chate that, lady," The Misfit said and drew a little circle in the ground with the butt of his gun.

"It'll take a half a hour to fix this here car," Hiram called, looking over the raised hood of it.

"Well, first you and Bobby Lee get him and that little boy to step over yonder with you," The Misfit said, pointing to Bailey and John Wesley. "The boys want to ast you something," he said to Bailey. "Would you mind stepping back in them woods there with them?"

"Listen," Bailey began, "we're in a terrible predicament! Nobody realizes what this is," and his voice cracked. His eyes were as blue and intense as the parrots in his shirt and he remained perfectly still.

The grandmother reached up to adjust her hat brim as if she were going to the woods with him but it came off in her hand. She stood staring at it and after a second she let it fall on the ground. Hiram pulled Bailey up by the arm as if he were assisting an old man. John Wesley caught hold of his father's hand and Bobby Lee followed. They went off toward the woods and just as they reached the dark edge, Bailey turned and supporting himself against a gray naked pine trunk, he shouted. "I'll be back in a minute, Mamma, wait on me!"

"Come back this instant!" his mother shrilled but they all disappeared into the woods.

"Bailey Boy!" the grandmother called in a tragic voice but she found she was looking at The Misfit squatting on the ground in front of her. "I just know you're a good man," she said desperately. "You're not a bit common!"

"Nome, I ain't a good man," The Misfit said after a second as if he had considered her statement carefully, "but I ain't the worst in the world neither. My daddy said I was a different breed of dog from my brothers and sisters. 'You know,' Daddy said, 'it's some that can live their whole life out without asking about it and it's others has to know why it is, and this boy is one of the latters. He's going to be into everything!'" He put on his black hat and looked up suddenly and then away deep into the woods as if he were embarrassed again. "I'm sorry I don't have on a shirt before you ladies," he said, hunching his shoulders slightly. "We buried our clothes that we had on when we escaped and we're just making do until we can get better. We borrowed these from some folks we met," he explained.

"That's perfectly all right," the grandmother said. "Maybe Bailey has an extra shirt in his suitcase."

"I'll look and see terrectly," The Misfit said.

"Where are they taking him?" the children's mother screamed.

"Daddy was a card himself," The Misfit said. "You couldn't put anything over on him. He never got in trouble with the Authorities though. Just had the knack of handling them."

"You could be honest too if you'd only try," said the grandmother. "Think how wonderful it would be to settle down and live a comfortable life and not have to think about somebody chasing you all the time."

The Misfit kept scratching in the ground with the butt of his gun as if he were thinking about it. "Yes'm, somebody is always after you," he murmured.

The grandmother noticed how thin his shoulder blades were just behind his hat because she was standing up looking down on him. "Do you ever pray?" she asked.

He shook his head. All she saw was the black hat wiggle between his shoulder blades. "Nome," he said.

There was a pistol shot from the woods, followed closely by another. Then silence. The old lady's head jerked around. She could hear the wind move through the tree tops like a long satisfied insuck of breath. "Bailey Boy!" she called.

"I was a gospel signer for a while," The Misfit said. "I been most everything. Been in the arm service, both land and sea, at home and abroad, been twict married, been an undertaker, been with the railroads, plowed Mother Earth, been in a tornado, seen a man burnt alive oncet," and he looked up at the children's mother and the little girl who were sitting close together, their faces white and their eyes glassy; "I even seen a woman flogged," he said.

"Pray, pray," the grandmother began, "pray, pray . . ."

"I never was a bad boy that I remember of," The Misfit said in an almost dreamy voice, "but somewheres along the line I done something wrong and got sent to the penitentiary. I was buried alive," and he looked up and held her attention to him by a steady stare.

"That's when you should have started to pray," she said. "What did you do to get sent to the penitentiary that first time?"

"Turn to the right, it was a wall," The Misfit said, looking up again at the cloudless sky. "Turn to the left, it was a wall. Look up it was a ceiling, look down it was a floor. I forgot what I done, lady. I set there and set there, trying to remember what it was I done and I ain't recalled it to this day. Oncet in a while, I would think it was coming to me, but it never come."

"Maybe they put you in by mistake," the old lady said vaguely.

"Nome," he said. "It wasn't no mistake. They had the papers on me."

"You must have stolen something," she said.

The Misfit sneered slightly. "Nobody had nothing I wanted," he said. "It was a head-doctor at the penitentiary said what I had done was kill my daddy but I known that for a lie. My daddy died in nineteen ought nineteen of the epidemic flu and I never had a thing to do with it. He was buried in the Mount Hopewell Baptist churchyard and you can go there and see for yourself."

"If you would pray," the old lady said, "Jesus would help you."

"That's right," the Misfit said.

"Well then, why don't you pray?" she asked trembling with delight suddenly.

"I don't want no hep," he said. "I'm doing all right by myself."

Bobby Lee and Hiram came ambling back from the woods. Bobby Lee was dragging a yellow shirt with bright blue parrots in it.

"Thow me that shirt, Bobby Lee," The Misfit said. The shirt came flying at him and landed on his shoulder and he put it on. The grandmother couldn't name what the shirt reminded her of. "No, lady," The Misfit said while he was buttoning it up, "I found out the crime don't matter. You can do one thing or you can do another, kill a man or take a tire off his car, because sooner or later you're going to forget what it was you done and just be punished for it."

The children's mother had begun to make heaving noises as if she couldn't get her breath. "Lady," he asked, "would you and that little girl like to step off yonder with Bobby Lee and Hiram and join your husband?"

"Yes, thank you," the mother said faintly. Her left arm dangled helplessly and she was holding the baby, who had gone to sleep, in the other. "Hep that lady up, Hiram," The Misfit said as she struggled to climb out of the ditch, "and Bobby Lee, you hold onto that little girl's hand."

"I don't want to hold hands with him," June Star said. "He reminds me of a pig."

The fat boy blushed and laughed and caught her by the arm and pulled her off into the woods after Hiram and her mother.

Alone with The Misfit, the grandmother found that she had lost her voice. There was not a cloud in the sky nor any sun. There was nothing around her but woods. She wanted to tell him that he must pray. She opened and closed her mouth several times before anything came out. Finally she found herself saying, "Jesus. Jesus," meaning, Jesus will help you, but the way she was saying it, it sounded as if she might be cursing.

"Yes'm," The Misfit said as if he agreed. "Jesus thown everything off balance. It was the same case with Him as with me except He hadn't committed any crime and they could prove I had committed one because they had the papers on me. Of course," he said, "they never shown me my papers. That's why I sign myself now. I said long ago, you get you a signature and sign everything you do and keep a copy of it. Then you'll know what you done and you can hold up the crime to the punishment and see do they match and in the end you'll have something to prove you ain't been treated right. I call myself The Misfit," he said, "because I can't make what all I done wrong fit what all I gone through in punishment."

There was a piercing scream from the woods, followed closely by a pistol report. "Does it seem right to you, lady, that one is punished a heap and another ain't punished at all?"

"Jesus!" the old lady cried. "You've got good blood! I know you wouldn't shoot a lady! I know you come from nice people! Pray! Jesus, you ought not to shoot a lady. I'll give you all the money I've got!"

"Lady," The Misfit said, looking beyond her far into the woods, "there never was a body that give the undertaker a tip."

There were two more pistol reports and the grandmother raised her head like a parched old turkey hen crying for water and called, "Bailey Boy, Bailey Boy!" as if her heart would break.

"Jesus was the only One that ever raised the dead," The Misfit continued, "and He shouldn't have done it. He thrown everything off balance. If He did what He said, then it's nothing for you to do but throw away everything and follow Him, and if He didn't, then it's nothing for you to do but enjoy the few minutes you got left the best way you can—by killing somebody or burning down his house or doing some other meanness to him. No pleasure but meanness," he said and his voice had become almost a snarl.

"Maybe He didn't raise the dead," the old lady mumbled, not knowing what she was saying and feeling so dizzy that she sank down in the ditch with her legs twisted under her.

"I wasn't there so I can't say He didn't," The Misfit said. "I wisht I had of been there," he said, hitting the ground with his fist. "It ain't right I wasn't there because if I had of been there I would of known. Listen lady," he said in a high voice, "if I had of been there I would of known and I wouldn't be like I am now." His voice seemed about to crack and the grandmother's head cleared for an instant. She saw the man's face twisted close to her own as if he were going to cry and she murmured, "Why you're one of my babies. You're one of my own children!" She reached out and touched him on the shoulder. The Misfit sprang back as if a snake had bitten him and shot her three times through the chest. Then he put his gun down on the ground and took off his glasses and began to clean them.

Hiram and Bobby Lee returned from the woods and stood over the ditch, looking down at the grandmother who half sat and half lay in a puddle of blood with her legs crossed under her like a child's and her face smiling up at the cloudless sky.

Without his glasses, The Misfit's eyes were red-rimmed and pale and defenseless-looking. "Take her off and throw her where you thown the others," he said, picking up the cat that was rubbing itself against his leg.

"She was a talker, wasn't she?" Bobby Lee said, sliding down the ditch with a yodel.

"She would of been a good woman," The Misfit said, "if it had been somebody there to shoot her every minute of her life."

"Some fun!" Bobby Lee said.

"Shut up, Bobby Lee," The Misfit said. "It's no real pleasure in life."

Questions for Writing or Discussion

1. How do the various character defects of the members of the doomed family contribute to their encountering the Misfit?
2. Explain the meaning of the title.
3. Explain the significance of the following quotations:
   a. "She would of been a good woman . . . if it had been somebody there to shoot her every minute of her life."
   b. "If He did what He said, then it's nothing for you to do but throw away everything and follow Him, and if He didn't, then it's nothing for you to do but enjoy the few minutes you got left the best way you can—by killing somebody or burning down his house or doing some other meanness to him. No pleasure but meanness."
   c. "I don't want no hep . . . I'm doing all right by myself."
   d. "I found out the crime don't matter. You can do one thing or you can do another, kill a man or take a tire off his car, because sooner or later you're going to forget what it was you done and just be punished for it."

Careful attention to details is necessary for
the success of your research project.

PART 3

RESEARCH

14
WRITING A RESEARCH PAPER

CHAPTER 14

WRITING A
RESEARCH PAPER

Not much is certain in this world—and that familiar truth includes Freshman English. When you begin Freshman English, you can't be certain if your instructor will be casual about grammar and spelling or care about nothing *but* grammar and spelling. Depending on which instructor you have, most of your papers may be essays based on personal experiences or formal analyses of class readings. Some instructors seem to show movies at every meeting; others seem to think they are making an audiovisual breakthrough when they write two words on the blackboard. At least one certainty does exist, however. Sometime during your year of Freshman English, you are going to be assigned a research paper.

A research paper (or "library paper" or "term paper") is a nearly universal assignment not merely because it's an academic tradition, but also because it serves a number of worthwhile, practical purposes:

1. The research paper teaches you how to handle substantially longer pieces of writing than does the normal classroom theme. At a bare minimum, the research paper will be five or six typed pages; most papers will probably be two or three times as long.
2. The research paper teaches you how to use the library. It's probably only a slight exaggeration to state that any adequate library contains most of the information in the world, all accessible and all free. You may not want to know everything, but when you want to know *something,* it's important to be able to find it.
3. The research paper makes you an expert on your subject. The satisfactions are deep and lasting. Few differences are greater than the difference between the dabbler and the authority.
4. The research paper prepares you for success in your other courses. To some extent, teaching how to write research papers is

a service the English department performs for other departments. As you go through college, particularly as you take more and more upper-level courses, you will find increasing stress being placed on research papers. At the upper levels, instructors tend to want students to demonstrate real mastery of the course materials—mastery that can come only through intense exploration of a subject rather than the dashing off of a fifteen- or thirty-minute essay during a mid-term or final exam.

THE REPORT AND THE THESIS PAPER

Virtually every research paper requires that you gather facts, alleged facts, and opinions (sometimes conflicting opinions) from a variety of sources and that you organize and present those facts and opinions in your own way through your own hard work. Every research paper requires that you *document* in footnotes and a bibliography whatever sources you have used. Still, there are two distinct kinds of research paper. The first is the *report.* In the report, you present objectively the information available about your subject; you are not concerned with expressing your own point of view. A paper titled *Recent Advances in Treating Leukemia* or *The World Series Scandal of 1919* might be a report: in such a paper you would present all the known facts, including impartial accounts of any differing opinions, but you would have no particular opinion of your own to offer to the reader. The second kind of research paper is one with a *thesis.* In a *thesis paper,* you do just as much research as for the straight report, but you feel that the facts about your chosen subject call for interpretation, and you try to persuade the reader that your interpretation or opinion is correct. Rather than merely stating the facts, you use them to back up your opinion. For example, on pp. 365–376, a student thesis paper strongly advocates going ahead with the building of nuclear power plants.

Many subjects, of course, can be dealt with either as a report *or* as a thesis paper. Reports titled *Custer's Last Stand* and *The Lizzie Borden Murder Case* [1] would give the reader information about two colorful episodes of the American past. Thesis papers on the same subjects would give the reader all or most of the same information, but the main purpose would be to argue, for example, that the battle of the Little Big Horn would never have taken place if it had not been for Custer's foolishness and vanity or that Lizzie Borden was really innocent of the murder charge brought against her.

Before you get deeply involved in your research project, make sure you know whether your instructor wants a report or a thesis paper, or if either will be acceptable.

CHOOSING A SUBJECT

The best subject for your research paper is often one that you are generally interested in and curious about. If you start out knowing everything or thinking that you know everything about your subject, all your research may be boring repetition of the familiar, and, if you are writing a thesis paper, you may not be sufficiently open-minded to evaluate fairly any views that conflict with your own. On the other hand, you'll naturally want to avoid subjects that may demand technical knowledge you do not possess. You may be vaguely interested in Einstein's theory of relativity, but that topic would surely be a poor choice for most students.

As you begin to formulate a subject, remember the importance of limiting it. *Custer's Last Stand* and *The Lizzie Borden Murder Case* might make good papers. No good paper of reasonable length could be written, however, on such topics as *Famous Battles* or *Great Trials.*

One final suggestion: Don't be too eager to settle on any single topic immediately. If you have two or three possibilities in mind, so much the better. There may not be as much information available on your first choice as you had hoped, and it's comforting to have something ready to fall back on.

PRELIMINARY READING AND THE PRELIMINARY OUTLINE

Once you have an idea of the topic or topics you might be interested in, it's time for a trip to the library. Your purpose is to do some fairly easygoing "reading around." You want to make sure that the subject that seemed so interesting when you were thinking about it is still interesting when you are reading about it. You want to acquire enough of a general perspective on your subject to be able to respond effectively when you begin more serious and detailed reading.

Usually, the most sensible place in which to begin reading around is a recent edition of a general adult encyclopedia such as the *Encyclopaedia Britannica* or the *Encyclopedia Americana.* No significant research paper is going to use an encyclopedia article as a major source; the article contains only a broad survey of its subject whereas a research paper explores its subject in depth. At this stage, however, a broad survey is all you want.

In fairness, some encyclopedia articles, especially the longer ones, may be written by leading authorities and contain much use-

---

1. "Lizzie Borden took an ax/And gave her mother forty whacks./When she saw what she had done,/She gave her father forty-one."

ful information. In such cases, you needn't be shy about using the articles as *minor* sources. If you come across an article that strikes you as potentially usable in your paper, make out a bibliography card for it (see pp. 338–344) and take notes (see pp. 344–349).

Some encyclopedia articles may also be valuable because they conclude with a brief list of outstanding books and articles on their subject. These references can help you to determine whether enough material is available for your paper, and they can give you some specific titles to look for immediately.

As good as or better than general encyclopedias for preliminary reading may be a number of specialized encyclopedias, dictionaries, and other reference works. For example, if you are writing about an American who is *no longer living,* the *Dictionary of American Biography* may have an excellent article. The *Dictionary of National Biography* supplies similar information about *English* figures who are no longer living. A brief list of some other specialized reference works follows:

ART

Britannica Encyclopaedia of American Art (1973)

Encyclopedia of World Art, 15 vols. (1959–69)

Bernard S. Myers, ed., *Encyclopedia of Painting,* 3rd ed. (1970)

BUSINESS

Douglas Greenwald, *The McGraw-Hill Dictionary of Modern Economics,* 2nd ed. (1973)

Glen G. Munn, *Encyclopedia of Banking and Finance,* 7th ed. (1973)

Harold S. Sloan and Arnold J. Zurcher, *A Dictionary of Economics,* 5th ed. (1970)

EDUCATION

Encyclopedia of Education, 10 vols. (1971)

Encyclopedia of Educational Research, 4th ed. (1969)

HISTORY

James Truslow Adams, ed., *Dictionary of American History,* 2nd ed., 6 vols. (1942–1963)

The Cambridge Ancient History, 3rd ed., 12 vols. (1970–75)

The Cambridge Medieval History, 8 vols (1911–36)

The Cambridge Modern History, 14 vols. (1902–26)

William L. Langer, *An Encyclopedia of World History,* 5th ed. (1972)

LITERATURE

Albert C. Baugh, *A Literary History of England,* 2nd ed. (1967)

John Buchanan-Brown, ed., *Cassell's Encyclopedia of World Literature,* rev. ed. (1973)

James D. Hart, *The Oxford Companion to American Literature,* 4th ed. (1965)

Phyllis Hartnoll, *The Oxford Companion to the Theatre,* 3rd ed. (1967)

Paul Harvey, *The Oxford Companion to English Literature,* 4th ed. (1967)

Robert Spiller and others, *Literary History of the United States,* 4th ed., 2 vols. (1974)

Roger Whitlow, *Black American Literature* (1973)

Percy Wilson and Bonamy Dobree, *The Oxford History of English Literature,* 12 vols. (1945–63)

MUSIC

Sir George Grove, *Dictionary of Music and Musicians,* ed. Eric Blom, 5th ed., 10 vols. (1955; supplement 1961)

The New Oxford History of Music, 10 vols. (1954–74)

Percy A. Scholes, *The Oxford Companion to Music,* 10th ed. (1970)

PHILOSOPHY

Frederick C. Copleston, *A History of Philosophy,* 8 vols. (1947–66)

Paul Edwards, ed., *The Encyclopedia of Philosophy,* 4 vols. (1973)

PSYCHOLOGY

H. J. Eysenck and others, *Encyclopedia of Psychology,* 3 vols. (1972)

Robert M. Goldenson, *The Encyclopedia of Human Behavior,* 2 vols. (1970)

RELIGION

F. L. Cross and Elizabeth A. Livingstone, *The Oxford Dictionary of the Christian Church* (1974)

The New Catholic Encyclopedia, 15 vols. (1967)

Geoffrey Parrinder, *A Dictionary of Non-Christian Religions* (1973)

Cecil Roth, ed., *The Standard Jewish Encyclopedia,* rev. ed. (1962)

SCIENCE

McGraw-Hill Encyclopedia of Science and Technology, 3rd ed., 15 vols. (1971)

Van Nostrand's Scientific Encyclopedia, 4th ed. (1968)

SOCIAL SCIENCE AND POLITICS

John P. Davis, ed., *The American Negro Reference Book* (1966)

Bert F. Hoselitz, ed., *A Reader's Guide to the Social Sciences*, rev. ed. (1972)

Barry T. Klein, ed., *Reference Encyclopedia of the American Indian*, 2nd ed. (1973–74)

E. R. A. Seligman and Alvin Johnson, eds., *Encyclopedia of the Social Sciences*, 15 vols. (1930–34)

David L. Sills, ed., *International Encyclopedia of the Social Sciences*, 17 vols. (1968)

Edward C. Smith and Arnold J. Zurcher, eds., *Dictionary of American Politics*, 2nd ed. (1968)

If all goes well in your preliminary reading, you should know enough to feel confident about your choice of subject and perhaps enough to be able to limit your subject further than you originally intended. Best of all, you should be in a position to draw up a *preliminary outline* or scratch outline indicating what the major divisions of your paper are likely to be. For a paper on the Lizzie Borden murder case, to mention one example, you might construct the following headings: The Crime, The Trial, The Controversy. Nothing elaborate is needed; the outline will be revised and expanded as you go along. In the meantime, the preliminary outline enables you to read and take notes as part of a systematic plan. You'll know what information is relevant and irrelevant, what divisions of the paper you need to work on more thoroughly, and so on.

When your preliminary outline is completed, it's time for some serious reading, and that brings us to the subject of *bibliography*.

A WORKING BIBLIOGRAPHY

A bibliography, in the sense that you will be using the term, is a list of books, articles, and other publications that serve as the sources of information for your paper. There are two kinds of bibliographies: the *working* bibliography and the *final* bibliography. The working bibliography is a set of cards listing any sources that might be useful to you. The final bibliography, which you will prepare after you complete your paper, is the list of sources you actually use in writing the paper. Since you cannot know in advance which books or articles will contain useful information, you will have to prepare *bibliography cards* for every source that looks useful. As you read, you will eliminate cards for those sources which turn out not to be helpful.

Finding Sources

The two best places to look for titles of books and articles are the book index and the periodical indexes. These, like the encyclopedias you have already consulted, are located in the reference room of the library.

THE BOOK CATALOGUE

The forms of book catalogues differ from library to library. Some libraries use computer printouts, bound into books, to list their holdings. Some libraries list their holdings on microfiche cards, sheets of microfilm about the size of filing cards. Since one microfiche card can list approximately a hundred titles, its use saves a great deal of library space. Its drawback to you as a researcher is that, to find the titles you want, you will have to learn to use the reading machine which will be located near the files of cards. Using the machine is not difficult, but you should probably get help from the librarian the first time you try it.

The most common method of listing books is by means of a *card catalogue*, an alphabetical filing system in which a separate card is used to index every book in the library. If you can use the card catalogue, you can use the other kinds of catalogues, since all provide essentially the same information. For this reason, we will limit our discussion of book catalogues to the *card catalogue.*

The library will list every book it holds three times: one card will list the book by its *subject,* one will list it by *author,* and the third will list the book by *title. A Swinger of Birches: A Portrait of Robert Frost* by Sidney Cox, for example, would be listed among the S's (for *Swinger*) in the title file—*A, an,* and *the* are not used in alphabetizing. The book would also be listed among the F's (for *Frost, Robert*) in the subject file, and among the C's (for *Cox, Sidney*) in the author file. A set of catalogue cards is shown on p. 336.

In addition to listing books by author, title, and subject, most card catalogues usually also contain *cross-reference cards* which suggest other subject headings. If, for example, you looked up *newspapers,* a cross-reference card might tell you to "see *journalism.*"

PERIODICAL INDEXES

To find magazine or journal articles, you will need to consult the *periodical indexes.* The most frequently used index is *The Readers'*

Guide to Periodical Literature, an index of articles that have appeared in popular American magazines during any given year since 1906. *The Readers' Guide* appears monthly in pamphlet form and is permanently bound every two years. If your subject is very current, you would, of course, use the most recent *Readers' Guide.* If, however, your subject deals with a particular period in the past, you would want to consult *The Readers' Guide* for the year or years that are appropriate for your subject. If, for instance, your subject is the presidency of Franklin Roosevelt, you would surely want to consult *The Readers' Guide* for the years 1933–1945, in addition to consulting guides of later years to see how Roosevelt's administration was evaluated after his death.

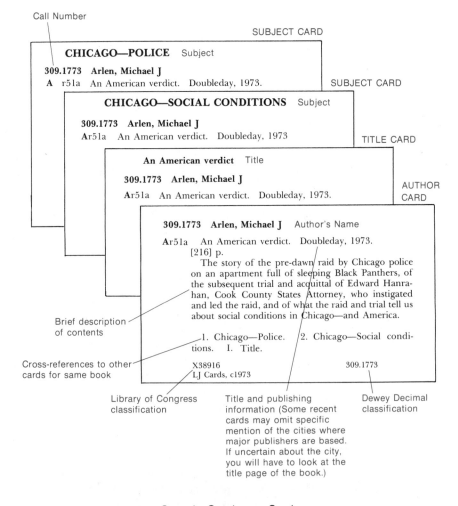

Sample Catalogue Cards

Although the guide does index authors, you will probably find it easier to look for subject headings. When you have located the heading or headings you need, you will find listed under the headings all the articles on that subject which have appeared in popular American magazines for the period covered by the particular guide.

Because *The Readers' Guide* indexes so much material, the entries must be printed in as little space as possible. That means, for one thing, that a number of abbreviations are used. If you do not understand an abbreviation, you will find keys and explanations of all abbreviations at the beginning of each issue. The need to conserve space also means that the editors will not punctuate titles, dates, and pages as you will in your paper. Here is an example of a *Readers' Guide* entry:

RESEARCH institutions
   Thumbs down on think tanks. N. Walsh. Science
    174:1008 D 3 '71

The first line (RESEARCH institutions) is the subject heading under which the index classifies articles on this topic. The next line begins the entry for one magazine article on the subject. "Thumbs down on Think Tanks" is the title of an article written by N. Walsh. The article appeared in *Science*, volume 174, page 1008, in the issue dated December 3, 1971.

The Readers' Guide is a good place to start, but it does, after all, index only popular American magazines. For most subjects, you will also want to read articles written by scholars in the field in order to get more specialized information. Almost every academic discipline has one or more journals to which specialists in the field contribute, and you would certainly want to look at their articles. To find them, you would consult the special index covering your subject. Most indexes are arranged in the same way as *The Readers' Guide,* so you will have no difficulty using the special indexes if you have mastered the use of *The Readers' Guide.*

Following is a list of some of the special indexes you might want to consult. It is by no means complete, but it will give you some idea of the kinds of indexes available. Should you want these or other special indexes, you will find them in the same area of the reference room that contains *The Readers' Guide.*

    Agriculture Index
    Applied Science and Technology Index
    Art Index
    Biological Abstracts
    Business Periodicals Index

Chemical Abstracts
Educational Index
Engineering Index
Index of Economic Journals
Index to Legal Periodicals
Music Index
Social Sciences and Humanities Index

NEWSPAPER INDEXES

Unfortunately, few newspapers are indexed. Some public libraries are now making the effort to index articles on local subjects that appear in their cities' major papers, but such indexes are far from complete. The only newspaper index that gives a complete listing of every article that has appeared in its newspaper during a given year is *The New York Times Index*. The *Times* has been thoroughly indexed since 1913. If your subject concerns a locality other than New York and you need newspaper articles from local papers, you must be prepared to page through or scan on microfilm the newspapers issued during the period your subject covers.

Making Bibliography Cards

In preparing your working bibliography, the most efficient method is to make out one three-by-five-inch card for each promising title you find. Obviously, you will not use all the sources for which you make cards, but it saves time to make cards for any title that might be useful before you begin your reading. Cards are easy to handle, and they permit you to add new sources or delete sources which turn out to be useless. Cards can also be alphabetized easily, and that will save you time when you make up your final bibliography, which must be alphabetized.

BIBLIOGRAPHY CARDS FOR BOOKS

It is important that you make proper bibliography cards as you go along because, again, following the correct procedure now will save time and frustration when you begin to write footnotes and bibliography entries for your paper. Make certain, then, that each of your book cards includes the following information and adheres to all the given instructions on matters of form:

1. The complete call number of the book. (See sample catalogue cards on p. 336.) If you do not copy the complete call number correctly, you cannot get the book.
2. The author's name (last name first), followed by a period.

3. For an essay, poem, short story, or a play in a collection, the title of the relevant selection, followed by a comma and enclosed in quotation marks.
4. The title of the book, underlined and followed by a period.
5. The city in which the book was published, followed by a colon.
6. The name of the publishing company, followed by a comma.
7. The copyright date, followed by a period.

Some books will require even more information. If the book is edited, the editor's name must also appear on the card, and if the book is translated, the translator's name must be given. If the book has more than one edition or has been revised, that information should appear on your card. Finally, if the work contains more than one volume, the number of volumes and the volume number you want should be indicated. (See p. 342 for sample bibliography cards.)

OTHER BIBLIOGRAPHY FORMS FOR BOOKS

A Book by Two Authors

Danziger, Marlies K., and W. Stacy Johnson. *An Introduction to Literary Criticism.* Boston: D. C. Heath and Company, 1961.

Only the name of the first author is inverted. The order of the names is the same as that on the title page.

A Book with Three or More Authors

Watkins, Fred C., and others. *Practical English Handbook,* 4th ed. Boston: Houghton Mifflin Company, 1970.

Only the name of the first author is given, and it is followed by the notation *and others.* The name given is the first name that appears on the title page.

A Book with an Editor

Kallsen, Loren J., ed. *The Kentucky Tragedy: A Problem in Romantic Attitudes.* Indianapolis: The Bobbs-Merrill Company, Inc., 1963.

The editor collected several documents about a famous murder case. No authors are given, and the editor's name is listed before the title.

An Edition of an Author's Work

Thoreau, Henry David. *Collected Poems,* ed. Carl Bode. Chicago: Packard and Co., 1943.

However, if the editor's work rather than the text is under discussion, place the editor's name first, followed by a comma, followed by "ed." or "eds."

Stauffer, Donald A., ed. *Selected Poetry and Prose of Coleridge.* New York: The Modern Library, 1951.

Editions Other Than the First

Decker, Randall E. *Patterns of Exposition.* 7th ed. Boston: Little, Brown and Company, 1980.

If the edition were a revised edition rather than a numbered edition, the abbreviation "rev. ed." would appear after the title.

An Edited Collection or Anthology

Schlesinger, Arthur, Jr., and Morton White, eds. *Paths of American Thought.* Boston: Houghton Mifflin Company, 1970.

Schlesinger and White collected essays written by several different authors.

A Translated Work

Böll, Heinrich. *End of a Mission.* Trans. Leila Vennewitz. New York: McGraw-Hill Book Company, 1974.

A Work of More Than One Volume

Adams, Wallace E., and others, eds. *The Western World: To 1770,* 2 vols. New York: Dodd, Mead & Company, 1968.

A Pamphlet

Treat a pamphlet as if it were a book, using the name of the committee or organization that put the pamphlet together as the author if no author's name is provided.

One Section of a Book Written by Several Authors

Mizener, Arthur. "To Meet Mr. Eliot," *T. S. Eliot: A Collection of Critical Essays,* ed. Hugh Kenner. Englewood Cliffs, N.J.: Prentice-Hall, Inc., 1962.

BIBLIOGRAPHY CARDS FOR MAGAZINE ARTICLES

A card for a magazine article should give the name of the author—if an author is listed—last name first and first name followed by a period; the title of the article in quotation marks with a comma before the closing quotation marks; the name of the magazine underlined and followed by a comma; the volume and issue number; the date in parentheses, followed by a comma; and the page numbers followed by a period. (See the sample bibliography card for magazine articles on p. 342.)

OTHER BIBLIOGRAPHY FORMS FOR MAGAZINES

Lewis, Bernard. "The Return of Islam," *Commentary*, 61, No. 1 (January 1976), 39–49.

> Both the volume and the issue number within that volume are given. The figures "61, No. 1" stand for "volume 61, issue number one."

Lamborn R. L. "Must They Be Crazy, Mixed-up Kids?" *The New York Times Magazine*, June 26, 1955, pp. 20–21.

> The sample card (p. 342) shows the standard form for a magazine article. The volume number appears before the date, which is placed in parentheses, and the page numbers follow. The words "volume" and "page" or "pages" (or their abbreviations, "vol.," "p.," "pp.") are not given when both volume and page numbers appear. In the entry above, however, no volume number is given. In this case, the date does not appear in parentheses, and the abbreviation "pp." is used.

"Thoughts from the Lone Cowboy," *Time*, 109, No. 9 (February 28, 1977), 20.

> No author is given. In such a case, the first part of the entry is the title of the article. The word "anonymous" (or its abbreviation, "anon.") should not be used.

BIBLIOGRAPHY CARDS FOR NEWSPAPER ARTICLES

A card for a newspaper article should give the name of the author—if an author is listed—last name first and first name followed by a period; the title of the article in quotation marks with a comma before the closing quotation marks; the name of the newspaper underlined and followed by a comma; the date followed by a comma; and the page numbers, followed by a period. (See the sample bibliography card for a newspaper article on p. 342.)

If the article is unsigned, the first part of the bibliography entry is the title of the article. If a newspaper has labeled sections, the section number in which the article appeared should also be given.

ANOTHER BIBLIOGRAPHY FORM FOR NEWSPAPERS

"Trudeau on Separatism," *The* [Cleveland] *Plain Dealer*, February 24, 1977, Sec. A, p. 22.

> If the name of the city is part of the title of the newspaper, as in *The New York Times*, it is underlined. If the name of the city is not part of the title, the city is inserted in brackets and is not underlined. If the city is not well known, the name of the state is also included in brackets.

809.892 Call Number
M694L

Moers, Ellen! Author

Literary Women! Title

Garden City, New York: City of Publication

Publishing
Company *Doubleday & Company, Inc.,*

1976 Copyright Date

BOOK WITH ONE AUTHOR

Arvin, Newton. Author

"Homage to Robert Herrick", Title of Article

New Republic, Name of Magazine

LXXXII Volume Number

(March 6, 1935), Date

93 - 95. Pages

MAGAZINE ARTICLE

Hess, John L. Author

*"A Sizzling Battle in the
Burger Business,"* Title of Article

The New York Times, Name of Newspaper

March 13, 1977, Date

Sec. 3, pp. 1, 9. Section and Pages

NEWSPAPER ARTICLE

Sample Bibliography Cards

BIBLIOGRAPHY CARDS FOR ENCYCLOPEDIA ARTICLES

Kealunohonoku, Joan W. "Hula," *Encyclopedia Americana*, 1971, 14, 542.

The above sample shows the standard form for a signed encyclopedia article. In many encyclopedias, the author's initials are given at the end of the article. You will have to check the list of abbreviations at the beginning of the volume to find the author's name.

A card for an encyclopedia article should give the name of the author, the last name first and first name followed by a period; the title of the article in quotation marks, with a comma before the closing quotation marks; the name of the encyclopedia, underlined and followed by a comma; the date, followed by a comma; the volume number, followed by a comma; and the page numbers, followed by a period.

ANOTHER BIBLIOGRAPHY FORM FOR ENCYCLOPEDIAS

"Massachusetts Bay Company," *The Columbia Encyclopedia*, 1963, p. 1317.

This encyclopedia has only one volume. When no volume number is given, use the abbreviation "p." or "pp." before the page numbers.

BIBLIOGRAPHY CARDS FOR OTHER KINDS OF SOURCES

Book Review. If the book review has a title, treat the review as you would any other magazine article. If the review is untitled, treat it as follows:

Adams, Phoebe-Lou. Review of *Black Sun*, by Geoffrey Wolff, *Atlantic*, 238, No. 3 (September 1976), 99.

Interview. The title or some indication of the authority of the person interviewed is given. It is also good to include the topic of the interview as well as the place and date:

Guhde, Barbara, Associate Professor of Modern British Literature, State University College at Brockport, New York, interview in Brockport, April 26, 1977, concerning Blake's influence on the works of Joyce Cary.

Letter. Give the author, the recipient, the place and date the letter was written, and the present location of the letter.

Bohi, John. A letter in my possession to Arthur H. Adams, dated at Hamburg, Germany, September 30, 1971.

Selection from a Casebook. Give the bibliography for the original printing and follow it with the documentation for the reprint.

Maclean, Hugh N. "Conservatism in Modern American Fiction," *College English*, XV (March 1954), 315–325. Reprinted in *J. D. Salinger and the Critics*, eds. William F. Belcher and James W. Lee. Belmont, California: Wadsworth Publishing Company, Inc., 1962.

Unpublished Dissertation. Give the author, the title of the dissertation, the location of the dissertation, and the date.

Alpern, Gertrude. "Women in Ancient Greek Political Thought." Diss. Case Western Reserve University, 1974.

Record Album. Give the composer, the title, the soloists, the orchestra, the conductor, the recording company, and the number of the album.

Verdi, Giuseppe. *La Traviata*. Beverly Sills, Nicolai Gedda, and Rolando Panerai. Royal Philharmonic Orchestra conducted by Aldo Ceccato. Angel SCLX-3780.

Television Program. Give the title of the show, the subtitle (if the show has one), the network, and the date of the show.

"Bill Moyer's Journal": Interview with Max Lerner, American journalist. PBS. May 30, 1980.

TAKING NOTES

When you have completed your bibliography cards, you are ready to begin taking notes, which will provide the evidence for your paper. Without good notes, you cannot hope to write a good paper. What, then, are the requirements for taking good notes?

Cards for Notes

To begin with, you should take your notes on cards. Opinions vary about the size of the cards. Some researchers prefer three-by-five-inch cards, believing that a note which requires more space is probably too long. Others prefer four-by-six-inch cards, believing that some notes must be long. In addition to extra space, the four-by-six-inch card offers the advantage of being obviously distinct from your bibliography cards. But size is a matter of personal choice. Taking notes any way other than on cards is not. Taking your notes in a notebook is simply not efficient. The idea is to be able to organize and reorganize your notes according to the facts and opinions they contain, not according to the books or magazines the material came from. You can shuffle cards, but you can't reorganize material in a notebook without a lot of cutting and pasting. Rule number one, then, is *take your notes on cards.*

Scope of Notes

Rule number two is *place only one note on a card.* One note is *one* fact, *one* idea, *one* opinion. If you put two facts or ideas or opinions on one note card, one of them is likely to get buried or lost among your accumulated notes. Either that, or as you organize and reorganize your notes, you may find that you will have to recopy that second fact, idea, or opinion, or take the time to cut notes into smaller units—all very inefficient. So put *one* fact, *one* idea, or *one* opinion on a card.

Content of Notes

What do you look for when taking notes? You should look for any fact, idea, or opinion not generally known that appears to relate to your topic. You will, of course, take far more notes than you need for your final paper, but if you plan to do an honest job of research, you should investigate your subject as thoroughly as you can and wait until later to start weeding out notes you don't actually need. It's easier to take a few extra notes than it is to go back to the library and reread a book or article when you discover, after you start writing the paper, that you don't have enough evidence to make a point.

Nevertheless, you should not simply take notes at random. You have begun your research with at least a vague idea of what you want to prove or report. The sooner the idea becomes definite, the more directed and less time-consuming your note taking will become. But don't worry if you find yourself taking many notes from the first sources you read. After all, the subject is fairly new to you, and everything seems important. You should soon get a focus on the material, and then you can become more selective in the notes you take.

Consider that example about the Lizzie Borden case. If you choose such a topic, you might, at first, be so fascinated by the story that you take notes on everything in the accused's life that could possibly have led to the crime: her mother made her stand in the corner for hours when she was only three; her father made harsh remarks about her appearance, etc. But soon you may decide that you will not try to provide Lizzie Borden with a motive; you will begin by simply describing the crime: what happened. Once you have made that decision, your reading will be focused. You will look specifically for information about what happened at the scene of the crime.

Similarly, you can restrict the other major topics of the tentative outline. A complete description of the trial could fill a book, as you

Melville, Moby-Dick, p. 165
"So that by no possibility could [Samuel Taylor] Coleridge's wild Rhyme ['The Rime of the Ancient Mariner'] have had ought to do with those mystical impressions which were mine, when I saw the bird upon our deck. For neither had I then read the Rhyme nor knew the bird to be an albatross."

A note containing a direct quotation and an insertion in brackets.

Melville, Moby-Dick, p. 165

Ishmael, while describing his feelings on first seeing an albatross, denies having read Coleridge's "The Rime of the Ancient Mariner" or even knowing the name of the bird he saw.

A note containing a paraphrase of the original material.

Melville, Moby-Dick, p. 165

Ishmael describes the first time he ever saw an albatross. He recounts that in "Antarctic seas," he found the bird "dashed upon the main hatches." The appearance of the bird caused him to believe he had "peeped to secrets which took hold of God" and made such an impression on him that, he says, "I bowed myself."

A note combining a paraphrase of the original and some direct quotation.

Melville, Letter to Hawthorne, pp. 557-559
"Let any clergyman try to preach the Truth from its very stronghold, the pulpit, and they [the mass of men] would ride him out of his church on his own pulpit bannister.... Why so? Truth is ridiculous to men. (557)
. . . .
The reason the mass of men fear God, and at bottom dislike Him, is because they rather distrust His heart, and fancy Him all brain like a watch." (559)

A note containing a direct quotation from which several paragraphs have been omitted.

Sample Note Cards

soon learn when you begin reading the evidence. You could decide, after a little reading, that you will not try to handle the testimony of character witnesses, that you will concentrate solely on physical evidence presented by the prosecution and its rebuttal by the defense. And you may decide to describe the controversy only in terms of Lizzie Borden's legal guilt or innocence, thus eliminating the need to deal with the sociological or psychological arguments that are sometimes raised in discussions of the case. Again, this kind of limiting of your topic will direct your note taking and save you a great deal of time because you will know exactly what kind of information you are looking for.

Limit your subject and your approach to it, then, just as soon as you can, so you can perform the job of note taking efficiently.

Documentation of Notes

Every note card should contain two kinds of information: the fact, idea, or opinion and the exact source of the information. (See the sample note cards on p. 346.) Since you have the complete data for the source on your bibliography card, you need to give yourself just enough information on the note card to refer you to the proper bibliographical reference. Usually, the author's last name and the page number from which you take the information will be sufficient. Occasionally, you will have two works by the same author. In that case, use the author's last name and an abbreviated form of the work's title to distinguish one source from another. If no author is given, use an abbreviation of the title of the book or article. Do not, however, use simply the name of the magazine. You could, for example, be using several articles from various issues of *Time*. If you simply write *"Time,* p. 118" on your note card, you won't have enough information to refer you to the bibliography card that lists the particular article from which you are taking notes.

Quotation of Sources

You may quote the actual wording used in your source, or you may *paraphrase*—that is, put in your own words—the facts or ideas contained in the original. If you do quote your source, be certain to put quotation marks around the material you quote. It may be a month or more between the time you take the note and the time you write your paper, and you don't want any uncertainty about which words are yours and which are those of the original author. Be certain, too, that you copy the quotation exactly as it appears in the original. If the original has an obvious error, copy the error and follow it in brackets with [*sic*], the Latin word for "thus." (Underline *sic* when you type or write the word. In print, the word is italicized.)

Occasionally, you may want to quote only parts of an entire passage. If you leave out a whole paragraph or two, indicate the omission by placing spaced dots all the way across the card. If you leave out a part of a sentence or one or two sentences, indicate the omission by placing three spaced dots (an ellipsis) where the sentence or part of the sentence has been left out. If you omit the beginning of a sentence, place the quotation marks *before* the ellipsis. If you omit the end of a sentence, place the quotation marks *after* the ellipsis and the end punctuation (period, question mark, or exclamation point).

A word or two of caution about using the ellipsis: Never alter the meaning of the original by using an ellipsis. If the original statement reads, "This is not the most exciting movie of the year," using an ellipsis to omit the word *not* would be dishonest. Secondly, be sure that you still have a complete sentence when you use the ellipsis. Don't omit from the sentence important elements such as subjects and verbs.

When quoting, you will sometimes find it necessary to clarify a word or date in the original quotation because you are taking the words out of context. Pronouns, for example, may need clarification. In context, "He suffered extreme hardships" may be perfectly clear. Isolated on a note card, however, the pronoun *he* may need to be explained. If you want to insert a word, phrase, or figure into the quotation, do so by putting the information in *brackets*—brackets, not parentheses: "He [Lincoln] suffered extreme hardships." Or the original might read, "In that year, he faced the greatest crisis of his life." The sentence, taken out of context, does not identify the year. You would want to insert it: "In that year [1839], he faced the greatest crisis of his life."

Paraphrase of Sources

Despite our lengthy advice on how to handle quotations, we urge you to quote sparingly. Most of your notes should be paraphrases— that is, summaries of the original material. Of course, if you are in a hurry and don't have time to think about the best way to paraphrase a note, rather than risk plagiarism (see "Plagiarism," p. 356), do quote the material and later decide how best to put it in your own words.

Disagreements: Facts and Opinions

One final warning on note taking: As you take notes, don't assume that just because something is in print, it must be true. Be careful to distinguish between a writer's statement of fact and expression of opinion. There is a world of difference between saying that Aaron Burr was the vice-president of the United States and saying that Aaron Burr was a scoundrel. In rare cases in which there appears to be an outright disagreement between authors on matters of fact, slam on your mental brakes and do some checking. One of the standard reference works or encyclopedias might be a good source for resolving such disagreements or disputes. When you don't feel you have sufficient basis for deciding which opinion is correct, it seems simple common sense to acknowledge frankly the difference of opinion and to present both opinions as honestly as possible.

OUTLINING

The research paper must meet the same requirements of good writing as any other paper you have written in your English course. It must have a thesis or purpose. It must support the thesis or purpose by using specific facts presented in specific language. And it must be organized; therefore, you must prepare a formal, written outline. The mental outline that may have been enough for a short theme will not be of any use for a research paper.

Although you may already have written outlines for many papers, we urge you, in case you have forgotten any important rules about outlining, to reread Chapter 3 of the text. A good outline is a good outline—whether it is for a four-paragraph essay or for a ten-page research paper. But we won't try to convince you that writing a good outline for a research paper is as easy as writing one for a four-paragraph paper. The research paper is certainly the longest and most complex paper you will write in your freshman English course, and it requires careful planning.

Making a Slug Outline

Start by reading and rereading all your notes very carefully. You have accumulated the notes over a period of weeks, and you may not have a precise picture of just what material you have gathered. Read the notes carefully, then. Some notes will have to be set aside. But in the others, you will begin to see a pattern. You will find that you have several groups of notes, each group relating to a single subject. If you had taken notes on the Lizzie Borden case, for example, you would probably have several notes which could be headed *reporting the crime*, let's say, or others which could be headed *clues at scene*. When you are familiar enough with your notes that you can arrange them in piles according to single headings, you are ready to write a *slug*—that is, a brief heading which indicates the content of the note—on each card. Don't try to be creative here and write a different heading for each card; you *should* have several cards with the same slug.

Because you may change your mind about the point that a particular note should support, it would be a good idea to write the slugs in pencil at first. That way you can easily change the slugs until you feel secure about the way the notes should be used. Once you have made a final decision, write a slug in ink in the upper right-hand corner of each card so that it can be seen quickly as you shuffle through your cards.

Writing a Formal Outline

If you have succeeded in writing slugs on each card, the outline will almost write itself. Either a topic outline or a sentence outline is acceptable, although if you plan to prove a thesis, it is probably wise to make a sentence outline; doing so will force you to state in a complete thought how each section of your paper contributes to the thesis. Observe all the conventions of good outlining as you write, using the slugs on your note cards as guides for topics and subtopics. (See the outline for the sample paper on p. 366.)

WRITING THE PAPER

All the rules of good writing that you have learned so far apply to the research paper. But the research paper presents a special problem: you must make borrowed material a part of your own statement. You have spent several weeks now taking notes; you have studied them and have decided how they can be organized, and that is half the battle. If, however, you simply string your notes together, you will not be writing a research paper; you will be merely transcribing your notes. The paper must be yours—your idea, your organization, and, for the most part, your words. The notes should be used to back up your ideas, which means the notes should be integrated into your statement. Otherwise, you do not have an honest research paper.

In the following excerpt from a student paper, the writer merely strings notes together.

> W. E. B. DuBois believed that "the problem of the twentieth century is the problem of the color line."[4]
> DuBois became aware of racial differences at an early age. He related this experience vividly:
>> The exchange [of children's calling cards] was merry, till one girl, a tall new comer, refused my card—refused it peremptorily, with a glance. Then it dawned on me with a certain suddenness that I

was different from the others; or like, mayhap, in heart and life and longing, but shut out from this world by a vast veil.[5]

DuBois felt that dreams of opportunities and fulfillment were reserved solely for whites.

The shades of the prison-house closed around about us all: the walls strait and stubborn to the whitest, but relentlessly narrow, tall, and unscalable to sons of night who must plod darkly on in resignation, or beat unavailing palms against the stone, or steadily, half hopelessly, watch the streak of blue above.[6]

When his infant son died, Du Bois was depressed, but yet he rejoiced because his son would not have to endure life "behind the veil."[7]

All that day and all that night there sat an awful gladness in my heart—nay blame me not if I see the world thus darkly through the veil, and my soul whispers ever to me, saying, "not dead, not dead, but escaped, not bound, but free." No bitter meaness now shall sicken his baby heart till it die a living death, no taunt shall madden his happy boyhood. Fool that I was to think or wish that this little soul should grow choked and deformed within the veil! . . . Well sped, my boy, before the world had dubbed your ambition insolence, had held your ideals unattainable, and taught you to cringe and bow. Better for this nameless void that stops my life than a sea of sorrow for you.[8]

---

[4]W. E. B. DuBois, *The Souls of Black Folk* (New York: Dodd, Mead, 1961), p. xiv.
[5]DuBois, p. 16.
[6]DuBois, p. 16.
[7]DuBois, p. 155.
[8]DuBois, pp. 155–56.

The student has simply copied his notes into his paper. The point could be made more clearly if it were phrased largely in the student's own words:

W. E. B. DuBois, who believed that "the problem of the twentieth century is the problem of the color line,"[4] learned as a child that he could be rejected simply because of the color of his skin. Later, he came to believe that dreams of opportunities and fulfillment were reserved solely for whites, and he compared the life of blacks in America with that of prison inmates. Indeed, he grew so bitter about the plight of blacks that he rejoiced when his infant son died because the child would never have to experience the prejudice that he had felt.[5]

---

[4]W. E. B. DuBois, *The Souls of Black Folk* (New York: Dodd, Mead, 1961), p. xiv.
[5]DuBois, p. 16 and pp. 155–56.

In this version, the writer has composed a unified paragraph which makes the point clearly without the use of so many quotations. (A good, safe rule of thumb is, unless the subject of your paper is an author's style, quote no more than ten percent of your paper.) The second paragraph also avoids the sin of overdocumentation. Five footnotes have been replaced by only two. This version shows a much greater mastery of the material than does the first version.

First Rough Draft

To remove the temptation of simply stringing notes together, you might try our method of writing a first rough draft. We suggest that you set your notes aside, put your outline in front of you, and start writing. In this draft, the point is to get your ideas down on paper. Don't worry about grammar or punctuation. Don't try to work in quotations. You should be familiar enough with the contents of your notes by now to remember the general ideas they contain. Just write, perhaps on every third line of a legal pad, until you have developed every point in your outline.

If you have really studied your notes, and if you have constructed a reasonable outline, following this procedure should assure that you will develop your own ideas in your own way.

Second Rough Draft

Now, write the paper again. This time you will consult your notes to add quotations where they seem appropriate and to fill in specific facts you might not have remembered in writing the first rough draft. You will check your notes, too, to be sure that the facts, ideas, or opinions you have reported are accurate. And in this second effort, you will make some attempt to correct any grammar or punctuation errors you made in the first draft and to rephrase awkward sentences. Then you will add footnotes. (See "Footnote Forms," pp. 358–362.)

Once you have completed this draft, go back through it several times to make certain that you have quoted accurately, that you have documented every source properly, and that you have polished your language as well as you can. Don't hesitate during this process to use scissors and scotch tape to add, delete, or shift passages as you go along.

Third Rough Draft

If you think you have polished the paper as much as you can, make a third copy, complete with quotations and footnotes. Many instructors will not accept a final copy of paper unless they have seen and approved the rough draft. If your instructor falls into this category, this is the rough draft you should submit. Your instructor will make suggestions, point out stylistic problems, and indicate the parts of your paper that are not developed as fully as they might be. Conscientious students heed their instructors' suggestions and make the appropriate changes on the third rough draft before typing the final paper.

Use of Quotations

The first rule regarding the use of direct quotations is use as few as you can. It is possible, in fact, to write an entire paper without using any direct quotations. There are, however, some cases in which direct quotations are called for:

1. If your subject is a literary one, you would, of course, want to represent the style of the author. Indeed, your purpose might demand an analysis of certain passages in the work. In that case, you certainly must quote the passages that you intend to discuss in detail.

Following is a section of a paper in which the writer argues that Herman Melville, in composing *Moby-Dick*, was influenced by Samuel Taylor Coleridge's "The Rime of the Ancient Mariner":

> One other image in Chapters 51 and 52 of *Moby-Dick* illustrates a slightly different way of adapting Coleridge's images. In this image, Melville incorporates both the image and the mood of the source in Coleridge's work. It occurs while the *Pequod* is still at the Cape of Good Hope:
>
> > Few or no words were spoken, and the silent ship, as if manned by painted sailors in wax, day after day tore on through the swift madness and gladness of the demoniac waves.
>
> Except that the ship is given motion, it is surely the Ancient Mariner's ship on which
>
> > Day after day, day after day
> > We stuck, nor breath nor motion;
> > As idle as a painted ship
> > Upon a painted ocean.

Clearly, the quotations are necessary to show Coleridge's influence on Melville's work.

2. If the original is so perfectly stated that much of its value is in the way it is worded, you may want to quote the original. The conclusion of Lincoln's second inaugural address might be such a quotation:

With malice toward none; with charity for all; with firmness in the right, as God gives us to see the right, let us strive on to finish the work we are in; to bind up the nation's wounds; to care for him who shall have borne the battle, and for his widow, and his orphan—to do all which may achieve and cherish a just and lasting peace among ourselves, and with all nations.

3. If your source has made a statement which is so outrageous or controversial that readers of your paper might question whether you have represented the idea correctly, quote the original statement.

Aside from the statistics, there are those in the nuclear field who make some rather strong accusations about the expertise of nuclear energy's critics. According to W. E. Cooper, the motives of the critics and the expertise of the technicians are "grossly unbalanced." Cooper states,

We are trying to balance the opposing motivations with groups which are grossly unbalanced in expertise. Here is the source of our present difficulties. We are trying to find the answers to difficult technical questions by using the adversary principal instead of impartial evaluations by experts, and the conflicts end up in the courts where decisions are made by people who have no technical competence at all!

When you do quote, make every effort you can to work the quotation into your own statement. It will be obvious, of course, that you are quoting, but the flow of your sentence should not be affected by the quotation:

Forster points directly to the need for myth: "Why has not England a great mythology?" he asks, and suggests that England's mythology "has not advanced beyond daintiness" because, unlike Greek mythology, it has not derived from the earth.

Because the quotations are worked out into the writer's own sentence, they require no special punctuation other than the quotation marks. If you want to introduce a longer quotation, punctuation depends on the words that precede the quote.

If the introductory words form a complete sentence, use a colon:

That Forster intended to establish man's need for connection with the earth is evident in his statement about London:

London was but a foretaste of this nomadic civilization which is altering human nature so profoundly, and throws upon personal relations a stress greater than they have ever borne before. Under cosmopolitanism, if it comes, we shall receive no help from the earth. Trees and meadows and mountains will only be a spectacle, and the binding force that they once exercised on character must be entrusted to Love alone. May Love be equal to the task!

If the introductory words do not form a complete sentence, imagine that the quote itself is the rest of the sentence and punctuate accordingly:

According to Forster,

London was but a foretaste of this nomadic civilization which is altering human nature so profoundly, and throws upon personal relations a stress greater than they have ever borne before. Under cosmopolitanism, if it comes, we shall receive no help from the earth. Trees and meadows and mountains will only be a spectacle, and the binding force that they once exercised on character must be entrusted to Love alone. May Love be equal to the task!

or

Forster writes that

London was but a foretaste of this nomadic civilization which is altering human nature so profoundly, and throws upon personal relations a stress greater than they have ever borne before. Under cosmopolitanism, if it comes, we shall receive no help from the earth. Trees and meadows and mountains will only be a spectacle, and the binding force that they once exercised on character must be entrusted to Love alone. May Love be equal to the task!

As all the above examples of quotations illustrate, you should put a *short quotation* into your own paragraph or sentence, indicating that the material is quoted by placing quotation marks around the quoted passage. Set *long quotations* off by themselves. The quoted matter should be blocked and single-spaced, as in the immediately preceding examples. When you block a quotation, *do not use quotation marks.* (See "Quotation Marks" in the "Handbook," pp. 484–486.) That the material is blocked and single-spaced *means* that it is quoted.

Use of Footnotes

Unless the material is something as well known as the Gettysburg Address, when you take facts or ideas from someone else, you must credit the source by footnoting the material. Such a statement often frightens students because their first assumption is that they will have to footnote almost every sentence in their papers. That is not the case.

You should, of course, footnote all direct quotations which are not well known. You should also footnote all facts and opinions which are not common knowledge—*even when you have put the facts or opinions into your own words.* Two kinds of facts or opinions come under the heading *common knowledge:* those facts which everyone in our culture should know (George Washington was the first president of the United States, for example), and those facts which are common knowledge in the field you are investigating. Suppose you are writing a paper on Custer's last stand. You might not have known, when you began reading, the name of the Indian tribe that fought Custer and his men. If every source you read, however, says that it was the Sioux tribe, you would not need to make a footnote for that fact. Your wide reading lets you know that the fact is commonly known to historians. Nor would it be necessary to footnote the opinion that Custer blundered; most historians agree that he did. But any theories about why Custer led his men into such a trap should be footnoted.

At this point you may be feeling vaguely disturbed by the fuss being made about apparent trivialities of quoting and footnoting. Unfortunately, these are the only devices by which your reader will be able to distinguish between the material drawn from other sources and the material that is your own. If you do not pay the most careful attention to the techniques of quoting and footnoting, you run the risk of being accused of plagiarism.

PLAGIARISM

Plagiarism is the use of facts, opinions, and language taken from another writer without acknowledgment. In its most sordid form, plagiarism is outright theft or cheating: a person has another person write the paper or simply steals a magazine article or section of a book and pretends to have produced a piece of original writing. Far more common is plagiarism in dribs and drabs: a sentence here and there, a paragraph here and there. Unfortunately, small-time theft is still theft, and small-time plagiarism is still plagiarism. For your own safety and self-respect, remember the following rules—not guidelines, *rules:*

1. The language in your paper must either be your own or a direct quote from the original source.
2. Changing a few words or phrases from another writer's work is not enough to make the writing "your own." Remember Rule 1. The writing is either your own or the other person's; there are no in-betweens.
3. Footnotes acknowledge that the fact or opinion expressed comes from another writer. If the *language* comes from another writer, quotation marks are necessary *in addition* to a footnote.

Now for a detailed example.

ORIGINAL PASSAGE

In 1925 Dreiser produced his masterpiece, the massively impressive *An American Tragedy.* By this time—thanks largely to the tireless propagandizing on his behalf by the influential maverick critic H. L. Mencken and by others concerned with a realistic approach to the problems of American life—Dreiser's fame had become secure. He was seen as the most powerful and effective destroyer of the genteel tradition that had dominated popular American fiction in the post-Civil War period, spreading its soft blanket of provincial, sentimental romance over the often ugly realities of life in modern, industrialized, urban America. Certainly there was nothing genteel about Dreiser, either as man or novelist. He was the supreme poet of the squalid, a man who felt the terror, the pity, and the beauty underlying the American dream. With an eye at once ruthless and compassionate, he saw the tragedy inherent in the American success ethic; the soft underbelly, as it were, of the Horatio Alger rags-to-riches myth so appealing to the optimistic American imagination [Richard Freedman, *The Novel* (New York: Newsweek Books, 1975), pp. 104–105].

STUDENT VERSION

There was nothing genteel about Dreiser, either as man or novelist. He was the supreme poet of the squalid, a man who felt the terror, the pity, and the beauty underlying the American dream.

COMMENT

Obvious plagiarism: word-for-word repetition without acknowledgment.

STUDENT VERSION

There was nothing genteel about Dreiser, either as man or novelist. He was the supreme poet of the squalid, a man who felt the terror, the pity, and the beauty underlying the American dream.[1]

  [1]Richard Freedman, *The Novel* (New York: Newsweek Books, 1975), p. 104.

COMMENT

Still plagiarism. *The footnote alone does not help.* The language is the original author's, and only quotation marks around the whole passage *plus* a footnote would be correct.

STUDENT VERSION

Nothing was genteel about Dreiser as a man or as a novelist. He was the poet of the squalid and felt that terror, pity, and beauty lurked under the American dream.

COMMENT

Still plagiarism. A few words have been changed or omitted, but by no stretch of the imagination is the student writer using his own language.

"Nothing was genteel about Dreiser as a man or as a novelist. He was the poet of the squalid and felt that terror, pity, and beauty lurked under the American dream."[1]

[1]Richard Freedman, *The Novel* (New York: Newsweek Books, 1975), p. 104.

Not quite plagiarism, but incorrect and inaccurate. Quotation marks indicate exact repetition of what was originally written. The student writer, however, has changed some of the original and is not entitled to use quotation marks.

"Certainly there was nothing genteel about Dreiser, either as man or novelist. He was the supreme poet of the squalid, a man who felt the terror, the pity, and the beauty underlying the American dream."[1]

[1]Richard Freedman, *The Novel* (New York: Newsweek Books, 1975), p. 104.

Correct. The quotation marks acknowledge the words of the original writer. The footnote is also needed, of course, to give the reader specific information about the source of the quote.

By 1925 Dreiser's reputation was firmly established. The reading public viewed Dreiser as one of the main contributors to the downfall of the "genteel tradition" in American literature. Dreiser, "the supreme poet of the squalid," looked beneath the bright surface of American life and values and described the frightening and tragic elements, the "ugly realities," so often overlooked by other writers.[1]

[1]Richard Freedman, *The Novel* (New York: Newsweek Books, 1975), pp. 104–105.

Correct. The student writer uses his own words to summarize most of the original passage. The footnote shows that the ideas expressed come from the original writer, not from the student. The few phrases kept from the original passage are carefully enclosed in quotation marks.

FOOTNOTE FORMS

When you are ready to add footnotes to your rough draft, you will have to consult your bibliography cards in order to change the brief notations you made on your note cards into proper footnote entries. As you will see by studying the examples of various kinds of footnotes below, footnotes contain essentially the same information as do bibliography entries, but the arrangement and punctuation of that information are a little different.

First References

A *first* footnote reference to a book should include the author, the title, the facts of publication, and the page or pages referred to. The author's name is not inverted in the footnote since you will not, of course, place footnotes in alphabetical order. Below are samples of *first* footnotes for the sources cited in the discussion of bibliography (pp. 334–344). Notice the differences in punctuation between a bibliography entry and a footnote entry.

A Book with One Author

[1]Ellen Moers, *Literary Women* (Garden City, New York: Doubleday & Company, Inc., 1976), p. 198.

A Book with Two Authors

[2]Marlies K. Danziger and W. Stacy Johnson, *An Introduction to Literary Criticism* (Boston: D. C. Heath and Company, 1961), p. 324.

A Book with Three or More Authors

[3]Fred C. Watkins and others, *Practical English Handbook,* 4th ed. (Boston: Houghton Mifflin Company, 1970), p. 73.

A Book with an Editor

[4]Loren J. Kallsen, ed., *The Kentucky Tragedy: A Problem in Romantic Attitudes* (Indianapolis: The Bobbs-Merrill Company, Inc., 1963), pp. 371–72.

An Edition of an Author's Work

[5]Henry David Thoreau, *Collected Poems,* ed. Carl Bode (Chicago: Packard and Co., 1943), p. 189.

If the editor's work, not the author's, is under discussion, use the following form:

[6]Donald A.Stauffer, ed., *Selected Poetry and Prose of Coleridge* (New York: The Modern Library, 1951), p. xii.

An Edition Other Than the First

[7]Randall E. Decker, *Patterns of Exposition,* 7th ed. (Boston: Little, Brown and Company, 1980), p. 87.

If the edition is a revised edition rather than a numbered edition, the abbreviation "rev. ed." should appear after the title.

An Edited Collection or Anthology

[8]Arthur Schlesinger, Jr. and Morton White, eds., *Paths of American Thought* (Boston: Houghton Mifflin Company, 1970), p. 23.

A Translated Work

⁹Heinrich Böll, *End of a Mission,* trans. Leila Vennewitz (New York: McGraw-Hill Book Company, 1974), p. 345.

A Work of More Than One Volume

¹⁰Wallace E. Adams and others, eds., *The Western World: To 1770* (New York: Dodd, Mead & Company, 1968), I, 548.

Notice that although the bibliography entry refers to a two-volume work, the writer has referred to only the first volume.

One Section of a Book Written by Several Authors

¹¹Arthur Mizener, "To Meet Mr. Eliot," *T. S. Eliot: A Collection of Critical Essays,* ed. Hugh Kenner (Englewood Cliffs, N.J.: Prentice-Hall, Inc. 1962), p. 20.

A footnote reference to a magazine should include the author, the title of the article, the name of the magazine, the volume and issue number, the date, and the page or pages referred to. A footnote to a magazine is almost identical to the bibliography entry except that the author's name is not inverted and, instead of giving all the pages of the article—as in a bibliography—you indicate only the specific page or pages referred to in your text.

¹²Newton Arvin, "Homage to Robert Herrick," *New Republic,* LXXXII (March 6, 1935), 94.

¹³Bernard Lewis, "The Return of Islam," *Commentary,* 61, No. 1 (January 1976), 41.

Both the volume and the number within that volume are given. The figures "61, No. 1" stand for " volume 61, number one."

¹⁴R. L. Lamborn, "Must They Be Crazy, Mixed-up Kids?" *The New York Times Magazine,* June 26, 1955, p. 21.

Because no volume number is given, the abbreviation "p." is used before the page number and the date is not placed in parentheses.

¹⁵"Thoughts from the Lone Cowboy," *Time,* 109, No. 9 (February 28, 1977), 20.

A footnote for a newspaper article should give the name of the author (if an author is listed), the title of the article, the name of the newspaper, the date, and the page. If the newspaper is divided into sections, the section number will also be given.

¹⁶John L. Hess, "A Sizzling Battle in the Burger Business," *The New York Times*, March 13, 1977, Sec. 3, p. 1.

¹⁷"Trudeau on Separatism," *The* [Cleveland] *Plain Dealer*, February 24, 1977, Sec. A, p. 22.

The name of the city is not part of the title of this newspaper and is indicated in brackets.

A footnote reference to an encyclopedia article is almost identical to the bibliography entry except that the author's name (if given) is not inverted.

¹⁸Joan W. Kealunohonoku, "Hula," *Encyclopedia Americana*, 1971, 14, 542.

¹⁹"Massachusetts Bay Company," *The Columbia Encyclopedia*, 1963, p. 1317.

Since this is a one-volume encyclopedia and no volume number is given, the abbreviation "p." appears before the page number.

OTHER FOOTNOTE FORMS

An Untitled Book Review

²⁰Phoebe-Lou Adams, Review of *Black Sun*, by Geoffrey Wolff, *Atlantic*, 238, No. 3 (September 1976), p. 99.

Interview

²¹Barbara Guhde, Associate Professor of Modern British Literature, State University College at Brockport, New York, interview in Brockport, April 26, 1977, concerning Blake's influence on the works of Joyce Cary.

Letter

²²John Bohi, a letter in my possession to Arthur H. Adams, dated at Hamburg, Germany, September 30, 1971.

Selection from a Casebook

²³Hugh N. Maclean, "Conservatism in Modern American Fiction," *College English*, XV (March 1954), 315–325. Reprinted in *J. D. Salinger and the Critics*, eds. William F. Belcher and James W. Lee (Belmont, California: Wadsworth Publishing Company, Inc., 1962), p. 13.

SUBSEQUENT REFERENCES

Thus far we have been dealing with the detailed first reference to any source. Subsequent references to the same source are much shorter and much simpler. For almost any material, the author's last name and a page number will be sufficient:

[4]Moers, p. 199.
[8]Mizener, p. 21.
[10]Lewis, p. 41.
[15]Hess, p. 1.
[16]Kealunohonoku, p. 542.

If your reference is to one volume of a multi-volume work, your footnote will need to include the volume number:

[6]Adams and others, II, 78.

If you have used more than one work by the same author, the page number and author's name will not give the reader enough information. Write the title of the work after the author's last name. If the title is long, you may use a shortened form. After first references, for example, to Ernest Hemingway's *For Whom the Bell Tolls* and *Across the River and into the Trees,* subsequent references may look like this:

[7]Hemingway, *Bell,* p. 30.
[9]Hemingway, *Across the River,* p. 127.

When the author is unknown or unnamed, subsequent references consist of the title and page number:

[13]"Thoughts from the Lone Cowboy," p. 20.
[17]"Trudeau on Separatism," p. 22.
[19]"Massachusetts Bay Company," p. 1317.

Two concluding comments: *first,* forget about the Latin abbreviations formerly common in footnotes, particularly in subsequent references—*Ibid., op. cit.,* etc. Such usages have largely become things of the past. *Second,* footnotes may appear at the bottom of each page of the text of your paper *or* in one long list on a separate page or pages immediately after the text. If the footnotes are on the bottom of each page, be sure to keep numerical sequence throughout the paper: *do not* begin with a new footnote number 1 on each page. Check with your instructor about the footnoting method you should use. If your instructor has no preference, you will probably find it easier to type all footnotes on a separate page.

FINAL BIBLIOGRAPHY

The final bibliography lists sources actually referred to in your paper. It may also include material that was of genuine value in adding to your insights and perspectives on the subject but which you did not have occasion to refer to specifically. (Such sources are sometimes listed separately under the heading "Supplementary Bibliography.") The final bibliography should not include titles that turned out to be of little or no value in your paper.

For a typed sample of a final bibliography, see the student paper, p. 376. Note in particular the following points:

1. Bibliography entries are arranged in alphabetical order according to the last name of the author.
2. For entries where the author is unknown or unlisted, alphabetical order is determined by the first important word of the title.
3. The first line of each entry begins at the left-hand margin. All other lines of each entry are indented five spaces.
4. The following form should be used in cases where more than one title by the same author is being used:

Melville, Herman. *Moby-Dick* in *Moby-Dick: An Authoritative Text, Reviews and Letters by Melville, Analogues and Sources, Criticism,* eds. Harrison Hayford and Hershel Parker. New York: W. W. Norton & Company, Inc., 1967.

––––––. *White Jacket or The World in a Man-of-War,* ed. Hennig Cohen. New York: Holt, Rinehart and Winston, 1967.

SAMPLE PAPERS

Our discussion of research papers concludes with two papers on a topic of current controversy, nuclear power plants. The first paper was written before the Three Mile Island accident and the second after.

While by no means perfect, the papers represent serious efforts by serious students to apply the lessons of this chapter. Whatever the final merits of the stands the authors take, the papers can serve as a ready reference for most matters of form.

When you write your own research papers, you may find the following checklist a handy guide to some easily forgotten fine points:

Title Page

Is your title in capital letters?

Have you included your name?

Outline

Is the title of your paper repeated at the top of your outline?

Have you included your thesis statement after the paper's title?

Have you used a consistent pattern of numbering and lettering?

Body

Are the pages correctly numbered?

Are all the footnotes included either at the bottom of each page or at the end of the paper? (Check with your instructor before deciding which form to use.)

Is the number of each footnote raised half a line?

Have you used the blocked form for long quotations?

Footnotes

Have your placed the author's first name first?

Have you indented the first line of each footnote, and is the second line of each at the left-hand margin?

Is the title of each work correctly marked with quotation marks or underlining?

Does each footnote end with a period?

Are the footnotes correctly numbered, with no numbers repeated or omitted?

Bibliography

Have you placed the author's last name first?

Are all the entries in alphabetical order?

Is the first line of each entry at the left-hand margin, and is the second line of each indented?

Does each entry end with a period?

THE RELIABILITY OF NUCLEAR POWER PLANTS

by

F. L. Fende

English 103

June 4, 1976

for

Professor Norlin

OUTLINE

THE RELIABILITY OF NUCLEAR POWER PLANTS

THESIS: Nuclear power plants are a safe and reliable source of energy
          and their further development should be continued in order to
          satisfy mankind's never-ending need for energy.

I.   Today's critics of nuclear energy question the need for nuclear
     power and would lead us to believe nuclear power can have a
     devastating effect on mankind.

     A.   Atomic energy is compared with the atomic bomb.

     B.   Atomic energy is seen as a poisoned power and is compared
          with toxic industrial agents.

          1.   Fission by-products released into the atmosphere are
               said to be the greatest danger to mankind.

          2.   Nuclear power plants are said to be defenseless against
               enemy attack.

     C.   Some critics feel we do not need the additional energy supplied
          by nuclear power.

II. The proponents of nuclear energy have strong arguments in favor of
     nuclear power plants.

     A.   Scientists have proven that it would be impossible for a
          nuclear power plant to explode like an atomic bomb.

     B.   The experts in nuclear energy say that radiation is a normal
          part of life.

          1.   They contend radiation is not new to us, and it has
               always been present in natural sources.

          2.   They feel that radiation released from nuclear power
               plants is negligible.

     C.   The overwhelming pressure from the critics has caused the A.E.C.
          to finance and study the reliability of nuclear power plants.

          1.   An excellent history of safety has supported the cause of
               nuclear energy.

          2.   Nuclear power is compared with other sources of energy.

     D.   Those in support of the cause of nuclear energy question the
          expertise and motives of the critics.

     E.   Simple economics point to a need for nuclear energy.

In 1957 the United States reached a new threshold in nuclear technology. The first commercial nuclear power plant went into operation in
Shippingport, Pennsylvania. Since that time, the number of operable
nuclear power plants has increased to forty-seven, and it is projected
that by the year 1986 there will be 206 commercially operated nuclear
power plants.[1] Along with this increase in nuclear energy, the magnitude
of the controversy dealing with the safety of nuclear power has increased.
The opponents of nuclear power contend that it is dangerous to mankind.
Some opponents question the need for nuclear energy on the basis that we
can live without it and its pitfalls. On the other hand, the proponents
of nuclear power argue that it is a safe form of energy, and they contend
that the additional nuclear energy is necessary in order to supplement
this country's never-ending need for energy. Each side in this controversy takes a firm stand on its beliefs; however, the facts, based on
the expertise of those in the nuclear field and on the safe history of
nuclear power, indicate that nuclear power plants are a reliable source
of energy, and that further development of nuclear power should be
continued.

Today's critics of nuclear power would lead us to believe that
nuclear power can have a devastating effect on mankind. Richard Curtis,
author of Perils of the Peaceful Atom, reports that Supreme Court
Justices William Douglas and Hugo Black consider nuclear power "the most
deadly, the most dangerous process man has ever conceived."[2] This sort
of attitude is not only conveyed by our high officials, but also carries
on down the ranks. There are those who have written extensive works
pertaining to the pitfalls of nuclear power, and it is not difficult to
understand how the attitudes of today's critics have developed. The
most common denominator associated with nuclear energy is the emotional
reaction most people have to the past history of devastation caused by
the atomic bomb. Richard Curtis displays this attitude when he states

1

2

that "each [nuclear power plant] will be fueled with a great many times the amount of uranium required to destroy Hiroshima."[3] The reference to the bomb is enough to place some doubt in the minds of most people, and it seems to have become a tool used by critics in their fight against nuclear power. John Gofman and Arthur Tamplin argue, for example, that "one percent of the inner radioactivity . . . from one plant could put as much harmful contamination . . . into the environment as 10 bombs."[4]

The claim of Gofman and Tamplin highlights another issue. There are those who feel that radioactivity may be the most critical pitfall of nuclear power. Curtis suggests that "the greatest potential hazard" in nuclear power plants is the radioactive by-products produced by fission and the possibility that these products can be released over the general populace. He goes on to say that these by-products are more toxic than any known chemical agent used in industry.[5] Although Curtis does not state any exact agent, one may assume he is referring to toxic agents such as chlorine used in our water systems or mercury, which has been cited for its toxic qualities.

Comparing these agents with the radioactivity of fission products is probably a fair comparison, although there are no facts which substantiate these allegations. On the other hand, Gofman and Tamplin contend that "no one has ever produced evidence that any specific amount of radiation will be without harm."[6] The critics' concern for the potential dangers of radioactive fission by-products is well taken, and no one will disagree that excessive doses of radioactivity are deadly. Then again, one cannot help but feel that most fears are based on past experience with atomic bomb tests and the devastation of Hiroshima.

Some of those who argue against nuclear energy take a more practical stand in their fight against nuclear power. Their concern is with the vulnerability of nuclear plants at the time of enemy attacks or the plants' exposure to natural catastrophe. Gofman and Tamplin state that "unprotected, above ground nuclear power plants . . . would certainly be large liabilities . . . under attack."[7] Their approach is sensible, and

3

their obvious concern is that the internal radiation present in a nuclear
plant would be exposed to the public, although one may ask which would
be of more concern, the nuclear plant radiation due to enemy attack or
the overall consequences of the enemy attack.

There are some critics who feel that the world should cut back on
its energy consumption rather than risk the perils of nuclear energy.
This has led one critic, Ralph Nader, a man who carries a great deal of
weight in the consumer market, to suggest that "Americans could willingly
accept a 40% reduction in energy consumption."[8] Nader has also suggested
that if the public had a choice between candles and nuclear power, the
public would be wise to choose the candles.[9] This seems like quite a
drastic measure. It would be interesting to see how many people would
be willing to burn wood in their stoves or go back to using the old-style
icebox.

The proponents of nuclear power have strong arguments in favor of
nuclear energy, and they present their case for nuclear energy in a
realistic and practical manner. The accusations of those who compare
nuclear power plants with the atomic bomb are countered with sound fact.
James Stokley, author of The New World of the Atom, has argued this point
about nuclear power and put his views in a form that the ordinary layman
can understand:

> Since the most peaceful application of nuclear energy has
> been in the production and distribution of electrical power
> from nuclear sources, let us consider the possible hazards.
> First of all the nuclear reactor cannot explode like a bomb.
> In the bomb pieces of essentially pure uranium 235, or some
> other fissile material must be brought together and held for
> an instant in one compact mass. But the power reactor, even
> with highly enriched uranium, has fuel elements that are
> small and scattered. Even an accident could not bring them
> together to form a critical mass . . . .[10]

Aside from Stokley's understanding of nuclear energy, he has a good
feel for the cause of the controversies regarding nuclear power. Stokley
points out that "we cannot forget the hundreds of thousands killed at
Hiroshima and Nagasaki . . . . The tendency of many to identify atomic
power plants . . . with the bomb has made people fear and oppose them."[11]

In answer to the critics' concern for the radiation emitted from
nuclear plants, the experts in nuclear energy say that radiation is a
normal part of life. They contend that radiation is not new to us, and
they explain that "it has always come from natural sources. Living
organisms on earth have always been exposed to it, even long before man
evolved."[12] Certain facts have been established by the Atomic Energy
Commission and other scientific institutes and used as a comparison to
evaluate the radiation emitted by nuclear power plants. It has been
established that the average dose of natural radiation from cosmic rays
and other natural sources is 125 millirems a year; however, airline
pilots receive an additional 5 millirems of natural radiation annually
because there is less resistance to cosmic radiation at high altitudes.
For the same reason, people in Denver, Colorado, receive an additional
75 millirems of natural radiation a year.[13] Any viewer of television
receives additional radiation from a television set; radiation is also
transmitted by a radium dial on a wristwatch and by medical X-rays.

After all is said about natural radiation, the answer to one question
remains: How dangerous is the radiation in nuclear power plants? In
Stokley's research, he found that the radiation emitted from nuclear power
plants is negligible. Stokley admits to the large amount of fissionable
products present in nuclear power plants; however, he discloses that
"more than 99.999 per cent are held in the fuel elements,..." and he
claims that the prime goal in the construction of nuclear plants is to
build them so they retain as much of the ten thousandth of a percent of
potentially harmful radiation as possible.[14]

Aside from Stokley's findings, the Toledo Edison Company has gone
one step further in answering the questions about the dangers of radioactivity. Using previous operating experience as a gauge, the Toledo
Edison Company insists that "if a person were to remain at the edge of
the Davis-Besse plant site for 24 hours a day for an entire year, he
would receive a maximum of five millirems a year of radiation."[15] This
is the same dose a pilot receives making coast to coast flights. Since

5

the National Committee on Radiation Protection has set 170 millirems per
year above natural radiation as the maximum amount of radiation to which
the general public should be exposed,[16] one can conclude that 5 millirems
does seem insignificant and surely will not exhaust man's bank of 170
millirems a year.

The overwhelming pressure by the critics of nuclear energy has caused
the Atomic Energy Commission to finance studies of the reliability of
nuclear power plants. One such report, directed by Norman C. Rasmussen,
professor of nuclear engineering at M.I.T., has stirred quite a bit of
enthusiasm among the proponents of nuclear power. W. E. Cooper has
concluded, on the basis of Rasmussen's report, that "the consequences of
potential reactor accidents are no larger, and in many cases, are much
smaller than those of non-nuclear accidents having similar consequences."
Cooper went on to explain that the non-nuclear accidents compared were
fires, explosions, toxic chemical releases, dam failures, airplane
crashes and earthquakes.[17]

Other experts in the nuclear field have come to similar conclusions
based on Rasmussen's report. R. Gillette feels that a loss-of-reactor-
coolant accident would probably be one of the worst consequences and
that it would be considered a severe catastrophe. However, he concluded
that the possibility of such an accident would be one chance in ten
billion.[18] Rasmussen's report and the conclusions reached by its
interpreters surely make a case in favor of nuclear power.

Even though Rasmussen's report and the conclusions of its interpreters
add to the case for nuclear power, they lead us to another area which shows
even more evidence that favors nuclear power. The historical safety record
of nuclear power plants is impeccable. In fact, most of the studies of
nuclear power plant reliability were based on their unmarred past. Con-
firming this point of view, one proponent of nuclear power declares,
"Counting commercial and military power reactors, there have been almost
2,000 reactor-years of experience with no nuclear accidents."[19] Then
again, there are those who feel that there are risks involved in any new

technology. J. J. O'Connor feels exactly this way; however, he has
observed that, to date, there have been no "appreciable uncontrolled"
radiation releases from commercial nuclear plants.[20]

Whether these statistics have any bearing on the case for nuclear
energy or not, there are those who rightly question the safety of nuclear
power plants as compared to other sources of energy. Statistics regarding
the safety of fossil-fired plants have been recorded long before the
nuclear age. As far back as 1890, records of boiler explosions have been
recorded with as many as twenty deaths attributed to these explosions.[21]
In a recent four-year study, using an evenly distributed sample of nuclear,
fossil and hydro-electric power plants, it was disclosed that there were
no fatal or permanently disabling accidents in nuclear power plants. On
the other hand, there were six fatal or permanently disabling accidents
recorded for the non-nuclear plants in this four-year period.[22] After
reviewing the most recent statistics, one might question the safety of
fossil-fired power plants rather than the safety of nuclear power.

Aside from the statistics, there are those in the nuclear field who
make some rather strong accusations about the expertise of nuclear
energy's critics. According to W. E. Cooper, the motives of the critics
and the expertise of the technicians are "grossly unbalanced." Cooper
states,

> We are trying to balance the opposing motivations with
> groups which are grossly unbalanced in expertise. Here
> is the source of our present difficulties. We are trying
> to find the answers to difficult technical questions by
> using the adversary principle instead of impartial
> evaluations by experts, and the conflicts end up in the
> courts where decisions are made by people who have no
> technical competence at all![23]

Although Cooper's analogy seems harsh, he does point out a glimmer
of hope. He feels that the production of voluntary standards such as
the ASME Boiler and Pressure Vessel Code Nuclear Rules will help balance
this communication gap between the experts and non-experts.[24] Indeed,
this sort of a system would surely answer the questions asked about
nuclear power and it certainly stands to reason that there is a need to
bridge the communication gap.

7

The facts outlined thus far make a case for nuclear power, but one question remains unanswered. Is there a need for nuclear power plants? The proponents of nuclear energy use basic economics to show a need for nuclear energy. The current energy crisis and predictions of future energy demand would lead us to believe that there is a definite need for nuclear power. John N. Nassikas suggests that 70 percent of our energy demand in 1990 will be supplemented by fossil fuel, and by the year 1980 "half of our oil consumption will be imported if foreign supplies are available . . . ."[25]

With this large demand for fossil fuels and our dependence on foreign oil, a good portion of the energy demand is left to be supplemented by other sources such as nuclear, hydroelectric, or possibly solar power. Certainly the dependence on foreign oil alone shows a need for a supplemental energy source. One observer has concluded that "competition from nuclear power plants will eventually have a stabilizing effect on world oil prices" and that nuclear energy will be one-half as costly as other sources by 1980.[26]

The projected energy demands and the dependence on foreign oil do show a need for supplemental energy of some kind. Solar energy and wind energy are certainly possibilities, but they are fairly new and untested. Nuclear power has proved to be a safe and reliable source of energy and should be slated to supplement our future energy demands.

8

FOOTNOTES

[1]James Stokley, The New World of the Atom (New York: Ires Washburn, 1970), p. 5.

[2]Quoted by Richard Curtis and others, Perils of the Peaceful Atom: The Myth of Safe Nuclear Power Plants (New York: Doubleday, 1969), p. ix.

[3]Curtis, p. ix.

[4]John William Gofman and Arthur R. Tamplin, Poisoned Power: The Case Against Nuclear Power (Emmaus, Pennsylvania: Rodale Press, 1971), p. 8.

[5]Curtis, p. 11.

[6]Gofman and Tamplin, p. 92.

[7]Gofman and Tamplin, p. 8.

[8]Quoted by S. Rippon, "Making the Case for Nuclear Power," Nuclear Engineering International, 19 (September 1974), 741.

[9]Quoted by Stanley C. Gualt, "Appliances and Energy: One Expert's Outlook, "The [Cleveland] Plain Dealer, April 22, 1975, Energy Supplement, p. 2.

[10]Stokley, p. 169.

[11]Stokley, p. 169.

[12]Stokley, p. 171.

[13]Facts About Radiation (Toledo, Ohio: The Toledo Edison Company, 1968), p. 5.

[14]Stokley, p. 170.

[15]Facts About Radiation, p. 5.

[16]Curtis, p. 151.

[17]W. E. Cooper and others, "Nuclear Vessels are Safe," Mechanical Engineering, 97 (April 1975), 19.

[18]Quoted by J. Anderson, "J.C.A.E. Recommends 20 More Years for Price," Electrical World, 182 (September 15, 1974), 26.

[19]R. Gillette, "Nuclear Safety: Calculating The Odds of Disaster," Science, 185 (September 6, 1974), 839.

[20]J. J. O'Connor, "Boiler Explosions Last Month--A Historical Perspective," Power, 119 (May 1975), 9.

[21]O'Connor, p. 9.

[22]A. D. Bertolett, "Accident-rate Sample Favors Nuclear," Electrical World, 182 (July 15, 1974), 41.

9

[23]Cooper, p. 21.

[24]Cooper, p. 21.

[25]John N. Nassikas, "National Energy Policy: Directions and Developments," Proceedings of The American Power Conference, ed. Betty Haigh (Chicago: Institute of Technology, 1973), pp. 4-8.

[26]Rippon, p. 742.

10

BIBLIOGRAPHY

Anderson, J. "J.C.A.E. Recommends 20 More Years for Price,"
    Electrical World, 182 (September 15, 1974), 26.

Bertolett, A. D., and others. "Accident-rate Sample Favors Nuclear,"
    Electrical World, 182 (July 15, 1974), 40-41.

Cooper, W. E., and others. "Nuclear Vessels are Safe,"
    Mechanical Engineering, 97 (April 1975), 18-23.

Curtis, Richard, and others. Perils of the Peaceful Atom: The Myth
    of Safe Nuclear Power Plants. New York: Doubleday, 1969.

Facts About Radiation. Toledo, Ohio: The Toledo Edison Company, 1968.

Gillette, R. "Nuclear Safety: Calculating the Odds of Disaster,"
    Science, 185 (September 6, 1974), 838-39.

Gofman, John William, and Arthur R. Tamplin. Poisoned Power:
    The Case Against Nuclear Power. Emmaus, Pennsylvania:
    Rodale Press, 1971.

Gualt, Stanley C. "Appliances and Energy: One Expert's Outlook,"
    The [Cleveland] Plain Dealer, April 22, 1975, Energy Supplement,
    p. 2.

Hauster, R. L. "Nuclear Power Plant Reliability," Combustion, 46
    (August 1974), 28-29.

Nassikas, John N. "National Energy Policy: Directions and Developments,"
    Proceedings Of The American Power Conference, ed. Betty Haigh.
    Chicago: Institute of Technology, 1973, pp. 4-17.

O'Connor, J. J. "Boiler Explosions Last Month--A Historical Perspective,"
    Power, 119 (May 1975), 9.

"Purdue's Expert Looks at U. S. Energy Options Today,"
    The [Cleveland] Plain Dealer, April 22, 1975, Energy Supplement,
    p. 10.

Rippon, S. "Making the Case for Nuclear Power," Nuclear Engineering
    International, 19 (September 1974), 741-43.

Stokley, James. The New World of the Atom. New York: Ires Washburn,
    1970.

NUCLEAR POWER, FOSSIL FUEL, AND ALTERNATIVES: 1980

by

Shirley C. Marlyne

English 103

March 19, 1980

for

Mr. Kaminsky

OUTLINE

NUCLEAR POWER, FOSSIL FUEL, AND ALTERNATIVES: 1980

THESIS: Based on evidence that a catastrophic nuclear accident can
          happen and that nuclear power as an economical source of
          electricity has failed, nuclear power plants should be phased
          out and replaced with fossil fuel plants until other sources
          of electricity can be mobilized.

I.   How did the country arrive at a point where Three Mile Island was
     possible?

     A.   After World War II, the nation began a search for peaceful
          uses of atomic energy.

          1.   The first production of nuclear-generated electricity was
               the beginning of a hopeful era.

          2.   The already dangerously close relationship between public
               power companies and government agencies was greatly
               intensified.

     B.   The demand for electric power grew in enormous increments until
          1973, with the U. S. using many times as much electricity as
          other industrial countries.

     C.   The use of fossil fuels to produce electricity creates a number
          of problems.

          1.   Dependence on foreign oil contributes heavily to an
               unfavorable balance of payments.

          2.   Pollution from fossil fuels is a serious threat to the
               environment.

          3.   The reservoir of fossil fuels is being depleted.

II. Nuclear energy has not proved to be a safe, reliable, or cheap
     source of electric power.

     A.   There are safety hazards in every phase of production.

          1.   Mining and preparing of radioactive elements are in
               themselves dangerous.

          2.   No adequate solution has been found for the disposal
               of radioactive wastes.

          3.   Scientists disagree over the undoubted harmful levels
               of radiation.

     B.   The possibility of terrorism is always present.

     C.   Nuclear power production has been subject to numerous inter-
          ruptions, some of them safety related and all contributing to
          poor and costly performance.

III.   Phase-out of nuclear power generation is imperative.

    A.   Petroleum and gas contributions could be maintained at their
       present level.

    B.   The use of coal could be gradually increased.

IV.   Mobilizing alternatives to both nuclear and fossil fuels will require
a long-term effort.

    A.   Numerous alternatives are in varying stages of research and
       development.

    B.   Caution must be exercised relative to safety, reliability, and
       economy of each alternative fuel source.

    C.   Conservation may be the most important alternative.

The first quarter of 1979 saw a rush of events that shook the nuclear establishment and stiffened the will of the anti-nuclear movement.

On New Year's Day, a court in the State of New York reached the conclusion that "it is impossible to answer in general terms the question of which is cheaper," after two years of testimony comparing nuclear and coal-fired power generation.[1] Less than a month later, the Nuclear Regulatory Commission (NRC) withdrew its endorsement of what is known as the Rasmussen Study, the preparation of which had been sponsored by the NRC itself at a cost of three million dollars and issued in 1975. Named for its director, Dr. Norman C. Rasmussen of MIT, the study had concluded that a nuclear power plant accident was approximately as remote as a meteor's striking and devastating a city.[2]

Two more blows to the nuclear establishment came on March 3, 1979: The NRC ordered five nuclear plants closed because of their possible vulnerability to earthquakes, and a special presidential committee questioned the safety of storing commercial nuclear wastes underground.[3] Finally, on March 29, 1979, Three Mile Island blew up--not physically, but certainly psychologically--for nuclear adherent and adversary alike. The "event,"[4] at Unit 2 of Metropolitan Edison's Three Mile Island complex, began a series of daily--sometimes hourly--conflicting announcements of what had happened and what could happen.[5]

Three Mile Island was the most striking of a number of occurrences that set the broad middle ground to thinking. Afterward, many who had been on neither side of the nuclear question joined the anti-nuclear community in the belief that, based on the evidence an extremely serious nuclear accident can happen and that nuclear power as an economical source of electricity has failed, nuclear power plants should be phased out and replaced with more fossil fuel plants.

Now, in 1980, it may be helpful to consider how the country arrived at a point where Three Mile Island was possible. Emerging from World

2

War II, scientist and layman alike gratefully embraced the potential for peaceful uses of the atom. Intense ethical doubts raised by Hiroshima and Nagasaki were sinking into the national conscience, and the discovery of a major use for nuclear energy that ostensibly caused no grotesque mutations or other destruction made the burden of nuclear knowledge more tolerable.

About the public mood after production of the first 200,000 watts of electricity from nuclear power in the United States, Joseph DiCerto comments: "Suddenly, atomic energy became beneficent magic; the atom would solve all our energy problems, providing unlimited clean energy forever. Or so many people believed."[6] In the continued euphoria, most people paid little attention to the further development and production of nuclear power and the attendant problems. R. A. Brightsen, now a senior executive at the NRC, writes,

> During the Fifties and Sixties, a very close working relationship developed between a small number of large private companies and the federal government. The federal organizations that financed and supported the early acquisition and development of nuclear expertise for the private corporations were principally the Navy, the Atomic Energy Commission, and the Joint Committee on Atomic Energy of the U. S. Congress. As time went on, the relationships between vendors and the AEC became even more intimate. This situation was protected from public scrutiny by apathy--and by secrecy when convenient--and shielded from congressional scrutiny by the all-powerful Joint Committee [on Atomic Energy] on Capitol Hill. In short, there was a closed nuclear club, and few voices were raised in objection.[7]

While experts were pressing to increase the nuclear contribution, the nation was using electricity at spectacular levels. Quoting from Department of Energy statistics, David Bodansky of the University of Washington Physics Department reports that from 1948 to 1978, electricity production by the utility industry "increased almost eightfold, while total energy consumption rose by a factor of 2.4."[8] It was an era when the electric slave was sent to perform every conceivable task, from the smallest to the most arduous. Americans were on a binge of electricity-consumption that would not begin to ease until the seventies. The growth rate has declined since 1973;[9] even so, in 1976, we were still "using twice as much [electric power] per capita as the British, two and one-half times as much as the Germans, and four and one-half times as much as the Japanese."[10]

As the power plants hummed away, producing electricity at a rate that doubled every decade, they themselves required a larger and larger share of the country's total energy supply, principally in the form of oil and gas but supplemented by coal (and in some areas by hydroelectric generation).[11] The burning of fossil fuels polluted the air and water with hundreds of tons of chemicals and solid particles while raising air and water temperatures with "wasted heat," a byproduct of all energy transfer.[12]

The troubles with fossil fuels did not end with the introduction of "scrubbers" that remove the more dangerous pollutants, such as sulfuric acid. As less domestic oil was pumped from the ground, more oil had to be purchased from the Middle Eastern countries, which had, by the mid-seventies, fully realized the demand for their product and had increased its price accordingly. By the late seventies, the difference between the dollar value of imports and exports (balance of payments) being made by the United States turned sharply unfavorable because of oil imports, thus weakening the dollar against other currencies and increasing the inflation rate.[13] Concurrently, environmentalists, geologists, and others were warning that the earth's reservoirs of fossil fuels, particularly oil and gas, were being rapidly depleted.

All these difficulties with fossil fuels helped to highlight nuclear energy as the answer to the demand for electric power.

The idea is attractive, for "one ounce of uranium has roughly the same potential as . . . 100 tons of coal."[14] The pellets of uranium in the fuel rods of a reactor are about twice as thick as a pencil and a little over half an inch long. They cost between five and ten dollars each, and each pellet contains the energy of a ton of coal or four barrels of crude oil.[15] Few would disagree that if a nuclear electric power plant could be made absolutely safe--from its outermost parts to the core of every nuclear reactor--and if the process

4

of preparing fuel from radioactive substances were totally free
from all hazards, then nuclear electric power would be the most
perfect power yet discovered. Unfortunately, neither of these
conditions has been met.

    Miners of uranium ore are exposed to radioactive gases and
solid particles that cause lung cancers at a rate six to nine times
greater than the rate in the general population. The milling process
causes lymphatic cancers from the breathing of uranium dust at a
rate four times greater than that in the general population.[16]

    If, before March 1979, one had asked whether there had ever
been an accident in a nuclear power plant, the reply would have
depended on the role of the person questioned. Brightsen, the NRC
executive, writing before Three Mile Island, said,

> Despite some minor accidents and close calls, and despite the
> growth and intervention of anti-nuclear groups in the reactor-
> licensing process and increasingly shrill demonstrations, the
> incontrovertible fact was that civilian nuclear power had been
> unblemished by a serious reactor accident during its entire
> two-decade existence.[17]

Even after Three Mile Island, power company officials seemed determined
to deny the possibility of accident, choosing, instead, to call the
occurrences an "event."

    But the literature of the anti-nuclear writers is full of references
to accidents before Three Mile Island. It was predictable that Ralph
Nader, gadfly of the establishment, would write about an accident at
the Fermi plutonium reactor located outside of Detroit.[18] Yet so did
David Inglis, professor of physics at the University of Massachusetts,
Amherst.[19]

    Perhaps the question of whether there has been a nuclear accident
is not as important as the question of whether one could happen and
what its consequences might be. Daniel F. Ford and Henry W. Kendall
have described what could happen:

> Layman might expect that a nuclear explosion could occur in
> some abnormal circumstance at a nuclear power plant, but this
> is not possible. Fissionable uranium represents only about
> 3% of the uranium in a power reactor and is too diluted to
> explode. The most serious accident a reactor can undergo is
> one that involves overheating and melting of the reactor core,

5

accompanied by leakage of radioactive materials into the
surrounding area. An accident that developed to melting would
involve breaching of all man-made structures with more than
100 tons of white-hot radioactive material melting its way
hundreds of feet into the ground. The molten mass would include billions of curies of radioactivity, more than one-fifth
of it gaseous or volatile. A large reactor prior to a periodic
refueling will contain about two tons of radioactive material
mixed within about 100 tons of slightly enriched uranium
dioxide. For comparison the Hiroshima atomic bomb produced
about two pounds of similar material. The accident is
colloquially referred to in the nuclear industry as the "China
syndrome," reflecting the direction, although not the destination,
of the molten material. Release of very large quantities of
radioactivity appears highly likely in a "China" accident owing
to the difficulty of retaining the gaseous materials as the
core melts downward.[20]

Added to the hazards of accident are the hazards of radioactive

wastes. The disposal of such wastes is a problem that is, so far,

without solution. Most of the elements used in and produced by the

nuclear fuel cycle are radioactive, but the time over which they

remain radioactive varies widely. Certain iodine isotopes lose their

radioactivity in about thirty days; plutonium 239 will be reasonably

safe after a quarter of a million years. Disposal methods up to now

have included raw dumping into the oceans, dumping in sealed containers

(now found by the Navy to be leaking), burial in cannisters in salt

mines, and temporary storage behind thick concrete walls, while

awaiting a "permanent" solution. Burial of the wastes in places that

are not subject to earthquakes, terrorism, underground seepage, or

accidental disturbance is believed to be the optimum solution, but

the earliest estimated time such a site might be available is 1988.[21]

Why is it so important to keep radioactive materials tightly

contained? The cells of the body--and within them, the chromosomes

that carry out genetic replication--are violated by radiation.

Radiation causes mutation, the loss of one or more molecules from

a chromosome. And mutations often cause cancer, leukemia, and

related diseases. The NRC has set a limit of five whole-body rems

(5,000 millirems) of radiation per year for workers in areas of

high radioactivity. (The average person in the United States gets

about 200 millirems a year from all sources, such as X-rays, emissions

from television sets, and the naturally occurring background

6

radiation.) Dr. Karl Z. Morgan of the Georgia Institute of

Technology, former director of the Health Physics Division of the

Oak Ridge National Laboratory, is one of the many experts who be-

lieve that there is no amount of radiation that is entirely harmless:

> An overwhelming amount of data shows there is no safe level of
> exposure and there is no dose of radiation so low that the risk
> of malignancy is zero. So the question is not: Is there a risk
> in low-level exposure? The question is: How great is the risk?
> Or how great may a particular radiation risk be before it exceeds
> the expected benefits, such as those from medical radiography or
> nuclear power?[22]

And the possibility of terrorism is always present. Although

nuclear fuel for power plant reactors is not of weapons grade, plutonium

that can be extracted from spent uranium pellets can be refined into a

strength sufficient to make an atomic bomb. Also, the newer so-called

"breeder" reactors such as power the Fermi power plant outside Detroit

use plutonium as their raw material.[23] Theft of materials for con-

struction of bombs is only one of the security threats. Among the

others are the possibility of a plant takeover by revolutionists or

other violent persons and the bombing of a plant either from inside

or from the air, with release of radioactive elements into the

surrounding area.

Another problem encountered in nuclear electric production is

that of keeping the plants in operation. In 1978, the average

capacity factor (the amount of power actually produced as a percentage

of that which could be produced at full capacity) was only 65% for 58

nuclear power plants in the United States. According to Robert Goble

and Christoph Hohenemser, the 1979 capacity factors, not yet avail-

able, will reflect the long period of outage of Three Mile Island's

Number 2 Unit.[24] Nuclear plants or parts of them are more frequently

shut down than are coal- or oil-fired plants. No one questions the

prudence of these measures, but every stoppage contributes to the

cost of producing nuclear power that ultimately must be borne by

the consumer.

Perhaps the nation can bear the money cost of nuclear power, but it

cannot risk the hazards. A phase-out of nuclear power, therefore, seems

imperative. With coal already contributing 44% of the nation's total
fuel for electricity production, it seems feasible to keep the petroleum
and gas contributions at the current level, 17% and 14%, respectively,
and to increase gradually coal's contribution while nuclear power is
phased out.[25] To be sure, the use of coal is not without risk. The
United States has a poor safety record in mining coal when compared
with that of other industrial countries. But these statistics are an
indication that we could, and should, carry out a much better program
of mining safety.[26] Furthermore, regrettable as a single mining
injury or fatality is, the threat of a nuclear accident that could
kill or cripple thousands seems the greater risk.

The task before us is a huge one. Finding alternatives to both
nuclear and fossil fuels will be an arduous undertaking. John Isaacs
and Walter Schmitt, for example, make this gloomy prediction:

> Man is rapidly emerging as a geophysical and geochemical force
> approaching the magnitude of other great natural systems.
> Energy consumption by humans in the early 21st century is pro-
> jected to exceed individually the natural energy flux of rivers
> and tides, that of all the waves and swells and currents of
> the oceans of the planet, as well as the total flux of geo-
> thermal heat.[27]

To effect a transfer of energy equalling the winds and waves, man
must find the resources for the task. Wind power, tidal power, and
geothermal energy are often mentioned as the "renewable" resources
that will take over as the fossil fuels run out. Also frequently
mentioned are solar power, solid waste, hydrogen fuels, nitrogen
fixation in the air, and lasars.[28] But according to scientists,
none of these sources is ready right now to make a significant
contribution to man's energy requirements. David Rose has said,
"Until about A. D. 2000, the major choices are nuclear power and fossil
fuels (of various sorts), or nothing, in varying proportions."[29]

Nevertheless, if the same human and fiscal resources as were
assigned to ready nuclear power are pledged to mobilizing these renewable sources, then surely some or all can be available in sufficient
quantity by the turn of the century. Extreme caution must be exercised
relative to safety, reliability, and economy of each alternative fuel
source. The nuclear experience must not be repeated.

8

    Finally, conservation may be the most important alternative. In its report, A Time to Choose, the Energy Policy Project of the Ford Foundation has put forth Zero Energy Growth (ZEG) as one of the alternatives of the future. The report describes ZEG as a condition not requiring austerity but one in which more emphasis would be placed on services and less on making things.[30] In the end, all of us have a responsibility for reaching decisions about the circumstances that affect us. As Goble and Hohenemser suggest, "Non-experts, including the general public and their elected representatives in Congress, must decide what constitutes the 'best buy,' both from economic and safety points of view."[31]

FOOTNOTES

[1]Harold Faber, "Cheapest Utility Fuel? Can't Decide, Court Says," The New York Times, January 1, 1979, Section A, p. 1.

[2]David Burnham, "Nuclear Agency Revokes Support for Safety Study," The New York Times, January 20, 1979, Section A, p. 1.

[3]Richard Halloran, "Five Atomic Plants Shut Down," The New York Times, January 20, 1979, Section A, p. 1, and David Burnham, "Safe Nuclear Waste Disposal Held as Still Unsolved," The New York Times, March 14, 1979, Section A, p. 19.

[4]"A Nuclear Nightmare," Time, 116, No. 17 (April 9, 1979), 8.

[5]"A Nuclear Nightmare," pp. 11-12.

[6]Joseph J. DiCerto, The Electric Wishing Well: The Solution to the Energy Crisis (New York: Macmillan Publishing Company, 1976), p. 61.

[7]R. A. Brightsen, "The Way to Save Nuclear Power," Fortune, 100 (September 10, 1979), 127.

[8]David Bodansky, "Electricity Generation for the Near Term," Science, 207 (February 15, 1980), 721.

[9]Bodansky, p. 721.

[10]Atlantic Council of the United States, Nuclear Fuels Policy Working Group, Nuclear Fuels Policy (Boulder, Colorado: Westview Press, 1976), p. 2.

[11]DiCerto, p. 60.

[12]DiCerto, pp. 17-19.

[13]Bodansky, p. 721.

[14]Ralph Nader and John Abbotts, The Menace of Atomic Energy, rev. ed. (New York: W. W. Norton & Company, Inc., 1979), p. 68.

[15]Kenneth F. Weaver, "The Promise and Peril of Nuclear Energy," National Geographic, 156, No. 4 (April 1979), 461.

[16]For additional commentary on this point, see Arell S. Schurgin and Thomas C. Hollocher, "Radiation Induced Lung Cancers among Uranium Miners" and Thomas C. Hollocher and James J. MacKenzie, "Radiation Hazards Associated with Uranium Mill Operations" in Union of Concerned Scientists, The Nuclear Fuel Cycle: A Survey of the Public Health, Environmental, and National Security Effects of Nuclear Power, rev. ed. (Cambridge: The M. I. T. Press, 1975), pp. 6-69.

[17]Brightsen, p. 128.

[18]Nader and Abbotts, p. 142.

10

[19]David Rittenhouse Inglis, <u>Nuclear Energy: Its Physics and Its Social Challenge</u> (Reading, Massachusetts: Addison-Wesley Publishing Company, 1973), p. 78.

[20]Daniel F. Ford and Henry W. Kendall, "Catastrophic Nuclear Reactor Accidents," Union of Concerned Scientists, pp. 71-73.

[21]Weaver, p. 483.

[22]As quoted by Weaver, p. 467.

[23]Nader and Abbotts, p. 142.

[24]Robert L. Goble and Christoph Hohenemser, "Nuclear Power Plant Performance: An Update," <u>Environment</u>, 21 (September-October 1979), 33.

[25]Bodansky, p. 722.

[26]Ford Foundation Energy Policy Project, <u>A Time to Choose</u> (Cambridge: Ballinger Publishing Company, 1974), p. 198.

[27]John D. Isaacs and Walter R. Schmitt, "Ocean Energy: Forms and Prospects," <u>Science</u>, 207 (January 18, 1980), 265.

[28]DiCerto, p. 60.

[29]As quoted by Bodansky, p. 722.

[30]Ford Foundation, p. 15.

[31]Goble and Hohenemser, p. 36.

11

BIBLIOGRAPHY

Atlantic Council of the United States, Nuclear Fuels Policy Working
    Group. Nuclear Fuels Policy. Boulder, Colorado: Westview
    Press, 1976.

Brightsen, R. A. "The Way to Save Nuclear Power," Fortune, 100
    (September 10, 1979), 126-218 .

Burnham, David. "Nuclear Agency Revokes Support for Safety Study,"
    The New York Times, January 20, 1979, Section A, p. 1.

    _____. "Safe Nuclear Waste Disposal Held as Still Unsolved,"
    The New York Times, March 14, 1979, Section A, p. 19.

DiCerto, Joseph J. The Electric Wishing Well: The Solution to the
    Energy Crisis. New York: Macmillan Publishing Company, 1976.

Faber, Harold. "Cheapest Utility Fuel? Can't Decide, Court Says,"
    The New York Times, January 1, 1979, Section A, p. 1.

Ford Foundation Energy Policy Project. A Time to Choose. Cambridge:
    Ballinger Publishing Company, 1974.

Goble, Robert L., and Christoph Hohenemser. "Nuclear Power Plant
    Performance: An Update," Environment, 21 (September-October 1979),
    32-36.

Gofman, John W., and Arthur R. Tamplin. Poisoned Power: The Case
    against Nuclear Power. Emmaus, Pennsylvania: Rodale Press, 1971.

Halloran, Richard. "Five Atomic Plants Ordered Shut Down," The New
    York Times, March 14, 1979, Section A, p. 1.

Inglis, David Rittenhouse. Nuclear Energy: Its Physics and Its Social
    Challenge. Reading, Massachusetts: Addison-Wesley Publishing
    Company, 1973.

Isaacs, John D., and Walter R. Schmitt. "Ocean Energy: Forms and
    Prospects," Science, 207 (January 18, 1980), 265-273.

Nader, Ralph, and John Abbotts. The Menace of Atomic Energy, rev. ed.
    New York: W. W. Norton & Company, 1979.

Union of Concerned Scientists. The Nuclear Fuel Cycle: A Survey of
    the Public Health, Environmental, and National Security Effects
    of Nuclear Power, rev. ed. Cambridge: The M. I. T. Press, 1975.

Weaver, Kenneth F. "The Promise and Peril of Nuclear Energy,"
    National Geographic, 156, No. 4 (April 1979), 461-465.

PART 4

STYLE

**Introductory Note:
Refining Your Use
of Language**

15
"PROPER WORDS IN
PROPER PLACES"

16
STYLISTIC PROBLEMS
AND THEIR SOLUTIONS

INTRODUCTORY NOTE
Refining Your Use of Language

Writing a well-organized theme is one thing. Writing a well-organized *good* theme is another, more complicated thing. Thousands of rusty filing cabinets and dusty shelves are filled with perfectly well-organized writings that got their authors nothing but bored and irritated readers—not to mention poor grades. These writings all had a thesis; they all attempted to prove the thesis; they all had an introduction, a body, and a conclusion. The paragraphs in these writings all had topic sentences, and the topic sentences were all connected to the thesis. In short, these writings followed all the directions and advice that this book has given so far. What went wrong?

The answer to that begins with another question. Do we waste time praising a relative's remodeled home because the sofa is in the living room, the stove in the kitchen, and the carpeting on the floors? We all know that if the sofa had been crammed into the bathroom and the stove dumped on top of the coffee table, we'd be faced with a disaster, but we generally take logical organization for granted. Like a home without this organization, an unorganized piece of writing is an obvious disaster. In a reasonably well-organized work, however, the reader simply assumes the structure is satisfactory and then concentrates on other matters. The reader is right, too. Few homeowners have ever received compliments for their good sense in putting the bed in the bedroom, and few writers have ever been praised for their superb mastery of topic sentences.

When we do praise writers, we generally praise them because they use language well, because they know how to work with words. We may think we liked a particular story or article because its ideas were powerful and interesting, but it was the words that *made* the ideas powerful and interesting. The same ideas expressed by a less skillful writer would appear flat and boring. Compare, for instance, the simple strength of the Christmas wish, "Peace on earth, good will to men," to this grotesque version of the same idea:

> All concerned and involved individuals at this point in time aspire to and wish for universal nonbelligerency militarywise and benevolence-oriented interpersonal relationships between persons.

A good writer knows how to handle language and can fascinate us with instructions on how to use automobile directional signals; a poor writer does not know how to handle language and can bore us with a passionate love letter.

This section of the book, then, discusses ways of "refining your use of language." We can assume that grammar and organization are no longer major problems and start to concentrate on style—how to write not only correctly, but *well*.

395

CHAPTER 15

"PROPER WORDS IN PROPER PLACES"

Jonathan Swift once defined good style as "proper words in proper places." Gustave Flaubert, the great French novelist, felt that the writer's craft was embodied in the quest for *le mot juste,* the right word. On one level or another, everyone who writes is involved in the same quest. Total success, if it has ever been achieved, probably depends on such vital but indefinable qualities as sensitivity, perceptiveness, creativity, and dozens of others. Fortunately, few people expect or demand total success. Nearly all writers can learn to hit the right word more often than they used to simply by becoming more alert to the possibilities of language.

DENOTATION AND CONNOTATION

Traditionally, the most logical place to begin thinking about right and wrong words is in the distinction between *denotation* and *connotation.* A few examples will help clarify that distinction.

Let's assume that you have finished with the drudgery of getting a diploma and are now the head of a successful advertising agency. A major motor corporation wants you to handle the campaign introducing a new compact car. Would you recommend calling the car the Giraffe, the Porcupine, or the Hawk?

Let's assume now that instead of becoming a big shot in an advertising agency, you've become a humble schoolteacher. You have almost finished writing reports to the parents of your fourth graders. You've saved the most difficult for last: what can you put down about your big problem, Suzy Mae? Do you write, "Suzy Mae has not done a single bit of honest-to-goodness work all year," or "Suzy Mae has not been working up to her full capacity"?

Now let's assume that, big shot or schoolteacher, you wound up making the wrong decision. You're depressed and annoyed. All you want to do is forget your problems. At a weekend party, you have too much to drink. "Oh, brother!" says your loyal spouse, "did you ever get looped last night!"

"Looped?" you answer. "Nonsense! I just got a little high!"

What do all these stories have in common? Just this: meaning comes as much or more from the *connotations* of words as from their *denotations*. The denotation of a word is its explicit, surface meaning, its bare "dictionary meaning." Call the new car anything at all; whatever name you come up with will *denote* a certain mechanical device with set wheelbase and rear headroom measurements, fuel tank capacity, engine size, and so on. Describe Suzy Mae harshly or kindly; your comments will denote that she does not do enough work. Think of yourself as "high" or "looped"; both words denote the condition of having had too much to drink.

But an advertising agency that thinks only of the denotations of words will soon go broke. A teacher who thinks it doesn't matter how Suzy Mae is described as long as the message comes through that she is lazy will soon be in serious trouble with the girl's parents. Married couples who don't realize that words like *looped* and *nag* and *scold* and *love* have meanings far beyond their denotations will probably find their lives turning into one long quarrel. Most words have connotations as well as denotations. The *connotation* of a word is its implicit meaning, the meaning derived from the atmosphere, the vibrations, the emotions that we associate with the word. The connotations are not always entered next to a word in the dictionary, but they are associated with the word in people's minds. Words such as *Las Vegas* or *South Africa*, for example, simply denote a particular city or country—a mere geographical location; but they also have an emotional significance for most people that has nothing to do with geography or dictionaries. Again, consider a word like *marijuana*. Its denotation is perfectly straightforward—a species of plant that can be used as a narcotic—but its connotations are endless, ranging from relaxation and self-expression on one side to crime and decadence on the other. Moreover, no one could have a valid idea of the full meaning of the word without being aware of these connotations.

Let's look more closely at how connotations work to determine our responses. We all probably agree that among Giraffe, Porcupine, and Hawk, the last name is the only reasonable choice for the new car. It may be no stroke of genius, as names go, but it wins easily against the competition. For most people, the idea of a hawk carries with it connotations of power, speed, and perhaps freedom and beauty as well. These are concepts that motivate people who buy cars, no matter how loudly they may proclaim that their sole interest is economy or "just transportation." Consider the animal names in recent use for car models and notice how many connote power, speed, or both: Cougar, Mustang, Impala, Bobcat, Skylark, Bronco, Colt, Rabbit, Thunderbird, Firebird, Roadrunner. The name Hawk, then, has certain connotations that might be helpful in marketing the car.

What are the connotations of Giraffe? We think of tremendous—even absurd—size, of something that basically looks funny. Zoologists may tell us that giraffes are actually capable of running extremely fast, but the average person associates the animals far more with awkwardness than with speed. What about Porcupine? When the average person bothers to think about porcupines at all, the connotations are likely to be of pesky creatures that sensible folks try to stay away from.

Giraffe, Porcupine, and Hawk denote the same product, to be sure. We can assume that whatever name is given to the new car, the car's performance will be the same. But people respond to the connotations of words, and it is hard to conceive of finding many buyers for the Giraffe or the Porcupine. One of Shakespeare's most famous lines is, "A rose by any other name would smell as sweet." From a strictly scientific point of view he was undoubtedly correct. In all other respects, he was dead wrong.

Developing a sensitivity to the connotations of words is a valuable asset for any writer. Was the person who had too much to drink *inebriated, intoxicated, drunk, looped, smashed, tipsy, high, crocked, pickled, loaded,* or *blotto?* You have all these words to choose from, and many more besides. Is an overweight person *plump, fat, pudgy, obese, chubby, portly, chunky, corpulent, stout,* or *stocky?* Few greater compliments can be paid to writers than to say that they have a knack for choosing the right word. That knack does not come simply from having a large vocabulary, but from sensing the fine distinctions in connotation that separate two words with similar denotations.

A well developed sense of the importance of connotations is also a valuable asset for any reader, especially any reader who happens to be taking an English course. Most English instructors, after all, ask you to write about the material you have read; you are probably licked before you start unless you have read that material alertly. We have seen how connotations determine meaning, and if you miss the connotations of many words, the basic meaning of a selection may easily elude you. Beyond this, once you begin discussing a writer's style, you are bound to feel rather helpless unless you know something about connotations. "Compare the tone in Love Poem A to the tone in Love Poem B." "How does the author's use of irony add to the effect of the story?" "Why does the author use the word 'drowsy' instead of 'sleepy' in line 7?" These may or may not be tough questions. Remember, though, that style gives life to language and that the fundamental element of style is the writer's choice of words.

Exercise A

Rearrange each group of words by connotation, from the least favorable term to the most favorable. In many cases opinions will differ; there are few purely right and purely wrong answers.

1. knowledgeable, bright, shrewd, smart, brainy
2. look, ogle, stare, glower, gaze
3. gaudy, loud, colorful, flashy, vulgar
4. unusual, crazy, weird, eccentric, odd
5. drink, cocktail, booze, rotgut, alcoholic beverage
6. plump, chunky, obese, chubby, fat
7. police officer, cop, fuzz, pig, smokey
8. handsome, cute, good-looking, sharp, attractive
9. pretty, gorgeous, lovely, stunning, beautiful
10. laugh, chuckle, giggle, guffaw, snicker

Exercise B

All the words in the parentheses can be used in the sentences in which they appear. Discuss how the meaning of the sentence changes, depending on which word is used.

1. His roommates thought his plan was (daring, foolhardy).
2. The football team needs a more (enthusiastic, strongly motivated) quarterback.
3. My father says that as a young man he (loved, adored) Marilyn Monroe.
4. This satire of American politics is unusually (funny, entertaining).
5. Investments in municipal bonds are likely to be more (dangerous, risky, insecure) than many people think.
6. Sometimes (solitude, loneliness, isolation) can be good for the soul.
7. Jean found the music (interesting, intriguing).
8. He was as smart as (a fox, a trained dog in a circus, Albert Einstein).
9. Congresswoman Saunders is a gifted (speaker, talker, orator).

10. Her excuse for being late was completely (unbelievable, fantastic).

ABSTRACT WRITING AND CONCRETE WRITING

The distinction between denotation and connotation, while valuable to a writer, can sometimes seem a bit remote and philosophical. It's easier to see the immediate, practical consequences to a writer's quest for the right word in the distinction between abstract writing and concrete writing.

Abstract writing is writing that lacks specific details and is filled with vague, indefinite words and broad, general statements. Every piece of writing needs generalizations, of course, and vague words such as *nice* and *interesting* can be useful. But writing that is dominated by such words is abstract writing, and abstract writing is the main cause of bored readers. It is often a reflection of lazy or careless thinking. It can interfere with full communication of meaning. It prevents many students from developing their themes adequately. ("I've already said all I have to say. How am I supposed to get 300 more words on this subject?")

Abstract writing occurs when someone writes:

Too much poverty exists in this country.
INSTEAD OF
I see one-third of a nation ill-housed, ill-clad, ill-nourished.

Mr. Jones is a tough grader.
INSTEAD OF
Mr. Jones flunked 75% of his class and gave no higher than a C to the students who passed.

Don't fire until they're extremely close.
INSTEAD OF
Don't fire until you see the whites of their eyes.

The story is quite amusing in places, but basically is very serious.
INSTEAD OF
Underneath the slapstick humor, the story presents a bitter attack on materialism and snobbishness.

Religious faith is important, but practical considerations are also important.
INSTEAD OF
Trust in God, and keep your powder dry.

Nothing is technically wrong with the above examples of abstract writing, but we need only compare them to the rewritten concrete versions to see their basic inadequacy. They convey less information. They are less interesting. They have less impact. There is nothing wrong with them except that they are no good.

Specific Details

The use of specific details is the most direct way to avoid abstract writing. We tend to get irritated with a politician—or college dean—who, when confronted by a crucial issue, releases a press statement declaring, "We will give this matter our careful consideration." We get irritated not because the matter doesn't require careful consideration, but because the abstractness of the statement makes us suspect that we have just received a strong whiff of hot air. That suspicion will probably decrease significantly if the statement goes on to tell us the names of the people who will confer on this issue next Monday under orders to present recommendations within two weeks, those recommendations to be acted on inside of forty-eight hours. In this case, the specific details have served to support the generalization, have given us a clear notion of what the generalization means, and have helped create an impression of seriousness and sincerity.

Politicians and college deans are not the only people who sometimes seem too fond of hot air. Much of the material we read every day is abstract: flabby, dull, vague, and essentially meaningless. Like hot air, it lacks real body, real substance. The sports columnist writes, "The team should do better this year," and leaves it at that, instead of adding, "It should finish in third or fourth place and even has a fighting chance for the pennant." The teacher writes an angry letter saying, "This school ignores all vital needs of the faculty," and sounds like just another crank unless the letter goes on and points to *specific* needs that have in fact been ignored.

Student writing, from essay exams to themes in composition courses, could be vastly improved if more attention were paid to eliminating excessive abstraction and adding specific details. The more specific details, the less chance of hot air. Students should not tolerate the same things in their own writing that antagonize them in someone else's. Our use of language, not to mention our level of thought, would probably improve a hundredfold if we established an informal rule *never* to make an unsupported general statement, a general statement not backed up by specific details.

This rule sounds easy enough, but it means what it says. It means a writer should never try to get by with sentences such as, "The day was too hot"; "The hero of the story was very ambitious";

"The establishment is corrupt"; "The Industrial Revolution brought about many changes." These sentences are neither ungrammatical nor necessarily incorrect, but if they are not backed up by specific details they are worthless. "The day was too hot" is uninteresting and unpersuasive. *Back it up.* The reader should know that the temperature was 93 degrees, that Bill's sweaty glasses kept slipping off his nose, that even the little kids who usually filled the street were inside trying to keep cool, that a cocker spaniel who had managed to find a spot of shade was too exhausted and miserable to bother brushing away the flies. Whatever the piece of writing—a letter of application for a job, an analysis of a short story, a final exam in history—specific details give the writing life and conviction that abstractions alone can never achieve.

One more point about specific details: within reason, *the more specific the better.* As long as the detail is relevant—as long, that is, as it backs up the generalization and is not instantly obvious as too trivial for consideration—the writer is unlikely to go wrong by being too specific. On a history exam, a student may generalize, "In the Revolutionary War, the Americans had many difficulties." As specific support for that statement, the student may go on to write, "The number of Tories was quite large." But better in all respects would be, "Tories numbered as much as 30% of the population." The more specific the better, and one can almost always be more specific. Eventually, it is true, one can defeat one's purpose; it would be a mistake to give the reader the names and addresses of all the Tories during the Revolutionary War. The writing would then become so overwhelmed by specifics that the major point would be lost. Elementary common sense is usually the best guide in preventing that kind of mistake, and in actual practice few student writers run up against the problem of being too specific.

To summarize: support all your generalizations with relevant specific details. Remember that, within reason, the more specific the details, the better the writing.

Abstract (weak)

The telephone is a great scientific achievement, but it can also be a great inconvenience. Who could begin to count the number of times that phone calls have come from unwelcome people or on unwelcome occasions? Telephones make me nervous.

More Specific (better)

The telephone is a great scientific achievement, but it can also be a great pain. I get calls from bill collectors, hurt relatives, salespeople, charities, and angry neighbors. The calls always seem to come at the worst times, too. They've interrupted my meals, my baths, my parties, my sleep. I couldn't get along without telephones, but sometimes they make me a nervous wreck.

Still More Specific (much better)

The telephone is a great scientific achievement, but it can also be a great big headache. More often than not, that cheery ringing in my ears brings messages from the Ace Bill Collecting Agency, my mother (who is feeling snubbed for the fourth time that week), salesmen of encyclopedias and magazines, solicitors for the Policeman's Ball and Disease of the Month Foundation, and neighbors complaining about my dog. That's not to mention frequent wrong numbers—usually for someone named "Arnie." The calls always seem to come at the worst times, too. They've interrupted steak dinners, hot tubs, Friday night parties, and Saturday morning sleep-ins. There's no escape. Sometimes I wonder if there are any telephones in padded cells.

Exercise

Invent two or three specific details to back up each of the following generalizations. Use some imagination. Remember, the more specific the better. Don't settle for a detail like "He reads many books" to support the statement, "My teacher is very intellectual."

1. Movies are my great escape.
2. Dr. Williams is the typical absentminded professor.
3. It's possible to tell a great deal about people from the way they shake hands.
4. The importance of a college education has been exaggerated.
5. The 55 mile per hour speed limit has added in some ways to the dangers of driving.
6. Our society systematically discriminates against left-handed people.
7. Essay examinations cannot be evaluated fairly.
8. My father has horrible taste in neckties.
9. Jackie is extremely unconventional.
10. Bill is a sloppy eater.

Specific Words and Phrases

Writers who take seriously our "the-more-specific-the-better" rule will find not only that their writing has more impact and meaning, but also that their style as a whole, their use of language, has started to change significantly. Specific details in themselves are not a guarantee of good writing. Something has to happen to the language, too. The words with which a specific detail is presented must *them-selves* be speciic. In fact, through using specific words, a good writer can make even the most tiresomely familiar abstractions take on new life.

For most writers, the biggest challenge is learning to recognize when a particular word or phrase is not specific enough, and why. Often the first word that pops into our heads doesn't really work as effectively as it should. "He smiled," for example, may seem the natural way to describe a common facial expression. What rational person could complain about such a straightforward phrase? But have we truly conveyed the exact expression we are trying to write about or have we just settled for a fuzzy approximation? Wouldn't our readers get a clearer picture of the face we have in mind if we tried to pin down the word that best describes *this* smile: He grinned? smirked? sneered? leered? simpered? turned up the corners of his mouth? smiled half-heartedly? smiled broadly? Once we develop the habit of checking our original word choices carefully, making sure we've come as close to our precise meaning as possible, our style will become at once more specific and more colorful.

Nobody, it is true, will ever be ridiculed or exposed to public disgrace for writing, "She went to the door." But surely our readers deserve to be told, and surely we should want them to know, if she ran or walked or strolled or strutted or shuffled or limped or stumbled or sauntered or trotted or tiptoed to that door. Only one abstract word needs to be changed here, but the person who habitually recognizes that abstract word, refuses to let it pass, and selects a specific word to replace it is no longer just someone who writes, but a *writer.*

Using specific words is a different matter from supporting generalizations with details, though specific words may sometimes help give us a more detailed picture. Selecting specific words is primarily a means of expression, a way of putting things, a style. "He wore a hat" becomes, "His top hat was tilted jauntily over one eyebrow." We are not backing up a previous statement about someone's clothing preferences here—we are making a statement that has a specific meaning in and of itself. Together, specific details and specific words are the primary means of eliminating boring and dreary abstractions from our writing.

Exercise

In the sentences below, the *italicized* words or phrases are abstract and dull. Find a specific word or short phrase that can substitute for the abstract one and will fit the meaning of the rest of the sentence.

1. The *official* said that *services* would be *reduced.*
2. The *large group* waited a *long time* to see the *candidate.*
3. The *small vehicle* crashed into the *big vehicle* at the *intersection.*
4. My parents gave me a *nice watch* for the *great event.*
5. *Certain tests* revealed that the *athlete* had a *serious injury.*
6. Since *the weather was good,* they decided on an *outing.*
7. Willie had been *in a low-income bracket* for *a long time.*
8. The *parent punished* the *child.*
9. Susan *acted wildly* and *talked strangely.*
10. *The local savings institution* has just *readjusted its interest rates.*

Comparisons

Another way of relieving the tedium of abstract writing and increasing the liveliness of concrete writing is to use effective figures of speech, particularly comparisons (see pp. 276–277 for a discussion of metaphors and similes). Sometimes a writer may have a hard time coming up with a forceful substitute for a humdrum expression like "it was very easy." There are plenty of synonyms for "very easy," of course, but the writer's best bet might be a comparison: *It was as easy as* (or *It was so easy it was like. . .) drinking a second glass of beer,* or *splattering toothpaste on the bathroom mirror,* or *forgetting the car keys.* Good comparisons are attention-getters. They provide a legitimate opportunity to show off a bit. They can demonstrate a writer's imagination or sense of humor. They can add a helpful spark to otherwise pedestrian writing.

Two cautions are in order. First, use comparisons in moderation. The more comparisons a piece of writing contains, the less impact each one is likely to have. Second, and more important, avoid the routine, trite comparisons with which our language is filled. Don't write "It was as easy as pie" or "It was as easy as taking candy from a baby." Try to be fresh and different. Rather than be trite, avoid comparisons altogether.

Make sure, by the way, that you phrase your comparisons correctly, whether you are using them for lively specific detail or as a simple means of making a point—"Alice is smarter than Sally," for example. Often, there is no problem, and we can do what comes naturally. But sometimes, through careless phrasing, we can appear to be comparing things that we had no intention of comparing, things that can't be compared because no relationship exists between them. None of us would think of writing "Eyebrows are better than hubcaps," but many of us have probably tossed off illogical sentences like the following:

INCORRECT	IMPROVED
Some of these horror stories are very similar to Edgar Allan Poe.	*Not what the writer meant.* He intended to compare the horror stories of one writer to the horror stories of another writer; instead, he pointlessly compared the horror stories of one writer to another writer—period. He should have written: Some of these horror stories are very similar to Edgar Allan Poe's. OR Some of these horror stories are very similar to those of Edgar Allan Poe.
His appetite was as huge as a pig.	His appetite was as huge as a pig's. OR His appetite was as huge as that of a pig. OR His appetite was as huge as a pig's appetite.
The new supermarket's prices are higher than the competition.	The new supermarket's prices are higher than the competition's. OR The new supermarket's prices are higher than those of the competition.

Another kind of illogical comparison unintentionally excludes an item of comparison from the group that it belongs to through the omission of the word *other:*

INCORRECT	IMPROVED
Lincoln had more detailed knowledge of the Bible than any American president.	Lincoln had more detailed knowledge of the Bible than any *other* American president.
My high school paid less attention to sports than any school in the city.	My high school paid less attention to sports than any *other* school in the city.

Sometimes, too, improper phrasing can result in confusion. What did the writer of these sentences want to say?

I like him more than you.	Did the writer mean *I like him more than you like him* or *I like him more than I like you?*
Hemingway is more indebted to Mark Twain than anyone else.	Did the writer mean *Hemingway is more indebted to Mark Twain than to anyone else* or *Hemingway is more indebted to Mark Twain than anyone else is?*

Exercise A

Make up *two* phrases to complete each of the following comparisons. Be prepared to tell which of your phrases is better and why.

1. Trying to study for this exam is like . . .
2. The long wait was as nervewracking as . . .
3. The dentist looked at me like . . .
4. Her old car was as dependable as . . .
5. Expecting common courtesy from him is like . . .
6. Her hair was such a mess that I was reminded of . . .
7. The Congressman's explanation was as plausible as . . .
8. A tender glance from my sweetheart is more precious to me than . . .
9. If you'd buy an insurance policy from him, you're the kind of person who . . .
10. The prospect of working for her has all the appeal of . . .

Exercise B

Rephrase the sentences below where necessary.

1. My mother loves me more than my father.
2. Henry Winkler's acting is not as skillful as Henry Fonda.
3. The use of nuclear energy arouses more emotions than any controversial issue.
4. I owe the bank less than you.
5. Rich's wonderful humor was like Harpo Marx.
6. He was as busy as a bee.
7. All things considered, Jane's bad luck has been worse than anyone's.

8. *Fiddler on the Roof* had a longer run than any Broadway musical.
9. Our gross national product is substantially larger than the Soviet Union.
10. She enjoys Dionne Warwick more than Diana Ross.

WORDINESS AND ECONOMY

Many human individuals use more words than are absolutely necessary and essential to express the thoughts and ideas which they (the human individuals) are attempting to communicate. They repeat the same thing constantly and say the same thing over and over again. Sometimes instead of actually repeating themselves they merely substitute various and sundry long phrases for a simple word due to the fact that it is their opinion that readers will be impressed by this writing method of procedure. But in the modern contemporary world of today, good writing should never be wordy. It should be economical; that is, it should say what it has to say, and then stop, cease, and desist.

In case you haven't noticed, the paragraph you just read violates all of its own good advice. You can find examples of wordiness everywhere: "human individuals" instead of "people," "thoughts and ideas" instead of "thoughts" *or* "ideas," "due to the fact that" instead of "because," "it is their opinion" instead of "they think." The whole paragraph could be cut to half its length without losing anything but a mass of nonfunctioning words:

> Many people use more words than are necessary to express their thoughts. They repeat the same things constantly or substitute long phrases for a simple word because they want to impress their readers. But good writing should never be wordy: it should say what it has to say, and then stop.

Wordiness is a major writing problem. It is hard to avoid because it can turn up for any number of reasons, and writers usually don't realize that they are being wordy. Nobody wants to be a windbag, yet unneeded words sneak into nearly everyone's writing.

Before discussing the different kinds of wordiness, we should clear up one point. Wordiness results from words that don't do anything—it has no direct connection to mere number of words. A poor writer can produce a wordy paragraph on the meaning of freedom; a good writer can produce a whole book on the same subject that is not wordy. If the words contribute to the effect the author wants, if eliminating any of them would sacrifice something valuable, then the author is *not* being wordy. Many pieces of writing with lots of specific details are longer than abstract versions of the same pieces would be, but getting rid of the details would mean a loss of interest and clarity. Only when words can be eliminated without any harm being done do we find real wordiness.

Deadwood

Some words are like "dead wood" on a tree or bush. Unless these words are removed, they sap the strength of the healthy words around them. Moreover, being dead, they can be removed with little or no tampering with the rest of the sentence, as in the examples that follow.

DEADWOOD	IMPROVED
His hair was red in color.	His hair was red.
Pollution conditions that exist in our cities are disgraceful.	Pollution in our cities is disgraceful.
The building has a height of 934 feet.	The building rises 934 feet.
She was in a depressed state of mind.	She was depressed.
Disneyland struck us as a fascinating kind of place.	Disneyland struck us as fascinating.
In this day and age we live in, people seem totally apathetic about everything.	People today seem totally apathetic.
The hero of the story was an individual in the high-income bracket.	The hero of the story was wealthy.
The validity of such statements should not be adhered to.	Such statements are invalid.
He spoke to her in a harsh manner.	He spoke to her harshly.
I am going to major in the field of sociology.	I am going to major in sociology.
The character had a hard type of decision to make.	The character had a hard decision to make.
Because of the fact that my teacher disliked me, he gave me a bad grade.	Because my teacher disliked me, he gave me a bad grade.
Sometimes the moral of a story is a very important factor.	Sometimes the moral of a story is very important.
The story "Quality," written by the author John Galsworthy, is a story with an unhappy ending.	"Quality" by John Galsworthy is a story with an unhappy ending.

The wise writer is always on the lookout for deadwood, especially in revision. Deadwood infiltrates nearly everyone's first draft, but there is no room for these tiresome words-without-purpose in a finished composition. As a general rule, it is safe to assume that if words can be removed without harming anything—as in the examples above—they should be removed.

Pointless Repetition of Meaning

Pointless repetition of meaning is a special kind of deadwood. Aside from adding useless words, such repetition reflects writers' lack of confidence in themselves—their fear that their point will not be clear unless they make it twice. Unfortunately, this overemphasis usually suggests sloppy thinking to the reader, rather than a desire for accuracy.

POINTLESS REPETITION	IMPROVED
The film was very interesting and fascinating.	The film was fascinating.
Our streams are filthy and dirty.	Our streams are filthy.
This approach could end in a catastrophic conclusion.	This approach could end catastrophically.
The author gives examples of different and varied criticisms of the novel.	The author gives examples of different criticisms of the novel.
To begin with, in the first place, the story has terrific suspense.	In the first place, the story has terrific suspense.
Some early critics of Jonathan Swift called him an insane madman suffering from the symptoms of mental disease.	Some early critics of Jonathan Swift called him insane.
There is no question about the worth and value of an education.	There is no question about the value of an education.
He has no emotional feelings.	He has no feelings.
Each and every person ought to read a newspaper.	Everyone ought to read a newspaper.
The new administration will make the exact same mistake as the old one.	The new administration will make the same mistake as the old one.

Exercise

Point out any instances of deadwood and pointless repetition in the following sentences.

1. The name of the game was blackjack, and the name of the dealer was Big Sam.
2. Gun-control legislation is a controversial kind of issue.
3. We need to get back to the basic fundamentals.
4. At the end of the program, the two competing contestants were tied.
5. The area of heredity still has many uncertain aspects to it.
6. I cannot give you a definite answer at this point in time.
7. Men and women of both sexes must join the combat to fight for a better world.
8. His race, color, and creed mean nothing to me.
9. This country has ignored the problems and difficulties of its elderly senior citizens.
10. I pledge to oppose the forces of godless atheism and disloyal treason.
11. He gave a forceful, energetic, and dynamic type of presentation of his opinion and point of view.
12. All day long, he took forever to make up his mind.
13. We would welcome hearing your comments and reactions.
14. She responded with a favorable attitude to the social life environment at the singles apartment facility.
15. A slow student who does not learn as quickly as other students needs to be singled out for special attention by the individual responsible for teaching.
16. The man her mother married was a cruel and unkind stepfather to her.
17. He disliked me due to the fact that I spoke to him in a sarcastic way.
18. Teenage young people can benefit from travel experiences.
19. Your car or automobile needs service and maintenance at regularly spaced intervals.
20. The class situation stimulates interpersonal communication between students.

Delay of Subject

There is, there has, it is, and *it has*—in all tenses—are frequent causes of wordiness. Nothing is wrong with these phrases in themselves; they are necessary parts of the language, and some thoughts might be inexpressible without them. Too often, however, they are used carelessly and delay a sentence or clause from getting down to business. In the following examples, the original sentences begin with words that have no more purpose than the throat-clearing noises made by a speaker before a talk. The revised sentences begin with important words, words that communicate the central concern of each sentence.

WORD DELAY	IMPROVED
There are too many people who care only for themselves.	Too many people care only for themselves.
It has often been commented on by great philosophers that philosophy solves nothing.	Great philosophers have often commented that philosophy solves nothing.
There have been a number of conflicting studies made of urban problems.	A number of conflicting studies have been made of urban problems.
It was on December 7, 1941, that the Japanese attacked the U.S. fleet at Pearl Harbor.	On December 7, 1941, the Japanese attacked the U.S. fleet at Pearl Harbor.
It is a fact that there has been a great increase in sensationalism in the theater.	Sensationalism in the theater has greatly increased.

Inadequate Clause-cutting

One of the most effective ways of reducing wordiness is to cut a cumbersome dependent or independent clause into a shorter phrase or, if possible, a single word. This clause-cutting can result in a tighter, more economical structure, with the phrase or word more firmly incorporated into the sentence than the original clause ever was. Sometimes, of course, a writer may choose to leave the clause alone for a perfectly valid reason, such as emphasis. But more often than not, such clauses are tacked on awkwardly and add unnecessary words; they should always be examined with a critical eye.

WORDY CLAUSE	IMPROVED
The girl who had red hair was a flirt.	The red-haired girl was a flirt.
Some of the students who were more enthusiastic wrote an extra paper.	Some of the more enthusiastic students wrote an extra paper.
The story was very exciting. It was all about ghosts.	The ghost story was very exciting.
Alexander the Great was a man who tried to conquer the world.	Alexander the Great tried to conquer the world.
The applause, which sounded like a thunderclap, shook the auditorium.	The applause shook the auditorium like a thunderclap.

No one who has a child of his or her own can fail to appreciate the charm of this poem.

No parent can fail to appreciate the charm of this poem.

Passionate love is a feeling that has inspired many great writers and artists.

Passionate love has inspired many great writers and artists.

He is an extremely ambitious man; he is scheming to replace his boss.

Extremely ambitious, he is scheming to replace his boss.

The two main characters in the play have similar attitudes toward other people and the way in which each feels about the conventions of society.

The two main characters in the play have similar attitudes toward other people and social conventions.

Exercise

Rewrite these sentences to make them more economical, cutting clauses and eliminating wordy delay of subject wherever possible.

1. The jeans that I had been admiring for several weeks magically appeared under the Christmas tree.
2. Alice Roosevelt Longworth was a woman who usually did exactly what she wanted to do.
3. There is no newspaper that has a better international reputation than the *New York Times*.
4. She is a woman who has always valued her career above her family.
5. It is no disgrace to apologize when you have done something wrong.
6. There are a number of flavors I love.
7. The idea of a guaranteed annual wage is a notion that conflicts with many traditional middle-class values.
8. Emerson had an extremely optimistic philosophy. It probably reflected the spirit of mid-nineteenth century America.
9. There was a chance she had to take.
10. Many nonconformists who are so proud of themselves are the worst conformists of all.
11. Cars that are made in Germany do not have the reputation for good workmanship that they used to have.
12. Roger Staubach, who used to play quarterback for the Dallas Cowboys, had a nickname which was "Roger the Dodger."
13. There have been many complicated plans that have been proposed to help New York City regain financial stability.

14. People who play practical jokes are people who are basically insecure.
15. People who do not know any better unthinkingly use chemicals that can be harmful to health on their backyard flowers and vegetables.
16. There are many professors who really are absentminded—except when it comes to due-dates for term papers.
17. She is such a successful terrorist that she is thinking of hiring an agent who can take care of public relations matters and a lawyer who can arrange advertising endorsements and guest appearances on talk shows.
18. When he was threatened with blackmail over letters he had written to the woman who had been his mistress, the Duke of Wellington replied, "Publish and be damned!"
19. The old show "Star Trek" still has thousands of loyal fans. They are affectionately known as "Trekkies."
20. On "Star Trek" Mr. Spock was played by an actor whose name was Leonard Nimoy. Mr. Spock was characterized as a completely rational being.

CHAPTER 16

STYLISTIC PROBLEMS AND THEIR SOLUTIONS

We have already outlined the general principles that writers should put into practice in developing their styles: choosing the word with the proper connotations, keeping the writing specific, and eliminating wordiness. But even writers who have mastered these ideas can still run into difficulty with particular stylistic problems. Often without realizing it, they may toss in a handy cliché, ignore a string of phrases that aren't parallel, repeat a word monotonously, or overlook an awkward passive verb. For such problems general principles are sometimes *too* general.

In this chapter, we define and discuss those problems that are most likely to arise so that you can either avoid them entirely or recognize and correct them if they do appear in your writing. We also explain which of these stylistic elements can serve a valid purpose when used consciously and carefully.

TRITENESS

A trite expression, or *cliché,* is a word or phrase that has become worn out through overuse. Many trite expressions may once have been original and even brilliant, but through constant repetition they have lost whatever impact they once had. If a writer uses many trite expressions, a reader may be tempted to assume that the thoughts are as secondhand as the language.

Triteness generally calls attention to itself in some way. Words like *the, a, man, come, go* are not trite even though they are used all the time, because they are simple, direct, and unself-conscious. Trite expressions are pretentious. They seem, on the surface, to convey a thought or feeling particularly well, and people who haven't read enough to recognize them sometimes think them clever, or elegant, or lively. Experienced readers, however, interpret them for what they usually are—evidence of a writer's laziness and lack of imagination.

The only way to handle triteness is to eliminate it. Apologetic little quotation marks do not help. If the writer has been trite, quotation marks call more attention to the fault and let the reader know that the triteness was no accident.

The list below contains a number of trite expressions. Avoid them. Choose fifteen from the list and try to think of original and effective ways to express the same ideas.

more fun than a barrel of monkeys	imperialist lackey
worth its weight in gold	Iron Curtain
over the hill	do unto others
stop on a dime	flat as a pancake
fresh as a daisy	dumb as an ox
happy as a lark	meaningful dialogue
hard as nails	turned on
have someone in a corner	red as a rose
make a long story short	tired but happy
no use crying over spilled milk	a good time was had by all
a penny saved is a penny earned	white as snow
cool as a cucumber	black as pitch
pretty as a picture	put it in a nutshell
in the pink	Mother Nature
hale and hearty	Father Time
apple-pie order	spread like wildfire
under the weather	the crack of dawn
devil-may-care attitude	spring chicken
go at it tooth and nail	dog-eat-dog
generation gap	survival of the fittest
every cloud has a silver lining	south of the border
sick as a dog	armed to the teeth
work like a dog	lean and lanky
easy as pie	flattery will get you nowhere
sweet as sugar	a matter of life and death
quick as a wink	male chauvinist pig

quick as a flash

greased lightning

tender loving care

sly as a fox

stubborn as a mule

rat race

Old Glory

trial and error

struggle for existence

the bigger they are the harder they fall

sad but true

a bolt from the blue

father of his country

signed, sealed, and delivered

open-and-shut case

flash in the pan

babe in the woods

not a cloud in the sky

feathered friends

slow as molasses

do your own thing

last but not least

In addition to the kind of phrases listed above, some familiar—and important—ideas have been expressed in the same language so often that the ideas themselves seem trite unless they are worded differently. No matter how much we believe in the need for stable human relationships, we are not going to get very excited when someone tells us "People must learn to get along with one another." If we are presenting one of these ideas, we must express it in a dramatic, forceful way, or at least show that we do not regard it as a profound new insight. Here is a partial list of such potentially trite ideas:

The older generation has made a mess of things.

A good marriage involves more than sex.

Getting to know people of different backgrounds is a good thing.

College is more difficult than high school.

Pollution is a major problem in the United States.

Education is necessary for many jobs.

We live in a technological society.

This problem could have been avoided by better communication.

This problem will be solved by better communication.

We need to think more about people who are less fortunate.

It is possible to have different opinions about a poem.

Nature is beautiful.

Adults have more responsibilities than children.

This issue is very complicated.

EUPHEMISMS

A euphemism is a word or phrase used as a polite substitute for a more natural but less refined word or phrase. Euphemisms can be handy to have around, especially in social situations. Chances are that clergymen and grandmothers will be happier and more comfortable to hear us react to a stubbed toe with "Oh dear" for "Oh damn" or "Good gracious" for "Good God." Chances are that the widow with two children will find her grief easier to bear if we say, "I was so sorry to hear about Fred," and thoughtfully omit the unpleasant medical details. As a rule, though, euphemisms should be avoided, especially in writing. They generally seem pretentious, fussy, and old-fashioned. They can make writers appear afraid to face facts and say what they mean. The natural, honest word is usually the best one, so long as honesty is not confused with exhibitionistic crudeness or vulgarity. In most cases, then, avoid writing both "He passed on to a better world" and "He croaked." Try "He died."

EUPHEMISMS	HONEST TERMS
low-income individual	poor person
urban poverty area	slum
sanitation worker	garbage collector
custodian *or* superintendent	janitor
mortician *or* funeral director	undertaker
conflict	war
distortion of the facts	lie
casualties	dead and wounded
senior citizen	old person
powder one's nose	go to the bathroom
financially embarrassed	in debt
reconditioned	used
to pass on	to die

Exercise

Locate trite expressions and euphemisms in the sentences below and suggest good alternatives.

1. It is sad but true that Corey is as slow as molasses running uphill in winter.
2. I told him to look before he leaped, but he insisted on doing his own thing.

3. She refused to see the handwriting on the wall because she was as stubborn as a mule.
4. As the sun sank slowly in the west, we bade a fond farewell to the Emerald Isle.
5. We live in troubled times.
6. The casket for the dear departed cost a pretty penny.
7. The army executed a strategic withdrawal.
8. Mr. Smith's immediate superior told him that his services would no longer be required.
9. After a long drive, the powder room at the gas station was a sight for sore eyes.
10. Our feathered friends sang their hearts out for us.

USE OF PASSIVE VERBS

In most English sentences, the subject performs an action.

> John likes this poem.
> The critic saw the movie.
> The senator is going to vote for the bill.

The verb in such sentences is said to be in the *active voice*. The active voice is direct, clear, and concise; in most sentences, it is what we expect.

Too often, however, instead of using the natural active voice, writers substitute the more stilted *passive voice*. A verb in the passive voice combines a form of *to be* with the past participle of the verb: *is given, has been delivered, was mailed*. Thus, instead of *acting*, the subject of the sentence is *acted upon*.

> This poem is liked by John.
> The movie was seen by the critic.
> The bill is going to be voted for by the senator.

Compared to the active voice, the passive is generally awkward, exceedingly formal, and wordy. It is better to write "This theme will analyze the story" than "The story will be analyzed in this theme." It is better to write "My sociology teacher offered some challenging insights into contemporary problems" than "Some challenging insights into contemporary problems were offered by my sociology teacher."

On occasion, the passive voice doesn't sound bad, of course. Such occasions may arise when the actor is unknown, insignificant, or nonexistent, or when a deliberately impersonal tone is required. Don't be afraid of the passive when it seems normal and unforced— as in the last part of the preceding sentence—but always be alert to its dangers. Here are a few examples of perfectly acceptable passives:

The game was delayed because of rain.

The eighteenth century has been called the Age of Enlightenment.

Your prompt attention to this request for payment will be appreciated.

The building will be finished in a few months.

We have been victimized time after time.

Exercise

In the sentences below, change the passive voice to the active voice wherever appropriate.

1. The extra-large pizza was eaten in six minutes by Mike.
2. The forms must be returned before April 15 by you.
3. Nothing tastes worse than cold lima beans.
4. Another perfect pass was dropped by the wide receiver.
5. The embezzler was imprisoned for his crimes.
6. The embezzler was imprisoned for his crimes by the court.
7. Don't believe everything that you are told.
8. The victim was pronounced dead on arrival.
9. The victim was pronounced dead on arrival by the coroner.
10. The exam was passed by me but failed by my best friend.

PARALLELISM

Essentially, parallelism means expressing ideas and facts of equal (or coordinate or "parallel") importance in the same grammatical form. We do it all the time, almost unconsciously.

The store was filled with *chairs, tables, sofas,* and *lamps.*	*a group of four nouns*
He *came home, ate dinner,* and *went to bed.*	*three verb phrases*
You can get there by *car, bus,* or *plane.*	*three nouns*

I thought the climactic episode in the story was *shocking, offbeat,* and *amusing.*	*three adjectives*

Parallel grammatical structure reinforces the writer's thought by stressing the parallel importance of the various sentence elements, and so makes life easier for the reader. Many of the most famous phrases in our language draw strength in part from effective use of parallelism:

. . . *life, liberty,* and the *pursuit* of happiness	*group of three nouns*
. . . *of the people, by the people,* and *for the people*	*three prepositional phrases*
love me or *leave me*	*two imperatives*
Early *to bed* and early *to rise* / Makes a man *healthy,* and *wealthy,* and *wise*	*two infinitives / three adjectives*
To be or not *to be*	*two infinitives*
Friends, Romans, countrymen . . .	*three nouns*
I come *to bury Caesar,* not *to praise him*	*two infinitives with objects*
I came, I saw, I conquered	*three independent clauses*
Peace on earth, good will toward men	*two nouns, each with prepositional phrase*
Better be *safe* than *sorry*	*two adjectives*
. . . *the land of the free* and *the home of the brave*	*two nouns, each with a prepositional phrase*

Now notice how faulty parallelism or lack of parallelism can sabotage a sentence.

You can get there by *car, bus,* or *fly.*	*two nouns, and suddenly a verb*
I thought the climactic episode in the story was *shocking, offbeat,* and *I found it very amusing.*	*two adjectives, coupled with an independent clause*
The teacher told us *to work fast* and *that we should write on only one side of the paper.*	*shift from infinitive to clause*
She *liked* people and *was liked* by people.	*shift from active to passive voice*

Bill was a *good husband,* a *loving father,* and *worked hard.*	*adjective-noun, adjective-noun, verb-adverb*

Descriptive words added to some of the parallel elements do not break the basic parallelism and can be valuable in avoiding monotony.

Judith had *brains, talent,* and an extremely charming *personality.*	*still parallel: a group of three nouns, even though one is modified by an adjective, and the adjective is modified by an adverb*
The man owned a *mansion* and a fine *collection* of modern etchings.	*still parallel: two nouns, even though one of them is modified by an adjective and followed by a prepositional phrase*
The baby has now learned how to *whimper, shriek, yell* loudly, and *cry* its head off.	*still parallel: four infinitives, even though one is modified by an adverb and one is followed by an object*

Parallelism, then, is an indispensable aid to style and meaning, but keep in mind that its value is limited to cases in which the various elements are of equal importance. If we try to parallel unequal elements, we can wind up with startling calamities, unless we are being intentionally humorous:

He had wealth, vitality, sophistication, and a short nose.

The story offers a profound message of inspiration and hope to mankind and occupies pages 152 to 170 of our textbook.

My friend John is a revolutionary activist and a former cub scout.

We must all work together to eliminate war, disease, hunger, and dirty movies.

Exercise

Which of the following sentences use faulty parallelism? Which use parallelism correctly? Which use inappropriate parallelism? Make corrections in the sentences that need them.

1. That concert will be expensive, exhausting, and something that is fun.
2. I am thinking of a career in law, medicine, or doing chemical research.
3. Percy Bysshe Shelley wrote some of the greatest poems in the English language, lived a spectacularly scandalous private life, and had a weird middle name.
4. A healthy family life can give a young person a feeling of security, a desire for excellence, and that most important of all qualities, a strong sense of identity.
5. Three kinds of weeds grow on people's lawns: weeds, more weeds, and nothing but weeds.
6. Food in the school cafeteria is tasteless and a ridiculous expense.
7. He was a snob about wine, food, clothing, and seeing people make grammatical mistakes.
8. Sister Philomena told us we were noisy, spiteful, and to pay more attention.
9. The repairman worked steadily, fixed the washer, charged a reasonable price, and was respected by Mrs. Clark.
10. Alfred Hitchcock had a nearly unbroken record of directing films that were suspenseful, original, and great successes.

SUBORDINATION

Which of these observations on that great new epic, *The Return of the Hideous Vampire,* is likely to be most significant?

It was produced by Paramount Brothers.

It is one of the best horror movies of the last ten years.

It was filmed in technicolor.

Which of these facts about Earnest N. Dogood deserves the most emphasis?

He is a Republican.

He has announced his candidacy for President of the United States.

He is a senator.

The answers are obvious; in both cases, the second item is the one you should have chosen. Neither set of statements would be appropriate as a list of parallel thoughts—because ideas and facts are not all created equal. This simple truth has tremendous consequences for our writing.

If we tried to present all the information we have as if it really were of equal, parallel importance, we would probably wind up with a form of baby talk. At one time or another, many of us have probably had to suffer through a young child's account of a movie or television show. To the child, everything is supremely fascinating. Distinctions between major and minor episodes mean nothing, and the child can easily make a plot summary seem to last as long as the show itself:

> First the cowboy woke up and he got dressed and then he went downstairs and he got on his horse and his horse's name was Big Boy and then he rode off on his horse to fight the bad guy.

Note that the child gives equal emphasis to all the facts by expressing each one as an independent clause, a unit that can stand alone as a separate sentence: *the cowboy woke up, he got dressed, he ate,* etc. This equality is further stressed by the use of *and* to tie the clauses together. *And* simply links new ingredients to a sentence or phrase—it doesn't help the reader decide which ingredient is more significant (*ham and eggs, boys and girls, war and peace,* for example). Essentially, the problem with the cowboy story is that important facts are forced to compete for our attention with relatively trivial ones.

Instead of giving equal weight to each fact, then, and creating a monotonous stream of unfiltered data, a skillful writer will *subordinate* some of those facts, arranging the sentence or paragraph so that some parts are clearly secondary to others.

> After waking up, eating, going downstairs, and getting on his horse, Big Boy, the cowboy rode off to fight with the bad guy.

We certainly have no specimen of prize-winning prose here, but we don't have the total mess we started out with either. This revision contains only one independent clause—*the cowboy rode off to fight with the bad guy*—and that clause contains the most important fact. None of the other independent clauses in the original sentence survives. They have all been subordinated grammatically and no longer clamor for the reader's primary attention.

Look again at the beginning of this section on subordination. We have three pieces of information about a movie. The writer with no sense of subordination merely smacks down each point as it comes to mind without attempting to differentiate between major and minor items' but, instead, giving each item a sentence to itself.

> *The Return of the Hideous Vampire* was produced by Paramount Brothers. It is one of the best horror movies of the last ten years. It was filmed in technicolor.

By contrast, with proper subordination the writer collects the three related observations, reserves the independent clause for the most important one, and tucks away the rest in a less conspicuous place.

> *The Return of the Hideous Vampire,* a technicolor film produced by Paramount Brothers, is one of the best horror movies of the last ten years.

We can see the same principle at work with Earnest N. Dogood.

UNSUBORDINATED	SUBORDINATED
Earnest N. Dogood is a Republican. He has announced his candidacy for President of the United States. He is a senator.	Senator Earnest N. Dogood, a Republican, has announced his candidacy for President of the United States.

Remember that related ideas can often be tied together in a way that shows their relationships more clearly. Remember that an independent clause, whether it stands alone as a single sentence or is incorporated into a complex sentence, is a loud cry for attention and should generally be saved for matters of importance.

Here are a few more examples of how subordination can improve your writing:

UNSUBORDINATED	SUBORDINATED
John is a wonderful person. He is very shy. He is extremely kind to everybody.	Although very shy, John is a wonderful person who is extremely kind to everybody.
	OR, IF YOU WANT TO EMPHASIZE THE SHYNESS Although he is a wonderful person who is extremely kind to everybody, John is very shy.
This play explores the fate of love in a mechanized society. It is highly symbolic, and it has two acts.	This highly symbolic play of two acts explores the fate of love in a mechanized society.

Professor Jones is terribly sarcastic. He is also a tough grader. It is true that he knows his subject. Most students dislike him, however.	Despite Professor Jones's knowledge of his subject, most students dislike him because of his terrible sarcasm and tough grading.

Exercise

Rewrite the following sentences, making effective use of subordination.

1. Jill was going up the hill to fetch a pail of water, and Jack was helping her. Then Jack fell down.
2. Shy people create many problems for themselves. I know this from experience. I am shy myself.
3. This film may be the worst one that has ever been made. The acting is bad. The humor is cheap. The exploitation of sex is disgusting.
4. It was sad to hear him say such harsh things about poor people. He had once been poor himself.
5. Money is not enough to make a person truly successful, but it certainly helps.
6. I am rarely confident about my work, but I thought I had done well on the exam.
7. The novel leaves its readers deeply shaken, and it is also very well written.
8. Scientists tend to laugh at voodoo as superstition. It is still a real religion, and it is taken seriously by many thousands of people.
9. Monty is spending a year shooting pool. It gets very boring, but it could turn out to be very profitable.
10. My uncle will never give up his dream of making a killing on the stock market. All his investments have been bad so far, and people laugh at him constantly.

SENTENCE MONOTONY AND VARIETY

Readers frequently find themselves struggling to concentrate on a string of sentences even though nothing obvious seems to be wrong. Sentence by sentence, in fact, the author may be writing perfectly well. Put the sentences together, though, and monotony sets in. The monotony can usually be attributed either to a series of sentences that are all, or nearly all, of the same *length* or the same *structure*.

Sentence Length

Sentences come short, medium, and long—and the simple principle for effective writing is to *try for variety.* Don't take this principle more rigidly than it's intended. Don't assume, for instance, that every single short sentence must be followed by a long one, and vice versa. A string of short or long sentences can sometimes be effective, providing that it is eventually followed by a sentence that varies the pattern. Common sense and alertness will tell you when variety is needed. Just remember that too many sentences of the same length bunched together can create a monotonous style and a restless reader.

MONOTONOUS	IMPROVED
He told us the car got good mileage. He said the tires were excellent. The engine was supposed to be quiet. The transmission was supposed to be smooth. He stressed that the brake linings still had plenty of wear. Everything he said was a lie.	He told us the car got good mileage and that it had excellent tires, a quiet engine, a smooth transmission, and sound brake linings. In other words, he lied.
I thought the course was going to be easy, but I was wrong, because after a two-week sickness early in the term I could never find the time to catch up with the assignments, and I kept getting poor grades. I wish I had had the foresight to see what was coming and had taken the initiative either to drop the course or to ask the teacher for an incomplete, but pride or vanity kept me plugging away, and nothing did any good.	I thought the course was going to be easy, but I was wrong. After a two-week sickness early in the term, I could never find the time to catch up with the assignments, and I kept getting poor grades. Why didn't I drop? Why didn't I ask for an incomplete? If I'd known for sure what was coming, I probably would have done one or the other. Pride or vanity kept me plugging away, however, and nothing did any good.

Sentence Structure

Regardless of sentence length, a group of sentences can become monotonous because each sentence uses the same basic structure. All the sentences begin with a present participle (-*ing* endings), for example, or the first word of each sentence is automatically the subject of that sentence, or the first word is *never* the subject. Perhaps every sentence turns out to be a compound sentence (two or more independent clauses) or a complex sentence (one independent clause and one or more dependent clauses). Now forget about the grammatical terms. Remember only that there are many different ways of structuring a sentence, and wise writers never limit themselves to one. Variety is again the key.

MONOTONOUS	IMPROVED
Entering the personnel manager's office, Bill wanted to make a good impression. Smiling, he shook hands. Sitting down, he tried not to fidget. Answering the questions politely, he kept his voice low and forced himself not to say "uh." Being desperate for a job, he had to be at his best. Wondering if his desperation showed, he decided to risk a little joke.	Entering the personnel manager's office, Bill wanted to make a good impression. He smiled, shook hands, and tried not to fidget when he sat down. He answered questions politely, keeping his voice low and forcing himself not to say "uh." Bill was desperate for a job. He had to be at his best. Wondering if his desperation showed, he decided to risk a little joke.
Red wine goes best with meat, and white wine goes best with fish. Red wine should be served at room temperature, and white wine should be chilled. Red wine should usually be opened about a half hour before serving, and the accumulated gases should be allowed to escape from the bottle. These rules are not meaningless customs, but they are proven by centuries of experience, and they improve the taste of the food as well as the wine.	Red wine goes best with meat, and white wine goes best with fish. Unlike white wine, which should be served chilled, red wine should be served at room temperature. Red wine also benefits from being opened about a half hour before serving to allow the accumulated gases to escape from the bottle. Proven by experience, these rules improve the taste of the food as well as the wine. They are not meaningless customs.

REPETITION, GOOD AND BAD

Repetition for Clarity

Repetition can help to clarify meaning and get the writer and reader from one sentence or clause to another. One of the simplest and most valuable transitional devices for a writer is the repetition of a key word or phrase, sometimes in slightly altered form, from a preceding sentence or clause:

> Five drug *companies* have been accused of misleading advertising. The first of these *companies* is . . .

> Critics tend to make too much of a fuss about *symbols. Symbols* are not obscure artistic tricks. Our own daily lives are filled with *symbols.*

Few people want to be thought of as extremely *conventional*, but respect for *conventions* of some sort is necessary for any society to function adequately.

Repetition for Impact

Repetition can often add effective emotional impact:

> We've shrugged at scandals. We've shrugged at violence. We've shrugged at overpopulation and pollution and discrimination. Now it's time to stop shrugging.

> When she lost her husband, she lost her friend, lost her lover, lost her confidant. She lost everything that gave meaning to her life.

> The decision must be made this week—not this year, not this month, not early next week, but this week.

If not handled skillfully and tastefully, repetition for impact can also lead to foolish emotionalism or unnecessary stress on the obvious:

> It's important to plan ahead in writing. It's really, really important.

> Must cruel developers have their way forever? What of the flowers? What of the trees? What of the grass? What of the homeless birds and squirrels and bunnies?

> There is too much violence on television. Bang, bang, bang, bang, bang—that's all we ever hear. Bang, bang, bang.

Undesirable Repetition of Meaning

This kind of repetition (already discussed under "Wordiness," pp. 408–413) involves stating a point that is already sufficiently clear:

> The American flag is red, white, and blue *in color.*

> She was remarkably beautiful. *She was, in fact, quite exceptionally good-looking.*

> The effect *and outcome* of all this was most unfortunate.

> In today's *modern contemporary* world . . .

Undesirable Repetition of the Same Word

We have noted that repetition of a word (either the same word or a different form of that word, as in *conventional/conventions*) can be helpful. It can also be monotonous and irritating, however, especially when the word itself is not crucial to the meaning of the passage; words such as *very, really,* and *interesting* are major offenders.

I am *very* pleased to be here on this *very* distinguished occasion. Your *very* kind remarks and your *very* generous gift have left me *very* much at a loss for words, but *very* deeply appreciative.

I *really* enjoyed reading this story. It was a *really* exciting story with *real* people in *real* situations. The suspense was *really* terrific.

We had a *wonderful* time in Florida. During the day we went swimming, and at night we saw some *really interesting* shows. The weather was great, the food was *really* just *wonderful,* and the sights were *very interesting.*

Beware of using different forms of the same word *through carelessness.* You can create an awkward and confusing sentence before you know it.

We had a *wonderful* time seeing the *wonders* of Florida.

The *beauties* of Shakespeare's sonnets are outstandingly *beautiful.*

People must be made more aware of the need for increased *awareness* of our environment.

One more menace to watch out for is repetition of words in the same sentence, or otherwise close together, *if there is a change in the meaning of the word.* Never commit this particular crime unless you are trying to be intentionally humorous.

Only a perfect *dope* would experiment with *dope.*

Gary *Player* is an excellent golf *player.*

If I *run* hard, my nose will *run.*

Our weekly games of *bridge* have helped build a friendly *bridge* of understanding between our two families.

Undesirable Repetition of Sounds

Save rhymes for poetry. Avoid horrors like these:

The condemnation of the administration was brought about by its own lack of ability and student hostility.

The church is reexamining its position on the condition of the mission.

The Allied troops' defensive stance stopped the German advance into France.

Go easy on alliteration, the repetition of sounds at the beginning of words. Every once in a while, alliteration can be effective, but when a writer is obviously pouring it on, the results are silly at best.

We must toss these sneering, snickering, swindling swine out of office.

The orchestra's bold blowing of the brasses thrilled me to the bottom of my being.

The main piece of furniture in the room was a dirty, damaged, dilapidated, and dreary old desk.

Exercise

Point out any undesirable repetition in the sentences below and make the necessary corrections.

1. He was amazed at her amazing feats on the trampoline.
2. This was a memorable short story; it will truly be hard to forget.
3. I think I prize my old running shoes more than the prize I won for finishing the race.
4. It's simply marvelous the way you can stand on the corner and simply pass out leaflets to hundreds of people who are simply passing by.
5. The supervisor's role is to train the applicant's brain to attain higher skills.
6. I am sure that ambition adds fuel to his already active aspirations.
7. A burglar stole Mrs. Plutocratz's jewelry and mink stole.
8. I asked her to marry me, and she said yes. She said yes!
9. The carpenter has such energy and drive that it's a pleasure just to watch him drive a nail into a piece of wood.
10. The really hard, really difficult goal is the one that is really most worth attaining and achieving.

SLANG

A carefully chosen, appropriate slang expression can sometimes add interest and liveliness to writing. It can be helpful in establishing a humorous or casual tone. More significantly, in a few cases, it can suggest an attitude or a shade of meaning that a more conventional expression could not. By and large, slang is inappropriate for the comparatively formal, analytical writing that college courses demand. But when you feel sure that a slang expression can genuinely communicate something you would not otherwise be able to get across, don't be afraid to use it. Incidentally, forget about the coy little quotation marks that many writers put around slang expressions to show that they are really sophisticated people who could use better language if they wanted to. Good slang should seem natural, and if it is natural, it doesn't need quotes.

> After spending their teens dreaming of chicks, broads, dames, dolls, and assorted foxy ladies, many young men are at a loss when they finally meet a real woman.
>
> Billed as a luxury resort, the hotel was just a high-priced dump.
>
> I don't think I'll ever be able to forget the creepy old busybody who used to live next door to us.

Be careful about using slang, however. Don't use it to show how up-to-date you are; slang changes so fast that what seemed current yesterday is often embarrassingly old-fashioned tomorrow. Don't use slang to show your reader what a folksy person you are; that technique almost always falls flat. Avoid crude sentences like these:

> In *Hamlet,* Hamlet's girl friend, Ophelia, goes nuts.
>
> This profound political allegory really turned me on.
>
> A good college devotes itself to academic excellence, social service, and intellectual stimulation. It can be a real hip place.
>
> Albert Einstein was one of the big brains of the twentieth century.

FANCY WRITING

For every writer who uses slang to show off, there are probably a dozen who show off by habitually using big or unfamiliar words. A large vocabulary is a splendid tool for any writer, of course, but that fancy word or phrase should be used only when it adds something valuable to tone or meaning that a more familiar word or phrase could not add. If the familiar word will do the job as well, use it; the unfamiliar word will seem stilted and pretentious.

FANCY	IMPROVED
Many of our new buildings suffer from inadequate fenestration.	Many of our new buildings have too few windows.
Some of the water we drink is insalubrious.	Some of the water we drink is unhealthy.
They raised their hands in the time-honored gesture of respect to the emblem of their nation's sovereignty.	They saluted their country's flag.
Human individuals who reside in abodes of glass should not hurl objects of masonry.	People who live in glass houses shouldn't throw bricks.

Charles Dickens's novelistic achievements are veritably unrivaled in English letters.	Charles Dickens wrote better novels than any other English writer.
We require an augmentation of interpersonal communications on substantive issues.	We need to talk more to each other about important issues.

MISCELLANEOUS DO'S AND DON'TS

Some special stylistic problems common to classroom writing don't fit conveniently under any of the big labels, so we've included brief comments about them here. Our comments are based on the assumption that you are writing for an audience of intelligent nonspecialists who have not yet made up their minds about your subject. You may argue that you're really writing for your instructor alone, but most English instructors have worked hard at training themselves to dismiss purely personal quirks and preferences from their reading of student themes. Despite the red pens or pencils in their hands, when they look at themes, they mentally turn themselves into an imaginary general reader—the intelligent, uncommitted nonspecialist just mentioned.

1. *Don't write a personal letter to your instructor.*

> This assignment at first confused me, but after several cups of coffee and too many cigarettes, I began to get an idea: I remembered that last week you said something about certain kinds of literature depending on formal patterns, and I think I've come up with an interesting notion about the two stories we just read. See what you think.

If that paragraph were read by anyone other than the teacher or the members of the class in which the stories were discussed, it would make almost no sense. What difference does it make to a general reader how much coffee the student drank? What assignment does the student refer to? What stories did the class just read?

2. *Don't make formal announcements of what you are going to do.*

> In this paper I am going to prove that Langston Hughes was attacking slum landlords.
>
> The thesis which I shall attempt to prove in this paper is that the energy crisis is an invention of the large oil companies.

It's distracting and unnecessary to begin a paper with a trumpet fan-
fare. Don't tell the reader what you are going to do. Get down to
business and do it.

> In "The Ballad of the Landlord," Langston Hughes attacks slum land-
> lords.
>
> The energy crisis is an invention of the large oil companies.

3. *Avoid a speechmaking tone.*

> In conclusion, let me simply say that . . .
>
> With your permission, I'd like to make a few observations on that point.

Such sentences introduce an irritating artificial quality into written
English.

4. *Don't hedge.*

> In my opinion, the Industrial Revolution was a major chapter in the
> history of civilization.
>
> I think that Dr. Watson is childishly impressed by Sherlock Holmes.

Go easy on terms such as *in my opinion, I think,* etc. Of course you
think, and the paper *is* your opinion, your interpretation of the
material—backed up by all the facts necessary to support it. An
apologetic or uncertain tone suggests that you do not have faith in
your ideas, and if you do not believe in what you say, your audience
probably won't either. Of course, you would not state a personal
theory as a universal truth; but don't weaken solid ideas by hedging,
and don't expect an *in my opinion* to make a shaky idea more acceptable.

5. *Don't bluster.*

> Anyone but an idiot can see that Hughes's poem protests against the
> treatment of blacks.
>
> Legalized prostitution is opposed mainly by neurotic hypocrites and re-
> ligious nuts.

Blustering is the opposite of hedging. Its effect on an intelligent audience is just as negative.

6. *Be careful about using "you" as an indefinite pronoun.*

> Even though you are a drug addict, you are not necessarily an evil person.
>
> Your constant arguments with your parents are part of the process of growing up.

You is the pronoun of direct address. In this book, for example, we, the authors, write to you, the students in a composition course, and thus address you directly. But in writing aimed at a general audience, it is preferable to use the indefinite pronouns: *anyone, one, each, either, neither, another, anybody, someone, somebody, everyone, everybody,* and *nobody.* And *you* cannot be substituted for *the speaker, the character, the average citizen, people, the student, the author, the reader,* and so on. Since you cannot be sure of the age, class, sex, or living conditions of your readers, you will not want to chance offending or unintentionally amusing them by attributing to them attitudes, strengths, vices, or talents they may not possess.

> Drug addicts are not necessarily evil.
>
> Constant arguments with parents are part of the process of growing up.

7. *Define unfamiliar terms.* This advice is especially important in any paper on technical subjects. An audience of nonspecialists can be expected to have the general knowledge of educated citizens, but nothing more. Avoid jargon—the special language of particular professions and activities—whenever you can. When you can't, see to it that your reader understands you. A paper on automobile repairs, for instance, would need to define terms such as *universal joint* and *differential.* A paper on legal problems would need to define *tort* and *writ of mandamus.* A paper on finance would need to define *cash flow* and *price-earnings ratio.*

Exercise

Comment on the stylistic problems in each of the sentences below.

1. From time immemorial, humanity has been faced with monumental choices.
2. Thus the poem clearly shows, in my humble opinion, that Dickinson was a shrewd observer.
3. I've really tried to do better in this paper, but I just can't seem to get the hang of it.
4. Cobalt treatment engendered remission.
5. This paper will show that jazz is an American phenomenon.

6. Recent government programs mean that you will no longer have to neglect your illegitimate children.
7. God is not dead. The rest of my paper will make an effort to establish a logical proof for this statement.
8. Let me add one further comment, if I may.
9. Roberts got bored with clipping coupons and went into commodities and convertibles.
10. It seems to me that our country's balance of payments problem has been grossly neglected.
11. Writing this comparison-and-contrast paper involved less drudgery than I first thought it would.
12. It is my intention, then, to provide my readers with information they will need to make up their own minds.
13. Being happy at one's job, to my way of thinking, is a truly important ingredient of a full life.
14. Your career as a ballerina demands that you practice every day no matter how tired you are.
15. The morons and crooks who oppose federal funding of research on solar energy ought to be exposed once and for all.

Repeated errors in grammar and mechanics
are often severely penalized.

PART 5

HANDBOOK
AND GLOSSARY

USING THE HANDBOOK
AND GLOSSARY

DEFINITIONS OF USEFUL
GRAMMATICAL TERMS

HANDBOOK

GLOSSARY OF PROBLEM WORDS

USING THE HANDBOOK AND GLOSSARY

This part of the book is intended as a quick guide to basic writing skills. Use it to check up on grammatical points that have become vague in your mind, to answer simple questions that may occur to you while writing, and to correct any mechanical errors that your instructor finds in your work. Most first-year English courses assume that you have already mastered grammar, punctuation, standard word usage, and the other basics. For the most part, you probably have—but even skilled professional writers sometimes need to use a reference book. Your instructor, at any rate, will probably devote little classroom time to mechanics; it is your responsibility to see that your papers are grammatically correct, and this Handbook and Glossary should help you do just that.

Both Handbook and Glossary are arranged alphabetically. The Handbook (pp. 446–502) discusses the most common areas of trouble: commas, fragmentary sentences, etc. Consult the relevant listing whenever your instructor calls attention to a writing mistake. A number of exercises on more difficult points have been provided so that you can test your understanding of these points. The Glossary (pp. 503–533) explains specific words and phrases that are a frequent source of confusion.

We have tried to keep this material as straightforward as possible. Our main assumption is that standard written English is an essential tool for educated people. In general, we have taken a direct yes-or-no, right-or-wrong approach, even though that approach may sometimes oversimplify complex and controversial issues. Our purpose is to give reasonable answers to common questions—not to write a dissertation on obscure grammatical details.

Immediately following is a special group of definitions of important grammatical terms. Some of these terms will turn up from time to time in the Handbook and Glossary, and if they are unfamiliar to you, this list may prove useful.

DEFINITIONS OF USEFUL GRAMMATICAL TERMS

Active voice. See *Voice.*

Adjective. A word that modifies or limits a noun or pronoun: the *tall* man, he is *tall,* the man with *green* eyes. Most adjectives have three forms: the basic form *(tall);* the comparative form, usually indicated by an *-er* ending *(taller);* and the superlative form, usually indicated by an *-est* ending *(tallest).* The comparative form is used for comparing groups of two, and the superlative form for comparing groups of three or more.

> A basketball center is taller than a guard.
>
> A basketball center is ordinarily the tallest person on the team.
>
> Sue is smarter than I.
>
> Ellen is smarter than she used to be.
>
> Sarah is the smartest person in the class.

Instead of having *-er* and *-est* endings for comparative and superlative forms, some adjectives—generally those of three or more syllables—are preceded by *more* and *most.* Still other adjectives have highly irregular forms.

> *Examples:* forgetful, more forgetful, most forgetful; perilous, more perilous, most perilous; good, better, best; bad, worse, worst; etc.

Adjective clause. A dependent clause that modifies a noun or pronoun. Adjective clauses are introduced by *who, which, that, whose,* and *whom.*

> The man *who lives next door* is my friend.
>
> The Titanic, *which was considered unsinkable,* went to the bottom of the sea on its maiden voyage.
>
> The car *that was stolen yesterday* was recovered by the police.
>
> The man *whom you addressed* is my father.

Adverb. A word that modifies a verb, an adjective, or another adverb.

442

John walked *slowly.*

The man had *very* green eyes.

She spoke *rather loudly.*

Most adverbs are formed by adding *-ly* to an adjective.

Adjective	*Adverb*
The sun was *bright.*	The sun shone *brightly.*
The *furious* lion roared.	The lion roared *furiously.*
The teacher told the class to be *more quiet.*	The teacher told the class to behave *more quietly.*

Adverbial clause. A dependent clause that functions as an adverb.

He was late for school *because he missed the bus.*

When he arrived, class had already begun.

Antecedent. The noun or pronoun to which a pronoun refers.

John left *his* lunch at home.

Here, the pronoun *his* refers to its noun antecedent, *John.*

Appositive. A noun or noun equivalent usually following another noun and further identifying it.

Napoleon, *the great French general,* was defeated by Wellington.

The first Chief Justice, *John Marshall,* is a towering figure in American history.

Auxiliary verb. A "helping verb," a verb used before another to form a verb phrase: forms of *to be* (*am* going, *were* going); modals (*can* go, *might* go); forms of *have* (*have* gone, *had* gone); forms of *do* (*does* go, *did* go).

Clause. A group of words with a subject and predicate. A clause can be *independent;* that is, it can stand alone as a separate sentence.

Maria went home.

A clause can also be *dependent;* that is, it cannot stand alone, but must depend on an independent clause to complete its meaning.

After I came home, I took a nap.

The man *who lived next door* died.

Complement. Usually a noun, pronoun, or adjective that follows a linking verb and is necessary for logical completion of the predicate.

Marilyn Monroe was an *actress.*

Who are *you?*

That proposal seems *sensible.*

Conjunction. A word used to join parts of sentences or clauses. *Coordinating conjunctions* (joining words or clauses of equal importance) are *and, or,* *but, for, nor, yet, so; subordinating conjunctions* (linking dependent and independent clauses) are *because, while, when, although, until, after,* etc.

Coordinating conjunction. See *Conjunction.*

Dependent clause. See *Clause, Adjective Clause, Adverbial Clause, Noun Clause.*

Direct object. See *Object.*

Expletive. A word that does not contribute directly to meaning but merely introduces a sentence or clause: *it, there.*

> *It* is raining.
>
> *There* are five boys here.

Independent clause. See *Clause.*

Infinitive. Simple form of a verb preceded by *to: to come, to go.*

Intransitive verb. See *Verb.*

Linking verb. See *Verb.*

Noun. Traditionally defined as the name of a person, place, thing, or concept, nouns are generally used as the subject, object, or complement of a sentence: *Roosevelt, Bill, accountant, California, Lake Ontario, Boulder Dam, desk, car, freedom, love.*

Noun clause. A dependent clause that performs the function of a noun.

> *That she works very hard* is beyond doubt.
>
> He said *that he would go.*

See *Clause.*

Object. The person, place, or thing that receives the action of a verb, or the noun or pronoun after a preposition.

> George shot *Joe.*
>
> Florence kissed *him.*
>
> All motives are suspect to *them.*
>
> You'll find your *gloves* in the *car.*

Passive voice. See *Voice.*

Person. The form of pronouns and verbs that indicates the speaker (*first person*), the person or thing spoken to (*second person*), or the person or thing spoken about (*third person*).

	Pronoun	*Verb*
First person	I, we	go
Second person	you	go
Third person	he, she, it	goes
	they	go

Predicate. The part of a clause that tells what the subject does, or what is being done to the subject.

> Sal *went home.*

See *Subject.*

Preposition. A connecting word such as *in, by, from, on, to, with,* etc., that shows the relation of a noun or a pronoun to another element in a sentence.

> The man *with* the gun shot the deer.

Pronoun. A word which takes the place of a noun. It may be personal (*I, you, he, she, it, we, they, me, him, her,* etc.), possessive (*my, mine, your, yours, his,* etc.), reflexive or intensive (*myself, yourself, himself,* etc.), relative (*who, which, that*), interrogative (*who, which, what*), or indefinite (*anyone, somebody, nothing,* etc.).

Sentence. A group of words beginning with a capital letter and ending with a period, question mark, or exclamation point that contains at least one independent clause.

> Birds sing.
>
> Do birds sing?
>
> Shut up, all you birds!

See *Clause, Subject, Predicate.*

Subject. A word, phrase, or clause that names the person, place, thing, or idea which the sentence is about.

> *Sal* went home.
>
> The president's *speech* was heard by 100,000 people.

See *Predicate.*

Subordinating conjunction. See *Conjunction.*

Transitive verb. See *Verb.*

Verb. A word that expresses an action, an occurrence, or a state of being. Verbs may be divided into three classes: *transitive* verbs, which require objects to complete their meaning (Mary *admires* him); *intransitive* verbs, which are complete in themselves (John *trembled*); and *linking* verbs, which join a subject to its complement (Phyllis *is* a beauty; Their actions *were* cowardly).

Voice. The quality of a verb that tells whether the subject *acts* or is *acted upon.* A verb is in the *active* voice when its subject does the acting, and in the *passive* when its subject is acted upon.

> *Active:* The Senate passed the new law.
>
> *Passive:* The new law was passed by the Senate.

HANDBOOK

Abbreviations. As a rule, avoid abbreviations.

WRONG	RIGHT
The financial ills of N.Y.C. and other municipalities can be cured only by aid from the federal gov't.	The financial ills of New York City and other municipalities can be cured only by aid from the federal government.
Thanksgiving comes on the fourth Thurs. of Nov.	Thanksgiving comes on the fourth Thursday of November.
I had trouble finding the proper st. & had to ask a taxi driver for directions.	I had trouble finding the proper street and had to ask a taxi driver for directions.

Even when abbreviations are permissible, it is nearly always acceptable in standard English to spell a word in its entirety; therefore, when in doubt, spell it out.

There are only a few cases in which abbreviations are required or preferred.

A. *Standard forms of address.* Before a person's name, it is standard usage to write *Mr., Mrs., Ms., Dr.,* or *St.* (for Saint, not street).

B. *Titles.* If both a person's surname (last) and given name (first) or initials are used, then it is acceptable to write *Rev., Hon., Prof., Sen.*

Rev. John Rice, Prof. A. J. Carr (but not Rev. Rice or Prof. Carr)

C. *Degrees.* After a name, abbreviate academic degrees, *Jr.,* and *Sr.* Academic degrees may also be abbreviated when used by themselves.

Thomas Jones, M.D.

He is now studying for a B.A.

D. *Organizations.* The names of many organizations and some countries are commonly abbreviated, often without periods.

NATO   NAACP   USSR   UN   USA   AFL-CIO

E. *Other.* Footnote references and bibliographical terms are nearly always abbreviated, as are a few common words.

446

etc.   pp. 137–140
ibid.   vol.
et al.   LSD
p. 23   DDT

Adjective-Adverb Confusion. Adjectives modify nouns.

> Getting a diploma takes *hard* work.
>
> The boxer's *left* jab is his *strongest* weapon.
>
> The *better* team won.
>
> The porridge was *hot.*

Adverbs modify verbs, adjectives, or other adverbs.

> We walked *carefully.*
>
> *Foolishly,* we kept arguing until midnight.
>
> The porridge was *very* hot.
>
> The doctor had to cut *quite* deeply.

Most adverbs are formed by adding *-ly* to adjectives:

ADJECTIVE:	nice	strong	poor
ADVERB:	nicely	strongly	poorly

When an adjective already ends in *y* or *ly,* the *y* may sometimes have to be changed to an *i* before the adverbial *-ly* ending is added. A few of the resulting adverbs may sound so awkward that an adverbial phrase is the preferred form:

ADJECTIVE:	pretty	messy	nasty
ADVERB:	prettily	messily	nastily

BUT

ADJECTIVE:	friendly	lovely	heavenly
ADVERB:	in a friendly way	in a lovely way	in a heavenly way

A few adjectives and adverbs are identical in form:

> ADJECTIVE: He is a *better* person for the experience.
>
> *Fast* drivers are dangerous drivers.
>
> ADVERB: He did *better* than I.
>
> I can type *fast.*

Some words are adverbs in themselves—adverbs to start with—and do not spring from adjectives: *very, quite, rather, somewhat,* etc. Other adverbs are irregular: the adjective *good,* for example, is expressed as an adverb by the word *well.*

ADJECTIVE: He was a *good* worker.

ADVERB: He did the work *well*.

Confusion of adjectives and adverbs is among the most common grammatical errors and is likely to turn up from one of the following causes.

A. *Misuse of an adjective to modify a verb.*

WRONG: I wish she acted *different*.

He answered *rude*.

Bill did *good* on his examination.

Let's speak *direct* to each other.

RIGHT: I wish she acted *differently*.

He answered *rudely*.

Bill did *well* on his examination.

Let's speak *directly* to each other.

B. *Misuse of an adjective to modify an adverb or other adjective.*

WRONG: The price was *sure* very expensive.

The patient is *considerable* worse today.

My teacher is *real* strict.

RIGHT: The price was *surely* very expensive.

The patient is *considerably* worse today.

My teacher is *really* strict.

C. *Misuse of an adverb after a linking verb.* The correct modifier after a linking verb is an adjective. The single most common linking verb is *to be* (*am, is, are, was, were, will be,* etc.). Verbs dealing with the senses—sight, touch, taste, smell, hearing—are often used as linking verbs: *feel, look, sound, taste, appear.* Other verbs frequently serving as linking verbs are *get, seem, remain, become.*

WRONG: I feel *prettily*.

The music sounds *beautifully*.

The food tastes *badly*.

He seems *cheerfully*.

RIGHT: I feel *pretty*.

The music sounds *beautiful*.

The food tastes *bad*.

He seems *cheerful*.

Some verbs, including many of those just listed, may be used as transitive or intransitive verbs, as well as linking verbs. In such cases, note how an adjective or adverb determines meaning.

I smell bad. (I need to buy deodorant.)

I smell badly. (My sinuses are stuffed up.)

He looks evil. (He looks like a wicked person.)

He looks evilly. (His glances are frightening.)

I feel terrible. (I am depressed or in ill health.)

I feel terribly. (My sense of touch has deserted me.)

Exercise

Choose the right adjective or adverb.

1. My employer has treated me very (shabby, shabbily).
2. My health is (good, well).
3. The teacher talked (rough, roughly) to the student.
4. The student's answer came back (furious, furiously).
5. The pathetic old man breathed (painful, painfully).
6. As (near, nearly) as I can determine, the first job offer seems the best.
7. All our products are (fresh, freshly) baked each day.
8. Speaking (personal, personally), I think the coach is the only real problem the team has.
9. My deep love for you becomes more (intense, intensely) each day.
10. If you act (bad, badly), you will be treated (bad, badly).
11. Please keep (calm, calmly).
12. Far from being a snob, Frank is a (real, really) fine person once you get to know him.
13. The potato salad tasted (unpleasant, unpleasantly).
14. My sister looks (splendid, splendidly) in her new three-piece suit.
15. When my candidate lost, I felt as (unhappy, unhappily) as could be.

Adjectives, coordinate. See *Comma, E.*

Adverbs. See *Adjective-Adverb Confusion.*

Agreement. See *Pronouns: agreement* or *Subject-verb agreement.*

Apostrophe. The apostrophe is used in forming contractions, plurals, and possessives.

A. *Contractions.* In contractions, the apostrophe indicates that a letter or letters have been left out.

> it is = it's   she is = she's   who is = who's   you will = you'll
>
> let us = let's   you are = you're   do not = don't   she would = she'd

B. *Plurals.* The 's is used to form the plural of lowercase letters and of abbreviations followed by periods: a's, x's, B.A.'s, Ph.D.'s, P.O.W.'s. Either 's or s may be used to form such plurals as the following, though 's is becoming less common:

the 1930s *or* the 1930's   the &s *or* the &'s

the three Rs *or* the three R's   several YMCAs *or* several YMCA's

C. *Possessives.* An apostrophe is used to form the possessive of nouns and indefinite pronouns. The first task is to determine whether a possessive apostrophe is needed. If one is needed, the second task is to use it correctly.

Difficulties for many people begin with the confusion of speaking with writing. In speech, *cats, cat's,* and *cats'* all sound identical. The meanings are all different, however, and in writing, those differences show up immediately. *Cats* is a simple plural—*s* is added to the singular and no apostrophe is used.

The cats howled all night.

Purring is a way cats have of showing affection.

Liver is a favorite food for many cats.

Cat's is a possessive singular, another way of expressing the thought *of the cat. Cats'* is a possessive plural, another way of expressing the thought *of the cats.* Note the simplicity of determining whether a word with a possessive apostrophe is singular or plural: just look at the part of the word *before the apostrophe.*

SINGULAR:	cat's claws	machine's speed	Mr. Smith's home
PLURAL:	cats' claws	machines' speed	the Smiths' home

Note, too, that in a phrase like *of the cats,* the word *of* takes care of the idea of possession, and no apostrophe is used.

POSSESSIVES WITH *OF* (NO APOSTROPHE)	POSSESSIVES WITH APOSTROPHES
The claws of a cat are sharp.	A cat's claws are sharp.
The name of my cat is Tigger.	My cat's name is Tigger.
The hunting abilities of cats are well known.	Cats' hunting abilities are well known.
The mysterious glow in the eyes of cats can be frightening.	The mysterious glow in cats' eyes can be frightening.

One more observation is necessary. Possessive pronouns—*my, mine, our, ours, your, yours, his, her, hers, its, their, theirs*—are already possessive in themselves and *never take apostrophes.*

When a possessive apostrophe is required, the rules are relatively simple.

A. Singular or plural nouns that do not end in *s* form their possessives by adding *'s:*

John's car	the boy's book	Women's Lib
the teacher's notes	New York's mayor	children's games

B. Plural nouns that end in *s* form their possessives by adding only an apostrophe:

the students' teacher   Californians' freeways

oil companies' profits   the two boys' mother

automobiles' engines   the two teachers' classes

C. Singular nouns that end in *s* ordinarily form their possessives by adding *'s*. The exceptions are words that already have so many *s* or *z* sounds in them *(Massachusetts, Jesus)* that a final *'s* would create awkward hissings or buzzings. The possessive of such words is often formed by adding only an apostrophe, and individual writers sometimes have to use their own judgment:

the octopus's tentacles   the press's responsibilities

Keats's poetry   the business's profits

Dickens's novels   Massachusetts' excise tax

Charles's bowling ball   Jesus' disciples

Mr. Jones's new roof   Moses' journey

D. Indefinite pronouns form their possessives by adding *'s:*

nobody's fool   someone's knock

anyone's guess   everybody's business

E. In the case of joint possession—possession by two or more—the possessive is formed by adding an apostrophe or *'s,* as appropriate, to the last noun:

the girls and boys' school   Jill and Bob's car

Note: To show individual possession, write "Jill's and Bob's cars" and "the girls' and boys' schools." Here Jill has a car and Bob has a car; the girls have a school and the boys have a school.

Exercise A

Rewrite the following phrases to form possessives, using an apostrophe or *'s*.

1. the roll of the drum
2. the roll of the drums
3. the suspense of the story
4. the suspense of the stories
5. the joy of the child
6. the joy of the children
7. the ambition of the actress
8. the ambition of the actresses
9. the orders of the boss
10. the orders of the bosses
11. the choice of the person
12. the choice of the people
13. the protest of the masses

14. the mother of Sarah and Jess
15. the mothers of Sarah and Jess (two mothers—individual possession)
16. the ending of the movie
17. the desire of one to excel
18. a break of an hour
19. a notice of a moment
20. the price of success

Exercise B

In the following sentences, decide which of the *italicized* words are simple plurals and which are possessives. Then make the necessary corrections and be prepared to justify them.

1. *Ballplayers* contractual *disputes* have achieved the impossible; they have aroused the *publics* sympathy for the *owners.*
2. *His* romantic *conquests* have stimulated his one *friends* envy and his hundred *enemies* disgust.
3. The *Devils* Triangle *refers* to a region in the Atlantic Ocean of many unexplained *accidents.*
4. *Beethovens* nine *symphonies* have intrigued *listeners minds* and enraptured *their souls.*
5. The *Smiths* went to the *Joneses* house for dinner.
6. Considering his record of *knockouts,* Muhammed *Alis* punching ability was consistently underrated by *sports commentators.*
7. Your behavior is worse than *theirs; yours* can't be excused by your *fathers* neglect.
8. It takes only a *moments* thought to realize that *televisions absurdities* are *reflections* of the *absurdities* of American society as a whole.
9. *Bettys plants* are late *bloomers,* but her *roses colors* are all sensational.
10. *Expenditures* for treatment of solid *wastes* will almost double the *towns* budget over the next five *years.*

Appositive. See *Comma, F.*

Blocked quotations. See *Quotation Marks, A, 1.*

Brackets. Use brackets ([ ]) to indicate comments or added information that you have inserted into a direct quotation. Do not use parentheses instead of brackets, or the reader will assume that the inserted material was part of the original quotation.

> "While influenced by moral considerations, Lincoln signed it [the Emancipation Proclamation] primarily to further the war effort."

> "The music column had the altogether intimidating title of *Hemidemisemiquavers* [sixty-fourth notes]."

Capital letters. Use a capital letter for the first word of a sentence or direct quotation, the first word and all important words of titles, the first word and all nouns of a salutation, the first word of a complimentary close, some pronouns, and all proper nouns—the names of particular persons, places, or things.

A. *The first word of a sentence or direct quotation.*

> A popular television show featured a detective whose most characteristic line was, "We just want the facts, ma'am."

B. *The first and all important words of titles of books, movies, radio and television programs, songs, magazines, plays, short stories, poems, essays, and chapters.* Unimportant words include *a, an, the,* and short prepositions such as *of, in, to,* etc.

A Streetcar Named Desire	"Ode to a Nightingale"
Time	"Such, Such Were the Joys"
Roget's College Thesaurus	"Basin Street Blues"

C. *The first word and all nouns of a salutation.*

> Dear Sir: My dear Ms. Hunt:

D. *The first word of a complimentary close.*

> Sincerely yours, Respectfully yours,

E. *Some pronouns.*

1. First person singular: I

2. References to the Judeo-Christian Deity, where necessary to avoid confusion:

   God told Moses that he must carry out His commandments.

F. *Proper nouns.*

1. Names and titles of persons and groups of persons:

   a. Persons: James Baldwin, Margaret Mead, Albert Einstein, President Roosevelt

   b. Races, nationalities, and religions: Caucasian, Chinese, Catholic

   c. Groups, organizations, and departments: League of Women Voters, Ford Motor Company, United States Senate, Department of Agriculture

   d. Particular deities: God, Allah, Buddha, Zeus

2. Names of particular places:

   a. Cities, counties, states, and countries: Cleveland, Cuyahoga County, Ohio, United States of America

   b. Particular geographical regions: Pacific Northwest, the South

   c. Streets: East Ninth Street, El Cajon Avenue

    d. Buildings: RCA Building, Union Terminal

    e. Heavenly bodies (except the sun and moon): Mars, Milky Way, Andromeda, Alpha Centauri

  3. Names of particular things:

    a. Days and months: Friday, August

    b. Holidays: Easter, May Day

    c. Historical events and periods: the Civil War, the Middle Ages

    d. School courses: Biology 101, History 102 (but "a *history* course")

    e. Languages: English, Russian

    f. Schools: Cornell University, Walt Whitman High School (but "I graduated from *high school.*")

    g. Brands: Buick, Peter Pan Peanut Butter (but "I had a peanut butter sandwich for lunch.")

Collective nouns. See *Subject-verb agreement, E.*

Colon. A colon (:) is commonly used after a clause introducing a list or description, between hours and minutes, in the salutation of a formal letter, between biblical chapter and verse numbers, and between the title and sub-title of a book. Less commonly, a colon may be used between independent clauses and before quotations.

A. *List.* A colon is used between a general statement and a list or description that follows:

> We shall never again find the equals of the famous three B's of music: Bach, Beethoven, and Brahms.

> He plans to take five courses: history, English, psychology, French, and physical education.

> *Note:* A colon should appear after a complete statement. A colon should *not* be used after a form of the verb *to be (be, am, is, are, was, were, been,* etc.) or after a preposition.

WRONG	RIGHT
Perennial contenders for the NFL championship are: Pittsburgh, Houston, Dallas, and Los Angeles.	Several teams are perennial contenders for the NFL championship: Pittsburgh, Houston, Dallas, and Los Angeles.
	OR
	Perennial contenders for the NFL championship are Pittsburgh, Houston, Dallas, and Los Angeles.

F. Scott Fitzgerald is the author of: *This Side of Paradise, The Beautiful and Damned, The Great Gatsby,* and *Tender Is the Night.*

F. Scott Fitzgerald wrote the following books: *This Side of Paradise, The Beautiful and Damned, The Great Gatsby,* and *Tender Is the Night.*

OR

F. Scott Fitzgerald is the author of *This Side of Paradise, The Beautiful and Damned, The Great Gatsby,* and *Tender Is the Night.*

B. *Time.* A colon is used between hours and minutes when a specific time is written in numerals:

8:00 P.M.   8:10 A.M.

C. *Salutation.* In formal letter writing, a colon is used after the salutation:

Dear Ms. Johnson: Dear Sir:

D. *Bible.* A colon is used to separate chapter from verse:

Genesis, chapter 1, verse 8—Genesis 1:8

E. *Title and subtitle.* A colon is used between the title and subtitle of a book:

Johnson's Dictionary: A Modern Selection

F. *Independent clauses.* A colon may be used between independent clauses when the second clause explains the first:

She brought up her children on one principle, and one principle only: do unto others what they would like to do unto you—and do it first.

G. *Quotations.* A colon *can* be used before a short quotation and often is used before a long block quotation:

Whenever I try to diet, I am reminded of the bitter truth of Oscar Wilde's epigram: "I can resist everything but temptation."

In commenting on his function as a writer, Joseph Conrad put every writer's dream into words:

My task which I am trying to achieve is, by the power of the written word to make you hear, to make you feel—it is, before all, to make you *see*. That—and no more, and it is everything. If I succeed, you shall find there according to your deserts: encouragement, consolation, fear, charm—all you demand—and, perhaps, also that glimpse of truth for which you have forgotten to ask.

Comma. Using a comma correctly is almost never a matter of taste or inspiration. It is even less a matter of following the ancient junior high school formula of tossing in a comma "to indicate a pause." Different people pause for breath and emphasis in different places. When errors turn up, they are most often the result of the writer's being comma happy—putting in too many commas. Our basic rule, then, is *never use a comma unless you know it is necessary*. It is necessary in the following cases:

* between elements in a list or series
* between independent clauses joined by *and, but, yet, for, or, nor, so*
* after long introductory elements
* before and after interrupting elements
* between coordinate adjectives
* before and after nonrestrictive elements
* before and after phrases that express a contrast
* before and after words of direct address, interjections, and *yes* and *no*
* between certain words to prevent misreading
* in conventional elements such as dates, numbers, addresses, titles, correspondence, direct quotations

A. *Series.* Three or more items in a list or series must be separated by commas for the sake of clarity.

> The potential buyer should take special care to inspect the roof, basement, and ceilings.

> Make sure you read parts one, two, and three before completing the assignment.

> The three novels in Dos Passos' *USA* trilogy are *The 42nd Parallel, Nineteen Nineteen,* and *The Big Money.*

> *Note:* In all three of these examples, the comma before *and* is optional. Most experienced writers use the comma, however, because it reinforces the idea of a series in the reader's mind.

B. *Independent clauses.* Independent clauses joined by a coordinate conjunction—*and, but, for, yet, or, nor, so*—require a comma *before* the conjunction:

> Connotations are not usually entered next to a word in a dictionary, but they still exist in people's minds.

> Each writing assignment requires a different kind of organization, and each may be a different length.

> *Note:* No comma would be used if the above sentences were rewritten to have only one independent clause:

> Connotations are not usually entered next to a word in a dictionary but still exist in people's minds.

> Each writing assignment requires a different kind of organization and may be a different length.

C. *Introductory elements.* A comma should be used after a long introductory element:

> *Because the student was having trouble with commas,* he read the section on punctuation.
>
> *In good writing,* there are few punctuation errors.

The *italicized* parts of these two sentences are introductory elements. When the introductory element is extremely short—one word, for example—the comma can sometimes be omitted if the meaning remains clear: *Soon* the term will end.

POOR	CORRECT
Because this is an introductory element it should have a comma after it.	Because this is an introductory element, it should have a comma after it.
Despite the best efforts of both parties no agreement was reached.	Despite the best efforts of both parties, no agreement was reached.
Never having seen her before I expected the worst.	Never having seen her before, I expected the worst.
As soon as he had showered he went straight to bed.	As soon as he had showered, he went straight to bed.

> *Note:* If any of the above introductory elements are moved so that they come *after* the independent clauses (and thus no longer introduce anything), no commas should be used:

No agreement was reached despite the best efforts of both parties.

He went straight to bed as soon as he had showered.

Exercise

Put a comma after the introductory element where necessary.

1. If I can forget about the senator's words, ideas, and personality I might actually vote for him.
2. Then I woke up.
3. Whenever I hear someone suggest that love is the answer to our problems I wonder why love has usually made me miserable.
4. Feeling as I do I have no alternative.
5. Bored and disgusted with the ballgame I thought bitterly that there were some peanut vendors in the stands who were better athletes than anyone on the field.
6. Frequently we worry about mistakes we never made.
7. Considering my shortcomings I have been luckier than I deserve.
8. Later we may need to discuss some exceptions to this rule.

9. If your essay falls apart it probably has no primary idea to hold it together.
10. After a long introductory clause or phrase use a comma.

D. *Interrupting elements.* A comma should be used before and after an interrupting element. Interrupting elements, while often needed for clarity and continuity, are those that break the flow of words in the main thought of a sentence or clause. In the previous sentence, *while often needed for clarity or continuity* is an interrupting element. Some writers find it helpful to think of interrupting elements as asides to the audience or parenthetical insertions. Interrupting elements may be words such as *indeed, however, too, also, consequently, therefore, moreover, nevertheless* and phrases such as *as the author says, of course, after all, for example, in fact, on the other hand.*

WRONG	RIGHT
Suppose for example that you decide to write about your own life.	Suppose, for example, that you decide to write about your own life.
We must bear in mind too that even the best system is imperfect.	We must bear in mind, too, that even the best system is imperfect.
Punctuation as we can see is not exactly fun.	Punctuation, as we can see, is not exactly fun.
The only thing wrong with youth according to George Bernard Shaw is that it is wasted on the young.	The only thing wrong with youth, according to George Bernard Shaw, is that it is wasted on the young.
His pledges for the future however could not make me forget his broken promises of the past.	His pledges for the future, however, could not make me forget his broken promises of the past.

E. *Coordinate adjectives.* A comma is used to separate coordinate adjectives—adjectives of equal rank—that come before the nouns they modify.

WRONG	RIGHT
This poet uses concrete believable images.	This poet uses concrete, believable images.
Her warm enthusiastic energetic behavior was often mistaken for pushiness.	Her warm, enthusiastic, energetic behavior was often mistaken for pushiness.

> *Note:* Coordinate adjectives have two features: you may put *and* between them (concrete *and* believable, warm *and* enthusiastic *and* energetic) and they are reversible (believable, concrete; enthusiastic, energetic, warm). Compare these examples to "This poet uses several concrete images." You cannot say "several and concrete" or "concrete several." Therefore, you do not use a comma between them. Note, too,

that if the coordinate adjectives had originally been joined by *and*, no commas would have been necessary: "Her warm and energetic and enthusiastic behavior was often mistaken for pushiness."

F. *Nonrestrictive elements.* A comma should be used before and after a nonrestrictive element.

Nonrestrictive modifiers. Commas are used before and after nonrestrictive modifiers. A nonrestrictive modifier gives additional information about the noun it modifies but *is not necessary to identify or define that noun:*

> The Empire State Building, which I visited last year, is a most impressive sight.
>
> My father, who has worked in a steel foundry for thirty years, has made many sacrifices for me.

A *restrictive* modifier is not set off by commas. It is a necessary part of the meaning of the noun it modifies:

> A person who is always late for appointments may have serious psychological problems.
>
> The novel that Professor Higgins praised so highly is very disappointing.
>
> People who live in glass houses shouldn't throw bricks.
>
> Many jobs for highly skilled technicians are still available.

Proper punctuation of restrictive and nonrestrictive modifiers often can affect meaning:

The sofa, with those huge armrests, is an eyesore.	The writer sees just one sofa. The nonrestrictive modifier merely conveys more information about it.
The sofa with those huge armrests is an eyesore.	The writer sees more than one sofa. The restrictive modifier is necessary to distinguish this sofa from the others.

A special type of nonrestrictive element is called the *appositive.* It is a word or group of words that means the same thing as the element that *precedes* it. In the sentence, "Joseph Terrell, *Mayor of Greenville,* will speak at graduation," the *italicized* phrase is an appositive; that is, it means the same thing as the first element, *Joseph Terrell.* The rules governing the punctuation of modifiers also govern the punctuation of appositives.

Nonrestrictive appositives. Commas are used before and after nonrestrictive appositives. A nonrestrictive appositive gives additional information about the noun it follows but *is not necessary to identify that noun:*

> Miss Susan Swattem, *the meanest person in town,* was my high school mathematics teacher.

Thomas Jefferson, *third president of the United States,* also founded the University of Virginia.

A *restrictive appositive* is not set off by commas. It is necessary to identify the noun it follows:

The expression *hitch your wagon to a star* was first used by Emerson.

He spoke to Susan *my sister,* not Susan *my wife.*

As with modifiers, proper punctuation of nonrestrictive and restrictive appositives often can affect meaning.

My brother, George, is a kindly soul.	The writer has only one brother, so the word *brother* is sufficient identification. *George* is nonrestrictive.
My brother George is a kindly soul.	The writer has more than one brother, so the name of the specific brother he has in mind is a necessary part of the meaning. *George* is restrictive.

Exercise

Use commas where necessary to set off nonrestrictive elements.

1. The person who left the notebook in the classroom went to the instructor's office before the next class.
2. Albert Einstein that legendary figure of modern science was a notable underachiever during his school days.
3. Exxon which is the largest oil company in the world used to be known as Standard Oil Company of New Jersey.
4. Swiss Army knives pocket knives with a dozen or so different blades have become extremely popular in recent years.
5. The Boy Scout knife that I had as a child will always remain my special favorite.
6. My sister Sonya has four children. My sister Judith has none.
7. The man who picked up the packages for the old woman had his wallet stolen when he bent over.
8. Republicans who support their party will try to support the policies of a Republican president.
9. Harold Arlen who wrote such songs as "Stormy Weather" and "Let's Fall in Love" also composed the classic score for *The Wizard of Oz.*
10. The baseball player who has the highest lifetime batting average in the history of the game is Ty Cobb.

G. *Contrast.* Commas should be used to set off phrases expressing a contrast.

She told him to deliver the furniture on Wednesday, not Tuesday.

Hard work, not noble daydreams, is what I believe in.

The money did not bring hope, but anxiety.

Note: The comma can sometimes be omitted before contrasting phrases beginning with *but: We have nothing to fear but fear itself.*

H. *Direct address, interjections,* yes *and* no. Commas separate words and phrases of direct address, interjections, and the words *yes* and *no* from the rest of the sentence.

1. Direct address:

   I tell you, ladies and gentlemen, that this strategy will not work.

   Jim, you're still not following the instructions.

2. Interjections:

   Well, it appears that the committee has finally issued its report.

   Oh, I'd say the new car should arrive in about three weeks.

   Note: Commas are generally used with mild interjections. More dramatic interjections may take exclamation points:

   Well! It was the worst mess I'd ever seen.

   Oh! How could she have made such a contemptible remark?

3. *Yes* and *no:*

   Yes, I plan to vote for Ruppert.

   I have to tell you plainly that, no, I cannot support your proposal.

I. *Misreading.* Apart from any more specific rules, commas are sometimes necessary to prevent misreading. Without commas, the following examples would be likely to stop readers in midsentence and send them back to the beginning.

CONFUSING	CORRECT
High above the trees swayed in the wind.	High above, the trees swayed in the wind.
High above the trees an ominous thundercloud came into view.	High above the trees, an ominous thundercloud came into view.
At the same time John and Arnold were making their plans.	At the same time, John and Arnold were making their plans.
Hugging and kissing my half-smashed relatives celebrated the wedding.	Hugging and kissing, my half-smashed relatives celebrated the wedding.

J. *Conventions.* Commas are used in such conventional elements as dates, numbers, addresses, titles, correspondence, and direct quotations.

1. Dates. Commas separate the day of the month and the year:

   April 24, 1938   January 5, 1967

If only the month and year are used, the comma may be omitted:

April 1938   *or*   April, 1938

If the year is used in midsentence with the day of the month, it should be followed by a comma. With the month only, the comma may be omitted:

World War II began for the United States on December 7, 1941, at Pearl Harbor.

World War II began for the United States in December 1941 at Pearl Harbor.

World War II began for the United States in December, 1941, at Pearl Harbor.

2. Numbers. Commas are used to group numbers of more than three digits to the left of the decimal point:

$5,280.00   751,672.357   5,429,000

When a number consists of only four digits, the comma may be omitted:

5,280   *or*   5280

3. Addresses. Commas are used to separate towns, cities, counties, states, and districts:

Cleveland, Ohio

Brooklyn, Kings County, New York

Washington, D.C.

Note: A comma is not used to separate the Zip Code from the state.

Pasadena, California 91106

4. Titles. A comma often separates a title from a name that precedes it:

Norman Prange, Jr.   Harold Unger, M.D.   Julia Harding, Ph.D.

5. Correspondence. A comma is used after the salutation in informal letter writing and after the complimentary close:

Dear John,   Dear Jane,

Respectfully yours,   Sincerely yours,

6. Direct quotations. See *Quotation marks, A.*

Comma splice. Often considered a special kind of *run-on sentence* (for which the Handbook provides a separate entry), a comma splice is a punctuation error that occurs when two independent clauses are joined only by a comma. To correct a comma splice, either use a comma *and* a coordinating conjunction, or replace the comma with a semicolon or a period.

There are only seven coordinating conjunctions: *and, but, or, nor, for, yet,* and *so.* When these are used between independent clauses, they should be preceded by a comma:

WRONG	RIGHT
The boy had been crippled since infancy, he still tried to excel in everything he did.	The boy had been crippled since infancy, but he still tried to excel in everything he did.
	OR
	The boy had been crippled since infancy; he still tried to excel in everything he did.
	OR
	The boy had been crippled since infancy. He still tried to excel in everything he did.
Each writing assignment requires a different kind of organization, each may be a different length.	Each writing assignment requires a different kind of organization, and each may be a different length.
	OR
	Each writing assignment requires a different kind of organization; each may be a different length.
	OR
	Each writing assignment requires a different kind of organization. Each may be a different length.

It is often tempting to use words such as *however, therefore, nevertheless, indeed,* and *moreover* after a comma to join independent clauses. *Don't!* The only words following a comma that can join two independent clauses are the seven coordinating conjunctions.

WRONG	RIGHT
We started with high hopes, however, we were disappointed.	We started with high hopes; however, we were disappointed.
She had been hurt many times, nevertheless, she always seemed cheerful.	She had been hurt many times; nevertheless, she always seemed cheerful.

Although any choice among coordinating conjunctions, semicolons, and periods will be technically correct, the best choice often depends on complex issues of style and thought. If the independent clauses under consideration are surrounded by long sentences, for example, the writer might choose to break the monotony with a period, thus creating two short sentences. If the independent clauses are surrounded by short sentences, the writer can sometimes achieve variety by creating a long sentence with a coordinating conjunction or semicolon. In addition, the more closely connected the thoughts in two independent clauses, the more likely the writer will be to show that connection by using a coordinating conjunction or semicolon. In such cases, two separate sentences would indicate too great a separation of thought. Obviously, no easy rules work here, and the writer's intentions have to be the main guide.

Comma splices can be acceptable in standard English when each clause is unusually short and when the thought of the whole sentence expresses an ongoing process.

> I came, I saw, I conquered.
>
> Throughout the interview, she squirmed, she stammered, she blushed.

Exercise

Rewrite the following sentences, correcting the comma splices where necessary.

1. The politicians complained bitterly, the company's profits had increased by 63 percent.
2. The company replied that figures have to be interpreted in context, the previous year's profits had been down 84 percent from the year before that.
3. It was impossible for him to express the full measure of his indignation, he bit his lip, and he clenched his fists.
4. As man learns to use machines more effectively, he has more leisure time.
5. Jack Nicklaus had a terrible golfing season recently, he won only $102,000.
6. Automation has cost many individuals their jobs, however, it has, on the whole, created jobs.
7. Tennis seems to have become an extraordinarily popular sport, personally, it leaves me cold.
8. Fear can prevent a person from acting, hate, on the other hand, will often cause action.
9. She was a human being. She was born, she lived, she suffered, she died.
10. Do not join two sentences with just a comma, use a comma and a conjunction, a semicolon, or a period to separate sentences.

Comparative and superlative forms. Comparative forms of adjectives and adverbs are used to compare or contrast groups of two—and only two. The comparative form of regular adjectives is formed by adding -er to the ending of the adjective or by using the word *more* before the adjective: *nicer, sweeter, more dramatic, more beautiful.* (Some adjectives are irregular: the comparative of *good* is *better;* the comparative of *bad* is *worse.*) The comparative form of adverbs is formed by using *more* before the adverb: *more nicely, more sweetly, more dramatically, more beautifully.*

Superlative forms of adjectives and adverbs are used to compare or contrast groups of three or more. The superlative form of regular adjectives is formed by adding -est to the ending of the adjective or by using the word *most* before the adjective: *nicest, sweetest, most dramatic, most beautiful.* (Some adjectives are irregular: the superlative of *good* is *best;* the superlative of *bad* is *worst.*) The superlative form of adverbs uses *most* before the adverb: *most nicely, most sweetly, most dramatically, most beautifully.*

In summary, *comparative forms apply to two, and superlative forms apply to more than two.*

WRONG	RIGHT
If I had to choose between Paul Newman and Robert Redford, I would have to say that Robert Redford is the *best* actor.	If I had to choose between Paul Newman and Robert Redford, I would have to say that Robert Redford is the *better* actor.
The high school girl and the junior high school girl competed on the parallel bars. The junior high school girl was given the *highest* scores.	The high school girl and the junior high school girl competed on the parallel bars. The junior high school girl was given the *higher* scores.
I like many people, but I like Betsy *more.*	I like many people, but I like Betsy *most.*
Although my first and second themes both required hard work, I wrote the second *most* easily.	Although my first and second themes both required hard work, I wrote the second *more* easily.

Comparisons. Comparisons must be both logical and complete.

A. *Logical.* Do not compare items that are not related. You would not compare horses to safety pins because they have nothing in common. Not all illogical comparisons are this obvious, however, since it is usually the phrasing rather than the thought behind it that is at fault.

WRONG	RIGHT
His appetite is as huge as a pig. (Here the comparison is between *appetite* and *pig.*)	His appetite is as huge as a pig's.
	OR
	His appetite is as huge as a pig's appetite.
	OR
	His appetite is as huge as that of a pig.

Mark Twain is more amusing than any American writer. (Here Mark Twain is excluded from the group that he belongs to.)

Mark Twain is more amusing than any other American writer.

B. *Complete.* A comparison must be complete: the items being compared must be clear, and both items must be stated.

1. Clarity:

    POOR: I like him more than you.

    RIGHT: I like him more than I like you.

      OR

      I like him more than you like him.

2. Both items stated:

    POOR: Old Reliable Bank has higher interest rates. (Higher than it had before? Higher than other banks have? Higher on deposits or higher on loans?)

    RIGHT: Old Reliable Bank has higher interest rates on savings accounts than any other bank in the city.

    Note: For further discussion of comparisons, see Chapter 15, pp. 405–407.

Exercise

Correct any faulty comparisons in the following sentences.

1. Alka-Seltzer commercials are more entertaining than Anacin.
2. Her marks were higher than anyone in the class.
3. Pale and deeply stirred, he looked like a dry martini.
4. *The Empire Strikes Back* was the best movie.
5. *Hamlet* is more interesting than any play ever written.
6. His great big sad eyes are like a cocker spaniel.
7. Her qualifications were as good as John.
8. I get along with my in-laws better than my wife.
9. My mother's temper is harder to deal with than my father.
10. Thomas Edison is more famous than any inventor in history.

Compound subjects. See *Subject-verb agreement, A.*

Conjunctions, coordinating. See *Comma, B* and *Comma splice.*

Conjunctions, subordinating. See *Fragmentary sentences, C.*

Coordinating adjectives. See *Comma, E.*

Coordinating conjunctions. See *Comma, B* and *Comma splice.*

Dangling modifier. See *Modifiers, A.*

Dash. A dash (—) is used primarily to emphasize a parenthetical or otherwise nonessential word or phrase. It can also highlight an afterthought or separate a list or series from the rest of the sentence. An *introductory* list or series may be separated by a dash from the rest of the sentence if it is summarized by a word that serves as the subject of the sentence.

A. *Parenthetical word or phrase.*

> Only when politicans are exposed to temptation—and rest assured they are almost always so exposed—can we determine their real worth as human beings.

B. *Afterthought.*

> The only person who understood the talk was the speaker—and I have my doubts about him.

C. *List or series.*

> The great French Impressionists—Manet, Monet, Renoir—virtually invented a new way of looking at the world.

> *The Scarlet Letter, Moby-Dick, Walden, Leaves of Grass, Uncle Tom's Cabin*—these American classics were all published during the incredible five-year span of 1850–1855.

Use dashes sparingly, or they lose their force. Do not confuse a dash with a hyphen. (See *Hyphen.*) In typing, indicate a dash by striking the hyphen key twice (--), leaving no space between the dash and the two words it separates.

Double negative. Always incorrect in standard English, a double negative is the use of two negative terms to express only one negative idea. Remember that in addition to obvious negative terms such as *no, not,* and *nothing,* the words *hardly* and *scarcely* are also considered negatives.

WRONG	RIGHT
I don't have no memory of last night.	I don't have any memory of last night.
	OR
	I have no memory of last night.
For truly religious people, money cannot mean nothing of value.	For truly religious people, money cannot mean anything of value.
	OR
	For truly religious people, money can mean nothing of value.
His mother could not hardly express her feelings of pride at his graduation.	His mother could hardly express her feelings of pride at his graduation.
Our troubles had not scarcely begun.	Our troubles had scarcely begun.

Ellipsis. An ellipsis (three spaced dots) shows omission of one or more words from quoted material. If the ellipsis occurs at the end of a sentence, there will be four spaced dots; one dot will be the period for the sentence.

ORIGINAL	USE OF ELLIPSIS
"The connotation of a word is its implicit meaning, the meaning derived from the atmosphere, the vibrations, the emotions that we associate with the word."	"The connotation of a word is its implicit meaning . . . the emotions that we associate with the word."

End marks. The three end marks are the period, question mark, and exclamation point.

A. *Period.* A period is used at the end of all complete sentences that make a statement, after abbreviations, and in fractions expressed as decimals.

1. Sentences. If a complete sentence makes a statement, use a period at the end:

   Please give unused clothing to the Salvation Army.

   Place pole B against slot C and insert bolt D.

   The class wants to know when the paper is due.

2. Abbreviations. A period is used after some abbreviations:

   Mr. R. P. Reddish   Mt. Everest   Ph.D.

   Note: A period is not used in abbreviations such as UNESCO, CORE, FCC, and AAUP. See *Abbreviations.*

3. Decimals. A period is used before a fraction written as a decimal.

   $\frac{1}{4} = .25$ $\frac{1}{20} = .05$

   Note: If a decimal is used to indicate money, a dollar sign is also necessary.

B. *Question mark.* A question mark is used to indicate a direct question or a doubtful date or figure.

1. Direct question. Use a question mark at the end of a direct question. Do not use a question mark with indirect questions such as "They asked when the paper was due."

   When is the paper due?

   Did the teacher say when the paper is due?

A question mark is also used when only the last part of a sentence asks a question, and when a quotation that asks a question is contained within a larger sentence.

I know I should go to college, but where will I get the money for tuition?

The student asked, "When is the paper due?"

After asking, "When is the paper due?" the student left the room.

Note: In the last example, the question mark replaces the usual comma inside the quotation.

2. Doubtful date or figure. After a doubtful date or figure, a question mark in parentheses is used. This does not mean that if you are giving an approximate date or figure you should use a question mark. Use it only if the accuracy of the date or figure is doubtful.

The newspaper reported that the government said it cost $310 (?) to send a man to the moon. (Here a question mark is appropriate because it is doubtful if $310 is the figure. Perhaps there has been a misprint in the paper.)

Chaucer was born in 1340(?) and died in 1400. (Here historians know when Chaucer died but are doubtful of exactly when he was born, even though most evidence points to 1340. If historians were completely unsure, they would simply write, "Chaucer was born in the mid-1300s and died in 1400.")

A question mark in parentheses should never be used to indicate humor or sarcasm. It is awkward and childish to write "He was a good (?) teacher," or "After much debate and sectarian compromise, the legislature approved a satisfactory (?) state budget."

C. *Exclamation point.* An exclamation point is used at the end of emphatic or exclamatory words, phrases, and sentences. In formal writing, exclamation points are rare. They most often occur in dialogue, and even there they should be used sparingly lest their effect be lost.

1. Word or phrase:

My God! Is the paper due today?

No! You cannot copy my exam.

2. Sentence:

The school burned down!

Stop talking!

Note: Comic book devices such as !?! or !! are signs of an immature writer. Words, not the symbols after them, should carry the primary meaning.

Exclamation point. See *End mark, C.*

Fragmentary sentences. A fragmentary sentence is a grammatically incomplete statement punctuated as if it were a complete sentence. It is one of the most common basic writing errors.

To avoid a sentence fragment, make sure that your sentence contains at least one independent clause. If it does not contain an independent clause, it is a fragment.

Here are some examples of sentences, with the independent clause *italicized;* sometimes the independent clause *is* the whole sentence, and sometimes the independent clause is part of a larger sentence.

> *Jack and Jill went up the hill.*
>
> *He sees.*
>
> If you don't stop bothering me, *I'll phone the police.*
>
> Tomorrow at the latest, *we'll have to call a special meeting.*
>
> *He straightened his tie* before he entered the room.
>
> Discovering that he had lost his mother, *the little boy started to cry.*

An independent clause is a group of words which contains a subject and verb and expresses a complete thought. This traditional definition is beyond criticism except that it can lead to messy discussions about the philosophical nature of a complete thought. Such discussions can usually be avoided by concentrating on the practical reasons for a missing independent clause. There are three major reasons: omission of subject or verb, confusion of verb derivatives (verbals) with verbs, and confusion of a dependent clause with an independent clause.

A. *Omission of subject or verb.* This is the simplest kind of fragment to spot:

> There are many events that take place on campus. *Such as plays, concerts, and many other things.*
>
> My father finally answered me. *Nastily and negatively.*
>
> Mrs. Jones has plenty of activities to keep herself busy. *Nagging, scolding, snooping, and drinking.*
>
> The new department head had a brand new pain in the neck. *In addition to the old ones.*
>
> We had many blessings. *Like love, nature, family, God, and television.*

These fragments should be obvious even without the italics, and the remedies should be just as obvious. Simple changes in punctuation will solve the problems. Here are the same sentences with the fragments eliminated:

> There are many events that take place on campus, such as plays, concerts, and many other things.
>
> My father finally answered me nastily and negatively.
>
> Mrs. Jones has plenty of activities to keep herself busy: nagging, scolding, snooping, and drinking.
>
> The new department head had a brand new pain in the neck in addition to the old ones.
>
> We had many blessings, like love, nature, family, God, and television.

B. *Confusion of verb derivatives (verbals) with verbs.* Verbals are words derived from verbs. Unlike verbs, they cannot function *by themselves* as the predicate of a sentence. Infinitive forms are verbals *(to do, to see, to walk)*. So are gerunds and present participles (-*ing* endings: *doing, seeing, walking*). Study the *italicized* sentence fragments below.

> I decided to take her to the game. *Susan enjoying football a lot.*
>
> Nobody ought to vote. *The government being corrupt.*
>
> We should take pleasure in the little things. *A boy petting his dog. Lovers holding hands. Soft clouds moving overhead.*
>
> *To make the world a better place. To help people be happy.* These are my goals.

In the last example, the fragments lack subjects as well as verbs and can readily be identified. Inexperienced writers, however, looking at the fragments in the first three examples, see a subject and what appears to be a verb. They assume, consequently, that the words make up an independent clause. They are wrong. A present participle all by itself cannot serve as a verb, and an independent clause must have a verb. Study these corrected versions of the fragments.

> I decided to take her to the game. Susan has been enjoying football a lot.
>
> Nobody ought to vote. The government is corrupt.
>
> We should take pleasure in the little things: a boy petting his dog, lovers holding hands, soft clouds moving overhead.
>
> I want to make the world a better place. I want to make people happy. These are my goals.

C. *Confusion of a dependent (subordinate) clause with an independent clause.* All clauses contain a subject and a verb. Unlike an independent clause, however, a dependent or subordinate clause does not express a complete thought and therefore cannot function as a sentence. A subordinate clause at the beginning of a sentence must always be followed by an independent clause. A subordinate clause at the end of a sentence must always be preceded by an independent clause. Fortunately, subordinate clauses can be readily identified if you remember that *they always begin with subordinating conjunctions*—a much easier approach than trying to figure out whether your sentence conveys a complete thought. Here, in alphabetical order, is a list of most of the subordinating conjunctions you are likely to encounter. *Whenever one of these words immediately precedes a clause (subject + verb), that clause becomes a subordinate clause and cannot stand alone as a complete sentence.*

after	as long as	before	if
although	as soon as	even if	in order that
as	as though	even though	once
as if	because	how	provided that

since	than	unless	whenever
so that	though	until	wherever
			while

Note: Except when used as question words, *who, which, when,* and *where* also introduce a subordinate clause.

In the left column, examples of subordinate clauses used as sentence fragments are *italicized*. In the right column, *italics* indicate corrections to repair these sentence fragments.

FRAGMENTS	CORRECTED
If I ever see home again.	If I ever see home again, *I'll be surprised.*
Keats was a great poet. *Because he was inspired.*	*Keats was a great poet* because he was inspired.
I will never apologize. *Unless you really insist.*	*I will never apologize* unless you really insist.
Provided that the contract is carried out within thirty days.	Provided that the contract is carried out within thirty days, *we will not sue.*
This is the man who will be our next governor. *Who will lead this state to a better tomorrow.*	*This is the man who will be our next governor,* who will lead this state to a better tomorrow.

The major difficulty anyone is likely to have with sentence fragments is in identifying them. They are usually child's play to correct. Sentence fragments occur, in many cases, because of a misunderstanding of complex grammatical issues, but they can almost always be corrected with elementary revisions in punctuation.

Sentence fragments should nearly always be avoided. In rare situations, they can sometimes be justified, especially if the writer wants a sudden dramatic effect.

I shall never consent to this law. Never!

Oh, God!

Scared? I was terrified.

Lost. Alone in the big city. Worried. The boy struggled to keep from crying.

Exercise

Some of the following are sentence fragments. Rewrite them to form complete sentences.

1. Whenever I go to the lake.
2. Because first impressions are often wrong impressions.
3. After she had gathered her information and written her paper.

4. Having extremely poor eyesight, I keep an extra pair of glasses at home.
5. The managing editor, an excellent journalist and former reporter.
6. Being the most popular actor of his generation.
7. At 5:00 P.M. the train was due.
8. Which he had lost several times before.
9. Before long, the fire died down.
10. Clearing away all of the wreckage, helping victims of the storm, and still finding time to operate the communications network.
11. Unless we all work together for a better world, we may have no world at all.
12. To mention just a few items of relatively minor importance.
13. A person who can approach problems with a unique combination of vision and practicality.
14. Shuffling papers and looking busy are the only requirements of the job.
15. Who does he think he is?

Fused sentence. See *Run-on sentence.*

Hyphen. A hyphen (-) is used in some compound words and in words divided at the end of a line.

A. *Compound words.*

1. As a general rule, you should consult a recent dictionary to check the use of the hyphen in compound words. Many such words that were once hyphenated are now combined. The following are some compound words that are still hyphenated:

   mother-in-law   court-martial

   knee-deep   water-cooled

2. All numbers from twenty-one to ninety-nine are hyphenated:

   forty-three   one hundred fifty-six

3. A hyphen joins two or more words that form an adjective *before* a noun:

   well-known teacher   first-rate performance

   but   *but*

   The teacher is well known. The performance was first rate.

B. *Divided words.* Divide words at the end of a line by consulting a dictionary and following accepted syllabication. A one-syllable word cannot be divided. In addition, a single letter cannot be separated from the rest of the word; for example, *a-bout* for *about* would be incorrect. The hyphen should come at the very end of the line, not at the beginning of the next line.

Indirect question. See *End marks, B, 1.*

Italics (underlining). In manuscript form—handwriting or typing— underlining represents printed italics. The rules for underlining and italics are the same. Underline titles of complete works; foreign words and phrases; words used emphatically; and letters, words, and phrases pointed to as such.

> *Note:* When a word or phrase that would usually be italicized appears in a section of text that is already italicized, the word or phrase is typed or written with no italics.

A. *Titles of complete works:*

1. Books: *The Great Gatsby, Paradise Lost, Encyclopaedia Britannica, Webster's New Collegiate Dictionary*

2. Newspapers: the *New York Times,* the *Chicago Tribune*

3. Plays: *Raisin in the Sun, Macbeth*

4. Movies: *Easy Rider, The Maltese Falcon*

> *Note:* The titles of poems are put in quotation marks except for book-length poems such as Milton's *Paradise Lost* or Homer's *Iliad.* The titles of small units contained within larger units, such as chapters in books, selections in anthologies, articles or short stories in magazines, etc., are put in quotation marks. See *Quotation marks, B.*

B. *Foreign words and phrases not assimilated into English:* vaya con Dios, paisano, auf Wiedersehen.

C. *Words used emphatically:*

Ask me, but don't *tell* me.

Under *no* circumstances can this be permitted to happen.

Except in special situations, good word choice and careful phrasing are far more effective than underlining to show emphasis.

D. *Letters, words, and phrases pointed to as such:*

Words such as *however* and *therefore* cannot be used as coordinating conjunctions.

The letter *x* is often used in algebra.

The phrase *on the other hand* anticipates a contrast.

Manuscript correction symbols. When you have finished writing a paper or examination in class and are reading it over, you will often find a number of small mechanical errors. For example, in your haste you wrote one word as two or two words as one; perhaps you left out a word here and there, or you forgot to indent for a paragraph. You might have reversed the letters in a word—*e* before *i,* for example. You need not copy the whole paper over. There are a group of neat and easy-to-use symbols for correcting these mistakes. On papers written at home, however, be careful! Correcting a *few* slips of the pen or typewriter is fine; making four or five corrections per paragraph is something else. If you have numerous corrections, it is best to recopy or retype.

A. ⌣ This device joins one word written as two or connects a word in which a space has mysteriously appeared:

Every one finished writing the paper on time.

Use manu script symbols where necessary.

B. / The slash line has two functions.

1. It can separate two words written as one:

Don't write two words as one.

2. It shows that a capital letter should be lowercased:

the English Language

the Museum Of Modern Art

C. ¶ This symbol means paragraph. Perhaps you forgot to indent a new paragraph or you simply ran two paragraphs together. Put a ¶ at the beginning of the new paragraph.

D. ∧ The caret indicates that the words written *above* the line are to be inserted at the point the caret is used. The caret is always inserted at the bottom of the line.

first published in 1851,
Herman Melville's *Moby-Dick*,∧is considered one of America's greatest novels.

E. ∽ This device indicates that letters or words are in the wrong order. It should be used *very* sparingly—usually it's better to erase and correct the error.

I recieved an A in the course.

I do always well in English.

F. ☰ Three lines under a lowercase letter show that it should be a capital.

He became a presbyterian minister.

I'll see you next friday.

Misplaced modifier. See *Modifiers, B.*

Modifiers. The most frequent errors involving modifiers are dangling modifiers and misplaced modifiers.

A. *Dangling modifiers.* A dangling modifier is a group of words, often found at the beginning of a sentence, that does not refer to anything in the sentence or that seems to refer to a word to which it is not logically related.

Dangling modifiers usually include some form of a verb which has no subject, either implied or stated. This construction results in statements that are often humorous and always illogical. To correct this error, either change the modifier into a subordinate clause, or change the main clause so that the modifier logically relates to a word in it. On occasion, it may be necessary to change both clauses.

INCORRECT	CORRECT
Climbing the mountain, the sunset blazed with a brilliant red and orange. (This sentence says that the sunset is climbing the mountain.)	As we were climbing the mountain, the sunset blazed with a brilliant red and orange. (Subordinate clause)
	OR
	Climbing the mountain, we saw the sunset blazing with brilliant red and orange. (Main clause)
After looking in several stores, the book was found. (In this sentence, the book is looking in stores.)	After looking in several stores, we found the book.
To become an accurate speller, a dictionary should be used. (In this sentence, the dictionary is becoming an accurate speller.)	If you want to become an accurate speller, you should use a dictionary.
	OR
	To become an accurate speller, you should use a dictionary.
While talking and not paying attention, the teacher gave the class an assignment. (This sentence says that the teacher is talking and not paying attention while giving an assignment. If that is what the writer meant, then this sentence is correct. If, however, the writer meant that the class was talking and not paying attention, then it is incorrect.)	While the class was talking and not paying attention, the teacher gave an assignment.
	OR
	While talking and not paying attention, the class was given an assignment by the teacher.

B. *Misplaced modifiers.* Since part of the meaning of the English language depends on word order—some other languages depend mostly on word endings—you must make sure that phrases serving as modifiers and adverbs such as *only, always, almost, hardly,* and *nearly* are placed in the position that will make the sentence mean what you intend. Misplaced modifiers, unlike dangling modifiers, can almost always be corrected simply by changing their positions.

1. Phrases serving as modifiers:

The teacher found the book for the student in the library.

This sentence indicates that the student was in the library. If, however, the writer meant that the book was found in the library, then the modifier *in the library* is misplaced. The sentence should read:

The teacher found the book in the library for the student.

The writer of the following sentence seems to be saying that the college is near the lake:

His parents met his friend from the college near the lake.

If, however, the writer meant that the meeting took place near the lake, the modifier is misplaced and the sentence should read:

Near the lake, his parents met his friend from the college.

2. Adverbs like *only, always, almost, hardly* and *nearly*. Words like these usually qualify the word that comes after them. Therefore, the position of these words depends on what the writer wishes to say.

Only is a notorious troublemaker. Observe how the sentence *I want a son* changes meaning significantly with the change in position of *only:*

I *only* want a son.	(I don't yearn for or long for a son; I only *want* one.)
I want *only* a son.	(I have no other wants.)
I want an *only* son.	(One son is as many as I want.)
I want a son *only*.	(I do not want a daughter.)

Exercise

Rewrite the sentences below, correcting any dangling or misplaced modifiers.

1. The man looked at the car he had just fixed while rubbing his hands with satisfaction.
2. Sitting on the edge of the bed, the blanket was wrinkled.
3. While driving through Yosemite, a bear stopped our car.
4. The student left for the college with excess baggage.
5. Running toward second base, we saw the runner make a daring slide.
6. John wants Judy to love him badly.
7. Walking through the park, the trees were in full bloom.
8. Speaking in a moderate tone, the lecture was much more successful.
9. The quarterback was removed from the game before he was permanently injured by the coach.
10. Leaving assignments until the last minute is bad policy.

Modifiers, nonrestrictive. See *Comma, F.*

Modifiers, restrictive. See *Comma, F.*

Nonrestrictive modifiers. See *Comma, F.*

Numerals.

A. *Numerals are used to indicate dates, times, percentages, money, street numbers, and page references.*

> On January 21, 1980, at 5:00 A.M., a fire broke out at 552 East 52nd Street, and before the Fire Department brought the flames under control, 75% of the building had been destroyed.

B. *In other cases, if a number is one hundred or under, spell it out; if it is over one hundred, use the numeral.*

> In the big contest yesterday, forty-five young boys were able to eat 152 hot dogs in two minutes.

C. *Spell out all numbers that start a sentence.*

> Four thugs assaulted an old lady last night.
>
> Three hundred thirty-one deaths have been predicted for the Labor Day weekend.

Parallelism. Ideas and facts of equal importance should be expressed in the same grammatical form:

INCORRECT	CORRECT
You can get there by *car, bus,* or *fly.* (noun, noun, verb)	You can get there by *car, bus,* or *plane.* (noun, noun, noun)
I thought the climactic episode in the story was *shocking, offbeat,* and *I found it very amusing.* (adjective, adjective, independent clause)	I thought the climactic episode in the story was *shocking, offbeat,* and very *amusing.* (adjective, adjective, adjective)
She *liked* people and *was liked* by people. (active voice, passive voice)	She *liked* people and people *liked* her. (active voice, active voice)
The teacher told us *to work* fast and *that we should write on only one side of the paper.* (infinitive, clause)	The teacher told us *to work* fast and *to write* on only one side of the paper. (infinitive, infinitive)

For further treatment of parallelism, see Chapter 16, pp. 420–423.

Parentheses. Parentheses can enclose incidental comments, provide explanatory details, and sometimes set off numerals that accompany the points of a paper. Parentheses are also used in footnotes. In many cases, parentheses serve to mark afterthoughts that should have been incorporated into the writing elsewhere. Therefore, use parentheses sparingly.

A. *Incidental comments:*

> The movie *The Killers* (its plot had little resemblance to Hemingway's short story) won an award.

B. *Explanation of details:*

The cornucopia (the horn of plenty) is a Thanksgiving symbol.

C. *Enumerated points:*

This essay has four main pieces of advice: (1) know your professors as people, (2) attend college-sponsored events, (3) attend student-sponsored events, and (4) use the library.

D. *Footnotes:*

Peter Straub, *Shadowland* (New York: Coward, McCann & Geoghegan, 1980), p. 10.

Period. See *End marks, A.*

Possessives. See *Apostrophe, C.*

Pronouns: agreement. A pronoun must agree with its antecedent in number (singular or plural) and gender (masculine, feminine, or neuter). The antecedent of a pronoun is the word or words to which the pronoun refers. For example, in the sentence *Jason lost his book,* the pronoun *his* refers to the antecedent *Jason.* Another example is *Jason could not find his book. He had lost it.* In the second sentence there are two pronouns—*he* and *it.* The antecedent of *he* is *Jason* and the antecedent of *it* is *book.* With the exception of constructions such as *it is nearly eight o'clock,* in which *it* has no antecedent, all pronouns should have antecedents.

A. *Gender.* If the gender of a singular antecedent is unknown or general, as in *student,* for example, then the antecedent is treated as if it were masculine. (This usage has come under attack in recent years. See Glossary, *He, his, him, himself,* pp. 516–517.)

Antecedent		*Pronoun*	
The boy	lost	his	book.
The girl	lost	her	book.
The briefcase	lost	its	handle.
The student	lost	his	book.
The students	lost	their	books.

B. *Number.* Most pronoun agreement errors occur when the pronoun does not agree with its antecedent in number. If the antecedent is singular, the pronoun must be singular; if the antecedent is plural, the pronoun must be plural.

1. Indefinite pronouns. Words like *anybody, somebody, everybody, nobody,* and *each* are always singular. Others like *few* and *many* are always plural. Indefinite pronouns such as *all, any, most,* and *more* can be either singular or plural, depending on the object of the preposition which follows them: *All of my concern is justified;* but, *All of my concerns are justified.*

INCORRECT: Somebody lost *their* books.

No one turns *their* paper in on time.

CORRECT: Somebody lost *his* books.

No one turns *his* paper in on time.

2. Collective nouns. Some singular nouns refer to more than one thing: *group, youth, family, jury,* and *audience,* for example. If the noun acts as a unit, it takes a singular pronoun. If the individuals within the unit act separately, the noun takes a plural pronoun.

The jury reached its decision.

The jury divided bitterly on their decision.

The audience rose to its feet to show its approval.

The audience straggled to their seats through the entire first act.

3. Antecedents joined by *either . . . or* and *neither . . . nor.* When two antecedents are joined by *either . . . or* or *neither . . . nor,* the pronoun agrees with the antecedent closer to it:

Either Ruby or Jan lost *her* album.

Either the mother or the daughters lost *their* albums.

Either the daughters or the mother lost *her* album.

Neither the boys nor the girls lost *their* albums.

4. Compound antecedents. Except when the words function as a single unit—*Macaroni and cheese is my favorite dish; I make it often,* for example—antecedents joined by *and* take a plural pronoun:

The owl and the pussycat shook *their* heads sadly.

Exercise

Correct any errors in pronoun agreement in the following sentences.

1. Nobody can ever tell what the future has in store for them.
2. Everybody passed their paper forward.
3. Neither the governor nor the mayors could explain their tax-reform proposal.
4. Everyone wants to feel some measure of control over their own life.
5. Each of the players signed their contracts.
6. All of the soup was tainted, so they were recalled by the manufacturer.
7. The crowd of sports fans shouted their disapproval of the umpire's decision.
8. Both Jenny and Marie had to make their plans carefully.
9. Either the boss or the workers will have to make up his mind about medical benefits.
10. Someone is certain to lose their temper.

Pronouns: case. Pronoun case refers to the change in form of pronouns which corresponds with their grammatical function. There are three cases, and their names are self-explanatory: *subjective* (when the pronoun acts as a subject), *objective* (when the pronoun acts as an object), and *possessive* (when the pronoun acts to show possession). Following is a list of case changes for the most common pronouns:

Subjective	Objective	Possessive
I	me	my, mine
you	you	your, yours
he	him	his
she	her	her, hers
it	it	its
we	us	our, ours
they	them	their, theirs
who	whom	whose

Case rarely presents problems for native speakers. Nobody says or writes *He gave I the album* or *Me like she.* Complications turn up in relatively few situations:

A. *Compound subjects and objects (subjects and objects connected by* and). Do not be misled by a compound subject or object. Use the pronoun case that shows the pronoun's grammatical role.

WRONG	RIGHT
My father scolded Jim and I.	My father scolded Jim and me.
Betty and her had many good times.	Betty and she had many good times.

A simple test for getting the right word is to eliminate one of the compound terms and see which pronoun works better. No one would write *My father scolded I*—so *My father scolded me* is correct. No one would write *Her had many good times*—so *She had many good times* is correct.

B. *Object of a preposition.* In a prepositional phrase, any pronoun after the preposition always takes the objective case.

WRONG	RIGHT
This match is just between you and I.	This match is just between you and me.
I went to the movies with she.	I went to the movies with her.
This present is for John and he.	This present is for John and him.

C. *After forms of* to be (*is, am, are, was, were, has been, had been, might be, will be,* etc.). A pronoun after forms of *to be* is always in the subjective case. This rule still applies rigorously in formal written English. It is frequently ignored in informal English and has all but disappeared from most conversation.

> It was she.
>
> This is he.
>
> The murderer might be he.
>
> The winners will be they.

D. *After* as *and* than. In comparisons with *as* and *than,* mentally add a verb to the pronoun to determine which pronoun is correct. Should you write, for example, *Bill is smarter than I* or *Bill is smarter than me?* Simply complete the construction with the "understood" verb. You could write *Bill is smarter than I am,* but not *Bill is smarter than me am.* Therefore, *Bill is smarter than I* is correct.

WRONG	RIGHT
I am just as good as *them.*	I am just as good as *they.*
Her mother had more ambition than *her.*	Her mother had more ambition than *she.*
Bill liked her more than *I.*	Bill liked her more than *me.* (Meaning *Bill liked her more than he liked me.*)
Bill liked her more than *me.*	Bill liked her more than *I.* (Meaning *Bill liked her more than I liked her.*)

E. We *or* us *followed by a noun.* Use *we* if the noun is a subject, *us* if the noun is an object. If ever in doubt, mentally eliminate the noun and see which pronoun sounds right. Should you write, for example, *The professor had us students over to his house* or *The professor had we students over to his house?* Mentally eliminate *students.* No one would write *The professor had we over to his house,* so *us* is correct.

WRONG	RIGHT
After the demonstration, *us* students were exhausted.	After the demonstration, *we* students were exhausted.
The company's reply to *we* consumers was almost totally negative.	The company's reply to *us* consumers was almost totally negative.

F. *Gerunds.* A gerund is an *-ing* verb form that functions as a noun. In *Swimming used to be my favorite sport, swimming* is a gerund. A pronoun before a gerund takes the possessive case.

WRONG	RIGHT
Us nagging him did no good.	*Our* nagging him did no good.
His parents do not understand *him* reading so poorly.	His parents do not understand *his* reading so poorly.

Them believing what she says does not mean that she is telling the truth.

Their believing what she says does not mean that she is telling the truth.

G. Who *and* whom. See Glossary, pp. 531–533.

Exercise ————————————————————————

Choose the correct pronoun, and be prepared to explain your choice.

1. You are fully as selfish as (I, me), but you do not have the courage to admit it.
2. To (he and she, him and her), the marriage counselor seemed to be speaking nonsense.
3. I think George and (I, me) will always be friends.
4. Twenty or thirty years from now, the president of the United States will be (she, her).
5. The judge then assessed an additional fine for (them, their) cursing.
6. Having to choose between (he and she, him and her) will make Election Day a worse burden than usual.
7. I honestly don't know what he expects (we, us) poor students to do.
8. The winning contestants were no brighter or quicker than (I, me).
9. (Him, His) lying had become part of his character.
10. Bennett hated Stephen and (she, her) with a jealous passion.

Pronouns: reference. A pronoun must not only agree with its antecedent, but that antecedent must be clear. An ambiguous antecedent is as bad as no antecedent at all. Generally two types of ambiguity occur: a pronoun with two or more possible antecedents, and one pronoun referring to different antecedents.

A. *Two or more possible antecedents. When Stanton visited the mayor, he said that he hoped his successor could work with him.* In this sentence, the pronouns *he, his,* and *him* can refer to either the mayor or Stanton. This problem can be avoided by making the antecedent clear: *When Stanton visited the mayor, Stanton said that he hoped his successor could work with the mayor.* Here the pronouns *he* and *his* clearly refer to Stanton. Be particularly careful of the potential ambiguity in vague use of the word *this.*

AMBIGUOUS

I received an *F* in the course and had to take it over again. This was very unfair. (Was the *F* unfair or having to take the course again? Were both unfair?)

IMPROVED

I received an *F* in the course and had to take it over again. This grade was very unfair.

Young people are unhappy today and are demanding change. This is a healthy thing. (What is healthy—being unhappy, demanding change, or both?)

Young people are unhappy today and are demanding change. This demand is a healthy thing.

B. *One pronoun referring to different antecedents. Mark received an* F *on his term paper and had to write a revision of it. It took a long time because it had many errors.* In these sentences the first *it* refers to the paper, the second to the revision, and the third to the paper. A reader could easily become confused by these sentences. In that case, simply replacing the pronouns with their antecedents would solve the problem. *Mark received an* F *on his term paper and had to write a revision of it. The revision took a long time because the paper had many errors.*

Exercise

Rewrite the sentences by correcting any errors in pronoun reference.

1. After the students left their papers on the teacher's desk, they remained in the classroom for an hour.
2. The students left the rooms in their usual order.
3. Cars break down so often because they don't make them the way they used to.
4. John told Bill that he could go.
5. John bought a new station wagon and a travel trailer. It needed several adjustments.
6. The teacher asked the student if he could read his writing.
7. He received his citizenship papers and registered to vote. This made him very happy.
8. It has been a long time since John left home.
9. The prosecutor disagreed with the judge. He felt he was guilty.
10. John's final grades were an *A* and an incomplete. This really saved him.

Question marks. See *End marks, B.*

Questions, indirect. See *End marks, B, 1.*

Quotation marks. Quotation marks are used to indicate material taken word for word from another source; to mark the title of a poem, song, short story, essay, and any part of a longer work; and to point out words used in a special sense—words set apart for emphasis and special consideration, slang and colloquial expressions, derisively used words.

A. *Direct quotations.* Quotation marks indicate what someone else has said in speech or writing:

> The mayor said, "The city is in serious financial trouble if the new city income tax does not pass."
>
> "No man is an island," John Donne once wrote.

If there is a quotation within a quotation, use single marks for the second quote:

> The mother commented wryly, "I wonder if Dr. Spock and the other great authorities on bringing up kids have ever seen one look at you, calm as can be, and say, 'I don't wanna.' "

Several rules must be observed in punctuation of direct quotations:

1. Blocked quotation. If a direct quotation other than dialogue is more than five lines long, it should be blocked. Blocked quotations *do not* take quotation marks. They are indented from the left margin and are single spaced.

   In the section of the text on quotation marks, the authors make the following observation:

   > Quotation marks are used to indicate material taken word for word from another source; to mark the title of a poem, song, short story, essay, and any part of a longer work; and to point out words used in a special sense—words set apart for emphasis and special consideration, slang and colloquial expressions, derisively used words.

   Note: Frequently a colon, rather than a comma, introduces a blocked quotation. See pp. 353–355.

2. Periods and commas. Periods and commas at the end of quotations always go inside the quotation marks.

   "The city will be in serious financial trouble if the city income tax does not pass," said the mayor.

   Although the producer used the word "art," the film was widely considered to be pornographic.

3. Other punctuation. An exclamation point or question mark goes inside the quotation marks *if it is part of the quotation.* If it is part of a longer statement, it goes outside the quotation marks.

   The student asked, "Is this paper due Friday?"

   Did Robert Frost write "Mending Wall"?

A colon or a semicolon always goes outside the quotation marks.

> The text says, "A colon or a semicolon always goes outside the quotation marks"; this rule is simple.

B. *Titles.* Use quotation marks to indicate the title of a work—a poem, a song, a short story, a chapter, an essay—that is part of a larger whole, or a short unit in itself.

> William Carlos Williams wrote the short story "The Use of Force."
>
> The chapter is called "Stylistic Problems and Their Solutions."

C. *Words.*

    1. Words used as words. Underlining is usually preferred. See *Italics.*

    2. Words used as slang or colloquial expressions. This usage is almost always undesirable. (See Chapter 16, pp. 431–432.)

    3. Words used derisively. The use of quotation marks to indicate sarcasm or derision is generally a primitive means of showing feelings, and should be avoided:

    The "performance" was a collection of amateurish blunders.

Run-on sentence. A run-on sentence is two or more sentences written as one, with no punctuation between them. It is most commonly corrected by rewriting the run-on sentence as separate sentences, by placing a semicolon between the sentences, or by placing a comma *and* a coordinating conjunction between the sentences. A comma alone would create a comma splice, often considered a special kind of run-on sentence. See *Comma splice.*

INCORRECT	CORRECT
This rule sounds easy enough putting it into practice is not so easy.	This rule sounds easy enough. Putting it into practice is not so easy.

OR

This rule sounds easy enough; putting it into practice is not so easy.

OR

This rule sounds easy enough, but putting it into practice is not so easy.

Exercise ────────────────────────────────

Correct the following run-on sentences by using a comma and a coordinating conjunction *(and, but, or, nor, for, yet, so)*, a semicolon, or a period.

  1. Machines do many jobs that people used to in the future, machines will replace even more people.
  2. Cramming is a poor method of studying many students, however, use it.
  3. Too few students use the library many do not even know its location.
  4. There may be life on other planets perhaps the new satellite will provide an answer.
  5. A community college may have students from all over the world most, however, come from the surrounding community.
  6. Drunk drivers are dangerous they killed 14,000 people last year.
  7. Many houses have hidden defects for example, the plumbing may be bad.

8. Miss Ohio won the title of Miss USA then she won the Miss Universe contest.
9. Make sure you separate sentences with a conjunction, a semicolon, or a period never just run them together.
10. Love does not mean just romantic love there can also be parental love, love of God, love of country, love for a book or a pet or a job.

Semicolon. A semicolon can be used between two independent clauses when the coordinating conjunction has been left out and between separate elements in a list or series when the elements contain punctuation within themselves.

A. *Between independent clauses:*

> Stating the problem is simple enough; solving it is the tough part.
>
> The girl wasn't precisely sure what the bearded stranger wanted; all she knew was that he made her nervous.

Observe that in both of these cases a coordinating conjunction preceded by a comma could be used to replace the semicolon. Under no circumstances could a comma alone be used between these independent clauses. In order to use a comma, you must have a coordinating conjunction *(and, but, or, nor, for, yet, so)* between independent clauses. See *Comma splice.*

B. *Between separate elements in a list or series:*

> The following American cities have grown enormously in recent years: Houston, Texas; Dallas, Texas; Phoenix, Arizona; and Denver, Colorado.

Shifts in time and person. Do not unnecessarily shift from one tense to another (past to present, present to future, etc.) or from one person to another (*he* to *you, one* to *I,* etc.).

A. *Tense shifts.* If you begin writing in a particular tense, do not shift to another unless a change in time is logically necessary. The paragraph below breaks this rule:

> In William Carlos Williams's "The Use of Force," a doctor *was called* to examine a young girl. The doctor *was concerned* about diphtheria and *needs* to examine the girl's throat. The girl *is* terrified and *begins* to resist. As her resistance *continues,* the doctor *is compelled* to use more and more physical force. Though he *knows* the force *is* necessary, the doctor, to his horror, *found* that he *enjoyed* it and really *wanted* to hurt the girl.

Here the writer starts in the past tense *(was called, was concerned),* shifts to the present tense *(needs, is, begins, continues, is compelled, knows, is),* and then shifts back to the past tense *(found, enjoyed, wanted).* Why? There is no reason. No change in time is needed. If writers view the events of a story as happening in the present, they should use the present tense consistently. Writers could also view the events as past actions—over and completed—and write entirely in the past tense. In either case, writers should decide which view they prefer and stick to it throughout.

ALL VERBS IN PRESENT TENSE	ALL VERBS IN PAST TENSE
In William Carlos Williams's "The Use of Force," a doctor *is called* to examine a young girl. The doctor *is concerned* about diphtheria and *needs* to examine the girl's throat. The girl *is* terrified and *begins* to resist. As her resistance *continues*, the doctor *is compelled* to use more and more physical force. Though he *knows* the force *is* necessary, the doctor, to his horror, *finds* that he *enjoys* it and really *wants* to hurt the girl.	In William Carlos Williams's "The Use of Force," a doctor *was called* to examine a young girl. The doctor *was concerned* about diphtheria and *needed* to examine the girl's throat. The girl *was* terrified and *began* to resist. As her resistance *continued*, the doctor *was compelled* to use more and more physical force. Though he *knew* the force *was* necessary, the doctor, to his horror, *found* that he *enjoyed* it and really *wanted* to hurt the girl.

B. *Shifts in person.* Write from a consistent point of view, making sure that any change in person is logically justified. If, for example, you begin expressing your thoughts in the third person (*he, she, it, they, one, the reader, the student, people,* etc.), avoid sudden shifts to the first person (*I, we*) or the second person *(you)*. Similarly, avoid sudden shifts from third or first person singular to third or first person plural.

POOR	IMPROVED
Most *average citizens* think *they* are in favor of a clean environment, but *you* may change *your* mind when *you* find out what it will cost. (Shift from third person *average citizens* and *they* to second person *you, your.*)	Most *average citizens* think *they* are in favor of a clean environment, but they may change their minds when they find out what it will cost.
The teenager resents the way *he* is being stereotyped. *We're* as different among *ourselves* as any other group in the population. *They* are tired of being viewed as a collection of finger-snapping freaks who say "cool" all the time. (Shift from third person singular *teenager* and *he* to first person plural *we* to third person plural *they.*)	*Teenagers* resent the way *they* are being stereotyped. *They* are as different among *themselves* as any other group in the population. *They* are tired of being viewed as a collection of finger-snapping freaks who say "cool" all the time.

Readers will find this suspense-filled mystery irresistible, just as *they* have found Mr. Stout's previous efforts. *You* should have a real battle keeping *yourself* from looking ahead to the last page. (Shift from third person *readers* and *they* to second person *you, yourself*.)

Readers will find this suspense-filled mystery irresistible, just as *they* have found Mr. Stout's previous efforts. *They* should have a real battle keeping *themselves* from looking ahead to the last page.

One wonders what is going on at City Hall. *We* have put up with flooded basements and lame excuses long enough. (Shift from third person *one* to first person *we*.)

We wonder what is going on at City Hall. *We* have put up with flooded basements and lame excuses long enough.

Spelling. Poor spelling can seriously damage an otherwise fine paper. Faced with any significant number of spelling errors, readers cannot maintain their original confidence in the writer's thoughtfulness and skill.

The one spelling rule every writer needs to know is very simple: *Use the dictionary*. Rules for spelling specific words and groups of words almost always have exceptions and are difficult to learn and remember. Good spellers, almost without exception, turn out to be people who read a great deal and who have the dictionary habit, not people who have memorized spelling rules. The most important spelling rule, then, as well as the quickest and easiest one, is *use the dictionary*.

Despite this good advice, it can sometimes be handy to have available a list of frequently misspelled words. For quick reference, we include such a list. Note that words spelled the same as parts of longer words are not usually listed separately: the list has *accidentally* but not *accident*, *acquaintance* but not *acquaint*.

absence	annual	belief	coming
accidentally	apartment	believe	commission
accommodate	apparatus	beneficial	committee
accumulate	apparent	benefited	comparative
achievement	appearance	boundaries	compelled
acquaintance	arctic	Britain	conceivable
acquire	arguing	business	conferred
acquitted	argument	calendar	conscience*
advice*	arithmetic	candidate	conscientious*
advise*	ascend	category	conscious*
all right	athletic	cemetery	control
amateur	attendance	changeable	controversial
among	balance	changing	controversy
analysis	battalion	choose	criticize
analyze	beginning	chose	deferred

*See Glossary

definitely
definition
describe
description
desperate
dictionary
dining
disappearance
disappoint
disastrous
discipline
dissatisfied
dormitory
effect
eighth
eligible
eliminate
embarrass
eminent
encouragement
encouraging
environment
equipped
especially
exaggerate
excellence
exhilarate
existence
existent
experience
explanation
familiar
fascinate
February
fiery
foreign
formerly
forty
fourth
frantically
generally
government
grammar
grandeur
grievous
height
heroes
hindrance

hoping
humorous
hypocrisy
hypocrite
immediately
incidentally
incredible
independence
inevitable
intellectual
intelligence
interesting
irresistible
knowledge
laboratory
laid
led
lightning
loneliness
lose
losing
maintenance
maneuver
manufacture
marriage
mathematics
maybe
mere
miniature
mischievous
mysterious
necessary
Negroes
ninety
noticeable
occasionally
occurred
occurrence
omitted
opinion
opportunity
optimistic
paid
parallel
paralysis
paralyze
particular
pastime

performance
permissible
perseverance
personal
personnel
perspiration
physical
picnicking
possession
possibility
possible
practically
precede*
precedence
preference
preferred
prejudice
preparation
prevalent
principal*
principle*
privilege
probably
procedure
proceed*
profession
professor
prominent
pronunciation
prophecy (noun)
prophesy (verb)
pursue
quantity
quiet*
quite*
quizzes
recede
receive
receiving
recommend
reference
referring
repetition
restaurant
rhythm
ridiculous
sacrifice
sacrilegious

salary
schedule
seize
sense
separate
separation
sergeant
severely
shining
siege
similar
sophomore
specifically
specimen
stationary*
stationery*
statue
studying
succeed
succession
surprise
technique
temperamental
tendency
than, then*
their, there,
   they're*
thorough
through
to, too, two*
tragedy
transferring
tries
truly
tyranny
unanimous
undoubtedly
unnecessary
until
usually
village
villain
weather
weird
whether
woman, women
writing

*See Glossary

Subject-verb agreement. A verb must agree with its subject in number and person. This rule has most practical meaning only in the present tense; in other tenses, the verb forms remain the same regardless of number or person. (The single exception is the past tense of *to be*; in that one instance the verb forms do change; *I was, you were, he was, we were, they were.*)

In the present tense, the third person, singular verb usually differs from the others—most often because an -s or -es is added to the verb stem. A third person singular verb is the verb that goes with the pronouns *he, she,* and *it* and with *any singular noun.*

TO DREAM

	Singular	*Plural*
First person	I dream	we dream
Second person	you dream	you dream
Third person	he she it } dreams	they dream

The lovers *dream* of a long and happy future together.

The lover *dreams* of his sweetheart every night.

People often *dream* about falling from great heights.

Jennifer *dreams* about being buried alive.

TO MISS

	Singular	*Plural*
First person	I miss	we miss
Second person	you miss	you miss
Third person	he she it } misses	they miss

The children *miss* their father more than they thought they would.

The child *misses* her friends.

The commuters *miss* the bus almost every morning.

The leftfielder *misses* more than his share of easy fly balls.

Even with highly irregular verbs, the third person singular in the present tense takes a special form (always with an *s* at the end).

TO BE

	Singular	*Plural*
First person	I am	we are
Second person	you are	you are
Third person	he she it } is	they are

TO HAVE

	Singular	*Plural*
First person	I have	we have
Second person	you have	you have
Third person	he she } has it	they have

The clowns *are* happy.

William *is* sad.

The Joneses *have* a lovely new home.

Mr. Jones *has* a lot to learn.

The few cases in which a present tense verb in the third person singular has the same form as in the other persons come naturally to almost every writer and speaker: *he can, he may, he might,* etc.

Once a writer realizes the difference between third person singular and other verb forms, the only problem is likely to be deciding which form to use in a few tricky situations:

A. *Compound subjects.* If the subject is compound (joined by *and*), the verb is plural unless the two words function as a single unit—*pork and beans is an easy dish to prepare,* for example—or unless the two words refer to a single person, as in *My cook and bottle washer has left me* (one person performed both jobs).

WRONG	RIGHT
Writing and reading *is* necessary for success in college.	Writing and reading *are* necessary for success in college.
The introduction and conclusion *does* not appear in an outline.	The introduction and conclusion *do* not appear in an outline.

B. *Neither . . . nor, either . . . or, nor, or.* If two subjects are joined by any of these terms, the verb agrees with the closer subject.

WRONG	RIGHT
Neither the students nor the teacher *are* correct.	Neither the students nor the teacher *is* correct.
Either the supporting details or the thesis statement *are* wrong.	Either the supporting details or the thesis statement *is* wrong.
Snowstorms or rain *cause* accidents.	Snowstorms or rain *causes* accidents.
Rain or snowstorms *causes* accidents.	Rain or snowstorms *cause* accidents.

C. *Time, money, weight.* Words that state an amount (time, money, weight) have a singular verb when they are considered as a unit *even if* they are plural in form.

WRONG	RIGHT
Two semesters *are* really a short time.	Two semesters *is* really a short time.
Five dollars *are* a modest fee for credit by examination.	Five dollars *is* a modest fee for credit by examination.
Five kilos of soybeans *are* about eleven pounds.	Five kilos of soybeans *is* about eleven pounds.

D. *Titles.* Titles of songs, plays, movies, novels, or articles always have singular verbs, even if the titles are plural in form.

WRONG	RIGHT
The Carpetbaggers were made into a movie.	*The Carpetbaggers was* made into a movie.
"The Novels of Early America" *were* published in *American Literature.*	"The Novels of Early America" *was* published in *American Literature.*

E. *Collective nouns.* Collective nouns such as *family, audience, jury,* and *class* have singular verbs when they are considered as a unified group. If the individuals within the unit act separately, the verb will be plural.

WRONG	RIGHT
The family *plan* a vacation.	The family *plans* a vacation.
The jury *is* divided on the verdict.	The jury *are* divided on the verdict. (The jury *are* acting as individual members, not as a unified group.)
The audience *are* going to give this show a standing ovation.	The audience *is* going to give this show a standing ovation.
The audience *is* divided in their opinion of the show.	The audience *are* divided in their opinion of the show.

F. *Indefinite pronouns.* Indefinite pronouns such as *one, no one, someone, everyone, none, anyone, somebody, anybody, everybody, each, neither,* and *either* take singular verbs:

WRONG	RIGHT
None of the ideas *are* correct.	None of the ideas *is* correct.
Each of the students *have* the time to study.	Each of the students *has* the time to study.
Either *are* a valid choice.	Either *is* a valid choice.

G. *Intervening elements.* No matter how many words, phrases, or clauses separate a subject from its verb, the verb must still agree with the subject in number.

1. Separated by words:

   WRONG: Many state capitals—Carson City, Augusta, Jefferson City, Olympia—is only small towns.

   RIGHT: Many state capitals—Carson City, Augusta, Jefferson City, Olympia—are only small towns.

   Here the plural *capitals,* not the singular *Olympia,* is the subject.

2. Separated by phrases:

   WRONG: A crate of oranges *are* expensive.

   RIGHT: A crate of oranges *is* expensive.

   Here *crate,* not *oranges,* is the subject.

   WRONG: Agreement of subjects with their verbs *are* important.

   RIGHT: Agreement of subjects with their verbs *is* important.

   Here *agreement,* not *subjects* or *verbs,* is the subject.

3. Separated by clauses:

   WRONG: Reading well, which is one of the necessary academic skills, *make* studying easier.

   RIGHT: Reading well, which is one of the necessary academic skills, *makes* studying easier.

   Here *reading,* not *skills,* is the subject.

H. *Reversed position.* If the subject comes after the verb, the verb must still agree with the subject.

1. There. If a sentence begins with *there* and is followed by some form of *be* (*is, are, was, were,* etc.), the number of *be* is determined by the subject. *There* is never the subject (except in a sentence like this one).

   WRONG: There *is* five students in this class.

   RIGHT: There *are* five students in this class.

   Here *students* is the subject, and it is plural. Therefore, the verb must be plural.

   WRONG: There *is* at least three systems of grammar for the English language.

   RIGHT: There *are* at least three systems of grammar for the English language.

2. Prepositional phrases. Sometimes a writer begins a sentence with

a prepositional phrase followed by a verb and then the subject. The verb must still agree with the subject.

WRONG. Throughout a grammar book *appears* many helpful writing hints.

RIGHT: Throughout a grammar book *appear* many helpful writing hints.

Here *hints*, not *book*, is the subject.

Exercise

Correct any subject-verb agreement errors in the following sentences.

1. *Smiles of a Summer Night* are among the best-known films of Ingmar Bergman.
2. Either the mayors or the governor has to take the blame for failure of the industrial development program.
3. There is suspense and laughter and romance in this marvelous new novel.
4. Watergate, like Teapot Dome and other political scandals, are turning out to have little impact on the long-range future of American government.
5. Each of the students in these schools are concerned about the recent tightening of the job market.
6. Compositions of this one special type requires a detailed knowledge of logical fallacies.
7. The whole board of directors are about to resign.
8. The League of Women Voters sponsor many worthwhile activities.
9. Neither John nor Bill have enough money to buy textbooks.
10. Federal judges and the president constitutes the judicial and executive branches of government.

Subjunctive mood. Once far more common English than it is now, the subjunctive mood is still sometimes used to express "conditions contrary to fact"—hypothetical conditions, conditions not yet brought about, suppositional ideas, and so on. In the subjunctive, the verb form is usually plural even though the subject is singular.

> If I *were* you, I would turn down the latest offer.
>
> I move that the chairperson *declare* the meeting adjourned.
>
> He looked as if he *were* going to be sick.

Subordinating conjunctions. See *Fragmentary sentences, C.*

Subordination. The most important idea in a sentence should be in an independent clause. Lesser ideas, explanations, qualifying material, and illustrations should be in subordinate clauses or phrases. See also Chapter 16, pp. 423–426.

POOR	IMPROVED
John is a wonderful person. He is very shy. He is extremely kind to everybody.	Although very shy, John is a wonderful person who is extremely kind to everybody. (The main idea is that John is a wonderful person.)
	OR
	Although he is a wonderful person who is extremely kind to everybody, John is very shy. (The main idea is that John is very shy.)
Professor Jones is terribly sarcastic. He is also a tough grader. It is true that he knows his subject. Most students dislike him, however.	Despite Professor Jones's knowledge of his subject, most students dislike him because of his terrible sarcasm and tough grading.
I am going to start on my new job and I am very optimistic.	I am very optimistic about starting on my new job.

Superlative forms. See *Comparative and superlative forms.*

Tense shifts. See *Shifts in time and person, A.*

Titles, punctuation of. See *Italics, A,* and *Quotation marks, B.*

Underlining. See *Italics.*

Verbs: principal parts. The form of most verbs changes according to which tense is being used, and to get the correct form a writer needs to know the principal parts of each verb. There are generally considered to be three principal parts: the *stem* or *infinitive* (the stem is the present tense form of the verb, and the infinitive is the stem preceded by *to*), the *past tense,* and the *past participle.* The past participle is the form used in perfect tenses (*I have seen, I had seen, I will have seen,* etc.) and in the passive voice (*I am seen, I was seen, I will be seen, I have been seen,* etc.)

The principal parts of *regular verbs* are formed by adding *-ed* or *-d* to the stem: *rush, rushed, rushed; love, loved, loved.* The past tense and past participle of regular verbs are always the same.

The principal parts of *irregular verbs* need to be learned separately—and even for the most experienced writer sometimes require checking in a dictionary or handbook. For quick reference, an alphabetical list of the principal parts of the most common irregular verbs follows:

Stem	Past tense	Past participle
arise	arose	arisen
be	was	been
bear	bore	borne, born
begin	began	begun
bind	bound	bound
blow	blew	blown

break	broke	broken
bring	brought	brought
burst	burst	burst
buy	bought	bought
catch	caught	caught
choose	chose	chosen
come	came	come
creep	crept	crept
deal	dealt	dealt
dig	dug	dug
dive	dived, dove	dived
do	did	done
draw	drew	drawn
drink	drank	drunk
drive	drove	driven
eat	ate	eaten
fall	fell	fallen
flee	fled	fled
fly	flew	flown
forbid	forbad, forbade	forbidden
freeze	froze	frozen
give	gave	given
go	went	gone
grow	grew	grown
hang	hung	hung
hang (execute)	hanged	hanged
know	knew	known
lay	laid	laid
lead	led	led
lend	lent	lent
lie	lay	lain
lose	lost	lost
mean	meant	meant
ride	rode	ridden
ring	rang	rung
rise	rose	risen
run	ran	run
see	saw	seen
seek	sought	sought
send	sent	sent
shake	shook	shaken
shine	shone, shined	shone, shined
sing	sang	sung
sink	sank, sunk	sunk
sleep	slept	slept
speak	spoke	spoken
spin	spun	spun

spit	spat	spat
spread	spread	spread
steal	stole	stolen
stink	stank	stunk
swear	swore	sworn
swim	swam	swum
swing	swung	swung
take	took	taken
teach	taught	taught
tear	tore	torn
thrive	thrived, throve	thrived, thriven
throw	threw	thrown
wear	wore	worn
weep	wept	wept
write	wrote	written

Confusion of the past tense and past participle of irregular verbs is a frequent cause of writing errors. Remember that the past participle is the correct form after *has, have,* and *had.*

WRONG	RIGHT
The mountaineers *had froze* to death.	The mountaineers *had frozen* to death.
The sprinter *has* just *broke* another track record.	The sprinter *has* just *broken* another track record.
I *begun* the book yesterday.	I *began* the book yesterday.
We *seen* that movie when it first came out.	We *saw* that movie when it first came out.

Verbs: tenses. What is the difference between *I eat* and *I am eating?* What is the difference between *I passed* and *I have passed?* Most verbs can be expressed in any tense, and the many different tenses enable the writer to present fine shades of meaning with great accuracy.

There are *six tenses.* Most verbs can take either the *active voice* or the *passive voice* (pp. 419–420) in any tense. To make matters even more varied, *progressive constructions* can be used for all tenses of active verbs and some tenses of passive verbs.

TO SAVE

	Active Voice	Progressive
Present	I save	I am saving
Past	I saved	I was saving
Future	I will (or shall) save	I will be saving
Present Perfect	I have saved	I have been saving
Past Perfect	I had saved	I had been saving
Future Perfect	I will (or shall) have saved	I will have been saving

Passive Voice

Present	I am saved	I am being saved
Past	I was saved	I was being saved
Future	I will (or shall) be saved	
Present Perfect	I have been saved	
Past Perfect	I had been saved	
Future Perfect	I will (or shall) have been saved	

TO DRIVE

	Active Voice	*Progressive*
Present	I drive	I am driving
Past	I drove	I was driving
Future	I will drive	I will be driving
Present Perfect	I have driven	I have been driving
Past Perfect	I had driven	I had been driving
Future Perfect	I will have driven	I will have been driving

	Passive Voice	
Present	I am driven	I am being driven
Past	I was driven	I was being driven
Future	I will be driven	
Present Perfect	I have been driven	
Past Perfect	I had been driven	
Future Perfect	I will have been driven	

The *present tense* indicates present action, of course, especially continuing or habitual action:

> I *save* ten dollars every week.
>
> I *eat* a good breakfast each morning.
>
> She *drives* carefully.

The present is also used to express permanent facts and general truths, and is often the preferred tense for discussing literary actions:

> The speed of light *is* faster than the speed of sound.
>
> Truth *is* stranger than fiction.
>
> In *The Great Gatsby,* all of the events *take* place during the 1920s.
>
> Nick Carraway *is* the only character in the novel who *understands* Gatsby.

The present can even be called upon to deal with future action:

> Tomorrow she *drives* to the convention.

The *present progressive* indicates actions occurring—actions "in progress"—at the specific instant referred to.

> I *am eating* a good breakfast, and I do not want to be interrupted.
>
> She *is driving* too fast for these icy roads.

The same principle of action *in progress at the time* applies to *all progressive tenses:*

> Past progressive: The criminal *was shaving* when the police arrested him.
>
> Future progressive: At this time next week, I *will be surfing* in Hawaii.

The *past* tense describes previous actions, generally actions over and done with.

> The lifeguard *saved* two children last week.
>
> She *drove* to Florida three years ago.

The *future* tense describes actions after the present:

> From now on, I *will save* fifteen dollars every week.
>
> Marlene says that her in-laws *will drive* her to drink.

The *present perfect* tense (*have* or *has* plus the past participle) refers to past actions, generally of the fairly recent past, that still go on or have bearing on the present:

> I *have saved* over one thousand dollars so far.
>
> She *has driven* this short route to work many times.

The preceding sentences expressed in the simple past would suggest different meanings. *I saved over one thousand dollars* would suggest that the saving has now stopped. *She drove this short route to work many times* would suggest that some other route is now being used.

The *past perfect* tense (*had* plus the past participle) is employed for actions previous to the simple past—"more past than past."

> The lifeguard saved two children last week and *had saved* three adults the week before.
>
> She *had driven* to Florida three years ago, so she felt quite confident about making the trip again.

The *future perfect* tense (*will have* or *shall have* plus the past participle) expresses action that will be completed before some future time.

> By this time next year, I *will have saved* two thousand dollars.
>
> When she gets to Florida, she *will have driven* through three time zones.

The proper *sequence of tenses* within a sentence or series of sentences when different verbs refer to different time periods is an important consideration for all writers. The simple rule that verb tenses need to express precisely the intended period of time is not always simple to apply to one's own writing.

IMPROPER SEQUENCE	CORRECT SEQUENCE
The witness *told* [past] the court that on the night of the crime he *saw* [past] the accused break the window of the liquor store.	The witness *told* [past] the court that on the night of the crime he *had seen* [past perfect] the accused break the window of the liquor store. (The past perfect *had seen* refers to events "more past than past.")
When I *will come* [future] to the lake, you *will* already *be* [future] there for two weeks.	When I *will come* [future] to the lake, you *will* already *have been* [future perfect] there for two weeks. (The future perfect *will have been* refers to events that will be completed before some future time.)
Although the coach *has set* [present perfect] new curfew hours, the players still *have refused* [present perfect] to comply.	Although the coach *has set* [present perfect] new curfew hours, the players still *refuse* [present] to comply. (The coach's rules were set a while ago. The present tense *refuse* is necessary to show that the players' refusal to follow the rules is current.)

Wordiness. Wordiness means using more words than are necessary to convey meaning. Wordiness never makes writing clearer, just longer. After writing a rough draft, be sure to look it over and remove all the unnecessary words you can find. For more information on wordiness, see Chapter 15, pp. 408–414.

A. *Deadwood.*

WORDY WRITING	ECONOMICAL WRITING
Her hair was red in color.	Her hair was red.
Pollution conditions that exist in our cities are disgraceful.	Pollution in our cities is disgraceful.
In this day and age we live in, people seem totally apathetic to everything.	People today seem totally apathetic.

B. *Pointless repetition.*

WORDY WRITING	ECONOMICAL WRITING
The film was very interesting and fascinating.	The film was fascinating.
The author gives examples of different and varied criticisms of the novel.	The author gives examples of different criticisms of the novel.
Some early critics of Jonathan Swift called him an insane madman suffering from symptoms of mental disease.	Some early critics of Jonathan Swift called him insane.

C. *Delay of subject.*

WORDY WRITING	ECONOMICAL WRITING
There are too many people who care only for themselves.	Too many people care only for themselves.
It is a fact that there has been a great increase in sensationalism in the theatre.	Sensationalism in the theatre has greatly increased.

D. *Inadequate clause cutting.*

WORDY WRITING	ECONOMICAL WRITING
The girl who has red hair was a flirt.	The red-haired girl was a flirt.
Some of the students who were more enthusiastic wrote an extra paper.	Some of the more enthusiastic students wrote an extra paper.

GLOSSARY OF PROBLEM WORDS

A, an. Use *a* when the next word begins with a consonant sound. Use *an* when the next word begins with a vowel sound.

a book	a horror film
a rotten apple	a use of soybeans
an element	an urgent request
an honest man	an added attraction

Note that it is the sound that counts, not the actual letter.

a hasty decision	an unusual picture
an hour	a usual routine

Accept, except. *Accept* is a verb meaning *to receive, to agree to, to answer affirmatively. Except* is usually a preposition meaning *excluding.* It is also used infrequently as a verb meaning *to exclude.*

> I accepted the parcel from the mailman.
>
> Senator Jones hoped they would accept his apology.
>
> Should she accept that rude invitation?
>
> I liked everything about the concert except the music.
>
> I except you from my criticism.

Adapt, adept, adopt. *Adapt* means *change or adjust in order to make more suitable or in order to deal with new conditions. Adept* means *skillful, handy, good at. Adopt* means *take or use as one's own* or *endorse.*

> The dinosaur was unable to adapt to changes in its environment.
>
> The new textbook was an adaptation of the earlier edition.
>
> Bill has always been adept at carpentry.
>
> They had to wait six years before they could adopt a child.
>
> The Senate adopted the new resolution.

Advice, advise. *Advice* is a noun. *Advise* is a verb.

> My advice to you is to leave well enough alone.
>
> I advise you to leave well enough alone.

Affect, effect. If you are looking for a noun, the word you want is almost certainly *effect,* meaning *result.* The noun *affect* is generally restricted to technical discussions of psychology, where it means *an emotion* or *a stimulus to an emotion.* If you are looking for a verb, the word you want is probably *affect,* meaning *impress, influence.* The verb *effect* is comparatively uncommon; it means *bring about, accomplish, produce.*

> Many of our welfare programs have not had beneficial effects.
>
> This song always affects me powerfully.
>
> The crowd was not affected by the plea to disband.
>
> We hope this new program will effect a whole new atmosphere on campus.

Affective, effective. The word you are after is almost certainly *effective,* meaning *having an effect on* or *turning out well. Affective* is a fairly technical term from psychology and semantics meaning *emotional* or *influencing emotions.*

> Only time will tell if Federal Reserve policy is effective.
>
> The affective qualities of sound are difficult to evaluate in laboratory conditions.

Aggravate. The original meaning is *worsen* or *intensify.* The more common meaning of *irritate* or *annoy* is also acceptable in all but the fussiest formal writing.

Ain't. *Ain't* should never be used in written English except in humor or dialogue. Use of the phrase *ain't I,* when asking a question in conversational English, is undesirable, as is the supposedly elegant but totally ungrammatical *aren't I. Am I not* is grammatically correct, but awkward and stuffy. The best solution to the problem is to avoid it by expressing the thought differently.

All ready, already. *Already* means *previously* or *by the designated time. All ready* means *all set, all prepared.*

> Professor Wills has already told us that twice.
>
> The plane is already overdue.
>
> The meal was all ready by six o'clock.

All right, alright. Many authorities consider *alright* to be nonstandard English. It is good policy to use *all right* instead.

All together, altogether. *All together* means *joined in a group. Altogether* means *thoroughly* or *totally.*

> For once, the citizens are all together on an important issue.
>
> The character's motivations are altogether obscure.

Allusion, illusion. An *allusion* is an *indirect mention or reference,* often literary or historical. The verb form is *allude.* An *illusion* is an *idea not in accord with reality.*

In discussing our problems with teenage marriages, the speaker made an allusion to *Romeo and Juliet.*

The nominating speech alluded to every American hero from Jack Armstrong to Neil Armstrong.

The patient suffered from the illusion that he was Napoleon.

At the end of the story, the character loses his pleasant illusions and discovers the harsh truth about himself.

A lot of. This phrase is more appropriate to conversation than to general written English. Use it sparingly. Remember that *a lot* is *two* words. Do not confuse it with *allot,* meaning *to give out* or *apportion.*

Alright. See *All right, alright.*

Altogether. See *All together, altogether.*

Alumna-alumnae, alumnus-alumni. An *alumna* is a female graduate. *Alumnae* is the plural. An *alumnus* is a male graduate. *Alumni* is the plural. Use *alumni* for a group of male and female graduates.

A.M., P.M. (*or* **a.m., p.m.**). Either capitals or lowercase letters are acceptable, but you should not alternate between the two in any one piece of writing. These abbreviations must be preceded by specific numbers:

RIGHT: His appointment is for 10:30 A.M.

WRONG: We expect him sometime in the A.M.

Among, between. Use *between* when dealing with two units. Use *among* with more than two.

WRONG: The company president had to make an arbitrary decision among the two outstanding candidates for promotion.

Tension has always existed among my parents and me.

Tension has always existed between my mother, my father, and me.

RIGHT: The company president had to make an arbitrary decision between the two outstanding candidates for promotion.

Tension has always existed between my parents and me.

Tension has always existed among my mother, my father, and me.

Amount, number. Use *amount* to refer to quantities that cannot be counted. Use *number* for quantities that can be counted.

No *amount* of persuasion will convince the voters to approve the new levy, though the mayor has tried a *number* of times.

An. See *A, an.*

And etc. *Etc.* is an abbreviation of *et cetera* which means *and so forth* or *and other things.* Using the word *and* in addition to *etc.* is therefore repetitious and incorrect. See *Etc.*

Anxious, eager. *Anxious* suggests worry or fear as in *anxiety. Eager* suggests enthusiasm.

> I waited anxiously for the telephone to bring me news of Joan's safe arrival.

> The whole town waited eagerly to greet the triumphant hockey team.

Anyone, any one. Use *anyone* when you mean *anybody at all.* Use *any one* when you are considering separately or singling out each person or thing within a group.

> Anyone can learn how to do simple electrical wiring.

> Any one of these paintings is worth a small fortune.

The same principle applies to *everyone, every one* and *someone, some one.*

As. Do not make this word mean *because* or *since.*

> POOR: I was late for my appointment as I missed the bus.
>
> As I am a shy person, I find it hard to make new friends.

As far as. This phrase should be followed by a noun *and a verb.* Without the verb, it is incomplete.

> POOR: As far as religion, I believe in complete freedom.
>
> BETTER: As far as religion is concerned, I believe in complete freedom.

Askance. This word is an adverb meaning *suspiciously, disapprovingly*— used for looks, glances, etc. It can never be used as a noun.

> WRONG: The sportswriters looked with askance at the coach's optimistic prediction.
>
> RIGHT: The sportswriters looked askance at the coach's optimistic prediction.

Aspect. An overused, pseudoscholarly word. Try to avoid it wherever possible. Where you feel you must use it, try to preserve the concept of *looking* as part of the implicit meaning of the word.

> We viewed the problem in all its aspects.

As to. Stuffy. Change to *about.*

> POOR: We need to talk more as to our late deliveries.
>
> BETTER: We need to talk more about our late deliveries.

Awful. The original meaning of this word is *awe-inspiring, arousing emotions of fear.* Some people insist that this is still its only valid meaning. We see nothing wrong, however, when it is also used to mean *extremely bad, ugly, unpleasant,* etc. The word *dreadful* has evolved in the same way, and we know of no objections to that word. See *Awfully.*

Awfully. Does not mean *very*.

> POOR: He's an awfully nice person.
> I'm awfully impressed by what you said.
> Jim felt awfully bad.

A while, awhile. *A while* is a noun. *Awhile* is an adverb.

> I thought I saw her a while ago.
> Take it easy for a while.
> Success comes only to those who are prepared to wait awhile.

Bad, badly. *Bad* is the adjective, *badly* the adverb. In some sentences, the verbs *look, feel,* and *seem* function as linking verbs and must be followed by the adjectival form.

> I play badly.
> *but*
> I feel bad.
> She looks bad.
> The idea seems bad.

Watch the location of *badly* when you use it to mean *very much.* It can often be misread as having its more familiar meaning, and comic disaster can occur.

> I want to act badly.
> He wanted her to love him badly.

Be. Not acceptable written English in constructions like *I be going, they be ready,* etc. Use *I am going, they are ready,* etc.

Beside, besides. *Beside* means *alongside of.* It can also mean *other than* or *aside from.*

> He pulled in beside the Volkswagen.
> Your last statement is beside the point.

Besides means *in addition to* or *moreover.*

> I'm starting to discover that I'll need something besides a big smile to get ahead.
> Besides, I'm not sure I really liked the dress in the first place.

Between. See *Among, between.*

Black, Negro. *Negro* is capitalized. *Black* is not, except for special emphasis.

> She was proud of being a black American, but she did not like to be called a Negro.
> He was a strong supporter of the Black Identity Movement.

The plural of *Negro* is *Negroes*. *Negro* is Spanish and Portuguese for *black*. *Black* is now considered preferable because *Negro* has a long history of use as a genteel social and political euphemism.

Blond, blonde. *Blond* is masculine; *blonde* is feminine. Use *blond* when dealing with both sexes or when sex is irrelevant.

> She is a blonde.
>
> His hair is blond.
>
> All the children are blonds.
>
> We chose blond furniture for the recreation room.

Brake, break. *Brake,* verb or noun, has to do with stopping a vehicle or other piece of machinery. For additional meanings, see dictionary.

> Frantically, he slammed on the brake.
>
> She braked her car to a complete stop.

Break, verb or noun, has many meanings, most commonly *destroy, damage, exceed, interrupt,* etc. The simple past is *broke;* the past participle is *broken.*

> Porcelain can break, so be careful.
>
> His left arm was broken.
>
> Henry Aaron broke Babe Ruth's home run record.
>
> The committee took a ten minute break.
>
> The attempted jail break was unsuccessful.
>
> The brake of the school bus has been broken.

Breath, breathe. *Breath* is a noun. *Breathe* is a verb.

> His statement was like a breath of fresh air.
>
> The soprano drew a deep breath.
>
> In some cities it can be dangerous to breathe the air.
>
> The soprano breathes deeply.

But however, but nevertheless, but yet. All these phrases are guilty of pointless repetition of meaning. Rewriting helps the logic and eliminates wordiness.

> POOR: Inflation is horrible, but however, the remedies are sometimes even more horrible.
>
> She loved her husband, but yet she feared him.
>
> Failure may be inevitable, but nevertheless we will do our best.
>
> BETTER: Inflation is horrible, but the remedies are sometimes even more horrible.
>
> Inflation is horrible; however, the remedies are sometimes even more horrible.

She loved her husband, yet she feared him.

Failure may be inevitable, but we will do our best.

But that, but what. Not acceptable standard English. Use *that*.

WRONG: I don't question but that you have good intentions.

          I don't question but what you have good intentions.

RIGHT: I don't question that you have good intentions.

Can, may. In formal English questions, *can* asks if the ability is there, and *may* asks if the permission is there.

May I intrude on your conversation? (Not *can* —anyone with a voice has the ability to intrude.)

Outside of formal contexts, few people worry about the distinction.

Can't help but. Wordy and repetitious. Avoid this phrase in written English.

POOR: I can't help but worry about what winter will do to my old car.

BETTER: I can't help worrying about what winter will do to my old car.

Censor, censure. *Censor*, as a verb, means *examine mail, art, etc., to see if it should be made public,* or *cut out, ban.* As a noun, *censor* means *a person engaged in censoring. Censure* can be a verb or noun meaning *condemn* or *condemnation, criticize adversely* or *adverse criticism,* etc.

Parts of the movie have been censored.

The prison censor examines all mail.

The Citizens for Good Citizenship Committee recently censured the mayor.

Dickens's deathbed scenes have long been singled out for censure.

Center around. Since a center is a single point in the middle of something, *center around* is an illogical phrase. Use *center on* instead.

The discussion centered on ways to increase productivity in the coming year.

Cite, site. *Cite,* a verb, means *mention. Site,* a noun, means *location.*

He cited many examples to prove his point.

The site of a new housing project has been debated for more than a year.

Climactic, climatic. *Climactic* is the adjectival form of *climax.*

The hero's death is the climactic moment of the story.

Climatic is the adjectival form of *climate.*

Climatic conditions in the Dakotas go from one extreme to the other.

Complected. Not standard English. *Complexioned* is preferable, but it's better to reword your sentence so you can avoid using either term.

ACCEPTABLE: He was a light-complexioned man.
BETTER: He had very fair skin.

Complement, compliment. The verb *complement* means *to complete* or *bring to perfection.* The noun *complement* means *the full amount. Compliment* means *praise* (noun or verb).

A string of pearls is an excellent complement to a black dress.

The ship had its required complement of officers.

Cheese and wine complement each other.

I don't appreciate insincere compliments.

Don't compliment me unless you mean it.

Compose, comprise. *Compose* means *to make up, to constitute.*

Thirteen separate colonies composed the original United States.

Comprise means *to be made up of, to encompass.*

The original United States comprised thirteen separate colonies.

If the distinction between these words gives you trouble, forget about *comprise* and use *is composed of* instead.

Conscience, conscientious, conscious. *Conscience* is the inner voice that tells us right from wrong, makes us feel guilty, etc. *Conscientious* means *painstaking, scrupulous,* or *ruled by conscience,* as in *conscientious objector. Conscious* means *aware.*

No one should ask you to act against your conscience.

I've tried to do this work as conscientiously as possible.

Jerry became conscious of a subtle change in Mary's attitude.

Conservative, reactionary. *Conservatives* are generally skeptical or cautious in their attitudes toward innovations. They tend to respect and rely on tradition and past experience. They are not against all progress but believe it is usually most effective when brought about slowly. *Reactionaries* are opposed to present conditions and want to restore the past. See *Liberal, radical.*

Console, consul, council, counsel. *Console:* As a verb (accent on second syllable)—*to sympathize with, to comfort.* As a noun (accent on first syllable)—*a radio, phonograph, or television cabinet, usually a combination, resting directly on the floor;* also *a small compartment, as found in an automobile between bucket seats;* for other meanings see dictionary.

Consul: A representative of a nation, stationed in a foreign city, whose job is to look after the nation's citizens and business interests.

Council: A governing body or an advisory group.

Counsel: As a verb—*to advise, to recommend.* As a noun—*advice, recommendation, exchange of ideas.*

> I could find no words to console the grieving widow.
>
> I've lived with this portable phonograph too long. I want a console.
>
> The French consul will answer any of your questions on import duties.
>
> The council met last week in a special emergency session.
>
> The tax expert counselled him on medical deductions.
>
> Sarah knew she could rely on her father's friendly counsel.

Continual, continuous. *Continuous* means *completely uninterrupted, without any pause.*

> The continuous noise at the party next door kept us awake.
>
> The patient received continuous round-the-clock care.

Continual means *frequently repeated, but with interruptions or pauses.*

> He had a bad cold and blew his nose continually.
>
> He changed jobs continually.

Costume, custom. *Costume* means *style of dress. Custom* means *conventional practice.* See dictionary for other meanings.

> He decided to wear a pirate's costume to the masquerade.
>
> Trick or treat is an old Halloween custom.

Could care less. See *Couldn't care less.*

Couldn't care less. Means *utterly indifferent to.* The phrase *could care less* is sometimes mistakenly used to mean the same thing. It does not mean the same thing; it makes no sense at all.

> WRONG: I could care less about his opinion of me.
>
> RIGHT: I couldn't care less about his opinion of me.

Could of, should of, would of. Not acceptable written English. Use *could have, should have, would have.*

Council. See *Console, consul, council, counsel.*

Counsel. See *Console, consul, council, counsel.*

Credible, creditable, credulous. *Credible* means *believable. Creditable* means *worthy of praise. Credulous* means *gullible, foolishly believing.*

> His lame excuses were not credible.
>
> Adam's behavior since his parole has been creditable.
>
> She's so credulous she still believes that the stork brings babies.

Criterion. This word (plural: *criteria*) is overused and frequently stuffy. Use *standard,* instead.

Cute. An overused word. Avoid it wherever possible in written English.

Data. Technically, a plural word, the singular of which is *datum*. The word's Latin origins, however, have nothing to do with its current usage. We believe that *data* can be treated as singular in all levels of English—and probably should be.

> CORRECT: This data is accurate and helpful.
>
> CORRECT (but very formal): These data are accurate and helpful.

Decompose, discompose. *Decompose* means *rot,* or *break into separate parts. Discompose* means *disturb, fluster, unsettle.*

> When the police found the body, it had already begun to decompose.
>
> His drunken foolishness discomposed all of us.

Definitely. Nothing is wrong with this word except that it is used far too often to add vague emphasis to weak thoughts and weak words.

Detract, distract. *Detract* means *belittle. Distract* means *divert, confuse.*

> Almost everyone tries to detract from television's real accomplishments.
>
> A mosquito kept distracting his attention.

Device, devise. *Device* is a noun meaning, among other things, *mechanism* or *special effect. Devise* is a verb meaning *to invent* or *to plot.*

> The safety pin is a simple but extraordinarily clever device.
>
> The person who devised the safety pin is one of humanity's minor benefactors.

Dialogue. In general, save this word for references to conversation in literary works.

> No creative writing class can give a writer an ear for good dialogue.
>
> Proper punctuation of dialogue requires knowledge of many seemingly trivial details.
>
> Some critics assert that Eugene O'Neill's plays have many great speeches but almost no believable dialogue.

Martin Buber, the great twentieth-century theologian, expanded the meaning of *dialogue* to refer to an intense, intimate relationship that can sometimes take place between God and human beings. Buber's influence, unfortunately, has led many people who should know better to corrupt the term into a pretentious, sometimes self-serving, synonym for normal conversation. Avoid this usage.

> POOR: At its meeting last week, the committee engaged in effective dialogue.
>
> The Singles Club provides its members with many opportunities for meaningful dialogue.

As if corruption were not enough, the word has been virtually destroyed through its faddish use as a verb. *Dialogue* is not a verb in standard written English. Never use it that way.

> WRONG: We dialogued about politics until two in the morning.
>
> Professor Briggs said that she enjoyed dialoguing with her students after class.

Different than. *Different from* is much better in all circumstances.

Discompose. See *Decompose, discompose.*

Disinterested, uninterested. Don't confuse these words. *Disinterested* means *impartial, unbiased. Uninterested* means *bored, indifferent.* An audience is uninterested in a poor play. A disinterested judge is necessary for a fair trial.

Disorientate, disorientated. Awkward and ugly variations of *disorient* and *disoriented.*

Distract. See *Detract, distract.*

Each. Takes a singular verb and a singular pronoun. See *He, his, him, himself.*

> Each breed of dog has its own virtues.
>
> Each actress was told to practice her lines.
>
> Each of the ballplayers is taking his turn at batting practice.

Eager. See *Anxious, eager.*

Economic, economical. Use *economic* for references to business, finance, the science of economics, etc. *Economical* means *inexpensive* or *thrifty.*

> We need to rethink our entire economic program to avert a recession.
>
> Economic conditions are improving in the textile industry.
>
> The economical shopper looks hard for bargains.
>
> It's economical in the long run to use first quality oil in your car.

Effect. See *Affect, effect.*

Effective. See *Affective, effective.*

Either. Use only when dealing with two units.

> WRONG: Either the Republican, the Democrat, or the Independent will be elected.

When *either* is the subject, it takes a singular verb and pronoun.

> The men are both qualified. Either is ready to give his best.

See *Neither.*

Elicit, illicit. *Elicit* means *draw out. Illicit* means *improper* or *prohibited.*

The interviewer was unable to elicit a direct answer.

Where would our modern novelists turn if they were suddenly prohibited from writing about illicit romance?

Ensure, insure. Both words mean the same. The more common spelling is *insure.*

Equally as. Not a standard English phrase. Eliminate the *as* or substitute *just as.*

> POOR: My grades were equally as good.
>
> The style was equally as important as the plot.
>
> BETTER: My grades were equally good.
>
> The style was just as important as the plot.

Establishment. Avoid this trite fad word. Basically, it should refer to a ruling group or structure that attempts to preserve the status quo. In practice, the word has become a term of vague abuse that interferes with discussion of complex issues.

Etc. Except where brevity is a major concern, as in this glossary, avoid *etc.* It tends to convey the impression that the writer doesn't want to be bothered with being accurate and specific. See *And etc.*

Every. This adjective makes the noun it modifies take a singular verb and a singular pronoun. See *He, his, him, himself.*

> Every businesswoman needs to learn how to deal with the prejudices of her male counterparts.
>
> Every Denver Bronco is required to report his weight upon arrival at training camp.
>
> Every idea has been put into its proper place in the outline.

Every day, everyday. *Every day* is the common phrase used for references to time.

> He loved her so much that he wanted to see her every day.
>
> Every day that we went to the pond that summer, we saw new signs of pollution.

Everyday is an adjective meaning *normal, ordinary, routine.*

> After the interview, Bill looked forward to changing into his everyday clothes.
>
> The everyday lives of many everyday people are filled with fears, tensions, and the potential for tragedy.

Everyone, every one. See *Anyone, any one.*

Except. See *Accept, except.*

Expand, expend. *Expand* means *increase, enlarge, fill out. Expend* means *spend, use up.*

The company needs to expand its share of the market.

The speakers will soon expand on their remarks.

Taxes must not be expended on visionary projects.

The student fell asleep during the final examination because he had expended all his energy in studying.

Explicit, implicit. *Explicit* means *stated or shown directly. Implicit* means *implied, not stated or shown directly.*

Cheryl's mother gave her explicit instructions to be home before dark.

Even by current standards, the movie goes to extremes in its explicit presentation of sex.

My wife and I have an implicit understanding that the first one who can't stand the dirt any longer is the one who does the dishes.

The diplomatic phrasing does not hide the implicit threat of war.

Facet. An overused, pseudoscholarly word. Avoid it wherever possible.

Farther, further. Not too many people worry about the distinction between these words anymore, but we think it is worth preserving. Use *farther* for geographic distance, *further* for everything else.

Allentown is five miles farther down the road.

Further changes need to be made in the curriculum.

Jim kissed her, but they were further apart than ever.

We need to go further into the subject.

Faze, phase. *Faze* means *disconcert, fluster.*

No great artist is fazed by critical sneers.

Phase means *a stage in development.* It is an overused word. Limit it to contexts in which the passage of time is especially significant.

POOR: One phase of the team's failure is poor hitting.

BETTER: The history of the team can be divided into three phases.

Fellow. As an adjective, the word means *being in the same situation* or *having the same ideas.* Make sure you do not use it to modify a noun that already implies that meaning.

RIGHT: My fellow workers and I voted to strike.

WRONG: My fellow colleagues have been hasty.

Fewer, less. Use *fewer* for references to amounts that can be counted individually, item by item. Use *less* for general amounts or amounts that cannot be counted or measured.

Fewer students are taking the course this term than last.

The company's advertising is less crude than it used to be.

Joe earned fewer dollars this year than he did five years ago.

Joe made less money this year than he did five years ago.

Figurative, figuratively. See *Literal, literally.*

Flaunt, flout. Flaunt means *show off arrogantly or conspicuously. Flout* means *treat scornfully, show contempt,* mostly in attitudes toward morality, social customs, traditions.

They lost no opportunity to flaunt their new-found wealth.

Those hoodlums flout all the basic decencies and then complain that we misunderstand them.

Foreword, forward. A *foreword* is a *preface* or *introduction. Forward* is the opposite of backward. It can also mean *bold* or *impertinent.*

The girl thought she was a swinger, but Mr. Tweedle thought she was a forward hussy.

Formally, formerly. *Formally* means *in a formal manner. Formerly* means *in the past.*

We were asked to dress formally.

People formerly thought that the automobile would turn out to be just another fad.

Former. Means *the first of two.* Don't use when dealing with more than two.

WRONG: Grant, McKinley, and Harding were poor presidents. The former was the poorest.

RIGHT: Grant, McKinley, and Harding were poor presidents. The first was the poorest.

Grant and McKinley were poor presidents. The former was the poorer.

See *Latter.*

Further. See *Farther, further.*

Gap. Phrases such as "generation gap," "missile gap," "credibility gap," etc. are media-spawned terms that have tended to lose their original meaning and impact through overuse. Avoid using them wherever possible.

Hanged, hung. Both are past participles of *hang;* technically, they are interchangeable. Traditionally, however, *hanged* is reserved for references to executions, and *hung* is used everywhere else.

The spy was hanged the next morning.

All the pictures hung crookedly.

He, his, him, himself. These common and seemingly inoffensive words have become the source of considerable controversy. Some people declare that the words contribute to sexual discrimination when used, as is traditional and grammatical, to refer to people who can be of either sex or when sex is irrelevant or unknown.

> The used-car buyer needs to be careful. In fact, *he* can hardly be too careful, for many dealers are waiting for the opportunity to swindle *him*.
>
> Each citizen, can make *his* choice known on Election Day.
>
> Everybody should protect *himself* from the dangers of alcoholism.

Defenders of these usages assert that in addition to being grammatically correct they are no more discriminatory in intent or effect than words like *mankind* or phrases like *no man is an island*. Both points of view are capable of being supported by legitimate logical arguments instead of the more usual hysteria and abuse.

For better or for worse, English has no distinct singular pronoun to refer to either sex. The *italicized* words in the three preceding examples are all technically correct—and if no means of revising them were available, they would have to remain as they are. At the same time, few writers want to run the risk of antagonizing a reader over the choice of pronouns, grammatical or not. Publishers of books, magazines, and newspapers have grown increasingly sensitive to the problem, and it seems safe to predict that the *he* usage will become less frequent as time goes by.

Like many problems, this one can often be solved by running away from it. We suggest that you *change singular phrasing to plural whenever possible.*

> Used car buyers need to be careful. In fact, *they* can hardly be too careful, for many dealers are waiting for the opportunity to swindle *them*.
>
> All citizens can make *their* choice known on Election Day.
>
> People should protect *themselves* from the dangers of alcoholism.

Sentences that do not lend themselves to a plural approach may have to be completely rephrased.

See *He or she, his or hers, him or her.*

He or she, his or hers, him or her. These efforts to achieve sexual equality in language are usually best saved for legal contracts. The phrasing is generally strained and pompous.

POOR: Everyone needs to make early plans for his or her career.

In cases of fatal illness, should a patient be told the truth about what is wrong with him or her?

BETTER: People should all make early plans for their careers.

In cases of fatal illness, should patients be told the truth about what is wrong with them?

Hopefully. *Hopefully* is an adverb, which means that it modifies and usually appears next to or close to a verb, adjective, or other adverb.

>   The farmers searched hopefully for a sign of rain.

>   Hopefully, the children ran down the stairs on Christmas morning.

Hopefully does not mean *I hope, he hopes, it is hoped that*, etc. Avoid using it in sentences like the following:

>   Hopefully, we can deal with this mess next weekend.

>   The new driver's training program, hopefully, will cut down on traffic fatalities.

In fairness, so many educated writers and speakers mishandle *hopefully* that the incorrect usage will probably worm its way into Standard English someday.

Human, humane. *Humane* means *kind, benevolent.*

>   Humane treatment of prisoners is all too rare.

I, me. *I* functions as the subject of a sentence or clause, and as a complement in the extremely formal but grammatically correct *It is I. Me* is the object of a verb or preposition.

>   He gave the book to me.

>   He gave me the business.

>   For me, nothing can beat a steak and French fries.

>   Why does she like me so much?

To determine which word to use in sentences like *Nobody is more enthusiastic than I* or *Nobody is more enthusiastic than me*, simply complete the sentences with a verb, and see which makes sense.

>   WRONG: Nobody is more enthusiastic than me (am).

>   RIGHT: Nobody is more enthusiastic than I (am).

Illicit. See *Elicit, illicit.*

Illusion. See *Allusion, illusion.*

Implicit. See *Explicit, implicit.*

Imply, infer. To *imply* means *to suggest or hint at something without specifically stating it.*

>   The dean implied that the demonstrators would be punished.

>   The editorial implies that our public officials have taken bribes.

To *infer* means *to draw a conclusion.*

>   I inferred from her standoffish attitude that she disliked me.

>   The newspaper wants its readers to infer that our public officials have taken bribes.

Incredible, incredulous. *Incredible* means *unbelievable*. *Incredulous* means *unconvinced, nonbelieving*.

> The witness gave evidence that was utterly incredible.
>
> I was incredulous at hearing those absurd lies.

Indict. To *indict* means *to charge with a crime*. It does not mean to arrest or to convict.

> The grand jury indicted Fields on a gambling charge.

Individual. Often contributes to stuffiness and wordiness.

> BAD: He was a remarkable individual.
>
> BETTER: He was a remarkable man.
>
> BEST: He was remarkable.

Infer. See *Imply, infer*.

Inferior than. Not standard English. Use *inferior to*.

Ingenious, ingenuous. *Ingenious* means *clever*. *Ingenuous* means *naive, open*.

> Sherlock Holmes was an ingenious detective.
>
> Nothing could rival the ingenuous appeal of the little girl's eyes.

Noun forms: *ingenuity, ingenuousness*.

In reference to. Stuffy business English. Use *about*.

In spite of. *In spite* is two separate words.

Insure. See *Ensure, insure*.

Inter-, intra-. *Inter* is a prefix meaning *between different groups*. *Intra* is a prefix meaning *within the same group*.

> Ohio State and Michigan fought bitterly for intercollegiate football supremacy.
>
> The English faculty needs a new department head who can control intradepartmental bickering.

Irregardless. Not standard English. The proper word is *regardless*.

Irrelevant, irreverent. *Irrelevant* means *not related to the subject*. *Irreverent* means *scornful, lacking respect*.

> Your criticisms sound impressive but are really irrelevant.
>
> America could use some of Mark Twain's irreverent wit today.

Confusion of these words may be responsible for the frequent mispronunciation of *irrelevant* as *irrevelant*.

Its, it's. *Its* is the possessive of *it*. *It's* is the contraction for *it is*.

The cat licked its paws. It's a wonderfully clean animal.

Its' is not a word. It does not exist, and it never has.

Job. Frequently overused in student writing. It is probably most effective when reserved for simple references to employment for wages.

> POOR: Shakespeare does a great job of showing Hamlet's conflicting emotions.
>
> RIGHT: Our economy needs to create more jobs.

Kind of. Means what it says: *a type of, a variety of.* It does not mean *somewhat* or *rather* except in the most informal writing.

> POOR: She was kind of pretty.
>
>   I was kind of curious about his answer.
>
> RIGHT: He suffered from an obscure kind of tropic fever.
>
>   He had a kind of honest stubbornness that could be very appealing.

Latter. Means *the second of two.* Don't use when dealing with more than two.

> WRONG: Washington, Jefferson, and Lincoln were great presidents. The latter was the greatest.
>
> RIGHT: Washington, Jefferson, and Lincoln were great presidents. The last was the greatest.
>
>   Washington and Lincoln were great presidents. The latter was the greater.

See *Former.*

Lay, lie. *Lay* is a transitive verb. It always takes an object *or* is expressed in the passive voice.

Present	*Past*	*Past Participle*	*Present Participle*
lay	laid	laid	laying

Lie is an intransitive verb. It never takes an object and never is expressed in the passive voice. This problem-causing *lie,* by the way, means *recline,* not *fib.*

Present	*Past*	*Past Participle*	*Present Participle*
lie	lay	lain	lying

Now I lay my burden down.

The hen laid six eggs yesterday.

The mason has laid all the bricks.

Our plans have been laid aside.

The porter is laying down our suitcases.

Now I am going to lie down.

Yesterday he lay awake for five hours.

The refuse has lain there for weeks.

Tramps are lying on the park benches.

Lead, led. As a noun, *lead* has various meanings (and pronunciations).

The student had no lead for his pencil.

The reporter wanted a good lead for her story.

Which athlete is in the lead?

The past of the verb *lead* is *led.*

The declarer always leads in bridge.

I led an ace instead of a deuce.

Is it possible to lead without making enemies?

Grant led the Union to triumph at Vicksburg.

Leave, let. *Let* means *allow,* etc. *Leave* means *depart.*

WRONG: Leave us look more closely at this sonnet.

RIGHT: Let us look more closely at this sonnet.

Lend, loan. *Lend* is a verb; *loan* is a noun.

Jack was kind enough to lend me ten dollars.

High interest rates have interfered with loans.

Less. See *Fewer, less.*

Liable, libel. *Liable* means *likely to* or *legally obligated. Libel* is an unjust written statement exposing someone to public contempt.

After a few drinks, that man is liable to do anything.

The owner of the dog was liable for damages.

Senator Green sued the newspaper for libel.

Libel, slander. *Libel* is written. *Slander* is spoken.

Liberal, radical. *Radicals* are extremists. They want drastic changes and usually want them immediately. They are inclined to accept extreme means for bringing about the changes. The word is most frequently used now with leftist connotations, but it need not be. A reactionary who wants to abolish Social Security is taking a radical position. *Liberals* tend to believe in reform more than in drastic change, though they are often strongly against the status quo. They are inclined to work within the system to achieve their goals. As an adjective, *liberal* is still used to mean *open-minded.*

See *Conservative, reactionary.*

Like, as. In agonizing over whether to use *like* or *as* (sometimes *as if*), look first at the words that follow. If the words make up a clause (subject plus verb) use *as;* if not, use *like.*

> He acted like a man.
>
> He acted as a man should.
>
> She treated me like dirt.
>
> She treated me as if I were dirt.

This rule is not foolproof, but it will handle almost all practical problems. *Like* in place of *as* is now fairly well accepted outside of formal written English, and we will have no overpowering regrets when it is accepted at all levels.

Literal, literally. These terms mean *in actual fact, according to the precise meaning of the words.* Some people use *literal, literally* when they mean the opposite: *figurative, figuratively.*

> WRONG: He literally made a monkey of himself.
>
> Some of our councilmen are literal vultures.
>
> I literally fly off the handle when I see children mistreated.
>
> RIGHT: The doctor said Karen's jealousy had literally made her ill.
>
> We were so lost that we literally did not know north from south.
>
> A literal translation from German to English rarely makes any sense.

Loan. See *Lend, loan.*

Loath, loathe. *Loath* is an adjective meaning *reluctant. Loathe* is a verb meaning *hate.*

> I am loath to express the full intensity of my feelings.
>
> I loathe people who use old-fashioned words like *loath.*

Loose, lose. *Loose* is the opposite of *tight* and *tighten. Lose* means *misplace.*

Mad. Use this word in written English to mean *insane,* not *angry.* Also, avoid it in its current slang senses of *unusual, wild, swinging,* etc.

> POOR: Please don't be mad at me.
>
> She wore a delightfully mad little hat.
>
> RIGHT: Shakespeare tends to be sympathetic to his mad characters.
>
> The arms race is utterly mad.

Majority, plurality. A candidate who has a *majority* has more than half of the total votes. A candidate who has a *plurality* has won the election but received less than half the total votes.

Masochist. See *Sadist, masochist.*

Massage, message. A *massage* makes muscles feel better. A *message* is a communication.

May. See *Can, may.*

May be, maybe. *May be* is a verb form meaning *could be, can be,* etc. *Maybe* is an adverb meaning *perhaps.*

> I may be wrong, but I feel that *Light in August* is Faulkner's finest novel.
>
> Maybe we ought to start all over again.

Me. See *I, me.*

Medal, metal, mettle. A *medal* is what is awarded to heroes and other celebrities. *Metal* is a substance such as iron, copper, etc. *Mettle* means *stamina, enthusiasm, vigorous spirit,* etc.

> The American team won most of its Olympic medals in men's swimming.
>
> Future metal exploration may take place more and more beneath the sea.
>
> Until the Normandy invasion, Eisenhower had not really proved his mettle.

Medium. An overused word in discussing communications. The plural is *media.* See the dictionary for its many meanings.

Mighty. Use this word to mean *powerful* or *huge.* It doesn't mean *very.*

> POOR: I was mighty pleased to meet you.

Moral, Morale. Moral, as an adjective, means *having to do with ethics* or *honorable, decent, upright,* etc. As a noun, it means *lesson, precept, teaching.* Morale means *state of mind, spirit.*

> Not all moral issues are simple cases of right and wrong.
>
> The story has a profound moral.
>
> The new coach tried to improve the team's morale.

More, most. Use *more* when two things are being compared. For any number over two, use *most.*

> Between Sally and Phyllis, Sally was the more talented.
>
> Of all my teachers, Mr. Frederic was the most witty.

Never use *most* as a synonym for *almost.*

> WRONG: Most everyone showed up at the party.
>
> I'll be home most any time tomorrow.

Mr., Mrs., Miss, Ms., etc. These titles should not be used in referring to figures from the historical, cultural, and scientific past. With living figures, the titles should be used in moderation; the better known the person, the less need for the title.

> POOR: Mr. John Adams was the second president of the United States.

The Scarlet Letter was written by Mr. Nathaniel Hawthorne.

The trial of Ms. Patty Hearst received worldwide press coverage.

BETTER: John Adams was the second president of the United States.

The Scarlet Letter was written by Nathaniel Hawthorne.

The trial of Patty Hearst received worldwide press coverage.

Ms. Now accepted in standard usage as a title for women, though Miss and Mrs. are still used occasionally.

Natural. Means *unartificial,* among other things. It is overused as a term of vague praise. It might be applied to someone's voice or manner, but it sounds absurd in a sentence like

Brand X eyelashes will give you that natural look.

Negro. See *Black, Negro.*

Neither. Use only when dealing with *two* units.

WRONG: I like neither collies nor poodles nor dachshunds.

When *neither* is the subject, it takes a singular verb and pronoun.

Both powers are responsible. Neither is doing its best for world peace.

See *Either.*

Nice. An overused word, generally too vague in meaning to have much value. Try to find more specific substitutes.

None. Means *no one* or *not one* and takes a singular verb and pronoun.

None of these police officers understands that she is a public servant.

Not hardly. A double negative. Not standard English. Use *hardly.*

WRONG: He couldn't hardly see his hand in front of his face.

RIGHT: He could hardly see his hand in front of his face.

Number. See *Amount, number.*

Often times. Wordy and pointless version of *often.*

Only. A tricky word in some sentences. Make sure that it modifies what you really want it to.

POOR: I only felt a little unhappy. (Only *felt!* Does the writer mean that he did not consciously *think* this way?)

I only asked for a chance to explain. (Does the writer mean that he did not insist on or strongly desire that chance?)

BETTER: I felt only a little unhappy.

I asked only for a chance to explain.

Orientate, orientated. Awkward and ugly variations of *orient* and *oriented.*

Passed, past. *Passed* is the past participle of *pass. Past* is used mainly as an adjective or a noun. Never use *passed* as an adjective or noun.

> We passed them on the highway.
>
> Valerie had a mysterious past.
>
> History is the study of past events.

Perpetrate, perpetuate. *Perpetrate* means *commit an evil, offensive, or stupid act. Perpetuate* means *preserve forever.*

> He perpetrated a colossal blunder.
>
> We resolve to perpetuate the ideals our leader stood for.

Perscription. No such word—you want *prescription.*

Persecute, prosecute. *Persecute* means *oppress, pick on unjustly. Prosecute* means *carry forward to conclusion* or *bring court proceedings against.*

> Persecuting religious and racial minorities is one of the specialties of the human race.
>
> The general believes that the war must be prosecuted intensely.
>
> We must prosecute those charged with crimes as rapidly as possible.

Perspective, prospective. *Perspective* has various meanings, most commonly *the logically correct relationships between the parts of something and the whole* or *the drawing technique that gives the illusion of space or depth. Prospective* means *likely to become* or *likely to happen.*

> Inflation is not our only problem; we need to keep the economy in perspective.
>
> Medieval painting reveals an almost complete indifference to perspective.
>
> The prospective jurors waited nervously for their names to be called.
>
> None of the prospective benefits of the Penn Central merger ever materialized.

Phenomenon. Singular; the standard plural form is *phenomena.*

Plurality. See *Majority, plurality.*

Precede, proceed. *Precede* means *go before. Proceed* means *go on.* See dictionary for other meanings.

> Years of struggle and poverty preceded her current success.
>
> Let us proceed with our original plans.

Prejudice, prejudiced. *Prejudice* is ordinarily a noun. *Prejudiced* is an adjective.

> WRONG: John is prejudice.

The neighborhood is filled with prejudice people.

RIGHT: John is prejudiced.

Legislation alone cannot eliminate prejudice.

Prescribe, proscribe. *Prescribe* means *order, recommend, write a prescription.* *Proscribe* means *forbid.* See other meanings in dictionary.

The committee prescribed a statewide income tax.

The authorities proscribe peddling without a license.

Principal, principle. As an adjective, *principal* means *foremost, chief, main.* As a noun, it can mean *a leading person* (as of a school) or *the amount owed on a loan exclusive of interest.* For other meanings see dictionary. *Principle* is a noun meaning *a fundamental doctrine, law, or code of conduct.*

The principal conflict in the novel was between the hero's conscious and subconscious desires.

For the third time that week, Jeff was summoned to the principal's office.

The interest on a twenty-five- or thirty-year mortgage often exceeds the principal.

Be guided by one principle: "Know thyself."

The candidate is a man of high principles.

Pronunciation. Note the spelling. There is no such word as *pronounciation.*

Quiet, quite. *Quiet* means *silence, to become silent, to make silent. Quite* means *rather* or *completely,* in addition to its informal use in expressions like *quite a guy.*

The parents pleaded for a moment of peace and quiet.

The crowd finally quieted down.

Throughout the concert, I tried to quiet the people behind me.

April was quite cold this year.

When the job was quite finished, Bill felt like sleeping for a week.

Radical. See *Liberal, radical.*

Raise, rise. *Rise* is an intransitive verb and never takes an object. *Raise* is a transitive verb.

I always rise at 8:00 A.M.

The farmer raises corn and wheat.

Rationalize. This word is most effective when used to mean *think up excuses for.* It can also mean *to reason,* but in that sense it is just a stuffy word for a simple idea. The noun form is *rationalization.*

The gangster tried to rationalize his behavior by insisting that his mother had not loved him.

All these rationalizations conceal the unpleasant truth.

Reactionary. See *Conservative, reactionary.*

Really. An overused word. It is especially weak in written English when it serves as a synonym for *very* or *extremely.*

> POOR: We saw a really nice sunset.
>
> That was a really big show.

When you do use *really,* try to preserve its actual meaning, stressing what is *real* as opposed to what is false or mistaken.

> The noises were really caused by mice, not ghosts.
>
> He may have been acquitted through lack of evidence, but everyone knew that Bronson was really guilty.

Reason is because. Awkward and repetitious. Use *reason is that.* Even this phrase is awkward and should be used sparingly.

> POOR: His reason for jilting her was because his parents disapproved of older women.
>
> BETTER: His reason for jilting her was that his parents disapproved of older women.
>
> EVEN BETTER: He jilted her because his parents disapproved of older women.

Relevant. An overused word, frequently relied upon to express shallow thought: "Literature is not relevant to our needs," for example. See *Irrelevant, irreverent* for note on pronunciation.

Respectfully, respectively. *Respectfully* means *with respect. Respectively* means *each in the order named.*

> Everyone likes to be treated respectfully.
>
> The speaker discussed education, medical research, and defense spending respectively.

Sadist, masochist. A *sadist* enjoys hurting living creatures. A *masochist* enjoys being hurt.

Seeing as how. Not standard English. Use *since* or *because.*

Seldom ever. *Ever* is unnecessary in this phrase. Avoid it.

> POOR: He was seldom ever angry.
>
> BETTER: He was seldom angry.

Set, sit. *To set* means *to place* or *to put.* The dictionary gives dozens of other meanings as well. Our main concern is that *set* does not mean *sit* or *sat.*

> Set the table.
>
> We sat at the table. (Not *We set at the table.*)

Set down that chair.

Sit down in that chair. (Not *Set down in that chair.*)

Shall, will. Elaborate rules differentiate between these words. Few people understand the rules, and no one remembers them. Our advice on this subject is to use *will* all the time except when *shall* obviously sounds more natural, as in some questions and traditional phrases. Examples: *Shall we dance? We shall overcome.*

Shone, shown. *Shone* is the alternate past tense and past participle of *shine.* Same as *shined. Shown* is the alternate past participle of *show.* Same as *showed.*

The sun shone brightly.

More shocking films are being shown than ever before.

Should of. See *Could of, should of, would of.*

Sic. Means *thus* or *so* in Latin. *Sic* is used in brackets within quoted material to indicate that an obvious error or absurdity was actually written that way in the original.

The author tells us, "President Harold [sic] Truman pulled one of the biggest political upsets of the century."

Site. See *Cite, site.*

Slander. See *Libel, slander.*

So. When *so* is used for emphasis, the full thought often needs to be completed by a clause. See *Such.*

POOR: The coffee was so sweet.

My sister is so smart.

RIGHT: That coffee was so sweet that it was undrinkable.

My sister is so smart that she does my homework for me every night.

So-called. This word has a specific meaning. Use it to complain about something that has been incorrectly or inaccurately named. Do not use it as a simple synonym for *undesirable* or *unpleasant.*

WRONG: These so-called jet planes make too much noise.

She wore a so-called wig.

RIGHT: Many of our so-called radicals are quite timid and conservative.

These so-called luxury homes are really just mass-produced bungalows.

Someone, some one. See *Anyone, any one.*

Somewheres. Not standard English. Use *somewhere.*

Sort of. Does not mean *somewhat* or *rather*. Means *a type of, a variety of*. See *Kind of*.

Stationary, stationery. *Stationary* means *unmoving, unchanging*. *Stationery* is paper for letter writing.

Story. A *story* is a piece of short prose fiction. Do not use the word when referring to essays and articles, poems, plays, and novels. Remember, too, that the action in any work of literature is *plot*, not story.

Such. When *such* is used for emphasis to mean *so much* or *so great*, etc., the full thought usually needs to be completed by a clause. See *So*.

> POOR: He was such a wicked man.
>
> RIGHT: He was such a wicked man that everyone feared him.
>
> We had such fun at the picnic, we had to force ourselves to go home.

Supposed to. Don't forget the *d*.

> This poem is supposed to be one of the greatest ever written.
>
> The students are supposed to have a rally tomorrow night.

Sure and. *Sure to* is preferable in writing.

> POOR: Be sure and cancel newspaper deliveries before leaving for vacation.
>
> BETTER: Be sure to cancel newspaper deliveries before leaving for vacation.

Than, then. *Than* is the word for expressing comparisons and exceptions. *Then* is the word for all other uses.

> Florida is more humid than California.
>
> John has nothing to worry about other than his own bad temper.
>
> At first I thought the story was funny. Then I realized its underlying seriousness.
>
> We must work together, then, or we are all doomed.

Their, they're, there. *Their* is the possessive form of *they*.

> They took their seats.

They're is the contraction of *they are*.

> The defensive linemen say they're going to do better next week.

For all other situations, the word you want is *there*.

They. Often used vaguely and meaninglessly, as in "They don't make things the way they used to," or "They really ought to do something about safety." Nowhere is the use of *they* more meaningless and weird than when applied to an individual writer. *Never* write:

This was an excellent mystery. They certainly fooled me with the solution.

I think it was sad that they had Othello die at the end of the play.

This, these. Frequent problem-producers when used imprecisely. Make certain that no confusion or vagueness is possible. To be on the safe side, many writers make a habit of following *this* and *these* with a noun that clarifies the reference: *this idea, these suggestions, this comment,* etc.

To, too, two. *To* is the familiar preposition used in diverse ways. *Too* means *also* or *excessively*. *Two* is the number.

Try and. Acceptable in conversation, but undesirable in print. Use *try to.*

POOR: We must all try and improve our environment.

BETTER: We must all try to improve our environment.

Type of. This phrase frequently contributes to wordiness.

WORDY: He was an interesting type of artist.

          I enjoy a suspenseful type of novel.

BETTER: He was an interesting artist.

          I enjoy a suspenseful novel.

Under way. Two words, except in special technical fields.

Uninterested. See *Disinterested, uninterested.*

Unique. This word means *one of a kind;* it cannot be made stronger than it already is, nor can it be qualified. Do not write *very unique, more unique, less unique, somewhat unique, rather unique, fairly unique,* etc.

Used to. Don't forget the *d.*

I used (not *use*) to like the tales of Jules Verne.

We are used (not *use*) to this kind of treatment.

Very. One of the most overused words in the language. Try to find one *exact* word for what you want to say instead of automatically using *very* to intensify the meaning of an imprecise, commonplace word.

very bright	*could be*	radiant
very bad	*could be*	terrible
very sad	*could be*	pathetic
very happy	*could be*	overjoyed, delighted

When. In using this word, make sure it refers to *time.*

WRONG: Basketball is when five men on opposing teams . . .

RIGHT: Basketball is a game in which five men on opposing teams . . .

WRONG: New York is when the Democratic Convention was held.

RIGHT: New York is where the Democratic Convention was held.

Where. In using this word, make sure it refers to *place.*

WRONG: I'm interested in seeing the movie where the motorcycle gang takes over the town.

RIGHT: I'm interested in seeing the movie in which the motorcycle gang takes over the town.

WRONG: The class is studying the time where the Industrial Revolution was beginning.

RIGHT: The class is studying the time when the Industrial Revolution was beginning.

Where ... at, where ... to. The *at* and the *to* are unnecessary. They show how wordiness can often sneak into our writing almost subconsciously.

POOR: Where are you staying at?

Where is he going to?

BETTER: Where are you staying?

Where is he going?

Whether or not. The one word *whether* means the same as *whether or not,* and is therefore preferable.

POOR: We wondered whether or not it would snow.

BETTER: We wondered whether it would snow.

Who, that, which. Use *who* or *that* for people, preferably *who*, never *which.* Use *which* or *that* for things, preferably *that*, never *who.*

Keats is one of many great writers who died at an early age.

There's the woman that I was telling you about.

Podunk is a town that people always ridicule.

The play which we are now studying is incredibly difficult.

Who, whom. Although the distinction between *who* and *whom* is no longer a major issue in the conversation of many educated speakers and in much informal writing, formal English still fusses about these words—and perhaps your instructor does, too. We will first discuss the traditional rules; then we will consider more casual approaches.

A. Formal English requires *who* to serve as the *subject* of verbs in dependent clauses:

She is a fine woman who loves her family.

Here is a person who should go far in this company.

I dislike people who can't take a joke.

Formal English uses *whom* as the *object* in dependent clauses:

> The drunk driver whom Officer Jerome had ticketed last night turned out to be Judge Furness.

> The teacher whom I feared so greatly last term has now become a good friend.

Note that it is the role played by *who* or *whom* in the *dependent clause* that determines which word is right; don't be distracted by connections *who* or *whom* may appear to have with other parts of the sentence. In cases of doubt, a sometimes effective tactic is to substitute *he, she, they* or *him, her, them* for the word in question and see which makes better sense. If *he, she, they* works, use *who*. If *him, her, them* works, use *whom*.

> *I dislike people (who, whom) can't take a joke.*

Take the dependent clause *(who, whom) can't take a joke.* Clearly, *they can't take a joke* works, and *them can't take a joke* does not work. Use *who*.

> *The drunk driver (who, whom) Officer Jerome had ticketed last night turned out to be Judge Furness.*

Take the dependent clause *(who, whom) Officer Jerome had ticketed last night. Officer Jerome had ticketed him last night* makes sense; *Officer Jerome had ticketed he last night* does not make sense. Use *whom*.

Special problems pop up when words intervene between *who* or *whom* and its verb. Don't be misled by expressions like *I think, they say, it seems, she feels,* and so on. These expressions should be thought of as interrupting words and do not affect the basic grammar of the clause.

> The minority leader is the man who I think should be the next president. (*Who* is the subject of *should be.*)

> No artist who he said was brilliant ever impressed us. (*Who* is the subject of *was.*)

B. Through the years, the complex traditional rules have confused many people, and we've tried to explore only the most frequent complications. As teachers, we confess that we feel distinctly uncomfortable when the old rules are broken. We also confess, however, that Theodore Bernstein, late stylist-in-chief of the *New York Times*, makes a strong case in declaring that the rules are more trouble than they are worth (see pp. 248–251). Check with your own instructor, and then consider the following guidelines and shortcuts:

A. Immediately after a preposition, use *whom*.

> He asked to whom I had been speaking.

> This is the man in whom we must place our trust.

B. At other times, use *who*.

> In my home, it's the man who does the cooking.
>
> Fred Smiley is the man who Ethel chose.

C. If *who* sounds "wrong" or unnatural, or if you are in a situation that demands formal writing and feel uncertain about the formal rules (the sample sentence about Fred and Ethel breaks the rules), try to eliminate the problem with one of these techniques:

1. Change *who* or *whom* to *that*.

> Fred Smiley is the man that Ethel chose.

2. Remove *who* or *whom*.

> Fred Smiley is the man Ethel chose.

Who's, whose. *Who's* is a contraction of *who is* or *who has*. *Whose* is the possessive form of *who*.

> Who's going to get the promotion?
>
> Fenton is a man who's been in and out of jail all his life.
>
> Whose reputation shall we attack today?
>
> Kennedy was a president whose place in history is still in doubt.

Will. See *Shall, will.*

Would of. See *Could of, should of, would of.*

INDEX

535